TheGreenGuide
Greece

D1248513

MICHELIN

THEGREENGUIDE **GREECE**

Editorial Director	Cynthia Clayton Ochterbeck
Book Packager	Azalay Media
Editor	Jonathan Gilbert
Contributing Writer	Mike Gerrard
Production Manager	Natasha G. George
Cartography	Stephane Anton, John Dear, Thierry Lemasson
Photo Editor	Sean Sachon
Design	Chris Bell, Christelle Le Déan
Layout	Michelin Travel Partner
Cover Layout	Natasha G. George

Contact Us

Michelin Travel and Lifestyle North America
One Parkway South
Greenville, SC 29615
USA
travel.lifestyle@us.michelin.com
www.michelintravel.com

Michelin Travel Partner
Hannay House
39 Clarendon Road
Watford, Herts WD17 1JA
UK
℘01923 205240
travelpubsales@uk.michelin.com
www.ViaMichelin.com

Special Sales

For information regarding bulk sales, customized editions and premium sales, please contact us at:
travel.lifestyle@us.michelin.com
www.michelintravel.com

Note to the reader Addresses, phone numbers, opening hours and prices published in this guide are accurate at the time of press. We welcome corrections and suggestions that may assist us in preparing the next edition. While every effort is made to ensure that all information printed in this guide is correct and up-to-date, Michelin Travel Partner accepts no liability for any direct, indirect or consequential losses howsoever caused so far as such can be excluded by law.

HOW TO USE THIS GUIDE

PLANNING YOUR TRIP

The blue-tabbed PLANNING YOUR TRIP section gives you **ideas for your trip** and **practical information** to help you organise it. You'll find tours, practical information, a host of outdoor activities, a calendar of events, information on shopping, sightseeing, kids' activities and more.

INTRODUCTION

The orange-tabbed INTRODUCTION section explores Greece's **Nature** and geology. The **History** section spans from ancient Greece to the European Union. The **Art and Culture** section covers architecture, art, literature and music, while **Greece Today** delves into the modern country.

DISCOVERING

The green-tabbed DISCOVERING section features Principal Sights by region, featuring the most interesting local **Sights**, **Walking Tours**, nearby **Excursions**, and detailed **Driving Tours**. Admission prices shown are normally for a single adult.

ADDRESSES

We've selected the best hotels, restaurants, cafés, shops, nightlife and entertainment to fit all budgets. See the Legend on the cover flap for an explanation of the price categories. See the back of the guide for an index of hotels and restaurants.

Sidebars

Throughout the guide you will find blue, orange and green-coloured text boxes with lively anecdotes, detailed history and background information.

😀 A Bit of Advice 😀

Green advice boxes found in this guide contain practical tips and handy information relevant to your visit or a sight in the Discovering section.

STAR RATINGS★★★

Michelin has given star ratings for more than 100 years. If you're pressed for time, we recommend you visit the ★★★ or ★★ sights first:

★★★   **Highly recommended**
★★   **Recommended**
★   **Interesting**

MAPS

- 🗺 Regional Driving Tours map, Principal Sights maps.
- 🗺 Region maps.
- 🗺 Maps for major cities and villages.
- 🗺 Local tour maps.

All maps in this guide are oriented north, unless otherwise indicated by a directional arrow. The term "Local Map" refers to a map within the chapter or Tourism Region. A complete list of the maps found in the guide appears at the back of this book.

DISCOVERING MAINLAND GREECE

© R. Mattès/MICHELIN

CONTENTS

5

Welcome to Greece

Greece gets into your blood. So many travellers return again and again. They may go for the remote islands and time spent lying on quiet sandy beaches. They may go for the country's wonderful archaeological sites like Mycenae or Knossos. Some go to climb its mountains or hike Europe's two longest gorges. Some enjoy a little of everything, and everyone wants to see the capital, Athens, one of the greatest cities in the world.

CENTRAL GREECE (pp106–179)

This region ranges from the peaks around Mount Parnassos to the pretty ports lining the Gulf of Corinth. Athens has the Parthenon, museums and city life, but a day trip to ancient Delphi reveals beautiful mountain scenery. Another attraction is Greece's second largest island, Euboea, which despite its size only attracts few foreigners to its mountains and wildernesses.

THESSALY & EPIRUS (pp180–201)

The Epirus region of northwest Greece is one of the most inspiring and surprising parts of the country. The Pindos Mountains are among the most dramatic in southern Europe and are dissected by the Vikos Gorge, one of the world's deepest gorges. There are beach resorts too, like the charming Parga; also the Epirus capital, Ioannina, which sits by Lake Pamvotis, is one of Greece's most fascinating cities. Pass through the mountain town of Metsovo to reach Thessaly, home to the cliff-clinging monasteries of Meteora, and the wooded hills and beaches of the Pelion Peninsula.

GREEK MACEDONIA (pp202–231)

Greece's second city, Thessaloniki, is a vibrant place as waterfront cities often are, offering museums and nightlife in equal measure. It's also the capital of Macedonia, which includes the country's highest mountain, Mount Olympus, and one of the mainland's most popular holiday areas, the Halkidiki Peninsula. By contrast, Halkidiki also has the private "Monk's Republic" of Mount Athos. There are important archaeological sites too, including Philippi, Dion, Pella and Vergina, mountain towns like Kastoria and the stunning Prespa Lakes.

THE PELOPONNESE (pp232–315)

Some of Greece's most beautiful and ancient places are found in the Peloponnese. The road from Athens passes over the engineering wonder of the Corinth Canal before reaching the royal tombs of Mycenae, ancient Tiryns and the theatre at Epidauros. Close by is Nauplion, one of the prettiest cities in Greece. Olympia is the site of the original Olympic Games, matched by impressive ruins at Mystras and the Temple of Apollo Epicurius at Bassae. There are excellent beach resorts too, plus the remote solitude of the Mani Peninsula.

CRETE (pp316–351)

Greece's largest island is like another country, with its own rugged individuality. It has numerous beach resorts, both for partying and for escape, and by contrast also has snow-capped mountains and Europe's longest gorge, the Samarian Gorge. Knossos is the best-known of its many archaeological sites, which also include Malia and Faistos, while Chania and Rethymnon are two beautiful harbour towns and the capital, Herakleion, has fine museums and a lively atmosphere.

THE CYCLADES (pp352–407)

The Cyclades have the archetypal Greek island look of white cube houses clustered under the deepest of blue skies. For this and other reasons they are among the most popular of the island groups, especially Mykonos and Santorini, with their beaches, nightlife, chic hotels and restaurants. Naxos and Andros offer mountainous terrain while the whole island of Delos is an archaeological site, and there are "get-away-from-it-all" islands too, including Analfi and Sifnos.

DODECANESE (pp408–435)

Attractions here range from religious sites to rampant party-going. The main island, Rhodes, has both party resorts and its UNESCO World Heritage Old Town. Little Symi oozes charm, as do other small islands like Nisyros and Lipsi. Kos has a string of beautiful beaches, while Karpathos is a step back in time as it clings to its traditions. Patmos steps back even further, where St John the Divine allegedly wrote the *Apocalypse*.

IONIAN ISLANDS (pp436–461)

A string of jewels down Greece's west coast, the Ionian Islands have some of the country's best beaches and, in Corfu Town, one of the more sophist-icated island capitals. Paxos is the perfect place to escape, while Ithaca lures with its peace and quiet. Beaches and windsurfing distinguish Lefkada, while Cephalonia is large enough to offer mountains, beaches, wineries, caves and a gem of a town in Fiskardo, and Zakynthos has beautiful beaches.

EASTERN AEGEAN ISLANDS (pp462–481)

This loose-knit group of disparate islands includes some of the least visited and strongly individual of all the Greek islands. From giant Lesbos with its wonderful beaches to little and lush Samothraki, these are very contrasting islands. Samos has modern resorts and traditional villages, while Chios relies as much on agriculture as on tourism. Thassos has wooded walks and golden beaches, while Icaria packs some dramatic mountains and deep gorges into its small size, and Lemnos has flamingo-filled lakes and other rewards for the more intrepid traveller.

SARONIC GULF ISLANDS (pp482–491)

These islands are easily reached from Athens, and though they can get crowded at times, they have lots of appeal. The closest, Salamis, is virtually a seaborne suburb of Athens, and most visitors bypass it to see Aegina and especially its 5C BC Temple of Aphaia. Poros is very much the popular holiday island, while Hydra bans cars and has always had a laid-back Bohemian feel. Spetses has just one main town, the rest being an island of beaches and pine forests.

SPORADES (pp492–497)

There may only be four main islands in this small group, but they offer lots of variety. Skiathos is a beautiful but busy island, the crowds attracted by its lovely beaches, while neighbouring Skopelos has fewer beaches but is covered with forests, olive groves, fruit trees and vineyards. Alonnisos is also covered in forests and orchards, and appeals more to walkers than to sun worshippers. The largest of the Sporades is Skyros, which is also the wildest and the one least affected by tourism, with a mountainous terrain and more than a touch of mystery.

Agios Pavlos, Lindos, Rhodes
© gallas/Fotolia.com

Michelin Driving Tours

REGIONAL DRIVING TOURS

See the Regional Driving Tours map on the following pages.

The suggested itinerary route maps at the beginning of this guide take into account the availability of accommodation along the way, the number of sites of interest, and the ease of travel along the route. Certain major sites do not have a convenient hotel; you may need to look for lodging in a nearby town of little interest to the visitor.

1 AROUND OLYMPUS

This itinerary explores the rugged peaks of northern Greece near the Albanian border. After seeing **Thessaloniki**, the second city of the country, head for the Macedonian tombs of **Lefkadia** (3–2C BC) before visiting the **Prespa Lakes** (a national park) and staying in the charming town of **Kastoria**, situated on a peninsula. Travel through the mountains, dominated by Olympus, to reach **Larissa**, the capital of Thessaly. Return along the coast with its fine beaches, making a point of stopping at the ancient city of **Dio**.

2 NORTHERN GREECE

Starting in **Thessaloniki**, this itinerary takes in the fertile plains and valleys of Macedonia. The **Sithonia Peninsula** is especially attractive with woodlands and beaches. To the north of **Kavala** is the site of **Philippi**, founded by Philip II of Macedon and greatly expanded by the Romans. Then cross to the island of **Thassos** with its fine archaeological remains for the final leg of the trip.

3 CENTRAL GREECE

This long circuit through some of the most beautiful countryside in Greece is best started from **Athens**. Along the way visit the monastery of **Óssios Loukás**, **Delphi** (where the

natural scenery is as breathtaking as the historical remains), and the island of **Lefkada** (linked by a bridge to the mainland) with its white cliffs (don't miss **Nidri Bay**, sheltered by a series of small islands). After an overnight stay at **Parga**, take a ferry from Igoumenitsa to the idyllic beaches and Italian influences of **Corfu**. Returning to the mainland head east to **Ioannina**, capital of Epirus, from where the natural beauties of the area, such as the Perama Cave and the Víkos Gorge, and the archaeological splendour of **Dodona**, may be easily reached. Farther east are the gravity defying monasteries of **Meteora**. Return to Athens via Trikala and Vólos; the route hugs the coast back to the capital.

4 PRINCIPAL ANCIENT SITES

The main monuments of classical Greece can be toured over the course of a week. Start in **Athens** with the Acropolis and its environs, and the big museums. Two days in the capital should suffice before taking to the road: the ancient city of **Corinth** is also the gateway to the Peloponnese, where many of the country's most important remains can be found. Here are **Mycenae** with its famous Lion Gate and the golden treasures of its tombs (now on display in Athens at the National Archaeological Museum), the ramparts at **Tiryns**, **Epidaurus** with its fine theatre, **Olympia** and the moving sight of its extensive remains where the Olympic Games began. Return to Athens via **Patras** and the unparalleled **Delphi**, with its Sacred Precinct and fascinating museum.

5 THE SOUTHERN PELOPONNESE

This programme takes in the main sites of the Peloponnese, including **Nauplion** with its fine citadel; close by are **Mycenae** and **Epidaurus**. Continue to the attractive resort of **Leonidío** and then on to unspoilt **Monemvassiá**, before exploring

Road through Meteora

© Maria Menshova/Bigstockphoto.com

the **Mani Peninsula**. Returning northwards, visit **Mystras** and the stunningly situated **Pylos**, prior to continuing to the ruins of **Olympia**, and finally stopping to admire the breathtaking sight of the temple at **Bassae**.

LOCAL DRIVING TOURS

Throughout the *Discovering* sections of the guide you can find local driving tours. Highlights include:

Arcadian Coast (Aktí Arkadías)
50km/31mi, allow 2hrs. From the agricultural centre of Ástros, past beaches and monasteries and ending at the little town of Leonídio★★.

Attica
65km/41mi round trip. The Apollo Coast to Cape Sounion★★.
Around 90km/56mi. West of Athens, ending at picturesque Egósthena★★ and its acropolis.

Ioannina
80km/49mi return journey.
Allow one day for this trip in the Zagória★★.

Kalamáta
80km/50mi one way. The West Coast of the Messanian Gulf★★★.

Herakleion (Iráklio), Crete
110km/69mi round trip. Idaian Massif★ to the southwest of the island.

Saint Nicholas (Ágios Nikólaos, Crete)
43km/27mi. Round trip of the Bay of Elounta★ from Ágios Nikólaos. Allow a day including Spinalónga island.
100km/63mi round trip. Head east out of Ágios Nikólaos. Follows the coast of Mirambélou Bay★★.

Naxos
80km/50mi. The Tragéa Valley★★ allow one day.

Rhodes (Ródos), The Dodecanese
200km/125mi. Round trip of the island★★ from Rhodes Town. Allow two days.

Cephalonia (Kefalonía), Ionian Islands
200km/125mi. Island tour★★; allow two days.

Corfu (Kérkyra), Ionian Islands
The south of the island★ or the north of the island★. Allow one day for each trip.

Lefkada, Ionian Islands
100km/63mi. Tour of the island★. Allow one day.

Chios
90km/56mi. Round trip of the Mastic Villages★★, south of Chios Town.

Thassos, Northern Aegean Islands
80km/50mi. Round trip of the island★★ clockwise from Liménas.

Regional Driving Tours

★★ *Limnes Préspes*

Édessa

★★ **Lefkádia**

Kastoriá ★★

Véroia

1

Flórina

Vjosë

★ Siátista

Kozáni

E 90

Aliákmonas

FARÁNGI VÍKOU ★★★

★ Monodéndri

METÉORA ★★★

★★ **PÉRAMA**

Métsovo ★★

Kalampáka

Ioánnina ★

Acheloós

Tríkala

E 92

Pineiós

★★ **Kérkyra**

E 90 E 92

Dodóni ★★

Igoumenítsa

E 55

Stena Pórtas ★

Tavropós

★★★ **KÉRKYRA**

Éfyras ★

E 952

★★ **Párga**

Kassópi ★

Árta ★

Sperchiós

★ Nikopólis

Préveza

Vónitsa

Lefkáda

Acheloós

LEFKÁDA Nydrí

I O N I A N

Náfpaktos

E 65

E 55

Mesolóngi

S E A

CÉPHALONIE

PÁTRA

Andravída

E 55

Pineiós

ZANTE

OLÝMPIA ★★★

Pyrgós

Karýtaina

Andrítsaina

★★ **Vassés**

Megalópo

Kyparissía

E 55

Alfeiós

5

Kalamáta

★*Anáktora Néstoros*

Pýlos ★★

★★ **Methóni**

MESSINIAKÓS KÓLPOS ★★★

TIRANA - SKOPJE

─── **Northern Greece**

1 : 750km/466mi
(6 days including 1 day in Thessaloníki and 1 day in Kastoriá)

2 : 700km/435mi
(4 days including 1 day in Thásos)

─── **Central Greece** 3 : 1750km/1087mi
(11 days including 1 day in Kérkyra, 1 day in Ioánnina and its environs, and 1 day in Vólos and its environs)

─── **Principal ancient sites** 4 : 900km/559mi
(7 days including 2 days in Athína and 1 day in Náfplio and its environs)

─── **Southern Peloponnese** 5 : 1100km/683mi
(7 days including 3 days for the environs of Gýtheio)

When and Where to Go

WHEN TO GO

Spring in Greece, with the mountains and islands covered in wild flowers, is brief but idyllic; the sea, however, can be chilly. In the northern mountains the night-time temperatures can also be cold, but in the more southerly islands the summer will usually be clearly on the way.

The best time of year to visit is June, with pleasant temperatures and gentle breezes. Accommodation is also cheaper as there are fewer visitors than in high season. September offers similarly favourable weather, and sea temperatures at their peak. In between, in July and August, the temperatures can soar and although many people enjoy travelling to Greece then, the occasional heatwave can make it almost unbearable. Athens can become a cauldron, while in more remote places air-conditioning is often not strong enough to cool the night-time heat.

Autumn is mild until mid-November, although many hotels close at the end of October. Days then begin to shorten significantly, and downpours revitalise the landscape, especially in the lush Ionian islands.

Note that most Greeks do not travel abroad for their holidays and further swell the tourist numbers in high season. Hotels and restaurants are full, and prices double or even triple. In the Aegean, there are strong winds throughout the summer which offer some relief from the heat, but they can blow violently and make sailing difficult.

In winter, Greece is a country of contrasts. In the north and at higher altitudes there is abundant snow, whereas the south and the islands remain mild. In January the average temperature is 11°C in Athens and 12°C in Herakleion, making winter vacations here very pleasant. Skiing is available just two hours' drive from Athens, where on sunnier winter days it is possible to dine outside.

WHERE TO GO
ATHENS (3–6 DAYS)

This great city was one of the most beautiful places in the ancient world.

DAY 1 – Top priority is a visit to the **Acropolis**, followed by a stroll through the **Plaka** district.

DAY 2 – Visit the **National Archaeological Museum**, with its unparalleled examples of Classical art, followed by a trip to the **Agora** and the **Keramíkos Cemetery**.

DAY 3 – Don't miss the **Benaki Museum** and **Museum of Cycladic Art**. Watch the changing of the guard before seeing the **Olympieion**, the **National Gardens** and **Odós Ermou**.

New Acropolis Museum, Athens

© Greek National Tourism Organisation

DAYS 4-6 – Rent a car to see the sights of the **Attica Peninsula**, **Delphi**, **Mycenae**, **Epidaurus** and **Nauplion**.

NAUPLION (3 DAYS)

In the eastern Peloponnese, Nauplion is an ancient city situated on a peninsula. It is also an excellent base from which to visit the archaeological sites of Mycenae, Epidaurus and Corinth.

DAY 1 – Discover **Epidaurus** and its stunning theatre, one of the great monuments of the classical world.

DAY 2 – A trip to **Mycenae** in the morning to admire the ruins of this great city founded in the second millennium BC; do not miss the famous **Lion Gate**. In the afternoon visit **Corinth**, remarkable for its citadel (Acrocorinth) and for its canal linking the Gulf of Corinth to the Saronic Gulf.

DAY 3 – Explore **Nauplion** itself, especially its citadel, and then relax at the beach.

GÍTHIO (3 DAYS)

This port on the Laconic Gulf is also the gateway to the Máni Peninsula. With numerous good quality hotels, it is the ideal base from which to explore the southern Peloponnese.

DAY 1 – Discover the wild mountains of the **Máni Peninsula** and its villages such as **Vathia**.

DAY 2 – Visit **Sparta** and continue up **Mount Taigetos** to **Mystra**, and its panoramic views.

DAY 3 – Explore the **Gulf of Messenia** with its many beaches. It is a short hop to the island of **Kythera**.

CORFU (4 DAYS)

This island is a Garden of Eden in the Ionian Sea, close to the coast of Epirus and the shores of Albania. **Corfu Town** shows a strong Italian influence with its tiled roofs and cypress trees.

DAY 1 – Wander through the streets of the old town, with its Baroque churches, museums and citadels.

DAY 2 – Make an early start to walk to the tip of the **Kanoni Peninsula** from where some of the finest landscapes in Greece can be seen, before visiting the **Achilleion**, a Neoclassical style villa built for Sisi, Empress of Austria.

DAY 3 – Discover the west coast of the island, including **Pelekas** (fine panoramic view) and **Paleokastrítsa Bay**.

DAY 4 – Take a trip to the north of the island; near **Sidari** are numerous inlets and rocky promontories caused by erosion. Inland, the countryside is dotted with ancient olive groves.

SANTORINI (3 DAYS)

The best-known island of the Cyclades, Santorini is also one of the most beautiful. Formed by a partially submerged volcanic crater, it possesses a breathtaking beauty.

DAY 1 – Visit **Thíra**, the principal town, and its environs before enjoying the sunset from the beautiful village of **Oia**.

DAY 2 –Take a boat trip round the submerged crater and visit the smaller island of **Thirasia**.

DAY 3 – Explore the **archaeological sites** of the island before ending the day with a visit to one of the fine beaches on the east coast.

CRETE (5 DAYS)

At the eastern end of Crete, the resort of **Ágios Nikólaos** is close to numerous places of interest, both natural and architectural.

DAY 1 – Wander round the town, constructed on the shores of a lake.

DAY 2 – Visit the tranquil island and peninsula of **Spinalónga**.

DAY 3 – Explore the Ancient Minoan city of **Mália**, and the picturesque village of **Krítsa**.

DAY 4 – Discover more of Crete by heading to **Ierápetra** and then turning west and following the coast before returning via Chersonisos.

DAY 5 – Start early and head to **Vai** at the eastern tip of Crete, pausing at **Sitía** on the way. At Vai, the palm-fringed beach is especially beautiful. If there is time turn south to visit the Minoan palace at **Káto Zákros**.

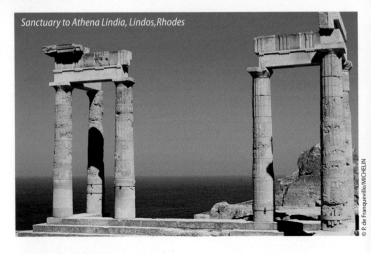

Sanctuary to Athena Lindia, Lindos, Rhodes

© P. de Franqueville/MICHELIN

RHODES (6 DAYS)

Rhodes is most easily reached by flying direct to the island. A six-day stay will allow time to discover not only Rhodes but also the beautiful neighbouring island of Sími.

DAY 1 – Explore **Rhodes Town** with its citadel, which in the Middle Ages was one of the great bastions against the Turks.

DAY 2 – Discover the east coast and stop by the town of **Lindos**, which has a medieval citadel.

DAY 3 – Head for the rugged west coast with its many inlets, which are ideal for swimming. Do not miss the fortress of **Monolithos** which dominates the landscape.

DAY 4 – Travel into the mountains, where there are many small churches and vineyards.

DAY 5 – Take a boat to the island of **Sími**, whose Neoclassical town is one of Greece's most beautiful.

DAY 6 – Enjoy the beaches of Sími before returning to Rhodes.

CEPHALONIA (3 DAYS)

DAY 1 – Explore the capital, **Argostoli**, and the **beach resorts** of the south, before driving and walking up **Mt Enos**, the island's highest peak.

DAY 2 – Drive north up the east coast, visiting the second town, **Sami**, and the **Melissani** and **Drogorati Caves** nearby.

DAY 3 – Visit the photogenic **Fiskardo** at the northern tip, drive down the west coast via picturesque **Assos**, and back to Argostoli.

MYKONOS (3 DAYS)

DAY 1 – Spend a full day in **Mykonos Town**, exploring its several museums and fine churches, a contrast to its hedonistic nightlife.

DAY 2 – Head by car, bus or boat to the famous south coast beaches like **Paradise** and **Super Paradise**, and be prepared for big crowds in the summer.

DAY 3 – Take a day trip to **Delos**, the sacred island that can only be reached by boat from Mykonos.

IDEAS FOR YOUR VISIT
ANCIENT SITES (4 DAYS)

There are so many wonderful ancient sites in Greece that it can be hard to choose which to see. Some of the best turn out to be the off-the-beaten-track places, where you find yourself alone with antiquity, and can connect with the past in a beautiful setting.

DAY 1 – Enjoy the sites of Athens, including the **Acropolis**, the **Agora**, and the **Kerameikos Cemetery** … and as many more as can be fitted in.

DAY 2 – Visit the sacred site at **Delphi**, in its magnificent mountain setting, either by driving or by taking an organised excursion from Athens.

DAY 3 – Drive to the Peloponnese, visiting **Acrocorinth**, **Mycenae**, **Tiryns** and **Epidauros**, and spend the night in the delightful town of **Nauplion**.

DAY 4 – An early start for a beautiful drive across the **Peloponnese** to the site of the original Olympic Games at **Olympia**, a very special ancient site indeed.

ISLAND HOPPING

See also Getting Around: By Ship, p32.
It's very easy to see several Greek islands on the same short trip, by using the ferries to go island-hopping. It's best to avoid the summer months of July and August, when accommodation may be in short supply – but also the temperatures can be unbearably hot.

Outside the hot high summer, though, travelling on from one island to another new discovery is one of the greatest pleasures of visiting Greece. It's best done in the Aegean, in the Cyclades and Dodecanese, or from Athens to the islands in the Saronic Gulf if time is limited. The Ionian Islands aren't great for hopping between, as moving from one to another sometimes involves a trip to the mainland and back, although Kefalonia, Zakynthos and Ithaca are all linked and can make for an enjoyable trip.

The best experiences are often to be had with no planned itinerary, but just to go where the ferries and the mood take you – and you may also want to allow for falling in love with one particular island, when you decide the hopping has to stop for a while. This is another reason for going in spring or autumn, and not booking accommodation ahead. Note too that ferry timetables are much more limited in the winter months.

BEACHES

You could travel to a different Greek island every week of the year, and to a different beach every day of the week, and still not run out of sand. Greece has some of the best beaches in the Mediterranean, and sun-worshippers should be sure to choose the right kind for them. On Santorini, for example, due to its volcanic origins, there are dramatic-looking beaches of red and black pebbles, and long beaches of black sand.

If you prefer the more conventional golden or silver sands, the Ionian islands also have some fine beaches. Several of them are used by the Greek National Tourism Organisation to promote the country, so you can be sure they're the most picturesque beaches you can find anywhere. Some islands, like Symi, have rather poor beaches … so plan ahead, or just move on to the next island.

THE MOUNTAINS OF THE NORTH

Anyone who thinks of Greece only in terms of beaches and islands is in for a wonderful surprise if they visit the north of the country. Here there are dramatic mountains, snow-covered for several months over the winter, and forests where wolves and bears still roam. Everyone has heard of Mount Olympus, home of the Gods and Greece's highest peak, in the east of the country, but fewer are familiar with mountains like Astraka (2,436m/7,992ft) and Gamila (2,497m/8,192ft) in the Pindus range, which offer challenges to climbers and hikers alike.

TOUR BY RAIL

See also Getting Around: By Train, p34.
The rail network isn't as extensive in Greece as in some countries, due in part to the rugged terrain, but it is possible to see some of the more beautiful parts by taking the train. There are two main networks, which connect in Athens. The northern network links Athens (Larissa Station) to Thessaloniki with branch lines to Halkída, Vólos, Tríkala and Kalambáka (Metéora), and northwest to Édessa and Kozáni; a line also runs from Thessaloniki to Alexandroúpoli

Gorge in Epirus

© Greek National Tourism Organisation

and Orestiáda on the way to Istanbul in Turkey. The southern network in the Peloponnese, which runs on a narrow gauge (982km/610mi), links Athens (Peloponnese Station) to Kalamáta via Patras and Pírgos (branch line to Olympia), or via Árgos–Nauplion and Trípoli. Some routes are very picturesque, especially the elevated section between Livadiá and Lamía (central Greece), which includes some impressive viaducts, and the rack railway through the Vouraïkós Gorge between Diakoftó and Kalávrita (Peloponnese).

MOTORCYCLE TOURS

Many Greeks use motorcycles as an economic form of transport, and visitors will find plenty of bikes, along with scooters and mopeds, to rent in all tourist areas. Motorcycles are relatively cheap, but care needs to be exercised. Only people already experienced in riding motorcycles should consider renting one. Greece has the highest death rate on the roads in the European Union, due in part to the rather reckless nature of Greek driving, and to the state of the roads in more rural places.

That said, taking to the open road as an easy rider will take you to many beautiful parts of the country, quickly and cheaply. Consider riding in the mountains of the north, heading east to the border with Turkey, or northeast to the Bulgarian border. Drive inland away from the beaches even on some of the smaller islands and you'll see a part of rural Greece not all visitors experience.

What to See and Do

OUTDOOR FUN

A trip to Greece conjures up sea, sun and historical sites, and it is easy to forget that it is also a mountainous country with ideal winter sports weather at altitude.

In many regions or islands, local tourist offices provide lists of the sporting activities available. Those looking for more specific information on a particular sport or activity should consult the appropriate federation.

BIRDWATCHING

Greece has a hugely varied birdlife and 196 Important Bird Areas (IBAs). The Hellenic Ornithological Society is a great place to get information about birds and their habitats in Greece *see Introduction to Greece: Fauna.* Specialist companies offer half-day and full-day tours to places like Athens and Mount Parnossos and longer trips of 5–7 days on Lesbos and Lemnos.

CANOEING AND KAYAKING

Several organisations propose trips either to **Lake Kremastá** or **Lake Plastira** in Thessaly. For further information, contact the Federation of Canoeing and Kayaking or specialist agencies.

- ◆ **Federation of Canoeing and Kayaking**
  📞 210 41 11 764 and 210 41 14 504, www.canoekayak.gr
- ◆ **Trekking-Hellas**
  📞 210 33 10 323, www.trekking.gr

CLIMBING AND MOUNTAINEERING

These activities are growing in popularity and provide an opportunity to have close contact with nature. And what could be more exciting than clambering over cliffs overlooking the Aegean Sea (well-maintained trails in Chios, Mílos, Kálimnos, Mykonos), the Kofinias peak in Crete, or happening upon a monk in meditation after climbing a rock in Metéora? Several associations organise relatively easy trips according to the number of participants. A number of agencies also offer day excursions or even longer trips. For information, contact:

- ◆ **Hellenic Federation of Mountaineering and Climbing**
  📞 210 36 45 904, www.eooa.gr
- ◆ **Trekking-Hellas**
  📞 210 33 10 323, www.trekking.gr

CYCLING

Greece is not one of the classic European bike destinations and part of the reason for this is that only 20 percent of the country is flat. This, though, makes for an exciting terrain with the benefit of not cycling along routes popular with large numbers of cyclists. A specialist company offering cycling tours at various levels of difficulty is **Bike Greece** (📞 210 45 35 567; www.bikegreece.com).

Their entry-level trips introduce the basics of mountain biking and are suitable for those seeking a few hours biking per day; three-quarters of the cycling time is spent off main roads.

The next level up is for mountain bikers with previous experience who are looking for a challenging ride across mountain ranges and along dramatic coastlines. Whatever your level, all travellers cycle in a group and stay in the same accommodation along the way.

Another company worth checking out for their cycling tour that explores the region around Mount Olympus is **Hooked on Cycling** (📞 01501 740 985; www.hookedoncycling.co.uk).

As a cyclist you have a van supporting you during the day and transferring your luggage; the region is hilly and will appeal to those with a good level of fitness.

By following the links at www.info hub.com you can find information on a number of other companies offering cycling tours in Greece.

GOLF

Golfing is not as popular a sport in Greece as elsewhere, but there are courses to discover and the sport continues to grow. One of the most sophisticated courses is the Glyfada Golf Club (www.ggca.gr), outside Athens in the seaside suburb of Glyfada. This pine-studded course with a view of the Saronic Gulf islands is open for most of the year. Other well-established courses are to be found on Corfu, on Rhodes and in northern Greece, at Halkidiki.

For further information contact the **Hellenic Golf Federation** at Glífáda (📞 210 894 1933; www.hgf.gr).

SAILING

Sailing is an excellent way to explore the Greek islands, provided that you are an expert sailor, and a holiday based around sailing is easy to arrange in a country with countless miles of coastline. There are a number of companies offering sailing holidays, and several agencies rent yachts equipped with a captain. You can also hire a yacht individually through specialised organisations. For information contact the **Federation**

Olympic Games

The Games, which the ancient Greeks traced back to 776 BC, were part of a religious festival devoted to Zeus. The event became so important that by the 7C BC, for the duration of the Games, a truce was declared by states at war so that athletes could not be prevented from journeying to Olympia in the Peloponnese. Only men participated and women had their own single running event, also at Olympia, called the *Heraea*. The first modern Olympic Games took place in Athens in 1896 and the next one will take place in London in 2012.

of Sailing, Marina Dimou Kallitheas, P.O. Box 78550, Athens, ℘210 94 04 825. Some companies offer **flotilla holidays** which take the form of a group of yachts travelling together, with each yacht equipped with berths for couples and singles. An example is Setsail Holidays (℘01787 310 445; www.setsail.co.uk) with their one- and two-week flotilla holidays starting in May and carrying on through to

October. Flotilla holidays are also available through Sunsail (℘0844 463 6495; www.sunsail.co.uk), a large company that also organises yacht charters and sailing schools.

At island resorts it is usually possible to find small boats and dinghies with their own motors available for rent by the day. The chartering of a yacht and crew (see, for example, www.anemos-yachting.gr or www.tenrag.com) tends only to make economic sense if you are able to form a group to share the expenses. Between the end of June and early September, however, there are strong Aegean winds (meltémi) that should be borne in mind by anyone new to sailing. The west coast of the Peloponnese is also affected by a northwest wind in the summer months, especially during the afternoons. If you are not in the hands of an experienced sailor, care and attention should always be exercised and expert knowledge sought before heading out onto the water.

Cruise Planners (℘0877 252 0508; www.seafarecruises.com) cover the world and this includes cruises in the eastern Mediterranean.

See also www.flotillasailing.co.uk.

Boat moored off the beach, Ithaca

©Alexander Hare/Dreamstime.com

SCUBA DIVING

This sport is strictly controlled to avoid theft of antiquities.

For information, contact the **Hellenic Centre for Scuba Diving** (☎210 41 21 708) or **Piraeus Diving Centre** (☎210 46 34 297), or consult the website www.greeka.com/greece/greece-diving.htm for a useful list of the some of the major diving schools in the country, Despite restrictions, it is possible to go on a cruise with special diving classes to enjoy the lovely underwater sights.

Before going on your own, contact the **Hellenic Institute of Marine Archaeology** (☎210 82 59 668; www.ienae.gr) to find out which sites are authorised.

Snorkelling is not as regulated and the necessary gear is not difficult to hire or purchase in Greece.

SWIMMING

With so many islands with sandy bays, swimming is always an option for visitors and nothing beats the open water for fun and an exhilarating sense of freedom. It makes good sense, though, to always check on the safety factor as regards any particular beach. On the more popular islands, beaches are monitored by lifeguards and a system of flags indicates where and when it is safe to swim.

Organised beaches, sometimes found close to the big cities on the mainland, may impose a daily charge and offer in return freshwater showers, changing rooms, umbrellas offering respite from the sun, toilets, bars, restaurants and lifeguards. Some organised beaches have a habit of not allowing visitors to bring their own food and drinks so check beforehand and ensure you know what the ground rules are.

On most of the islands, the spectacular beaches and coves are free of charge to everyone and the only cost will occur if you choose to hire a deckchair or parasol.

Beware of the heat of the sun between midday and around 4pm; the best time to swim is before or after these hours. The use of a sunscreen is essential, especially for the first few days on a beach.

Topless swimming and sunbathing is widespread and many resort areas will have a particular beach, or a section of one, that is unofficially devoted to nude swimming and sunbathing. SwimTrek (www.swimtrek.com) claims to be the world's leading swimming holiday operator and its swimming tours include Greece. The tours involve island hopping, with an emphasis on locations where swimming opportunities are at their best. One of their well-established holidays is to the island of Naxos, and it includes swimming along the coast with opportunities to swim alongside monk seals, sea turtles and dolphins.

WALKING

Some companies offer dedicated walking holidays and one of the best in this respect is Exodus (☎ 020 8675 5550; www.exodus.co.uk). The company has programmes in different parts of Greece, including the Cyclades and Evia. Also worth checking out is **Ramblers** (☎01707 331133; www.ramblersholidays.co.uk) and their trips feature a variety of destinations like the Sporades, Cyclades and Crete. There is also the option with Ramblers of a walking holiday based around some of the Classical sights of ancient Greece. **Headwater** (☎016 0672 0199; www.headwater.com) is a company specialising in walking holidays including one on Crete. **ATG Oxford** (☎01865 315 678; www.atg-oxford.co.uk) have a variety of walking tours, one of which is an 11-day escorted walk in the west of Crete. **Explore** (☎0845 013 1537; www.explore.co.uk) offer walking holidays on Corfu, Crete and the Aegean islands.

Jonathan's Tours are based in France (☎00 33 561046447; www.jonathans tours.com) and this family business organises guided walking tours in Greece, including one on Crete that focuses on the role of Cretan and British resistance fighters on the

Kayaking in Vikos Gorge

© Antonis-Nikolopoulos/Greek National Tourism Organisation

island during the German occupation in World War II. For walks on Symi, contact **Marengo Guides Walks** (*℘01485 532 710; www.marengo walks.com*).

Walking Plus (*℘020 8835 8303; www.walkingplus.co.uk*) offer one-week guided walking holidays based on either Naxos or Tinos as well as two- and three-week trips that combine Amorgos, Tinos and Naxos. Self-guided walks organised by travel companies are not very common but Walking Plus offers this on Tinos and Naxos. They are longer and more challenging than their guided counterparts but are also more adventurous, as many of the paths are not marked.

WHITE-WATER RAFTING

Trips varying in length from a weekend to three weeks are organised on different class rivers and are coupled with theoretical and practical lessons on site (*essential*).
The most popular areas to practise this sport are Evritania (in the Karpensíssi region) or in Grevená and Arachtos

(contact **Trekking-Hellas** *℘210 33 10 323; www.trekking.gr*) as well as Evinos and in the Alfiós gorges. September–November and March–May are the best months for rafting in Greece.

WINDSURFING AND WATERSKIING

The many bays that characterise Greek islands are perfect for learning to windsurf and any resort worth its salt will have a choice of places offering to rent boards and tutor beginners. Especially good in this respect are the islands of Kos, Lefkada, Samos, Lesbos, the west coast of Corfu and the resorts on Crete. Waterskiing tends to be confined to the larger resorts and instructional courses are nearly always available. Parasailing is also available in the more popular island resorts. **Sportif** (*℘01273 844 919; www. sportif.travel*) is a travel company specialising in watersports and one of their packages is a windsurfing-based holiday on Karpathos, one of the most southerly of the Greek islands. The island has acquired a reputation as an excellent high-wind venue and is able to offer challenges for the experienced as well as shallow, flat water that is ideal for beginners. Other windsurfing holiday packages are available in Rhodes, Kos, Crete and Samos. **Peligoni Club** (www.peligoni.com) is an upmarket resort on the island of Zakynthos that concentrates on water sports like windsurfing, sailing, wakeboarding and waterskiing. With good winds on a daily basis, watersports enthusiasts are kept busy and the prevailing summer winds along the island's northeasterly coast are ideal for outdoors fun.

WINTER SPORTS

Greece isn't one of Europe's major winter sports destinations, but nevertheless its mountainous landscape ensures that there are plenty of ski resorts to choose from.

Skiing

Greek ski resorts have expanded rapidly, but they still lack the services provided by many large ski stations. They are nonetheless of high quality and most of them are relatively inexpensive. On-site lodging is still sparse, and it is often necessary to stay in villages far from the slopes. For information, contact the **Hellenic Ski Federation**, 7 Odós Karagiorgi Servias, 105 63 Athens ✆ 210 32 30 182, www.eox.gr.

Centres for skiing range from small ones like the four slopes at Mount Helmos (✆ 0692 22661) near Kalávrita, to the 16 slopes at Mount Parnassos (✆ 0234 22694) which are divided according to difficulty and types of running. The slopes at Mount Parnassos are the most popular in Greece, partly because they can be easily reached from Athens. If you want to ski with the gods then there are two slopes at Mount Olympus but, because they are run by the Greek army, you need to obtain advance permission (✆ 0493 23467). Information on all the skiing centres in Greece can be found at www.greek travel.com/winter/ski.html.

Snowboarding

Snowboarding was virtually unknown in Greece before the 1980s but the sport has spread rapidly over the last few decades. The first Panhellenic Slalom took place in 1994 with around 60 Greek athletes taking part in the event. Two years later the Hellenic Ski Federation gave its official blessing and the first snowboard national team was organised.

One of the best places for snowboarding is the Kalavrita Ski Resort on Mount Helmos. Here you will find a snowboarding park and all the facilities of a well-developed ski centre. The ski centre is open daily throughout the ski season (Dec–Apr).

ACTIVITIES FOR KIDS

In this guide, sights of particular interest to children are indicated with a ▲▲ symbol. Some attractions may offer discount fees for children. Greece is a great country for kids, especially the Greek islands with sandy beaches and safe sheltered coves and the near certainty of finding other holidaymakers of a similar age. Depending on age, of course, activities like snorkelling, sailing, waterskiing, horse riding and beach volleyball are all options for young travellers. Greek people love children and bringing them along to a restaurant is rarely a problem.

SHOPPING

Local dealers have succeeded somewhat in adapting items of traditional provenance to the tourist market … but beware. Most souvenirs marked "traditional" are mass-produced elsewhere. It's worth seeking out authentic items made locally.

Good shopping begins in **Athens** because of the sheer range of available merchandise; see the Address Book section for Athens for more details. Find time to wander through the Central Market on Athinás St (open daily except Sunday) and, for the latest consumer goodies, the

Attica Mall on Panepistimiou St. **Crete**, and Rethymnon in particular, has a good weekly market and an arts and crafts bazaar in Souliou St. **Corfu Town** has a good range of shops, especially jewellery and leather goods. The island of Santorini is hard to beat when it comes to quality jewellery and arts and crafts and there is a better range of shops here than on any other of the Greek islands.

WOOD

Some islands such as the **Northern Sporades** are renowned for their furniture, and in the Peloponnese there is a tradition of making objects in wood, especially in the town of **Vitína** between Tripoli and Olympia.

JEWELLERY

In the 1950s, **Ilias Lalaounis** introduced themes from classical times into contemporary jewellery design. A goldsmiths' school was founded to train artisans in the necessary techniques. Since then, some extraordinary pieces drawing their inspiration from Minoan civilisation, Macedonia, classical Greece and Byzantium have been created. When buying jewellery it can be difficult at first glance to distinguish between the mass-produced and the hand-crafted, but the asking price should offer a good indication. In the areas popular with tourists there are many jewellery shops, most of which sell mass-produced items, which can make good-value souvenirs.

CARPETS AND TEXTILES

A legacy of Ottoman domination, there is a strong tradition of carpet weaving in **Thessaloniki**. Elsewhere in Greece, most notably in **Crete**, **Delphi** and **Epirus**, decorative textiles have been made incorporating traditional patterns for generations.

EVERYDAY OBJECTS

Ideal items to take home include *tavli* (game of Ottoman origin), *flitzanakia* (porcelain coffee cups), *keramika* (ceramic items from Siphnos, Rhodes and neighbouring islands), *bouzoukia* (the traditional stringed instrument) and the famous *kombolói* (worry beads).

CULINARY SPECIALITIES

Those looking to take home some of the memorable flavours of Greece have a wide choice: honey, fig or cherry jam, Aegina pistachios, Muscat from Samos or, of course, a bottle of ouzo or retsina. Greece's olive oil is world-renowned; the most famous comes from Crete.

BOOKS
ART AND ARCHAEOLOGY

Minoan and Mycenaean Art –
Reynold Higgins, Lyvia Morgan. (1997).
> A useful accompaniment if visiting Crete and Mycenae.

The Oxford Dictionary of Classical Myth and Religion – Simon Price. (2004).
> An authoritative guide to all aspects of ancient religious life and thought.

Classics: A Very Short Introduction – John Henderson. (2000). A very readable guide to how the Classics continue to influence our culture.

The Elgin Marbles: Should They Be Returned to Greece? – Hitchens, Browning, Binns. (1997).
> The background, the controversy and a point of view.

Illustrated Encyclopaedia of Ancient Greece – Sean Sheehan. (2003).
> Good, illustrated guide for young readers.

GEOGRAPHY AND HISTORY

The Spartans: An Epic History – Paul Cartledge. (2002). An exciting account by a noted historian.

The Ancient Olympic Games – Judith Swaddling. (1999). The history behind the Games.

Ill Met by Moonlight – W Stanley Moss (1999). The kidnapping of a German General from occupied Crete by two British officers and Cretan partisans.

The Flame of Freedom: The Greek War of Independence, 1821–1833 – David Brewer. (2001). An evenhanded account of courage and barbarism by Greeks and Turks alike.

Alexander the Great – Robert Lane Fox. (2004). The passion and the achievements of the great Greek warrior.

Atlas of Classical History. Richard Talbert. (1985). Over 100 maps of the ancient world.

Modern Greece: A Short History, CM Woodhouse. (1999). Exactly what the title indicates.

The Greeks: Crucible of Civilization. Paul Cartledge. (2001). Ancient history but told by a modern historian.

TRAVEL BOOKS: NON-FICTION

The Greek Islands – Lawrence Durrell. (2002). An evocative mix of memories, myth and history.

Reflections on a Marine Venus – Lawrence Durrell. (2000). A classic account of the island of Rhodes.

Roumeli: Travels in Northern Greece – Patrick Leigh Fermor. (2003). The ideal accompaniment when travelling in this corner of Greece.

Máni: Travels in the Southern Peloponnese – Patrick Leigh Fermor. (2003). The sister volume to the above.

Heart of Crete – Christopher Somerville. (2007). An absorbing memoir of Crete.

TRAVEL LITERATURE

Captain Corelli's Mandolin – Louis de Bernières. (2001). An engaging novel to read on the beach.

Zorba the Greek – Nikos Kazantzakis. (1946 or 2008). Also a classic film about Greece starring Anthony Quinn and Alan Bates, the original book is an equally lively read. Any of Kazantzakis' fiction makes for suitable reading for a visit to Crete.

FILMS

see Introduction to Greece: Cinema.

Never on Sunday – Jules Dassin (1959). Set in 1950s Piraeus, the story of an encounter between a prostitute and an American trying to comprehend the mysteries of Greek society. Dassin's finest Greek film, here directing his future wife Melina Mercouri.

Stella – Michael Kakoiánnis (1955). The film that launched Mercouri's career. A tender and tragic evocation of the poverty experienced by so many in Greece. Also by the same director: *Electra* (1962) and the famed *Zorba the Greek* (1964).

Z – Costas Gavras (1968). Inspired by the assassination of a Left-wing politician, this political thriller charts the rise of the Far Right in Greece.

Eternity and a Day – Theo Angelópoulos (1998). Contemporary Greek filmmaker with international reputation explores themes of identity, frontiers and memory.

300 – Zack Snyder (2006) Based on Frank Miller's graphic novel, *300* portrays a fictional and violent account of the Battle of Thermopylae, where King Leonidas and 300 Spartans fought against the invading Persian army.

Calendar of Events

For exact dates apply at tourist offices. In the Orthodox Church, Lent, Easter and Whitsun are fixed according to the Julian Calendar and may fall from one to four weeks earlier or later than in the Western church.

SPRING

MONDAY BEFORE LENT
Athens – Popular songs and dances near the temple of Zeus; kite-flying competition.

PALM SUNDAY AND HOLY SATURDAY
Corfu – St Spiridon's procession.

GOOD FRIDAY
Throughout Greece – Procession of the Epitáfios (image of Christ).

EASTER SATURDAY/SUNDAY
Throughout Greece – Midnight mass.

EASTER WEEK
Kálimnos – *Voriatikí* (North Wind), a men's dance.

Mégara (Attica) – Local festival: traditional dances in costume.

23 APRIL (ST GEORGE'S DAY)
Skála (Cephalonia) – Local festival.

MAY
Lesbos – Animal sacrifices, horse racing, dancing, religious festival (♿*see Lesvos*).

21–23 MAY
Langadás (NE of Thessaloniki and Agiá Eléni in Séres (NE of Thessaloniki) – Ritual ceremonies: the *Anastenarídes*, dance barefoot on hot coals holding icons of Saints Constantine and Helena.

29 MAY
Mystras – Commemoration of the death of Emperor Constantine Palaiologos on 29 May, 1453.

SUMMER

MAY–SEPTEMBER
Athens – Folkloric dancing by the Dora Stratou company.

JUNE–EARLY SEPTEMBER
Rhodes – Cultural Summer. Theatre, dance and music events.

Good Friday procession, Corfu Town

© World Illustrated/Photoshot

Athens Festival at the Odeon of Herodes Atticus

© Greek National Tourism Organisation

MID-JUNE–EARLY OCTOBER
Athens – Athens Festival: Greek drama, concerts, ballet. www.greekfestival.gr

SATURDAYS AND SUNDAYS, END JUNE–END AUGUST
Epidaurus – Festival of Ancient Drama. www.greekfestival.gr

MID-JUNE–EARLY OCTOBER
Patras – Cultural Festival.

END JUNE–END SEPTEMBER
Herakleion (Crete) – Festival.

19 JULY
Throughout Greece – Pilgrimages to peaks dedicated to St Elijah (Ilías).

JULY–AUGUST
Rethymnon – Renaissance Festival. www.rethymnon.biz/Reth/event/renaissance.htm
Delphi – Arts demonstrations.
Thassos – Ancient Drama Festival.

MID-JULY–SEPTEMBER
Rethymnon (Crete) – Wine festival.

AUGUST
Lefkada – Arts and folk festival.

6 AUGUST
Corfu – Procession of boats to the Isle of Pondikonísi.

11 AUGUST
Corfu – St Spiridon's procession.

12–15 AUGUST
Arhanés and Neápoli (Crete) – Art festival; wine tasting.

AUGUST–SEPTEMBER
Patra – Wine festival.
Dodona – Performances of Ancient Greek drama. ✆ 26510 82287.
Ioannina – Various arts events.

15 AUGUST
Tenos – Pilgrimage to the miraculous icon of the Virgin.

FIRST SUNDAY AFTER 15 AUGUST
Portariá (Mount Pelion) – Representation of a traditional country wedding.
Skiathos – Procession of the Epitáfios (image of the Virgin).

LAST SUNDAY IN AUGUST
Kritsá (Crete) – Representation of a traditional country wedding.

27

Float in the Carnival, Patra

© Greek National Tourism Organisation

END AUGUST–EARLY SEPTEMBER
Zakynthos – Zakynthos
  Environmental Film Festival
  ✆695 29870.

SEPTEMBER
Thessaloniki – International
  Trade Fair. www.tif.gr
Xánthi – Carnival.

*Thessaloniki International
Film Festival*

© MotionTeam/Thessaloniki International Film Festival

14 SEPTEMBER
Préveli – Religious festival of the
  True Cross; pilgrimage.

AUTUMN

OCTOBER
Thessaloniki – Film Festival.

OCTOBER–NOVEMBER
Thessaloniki – St Demetrios'
  procession; Dimitria festival.

WINTER

8 NOVEMBER
Arkádi (Crete) – Parade and
  traditional dances in memory of
  the sacrifice of the defenders of
  the monastery.

30 NOVEMBER
(ST ANDREW'S DAY)
Patra – Procession in honour of
  the patron saint of Patras.

24 AND 31 DECEMBER
Throughout Greece – Children
  sing *Kálanda* in the streets.

6 JANUARY (EPIPHANY)
Piraeus and other ports – Blessing of
  the sea and immersion of a cross,
  retrieved by swimmers.

FEBRUARY–MARCH
Patra – Carnival, the most
  important in Greece: procession
  of floats. www.carnivalpatras.gr
Athens – Carnival with masks and
  disguises.
Skyros – Carnival; costume
  procession; traditional dances.
Náoussa (Macedonia) – Carnival of
  the *Boúles*, masked dancers.

Know Before You Go

USEFUL WEBSITES

The Internet enables visitors to contact tourist offices, consult programmes and brochures, and make bookings online.

www.gnto.gr
Greek National Tourist Office.

www.culture.gr
Website of the Ministry of Culture, with lists of sites and museums, and numerous links; in English and Greek.

www.travelinfo.gr
Good source of information for the Cyclades, Dodecanese and Crete.

www.gtp.gr
Connection and timetable details for ferry services; links to operators' sites for booking.

www.ferries.gr
Schedules, connections and prices for ferry services from mainland Greece to the islands and Europe.

www.greek-tourism.gr
General information for travel to and from Greece.

www.phantis.com
Comprehensive search engine for all aspects of Greece.

www.greek-islands.org
Site created by a devotee of the Cyclades; good tips and addresses.

www.greece-travel-secrets.com
Two travel writers share their love of Greece.

www.explorecrete.com
Links, blogs and general information about Crete.

TOURIST OFFICES

GREEK NATIONAL TOURIST ORGANISATION (GNTO), ELINIKÓS ORGANISMÓS TOURISMOÚ (EOT)

Information and brochures on all regions of Greece are available from the following official tourist offices:

- 4 Conduit Street,
  London W1S 2DJ
  ℘020 7495 9300; Fax 020 7495 4057; info@gnto.co.uk; www.visitgreece.gr
- 645 Fifth Avenue, Olympic Tower,
  New York, NY 10022
  ℘212 421 5777; Fax 212 826 6940;
- 91 Scollard Street, 2nd Floor,
  Toronto, Ontario M5R 1G4
  ℘416 968 2220; Fax 416 968 6533
- 37–49 Pitt Street,
  Sydney, NSW 2000
  ℘00612 9241 1663, 9252 1441; Fax 00612 9241 2499

LOCAL TOURIST OFFICES

Local tourist offices generally supply information on accommodation, sightseeing and transport. The addresses and telephone numbers of these offices appear after the 🛈 in the introduction section for each entry in the Discovering Greece section.

INTERNATIONAL VISITORS
EMBASSIES AND CONSULATES ABROAD

- **United Kingdom**
  1A Holland Park, London W11 3TP
  ℘020 7229 3850;
  Fax 020 7229 7221;
  www.mfa.gr/london

- **USA**
  2217 Massachusetts Avenue NW, Washington, DC 20008
  ℘202 939 1300; Fax 202 939 1324;
  www.mfa.gr/washington

- **Canada**
  80 MacLaren Street, Ottawa, Ontario, K2P 0K6
  ℘613 238 62 71/3;
  Fax 613 238 5676;
  www.mfa.gr/ottawa

♦ **Australia**
9 Turrana Street, Yarralumla,
Canberra 2600
☎00612 62733011
Fax 0061262 732 620;
www.mfa.gr/canberra

IN GREECE

Information on all embassies and
consulates is available from the
Ministry of Foreign Affairs ☎(210) 36
11 058 (8am to 2pm).

♦ **Australian** Embassy and
Consulate, Level 6, Thon Building,
Kifissias & Alexandras Ave,
Ambelokipi, Athens 115 23
☎210 870 4000; Fax 210 870 4111.
www.greece.embassy.gov.au
♦ **Canadian** Embassy, 4 Ioannou
Gennadíou, 115 21 Athens
☎210 727 3400; Fax 210 727 3480.
www.athens.gc.ca
♦ **Irish** Embassy, 7 Leofóros Vasileos
Konstantinou, 106 74 Athens
☎210 723 2771; Fax 210 729 3383
♦ **New Zealand** General Consulate,
268 Kifissias Ave, 152 32 Halandri
☎210 687 4700
♦ **South African** Embassy and
Consulate, 60 Leofóros Kifissias,
151 25 Maroussi
☎210 610 6645; Fax 210 610 6640
♦ **USA** Embassy and Consulate,
91 Leofóros Vassilissi Sofías,
101 60 Athens
☎210 721 2951.
http://athens.usembassy.gov
♦ **UK** Embassy and Consulate,
1 Odós Ploutárchou, 106 75 Athens
☎210 727 2600.
http://ukingreece.fco.gov.uk

ENTRY REQUIREMENTS

A **passport** or (for EU residents) a valid
identity card is required for a stay not
exceeding 90 days. For stays of longer
than 90 days a visa must be obtained
and this can be done either at the
Greek embassy in your own country
before you depart, or, if already in
Greece, by contacting the Bureau
of Aliens in Athens at 173 Leofóros
Alexandras, ☎(210) 770 5711.

A national driving licence is sufficient
for citizens of EU member countries
and for US drivers for up to 90 days
but an international driving licence
is necessary for other drivers. An
international **green insurance card**,
covering vehicles driven outside their
country of origin and issued by the
Motor Insurers' Bureau, is required
if you drive your own car in Greece;
check with your insurance provider or
www.mib-hellas.gr.

CUSTOMS REGULATIONS

EU travellers can bring into or out
of Greece any amount of goods,
including drinks, for their personal
use. More than 10 litres of spirits in
your luggage would not be accepted
as goods for personal use.

Non-EU travellers, when leaving
Greece, are subject to a duty-free
allowance of 1 litre of spirits or 2
litres of liquors (sherry or port), plus
2 litres of wine, 200 cigarettes and
50 grammes of perfume.

Vehicles can be imported by visitors
without payment of duty if the vehicle
is intended only for personal use and
for the duration of the period of the
visit. In this context, a visitor is defined
as someone arriving in Greece who
has their habitual residence abroad
and stay abroad for at least 185 days
in a period of 12 months.

The spouse, parents, and children
of the vehicle owner may use the
vehicle, provided they are also visitors
as defined above. The vehicle cannot
be transferred, leased, loaned or
donated and heavy fines are imposed
if these rules are broken.

Prohibited Items

Prohibited items include weapons,
explosives and drugs. Greece is very
strict on drug use and anyone found
with drugs in their possession will be
dealt with severely. Anyone taking
medication should have a certificate
from their doctor, and codeine is
banned in Greece unless you have a
medical certificate.

Domestic Animals

An **international vaccination card** and a **certificate of good health** issued in the country of origin 15 days before departure, are required for all animals entering Greece.

HEALTH

International visitors from EU countries should acquire a **European Health Insurance Card** *(available online at www.ehic.ie or ℘0871 434 9073)* which entitles the holder to urgent treatment for accident or unexpected illness. Any such treatment would be available at the most basic level provided for in IKA hospitals (the Greek equivalent to National Health Service hospitals in the UK) and EU travellers should consider taking out health cover as part of a travel insurance policy. Such a policy would allow treatment at a private hospital or from a private doctor. With or without a European Health Insurance Card, visitors can expect to be charged part of the cost of X-rays, special tests and prescription drugs; be sure to keep receipts for any payments made as you will need these to make a claim on any health insurance policy.

Nationals of non-EU countries should check that their insurance policy covers them for overseas travel, including doctor's visits, medication and hospitalisation in Greece (you may need to take out **supplemental insurance**).

All prescription drugs should be clearly labelled; carry a copy of the prescription with you. There are no compulsory **inoculations** for Greece but it makes sense to check that you are up to date with tetanus and polio injections.

ACCESSIBILITY

Away from Athens, facilities for disabled travellers are limited, although the helpful and friendly nature of the Greeks can sometimes be relied upon to minimise any problems. Visitors cannot expect to find wheelchair ramps at street corners and road crossings; beeping systems for the sight-impaired at road crossings are rare.

Some ferries and aircraft serving the islands offer access for wheelchairs but this is more often the exception than the rule. On some of the more popular islands, like Rhodes and Kos, it is possible to find hotels with facilities for the disabled but do not take anything for granted and always check ahead of your visit.

For UK travellers, **advice for the disabled** is available from RADAR *(12 City Forum, 250 City Road, London EC1V 8AF; ℘020 7250 3222, www.radar.org.uk)* and one of their publications, *There & Back*, is about travel issues for the disabled.

Tourism for All *(℘0303 303 0146, www.tourismforall.org.uk)* is another organisation with useful advice and information. Disability Now *(www.disabilitynow.org.uk)* has some information for travellers going to Greece and, in particular, suitable accommodation in Crete.

US and Canadian travellers can access information and advice from Mobility International USA *(132 E Broadway, Suite 343, Eugene, Oregon USA 97401; ℘541 343 1284, www.miusa.org)*. There is also a very useful link at www.emerginghorizons.com for travellers to Greece and this has information on relevant tour companies and locations in Greece of interest to disabled travellers.

Other **useful websites** for disabled travellers planning a trip to Greece include www.greekhotel.com. This site is devoted to information about suitable hotels and accommodation in general. Using the search function at www.gogreece.about.com brings up useful links providing information on wheelchair-friendly resorts and hotels, access for the disabled at some of the major archaeological sites, use of the metro system in Athens and various other issues of interest.

Getting There and Getting Around

BY PLANE

There are daily flights to Athens from many cities by international carriers and by **Olympic Air**, the national air carrier of Greece (96 Leofóros Singrou, 117 41 Koukaki, Athens, ℘210 92 69 111; reservations 210 9 666 666; www.olympicair.com).

Reserve well in advance, especially in summer. International flights also serve Herakleion, Rhodes and Thessaloniki.

Some of the best deals on airfares to Greece are likely to be available online and any search engine will bring up all the websites of all the main companies. An instant fare quotation is usually available.

OLYMPIC AIR OFFICES:

♦ 11 Conduit Street, **London** W1S 2LP ℘0871 2000 500 or 020 7399 1500; Terminal 2, Heathrow Airport ℘020 8745 7339 or 8759 5884; Gatwick Airport ℘01293 535 353 or 01293 502 469
♦ 1 Penn Plaza, Suite 1416, **New York** 10119 ℘855 359 6200 (toll free)
♦ Breakaway Aviation Services, P.O. BOX R183, **Sydney**, NSW 2000 ℘2 9250 9450

INTERNATIONAL CARRIERS:

♦ **British Airways**
Reservations
℘0844 493 0787 (from the UK);
1-800-AIRWAYS (from the US).
www.britishairways.com
♦ **Brussels Airlines**
Reservations
℘0905 6095 609 (UK);
℘02 723 2362 (outside the UK).
www.brusselsairlines.com
♦ **Delta Airlines**
Reservations ℘800 221 1212 (in the US); ℘404 765 500 (outside

Athens	Mykonos
Cephalonia	Patra
Corfu	Préveza
Chania (Crete)	Rhodes (Dodecanese)
Herakleion (Crete)	Samos
Kalamáta	Santorini
Kavála	Skiathos (Sporades)
Kos (Dodecanese)	Thessaloniki
Lemnos	Zakynthos
Lesbos	

the US); ℘0845 600 0950 (UK); www.delta.com
♦ **Aegean Airlines**
www.aegeanair.com
♦ **Olympic Air**
www.olympicair.com

In summer there are **charter flights** from the UK to dozens of Greek destinations, mainly in the islands but also to the mainland. The **domestic airline network** (*see Aegean airlines and Olympic Air, above*) is extensive. Fares that are equal to a first-class boat ticket are good value. It is advisable to book early in season as domestic services are very popular with both Greeks and tourists, particularly during Greek public holidays. Some lines operate small planes which may suffer long delays in the event of strong winds and bad weather.

BY SHIP

In general there is daily **ferry service** from Piraeus to the well-frequented islands with a weekly or twice-weekly service to the other islands. Vessels include large ferries, which are very dependable and travel all year even in rough weather; hydrofoils or catamarans (twice as fast as traditional ferries); and launches or caiques operate in season between the islands. *See the Address Books in* the Discovering Greece *sections for further information*. Ships on the major routes have two, three or four classes. Tourist (C) class accommodation consists of a lounge fitted with

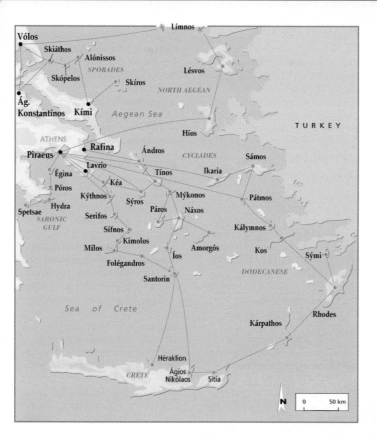

armchairs and a bar-cafeteria, with easy access to the upper deck for a good view.

Timetables (which may vary from week to week, especially in mid-season) are available from tourist offices (GNTO/EOT) abroad and in Athens; they are published every month by the GNTO (EOT) and by the excellent website **Greek Travel Pages**, **www.gtp.gr**. Timetables are also available at www.greekferries.gr. The timetables of ships operated by private companies are sometimes unreliable. The list of services posted on information boards on the dockside is not always exhaustive or up to date; it is advisable to enquire in the offices of the different shipping-lines round the harbour.

Be aware that ferry crossings are always subject to delay or cancellation due to weather, so plan accordingly. It's best to return to Athens at least one day before your flight home, for example.

Tickets for all trips (ferries and hydrofoils) are issued in the shipping-line offices or at mobile counters on the dockside. Be sure to book in advance for car ferries in season and for berths on night ferries (Crete and Rhodes). The ferries are likely to be crowded during Greek public holidays.
Piraeus Central Port Authority
℘ 210 45 11 310-17.

Information also available from:
- **Blue Star Ferries**,
  www.bluestarferries.com
- **Minoan Lines**
  ℘ 210 414 5700;
  www.minoan.gr

PLEASURE CRUISING

For the hire of yachts, motor cruisers and caiques, with or without crew, apply to the GNTO (EOT). The Cyclades and the Sporades Islands are the most popular for pleasure cruising. The Ionian Islands, protected from the wind, are less popular. The main moorings for pleasure craft are shown on Michelin map 737.

BY TRAIN

See also Ideas For Your Visit: Tour By Rail p18.

There are rail links from northern Europe to Athens changing at Munich, Cologne or Venice. For information apply to **GNTO (EOT)**, or to **Greek Railways (OSE)** 1–3 Odós Karolou, Athens ☎210 529 7005, www.ose.gr. Also consult www.seat61.com for advice on train travel to and within Greece.

The Greek railway system is not very extensive. Fares are inexpensive and trains run frequently, but travel is slower than by bus. There are ordinary trains and wagon-lits organised by the **Hellenic Railways Organisation (OSE)**.

BY CAR

Travellers wishing to visit Greece by car from Western Europe are advised to travel by ferry from Italy. Crossings have become more popular and more frequent in recent years. From Italy, ports include Venice, Trieste, Ancona, Bari and Brindisi; ports in Greece include Corfu, Igoumenitsa, Patras and Piraeus.

Reserve at least two months in advance in summer. For information, contact **www.greekferries.gr**, or **www.ferries.gr**.

DRIVING IN GREECE

The speed limit is 100kph (62mph) or 120kph (74mph) on motorways, 80kph (50mph) on trunk roads, and 50kph (31mph) in built-up areas. Seatbelts are compulsory.

Drive with caution; Greece has the highest rate of fatal accidents in Europe. The Greek road network, which now consists of over 117,000km (72,700mi) of roads, has improved considerably during the past 30 years. There are two motorways (with tolls) linking Athens to Patras and Thessaloniki. The other roads tend to be slow and winding because of the terrain and relief. There are still some unsurfaced local and regional roads which carry heavy traffic including buses. Roads are frequently under repair, and delays are inevitable as there are often no alternative routes.

Extra care is required in the countryside, as there are numerous flocks of sheep or goats as well as donkeys in mountain areas.

Donkeys on road near Kritsá, Crete

© P. de Franqueville/MICHELIN

The roads are sometimes poorly signposted, although many of the signs are written in Roman as well as Greek lettering; the main sights are indicated in English. Off the beaten track, road signs are often rudimentary and are only in Greek; it's a good idea to familiarise yourself with the Greek alphabet.

The Greek Automobile Touring Club (ELPA) has about 40 offices throughout the country and runs a roadside breakdown service (OVELPA – ☎104) which is free to members of other national Automobile or Touring Clubs.

PARKING

There is no metered parking in central Athens and finding a space during the day can be difficult. The bus or metro is an easier way of getting around. Illegal parking can result in the confiscation of a number plate, returnable only upon payment of a fine.

ACCIDENTS

In the event of a road accident, a police officer must compile a report, a copy of which is given to the parties involved. Greece's many garages are usually well equipped to deal with incidents of minor damage.

PETROL STATIONS

These are frequent enough except on some mountain roads. The price of petrol tends to be less than in other European countries. Most service stations do not accept credit cards; wait for an attendant, as self-service is not available in Greece.

RENTAL CARS

It is possible to hire a car from rental offices in the cities and towns, at airports and railway stations, and at large hotels. Rentals are by the day; be sure to check the condition of the vehicle before signing the contract:

- **Avis** www.avis.gr
- **Europcar** www.europcar-greece.gr/en/
- **Hertz** www.hertz.gr

JOURNEY TIMES FROM ATHENS	
Argos	5hrs
Cephalonia	8hrs
Corfu	11hrs
Corinth	1hr 30min
Delphi	3hrs
Epidaurus	2hrs 30min
Ioannina	7hrs 30min
Halkída	1hr 30min
Kalamáta	4hrs 30min
Kavála	10hrs
Lamía	3hrs 15min
Monemvassiá	6hrs
Nauplion	2hrs 30min
Olympia	5hrs 30min
Patra	3hrs
Sparta	4hrs
Thebes	1hr 30min
Thessaloniki	7hrs 30min

BY TAXI

Metered taxis can be hired at a taxi stand or will stop on request. Always ask the price before riding. Other passengers going in the same direction may share the taxi but will pay their own fare. Drivers will stop to pick up passengers going in the same direction, so don't hesitate to hail a taxi that is not completely full. When paying it is advisable not to offer a high-value note but to give the right (or nearly right) amount in change. The driver is allowed to add a supplement onto fares between Athens–Piraeus and Athens–airport. Taxis are yellow in Athens and grey or burgundy in the rest of the country.

MOPEDS

Renting a moped requires a valid driving licence. Clarify with the hirer whether rental is for a 24-hour period or only for the duration of the day (this has caused some confusion in the past). Check the condition of the vehicle and fuel quantity. Request a crash helmet, as they are compulsory.

BY COACH/BUS

The bus network is very extensive and the buses, some of which have air-conditioning, are a cheap and colourful way of exploring the country as they run to even the most remote places. Information is available at all bus stations.

The OSE railway company also runs bus services to the provinces. Information on services for the Athens region and intercity connections is available from local tourist offices and the GNTO (EOT). Intercity services are run by KTEL (a group of private bus companies). In principle, there are daily services with frequent express buses from Athens to the regional capitals. Journey times from Athens are indicated in the table below:

MAPS

For journey preparation and selection of your itinerary, refer to the listing of Michelin maps and plans at the back of this guide.

Where to Stay and Eat

WHERE TO STAY
USEFUL WEBSITES

www.greekhotel.com

Very comprehensive site with several thousand pages of entries that have detailed descriptions of Greek accommodation options.

www.travelguide.gr

Reviews of over 2,000 hotels throughout Greece and the islands, including current rates and online booking option.

www.hotelsofgreece.com

Personal reviews of recommended hotels by Greek travel guru Matt Barrett.

CATEGORIES

Hotels are described in the Address Books within the Discovering section of this guide.

Comfort, location, quality of service and value were our criteria when selecting establishments. All have been visited and carefully chosen. Note that in popular destinations such as Athens or Mykonos, it can be difficult to find good-value accommodation. Always reserve well in advance in high season.

Our selection is divided into four price brackets: ☺ (under €65 in large cities and high-demand areas; under €45 elsewhere); ☺☺ (€65 to €100 in large cities and high-demand areas; €45 to €65 elsewhere); ☺☺☺ (€100 to €160 in large cities and high-demand areas, €65 to €100 elsewhere); and ☺☺☺☺ (more than €160 in large cities and high-demand areas; more than €100 elsewhere). These categories appear in the Legend on the cover flap.

GNTO SCHEME

The Greek hotel sector is well developed, offering everything from luxury hotels to rooms in private houses.

Prices vary according to categories established by the GNTO (EOT). B- and C-class hotels are usually clean and reasonably comfortable; all rooms have facilities. D hotels are simpler but often have rooms with facilities. D and E hotels do not serve breakfast but there are usually cafés nearby.

The following price categories apply:

- ◆ **Luxury** €180 upwards
- ◆ **A** €130 to €300
- ◆ **B** €90 to €170
- ◆ **C** €60 to €135
- ◆ **D** €40 to €65
- ◆ **E** €25 to €50

This classification applies to establishments approved by the GNTO (EOT), which display a blue and yellow plaque, and a full list of prices. Details can be obtained from local tourist offices. Note that prices often halve out of season.

HOTELS

Rooms are available by the night; credit-card details may be requested when the reservation is made. If staying on the islands, tell your hotel on which ferry you will arrive and they may come to meet you.

ROOMS IN PRIVATE HOUSES

Outside large towns and resorts it is common to take a room in a private house, particularly on the Aegean Islands where the boats are met by homeowners offering rooms. Signs reading Rooms or *Domatia* are also found on the roadsides. You can also check www.familyhotels.gr, an excellent website with links to organisations arranging this type of accommodation. Breakfast is not normally included. Credit cards are not widely accepted.

SELF-CATERING

Good value when travelling with a group of family or friends, this type of accommodation is generally of a high standard.

HOSTELS

There are youth hostels throughout Greece. Holders of an International Youth Hostel Federation card should get a list from the International Federation or from the **Greek Youth Hostels Association**, 75 Odós Damareos, Athens ✆ 210 751 9530, y-hostels@otenet.gr.

CAMPING

The Panhellenic Camping Association, 24 Odos Stadiou, Athens ✆ 210 362 1560, www.panhellenic-camping-union.gr, has information on all the official campsites operating in Greece. There are about 350 of these, though they are mostly only open in the summer months.

USEFUL WEBSITES

www.greecefoods.com
Matt Barrett's guide to Greek food, with links to reviews of restaurants in the areas of Greece he knows best, including Athens.
www.tripadvisor.com
TripAdvisor carries reviews by travellers to hundreds of restaurants in Greece, as well as their comprehensive hotel reviews.
www.ultimate-guide-to-greek-food.com
Very detailed guide to Greek food including many recipes, compiled by an Anglo-Greek couple from their traditional family recipes.

CATEGORIES

Selected restaurants are described in the Address Books within the Discovering section of this guide.
Eating places have been chosen based on a combination of atmosphere, location, quality of food and value for money. Some of the best food is found in very ordinary-looking places, so don't be put off by initial impressions. Our selection is divided into four price brackets: ⊜ (under €16 in large cities and high-demand areas; under €14 elsewhere); ⊜⊜ (€16 to €30 in large cities and high-demand areas; €14 to €25 elsewhere); ⊜⊜⊜ (€30 to €50 in large cities and high-demand areas, €25 to €40 elsewhere); and ⊜⊜⊜⊜ (more than €50 in large cities and high-demand areas; more than €40 elsewhere). These categories appear in the Legend on the cover flap.

RESTAURANTS

Restaurants in Greece cater to all tastes and budgets. **Tavernas** serve simple, inexpensive traditional cuisine. **Ouzeries** (and *mezedopólio*) are different from tavernas because their menus feature *mezédes* (savoury snacks) instead of cooked dishes.

The Michelin Red Guide

The *Michelin Red Guide Main Cities of Europe* is updated annually; this includes numerous establishments in Athens with full details of price, standards of service and levels of comfort. Selections for inclusion are made after research and visits by Michelin experts. Hotels of an especially high standard are distinguished by a red symbol. The guide also lists a selection of restaurants; those offering truly remarkable cuisine are graded between one and three stars.

Restaurants *(estiatória)* offer both Greek and international cuisine, even elaborate specialised dishes. In tourist resort areas, the quality of food is much as one might expect and unwholesome pizzas and pasta-based dishes are all too common. For the best of local cuisine, look for places where Greeks are eating and avoid places with large menus in English. Greeks like to eat out and prices are generally affordable and good value. Greeks rarely lunch before 1pm, and 9pm is the preferred dinner hour. Breakfast is not a noteworthy meal in traditional Greek cuisine; hence the desultory offerings that are common in all but the better hotels. Tea is especially disappointing and dedicated tea-drinkers may want to consider bringing their own brand. Often listed on a blackboard, dishes in Greek restaurants can usually be chosen by diners direct from the kitchen. Greek cuisine relies heavily on numerous side dishes and starters, which tend to be served all at once (be sure to request otherwise if you want them served one after another). Meals are often concluded with fruit; for a proper dessert go to a *zaharoplastio* (patisserie); for coffee visit a *kafenion* (café).

CAFÉS AND BARS

Every Greek village has a *kafenion*, usually dominated by male customers playing cards, chatting or reading newspapers, and the coffee is usually of a thick variety. Soft drinks and beer are also available. More modern cafés are becoming increasingly common, especially in areas popular with overseas visitors, and here you can expect to find better quality coffee and tea as well as breakfast and yogurts.

Bars are always to be found, especially ones with music on the islands in the summer months, serving a variety of drinks. The *apéritif* of choice is the anise-flavoured ouzo, diluted with water.

Table with a variety of Greek specialities

© Greek National Tourism Organisation

Useful Words and Phrases

Many Greeks who live and work in the tourist areas speak English and other languages, especially the younger people who learn languages at school. Once you get out of those areas, though, it certainly helps to know some basic Greek. An ability to read the Greek alphabet also helps, when travelling around, so that you can read road signs, destinations on buses and ferries, and other basic information.

Greetings

	Translation
Good morning	KaleeMEra
Good evening	KaleeSPERa
Good night	KaleeNIKta
Hello	YahSU
Goodbye	Ah-DEE-oh

Numbers

	Translation
One	AYnas, MEEa or AYna
Two	THEE-oh
Three	Tris or TREE-ah
Four	TESeris
Five	PENday
Six	EXy
Seven	EPta
Eight	OCH-tow
Nine	Eh-NAY-ah
Ten	THEH-ka
Twenty	I-KO-si
Thirty	Tree-AN-dah
Forty	Sah-RAN-dah
Fifty	Peh-NIN-dah
Sixty	Ex-IN-dah
Seventy	Evdo-MIN-dah
Eighty	Og-DON-dah
Ninety	Eneh-NIN-dah
One hundred	Eh-KAH-toh

General Phrases

I understand
  Kata-la-VAY-no
I don't understand
  THEN Kata-la-VAY-no
Please Paraka-LOW
Thank you EfcareeSTO
Yes Neh
No OH-hee
Sorry/Excuse me Sig-NO-mee
My name is Meh LEH-neh …
Do you speak English?
  Mih-LAH-tay An-GLI-ka?
How much is …?
  POH-so EE-nay …?
A room AY-nah tho-MAH-tia
Where is …? Poo EE-neh …?
Airport Aero-THROH-mio
Bank Tra-PAY-zah
Hotel Xenotho-KEE-oh
Post office Taki-throw-ME-oh
Restaurant Esty-ah-TOW-rio
Pharmacy Phar-mak-EE-oh
I want ThELL-oh

Days

	Translation
Today	SIM-merah
Tomorrow	AV-rio
Monday	Thef-TER-ah
Tuesday	TrITi
Wednesday	Tet-ART-ee
Thursday	PEM-pti
Friday	Para-skay-VI
Saturday	SAVV-attoh
Sunday	Kiria-KEY

Basic Information

BUSINESS HOURS

Opening hours are idiosyncratic and vary from town to town, but the following can be taken as guidelines:

- In towns, shops are open from 9am–2pm on Mondays, Wednesdays and Saturdays, and from 9am–2pm and 5–8pm on Tuesdays, Thursdays and Fridays. On Sundays, bakeries and drinks retailers are open, in some cases until 8pm.
- In tourist villages, shop opening hours vary widely. In summer, some shops stay open until 10pm or later all week.

Throughout the day and for much of the night, chilled cabinets are available for the purchase of drinks outside restaurants and bars.

MUSEUMS

Visiting times for museums and monuments are given throughout this guide, and are subject to change.

MUSEUMS AND ARCHAEOLOGICAL SITES

Generally speaking these are open between April and October from 8am to late afternoon or early evening. They are closed on Mondays and public holidays. Between November and March, opening hours tend to be 8.30am–3pm. For more specific information, consult www.culture.gr.

CHURCHES

Local churches are open daily, in the mornings and late afternoons. The larger churches tend to stay open all day. The numerous private chapels are usually closed, as are some establishments of historical significance (usually for their preservation). These may be visited on the feast days when they are opened for services, by finding the local key-holder or by application to the tourist office.

COMMUNICATIONS

The **OTE** offices are generally open from 8am to 2pm Monday–Friday. There are telephone booths in the streets and also at newspaper stands (*períptera*). Telephone cards can be purchased from the OTE offices or in kiosks.

DOMESTIC CALLS

All numbers are 10 digits long and start with a 2; all mobile numbers are prefixed by a 6.

INTERNATIONAL CALLS

To ring a foreign number directly from Greece, dial **00** followed by the country code, the city or district code and the person's number.

162 Information on calling abroad
169 Instructions for international calls (English, French)
161 Announcements on telephone calls abroad

INTERNATIONAL DIALLING CODES:

6 for Australia
64 for New Zealand
1 for Canada
44 for United Kingdom
353 for Ireland
1 for United States of America
When telephoning Greece from abroad dial **00 30**.

MOBILE PHONES

If you live in a EU country there are now reasonable rates for using your mobile phone to call home or receive a call in any EU country.
If coming from a non-EU country, check whether your mobile will work in Greece and, if so, what are the rates.

Pay-as-you-go SIM cards – You can purchase SIM cards from any of the mobile phone outlets that are to be found everywhere in Greece. Mobile shops can legally unblock your mobile for a small charge.
Mobile phones can also be rented in Greece (*see www.cellularabroad.com or www.planetomni.com*).

PAY PHONES

You can purchase phonecards of various denominations (from kiosks and newsagents) to use in call boxes. It is not usually possible to have someone phone you back on these phones. For international calls from pay phones, purchase an international calling card and follow the instructions to activate the card.

ELECTRICITY

The voltage is 220AC, 50 cycles per second; the sockets are for two-pin plugs. It is therefore advisable to take an adaptor for hairdryers, shavers, computers, etc.

EMERGENCIES

General police: ☎100
Tourist police: ☎171
Ambulance: ☎166
Emergency: ☎112

MAIL/POST

Post offices can be recognised by their yellow **ELTA** signs displaying the figure of Hermes. They are usually open Monday to Friday, 7.30am–2pm. In the bigger branches a numbered ticket system operates. In addition to

Postal Services

The Greek postal service is good, if sometimes a little bit slow. When using a larger post office note that there are often different queues for different services, so make sure you join the right queue.
A bright yellow sign indicates a post office, and post boxes are also yellow. Bear in mind that there are sometimes two post boxes side by side in some places. The box for domestic mail will say *esoteriko* on it, and international mail should go in the box with *exoteriko* written on it. If mailing a parcel, you must leave it open in case the clerk needs to examine the contents, so be sure to take some sticky tape and maybe scissors with you, to seal it before mailing.

standard mail, the Greek postal service offers an express service.

MEDIA
NEWSPAPERS

Most foreign papers are available the day after publication or on the same day, in some places. Alternatively, *Athens News* (printed in English, on sale in the capital and major tourist resorts) reports on local stories.

TELEVISION/RADIO

Private television stations offer a more mixed fare of programmes than the state-funded channels although you may be pressed to find anything worth watching apart from the occasional film or sports event. Foreign films are broadcast in their original language with Greek subtitles. Available satellite channels include BBC World and CNN. There are countless radio stations offering a mixture of music and chat.

MONEY

The unit of currency is the **euro** which is issued in notes (€5, €10, €20, €50, €100, €200 and €500) and in coins (1 cent, 2 cents, 5 cents, 10 cents, 20 cents, 50 cents, €1 and €2).

TAXES

The usual rate of value-added tax (VAT) on goods and services in Greece is 19 percent. There is a reduced rate of 9 percent that applies, in the main, to food and medicines, and on books and newspapers the rate is 4.5 percent.

CURRENCY CONVERSION

At time of print, one pound sterling was worth 1.2 euro, which makes 1 euro worth 84 pence. The US dollar is currently worth 0.75 euro, which makes 1 euro worth 1.33 US dollars. For the most up-to-date exchange rates, see www.oanda.com.

BANKS

Banks are usually open Monday to Friday, 8am–2/2.30pm. Most branches operate on a numbered ticket system so be sure to obtain a ticket on arrival.

CREDIT CARDS

Payment by credit card is widespread in the cities and larger resorts but is often not accepted on the islands or off the beaten track.

NOTES AND COINS

The designs on euro banknotes were inspired by European architecture. Windows and gateways feature on the front of the notes, and bridges on the reverse, symbolising openness and cooperation. Euro coins have one face common to all 16 countries in the Eurozone, and a reverse side specific to each country.

TRAVELLERS' CHEQUES

The safest way to carry money around, cheques are widely available from American Express, Thomas Cook, Visa, Travelex, Citicorp (Canada) and other providers. Some establishments may charge a small commission when accepting them. Although very common in the cities and larger resorts, they are not widely used in quieter parts of Greece. All banks, however, will accept them.

REDUCED RATES
BY TRAIN: ALL AGES

The InterRail ticket allows the holder (who must have been an EU resident for at least six months) to travel through 30 countries divided up into eight geographical areas: zone G includes Italy, Slovenia, Greece, Turkey, and ferry travel between Italy and Greece.

Those under 26 benefit from a reduced price. For details contact **Rail Europe Direct** 08705 848 848; www.raileurope.co.uk/inter-rail; or www.raileurope.com.

FOR YOUNGER TRAVELLERS

The International Student Identification Card (ISIC) entitles the holder to various travel-related discounts. Contact **STA Travel** 800 781 4040 (US); 0871 230 0040 (UK). www.statravel.com or www.statravel.co.uk.

PUBLIC HOLIDAYS	
1 January	New Year's Day
6 January	Epiphany. All coastal towns and villages hold a blessing-of-the-sea ceremony.
First Monday in Lent	(variable, celebrated 41 days before the orthodox Easter)
25 March	Independence Day and Feast of the Annunciation, marked by military parades in Athens and Thessaloniki, and children's parades throughout Greece.
Easter	Good Friday sees processions in many towns. The Resurrection is celebrated at midnight on Saturday with fireworks. On Easter Sunday, it is traditional to eat roast lamb. The Monday is also a public holiday.
1 May	Labour Day.
15 August	Feast of the Assumption.
28 October	Ohi Day, with military parades, marks Greece's defiance of Italian territorial demands in 1940.
25 - 26 December	Christmas.

SMOKING

Smoking is already outlawed on public transport and in train and bus stations. Restaurants and cafés must designate at least 50 percent of their establishments as non-smoking areas. A complete ban on smoking in public places, including cafés and restaurants, came into effect in 2009 though it is widely ignored.

TIME

Greece is two hours ahead of the United Kingdom; only one time zone applies across the country.

TIPPING

Although not compulsory, it is customary to leave a tip of up to 10 percent at the end of a meal. When using taxis, the normal procedure is to round up the bill in the driver's favour.

CONVERSION TABLES

Weights and Measures

1 kilogram (kg) 6.35 kilograms 0.45 kilograms	**2.2 pounds (lb)** 14 pounds 16 ounces (oz)	**2.2 pounds** 1 stone (st) 16 ounces	*To convert kilograms to pounds, multiply by 2.2*
1 metric ton (tn)	**1.1 tons**	**1.1 tons**	
1 litre (l) 3.79 litres 4.55 litres	**2.11 pints (pt)** 1 gallon (gal) 1.20 gallon	**1.76 pints** 0.83 gallon 1 gallon	*To convert litres to gallons, multiply by 0.26 (US) or 0.22 (UK)*
1 hectare (ha) **1 sq kilometre (km²)**	**2.47 acres** 0.38 sq. miles (sq mi)	**2.47 acres** 0.38 sq. miles	*To convert hectares to acres, multiply by 2.4*
1 centimetre (cm) **1 metre (m)**	**0.39 inches (in)** 3.28 feet (ft) or 39.37 inches or 1.09 yards (yd)	**0.39 inches**	*To convert metres to feet, multiply by 3.28; for kilometres to miles, multiply by 0.6*
1 kilometre (km)	**0.62 miles (mi)**	**0.62 miles**	

Clothing

Women				Men			
	35	4	2½		40	7½	7
	36	5	3½		41	8½	8
	37	6	4½		42	9½	9
Shoes	38	7	5½	Shoes	43	10½	10
	39	8	6½		44	11½	11
	40	9	7½		45	12½	12
	41	10	8½		46	13½	13
	36	6	8		46	36	36
	38	8	10		48	38	38
Dresses	40	10	12	Suits	50	40	40
& suits	42	12	14		52	42	42
	44	14	16		54	44	44
	46	16	18		56	46	48
	36	6	30		37	14½	14½
	38	8	32		38	15	15
Blouses &	40	10	34	Shirts	39	15½	15½
sweaters	42	12	36		40	15¾	15¾
	44	14	38		41	16	16
	46	16	40		42	16½	16½

Sizes often vary depending on the designer. These equivalents are given for guidance only.

Speed

KPH	10	30	50	70	80	90	100	110	120	130
MPH	6	19	31	43	50	56	62	68	75	81

Temperature

Celsius (°C)	0°	5°	10°	15°	20°	25°	30°	40°	60°	80°	100°
Fahrenheit (°F)	32°	41°	50°	59°	68°	77°	86°	104°	140°	176°	212°

To convert Celsius into Fahrenheit, multiply °C by 9, divide by 5, and add 32.
To convert Fahrenheit into Celsius, subtract 32 from °F, multiply by 5, and divide by 9.
NB: Conversion factors on this page are approximate.

Roussánou Monastery, Meteora, Piniós Valley
© Marc Dozier/hemis.fr/Photoshot

INTRODUCTION TO GREECE

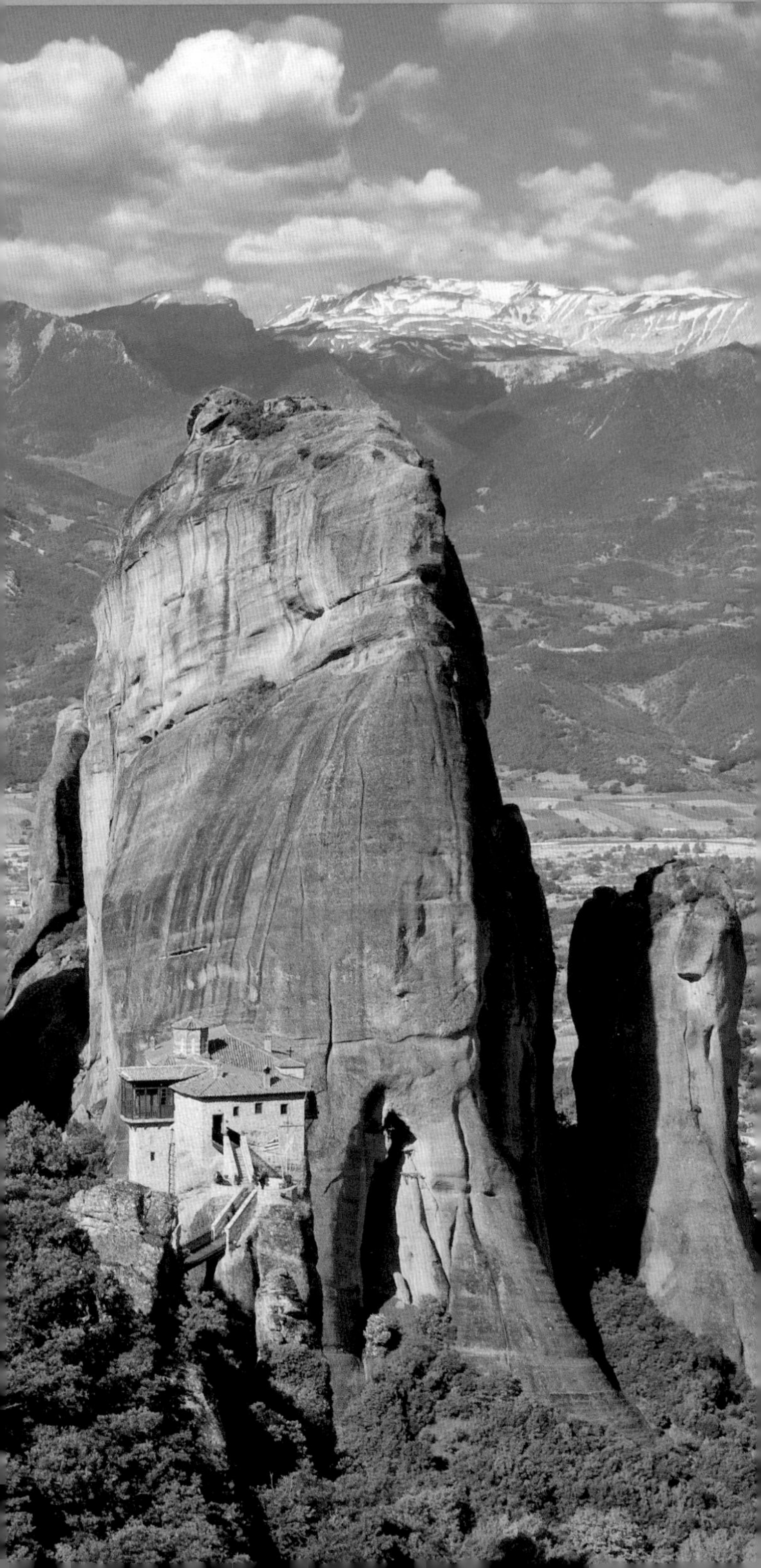

Greece Today

Travellers to Greece expect to discover and enjoy the country's intriguing traces of past civilisations. In doing so, they encounter the Greeks of today, a warm and welcoming people who are remarkably friendly and open to visitors. Who are they, the Greeks of today, and how do they live? Answers lie not just in the past, but in the present: in Greek music, crafts and popular arts, and in the delectable Greek cuisine.

21ST CENTURY GREECE
LIFESTYLE

Greece is the most homogeneous country in the Balkans – the result of the early 20C population exchanges with Bulgaria and Turkey. Modern Greeks have a very strong sense of culture and history, based on their language and the Orthodox religion, both subjects that are taught in the school syllabus from an early age. Instinctively, the Greeks look to the West for the values they helped disseminate, but this natural inclination is tempered with suspicion based on centuries-old interference of the various Great Powers in Greek politics. Despite globalisation, regionalism thrives and the best opening line to start a conversation with a Greek is always "Where do you come from?" Like the wider homeland (patrída) of Greece, the specific native town or village is always a source of pride.

Like many cultures along the Mediterranean, the Greek family is the most important social unit. It is the family that is expected to shield an individual against unemployment, help the children's education and provide health care for the elderly. Such family ties can be extended sideways with the tradition of godparenting which is still important in Greek society. As a result, there is an unwritten but succinct set of relationships which determine individual behaviour towards parents, uncles, siblings, grandparents and even strangers. Tourists will benefit from this since treating guests as anything less than royalty would be unseemly. In return, Greeks, who are very keen on their individual and the national reputation, will expect some sign of appreciation. A smile and a thanks (efcharistó) goes a long way.

RELIGION

The importance and influence of the Orthodox religion on the average Greek cannot be underestimated. The removal of religious affiliation on Greek ID cards, under pressure from the EU, was met with an unprecedented wave of protests from a people who could not comprehend how someone could be Greek and non-Orthodox. In 2010 only 2 percent count themselves of a different religion, with 1.3 percent being the Muslim minority of Thrace. This dependency on the Orthodox church stems both from the tradition of Byzantine theocracy, but also from the long Turkish occupation. The Ottoman Empire was divided into religious streams with different laws, taxes and obligations for Muslims, Christians and Jews; even the exchange of populations in 1922/23 was based on religious lines and not ethnicity. Ultimately it was the Orthodox church, dominated by Greek speakers, that instilled the sense of a nation and led to the War of Independence in 1821.

SPORT
Sporting Successes

The sports facilities throughout Greece are excellent and they have staged many international competitions including the Olympics (twice). Like in many countries, football is the most popular sport and the two big teams of Panathinaïkós (based in Athens) and Olympiakós

© R. Mattes/MICHELIN

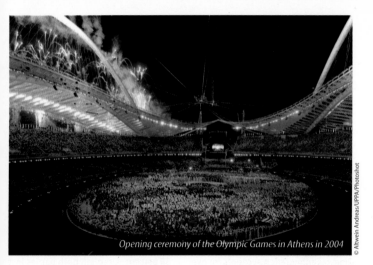

Opening ceremony of the Olympic Games in Athens in 2004

© Altvein Andreas/UPPA/Photoshot

(based in Piraeus) are regular players in the Champions League. Panathinaïkós is the most successful, having played in the European final against Ajax in 1971 (lost 2–0). The Greek national team currently lies 13th in the FIFA rankings, having pulled off a remarkable win in the 2004 European Championship, beating Portugal 1–0 in the final in Lisbon. However, basketball, volleyball and water polo also draw regular crowds of 10,000-plus. The Greek Basketball League is considered the strongest in Europe and its teams have won the European league about a dozen times whereas the national basketball team has won the European Championship twice, in 1987 and 2005. Greek volleyball and water polo are also strong with many silver and bronze medals in world competitions. Sailing is both popular and successful with the then Crown Prince Constantine's Olympic gold win in 1960 kicking off a series of several Olympic medals.

The Olympics

Greece gave the world the concept of a sports competition with its various games in the ancient world, of which the Olympics are the most famous. As the birthplace of the Olympic ideal – a world united in sport – the first ever modern Olympics were revived in Athens in 1896. As a mark of recognition, the Olympic flame is lit at Olympia before it journeys around the world, and the Greek team is the first to march during the Olympic opening ceremony. Greece fought very strongly for holding them for the 1996 centenary; the bitterness of losing them to Atlanta was palpable. In the end, Athens held them again in 2004, and Greece was the smallest country in 50 years to be burdened with such a task. Although the degree of preparedness for the Games was under constant scrutiny, everything was great on the night, and the Games were a resounding success. There is a feeling among Greeks – shared by sports enthusiasts – that maybe Greece should be their permanent home, but this opinion is not endorsed by the IOC.

POPULATION AND LANGUAGE

Greece's population, approaching 11 million, is spread out unevenly across the country's *nomoí*; some of these administrative regions are vast and almost void of people, others cover a tiny area but are crammed with inhabitants. The Athens metropolitan area, composed of the two *nomoí* of Athens and Piraeus, continues to extend its sprawl and is now home to around a third of all Greek citizens; Thessaloniki in Macedonia has a population of 800,000. At the other extreme, an exodus from agriculture means that the mountain areas and some of the islands now have fewer than 10 inhabitants per square kilometre.

The only minority in Greece that has some degree of legal recognition is a Muslim one in Thrace that accounts for less than 1 percent of the total population. Its members are predominantly of Turkish and Roma ethnic origins. The country, though, is also home to minorities of Armenians and Jews, as well as speakers of non-Greek languages. The latter include Arvanites, who speak a form of Albanian known as Arvanitika, and Aromanians and Moglenites (known as Vlachs) who speak a language related to Romanian. In northern Greece there are also Slavic-speaking groups.

Non-EU immigration accounts for over 15 percent of the population in and around Athens, with Albanians making up more than half the total. Smaller numbers of Bulgarians, Georgians and Romanians contribute to the racial mix and these minorities are mostly employed as cheap labour by better-off Greeks.

Greek is the official language of the country and, because it is spoken by just about everyone, Greek society is linguistically homogeneous to a remarkable degree. Even more remarkable, though, is the fact that the language has an unbroken literary tradition that goes back almost 3,000 years, a unique achievement among European languages (*See Literature and Language, p91*).

MEDIA

With over 100 radio stations, 35 TV stations and 40-odd national newspapers, there is an unprecedented degree of plurality of expression in the Greek media. This reflects the large number of political parties as there are few truly independent voices, since the press is usually tied to a political party (or in the cases of sports papers to a particular sports team) whereas TV stations tend to take the government line for whichever party is in power.

A list of online Greek newspapers can be found in http://www.onlinenewspapers. com/greece.htm.

GOVERNMENT

The constitution of 1975 confirmed Greece as a parliamentary republic. The prime minister is the head of government, and of a multi-party system, with a president with largely ceremonial functions. The president is elected by the parliament for a five-year term and can only enjoy two terms in office. The party system is dominated by two main parties: the right-wing New Democracy and the socialist Panhellenic Socialist Movement. A New Democracy government won power in the 2004 elections, for the first time in 11 years, and in the 2007 elections won the largest share of votes, 42 percent, followed by the Panhellenic Socialist Movement with 38 percent. Although both parties lost around 15 percent of the votes that they had collected in 2004, New Democracy managed to secure an absolute but narrow majority of 152 out of the 300 parliament seats. The Communist Party increased their share of the vote by 10 percent in 2007 but the election also saw the emergence of the Popular Orthodox Rally party, a nationalist grouping of the far-right led by a controversial journalist Georgios Karatzaferis after he was expelled from New Democracy in 2000.

Konstantínos Alexandrou Karamanlís remained prime minister of the country, as leader of the New Democracy party which his uncle Constantine Karamanlis had founded. Regional government is organised around 13 administrative districts, further divided into 51 prefectures called the *nomoí*.

Greece became a member of the EU in 1981 and of the euro in 2002.

ECONOMY

Greece remains a predominantly rural country, especially in Boeotia, Macedonia, Thessaly and Thrace. Farms are generally small (except in the north); the main crops are olives, citrus fruits, maize, cotton, tobacco, sugar beet, barley and rice. Agriculture and associated activities employ around 20 percent of the workforce; half this number work directly in farming.

Greece has several hydroelectric and thermal power schemes. There is an active bauxite mining industry around Mt Parnassos (the raw material is used to make aluminium); the building sector is also significant to the economy.

The nation's two greatest sources of income are merchant shipping and tourism. Greek mecrhant shipping is the largest in the world, with over 3,200 vessels registered, comprising 12 percent of the world's capacity. The tourist industry, evident everywhere across the country, accounts for 17 percent of GDP. With nearly 20 million visitors a year, Greece has more tourists than inhabitants. The excellent weather, warm sea, beautiful countryside and countless historic sites account for this success.

Greece is part of the European single currency area or "Eurozone" (*see Money*) and interest rates are governed by the Central European Bank. The organisation of the Olympic Games held in 2004 led to substantial modernisation of the country's infrastructure, with aid from the European Union, and the result was an increase in income levels for many Greeks. The Greek economy grew by nearly 4 percent per year between 2003 and 2007. Immigrants make up nearly one-fifth of the country's workforce, mainly in agricultural and unskilled jobs, and as in other European countries this has provoked some extreme responses from right-wing, nationalist groups.

An aspect of Greece's economy that may grow in importance over the coming years arises from its access to the sizeable emerging markets in the Balkan, Black Sea, eastern European and eastern Mediterranean regions. One healthy economic statistic points to the existence of over 3,000 export and investor Greek companies and a growing proportion of these are concerned in trade with Bulgaria, Romania, Serbia, Albania and the Republic of Macedonia (though the fact that Macedonia is also the name of a region in northern Greece is a source of contention between the two countries).

The Conservative governments that were in power between 2004 and 2009 pursued economic reforms in the areas of social insurance, welfare and the labour market. Such measures were supposed to encourage further investments, lower the country's high unemployment and promote growth and economic stability. Laws liberalising working hours in retail trade and employment and providing for public–private financing initiatives followed in the teeth of opposition. However, when the Socialist PASOK party came to power in the elections of October 2009, called early, Prime Minister Geórgios Papandreou discovered a dire economic situation masked by dubious statistics. To his credit, he tried to give a true picture of the economy which revealed that Greece was hit both by a large public debt (115 percent of GDP at the latest count) and a 13 percent deficit. Despite two rounds of cuts in 2010, the economy did not recover, as markets imposed a high premium for lending to the Greek government. This was reflected in a weakening of the euro itself, as fear of default and, contamination of other Mediterranean economies spread in the markets. After original European (mostly German) refusal to bail Greece out, a joint IMF/EU rescue package was agreed in May 2010.

ARTS AND TRADITIONS

For centuries the social and political situation in Greece ensured that a large number of traditions and practices with roots going back to Ancient Greece were preserved, but rural folk traditions have now almost entirely disappeared because of the combined effect of modernisation of agriculture and the revolution in means of communication, which has brought the villages out of isolation. Many of the Greek customs and traditions have their roots in the Greek Christian Orthodox religion and as long as the church continued to play an important part in people's lives customs and traditions were preserved accordingly. Gradually, however, the influence of the Church is declining, a process inseparable from the increasing modernisation of the country, and the result is a notable decline in traditional practices. Two aspects of cultural life – music and weddings – are proving resistant to this seemingly inevitable process and for many families events like the birth of a child or the coming of Easter remain occasions for the observance of centuries-old customs. Superstitions (see below) are also testimony to the continuing hold of the past on the increasingly modern consciousness of Greeks.

CRAFTS

During the last decade a craft revival has been promoted by government organisations and private associations. Schools and workshops have been set up throughout the country and about 100 workshops produce **carpets** in beautiful designs, reviving the making of *flokáti* from shaggy wool, which was formerly widespread in Thessaly. In the country practically all households had a loom in the past and **weaving** is still a common pursuit. The methods, materials (wool, silk or cotton) and designs (floral or geometrical) vary from region to region; bags, cushions and bedspreads are the most common articles produced. **Embroidery**, which enhances garments, curtains and bed valences, is highly decorative and red is usually the dominant colour; the floral designs denote the oriental influence of Greeks from Asia Minor; in Epirus, Skyros and Crete, scenes from everyday life are also included. Weavers and lacemakers are often seen at work on their doorstep.

Ceramics remain a male preserve except for decoration. Huge jars made in Crete, Attica and the western Peloponnese that were used in the past to store oil or cereals now serve as garden ornaments. The richly decorated glazed pottery found in the eastern Aegean Islands and Rhodes recalls the influence on Greek art of Asia Minor. Skyros has beautiful decorative plates; Aegina and Sifnos have produced high-quality pottery for centuries.

Wood carving remains a special tradition in Epirus, Skyros, Thessaly and Crete (pews, iconostasis, wedding chests).

Votive offerings and painted shop signs are popular forms of naive art.

TRADITIONAL DRESS

Traditional dress is hardly worn except for patronal festivals or feasts of the Virgin (processions), at weddings, during the carnival or, in a simpler form, on market day. The women are resplendent in embroidery and chased ornaments chiefly displayed on their bodices and skirts. However, no one still wears the heavy pleated **kilt** (*foustanélla*), which is the uniform of the soldiers (*évzoni*) of the Guard, as well as the **pompom shoes** (*tsaroúhia*). Local costumes are most common at Métsovo in Epirus, on Lefkada, in the northern Sporades, occasionally in the Peloponnese, on Kárpathos and Astipálea in the Dodecanese and also in Crete; women spinning are often to be seen in the country districts. Costumes are also displayed in the museums of traditional art such as those of Nauplion, Thessaloniki, Chios and Athens.

SUPERSTITIONS

The Evil Eye – the most famous of all Greek superstitions, with a lineage stretching back two millennia (ancient Greek paintings of Greek triremes show an eye painted on them), the Evil Eye is able to strike anywhere without notice and the best defence is to wear or carry an eye painted in the middle of a blue charm (a clove of garlic is helpful too in warding off the bad luck associated with the Evil Eye).

Curses – a parent's curse is said to be a dangerous thing and showing respect to one's parents is considered the best way to minimise the afflictions it may bring. **Tuesday 13th** – the equivalent of the Anglo-Saxon Friday 13th. Tuesday is the unluckiest day for the Greeks, because Constantinople fell to the Turks on a Tuesday.

FOOD AND DRINK

The Greek soil seems to have been blessed by the gods, who since antiquity have ensured a plentiful supply of grapes for wine, olives for oil, goat's

The Perfect Moussaka

Serves 6

Ingredients: 1kg aubergines (eggplants), 1 large onion, 2 cloves of garlic, 400g minced lamb, 1 glass of white wine, 4 tomatoes, 1 bunch of parsley, olive oil, butter, milk, salt, pepper, a little flour, grated cheese.

Slice the aubergines into long thin slices and soak them in salted water for 1 hour. Soften the chopped onion and garlic in butter before adding the minced lamb and 4 tablespoons of water. Cook for 5 minutes on a low heat, stirring regularly. Add the chopped and peeled tomatoes, parsley and wine, and flavour with salt and pepper. Cover and simmer for 15 minutes. Pat the aubergines dry, and fry lightly in olive oil before draining on paper towels. Line a greased dish with half the aubergines, then add the meat and tomato mixture before covering with the remaining aubergines. Make a thick roux sauce with butter, flour and milk and add on top of the aubergines. Sprinkle with grated cheese before placing in a preheated oven at 180°C / 350°F until golden.

and sheep's milk for cheese. The influence of the Venetian occupation can still be tasted in the cuisine of the Ionian Islands, while the flavours of the Ottoman Empire remain in the sweet pastries and the use of spices. The island of Crete in particular is renowned for its supremely healthy dishes.

DISHES

Greek cuisine is simple but full of flavour. The main elements are Mediterranean: olive oil, tomatoes, lemons, herbs (oregano, mint, dill) and aromatic spices (allspice). The pastries and cakes, which are very sweet and flavoured with honey and cinnamon, evoke the Orient. Authentic but inexpensive Greek dishes are to be found in the tavernas and some more modest restaurants *(estiatório)* in the towns and the country.

A favourite aperitif and the national drink is a colourless aniseed spirit *(ouzo)*, served in tiny glasses accompanied by a glass of water or diluted in a glass of water which turns cloudy.

Aperitifs are usually accompanied by *mezédes* or *meze*. These include vine leaves stuffed with meat and rice *(dolmádes)*, spit-roasted offal sausages *(kokorétsi)*, aubergine purée with black olives *(melitzanosaláta)*, yogurt with chopped cucumber and garlic *(tzatzíki)*, purée of fish roe and breadcrumbs or potatoes *(taramosaláta)*, rice with toma-

toes *(piláfi)*, stuffed tomatoes, peppers and aubergines *(gemistá)*.

When in season, melons and watermelons are popular starters, as is the famous Greek salad, which contains tomatoes, cucumbers, feta cheese, onions and olives, all generously doused in olive oil.

Main courses are usually selected from a board or direct from the kitchen. If you want your dishes to arrive in sequence rather than all at once, it is best to specify this. On the coast, fish dishes are weighed prior to cooking and sold at cost per kilo. It is sadly not uncommon now for frozen fish to be used; this should be described as such *(katepsigmenos)* on the menu. The staple seafood dishes include prawns *(garídes)*, sword-

Octopus - one of the Greek specialities

© Greek National Tourism Organisation

fish *(ksifías)*, squid *(kalamári)*, octopus *(chtapódi)*, and sardines *(sardéles)*.

The food resources of mainland Greece are ample: in Thessaly and the Peloponnese there are countless orchards and farms producing tomatoes, aubergines, pistachios, chestnuts and olives. Pelion is renowned for its meat and especially game sausages. Against this backdrop, it is easy to forget that Greece is essentially a frugal country. Dishes are predominantly seasonal, and meat can be roasted, grilled or fried. Vegetable dishes are often stuffed or fried.

The Greeks eat a lot of cheese. The best known is goat's or sheep's milk cheese *(féta)* which may be served with olive oil and olives; also popular is a sort of Gruyère *(graviéra)* and a mild cheese similar to Cheddar *(kasséri)*.

Desserts tend to be eaten separately, often as a mid-afternoon snack. These include millefeuilles with walnuts or almonds and cinnamon *(baklavá)*; rolls of thread-like pastry with honey and walnuts or almonds *(kadaïfi)*; mini doughnuts with honey and sesame or cinnamon *(loukoumádes)*; flaky pastry turnover with cream and cinnamon *(bougátsa)*; and almond or sesame paste *(halva)*.

DINING ETIQUETTE

Apart from obviously formal restaurants of the kind to be found in the better hotels the general rule is one of relaxed informality. It is not rude to go to the kitchen and see what is cooking and, if necessary, you may point out to a waiter what you wish to eat. Service tends to be an easygoing process as well and if you want something it is usually up to the customer to attract the waiter's attention.

Wine is common at both lunch and dinner and an often used toast is *stin igeía sou* ("good health").

Waiters in tourist areas are keen to attract customers into their restaurant (their pay is often related to the number of customers and the amount they spend) and work persuasively to entreat you to take a table. When the bill arrives it is not always itemised and there is scope for being overcharged. Greeks are hospitable people and guests are often treated generously when it comes to eating out and sharing a meal. If invited to a meal by Greeks treat the scheduled time with some leeway; turning up punctually may well cause some surprise.

WINES AND SPIRITS

With its dry, warm climate and limestone or volcanic soil Greece is an excellent country for producing wine; the main wine regions are the northern Peloponnese, Attica, Crete, Rhodes and Samos. Twenty-six regions now have recognised status as winemaking districts. Elsewhere matters are less strictly controlled, and the wine is sold under the name of the grower or a cooperative. The best-known Greek wine is probably *retsina*, a white wine to which pine resin has been added as a preservative; served chilled as it usually is, it is very refreshing without being heavy.

Among the unresinated wines *(aretsínoto)*, some have earned a particular reputation: the full-bodied reds from Náoussa in Macedonia, the fruity reds from Neméa in the Argolid, the scented rosé from Aráhova near Delphi, the well-rounded dry white wines of Hymettos and Palíni in Attica, the sparkling dry white wine of Zítsa in Epirus, the white wines of Chalcidice, which preserve their quality well, and the popular white wines of Achaïa (Demestica, Santa Laura, Santa Helena).

In the islands there are the generous reds and rosés from Crete, dry whites from Lindos in Rhodes, sweet reds from Samos, the heady and scented wines from the Cyclades, particularly Naxos and Santorini, and from the Ionian Islands: Zakynthos (Verdéa, Delizia), Cephallonia (Róbola, fruity and musky) and Leukas (Santa Maura).

Wine from the vat *(krassí híma)* is served in carafes or copper pitchers.

Coffee and Liqueurs

Greek coffee has a strong aromatic flavour and is usually served with a glass of water. Greek coffee leaves a grainy deposit at the bottom of the cup which should not be consumed. Order it *glikó* (plenty of sugar), *métrio* (a little sugar), or *skéto* (no sugar). **Frappé** is a popular frothy cold coffee.

Samian wine is normally drunk as a liqueur at the end of the meal, as is the Greek brandy **Metaxa**.

There is also the Cretan **rakí**, a very strong spirit (not to be confused with Turkish raki which is similar to ouzo), and **mastícha**, a sweet resin drink from Chios.

Ouzo is the national drink; aniseed-flavoured, it is either consumed neat or diluted with water.

WHAT TO EAT

Starters

Dolmádes: vine leaves stuffed with meat and rice.

Tzatzíki: yohurt with chopped cucumber and garlic.

Melitzanosaláta: aubergine purée.

Moussaká: aubergine and minced lamb with a béchamel sauce.

Piláfi: rice with tomatoes.

Taramosaláta: purée of fish roe and breadcrumbs or potatoes.

Saláta horiátiki: classic Greek salad.

Soups

Psarósoupa: fish soup.

Soúpa avgolémono: broth with rice, egg and lemon.

Fish

Fish *(psari)* is served boiled *(vrasto)*, fried or grilled *(scharas)*.

Garídes: prawns.

Glóssa: sole.

Ksifías: swordfish.

Kalamári: squid.

Chtapódi: octopus.

Meat

Meat can be roasted, grilled *(scharas)*, boiled or braised *(stifado)*. The words *tis oras* next to a dish mean that it will be cooked to the client's wishes.

Arní and **arnáki**: lamb and mutton.

Biftéki: minced beef patty.

Choirinó: pork.

Kotópoulo: chicken.

Moschári: veal.

Soutzoukákia: meatballs in tomato sauce.

Souvlákia: meat on a skewer served with tomatoes and onions.

Kokorétsi: spit-roasted offal sausages.

Cheese

Féta: goat's or sheep's cheese.

Graviéra: similar to Gruyère.

Kefalotíri: similar to Parmesan.

Kasséri: mild cheese similar to Cheddar.

Fruit

Fráoules: strawberries; **Karpoúzi**: watermelon; **Kerássia**: cherries; **Pepóni**: melon; **Portokáli**: orange; **Rodákina**: peaches; **Síka**: figs; **Stafília**: grapes; **Veríkoko**: apricot.

Desserts

Baklavá: millefeuille with nuts.

Bougátsa: flaky pastry turnover with cream and cinnamon.

Halvá: almond or sesame paste.

Kadaΐfi: rolls of threadlike pastry with honey and walnuts or almonds.

Loukoumádes: mini doughnuts with honey and sesame or cinnamon.

Rizógalo: cream rice.

Yaoúrti me méli: yogurt with honey.

Amigdalotá: macaroons.

Kourabiédes: almond cakes.

Snacks

Mezés (pl. mezédes): small dishes of olives, seafood, meat and cheese, best enjoyed with a glass of ouzo at an **ouzerí** or as a big meal at a restaurant.

Eliés: olives (Vólos, Kalamáta and Amfissa ones are especially good).

Spanakópita: spinach pastry.

Souvlakópita: grilled meat pastry.

Tirópita: cheese pastry.

History

The origins of Greece are buried in legend, and it can be difficult to determine where myth leaves off and reality begins. The nation's complex and turbulent history was born of many waves of invasion and conflict: the city-states of the classical period; the empires of Macedonia and of Rome; and the long period when Greece virtually disappeared within the Byzantine and Ottoman empires before finally taking its place as an independent European nation.

ANTIQUITY

Although Greece was definitely inhabited from the Palaeolithic period (around 40000 BC), it was not until the Neolithic period (around 6000 BC) that settled communities established themselves, as is evident from excavations in Epirus, Macedonia and Thessaly. It was the Bronze Age (3000 BC), however, that was to witness the development of civilisation, founded largely on a common Indo-European language.

LEGENDARY ORIGINS

In his poem *Works and Days*, **Hesiod** (second half of 8C BC) laid down a chronology associating metals with the generations who had lived before. If the golden age was lost in time, the age of silver corresponded to the Neolithic period (6000–2600 BC), while the age of bronze witnessed the Ionian and Achaean invasions (2600–1500 BC). Hesiod's own period (the Archaic era) was the age of iron.

The Myth of the Flood

According to legend, Zeus sent a great flood to punish the impious people of the Bronze Age. Only two were saved: Deucalion, son of Prometheus, and his wife Pyrrha, who had been advised by Prometheus to ride out the flood in an Ark. After nine days and nights, the vessel came to rest in the mountains of Thessaly. Zeus sent Hermes to make the survivors swear their fidelity to him. Deucalion asked for companions, and the two survivors were told to throw the bones of their mother over their shoulders. Their mother being the Earth, they threw stones as instructed. Deucalion's stones became men, and Pyrrha's became women.

Deucalion and Pyrrha had many children, including Helen whose sons were Doros, Xouthos and Eole; Xouthos in turn fathered Achaeos and Ion. Thus the main groups of invaders – Dorians, Aeolians, Achaeans and Ionians – were legitimised in mythology.

THE MYCENAEANS (1600–1100 BC)

While a culture developed in Crete, known today as **Minoan**, using a pictogram script known as **Linear A** (which subsequently evolved into the syllabic **Linear B** script, finally deciphered in 1952), continental Greece was being settled by groups of Caucasian origin: the **Ionians** and **Aeolians** (around the beginning of the second millennium), and later the **Achaeans** (c.1600 BC); this last group settled in the Peloponnese. This era witnessed the establishment of fortified settlements centred on a *megaron*, administered by the *anax* (king). Society was dominated by a military aristocracy. This **Mycenaean** culture, of which much is known (both from the works of **Homer** and from archaeological evidence), used the Linear B script to

Detail of a teracotta tablet with the Mycenaean Linear B inscription from Pylos (2nd millennium BC)

© The Art Archive/Alamy

record commercial transactions, practised ancestor worship and were able to work in non-ferrous metal. It's likely that their common language allowed communities to cooperate, as evidenced by colonisation of Crete (15C BC) and Rhodes, and the sack of Troy (around 1230 BC).

THE DARK AGE (LATE 12C–EARLY 8C BC)

According to Thucydides, author of the *History of the Peloponnesian War*, the end of Mycenaean culture was caused by the arrival of the **Dorians**, a new wave of invaders originating from the valleys of the Danube. Driving out the established inhabitants, the Dorians brought with them iron, ceramic wares and the first identifiable sacred sites. Over the course of the 9C and 8C BC, the Phoenician alphabet was adapted to become the Greek alphabet, engendering a literary civilisation with a common language. Within a few decades, the great epics the *Iliad* and the *Odyssey* were to be written.

THE ARCHAIC ERA (MID-8C–6C BC)

This period was a cultural re-awakening, with the development of political institutions centred on the *polis*, a spirit of commercial dynamism which fuelled colonisation throughout the Mediterranean world, and eventually a religious apogee, ample evidence of which exists in the holy places (Olympus, Delphi, Epidaurus) and temples of this date. Plutarch (1C) relates how "Theseus had a grand plan to gather together all the peoples of Attica in one great city, creating one state for one people." This structure, increasingly prevalent from the 8C BC, resulted in the emergence of autonomous **city states**, each constituting an urban settlement presiding over its surrounding lands. Árgos was probably the first of these, but they soon proliferated to include Sparta, Corinth, Thebes and Athens. This parcelling up of land led to incessant disputes over territory. From such conflict came the Lelantine War (between Halkída and Eretria in Euboia), the Messenian War (between Sparta and her neighbours), and many others. Over the years these societies evolved (although there were exceptions to this rule, such as Sparta) from royalties, to oligarchies, then tyrannies, before emerging as democracies. An important development was the emergence of legislators like Solon of Athens. Their contribution did much to assuage unrest among ordinary citizens who were concerned by the arrogant ambitions of the aristocracy. This was also a fundamental reason for the emergence of tyrant rulers, many of whom established dynasties.

September 776 BC Inauguration of the **Olympic Games**. This date represents a key milestone in the chronology of Ancient Greece. The Olympic Games were to form the model for the Phytic Games at Delphi (c.675 BC), the Isthmic Games held in northern Corinth and the Nemean Games.

c.775 BC Beginnings of colonisation. Colonisation enabled greater control of maritime trade routes for Greece. New settlements were daughter cities of the mother cities from which they originated. Although politically independent, these new colonies retained strong cultural and religious links with their mother cities. Four great waves of colonisation are recorded: between 775 BC and 675 BC, when Sicily and southern Italy were settled; 675 BC to 600 BC, when the Black Sea, Egypt and Cyrenaica were colonised; 600 BC to 545 BC, when colonists arrived in Etruria, southern Gaul and the east coast of Spain; and from 545 BC onwards when Thrace and the islands were colonised.

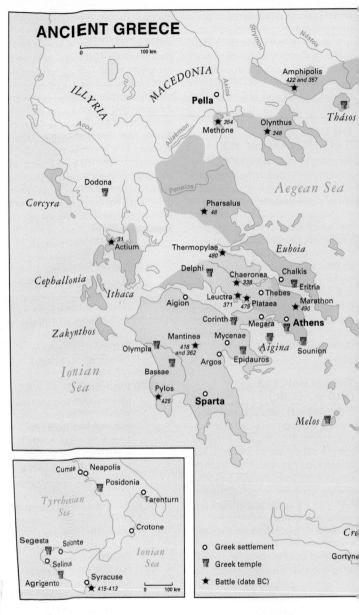

ANCIENT GREECE

0 ___ 100 km

ILLYRIA

MACEDONIA

Strymon

Néstos

Pella

Axios

Amphipolis
422 and 357

Thásos

Aoos

Aliakmon

Methone
★ *354*

Olynthus
★ *348*

Dodona

Peneios

Aegean Sea

Corcyra

Pharsalus
★ *48*

Actium
★ *31*

Thermopylae
★ *480*

Euboia

Cephallonia

Delphi

Chaeronea
★ *338*

Chalkis

Eritria

Ithaca

Aigion

Leuctra
★ *371*

Thebes

Plataea
★ *479*

Marathon
★ *490*

Zakynthos

Corinth

Megara

Athens

Ionian
Sea

Olympia

Mantinea
★ *418
and 362*

Mycenae

Aigina

Sounion

Argos

Epidauros

Bassae

Pylos
★ *425*

Sparta

Melos

Cumae

Neapolis

Posidonia

Tyrrhenian
Sea

Tarenturn

Crotone

Segesta

Solonte

Ionian
Sea

Cre

Gortyn

Selinus

Syracuse

Agrigento

★ *415-413*

0 ___ 100 km

○ Greek settlement

▥ Greek temple

★ Battle (date BC)

c.750 BC Homer's epics, the *Iliad* and the *Odyssey*, are written.

c.740 BC Lelantine and Messenian Wars.

621–620 BC Edict of Draco in Athens lays down legislative framework to deal with criminal acts.

594–593 BC Archonate of Solon introduces social reforms and political structures.

560–510 BC Tyranny of Pisistratos and his sons.

508 BC Reforms of Cleisthenes.

conflicts, however, Athens was to experience a golden age of artistic and political pre-eminence.

499–494 BC Revolt of the Ionian Greeks. A contingent of Athenians destroy Sardes, the Persian capital. Miletus is sacked in reprisal and the Ionian cities are obliged to swear allegiance to the Persian king Darius.

492 BC First Persian War.

490 BC Darius lands in eastern Attica, but is defeated by the Athenians at Marathon.

482 BC Themistocles builds a fleet of 200 triremes to defend Athens.

481 BC Formation of the League of Corinth: at the request of Athens, the Greek states (except Thessaly and Boeotia) form an alliance under the command of Sparta.

480 BC Second Persian War.
The army of Darius' successor, Xerxes, is stalled by Leonidas' heroic Spartans at Thermopylae. After the Spartans' defeat, the Persians burn down the Acropolis of Athens, but their fleet is comprehensively destroyed at Salamis.

478 BC Formation of the League of Delos.
The cities of the Ionian and Aegean islands unite with Athens against the Persians. Each city contributes towards a common war chest to maintain an army and navy.

454 BC Transfer of the League's treasury from Delos to Athens.

449–448 BC Peace of Callias ends the Persian Wars: autonomy

THE CLASSICAL PERIOD: THE TRIUMPH OF ATHENS (5C BC)

This was a bloody time in Greek history, starting with the revolt against Persian domination in the Ionian colonies, which was followed by the Persian Wars, and later in the century the long Peloponnesian War. Between these two great

The Impiety of Socrates?

In classical Greece, where religion was founded on practicality rather than dogma, the accusation of impiety was a serious one. Numerous philosophers suspected of questioning the accepted beliefs were banished and some, like Socrates, were condemned to death for having corrupted society's youth. The charges levelled at Plato's teacher stated that "Socrates is guilty of not believing in the deities in which the city believes, and of proposing new gods". In reality, it was fear of his philosophical teachings and their potential impact upon the State's political cohesion, rather than any spiritual considerations, which prompted his demise. As ever in Greece, behind the façade of religion lurked the machinations of politics.

of the Greek cities of Asia Minor is recognised by Persia.

446 BC Thirty Years' Peace agreed between Athens and Sparta.

444–428 BC Pericles at the forefront of Athenian affairs: affirmation of democracy, strengthening of naval power, and a vibrant political scene.

Pericles

© Scala, Florence/Plus-Clementine Museum, Vatican City

431–404 BC Peloponnesian War. Athens' attempt to spread her power results in Corinth and other cities of the isthmus appealing to Sparta. War is declared and the lengthy struggle which ensues involves the whole Greek world. Athens is finally defeated in 404.

404–403 BC Tyranny of the Thirty: rule by oligarchy until democracy re-established in 402 BC.

MACEDONIAN HEGEMONY AND HELLENISTIC GREECE (4C–3C BC)

Under the watchful eye of the Persian Empire, Sparta and Thebes vied for supremacy in the aftermath of the Peloponnesian War.

The intervention of the kingdom of Macedonia brought greater stability; this was the prelude to the reign of Alexander the Great and his empire which was to extend to the Indus and the foothills of the Himalayas.

399 BC Socrates is condemned to death.

395–387 BC Corinthian War. Thebes occupied by the Spartans (382 BC). Peace negotiated under the auspices of Artaxerxes II of Persia.

377 BC Formation of the second League of Delos: Athens and other cities unite against Spartan hegemony. Unlike the first such coalition, Athens is not able to impose her wishes unilaterally.

376 BC Reorganisation of the Boeotian League centred on Thebes. Theban hegemony under Pelopides and Epaminondas. After the defeat of the Spartans at Leuctra (371 BC), the Boeotians invade the Peloponnese, ravage Sparta and occupy Messenia.

356 BC Mausolus, Statap of Caria in Asia Minor, forms an alliance including Chios, Rhodes and Byzantium, destroys the Athenian fleet, and forces Athens to accept the independence of the rebel Aegean cities.

356–336 BC Philip II of Macedon conquers the territories neighbouring his kingdom. Exploiting the disarray among the city states, he advances into central Greece and defeats the Athens–Thebes coalition at Chaeronea (338 BC). Demosthenes, who had worked tirelessly to foil the Macedonian invaders, railed against his fellow citizens: "It is shameful, a slur on your reputation, that of Athens and of your ancestors, to allow Greece to become enslaved." Philip negotiated a treaty with Athens that was more generous than in the case of other Greek states; he did, however, appoint himself commander-in-chief of the Hellenic League, the alliance formed to tackle the Persian threat. In 336 BC Philip was assassinated at Pella.

336 BC Alexander, son of Philip, is acclaimed king by the army. Conflict with neighbouring northern states, and the Theban revolt (335 BC).

Crown of gold oak leaves of Philip II of Macedon from Royal Tombs, Véria

© Greek National Tourism Organisation

334–323 BC Alexander's Asian campaigns fulfil his father Philip's ambitions. The young king's army sweeps across Asia Minor, defeating the Persians at Granicus. After conquering the cities of the south and west coasts, he stops at Gordium, where he severs the famous knot (according to legend, whoever achieved this feat would become master of all Asia). Halicarnassus was taken, before Darius and the Persians were defeated at Issus (333 BC). The Phoenicians were next to crumble before Alexander, after Tyre was besieged (332 BC). Egypt was added to his dominions (Alexandria was founded in 331 BC) before Alexander crossed the Tigris and Euphrates, defeated Darius

The Heroic Defence of Thermopylae

The narrow defile of Thermopylae was protected by a wall built in the 6C BC and is the main access between Thessaly and central Greece. It was here that Leonidas deployed his meagre force of Spartans and Thebans to halt the advance of Xerxes' 130,000 Persian troops. Despite their superior numbers, they were not to succeed. Although the Greek forces were surprised by a Persian attack from the rear, Leonidas ordered the bulk of his force to withdraw and made a last stand with just 800 soldiers committed to fighting to the death. The Spartans "fought with their swords, their hands, their teeth" and took a heavy toll on the attacking Persians, who finally prevailed but at a heavy cost. Thermopylae entered the annals of Greek legend. A monument at the site bears the inscription from the text by Herodotus: "Go, tell the Spartans, thou who passest by, that here obedient to their laws we lie."

Ancient Greeks at War

From the Homeric wars to the Macedonian conflicts, war is an omnipresent feature of Greek life, marked by evolving strategies and tactics. The first big development came in the 7C BC with the emergence of the phalanx, which allowed troops to advance in tight formation with their weapons drawn. Composed of infantry troops known as *hoplítes* armed with a javelin or sword, and protected by a shield, helmet, leather breastplate and gaiters, the phalanx is in stark contrast to the concept of the aristocratic mounted warrior, as depicted in the *Iliad*, in quest solely of individual glory. Philip of Macedon added archers and javelin-throwers, and developed the *sárissa*, a steel-tipped pike which could be as long as 5m/16ft. Full-time soldiers in the pay of the king, Macedonian troops were to incorporate Greeks among their ranks, as well as using mercenaries when necessary.

again at Gaugamela and annexed Babylon and Susa. Persepolis was destroyed, Media and Parthia were then conquered and by 329 BC Alexander's army had reached Bactria. Crossing the Indus in 326 BC, Alexander reached his furthest point, before his troops' unwillingness to proceed obliged him to retrace his steps. In 324 BC he married Roxane of Bactria, and then set about building a fleet to conquer Arabia. This ambition, however, was cut short by his death on 13 June 323 BC.

323 BC The compromise of Babylon: Alexander's generals divide up the empire between themselves and conflict ensues among them. The Antigonid dynasty become rulers of Greece. Various alliances are formed, either to fight Macedonian control, or to preserve a Panhellenic status quo.

280–275 BC Pyrrhus, king of Epirus, aids Tarentum against Roman expansionism and wins a number of victories.

279–278 BC Delphi attacked by the Gauls.

228 BC Athens expels the Macedonian garrison from Piraeus.

227 BC Cleomenes III of Sparta implements reforms.

212 BC Fall of Syracuse to Rome.

Detail of a mosaic of the Battle of Issus showing Alexander, National Archaeological Museum, Naples

ROMAN GREECE (2C–1C BC)

After Philip V of Macedon (221–179 BC) had supported Hannibal in the Second Punic War, Rome began to take an interest in the Hellenic world which had developed from the empire of Alexander. Having defeated Philip V at Cynoscephalae, Rome declared the freedom of Greece in 196 BC. In fact, the Greeks recovered only part of their independence under Roman control. The continuing intervention of Rome in Greek affairs led in 146 BC to a rebellion by the Achaean League headed by Corinth, which was laid waste by the Roman legions. The various city leagues were then broken up and Greece came under Roman occupation, which subsequently spread to the rest of the Hellenic world; this was annexed completely after the triumph of Augustus over Antony and Cleopatra at Actium in 30 BC. In 27 BC the Romans united the Greek lands to form a single province, the province of Achaïa. Some cities were given the status of free cities (e.g. Byzantium), while others had federated or allied status.

COMING OF THE BYZANTINE EMPIRE (1C–4C AD)

Although the Greek city states lost power and prestige, **Hellenism** flourished and Greece retained its cultural, literary and artistic influence. No doubt this was largely due to the political and religious tolerance practised by the Romans, for whom Greece held a strong fascination (the Emperor Hadrian visited Athens three times). Administration was largely in the hands of the local population and the practice of the Greek religion was permitted. This relative autonomy granted by Rome gradually created two spheres of influence in the Roman Empire: on the one hand a Greek East combining the Greek world proper and the Hellenistic areas of Asia Minor, and on the other a Latin West.

From the 3C AD, Greece, in common with the rest of the Empire, had to face barbarian invasions, which were more successfully resisted by the eastern Empire than the western part. These

Constantine the Great

©Hip/Scala, Florence/Musei Capitolini Rome

dangers made Rome's loss of influence more palpable and in 330 the **Emperor Constantine** made Byzantium, a former Greek colony on the Bosphorus, the capital of the Empire. Initially called New Rome, the city was soon to bear the name **Constantinople** in his honour.

In 380, during the reign of **Theodosius the Great**, Christianity became the official religion, pagan cults were banned, and in 393 the Olympic Games were abolished. In order to resist the barbarian invasions in its western part, he divided the Empire at his death in 395 between his two sons: Arcadius inherited the East and Honorius the West. Constantinople remained the capital of the Eastern Empire.

LIFE IN THE 5C BC

Prior to the 6C BC there is very little documentary evidence to help historians reconstruct daily life. From this date onwards, however, there is ample material: ceramic wares, written texts, coinage and other archaeological finds. The most data has been gathered for Athens and Attica, Sparta, Thebes and Boeotia; more than enough to give a picture of daily life in classical times. Attica's population numbered between 250,000 and 300,000. Sparta, covering a larger but harsher territory, had slightly fewer inhabitants. Around 150,000 lived in the Theban province of Boeotia. Excluding Macedonia and the colonies of Asia Minor and greater Greece, the total population was close to 2,000,000.

BEHIND THE FAÇADES

The great legends give the impression of a society of luxurious villas, streets paved with marble, rigorous order and impeccable cleanliness. The reality, however, was rather different. One visitor observed: "The city has no water supply, and signs of its decrepitude are everywhere." To conclude, he stated: "It is difficult to believe that this place is truly Athens." Although the great monuments such as the Acropolis or the Agora were very elegant sites, the rest of the city was a dirty, malodorous mass of confused streets and alleys. The first real town planner was **Hippodamos of Miletus** (mid-5C BC) who introduced a more ordered approach. To him is attributed the reconstruction of Piraeus (as decreed by Themistocles) and Miletus, among other projects.

Houses were built in adjoining terrace fashion, separated by thin dividing walls (so thin that when the Thebans attacked the Plataea in 431 BC, the inhabitants fled their attackers by knocking through the walls from house to house). In Athens, the poor lived in cave dwellings carved into the hillsides. The more prosperous lived in houses, each built around a central courtyard, sometimes embellished with a portico and a well. In areas of dense habitation, some houses were divided up into numerous apartments, each rented to a separate family. Flooring was usually plain earth at ground level, with wood boards used for the upper storeys. Windows were small and doors opened directly into the street.

FOOD AND CLOTHING

Although the Greeks had been able to tell the time accurately from the 5C BC, the ordering of the days was largely dictated by meals. Breakfast (usually barley bread soaked in wine) was eaten at dawn. Lunch at noon was a light affair, with supper as the main meal of the day. Away from mealtimes, there would be trips to the market, and for more prominent citizens, involvement in public affairs. A ubiquitous feature of the Greek diet was the *maza*, made from barley flour. Fish and game were also common; meat, though, was reserved for sacrificial purposes. The many Greek states had differing attitudes towards food, from the austere Spartans (who existed almost exclusively on a diet of black gruel) to the opulent Boeotians (whose gluttony was widely observed). In addition to water, the Greek drank goats' milk, and, of course, wine, often diluted with sea water or flavoured with thyme or cinnamon. Certain Greek wines, notably those from Lesbos, Chios and Thasos, were highly regarded and exported throughout the Mediterranean. Wine flowed freely at Greek banquets *(symposia)* where diners, served by slaves, reclined at low tables and ate with their hands.

Evening meals would often be preceded by a bath (at the public bathhouse, at home for the better off, or indeed in the river for the austere Spartans). Beards were the norm (until the reign of Alexander the Great at least), hair was cut short in Athens and usually dispensed with altogether in Sparta. Women had elaborate hairstyles and wore make-up. Clothing was similar in style across the social classes, although the better off had theirs made of finer fabrics. A short tunic *(cheiton)* fastened at the shoulders was the norm; on more formal occasions a larger cloak *(himateion)* was also worn. Women wore a longer tunic-type garment fastened with a belt at the waist.

CRADLE TO GRAVE

According to Greek literature, courtesans were for pleasure, concubines for the fulfilment of everyday needs, and wives for the production of legitimate heirs and the running of the household. The Athenian wife lived a secluded existence (unlike Sparta's women, who scandalised the world with their relative freedom), in the company of her mother-in-law and other female members of the family, and played no part whatsoever in public life. Dedicated to procreation alone, few marriages were based on romance. The emphasis on breeding a strong next generation was particularly accentuated in Sparta, where ruthless weeding out of the weak was practised. Babies deemed in any way deficient were thrown to their deaths over a cliff. Those who were fit and healthy underwent a rigorous upbringing: at the age of seven they were taken from their mothers and entered state academies where they learnt the martial skills necessary for Sparta's continued military pre-eminence. This training culminated in a period of living wild in the forests when, according to tradition, the young Spartans were expected to hunt down and kill a slave to prove themselves. Young Athenians, on the other hand, received a wide and cultivated education which included the study of grammar and music. Those who sought further education could then become pupils of one of the seats of learning founded by the philosophers, such as Plato's Academy or Aristotle's Lyceum. All Greeks were duty-bound to assist and care for their parents; failure to do so could result in loss of civil liberties or even imprisonment. The elderly were an object of veneration. Funeral rites were complex, involving ceremonial purification, mourning and processions; both burial and cremation were practised.

WORK AND PLEASURE

The 5C BC saw a decline in the economic importance of agriculture and a corresponding increase in the importance of manufacture and trade. Money replaced bartering, the **drachma** becoming a universal currency as Athens' power grew. Status in society, however, remained largely dictated by the role played by the individual rather than based on personal wealth.

Manufacture and trade were highly diversified, with potters, linen merchants, food producers and many other retailers in the city markets. Industrial activity such as mining was well established, with some operations functioning 24 hours a day; the ready availability of large numbers of slaves facilitated this and, indeed, all aspects of life for the Greeks.

Detail of a vase depicting a courtesan tying up her himation in front of her client (c.500 BC)

© Marie-Lan Nguyen/Wikimedia Commons

For free citizens, there was plenty of time for relaxation. In Athens there were 152 public holidays a year, days dedicated to games, hunting, fishing and theatrical events.

BYZANTINE GREECE

In the late 4C AD, the eastern territories of the Roman Empire included the Balkans, modern Greece, Asia Minor and Egypt. Greek, the language of the Church and the vernacular of the peoples of the eastern Mediterranean, gradually superseded Latin as the official language. Thus a totally Hellenised empire emerged which was to perpetuate the traditions of Rome long after the fall of the Western Empire in 476.

RELIGIOUS CONFLICT AND EXTERNAL THREATS

AD 395	Division of the Roman Empire between the sons of Theodosius: a Latin empire in the west, and a largely Greek empire centred on Constantinople (formerly Byzantium) in the east.
451	**Council of Chalcedon**: confirmation of the position of the Patriarch of Constantinople as second in honour only to the Pope.
476	The last western emperor is deposed by Odoacer. **Constantinople** becomes sole capital of the Empire. Byzantium was a theocratic empire, where the emperor (known by the Greek

title of *basileus* from the 7th century onwards) and patriarch exercised interdependent functions (symbolised by the twin-headed eagle, Byzantium's emblem); the former as protector of the empire's status as the ultimate manifestation of God's kingdom on Earth, and the latter as guardian of the Christian faith. Doctrinal issues were of concern to everyone in society, since not only did such matters jeopardise the chances of the individual soul's entry into heaven, but they could also threaten the very fabric of society. Indeed, the history of Byzantium is largely dictated by religious debates.

Throughout its thousand-year existence, the Empire was under constant threat of invasion. From the west came barbarians, Normans, Franks and Venetians; from the north the Slavs, who occupied mainland Greece and the Peloponnese from 6C to 8C; from the east the Persians, the Arabs and finally the Turks. The erosion of the Empire over time resulted in shortages of food, manpower and revenue, so necessary for the operation of the vast bureaucratic machine which Byzantium had become. The Byzantines were fine soldiers, but just as importantly they used diplomacy skilfully, paying off one group of aggressors while receiving tribute monies from other adversaries. They also spread Christianity, converting their northern neighbours, the Slavs.

Emblem of the Byzantine Empire and the Paleologus Dynasty

© Dragases/Wikimedia Commons

527–65 Reign of Justinian I. In 529 he closed the great Athenian seats of learning, the Academy and the Lyceum, suspecting them of propagating paganism. He retook Italy from the Ostrogoths and a large part of Spain from the Visigoths, but the barbarians invaded Thessaly and reached the Isthmus of Corinth. During his reign the Corpus Juris Civilis legal texts were compiled, subsequently known as the Justinian Code.

532–37 Construction of Hagia Sophia in Constantinople.

580 onwards Slavic invasion: siege of Thessaloniki and occupation of the Peloponnese.

610–41 Reign of Heraclius. He defeated the Persians, and saw off the Avar siege of the capital (626), but could not prevent the conquest of Syria and then Egypt by the Arabs (636).

717–41 **Reign of Leo III** the Isaurian, who, in 726, forbade the cult of icons and ordered their destruction (iconoclasm); he also stemmed Arab expansionism.

754 Iconoclast Council of Hiera.

783 Victory of General Stavrakios over the Slavs, who were subsequently defeated at Patras (805).

813 The Bulgars lay siege to Constantinople.

827 Crete falls to the Arabs.

11 March 843 Affirmation of orthodoxy and rehabilitation of icons.

856–87 and 877–86 Patriarchate of Photius who sought to convert the Slavs, sending out the missionaries Cyril and Methodius, pioneers of the Cyrillic alphabet.

Mosaic depicting Emperor Constantine, Hagia Sophia

© Scala, Florence

860 The Russians attack Byzantium, laying siege to Constantinople.

885 Decree by Basil I consecrating Mount Athos to monastic life.

904 Fall of Thessaloniki to the Arabs.

961 Crete recaptured from the Arabs by Nicephoras Phocas, who, in 969, also takes Antioch.

991–1018 Basil II campaigns against the Bulgars: in the narrow defile of Cleidion (1014) the Byzantines inflict a heavy defeat on Samuel's Bulgarian army.

c.1050 Michael Psellus reintroduces the study of philosophy at the University of Constantinople. Through his pupils he was to exert enormous influence on Byzantine thought and is seen as a proto-humanist.

1054 Schism between the Catholic and Orthodox Churches.

1071 Battle of Mantzikert: the Byzantines are defeated by the Seljuk Turks, denoting the end of the Byzantine Empire in Anatolia.

1081–1185 The Comnenus dynasty: through their oligarchic rule, neglect of the army and imprudent expenditure, they heralded the decline of the Empire.

FROM THE CRUSADES TO THE OTTOMANS

The Crusades were unleashed in the east by 11C and 12C popes on the pretext of aiding the Byzantines in their efforts to recover the Holy Land from the Muslims; the Franks, however, were clearly more interested in carving out territory for themselves and the Venetians saw commercial opportunities aplenty.

1185 Thessaloniki taken by the Normans.

1204 Constantinople taken on the pretext of resolving the issue of succession to the imperial throne. On 13 April, the troops of the Fourth Crusade sack the city, desecrating its churches. This event and the subsequent occupation, aggravated no doubt by the stark doctrinal differences between the Catholic and Orthodox Churches, served to intensify Greek hostility towards the west.

The Latin Empire of Constantinople

A college of six Venetians and six Frenchmen elected Baldwin of Flanders emperor. With the exception of Epiros, Greece was divided along feudal lines: the Venetians took the islands and the main coastal sites, while the French and Lombards controlled the bulk of the mainland. The Emperor Baldwin held Constantinople, which he shared with the Venetians, Thrace and the adjacent parts of Asia Minor. After his death, he was succeeded by his brother Henry of Flanders, then by Peter and Robert de Courtenay, and finally by Baldwin II de Courtenay in 1261.

This Latin incursion into the Byzantine world brought with it feudal structures: a Latin empire around Constantinople was established, encompassing Thrace and the northwest of Asia Minor (1204–61); the kingdom of Macedonia, taking in Thessaloniki and Macedonia (1204–24); central Greece was carved up into baronies, and the Peloponnese became the Principality of Achaïa. Confronting this Latin hegemony were three independent states preserving the Greek traditions: the Empire of Nicea (1204–61), the despotic State of Epirus (1205–1318), and the Empire of Trebizond (1204–1461), geographically isolated to the east of what is now modern Turkey.

1249 Foundation of Mystra. Originally a simple defensive fort, it became a leading centre of cultural and spiritual affairs under the influence of the philosopher George Gemistos Plethon.

1261 The emperor of Nicea, Michael VIII Paleologus, recaptures Constantinople, and over subsequent years part of the Peloponnese is retaken. The despotic State of Morea in the southern Peloponnese is founded at Mystra in 1348; it is to last until 1460.

1331 Nicea captured by the Ottoman Turks marking the beginning of Ottoman expansionism.

Late 14C Exodus of Byzantine academics and intellectuals to the west: Manuel Chrysoloras to Florence, where he taught Greek

*Detail of Crusaders conquer Constantinople (1840)
by Eugène Delacroix, Musée du Louvre*

© World Illustrated/Photoshot

language and literature, and George Ermonymos to Paris, where he taught Erasmus. The spread of Greek ideas contributed to the development of humanism.

1439 Council of Florence: proclamation of an alliance between the Catholic and Orthodox Churches (subsequently condemned by Patriarch Gennadius II Scholarius in 1456).

29 May 1453 Constantinople finally falls to the Ottomans, despite the valiant efforts of the last emperor Constantine Paleologus, who waited in vain for assistance from the west.

1460 Mystra taken by the Turks.

OTTOMAN DOMINATION AND INDEPENDENCE

For four centuries, Greece formed part of the Ottoman Empire. The Turks inherited the Byzantine machinery of government and ruled their dominions firmly. During this era there was a revival in Hellenistic sentiment, which was to reach its climax in a bloody struggle for independence, drawing in other European nations and giving birth to a modern state.

The Principality of Morea

The prince of this state was styled Duke of Achaïa, who had 12 barons as his principal vassals. The first rulers were from Champagne; originally in the hands of Guillaume de Champlitte, it then passed to the Villehardouin family before becoming property of the Anjou–Sicily dynasty in the person of Charles I of Anjou, brother of King Louis IX of France. After the Byzantines retook Constantinople in 1261, they gradually won back the Peloponnese. The princes of Morea, whose story is told in the *Chronicle of Morea*, also held sway over the duchies of Thebes and Athens, which had devolved to the La Roche, who were succeeded by the Brienne. When Gautier de Brienne and his knights were killed at the Battle of Kephisos in 1311, the duchy fell into the hands of the Catalans; from there it passed in 1388 to the Acciaiuoli, Florentines allied to the Anjou–Sicily dynasty.

TWO CENTURIES OF CONQUEST

It would be wrong to imagine the Turks descending as a horde upon the Empire of Byzantium.

Their process of conquest started in the Balkans in the 14C, peaked with the capture of Constantinople in 1453, and was not concluded until 1669, when Herakleion was captured from the Venetians, who continued to maintain a presence in the Ionian Islands, notably Corfu, until the 18C.

1444–81 Reign of Mehmet II who, after taking Constantinople, conquers eastern Greece.

1456–75 Fall of the Duchy of Athens, Boeotia, Lesbos, Halkída in Euboia, and Sámos.

1480 Siege of Rhodes; the Knights of St John successfully defend the island against the Turks. Mehmet II's heirs continue his expansionist strategy, taking the Peloponnese and numerous islands, gaining mastery of the eastern Mediterranean.

1500 Sack of Naupacte.

1522 Suleiman the Magnificent takes Rhodes and the Dodecanese.

1537 onwards Nauplion, Monemvassía and the Aegean Islands fall to the Ottomans. Only Timos,

Suleiman Mosque, Rhodes Town

© Bill Stamatis/iStockphoto.com

under Venetian control, remains unconquered. The former corsair Khair al Din, originally from Lesbos, now Suleiman II's grand admiral, defeats Charles V's fleet off Prévesa.

1566 Capture of Chios.

1571 Cyprus taken. **Naval Battle of Lepanto**; Don John of Austria and the Venetians defeat the Turkish fleet, thereby curbing Ottoman expansion.

1669 The fall of Herakleion ends Venetian control of Crete.

Battle of Lepanto (1603) by Andrea Vicentino

© AISA/World Illustrated/Photoshot/Palazzo Ducale, Venice

ORGANISATION OF THE OTTOMAN EMPIRE

The Turks allowed Christians and Jews to worship freely, but as non-Muslims their status was inferior; known as *rayas*, their continued existence was deemed necessary in order to meet the Empire's manpower requirements.

Large towns were administered by governors, **pashas**; smaller towns and villages were effectively ruled by the Muslim landowners, the **agas**. The government exacted heavy taxes from the Muslim and non-Muslim communities alike, but the latter had to perform all sorts of additional duties imposed by the local rulers in the rich agricultural regions. According to Ottoman law, all lands belonged to the sultan, who often delegated their administration to his great generals. They acted as tax gatherers, keeping large amounts of revenue for themselves.

The harshest aspect of the occupation, especially during the first 200 years, was the abduction of young boys. The strongest were chosen to serve as mercenary soldiers, **Janissaries**, the sultan's personal guard. The brightest were raised in the harem and became devoted government officials. Some Christians converted to the Islamic faith to escape poverty. Many more took refuge in the harsh, wild mountains where the Turks hardly ventured and succeeded in forming prosperous and largely autonomous communities. From the 17C **Phanariots**, natives of the Phanar district in Constantinople, who were often descendants of the Byzantine imperial families, were appointed as governors *(hospodar)* of the Romanian provinces, as interpreters *(dragoman)* for the sultan and often as ambassadors to the Western powers. Many of those Christians who could afford to leave chose exile; this Greek diaspora was to make a significant contribution towards the emergence of humanism in the west, and keep alive Hellenic aspirations which would subsequently lead to an independent Greece.

After the fall of Byzantium, the sultan not only confirmed the authority of the **Patriarch of Constantinople** in religious matters, but also appointed him as temporal leader *(ethnarches)*, responsible for the internal affairs of all the Orthodox communities throughout the Empire. He was also answerable to the Turkish authorities for the loyalty and good behaviour of the Christian population. In spite of, or perhaps because of, this dual function, the **Orthodox Church** succeeded in maintaining the Greek religion, language and traditions in these difficult times. The monasteries, in particular those on Mount Athos, the Meteora and Patmos, were the principal centres of Greek culture.

The Struggle for Liberty

There had been revolts in the 17C, but it was in the 18C that a feeling of nationalism began to develop with the full support of the Orthodox Church. Meanwhile, the Venetians continued to maintain a strong presence in the eastern Mediterranean; in 1687 they retook the Peloponnese and the island of Aigina. Following the Treaty of Karlowitz, the Ottomans ceded Morea to Venice.

It was from outside Greece, however, that the strongest impulses came. Among émigré Greeks there were numerous secret societies that raised funds and laid plans to bring an end to Ottoman occupation. The largest was the **Filikí Etería**, founded in Odessa in 1814 by **Alexander Ypsilantis**, aide-de-camp to the Russian Czar. These societies consisted of merchants and civil servants like the **Phanariots** (natives of the Phanar district in Constantinople), ship owners from the islands and businessmen, bankers and writers living in Greece or abroad, where they were influenced by the ideals of the Age of Enlightenment and later of the French Revolution.

In the mountains, bands of *kléftes* (the word literally means "robber" in Greek) began to harass the Turks; they were joined by the militia *(armatoloi)*, composed of Greek citizens armed by the Turks to fight the rebels but who took up their cause.

The intellectuals of the secret societies and the rebels of the mountains had little in common except a desire to overthrow Ottoman rule; there was no clear agenda as to how it should be replaced, with some favouring a republic, others a monarchy. The hunger for liberation, however, was the factor which overrode all others.

The Grand Revolution

1797 End of the Venetian Republic. The Ionian Islands come under French control.

1800 Ionian Islands taken by Russia and handed over to Turkish rule.

1807 Treaty of Tilsit – Ionian Islands revert to French control.

1809 The British occupy the Ionian Islands, except Corfu which resists occupation until 1814.

1818 Ionian Islands declared independent, under a British protectorate. Greek confirmed as the official language.
The first uprisings begin in the Danube districts in 1821, but a lack of wider support results in failure.

25 March 1821 The Metropolitan of Patras, **Germanós**, raises the flag of revolt, a white cross on a sky-blue background, against Sultan Mahmoud II at the Agía Lávra Monastery near Kalávrita. The revolt spreads throughout the Peloponnese, into Epirus, ruled by Ali Pasha, and to the islands of the Saronic Gulf; 40,000 Turkish troops are massacred. This was the start of the War of Independence, also known as the **National Revolution**. By 1822 **Theodore Kolokotrónis** and his troops were in total control of the Peloponnese.

1 January 1822 Unilateral declaration of independence. The provisional government under Alexandros Mavrocordátos is established at Missolonghi. Following the insurrection on Sámos, the Turks massacre 20 000 men, enslaving their women and

Heroes of the Struggle for Independence

Lascarína Bouboulína (1771–1825): Originally from Spetsae, she fought the Turks at sea and in the Peloponnese.

Márkos Bótsaris (1788–1823): Of Souliot origin, he led the defenders of Missolonghi and was killed near Karpeníssi.

Germanós (1771–1826): He blessed the standard of Greek independence at the monastery of Agía Lávra, and preached the cause at Patras on 25 March 1821.

Konstantinos Kanáris (1790–1877): A fire-ship expert, later a politician.

Giorgios Karaïskakis (1780–1827): Leader of the *palikares* on the mainland; he was killed at the Battle of Phaleron near Athens.

Theodore Kolokotrónis (1770–1843): Originally from the Peloponnese, he inflicted the first major defeat upon the Turks in the Dervenáki Gorge in 1822.

Yannis Makriyánnis (1797–1864): A native of Thessaly and military leader. His memoirs are a precious and picturesque testimony to the popular uprising.

Andréas Miaoúlis (1769–1835): Sailor who fought numerous battles against the Turkish navy between 1822 and 1825.

children. Discord between the provisional government and Kolokotrónis in the Peloponnese, with a second assembly being established at Kranidi.

1823 New government in place, first under Petros Mavromichalis, and subsequently Georgios Coundouriotis.

1825 End of civil war between monarchist and republicans. Turkish victory at Methóni; the troops of Mehmet Ali, Sultan of Egypt, ravage the Peloponnese.

Having failed to storm **Missolonghi**, the Turks besiege the city in April 1822. In 1824 **Lord Byron** visits the city and resolves to do everything in his power to help the cause of Greek independence, but he dies prematurely the following year. The city falls in 1826 and the resultant loss of life has a great impact in Europe.

1826 St Petersburg protocol; Britain and Russia decide to intervene to enforce an armistice "without however taking any part in the hostilities". The allied fleet goes to parley with the Turkish fleet anchored off Chios in Navarino Bay and ends up destroying it.

1827 National assembly convenes and proposes a republican government headed by a president to hold office for seven years, and the election of a chamber of deputies. Subsequently the London convention upholds the St Petersburg protocol. The Ottoman Empire refuses to comply and its fleet is blockaded, then destroyed, by the allies in October that year.

1828 **John Kapodístrias** becomes governor of Greece, reorganising the state and army, but his republican leanings alienate many.

1829 Treaty of Adrianople grants autonomy to Greece.

1830 **Treaty of London**; Greece's independent status recognised by the Great Powers.

9 October 1831 Assassination of John Kapodístrias.

1832 Exploiting a clause in the Treaty of London, the allies decide on a monarchy for Greece and ask Otto von Wittelsbach to become king.

DEMOCRACY AND A EUROPEAN IDENTITY
OTTO I AND GEORGE I

1833–62 Reign of **Otto I** of Bavaria.

1834 Athens becomes capital of independent Greece. Foundation of first state university in 1837.

1854 Crimean War. Greece sides with Russia, provoking an Anglo-French attack on Piraeus.

1863–1913 Reign of **George I** of Denmark, a constitutional monarch along the British model.

1864 The **Ionian Islands**, British possessions since 1814, become part of Greece. Proclamation of a new liberal constitution: George I declared "King of Greeks".

1881 Congress of Berlin: Greece recovers Thessaly and most of Epirus.

1882–93 Construction of **Corinth Canal**.

1896 First modern Olympic Games.

1908 Elefthérios Venizélos proclaims the unification of Crete with Greece.

1912–13 **Balkan Wars**. Macedonia and Epirus liberated from the Turks by the Greek army.

Opening ceremony of 1896 the Olympic Games

© UPPA/Photoshot

After **John Kapodístrias**, the prime minister, was assassinated in 1831, the Great Powers (Russia, Britain and France) imposed an absolute monarchy upon Greece, in the shape of a Bavarian prince, **Otto I**, who was not even 18 years old at the time of his accession. A Catholic himself, his wife (also Catholic) was vehemently opposed to Orthodoxy, and he presided over a cabinet made up of Bavarian ministers and a German-speaking court. A coup on 3 September 1843 forced him to choose a Greek cabinet and approve a constitution. Even so, as the king continued to intervene in political life, the wave of liberal opposition – secretly supported by the British who disliked the king's close relationship with Russia – culminated in a second coup and Otto was deposed. On 6 June 1863 Prince William of Denmark (1845–1913), suggested by Britain as a possible candidate for the throne, accepted the crown and became king with the title of **George I**. For its part, Britain gave up its protectorate of the Ionian Islands, which restored Greek territorial integrity. The role of the new dynasty was in fact to bring Greek policy into line with that of the British in eastern Europe. Pressure from an increasingly influential middle class led the new king to grant a more liberal constitution in 1864, then to introduce parliamentary government in 1875.

The main problem, however, remained the territorial issue, as significant areas of Greek population were still under Turkish occupation. In 1866 the king backed a Cretan uprising against the island's Ottoman overlords but, lacking support from the big powers, he had to leave the island in the hands of the sultan. When the Russo-Turkish war began in 1877, Greece invaded Thessaly but, although the Treaty of San Stefano recognised the independence of Serbia, Romania and Bulgaria, it maintained Turkish rule in Macedonia. It was not until 1881 and the Congress of Berlin that Thessaly became part of Greece. In March 1896 Crete, with the support of Greek volunteers, again

Corinth Canal

©Styve Reineck/Bigstockphoto.com

rebelled against the sultan. The Greek government landed troops there in February 1897 and an army commanded by the Crown Prince Constantine invaded Macedonia, where it was defeated. The mediation of the big powers led to the signature in December of the Treaty of Constantinople, which granted Crete autonomy under the rule of the king's second son, Prince George.

Dissatisfied with the lack of territorial recovery, discontent developed and was aggravated by the Balkan crisis. The first sign of this potent nationalism occurred in 1908, when the Cretan **Elefthérios Venizélos** (1864–1936) proclaimed the unification of Crete with Greece. An army revolt in 1909 forced the king to call on Venizélos to form a government in 1910. The aim of Venizélos was to unite all territories with Greek populations and to reorganise the administration, army and economy. In 1911 he gained approval for a new constitution with better guarantees for individual freedoms. In 1912, together with Bulgaria, Serbia and Montenegro, he founded the **Balkan League**, which declared war on Turkey on 18 October. Greece invaded Macedonia, and in November took Thessaloniki, where King George was assassinated in March 1913.

The London Conference in May 1913 put an end to this first conflict, but the arguments over the partition of Macedonia started a second one, with Bulgaria this time fighting its former allies. The Treaty of Bucharest in August 1913 sanctioned the annexation of southern Macedonia, southern Epirus and most of the Aegean Islands by Greece, as well as her sovereignty over Crete, but gave northern Macedonia to Serbia. In the same year, the Protocol of Florence ceded northern Epirus to the newly formed state of Albania. Even today, territorial issues remain hotly debated.

WAR FOLLOWS WAR

1913   Constantine I comes to the throne.

1914–18   First World War. Greece brought into the war by Venizélos on the side of the Allies. Thrace and Smyrna awarded to Greece in 1919.

1917   Abdication of Constantine I; his younger son Alexander I succeeds him.

1919–22   New Greco-Turkish conflict; the **Great Catastrophe**. After the defeat of the Greek army, 1.5 million ethnic Greeks from Asia Minor become refugees.

1920   Following a referendum, Constantine returns to the throne.

1922   Constantine abdicates again in favour of his elder son George II.

Greeks landing at Smyrna, escorting Turkish prisoners on to the ships on 15 May 1919

© UPPA/Photoshot

1923 Treaty of Lausanne redraws Greece's frontiers: Turkey takes Smyrna, Italy the Dodecanese, and Britain takes Cyprus. A formal population exchange with Turkey strengthens the homogeneity of the Greek state.

25 March 1924 Declaration of a republic; Admiral Pavlos Coundoriótis elected president.

1935 After a number of coups, a monarchist government is elected; following a referendum George II returns to the throne.

1936–41 Dictatorship of General Metaxas.

1940–41 Italian troops invade Epirus on 28 October 1940. The Greek army repulses this attack, pushing the Italians back into Albania.

1941–44 German occupation.

When war broke out in 1914, the Greek government was split between the patriots with Venizélos at their head and the Germanophiles grouped around King Constantine I (1868–1923), brother-in-law of Kaiser Wilhelm II. Venizélos suggested that the king should align himself with the Allies but he was forced by the king to resign in March 1915. Returned to power by the electors, Venizélos tried to make a secret pact with the Allies but again the king demanded his resignation. The army then gave its backing to the prime minister and together they formed a republican government at Thessaloniki in September 1916.

The king started to form partisan battalions, so the French occupied Thessaly and demanded his abdication. Venizélos returned to Athens in June 1918. The new king, **Alexander I** (1893–1920), asked him to form a government and on 15 Sept aligned himself with the Allies. In the Treaties of Neuilly (1919) and Sèvres (1920), Greece gained eastern Thrace and the Smyrna region of Asia Minor came under its administration. Then Britain, playing on Venizélos' impe-

rialist ambitions, caused the Greek leader to start a new war with Turkey by annexing the Smyrna region. This proved very unpopular and brought about the downfall of Venizélos at the polls in November 1920, immediately after the death of the king. A plebiscite followed, recalling Constantine I. Abandoned by its allies, Greece was unable to hold out for long against the Turks. Military failures led to Constantine's second abdication in September 1922, in favour of his son **George II** (1890–1947), and to the evacuation of Asia Minor and the tragic forced emigration of the ethnic Greeks living there. This massive influx of new population could only aggravate an already difficult economic situation. The elections returned the Venizélos party to power and the king preferred to abdicate (in December 1923). A republic was proclaimed on 25 March 1924 and confirmed by a plebiscite. It experienced numerous crises, with a succession of alternating dictatorships and republican union governments. July 1928 saw the return of Venizélos as head of government until his resignation in 1932. Numerous domestic problems accentuated the political divide between the Right and the Communist Left. Consequently a further coup in March 1935, supported by Venizélos himself, abolished the republic; a plebiscite soon restored the monarchy and reinstalled George II. The king asked **General Metaxás** to form a government, although, to all intents and purposes, he acted as dictator until his death in 1941. With the king's agreement, Metaxás abolished the constitution, dissolved parliament and adopted Fascist policies. Greece had, however, felt threatened by the annexation of Albania by Italy under Mussolini. When in October 1940 Italy demanded free passage for its troops, Greece rejected the ultimatum and came over to the British side. The Italians crossed the border into Greece but the Greek army succeeded in pushing them back towards Albania. German troops then came to Mussolini's aid. The king fled first to Crete and then, under British occupation, to Cairo; Greece was divided between the Italians, Germans and Bulgarians. Resistance groups, in particular the fiercely Marxist National Liberation Front (EAM), waged active guerrilla warfare against the occupiers with ever-increasing support among the population. The Russian offensive in Romania caused the Germans to evacuate Greece in October 1944. The king, George II, had meanwhile set up a government in exile under Papandréou, and promised not to return until there had been a plebiscite.

THE CIVIL WAR AND ENTRY INTO EUROPE

1947–49 Civil War.

1952 Greece joins NATO.

1953–63 Period of Conservative governments under Pagagos and **Konstantínos Karamanlís**.

1967–74 Dictatorship of the Colonels.

1974 **Karamanlís** returns. Referendum decides in favour of a republic.

1981 Greece joins the EEC, later the European Union.

2004 Athens hosts the Olympic Games.

2006 The Council of the European Union names Patras, Greece the European "Capital of Culture" for 2006.

2010 European debt crisis

As the Germans evacuated Greece to the north, the British army was disembarking at Piraeus. The British were particularly worried about the influence exerted by the EAM and asked in vain that their partisan army should be disarmed. In the elections of March 1946, massive abstentions on the part of the republicans gave the victory to the royalists, who pressed forward with a plebiscite which came out in favour of the king's return. When he died soon after, he was succeeded by his brother, **Paul I** (1901–64). While the Treaty of Paris of February 1947 gave the Dodecanese Islands to Greece, the interior of the country faced an extremely critical situation since the left-wing parties refused to support the monarchy. In December 1947, with Soviet support, General **Márkos Vafiádis** formed a provisional government of Free Greece and took refuge in the mountains of the north; from there he waged a guerrilla campaign against the royalist government. The Civil War lasted until October 1949 and was ended only by the capture, with the help of the United States, of the rebels' main stronghold in the Grámmos Mountains.

The ensuing elections were a victory for the moderate parties but successive governments up to 1963 were, in fact, controlled by extreme right-wing forces, which in effect formed a parallel government. The emergency laws passed at the time of the Civil War were never repealed and remained in force. When the elections of 1963 gave power to the democratic parties, **Giórgos Papandréou** (1888–1968) was asked

Konstantínos Karamanlís swears in as Prime Minister in July 1974

© DeAgostini/Photoshot

Ceremonial changing of the guards, 'Evzones' at the Parliament Building, Athens

© Eye Ubiquitous/Hutchison/Photoshot

to form a government; however, the positions he adopted were not always in line with US policy, and the extreme right in Greece saw in his premiership a threat to their privileges. Badly advised, the young King **Constantine II** (b.1940) disagreed with his head of government, who resigned. This gave rise to a political crisis, in the course of which every attempt to form a legitimate government failed. On 21 April 1967, before new elections scheduled for May could take place, a **junta** led by a number of colonels, who did not even represent a majority within the army, took power in the name of the king.

The colonels set up a regime based on terror; opponents were dragged before a military court and either imprisoned or deported. Constantine II tried to remove the colonels in a coup but failed; he fled from Greece on 13 December 1967. A new constitution restricted individual freedom and gave excessive powers to the army. The hostility of the majority of the population steadily increased and, in spite of some measures intended to give an illusion of liberalisation, such as the deposition of the king and proclamation of a republic in July 1973, demonstrations against the regime grew in scale. They reached a climax in the Athens Polytechnic uprising of 17 November 1973 which left at least 24 dead. A new coup by army hardliners

followed that proclaimed martial law and set up special courts in response. However, in 1974, because of the Cyprus crisis and squabbles within the junta, those in power were obliged to call on **Konstantínos Karamanlís**, leader of the right-wing parties and an opponent of the regime. He abolished all the institutions of dictatorship and reintroduced the constitution of 1952, with the exception of the clauses relating to the monarchy. Fundamental liberties were restored, political parties legalised, and the main figures involved in the dictatorship brought to justice. The referendum of 8 December 1974 decided in favour of a **republic**, and a new constitution was promulgated in June 1975.

Since then, the return to democracy has been clearly demonstrated by the alternation in power of right- and left-wing parties, and further reinforced by Greece's membership of the EU, which it joined in 1981. In 2002 Greece also joined the euro.

Despite a continuous spat with Macedonia – officially known as FYROM at the insistence of Greece – whose name it sees as usurping its history, post-Cold War foreign relations continue to be dominated by the arms race with Turkey which, along with the 2004 Olympics and the endemic corruption almost bankrupted the state in 2010, causing an intervention by the EU and the IMF.

Architecture

The architecture of Ancient Greece – airy, buoyant and graceful – stems from and celebrates the omnipresent Mediterranean sunlight. It served as the chief archetype of the Roman building style and, when rediscovered in the Renaissance, led to several styles collectively deemed "Neoclassical".

CONSTRUCTION TECHNIQUES

The chief building material was stone: limestone tufa (often shell limestone), and marble from the quarries on Pentelikon, Thassos and Naxos. The stone blocks were quarried with a pickaxe and extracted with the aid of metal or wooden wedges; the latter soaked to make them expand. Often the blocks were then shaped on the spot into architectural elements: columns, capitals and models of statues.

The blocks were removed from the quarry down a slipway built so as to have a regular gradient. Weighing on average 5 tons, the blocks were loaded onto wooden sledges which were lowered on ropes hitched round fixed bollards. The blocks were then moved to carts or drays drawn by bullocks for transport to the actual building site. On the site the rough or prepared blocks were unloaded with the aid of levers and rollers and sent to the workshop to be dressed or decorated (fluting or moulding) or carved (capitals, pediments and *metopes*). The blocks were raised into position with a block and tackle and hoist or derrick. The dressed stones, which were placed one upon another without mortar, were held in place by H or N clamps. Wooden or metal pins were used to secure the piles of drums which made up a column: the holes which held them can still be seen. Stone columns received a coat of stucco.

In large-scale constructions the blocks of stone were cut and placed in various ways according to the purpose and period of the building and the means and time available. No bonding material was used. This gives Greek stonework an almost unrivalled aesthetic and functional value. The **Cyclopean** style of construction, rough but sturdy, is found in some **Mycenaean** structures, especially at Tiryns. Polygonal bonding was used in all periods, often for foundations; at first the blocks were rough hewn, then came curved surfaces and finally flat ones. Trapezoidal bonding, with varying degrees of regularity, was widespread in the 4C BC. Rectangular bonding, which occurred in all periods, was used most frequently in the classical period.

MYCENAEAN PERIOD (1550–1100 BC)

The Mycenaean palace stood within a fortified city *(acropolis)* surrounded by so-called Cyclopean walls (according to legend they had been built by the Cyclops, a mythical race of giants). The palace had a simple and logical plan: one entrance, a courtyard with the throne room on one side, preceded by a vestibule and the main reception rooms on the other. The largest room was the **megaron** with four columns supporting the roof and surrounding the central hearth; it had both domestic and religious purposes. Beyond lay the king and queen's private apartments, usually with baths. The best examples of Mycenaean palaces are in Mycenae, Tiryns and Pylos.

The dead were buried on the edge of the city in either a pit grave, a rock sepulchre or a circular domed chamber *(thólos)* with an entrance passage *(drómos)*. The skilled craftsmanship of the objects found in these **tombs** indicates that the princes buried in them were astonishingly rich; for many years the graves were known as "treasuries". The best examples of Mycenaean graves are at Mycenae, Chios, Vapheio, Peristéria (in Peloponnese) and Orchomenos (in Boeotia).

TEMPLES (700 BC ONWARDS)

The temple was the dwelling place of the god or goddess to whom it was dedicated and housed his or her statue; some temples were dedicated to more than one divinity. Thought to represent the architectural ideal, they are essentially a blend of structural simplicity and harmonious proportions. The proportions were governed by the module, the average radius of the column, which determined the height since the column was the basic element in the elevation of the building.

In some buildings the architects departed from rigid verticals and horizontals to correct optical distortion. The horizontal entablatures were slightly bowed, making the centre imperceptibly higher than the ends; each column was inclined towards its inner neighbour as it rose, the angle of incline increasing from the centre of the colonnade towards the outer corner.

Sculpted figures, often didactic, were placed on the secondary architectural features: the *tympanum* (pediment) and the *metopes* (architrave).

The temples were painted: the background was generally red with the prominent features in blue to form a contrast. These brilliant colours made the stone or white marble sculptures stand out. A gilded bronze colour was used to pick out certain decorative motifs such as shields or *acroteria*. There were three main types. The large peripteral temple consisted of a central oblong chamber *(naos)* containing the divinity's statue, with a porch at either end screened by two columns; one porch *(prónaos)* led into the **naos**, the other *(opisthódomos)* contained the temple's most precious offerings.

The roof of the *naos* might be supported on two rows of columns. Behind the *naos* there was occasionally an inner chamber *(adyton)* which only the priest could enter. This was surrounded by a colonnade *(peristyle)* and the temple was described in terms of the number of columns in the front and rear colonnades: *hexastyle* (six). A temple's length was usually twice its width. The "in antis" temple consisted of a *naos* and *pronaos* screened by two columns between two pilasters at the ends of the extended walls of the *naos*. The **thólos**

was a votive or commemorative circular building with a peristyle.

The main elements of a temple were the base *(stylobate)*, the columns, the entablature supporting a wooden roof frame covered with tiles and a pediment at either end. The articulation of these elements gave rise to the orders.

Developed on the mainland among the Dorian people, the **Doric** Order was the most common style in Greece from the 7C onwards. The columns, which had 20 flutes, rested directly on the stylobate without bases; the capitals were plain. The entablature consisted of three parts one above the other: the architrave, the frieze and the cornice; the frieze was composed of *metopes*, panels often carved in high relief, alternating with triglyphs, stone slabs with two vertical grooves. The triangular pediments were sculpted with scenes in high relief and also adorned with decorative motifs *(acroteria)* at the angles. Along the sides above the cornice were sculpted ornaments *(antefixa)* which served as gargoyles. The Ionians who had settled in Asia Minor in the 5C BC created the **Ionic** Order, which was considered a feminine style; its delicate grace and rich ornament contrasted with the austere strength of the Doric Order. Its main characteristics are tall slim columns with 24 flutes resting on moulded bases and crowned by capitals in the form of a double scroll; an entablature consisting of an architrave, a continuous sculpted frieze, a cornice decorated with egg and dart, and leaf and dart moulding; a pediment with *acroteria* shaped like palm leaves at the angles. The **Temple of Athena Nike** in the Acropolis is the best example.

Invented in Corinth in the 5C BC the **Corinthian** Order did not spread until the 4C BC; it was very popular in the Roman period. It is a derivative of the Ionic Order and its chief distinction is the scroll capital almost entirely covered in curled acanthus leaves. The best examples are the **Olympoeion** and **Hadrian's Arch** in Athens and the **Temple of Octavian** in Corinth. The capital was invented by **Kallimachos**, a sculptor and contemporary of Pheidias.

Odeon of Herodes Atticus, Athens
© J Malburet/MICHELIN

THEATRES

Nearly all religious sites in Ancient Greece included a theatre originally designed for the Dionysiac festivals that included hymns or dithyrambs, which later developed into tragedy. The original wooden structures were later built of stone and from the 4C BC comprised:

◆ a central circular area *(orchestra)* where the chorus performed round the altar of the god and the actors wearing the appropriate masks acted their parts;

◆ tiers of seats *(koilon or theatron)* extending round more than half the orchestra to form the segment of a circle; the first row of seats was reserved for the priests and officials; a promenade *(diázoma)* ran round between the upper and lower tiers of seats. The audience reached their seats from above, from the diázoma or through passages *(parodos)* leading into the orchestra;

◆ a proscenium *(proskenion)*, a sort of portico forming a backdrop, and a stage *(skene)*, originally a storeroom. In the Hellenistic period the stage was incorporated into the performing area; the back wall improved the acoustics.

Odeons were covered theatres, which grew in number in the Roman period. The major theatres are in Athens, Delphi, Argos, Epidaurus and Dodona.

BYZANTINE ARCHITECTURE

After Christianity's establishment there was impetus for an architectural form that would differentiate the new religion from the pagan Greek temples. Although continuity with the Roman styles persisted in the simple basilica (a central nave divided from the aisles through two colonnades), Orthodox Christianity extended this design fairly quickly through the characteristic shape of a dome lying on a Greek cross, as the central transept was broadened and widened to carry the cupola's weight. The dome itself symbolised the celestial sphere, dominated by the figure of Christ, while the iconostasis (a wall of icons separating the nave from the sanctuary) presented the faithful with soul-uplifting imagery. Byzantine architecture reached its peak in the 6C BC with Agia Sophia and never looked back – or forward. While in the West it evolved into the Romanesque and in the East became the blueprint for Islam, the format remained frozen and proscriptive within Byzantium: today's immediately recognisable Greek churches are built in the same style as their predecessors 1,000 years ago. Because of the long Turkish and Venetian occupations of Byzantium there are few examples of secular architecture (e.g. palaces, villas, forts). Many that have survived are concentrated on Mt Athos and, most notably, Mystras, where the whole town serves as a unique window to the Byzantine era.

Art

Classical Greek art dominated the ancient world for about 1,000 years, while Byzantine architecture and iconography impacted on Orthodox Eastern Europe and Russia for another 1,000 years. Such traditions have survived and flourished in post-independence Greece, when it opened up to the world and reflected Western artistic influences.

ARCHAIC PERIOD (700–500 BC)

In the 7C BC the Greek world began to produce its first full-size statues, strange, rigid figures made of wood *(xoanon)*, with ecstatic expressions inspired by Asiatic, particularly Egyptian, models.

In the 6C BC two well-known and distinctive types of statue were produced: the **kouros**, a naked young man, and the **kore**, a young woman dressed in a tunic, Doric **peplos** or Ionian **cheiton**. The figures, which were life size or larger, were sometimes made of bronze, like the Piraeus Apollo discovered in 1959, but more often of limestone *(poros)* or marble and then painted with vivid colours.

The high reliefs, carved in stone and also painted, mostly come from pediments and are impressive for their realistic and expressive appearance; the bronze sculptures are more stylised.

The Acropolis Museum in Athens has an important series of Archaic figures (*kouroi* and *korai*, high-relief pedimental sculptures, *moschophoroi*); the National Museum displays the **Warrior of Marathon** and several *kouroi* including the Kouros of Sounion, the oldest known (600 BC), and the Kouros of Anávissos; the **Piraeus Apollo** (late 6C BC) is to be found in the Piraeus Museum.

Other examples typical of Archaic art are the stone gorgon from the Temple of Artemis in Corfu (Corfu Museum), the marble frieze from the Sifnian Treasury and two *kouroi* representing Cleobis and Biton (Delphi Museum).

CLASSICAL PERIOD (500–300 BC)

There was a transition period, marked by the **Charioteer of Delphi** (475 BC), where the figure turns slightly to the right and takes his weight on one hip; passing through two distinct phases, Classical statuary then freed itself from the rigid frontal stance.

In the idealistic phase (5C BC) Greek sculpture reached its height in the work of **Polykleitos** and **Pheidias**. The former established a standard model, the **canon**. The latter created an ideal standard of beauty composed of strength, majesty and serenity in the delicately carved lines of his marble figures: his genius is expressed in the Parthenon sculptures (Acropolis Museum, British Museum, Louvre); unfortunately the famous chryselephantine (gold and ivory) statue of Zeus at Olympia was destroyed. Other typical works of the period include **Athena Mourning** in the Acropolis Museum and *Poseidon* from Artemision in the National Museum.

During the "naturalist" phase (4C) majesty gave way to grace and the female nude made its appearance. Artists began to compose from nature giving their figures expressive faces; the best known are Skopas, Lysippos and Praxiteles who produced tall figures such as the Hermes of Olympia.

The *Apollo Belvedere* (Vatican) also dates from this time as do the great bronzes in the Athens Museum: the *Ephebe* from Antikythera and the *Athena* and *Artemis* in the archaeological museum in Piraeus.

Tanágra in Boeotia produced the famous funerary figurines in terracotta.

HELLENISTIC PERIOD (300–100 BC)

Sculpture began to be influenced by expressionism and orientalism. Realism, sometimes excessive, was used to express not only pain but also movement as in the *Laocoön* (Vatican) and the *Victory of Samothrace* (Louvre); at the same time it could produce the beautiful serenity of the *Melos Aphrodite (Venus de Milo)*. Artists took delight in repre-

Detail of frescoes in Knossós, Crete

© P. de Franqueville/MICHELIN

senting old people and children, such as the bronze jockey from Artemision in the National Archaeological Museum, Athens.

PAINTING AND CERAMICS

Except for the Minoan frescoes in Crete or Thíra (Santorini) and the Hellenistic funerary paintings in Macedonia (👁 *see Véria*) few examples of Ancient Greek painting have survived. In fact, although painting played a major role in the decoration of sculptures and monuments, it was less important as an art form in its own right and the works of the great painters of the 4C BC – Zeuxis and above all Apelles, Alexander the Great's favourite artist – have not survived the passage of time. For a knowledge of Greek painting one must study the decoration of pottery on the many vases which have come down to us.

The ornamentation painted on vases is one of the major sources of information about Greek religion and civilisation. These vases had specific functions: the *pithos* was used for storing grain, the *amphora* for the storing and transport of oil or wine. The *pelike*, *krater* and *hydria* were used as jars for oil, wine and water respectively. The *oinochoë* was used as a jug for pouring water or wine into a *kantharos*; the *kylix* was a drinking cup and the *rhyton* was a vessel shaped like a horn or an animal's head. The *lekythos* was a funerary vase.

Styles developed in step with the great artistic periods; there were several types.

Creto-Mycenaean vases (1700–1400 BC): scenes of flora and fauna treated with great freedom and decorative sense. Typical examples: octopus *amphora*; Phaistos *krater* (Herakleion Museum); Santorini vases (National Museum in Athens).

Archaic vases (1000–600 BC): geometric style in the Cyclades and Attica with large *kraters* or *amphorae* decorated with dotted lines, the key pattern, checks, lozenges and sometimes animals; orientalising style in Rhodes and Corinth where small vessels were decorated with oriental motifs: roses, lotus sprays, sphinxes and deer.

© Scala, Florence/Archaeological Museum, Florence

Detail of a kylix showing Athena building the Trojan Horse

Typical examples: *amphorae* from the Kerameikos and the Dipylon (National Museum in Athens); perfume flasks (Corinth Museum).

Black-figure vases (600–480 BC): subjects for decoration drawn from mythology or history: silhouettes in black painted on a red ochre ground. Typical examples: *krater* showing Herakles and Nereus (National Museum in Athens).

Red-figure vases (480–320 BC): subject for decoration not only mythological (so-called "severe" style – 5C BC) but also familiar and more light-hearted: scenes and figures drawn in detail and accentuated by a black or white ground (*lekythoi*). Typical examples: *krater* from Kalyx and *lekythoi* from Erétria (National Museum in Athens).

BYZANTINE ART

Byzantine art revolves mostly around religion. The Orthodox Churches interpreted the Second Commandment "Thou shalt not make unto thee any graven image" as a prohibition against sculpture, which explains the lack of statues in Orthodox churches, but thankfully not against painting. Thus Eastern creative energy was channelled towards the production of mosaics, frescoes and, mainly, icons. The first two can be considered as a continuation of the Roman tradition and it is no coincidence that

Virgin and Child, Benáki Museum, Athens
© Scala, Florence

the best examples are found in Italy such as in San Vitale in Ravenna.

Icons, however, are a genuine product of Orthodoxy, being considered an intermediate layer between the veneration of God and the saints, and the faithful. As St Basil asserted, the honour bestowed upon the holy image passed on to the archetype. It is for this reason that the format of the icon is stylised and symbolic with the emphasis on the supernatural, ethereal and otherworldly, as opposed to the verisimilitude of Western religious painting. It is also why upon encountering the ghostly, hauntingly gaunt figures of the iconostasis one feels an appreciation of the Sacrosanct and an insight into the Holy.

Byzantine music and composition was also mostly liturgical and choral, employing chromatic scales which sound positively oriental to the Western ear and based upon powerful religious poetry. The best examples of Byzantine hymnody can be heard in any Greek church during Fridays in Lent ("Chairetismoi") and in the Holy Week ("Tropario tis Kassianis" on Tuesday).

TRADITION AND INFLUENCE

The accession to the throne of Otto of Bavaria in 1832 heralded the arrival of foreign artists who taught at the College of Fine Arts, founded in 1843. They influenced numerous Greek artists; other Greek painters studied abroad, notably in Munich, like **Nikifóros Lýtras** (1832–1904) who concentrated on painting portraits and scenes from daily life. Another famous name of the "Munich school" was **Konstantínos Volonákis** (1839–1907), who made his name as a marine artist, although his *Munich Circus* exhibited at the National Gallery in Athens shows a move towards Impressionism. In all spheres of art, the second half of the 19C in Greece bore the stamp of officially approved academicism.

At the turn of the century art in Greece underwent an important evolution under the influence, in painting, of **Konstantínos Parthénis** (1878–1967), who followed the path of post-Impressionism

Cycladic Art and Idols

The brilliant civilisation that flourished at the end of the third millennium BC in the Cyclades left behind a great deal of artistic evidence. This included painted and engraved ceramics, jewellery, elaborate weapons, but, above all, astonishing marble statuettes, the famous Cycladic idols, whose function remains shrouded in mystery.

They mainly represent women, arms crossed over naked bodies, with oval, flat and perfectly smooth heads and only a nose protruding. Less common forms include musicians, flautists or harpists sitting cross-legged.

These surprisingly modern artworks, with their perfect proportions, bold curves and acute sense of stylisation, influenced many 20C artists, especially the Cubists.

© Albert B. Knapp MD/Pictures Colour Library

Cycladic marble female figurine (2800–2300 BC), Museum of Cycladic Art, Athens

taught at the College of Fine Arts, and of the sculptor **Konstantínos Dimitriádis** (1881–1943), who was inspired by Rodin. They opened the way for Greek art to embrace modern forms and the most advanced movements of the time, as seen in the work of the expressionist painter **Giórgos Bouziánis** (1885–1959), cubist **Níkos Gíkas** (1906–1994), and the internationally acclaimed surrealist **Níkos Engonópoulos** (1910–1985).

After the Second World War, Greek art flourished again, following two principal directions. Together with the search for a true Greek spirit, of which the main exponent was **Yánnis Móralis** (1916–2009), there developed a strong movement concerned with contemporary forms. Its most notable members were the following abstract painters: **Alékos Kontópoulos** (1905–1975), **Chrístos Lefákis** (1906–1968) and **Yánnis Spyrópoulos** (1912–1990); and the sculptors **Giórgos Zogolópoulos** (1903–2004) and **Achilleús Apérgis** (1909–1986). Although on the one hand there is a clear return to representative art, notably with the painter **Yánnis Gaitis** (1923–1984) and the sculptor

Giórgos Giorgiádis, those Greek artists working in a contemporary vein are ever more closely linked with the various Western artistic movements, many of them working abroad.

In addition to figures such as **George Candilis** (1913–1995), the architect who designed the urban development at Toulouse-le-Murail and also worked in Berlin, and **Marios Prássinos** (1916–1985), well known for his pointillist works in black and white and the cartoons he produced for the Aubusson weavers, two names have gained international recognition.

Yánnis Kounéllis (b.1936) lives and works in Italy, where he has been active in the **Arte Povera** movement; after offering performances and installations, he has taken a more minimalist line which purports to be close to poetry in its original form.

Panayótis Vassilákis, known as **Takis** (b.1925), has been living in Paris since 1954. His name is associated with technology in art, with his research into magnetism using constructions of metal rods, indicator lights and electromagnets, and making musical clocks.

Classical Civilisation

Modern Western civilisation finds its origins in Ancient Greece. Almost everything recognised in the West as art has its roots in a few centuries of Greece's history. Ancient Greece witnessed the dawn of poetry with Homer's great epics the *Iliad* and the *Odyssey*; the Acropolis of Athens defined architectural and sculpture standards for centuries; theatre was born with the tragedies and comedies of Aeschylus, Sophocles and Euripides; history started being written with Herodotus; while the meticulous examination of nature ignited Western philosophy, mathematics, geography, physics and astronomy.

The First Storytellers

Two poets are identified with the origins of Greek literature: **Homer** (late 9C to mid-8C BC), although there is little firm evidence of his existence and many believe his oeuvre to be the work of various authors, and the peasant poet **Hesiod** from Boeotia (late 8C BC), of whom more is known from the contents of his work.

Homer's two great epics are the *Iliad* and the *Odyssey*, which include some of the most famous characters of the Greek imagination. The *Iliad* does not simply recount the story of the Trojan War; it focuses on the anger of Achilles and how it jeopardises the whole of the Greek attack on Troy. Less warlike in tone, the *Odyssey* recounts a long journey during which the hero Odysseus (Ulysses) has to overcome many dangers before returning home to his love. Both are tales of the struggles of man, but the gods play significant roles, siding with one party or another.

Hesiod recounts the origins of the gods and their conflicts in the *Theogony*; his other great poem, *Works and Days*, traces the origins of humankind and depicts a rustic ideal.

History

Tragedy treated the the past with a dramatic sensibility, while history sought to keep records of fact. The pioneer historians of the 5C BC worked to transcribe the mythical past and bear full witness for the benefit of future generations.

Herodotus (mid-5C BC) is generally acknowledged to be the first historian. He was born in Halicarnassus in Asia Minor at a time when the city was ruled by the Persians. An avid traveller (to the Greek mainland, Egypt and Scythia), he gathered vast amounts of information on his journeys for his work on the history of the Persian War. Unlike previous storytellers, Herodotus tried to explain historical change.

Thucydides (c.460–404 BC) produced a history of the Peloponnesian War; this relied on analytical methods (notably eyewitness accounts) explained by the author at the beginning of the work, which have a remarkable modernity. Thucydides was an Athenian and, unlike Herodotus, avoids myth and digressions in his single-minded pursuit of the cause and course of the war between his native city and Sparta.

In the 4C BC **Xenophon** (c.430–350 BC), a pupil of Socrates, produced historical works which were narrative rather than analytical in style. He completed the history of the Peloponnesian War which Thucydides, whose work breaks off in the middle of a sentence, was not able to complete.

Philosophy

Tracing its origins to Greek cities in Asia Minor in the 6C, philosophy (a Greek word literally meaning "love of wisdom") sought to explain the mysteries of the universe without resort to myth. The earliest philosophers were active at Miletus in Asia Minor: among them was **Thales** (c.620–546 BC), who looked for general principles governing the cosmos and famously predicted a solar eclipse. The Greek-Italian philosopher **Parmenides** (515–445 BC) introduced another revolutionary idea with the theory that the ultimate source of reality lay outside the material world.

Pythagoras, a Greek philosopher whose writings have not survived, worked in the late 6C BC and pioneered the study of mathematics. Today he is probably best remembered through the theorem that was named after his discovery that the square of the length of the hypotenuse of a right-angled triangle is equal to the sum of the squares of the other two sides. Pythagoras was born on Samos but emigrated to Croton in southern Italy, and it was there that his reputation was established.

It was with **Socrates** (470–399 BC) that philosophy began to make its mark; he endeavoured to lay bare the falsehoods distorting public opinion, refute the claims of politicians and reveal their ignorance. Socrates left no written documentary evidence, but his pupil Plato (428–347 BC) ensured that his ideas would survive and thrive.

Plato remains a hugely important figure in philosophy. A citizen of Athens, he founded the world's first institution of higher learning with his Academy. Plato's theory of eternal Forms, underlying the world of appearance, was of tremendous consequence for Western philosophy. After the execution of Socrates following his trial for subversion in Athens, Plato fled the city in fear of his own life. He travelled to Greek colonies in the south of Italy and Sicily, returning to Athens around 360 BC. These were the years of his Academy and his most brilliant student there was Aristotle.

© J. Malburet/MICHELIN

Aristotle, National Archaeological Museum, Athens

Aristotle (384–322 BC) was Plato's pupil but his pragmatic ideas represented a departure, drawing their inspiration from reality rather than abstract concepts. He distinguished between the different disciplines, identifying logic, rhetoric, ethics, politics and physics in their own right.

Men like Thales and Pythagoras are seen as the fathers of mathematics, but their achievements also included discoveries in astronomy and physics. Other philosophers also made great discoveries, such as **Hippocrates** (c.460–377 BC), whose work in the field of medicine was to remain the backbone of the subject until the Middle Ages.

Numerous philosophical schools were active between the 4C and 2C BC: the Epicureans, the Stoics, the Cynics and the Sceptics. Philosophy's basic tenet, which was the nature of the individual, was in contrast to the traditional social structure of the city state and served to hasten its demise.

Religion

Whereas Greek Antiquity has given us divine myths which have become the subject of art for centuries, modern Greeks define their nationhood by their language and especially by their Orthodox religion, which kept them distinct from the Muslim Turks during 400 years of occupation.

MYTHOLOGY

Gods who mixed with men, watching over them, sharing their feelings, their sorrows as well as joys; such are the divinities who inhabited the Greek pantheon. This interweaving of mortal and immortal forms the inspiration for the religion of Ancient Greece.

What the modern world understands as classical religion involved a series of rituals performed in specific locations or in private involving persons of status. These well-defined rites commemorated divinities or heroes whose exploits form a complex and remarkable web which we call **mythology**.

Originally a purely oral tradition, this series of tales came to be recorded in writing, starting with Hesiod's *Theogony*.

THE PANTHEON OF GODS

Unlike biblical tradition, which presupposes a god outside and above the world, the Greek creation myth involves a separation of primitive forces from which the gods were born.

From **Chaos** (a chasm of darkness) emerged **Gaia** (the Earth, mother of all) and then Eros. To the Greeks, Chaos was neuter, Gaia feminine, and Eros masculine; between them, they constituted the three primitive forces. Also to emerge from Chaos were Erebe (total darkness) and Nyx (the night) who begat Ether (light) and Hemera (the day). Gaia then begat Ouranos (the sky) and Pontos (the oceans). Ouranos and Gaia went on to have numerous offspring, including Kronos and Rhea who were parents to the principal Olympian gods and goddesses.

Zeus is the king of the Olympian divinities; his name appears on Linear B tablets dating back to 1400 BC. A weather god originally, Zeus dispatches thunderstorms against his enemies and is often depicted hurling a thunderbolt. **Hera** is his wife and sister, independent in spirit but jealous of her husband's philandering and capable of exacting cruel vengeance against women who catch his eye. **Demeter** is the goddess of fertility and grain and she had a daughter with Zeus, who in myth became assimilated with **Persephone** who was carried to the Underworld by the god **Hermes** and made his wife. Desperately seeking her daughter, Demeter let the earth go barren until Zeus decreed that her daughter be allowed to return. However, because Persephone had eaten some pomegranate seeds while in the Underworld, she was obligated to Hades and had to spend a part of every year with him (the four hot months of the Greek summer when the soil is unproductive). **Poseidon** is another one of the more important gods, governing the sea and as patron of seafarers had temples devoted to him in coastal regions of Greece. Poseidon, often portrayed in myth as rather brutish, was the lover of Medusa, a winged monster with hair of snakes and a face capable of turning men who gazed on it to stone. His mistress was Scylla, turned into a ferocious sea monster by a jealous rival for the attention of the sea god. Very different to Poseidon is the goddess **Athena**, patron of the city of Athens, born from the head of Zeus with the help of the smith god **Hephaestus**. Athena was worshipped in Sparta and other cities but her principal temple was the Parthenon in Athens. The goddess of wisdom and disciplined warfare, her orderly nature is opposed to the bloodthirsty **Ares** who is the god of murderous war.

The gods and goddesses lived in majesty on Mount Olympus hidden in the clouds with Zeus the thunderer at their head. There was also a host of lesser divinities: local gods, Egyptian and Syrian gods, demi-gods born of the love affairs between the greater gods and mere mortals, and heroes; they all peopled an

Statue of Athena, National Archaeological Museum, Athens

ever-growing pantheon where divinities from the Creto-Mycenaean period gradually became confused with the great gods whose cult was reduced to catering for special needs.

RITUALS

Religious celebrations took various forms depending on the purpose of the ceremony, which could be adjusted for individual circumstances and used for initiation. The complex **mysteries** which made use of symbolic objects such as representations of sexual organs were supposed to bring eternal salvation and ensure an afterlife; the most famous were performed at **Eleusis** (Elefsína). Another purpose of the ceremonies was to foretell future events, and so the faithful also came to consult the **oracles**, replies which the gods sent through the medium of the priests. The sanctuary of Apollo at **Delphi** (Delfí) is famous for the predictions made there by the **Pythia**. The rites could, of course, involve the whole community, and the most important ceremonies took place on the occasion of particular festivals. They were accompanied by activities which for us today have no connection with religion,

such as poetry competitions or games and sporting events. The athletic and horse-riding competitions also had an aspect of initiation, since the winner (for example at the **Panhellenic Games** held annually at Olympia) received a sacred olive branch brought by **Herakles** (Hercules). The cult of **Dionysos** was accompanied by choruses, originally not written down, which are considered to have been the origin of all forms of theatre, whether tragedy, comedy or satire (the Satyrs were the companions of Dionysos). The prayers were usually accompanied by an offering: libations of milk or wine, and cakes and fruit placed before the altar. In return for a favour from the god a commemorative stele or a small votive statue would sometimes be promised. For a more important request animal sacrifice was used, part of which was burnt on the altar and the rest divided between the priests and the faithful. There were also purification rites with the purpose of cleansing the persons or objects considered impure by sprinkling them with water.

The temple *(hieron)*, dedicated to the god or goddess, stood within a sacred precinct *(témenos)* which was entered by a grand gateway *(propylaia)*. Purified with consecrated water, the worshippers entered the precinct and proceeded along the sacred way past the treasuries, small buildings for the reception of offerings, the semicircular bench seats *(exedra)* and the votive offerings (inscriptions, statues) which also surrounded the temple. The altar, where the libations were poured and the animals were sacrificed, stood in the open in front of the temple. After the sacrifice the people entered the temple vestibule to see the statue of the divinity through the open door of the inner chamber *(naos)*.

BYZANTINE ORTHODOX CHURCH

Actively involved in state politics, eastern Christianity evolved through numerous heresies and schism with Catholicism into Orthodoxy, strictly interpreting the teachings of the Gospels. Close to the ordinary people, it is

The Roles of the Gods

(Latin names in brackets)

Name	Sphere	Attributes
Aphrodite *(Venus)*	Amorous love	Doves, shells
Apollo *(Apollo)*	Light, the arts	Lyre, arrows, laurel, sun
Ares *(Mars)*	War	Helmet, arms and armour
Artemis *(Diana)*	Chastity, hunting	Bow and quiver
Athena *(Minerva)*	Wisdom, arts and crafts	Shield, helmet, owl, olive branch
Demeter *(Ceres)*	Farming, motherly love	Ear of wheat, sceptre, scythe
Dionysos *(Bacchus)*	Wine, joy	Vine, thyrsus, goat, panther
Hades *(Pluto)*	Underworld	Throne, beard
Hephaistos *(Vulcan)*	Fire, metal	Anvil, hammer
Hera *(Juno)*	Marriage (Zeus's wife)	Peacock, diadem
Hermes *(Mercury)*	Commerce and eloquence	Winged sandals and helmet, caduceus, ram
Hestia *(Vesta)*	Family hearth	Fire
Poseidon *(Neptune)*	Sea and storms	Trident
Zeus *(Jupiter)*	King of gods and the world	Eagle, sceptre, thunder

ever present in the landscape through its countless churches and monasteries. Fundamental to the faith is the cult of images and relics; the domes of its churches have since the earliest times been decorated with beautiful mosaic work by anonymous artists seeking to glorify God.

HERESY, SCHISM AND RECONCILIATION

It is impossible to dissociate the Hellenisation of the Eastern Empire and its conversion to Christianity. Just as **Hellenism** was gaining ground, the Christian religion was spreading throughout the territory. In the early days of Christianity, its adherents were only united on a few articles of faith and worship. Its evolution was marked by the gradual growth of an internal hierarchy with the creation of bishops and archbishops. When in AD 380 Theodosius the Great made Christianity the official religion and out-

lawed pagan cults, his intention was to consolidate the temporal structure of the Empire by insisting on its spiritual unity. But the distance between **Rome**, the religious capital and Constantinople, the political capital, made communication between the emperor and the head of the Church difficult. So **Constantinople** was raised to the status of metropolis, the same title as Rome, by a Council of 381, a decision confirmed and reinforced by the Council of Chalcedon in 451, which gave Constantinople primacy throughout the east.

Although the link between the emperor and the patriarchate in Constantinople and the dependence of the one on the other was confirmed, the Church of Rome maintained its supremacy over ever more vast territories beyond the control of the eastern emperor and insisted ever more firmly on its divine right to rule, inherited from its first bishop, St Peter.

Differences of interpretation between the two Churches also came to the surface. In addition, numerous heretical sects were popular: **Arianism** followed the tenets laid down by the early-4C Alexandrian bishop Arius (Christ's divinity was secondary to that of God); the **Nestorians** adhered to the teachings of the 5C bishop Nestorius (Christ was simply a man, not a God-made man); the **Monophysites** (5C–6C), on the other hand, emphasised Christ's divinity rather than humanity. All these sects were condemned at the Council of Ephesus in 431, and again at the Council of Chalcedon 20 years later, but their influence remained strong in some regions of the Empire. More important was the issue of **iconoclasm**, promoted by Emperor Leo III from 726 with the aim of bringing the eastern peoples back into the Orthodox fold; this required the destruction of all images (icons and other representations of the godhead). The long internal conflict resulting from this prohibition also aggravated the divisions between the Eastern and Western Churches. Iconoclasm was finally abandoned in 843, and icons have remained a prominent feature of Orthodox worship to this day. In the temporal sphere, the crowning of Charlemagne as Emperor of the West by the Pope in 800 made him a usurper in the eyes of the Byzantines, who regarded their emperor as the sole legitimate heir to the Roman Empire. In the religious field the main subject of dispute was the Filioque issue (the use in the "Credo" of the doctrine that the Holy Ghost proceeds from the Father and the Son). Despite many attempts to restore unity, a gulf gradually opened up between east and west, between Orthodoxy and Roman Catholicism. The final break came in 1054 when the Patriarch of Constantinople, Michael I Cerularius, and Pope Leo IX excommunicated one another.

The Crusades brought Roman Catholic monks to Greece, especially **Cistercians**, whose task was to work towards oecumenism ("union"). At the same time, the critical situation in which the Empire found itself meant it had to seek a rapprochement with Rome, already indispensable in view of the capture of Constantinople by the **Crusaders** in 1204. The plan was to take on more concrete form with the **Council of Lyon** (1274), held by Pope Gregory X in the presence of the Latin Emperor Baldwin II de Courtenay and the Byzantine Emperor Michael VIII Paleologos, who accepted the conditions laid down by Rome. The plan failed because of the sustained opposition by the Orthodox Christians. A second attempt to achieve oecumenism in Greece was made in 1439 at the **Council of Florence**, which brought together Pope Eugenius IV, the Emperor John VIII Paleologos, Cardinal Bessarion and the philosopher Georgios Gemistos Plethon. After agreement had been reached on the Filioque clause, Purgatory, the primacy of the Pope and the freedom of liturgical practices, the act of union was signed by all Orthodox bishops present but one, but this propitious project was wrecked again by the Eastern clergy and civil authorities back home.

MONASTIC PRESTIGE

The strictly hierarchical Eastern clergy had at its head the patriarch, chosen by the emperor from a list of three candidates put forward by the Synod, composed of senior clergy drawn from the aristocracy. The position was as important as that of any of the great offices of state. At the other extreme, the local clergy, usually peasant-priests, performed an administrative role in the villages of the Empire. Their role was more functional than spiritual. The ordinary population, whose zeal focused on images and relics, looked to the monastic communities for religious guidance.

The earliest monks were hermits who sought out the isolation of desert life. It was St Pacomas who developed a new means of withdrawal from society by bringing together communities of monks to live in monasteries. Geographically, visually and spiritually, monasticism came to occupy centre stage in Greek life. The monk was cast in the role of holy man, whose wisdom was in demand as much for practical advice as for religious guidance. Unsurprisingly, the tombs of exceptional examples of such figures became local sites of pilgrimage, often marked by the construction of a church or monastery. Every detail of their lives was perpetuated through oral tradition, thereby creating characters of legendary status, and their relics were invested with miraculous powers.

As with icons, relics were perceived to be sacred and became objects of unparalleled veneration. Around such items grew up cult places of worship which made the monasteries rich, incurring the resentment of the temporal authorities who realised, however, that relics, unlike icons, could not be banned.

CHURCH DOMES AND THE APOGEE OF MOSAICS

The confluence of Roman civilisation and the traditions of Asia Minor give rise to a distinctive Byzantine style most clearly expressed in religious architecture. Certain features are ubiquitous, such as the centralised plan and the dome decorated to resemble the heavens (the ability to construct domes on rectangular structures was the great architectural triumph of the age).

Inheriting the layout of Classical buildings, early Christian churches (5C–6C) were preceded by an atrium. The design was either a basilica or had a Greek cross layout, with an imposing dome at the centre and galleries for women worshippers. Only the ruins of such churches remain now at Philippi, Lechaion in Corinth, and Thessaloniki.

A second golden age of architecture (9C–12C) saw the construction of many more churches, often small in scale but of perfect proportions, built to a cross-in-square design, most striking when viewed from the exterior. These buildings, usually entered through a narthex, have domes resting on drums to give them greater height, and are decorated with low-relief carvings, marble and mosaic work. Fine examples may be seen at Daphne, Óssios Loukás in Boeotia, Néa Moní in Chios and Agia Sophia in Monemvassía.

RENAISSANCE UNDER THE PALAEOLOGUES (13C–16C)

More elaborate schemes combining basilica and Greek cross designs, multiple domes and increased fresco decoration were the features of this period, as can be seen in the churches of Thessaloniki, Árta, Kastoriá and Mystras. Churches were ornately decorated with polychrome marble pavements, frescoes (from 13C), and mosaics using gold and warm colours. The subject matter was strictly defined by religious dogma: in the dome, Christ *Pantocrator* (the Creator) surrounded by archangels, Apostles and Evangelists; the Virgin *Theotokos* (Mother of God) or *Galactophoroussa* (Suckling the Christ Child) between the archangels Michael and Gabriel in the apse; scenes from the life of Christ or the Virgin, usually following the sequence of feast days rather than chronological order. Some of the finest Byzantine mosaics may be observed in the monasteries of Daphne, Néa Moní at Chios and Óssios Loukás.

Alongside these dazzling works of art, the tradition of **icon** painting and its significance to the eastern Christian tradition must be considered. Painted on wood, these images are displayed in churches on the iconostasis but are equally common in private homes. Objects of veneration once accused of being idolatrous, their purpose was confirmed by the Council of Nicaea in 787 ("God the Son is the living icon of God the Father"). Among the commonest subjects of icon painting are the Last Judgment, the Dormition of the Virgin and the Nativity. The archangels Michael and Gabriel are often depicted at the head of celestial armies. The most venerated saints are the hierarchs or doctors of the Church, namely John Chrysostom, Basil and Gregory of Nazianzus. Other popular saints are John the Baptist (known as Prodromos, the forerunner), George (depicted slaying the dragon), Andrew of Patra, Dimitrios of Thessaloniki, Nicolaos, Athanasios, Stylianos of Corfu, the two Theodores of Egypt and the Studite, Cosmas and Damian, St Constantine and Nektarios.

Literature and Language

Although the Greek language has been spoken without interruption through the ages, it has undergone profound changes. A scholar of Classical Greek needs special studies to understand the Homeric epics; the language of Plato is very different to the simpler, Hellenistic Greek of the Bible; and modern Demotic Greek has progressed a long way from the language of the Byzantine liturgy.

LINGUISTIC CHANGES

Throughout the Ottoman period, the patriarchate preserved a formal Greek speech which was used by the elite, while the majority of the population spoke various dialects. **Dimitrios Katardzis** (1730–1807) was the first public figure to propose a policy of teaching and promoting a correct form of the language to the general population. Subsequently **Adamantios Koraïs** (1748–1833) adopted a simple and sober form of the educated language *(katharévoussa)*, enriched it and brought it up to date. This was used as the official language, appearing in administration, media, and schools. The language used by the ordinary people, known as Demotic, remained unchanged by these developments. After the Second World War, the socialist press began to print their newspapers in Demotic Greek as a reaction against the bourgeois sentiments of other papers. In 1974, Demotic Greek was recognised as the official language of the country, although certain official documents still employ the formal style. Thus the law followed the lead of the country's authors, who for many years had written their books in the language of the people.

A LITERARY RENAISSANCE
THE IONIAN SCHOOL

In the Ionian Islands, the Greek uprising inspired the first Neohellenic poetry. Originally from Zakynthos, **Andreas Kalvos** (1792–1867) holds an important place in the history of Greek literature because of his publication of 20 odes in two volumes in Geneva and Paris in Greek and French: *La Lyre* (1824) and *Odes Nouvelles* (1826). The leader of this "Ionian School" was another native of Zakynthos, **Dionysios Solomos** (1798–1857); he blended romantic feelings with Classical rigour. Part of his *Hymn to Liberty* (translated into English by Rudyard Kipling) is now the Greek national anthem.

ROMANTICISM OF THE ATHENS SCHOOL AND CONTEMPORARY MOVEMENTS

As Europe's intellectuals encouraged the Greek uprising, so Greece's authors drew upon foreign works for their inspiration: *The Prince of Morea* (1850) by Kleon Rizos-Rangavis, for example, shows the influence of Sir Walter Scott. The unbridled romanticism of the **Athens School** is characterised by a reactionary chauvinism mixed with foreign influences from writers such as Musset and Byron. The memoirs of **Yannis Makriyannis** (1797–1864), a merchant who took up arms to fight for liberation from the Ottomans, provide an insight into the realities of the struggle of ordinary people against the occupiers, and have an essential humanity untainted by preoccupation with stylistic issues.

Another important figure in 19C Greek literature is **Emmanuel Roïdis** (1836–1904), author of *Pope Jean* (1866), a stylishly satirical work which defied the romantic status quo.

POETRY AND PROSE
POETRY

As a reaction to the often mediocre realism of the Romantics, Symbolism became popular. A pioneer of the new style was **Ioannis Papadiamantopoulos** (1856–1910), who wrote in the French language under the pseudonym **Jean Moreas**; a classic Symbolist poet/author, his themes were vanity, glory, solitude and old age. On the margins of the symbolist movement was **Constantine Cavafy** (1863–1933), an educated

Cover of Meres (Days–diaries)
by Georgios Seferis

and private man, born in Alexandria in 1863, who spent seven years in England in his youth and returned to Alexandria in 1885. His widely translated verse reflects two worlds: contemporary Alexandria and Ancient Greece.

Georgios Seferis (1900–1971), influenced by Symbolism, expressed his anguish in confronting existence with poems imbued with an evocative power. He was awarded the Nobel Prize for literature in 1963. **Odysseas Elytis** (1911–1996) reveals through his surrealist poetry the sacred feeling Greeks have for their natural environment: the land, the sea and above all the light. He was awarded the Nobel Prize in 1979.

PROSE

John Psycharis (1854–1929), who lived in Paris for many years, contributed to the pre-eminence of the Demotic language in Greek literature and also wrote several novels. **Georgios Vizyinos** (1849–1896) was one of the first writers to launch out into new fields. Most of his themes are connected with Thrace, his birthplace, and with the study of contemporary manners. He initially published collections of poetry (*My Mother's Sins and Other Stories*, available in English).

Alexandros Papadiamantis (1851–1911) was one of the great classical writers of Greek prose. His novels describe the humble and often tragic lives of fishermen and peasants in elegant but comprehensible language (*The Murderers* is translated into English).

By far the best known Greek writer is the Cretan **Nikos Kazantzakis** (1883–1957) if only because of the film versions of two of his books: *Zorba the Greek* (1943) and *The Last Temptation of Christ* (1951). The latter, where Kazantzakis has Jesus contemplate a normal life with Mary Magdalene, turned him into a hate figure for the Orthodox Church who excommunicated him in 1955; the Vatican also placed the book in its Forbidden Index. The controversy was re-ignited when Martin Scorsese filmed the book (1998) with worldwide protests against the film.

Vassilis Vassilikos (b.1934) also deserves a mention; his screenplay for the film *Z* won a Palme d'Or at the Cannes film festival. In 2008 he was one of a group of Greek intellectuals to condemn the withdrawal of a novel by **Ersi Sotiropoulou**, *Zig-Zag Through the Bitter-Orange Trees*, from Greek school libraries due to its alledged indecency. The book is available in English and is an imaginative work of fiction that deserves to be better known.

The Chorus

The various genres in Classical theatre were set-pieces; the chorus, manifestation of the city, selected its members from the leisured classes of society, and was directed by a professional dramatist. The development of tragedy can be traced through the titles of works: collective names such as *The Persians*, *The Choephori* and *The Eumenides*, or more frequently, titles focusing on a principal character such as *Electra*, *Hercules* and *Iphegenia*. As the tragic mode of drama developed, the role of the chorus gave way to some extent to individual actors. Aeschylus introduced a second speaking actor and Sophocles introduced a third as well as dimishing the role of the chorus.

Origins of Theatre

There is convincing evidence to suggest that Greek theatre derives from religious rituals associated with the cult of Dionysos, whose places of worship formed the backdrop for the first plays. Aristotle relates the origin of tragedy with a narrative choral song, known as the dithyramb, that was performed at particular festivals of Dionysus. At some stage, an individual performer must have stepped out of the chorus and sang or spoke in the role of a character from the mythical story that was the subject matter of the dithyramb.

It was in Attica in the 5C BC that the theatre began to come into its own, with the appearance of the first purpose-built structures, and the emergence of tragedy and comedy as the two main genres for dramatic performances. With myths as the narrative basis for tragedy, an ancient Greek audience was familiar with the plot beforehand and the interest lay in the manner of the playwright's handling of the known story.

Sculpture of a theatrical mask

The pioneer of Greek tragedy is believed to be Thespis of Icaria (6C BC); three great names, however, were to dominate in the following century: **Aeschylus** (525–455 BC), whose life coincided with the rise to greatness of Athens, focused on the frailties of men and gods alike as his main theme; **Sophocles** (497–406 BC), who lived at the time of Athenian pre-eminence, dwelt upon the notion of humanity and the liberty of man; and **Euripides** (480–406 BC), who looked beyond a society dominated by deities, produced an oeuvre characterised by psychological and ideological issues.

In the field of comedy, **Aristophanes** (c.450–c.388 BC) was a wry observer of politics and society, who did not hesitate to combine vulgarity and farce with serious sociological and political comment. The deaths of Sophocles and Euripides in 404 BC and the defeat of Athens in the Peloponnesian War led to the decline of great Athenian drama. In the late 4C BC, Menander (342–293 BC) produced comical works which blended intrigue with sentimentality.

Ruin of a theater in Dodona

Performing Arts

MUSIC AND DANCE

Modern Greek music has three main strands: traditional folk music now only performed in village weddings and at saints' feasts; popular music based on the style of Asia Minor, which entered Greece with the refugees of the 1920s; and Western rock music which thrives in the "alternative" scenes of Thessaloniki and Athens.

Folk music is played at festivals and other ceremonies (weddings and funerals), in the cafés and squares. On these occasions the traditional instruments are used: the **bouzoúki**, a sort of lute with a very long neck, three or four pairs of strings, and a shrill tone imported from Asia Minor, the **baglamás**, which is a small bouzoúki, the **Cretan lyre** (lyra), a three-stringed viol played with a bow, the **sandoúri**, which is played by striking its steel strings with small hammers, and the **Epirot clarinet**. There are also various rustic wind instruments, such as the **floyéra**, a transverse flute from Epirus, the **dzamára**, a straight pipe, and the **pípiza**, a kind of high-pitched oboe. These instruments accompany singers, whose plaintive style owes much to oriental music. Many folk dances are also of oriental origin such as the zeïmbékiko,

improvised by a man on his own, or the hassápiko, the butchers' dance, performed by men who lay their hands on one another's shoulders. Others such as the Cretan pendozáli imitate war; a clarinet accompanies the mirológia, funeral dances and dirges, often improvised and danced in turn to the point of exhaustion by the women taking part in the wake (Mani and Crete). The national dance, kalamatianós, is danced in a ring and recalls the sacrifice of the Souliot women. The lively sirtáki devised for the film Zorba the Greek is aimed more at tourists (its name was even invented outside Greece); it was based on the hassápiko. The list would not be complete without the anastenária, a dance with a constantly accelerating rhythm performed in Macedonia and Thrace in May on St Constantine's Day, in which the dancers achieve a trancelike state.

After the exchange of populations in 1923, the famous **rebétika songs** were dramatic accounts of the terrible conditions in the refugee slums, mostly of Thessaloniki, or the search for an impossible love. Termed the Greek Blues, their greatest exponent was **Vassilis Tsitsanis** (1915–1984), who succeeded in transcribing them in a very pure form. After 1945 Greek composers turned to traditional forms for rhythm and melody and began to take an interest in rebétika. The leading lights in this musical

Musicians celebrating the Feast of the Assumption, Amorgos

renewal, who had different techniques but both exhibited the same attachment to popular Greek music, were **Manos Hatzidakis** (1925–1994) – romantic, lyrical and elegant *(5 laîkos zografies, O megálos eroticós, I epochi tis Melissanthis)* – and **Mikis Theodorakis**, with his passion for social problems (*Axion Esti*, a setting of extensive extracts from the verse work of this name by **Odysseas Elytis**, Romiosini, Canto General, film music for *Zorba the Greek* and *Z*). In mentioning this folk-inspired music, we must not forget that several composers working in a more experimental vein also did much to put Greek music on the map, notably **Nikos Skalkottas** (1904–1949) and **Ioannis Xenakis** (1922-2001).

However, during the last three decades, young musicians and bands in the major cities of Greece seem to keep a distance from all the above, creating their own music that owes a lot to Western rock. Independent radio, with long-standing DJ and producer **Chris Daskalopoulos** (b.1956), has played a big role in creating such an alternative scene, which can be heard at www. stokokkino.gr/ekpompes/25.

CINEMA

Contemporary Greek cinema has had only limited impact abroad. Although certain actors and directors have become international names, Greek film remains firmly on the art-cinema circuit rather than in the mainstream.

The theme of many of the films made between 1946 and 1949 was wartime resistance, but as they were divorced from their social context they lack objective comment. There were also several comedies, the most daring being *The Germans are Back* by **Alekos Sakellarios** (1913–1991), which pleaded for national unity at a time when the government was actively anti-Communist. The scenario used the return of the Germans to promote reconciliation among the divided Greeks.

The dominant influence during the 1950s was **Italian neo-realism**. In 1953 **Michalis Kakoyannis** made *Sunday Awakening*, a neo-realist comedy,

Still from Eternity and a Day *(1998) by Theo Angelopoulos*

© Theo Angelópoulos/The Kobal Collection

the first of many remarkable films including *Stella* (1955), *Electra* (1962), *Zorba the Greek* (1964), *The Trojans* (1971) and *Iphigenia* (1977). During those formative 1950s *Magic City* (1952) and *Serial Killer* (1956) were released , two masterpieces by the Cretan film-maker **Nikos Koundouros** (b.1926).

The great majority of the Greek films produced in the 1960s were musical romantic comedies for domestic consumption from the studios of **Finos Films** and **Damaskinos/Michailides**. The big "national" star in those highly popular films was **Aliki Bougiouklaki** (1933–1996) whose marriage and subsequent divorce to her regular co-star **Dimitris Papamichaïl** (1934–2004) was the equivalent of the Liz Taylor–Richard Burton love affair for Greek media circles. When Bougiouklaki died in 1996, she was given a state funeral attended by the Greek political and artistic establishment.

In the 1970s Greek cinema reflected a social and political approach. **Theo Angelopoulos** (1935-2012) produced a historical trilogy covering 1936 to 1977, followed by *Alexander the Great* (1980) which won the Golden Lion in Venice, *Voyage to Kythera* (1984), which won the prize for best scenario at the Cannes Festival (1984), *The Bee-keeper* (1986) and *Foggy Landscape* (1988), which won nine international prizes.

Melina Mercouri and Jules Dassin in 1971

The Legendary Couple of Greek Cinema

Jules Dassin was born in 1911 in the USA; he began his career in New York and in barely three years achieved fame with four major films: *Brute Force* (1947), *The Naked City* (1948), *Night and the City* (1949) and *Thieves' Highway* (1950). After making *Rififi* (1955), a thriller set in Paris, he met Melina Mercouri and made her an international star with roles in *Never on Sunday* (1960); they married in 1960.

Born in 1923, Melina Mercouri began her career in theatre, then appeared in Kakoyannis' film *Stella* (1954). Her reputation was established with roles in *Phaedra* (1962), *Topkapi* (1964), *Promise at Dawn* (1971) and *A Dream of Passion* (1977), all by Jules Dassin. She was also a popular singer, before becoming involved in politics as an ardent opponent of the regime of the Colonels. This forced her into exile for a time, but she returned to become Minister of Culture in the subsequent Socialist administrations between 1981 and 1989 and again from 1993 until her death in New York a year later. The couple acquired legendary status among young Greeks, who were captivated by her beauty and courage, and by his charm.

He continued his award-winning career with *The Glance of Odysseus* (1995), for which he won the Grand Prix at the Cannes festival. He was awarded the Palme d'Or in 1998 for *Eternity and a Day*, a deeply moving meditation on the passage of time, opportunities missed and vanished hopes.

The most successful and popular film of recent years is *A Touch of Spice* (2003), a bittersweet tale about life for the Greek minority community in Istanbul. Some 30,000 Greeks "left" Istanbul – deported might be more accurate – in 1964 and the family of the film's director, Tassos Boulmetis, was one of those uprooted from the city. The film boldly confronts the prejudices of both Greeks and Turks

in a spirit of reconciliation and touched a chord with Greek audiences who flocked to see it in preference to the latest Hollywood blockbuster. Since *A Touch of Spice* there has been a lively resurgence in Greek cinema. *Nyfes (Brides)* came out in 2004, directed by Pantelis Voulgaris, starring Victoria Haralabidou and Damian Lewis. The story is about a mail-order bride in the 1920s who falls in love with an American photographer while on her way to her arranged marriage in Chicago. *Loafing and Camouflage: Sirens in the Aegean* (2005), about a group of Greek soldiers assigned to the island of Kos to guard against alleged invasion from Turkish troops, handles a sensitive topic with humour and grace.

Nature

The combination of sea and mountains, the many peninsulas and deep bays all contribute to Greece's unusual geography; no stretch of coastline is far from a mountain.

LANDSCAPE
A MOUNTAINOUS PENINSULA AND THOUSANDS OF ISLANDS

Lying at the southern end of the Balkan peninsula, Greece is a mountainous country with a landmass of 131,944sq km/50,944sq mi (a little over half the size of the United Kingdom).

Its geography gives it a feeling of vastness: the mainland broken up by mountain ranges, and its many islands scattered across the sea. A total of 1,000km/621mi separate Corfu from Kastellorizo, and the eastern end of Crete is 800km/497mi from the northern boundaries of Thrace.

The country, with its highest point at Mount Olympus (2,917m/9,577ft), presents a fragmented and complex topography, with numerous peaks over 2,000m (notably Mount Smólikas in the Pindus range at 2,637m, Mount Parnassos at 2,457m, Mount Ida on Crete at 2,456m, Mount Taýgetos in the southern Peloponnese at 2,407m, and Mount Falakró in Macedonia at 2,182m). The country's geology forms two main zones. In the east, an ancient primary substratum has been raised by movements of the earth's crust: this includes the mountain ranges of Thrace and Macedonia, Mounts Olympus and Pelion, and Euboia; the Aegean Islands are traces of a continent (the mythical Atlantis) submerged at the end of the Tertiary era by earthquakes. Volcanic activity is still evident, especially on Níssiros in the Dodecanese, and Santorini in the Cyclades, where a catastrophic eruption was the most likely cause of the disappearance of the Minoan civilisation. In the west, a tertiary chain, the Balkan Dinaric Alps, continues south to form the spine of Greece, composed mainly of karst, a limestone rock eroded by running water to form caves, chasms and swallow-holes *(katavóthres)*. This mountain range includes the peaks of the Pindus, **Mount Parnassos** (2,457m/8,061ft), the Peloponnese and terminates in the mountains of Crete.

CONTINENTAL GREECE
Central Greece and Euboia

The heart of historic Greece, **Attica** is a promontory consisting of low hills and plains. Population density is high, even outside the Athens metropolitan area. To the north of Attica, between Mounts Parnes and Parnassos, lies **Boeotia**; its main towns, Thebes and Livadiá, are important agricultural markets. The area once belonging to Lake Copaïs has been drained and is a huge cotton plantation. The island of **Euboea** (Évia) lies parallel to the east coast of the Attic Peninsula, to which it is linked by a bridge. Like the mainland, it is very mountainous.

Phocis, the region lying between Boeotia and Etolía, is dominated by Mount Parnassos with its ski resorts; to the west lies the lake formed by the dam on the Mórnos, which supplies water to Athens. Phocis is particularly famous for the sanctuary at Delphi and the sea of olive trees which fills the Ámfissa Basin. **Aetolia** on the west coast comprises a cool mountainous district clothed with holm oaks round the huge reservoir, Lake Trihonída, and the River Ahelóos expanding into the Agrínio Basin; the gleaming lagoon at Messolónghi (salt marshes) lies on the north coast of the Gulf of Patras.

The wooded highlands of **Eurytania** in the north of central Greece are still impenetrable in parts. Karpeníssi, dominated by Mount Timfristós, is the main town in the region, where forestry is the principal activity. On the western boundary with Etolía lies the vast Kremastón reservoir formed by the dammed waters of the River Ahelóos, which has a great energy production capacity. To the northeast of Phocis, the region of **Fthiotis** is largely agricultural and is bisected by the beautiful Sperhiós Valley. The only large town, Lamía, is an important road and rail junction.

Peloponnese

The **Peloponnese**, linked to Attica by the Isthmus of Corinth (now breached by the Corinth Canal), is a mountainous peninsula made up of high peaks, inland basins caused by subsidence and irrigated coastal plains.

The eastern coastal plain is known as the **Argolis**. To the north lies a fertile coastal strip between the mountains and the gulf of Corinth; this area comprises **Corinth** (east) and **Achaïa** (west). **Patra**, which is the third largest city in Greece and an important centre for wine merchants, is also a popular port. Down the west coast extends the verdant agricultural plain of **Elis (Ilía)**. The southern coast is split into three promontories: the longest, an extension of the Taÿgetos massif, is **Mani**, a wild limestone region. Taÿgetos is flanked by two alluvial plains: **Laconía** and **Messenia**.

At the centre of the Peloponnese lie the pasturelands of **Arcadia** (between 600m and 800m/1,968ft and 2,625ft above sea level), home to the town of Tripolis.

Epirus

Between the Ionian Sea and the western border of Thessaly rise the mountains of **Epirus**; the landscape is majestic and harsh, furrowed by valleys and gorges. The capital, **Ioannina**, is situated by a lake. To the northeast rise the limestone heights of Zagória. To the south extends the plain of Árta.

Thessaly

Thessaly, which has two main centres at Lárissa and the port of Vólos, is composed of a rich agricultural basin, watered by the River Piniós and surrounded by high peaks: Pindus, Olympus, Pelion and Timfristós. The region is cold and damp in winter and very hot in summer.

At the foot of Mount Pelion lies the port of Vólos providing maritime communications. Road and rail links with Macedonia to the northeast pass through the famous Vale of Tempe at the foot of Mount Óssa; the road to Ioannina and Epirus in the northwest climbs over the Métsovo Pass (1,705m/5,594ft), the highest road pass in Greece. As it rises into the Pindus range the road passes the curious pillars of rock created by erosion which are known as the Meteora.

Macedonia

This vast province stretches along the border with Albania and Bulgaria. At the centre of the province lies the alluvial plain of the River Axiós, also known as the Vardar. East of the mouth of the Axiós lies the port of **Thessaloniki** (Salonica), the capital of Macedonia and the second largest city in Greece. **Chalcidice** (Halkidikí), the region southeast of Thessaloniki, consists of three wooded peninsulas, the most easterly of which is the site of the famous monasteries of Mount Athos.

The country farther east round Kavala is composed of broad valleys and inland depressions overlooked by high plateaux and Mount Pangaion with its famous goldmines.

In the mountains of western Macedonia there are some fine lakes, particularly Préspa, a nature reserve on the border with Albania.

Thrace

Reunited under the Greek flag after the Second World War, Thrace is the easternmost province of mainland Greece, flanked by Bulgaria and Turkey. The country consists of hills and cultivated plains. There is still a Muslim minority, particularly round Komotiní, Álexandroúpoli and Souflí, where Turkish is taught in primary schools.

THE SEA AND THE ISLANDS

The sea is never far away in Greece; its long coastline is extended by countless bays and gulfs. The lack of tide, the transparent blue water and the excellent visibility are favourable to navigation.

Ionian Islands

Strung out in the Ionian Sea off the west coast of Greece and not far from Italy, these islands are as Latin as they are Greek. There are seven main islands: Corfu, Paxós, Leukas, Cephallonia, Ithaca, Zakynthos, also known as Zante, and Kythera which falls within the Attica

Paleokastritsa coastline, Corfu

© Roman/Fotolia.com

administrative region and lies off the southern tip of the Peloponnese.

Aegean Islands

Although some form part of regions administered from the mainland, these islands strung out towards Turkey are a world apart from the rest of Greece. In the Cyclades and the Dodecanese the cuboid houses under their dazzling whitewash contrast starkly with the barren rock-strewn land. Close to the Turkish coast, the Dodecanese is a group of 12 islands, the principal one being Rhodes. The islands of the northern Aegean – Lemnos, Lesbos, Chios and Sámos – are green and fertile.

Crete

Dominated by three mountain ranges, and ringed by fabulous beaches, Crete is the largest island in the Greek archipelago. Although the north coast is relatively flat, sheer cliffs plunge into the sea along the south of the island. The island gets drier as one travels west to east, from the lushness of the Samariá Gorge to the palm beam at Váï.

EUROPE'S MOST MEDITERRANEAN COUNTRY

The Greek climate is hot in summer and mild in winter (except in the mountains). Inland, particularly in northern Greece, the climate is more continental: stifling in summer, cold in winter, with some areas experiencing sudden and heavy rainfall. At altitude, snow is frequent between November and April.

Bathed in brilliant light, the islands of the Aegean are exposed to the prevailing wind, which blows from the north. In winter it is known as the *voriás* but in spring and summer it becomes the *meltémi* which can blow for two or three days at a time, roughening the sea but refreshing the air. The sea temperature is warm and swimming is possible everywhere between May and October; the water is warmest in September.

Average temperatures (January and July, degrees Celsius): Athens 12 and 32, Corfu 10 and 25, Herakleion 11 and 27, Lesbos 9 and 26, Rhodes 13 and 27.

A LAND OF VILLAGES

In the mountains of the north the building style, typified by stone houses with sloping roofs, has not changed for centuries. Greece's most beautiful villages are found on the islands of the Aegean. Most of them have a port or a landing place called *skála* (steps) in a sheltered bay, a town called *hóra* (place) on a hill out of reach of marauders and a fortified site *(kástro)*, which may have begun as an Ancient Greek acropolis and subsequently became a castle or citadel.

FLORA

Greece boasts over 6,000 botanical species, of which about 600 are unique to Greece including 130 in Crete alone. More generally it is the island of Crete

ABC of Greek Flora

Acanthus: Its curved, spiny leaves are often represented in Classical architecture.

Almond tree: Widely cultivated in the plains and valleys; early pink blossom.

Bougainvillea: Climbing plant with vivid clusters of flowers.

Holm oak: Evergreen oak growing in calcareous soil below 800m/2,620ft.

Cistus: Dark-green foliage contrasts with its white or pink flowers drunk as tea.

Juniper: Purplish berries are a favourite of birds like quails and blackbirds.

Lentisk: Dense evergreen foliage with small round fruits which turn black when ripe; its resin is used to make an aromatic chewing gum and a liqueur, "Masticha".

Myrtle: White flowers and blue-black berries symbolise passionate love.

Olive tree: Twisted trunk and silvery foliage; a symbol of Greece since antiquity.

Aleppo pine: Found on calcareous coastal slopes, this tree has light foliage, a twisted trunk and grey bark. Its resin is used to flavour retsina wine.

Tamarisk: Small tree also called the salt cedar, often found on the fringes of beaches.

and the Peloponnese where the visitor will encounter the largest variety and profusion of wild flowers. The country boasts over 100 varieties of orchids, and violets, peonies, narcissus, primroses and anemones abound from early March.

The native forests that once covered much of the country have now largely disappeared other than for disparate areas in the far north. Here you will see various pine trees as well as fir, white poplars, spearheaded cypresses and chestnut. The tree most commonly seen in the village squares across Greece is the Cyprus plane tree.

Cultivated trees are found on farmland, in the plains and on the lower slopes of the hills, grown in plantations: olives more or less everywhere up to 600m/1,969ft, citrus fruits on irrigated land, almonds in sheltered spots and mulberries, figs and pomegranates. Olive trees have been cultivated since antiquity and have always had a special place in Greek culture. Highly drought-resistant and easily propagated by cuttings, ovules or by grafting (a technique perfected in ancient times), the tree's olives are harvested in autumn and winter and processed for table olives and oil (in their raw state they are inedible). The popularity of the olive, however, carries a high ecological price. In order to profit from the oil, large tracts of native forest were cut down to make way for olive groves and this led to the gradual dis-

Olive trees

Rock rose (Cistus ladaniferus), Myrtle

National Parks

Greece has 10 National Parks, covering a total area of 69 000ha/170 500 acres, established to protect flora and fauna: the Prespa Lakes (Macedonia), Mount Olympus (Thessaly and Macedonia), the Pindos Chain (Epiros), Mount Parnassus (central Greece), Cape Sounion (Attica), Mount Ainos (Cephallonia), the Samaria Gorge (Crete), the Vikos Gorge (Epiros), and Mount Oitis (Phocis). They are sparsely populated, and camping, touring by car, picking flowers, and hunting are forbidden. Each of these unspoilt areas is ecologically important for its local flora, fauna or geology. The Prespa Lakes, for example, have more than 30 species of rare birds; the Samaria Gorge, aside from its natural splendour, has the only wild goats left in Europe; Mounts Olympus and Parnassus have rare and beautiful plants. There are now also two National Marine Parks.

appearance of the surface root systems of the native trees. The consequence was massive soil erosion. Here in the land of Dionysos, the vineyard is ubiquitous, either cultivated for winemaking (as in the Peloponnese, Attica, Macedonia, Samos, Euboea, Crete and Santorini) or for grapes.

FAUNA

Foxes, squirrels, weasels, otters and the suslik, a relatively rare type of ground squirrel, are common on the mainland. There are several species of snakes and while most of them are poisonous they do not pose any danger if left alone. Resident birds include thrushes, swallows, bee-eaters and wagtails and there are a large number of migratory birds passing though on their way to Africa and Europe. The largest one you are likely to see is the stork. Herons, cormorants and the rare Dalmatian pelican are to be found in the inland waters of northern Greece. Contact the Hellenic Ornithological Society (www.ornithologiki.gr) for more information.

Bears and Wolves – The habitats of the brown bear and the wolf are to be found in central and northern Greece. A good source of information for the problems facing these large carnivores is the website of Arcturos, a Greek organisation founded in 1992 and working for the conservation of the country's bears and wolves (www.arcturos.gr). Another organisation is Callisto (www.callisto.gr), founded in 2004 and also striving to protect the natural environment of Greece

and its flora and fauna. Europe 's rarest mammal, the Mediterranean monk seal, exists in small numbers in the waters around Greece.

The loggerhead turtle, with nesting sites on Crete, Zakynthos, Cephalonia and around the coast of the Peloponnese, is also endangered. The turtles need clean and undisturbed beaches to lay their eggs and the development of tourist facilities on the islands has proved to be a major hazard. Contact The Sea Turtle Protection Society of Greece (www.archelon.gr) for more information.

Forest Fires

In the summer of 2007 a series of forest fires broke out across Greece, caused by a combination of arson and negligence in an exceptionally hot summer. Over 80 people lost their lives and some 2,700 square kilometres (670,000 acres) of forest, olive groves and farmland were destroyed. Environmentalists point to global climate change as the cause of long-term changes in Greek microclimates, positing Athens as an example of how this will adversely affect the quality of life for its citizens. In the fires of 2007, Mount Parnitha, only about 20km/12mi northwest of the city centre, burnt for five days and conservationists issued dire warnings of how such events are likely to recur.

Theatre ruins, Dodona, near Ioánnina
© R. Mattès/MICHELIN

Central Greece and the Peloponnese

Porch of the Caryatids, Eréhthio, Acropolis, Athens

CENTRAL GREECE

The serene Parthenon rises majestically over Athens' hectic streets, casting an evocative image over the rambling city. Add to this the magnificent National Archaeological Museum, the impressive new Acropolis Museum, numerous archaeological sites and museums, restaurants and tavernas, and you have a very special city indeed. One of the most common day trips from Athens is into Central Greece, to the sacred ruins at Delphi, arguably the second most important site in Greece. Aside from its historic resonance as the place where the Delphic Oracle gave her advice, it has a breathtakingly beautiful setting. Easily visited on the way are the characterful mountain village of Arahova,

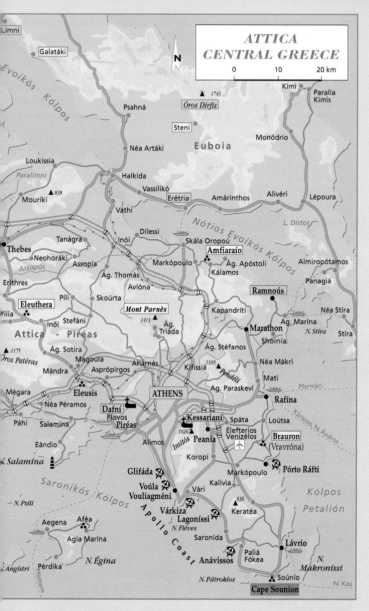

nestling, like Delphi, below the slopes of Mount Parnassos, the city of Thebes (home of Oedipus), and the monastery of Ossios Loukas. Here are some of the best-preserved mosaics in Greece, dating from the 11C, housed in one of the country's most atmospheric monasteries. The fishing ports that line the northern coast of the Gulf of Corinth are another attraction here, while further east the mountainous and wooded island of Euboea is also a relaxing rural contrast to the bustle of the capital. Its mix of ancient sites and sandy beaches make it an appealing retreat for many Athenians, but far fewer foreigners venture here, where you may seek out that elusive "real Greece".

ATHENS★★★ *Athína – Αθήνα*

The attractive site, the brilliant light, the beauty of the ancient monuments and the quality of the museums all contribute to the pleasure of visiting Athens, the city of Athena, the cradle of Western civilisation. Athens also has many Roman, Byzantine and Neoclassical remains, and certain districts, such as the old bazaar, have an enticing oriental flavour. With a population of over three million, Athens is also a modern metropolis. The ambitious programme of improvements for the 2004 Athens Olympics spearheaded a new wave of commercial optimism. Today, Athens fights again, this time against recession.

Highlights

1 Marvel at the **Parthenon** on the Acropolis (p120)
2 Discover the new **Acropolis Museum** (p122)
3 Stroll through **Plaka** (p124)
4 Take in the panorma of the city from the summit of **Mount Lycabettus** (p130)
5 Treasures of the **National Archaeological Museum** (p132)

Ancient Athens

Birth of Athens – The Acropolis was built on a natural defensive site consisting of a steep-sided hill, the approaches protected by two rivers – **Kifissós** *(west)* and **Ilissós** *(east)* – with a circle of hills forming outposts. Athens is thought to have been founded by **Cecrops**, the king of a prehistoric race. Erechtheos, a descendant of Cecrops, established the cult of Athena, the goddess who was associated with the olive and the owl: the cult was practised on the site where the Erechtheion now stands.

Aigeus' son, **Theseus** (12C or 11C BC), made Athens the capital of a coherent state covering present-day Attica and afforded great importance to the processions in honour of Athena, called the Panathenaia. In his reign the city was scarcely larger than the Acropolis.

Athens in her glory (6C–5C BC) – After the great urban reforms introduced by **Solon** and the enlightened dictators, **Peisistratos** and his sons (561–510), the city developed extensively. A new circuit wall was built enclosing the Areopagos Hill northwest of the Acropolis, as well as the two *agoras* of Theseus and Solon. At the same time various municipal undertakings were being carried out in the lower town: public buildings, a water system, sewers and roads. The first coins were struck bearing the effigy of Athena and the owl; the Lyceum and the Academy – famous *gymnasia* surrounded by gardens – were established.

When **Kleisthenes** rose to power in 508 BC he organised Athens into a direct democracy. Legislative power was exercised by an Assembly of the people *(Ecclesia)* which met three or four times

View of the Acropolis with Likavitós Hill in the background

© Greek National Tourism Organisation

a month on the Pnyx; a Senate *(Boule)* of 500 members which was subordinated to the Assembly; and a Tribunal *(Heliaia)* comprising elected magistrates and juries chosen by lot. Executive power was exercised by *archons* and *strategi*; the latter in command of the army.

Following the Persian Wars in 479 BC, Themistocles, the victor of the Battle of Salamis, gave orders for the construction of the wall which bears his name; he also built the "Long Walls", a fortified corridor linking Athens and Piraeus.

In the **Age of Pericles**, that great Athenian statesman devoted himself to the reconstruction of Athens with the advice of the sculptor Pheidias. An overall plan was drawn up for the Acropolis, and the Propylaia, the Parthenon, the Erechtheion and the Temple of Athena Nike were constructed. Almost the whole area within the walls was covered by brick houses.

Athens in Decline (4C–2C BC) – The Peloponnesian War (431–404), in which Athens was defeated by Sparta, marked the beginning of a decline in the moral sphere which is illustrated by the death of the philosopher **Socrates**.

Despite the exhortations of the orator **Demosthenes**, the Greeks never agreed a concerted policy, and after the Battle of Chaironeia (338 BC) Athens became subject to Philip of Macedon, who was succeeded by Alexander the Great.

Secure under Macedonian "protection", which lasted until the end of the 3C BC, the Athenian municipal authorities embarked on public works of embellishment: the Theatre of Dionysos and the Choregic Monument of Lysicrates. The Hellenistic period, which began with the death of Alexander (323 BC), was marked by the division of the Macedonian Empire into several kingdoms. Athens vegetated; only the building of a few porticoes and *gymnasia*, in the reigns of the kings of Antioch and Pergamon, reveal the city's continuing intellectual power.

Conquered by Rome (1C BC–4C AD) – The political independence of Athens came to an end in 86 BC when the city was captured by **Sulla** and the walls

▶ **Population:** 745,514 (Greater Athens 3,130,841).

Michelin Map: 737 I 9 – Attica.

Info: 18-20 Dionysiou Areopagitou (near the Acropolis Museum). ☏ 210 33 10 392. Arrivals Hall at the airport. ☏ 210 3530445-8. www.breathtaking athens.com.

Location: Athens is close to the Saronic Gulf and the port of Piraeus, where ferries and hydrofoils offer service to most of the Greek Islands. The new Athens airport is located at Markopoulos *(27km/17mi northeast of the city)*. The main historic areas of Plaka and Monastiráki lie north of the Acropolis. From there the immense modern city spreads forth, scored by wide, busy avenues.

Parking: Traffic can be infernal in Athens, especially at rush hours; it's best to park your car quickly and move about on foot or by public transport. There's a large underground garage on Odós Rizari near the Ethniki Pinakothiki.

Don't Miss: The Acropolis and the Acropolis Museum; a stroll through the Plaka district; the National Archaeological Museum, and the Benaki Museum.

Timing: Hit the highlights in two days, but stay five days or longer for a better picture of the city.

Kids: The zoo in the National Garden; the Museum of Popular Musical Instruments.

GETTING THERE GETTING AROUND

BY AIR – Athens International Airport (E. Venizelos) is located at Markopoulos, 27km/17mi northeast of the city (www.aia.gr).

The simplest way to get to the centre of Athens is via the **metro** (€8) from the airport *(Aerodromio)* station. Trains depart every 30min to Syntagma and Monastiraki stations, which connect to other metro lines. If returning to the airport via metro, note that not all trains go all the way to the airport; make sure that Aerodromio is the destination listed on the front of the train.

Suburban trains (www.oasa.gr) link the Aerodromio station to Larisa Station with stops at Nerantziotissa near Maroússi. Departures every 30min (€8). Allow one hour or more to travel from the airport to the centre of Athens by **bus** or **taxi**. Buses from the airport terminate at Ethniki Amyna underground station (bus X 94), Sindagma Square (X 95) or Piraeus (X 96); they operate seven days a week and every 10 minutes during the day; check schedules for evening operation. A ticket to or from the airport costs €3.20 and is available from ticket kiosks and bus and underground stations. Taxis €30.

Car rental agencies are located in the lower level arrival hall.

BY TRAIN (OSE) – Two stations are linked by underground line 2: **Lárissa Station**, *31 Odós Deligiani*, ☏ *21052 97 777* for northern and eastern Greece (Thebes, Larisa, Thessaloniki) and **Peloponnese Station**, *3 Odós Sidirodromon*, ☏ *21051 31 601*, for the southwest of the country. There is also a train station at Piraeus. For information and reservations (two days before departure), contact **OSE**, *6 Odós Sina*, ☏ *21052 97 313, www.ose.gr*.

BY BUS (KTEL) – There are 3 main bus terminals in the centre of Athens: **Terminal A or KTEL Kifissou**, *100 Odós Kifissou*, ☏ *21051 50 785 /*

24 910: for the Peloponnese, Etolía, Epiros, Macedonia and the Ionian Islands.

Terminal B or KTEL Liossion, *260 Odós Liossion*, ☏ *21083 17 147/53*: for central Greece, Euboea and Thessaly. **KTEL Attica**, *Pedio Areos, to the north of the National Museum*, ☏ *21082 13 203/(21088) 43 250*: Sounion, Lávrio, Rafína, Marathon, Markópoulo and Thessaloniki.

BY SEA – From Athens, take metro line 1 to the port at Piraeus (green line; 20min from Monastiraki station) or by bus X 96 from the airport.

BY METRO – The Athens underground network is the easiest way to get around the principal tourist sites (Acropolis, Sindagma, Monastiráki, Omónia, Thissío, Piraeus). It runs every day 5am–11.30pm. A one-use ticket costs €0.80, but you can buy a ticket good for one day, €3, or one week, €10, covering the whole public transport network (bus, trolley bus, trams and metro). Validate your ticket before boarding. Maps and information available in English at ticket counters or at *www.amel.gr*.

BY BUS AND TROLLEY – There are 320 bus routes in Athens. Information and maps are available from the OASA office, *15 Odós Metsovou*, behind the National Archaeological Museum. Tickets, priced from €0.50, are also available from the office.

TRAMS – The tramway links the centre of Athens with western Attica (Faliro, Agios Kosmas).

SUBURBAN TRAINS – Interchanges with the underground network at Aerodromio, Doukissis Plakentias (line 3) and Neratziotissa (line 1).

TAXI – Radio Taxi, ☏ *21092 179 42*.

TOURS – An easy, if less scenic means of getting from place to place, the **Sightseeing Public Bus Line** (€5 ✕ for 24hrs) departs from the National Archaeological Museum every 30min and passes by 20 tourist sights; visitors alight at will, visit the sights and continue on the next convenient bus.

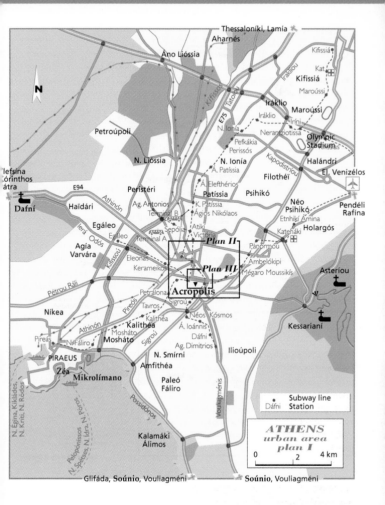

ATHENS
urban area
plan I

0   2   4 km

were razed. Nonetheless, the "Roman peace" enabled Athens to retain its leadership in cultural affairs in the Mediterranean world; the Romans carried away or copied her works of art, imitated her citizens' way of life and sent their sons to Athens to complete their education. In the 1C BC a temple to Rome and Augustus (Naós Rómis ke Avgoústou) was built on the Acropolis hill and a Roman forum and a hydraulic clock, known later as the "Tower of the Winds", were built at the foot; a covered theatre *(odeon)* was built on the old *agora*.

In AD 53 Christianity was brought to Athens by **St Paul** who preached the gospel and exalted the "unknown god" on the Areopagos. Later, in the 2C AD,

the **Emperor Hadrian**, who cherished all things Greek, completed the temple of Zeus (Olympieion) begun by Peisistratos, built a library and aqueducts and a new district east of the Acropolis protected by a wall. Herodes Atticus, a wealthy Athenian, constructed a theatre *(odeon)*, which still bears his name, on the southern slope of the Acropolis, and a splendid white-marble stadium on the east bank of the Ilissós.

Byzantine, Medevial and Ottoman Athens
Rise of Christianity (5C–13C) – Following the Germanic invasions in the middle of the 3C the Roman Empire was split in two in 395, with Athens in the eastern

111

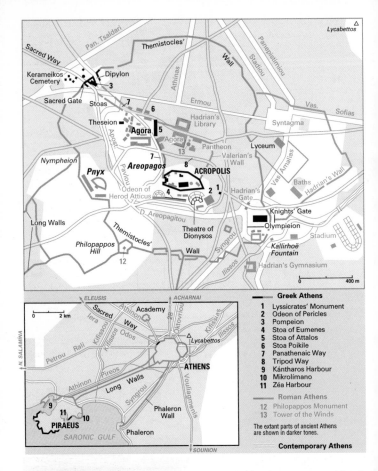

New Acropolis Museum

© Greek National Tourism Organisation

part ruled by the emperor residing in Byzantium (Constantinople). The Edict of Milan in 313 allowed Christians to practise their religion legally and their proliferation from the 5C to the 7C led to the suppression of the schools of philosophy and the establishment of basilicas in the Parthenon and other pagan temples. The majority of the Byzantine churches date from the 9C and often incorporated fragments of ancient buildings; many have survived. Until the late 12C when Athens was sacked by the Saracens, it was a flourishing city with a stable population protected by the castle on the Acropolis.

Dukes of Athens (13C–15C) – The Fourth Crusade, which captured Constantinople in 1204, caused Athens to fall into the hands of the Frankish knights who also held Thebes. Athens passed to a family of Burgundian origin, the **La Roche**. During their tenure Athens was raised to a duchy by Louis IX of France (1260). The Franks fortified the Acropolis and altered the Propylaia to form a palace guarded by the Frankish Tower, which stood until it was demolished in 1875. The Frankish domination of Athens came to an end in 1311 after the Battle of Kephisos.

The Catalans then occupied the region but established their stronghold in Thebes. In 1387 Athens was captured by a Florentine, Nerio Acciaiuoli. After a brief Venetian interlude, 1394–1403, the Acciaiuoli reigned until 1456, when they were obliged to submit to the Turks who had captured Constantinople.

Athens at its Lowest Ebb (1456–1821) – Sultan Mehmet II, the Turkish ruler, granted a certain degree of autonomy to Athens and allowed several churches to be built; in the 17C the Turks even permitted the Jesuits and Capuchins to found monasteries. The Acropolis was fortified to form the kernel of the Turkish fortress; in 1466 the Parthenon was converted into a mosque with an adjoining minaret; the Propylaia was used as a powder magazine and the Erechtheion housed a harem.

Venetian troops laid siege to Athens in 1687; during the bombardment a powder magazine on the Acropolis exploded, causing grave damage to the Parthenon. The Turks surrendered but recaptured the town a year later.

From then until independence Athens was a town of about 10,000 to 15,000 inhabitants living on the northern slopes of the Acropolis Hill. The city began to attract many visitors from Western Europe. In 1762 **"Athenian" Stuart** and Revett published the first volume of "an accurate description of the Antiquities of Athens". Richard Chandler, who visited Athens some 10 years later, remarked that it was "to be regretted that so much admirable sculpture as is still extant … should be all likely to perish …" **Lord Elgin**, British Ambassador in Constantinople at the time, is famous for his acquisition of marble sculptures.

Greek Capital

Independence (1821–34) – On 25 April 1821 the Athenians rose in rebellion and occupied the town except for the Acropolis, which held out until 10 June. A counter-attack in 1826 enabled the Turks to capture Missolonghi and to lay siege to Athens. The Greek troops were forced to surrender on 24 May 1827.

Independence Day Parade in Athens on 25th March

© ANE/Andreas Neumeier/Greek National Tourism Organisation

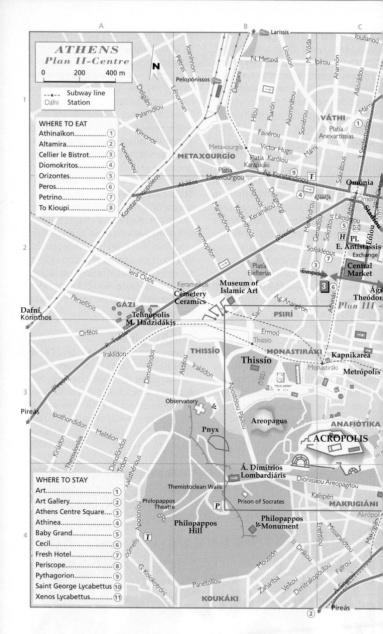

Subway line
Dáfni Station

WHERE TO EAT
Athinaïkon................①
Altamira...................②
Cellier le Bistrot.......③
Diomokritos.............④
Orizontes.................⑤
Peros......................⑥
Petrino....................⑦
To Kioupi................⑧

WHERE TO STAY
Art............................①
Art Gallery................②
Athens Centre Square....③
Athinea....................④
Baby Grand..............⑤
Cecil.........................⑥
Fresh Hotel...............⑦
Periscope..................⑧
Pythagorion.............⑨
Saint George Lycabettus ⑩
Xenos Lycabettus...........⑪

Eleven months of fighting and bombardment had devastated the town.
Although the War of Independence ended in 1829, the Acropolis remained in Turkish hands until 1834 when Athens succeeded Nauplion as the capital of the new State of Greece; the population numbered barely 4 000.

First Neoclassical era (1834–1900) – In 1832 the Great Powers imposed on Greece a German king, the young **Otto of Bavaria**, son of Ludwig I of Bavaria. In the reign of Otto and Queen Amalia, a policy of great works was inaugurated under the aegis of the Bavarian architect, Leo von Klenze. A new town

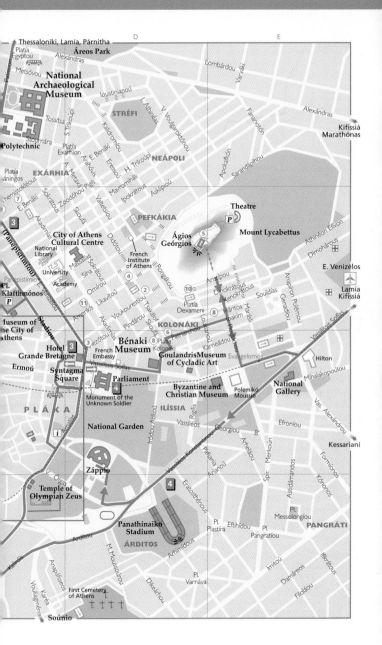

with straight streets was traced out in a triangular area based on Odós Ermoú with Odós Pireós (Panagí Tsaldári) and Odós Stadíou forming the two sides and meeting in Omónia Square. In 1861 the population of Athens had reached 41 298.

Many of the buildings from this period were in the Neoclassical style. The main German contributions were the Royal Palace, the University, the Academy and the Observatory. **Kleanthes**, a Greek architect, worked more on houses for private clients: the Duchess of Plaisance's residence in Ilissia (⟲see

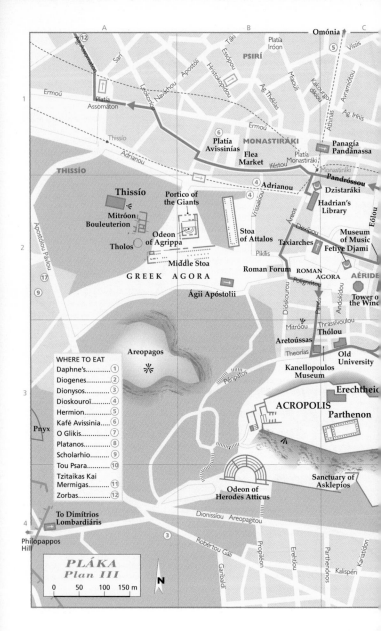

Byzantine Museum) and his own house in Plaka.

Expansion (after 1900) – When the Greeks from Smyrna in Asia Minor were expelled by the Turks in 1922, a wave of refugees settled in Athens, mainly in the district north of Piraeus. The city has continued to expand. The lower slopes of Lycabettos have been covered by the elegant Kolonáki district; the Ilissós now runs underground beneath a broad highway, and the outer districts of detached houses now extend from Kifissiá in the north to Fáliro (Phaleron) in the south. After the Second World War new buildings were concentrated

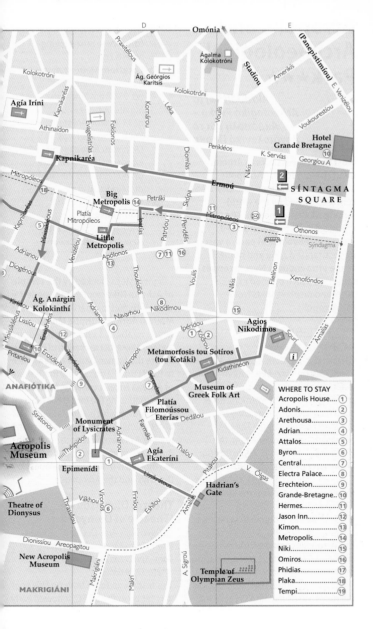

along Leofóros Venizélou. The Hilton Hotel and the American Embassy by Gropius, the Athens Tower at Ambelókipi, and the more recent Olympic Stadium at Maroússi are the most striking constructions.

In the early 1980s, measures were put in place to protect and restore the traditional buildings of Plaka and the city centre. Part of Plaka and many streets in the centre are pedestrianised and planted with trees; the problem of atmospheric pollution remains an issue which the authorities continue to tackle.

Acropolis and Archaeological Park★★★

Akrópoli kai to Arheologikó Párko – Ακρόπολη και το Αρχαιολογικό Πάρκο

Most first-time visitors to Athens head straight for the Acropolis, a rocky mound rising in the city centre, crowned by the world-famous 5C BC Parthenon. The area has recently been transformed into an archaeological park, a vast pedestrianised zone and home to the ultra-modern New Acropolis Museum, which opened in June 2009 and displays finds from the Acropolis.

WALKING TOUR
ACROPOLIS★★★

🕐*Open Apr–Oct 8am– 7.30pm (Mon 11am-7.30pm), Nov–Mar 8.30am–3pm. ⊚€12 (see http://odysseus.culture. gr for days with free admission), ticket good for four days allows entry to all Acropolis sites plus the Theatre of Dionysos, the Ancient Agora, the Olympieion, the Roman Agora and the Keramíkos Cemetery. 𝄞210 32 10 219.*

The artistic climax of Greek architecture, the Acropolis stands on the summit of a steep rock platform. Covering an area of 4 ha/10 acres, it dominates the lower town by 100m/329ft.

The Acropolis comprises traces of construction from various periods dating back to the second millennium BC (Mycenaean period), but the principal buildings are all in white Pentelic marble and belong to the Age of Pericles (5C BC). The 1981 earthquake, coupled with air-pollution problems in recent years, has made it necessary to take steps to protect the stone and to replace the remaining sculptures with copies. The entrance to the Acropolis is known as the **Píli Beulé (Beulé Gate)** since it was discovered in 1853 by French archaeologist Ernest Beulé. Beyond is

---

ℹ **Info:** www.breathtaking athens.com.

▶ **Location:** Metro station Acropoli (red line), bus no. 230 from Síndagma Square or trolleys 1, 5 or 15 (Makrigiani stop). Walk along Leofóros Dioníssou Areopagitou which passes the Theatre of Dionysos and the Odeon of Herodes Atticus.

👥 **Kids:** Philopappos Hill.

☺ **Don't Miss:** The Parthenon and the New Acropolis Museum.

---

a flight of steps, flanked by the **Temple of Athena Nike** *(south)* and a pedestal of grey Hymettos marble *(north),* the **Mnimío Agrípa (Agrippa Monument)**, which in about 15 BC supported the *quadriga* (four-horse chariot) of Agrippa. Before the Roman period the entrance to the Acropolis was below the Temple of Athena Nike; it consisted of a steep ramp continuing the **Ierá Odós (Sacred Way)** along which the Panathenaic processions made their way up to the temple. A projecting terrace north of the Agrippa monument gives a good view of the three hills to the west: Philopappos, the Pnyx and the Areopagos.

Théatro Dioníssou★★ (Theatre of Dionysus)

🕐*Open daily Apr–Oct 8am– 7.30pm (Mon 11am-7.30pm), Nov–Mar 8am–5pm. ⊚€2 (Sun ⊚no charge). 𝄞210 32 24 625.*

The first stage to be built on this spot was set up in the 6C BC, followed early in the following century by a real theatre equipped with wooden terraces, where the great Classical dramas were played: *The Persians* by Aeschylus, *Oedipus Rex* by Sophocles, *Medea* by Euripides and the *Wasps* by Aristophanes. The present stone structure (4C BC) provided 17,000 seats. It was restored early 19C. Beyond the remains of a temple to Dionysos and a portico lies the stage of

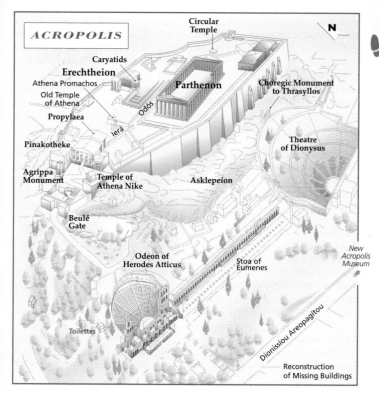

ACROPOLIS

Circular Temple

N

Caryatids
Erechtheion
Athena Promachos
Old Temple of Athena
Parthenon
Choregic Monument to Thrasyllos

Propylaea

Odós

Ierá

Pinakotheke

Theatre of Dionysus

Agrippa Monument
Temple of Athena Nike

Asklepeíon

Beulé Gate

Odeon of Herodes Atticus
Stoa of Eumenes

New Acropolis Museum

Toilettes

Dionissiou Areopagitou

- - - - Reconstruction of Missing Buildings

the theatre. Its foundations date from the 4C BC but it was rebuilt under Nero (1C AD): the sculptures at the front of the stage date from this period. The terraces (4C BC) are partially preserved; they rose as high as the monument to Thrasyllos, 30m/98ft. In the first row were the seats reserved for individuals, bearing the names of the those who occupied them in the 2C AD.

From the top there is a good view of the site; on the left are traces of the **Odeon of Pericles**, a covered theatre.

There is nothing left but the pedestal of the **Mnimío Thrassílou (Choregic Monument of Thrasyllos)**, a votive monument set up by Thrasyllos a chorus-leader *(choregós)* in 4C BC, in honour of Dionysos, who was worshipped in the cave *(below)*.

Asklepeíon

A long terrace west of the upper part of the Theatre of Dionysos bears the remains of two sanctuaries to Asklep-

eios (Aesculapius); one dates from the 4C BC *(east)* and the other *(west)* from the 5C BC.

Below the Asklepeion, facing south, is the **Stoa of Eumenes**, built in the 2C BC by **Eumenes II**, King of Pergamon; the **façade**★ is especially noteworthy.

Odío Iródou Atikoú ★ (Odeon of Herodes Atticus)

🕐*Not open except for performances.*

The Odeon (161 BC) was built by Herodes Atticus in memory of his wife. The **façade**★ is fairly well preserved. It can accommodate 6 000 spectators and today hosts performances of the Athens Summer Festival. From the Odeon, a path leads to the Beulé Gate and thence to the Acropolis.

Propylaea★

👁*The marble steps are very slippery.*

The monumental gates to the Acropolis, the **Propylaea**, were built by the architect Mnesikles. From the 12C to the 15C they were adapted as a palace. The Turks reinforced the gates with bastions, and it was not until 1836 that the Propylaea were stripped of their military accretions.

On passing through the Propylaea, one comes face to face with the graceful silhouette of the Erechtheion *(left)* and the majestic golden pile of the Parthenon *(right)*. Opposite the Propylaea stood the **Athena Promachos** (9m/30ft high), an impressive warrior figure of Athene, designed in bronze by **Pheidias** to commemorate the Athenian victory over the Persians.

Parthenon★★★

This Doric temple was constructed by **Iktínos** under the direction of Pheidias in the Age of Pericles. The Parthenon was dedicated to Athena, whose statue by Pheidias adorned the sanctuary. Pheidias was also responsible for the sculptures decorating the pediments, friezes and *metopes*.

The statue of Athena was removed to Constantinople in the Byzantine period and destroyed in 1203. The Parthenon was converted into a church and richly decorated with frescoes and mosaics. After eight centuries of Orthodox worship, the Franks styled it St Mary of Athens, in the Roman rite.

The Turks converted the Parthenon into a mosque and built a minaret at the southwest corner. The building still retained the majority of its sculptures before the explosion of the powder magazine in 1687 destroyed many of them and brought down the Parian marble roof slabs, the walls of the *naos* and 28 columns.

Since 1834 efforts have been made to restore the structure, particularly the re-erection of the colonnades, a difficult operation known as **anastylosis**, which was carried out by Greek archaeologists after the First World War.

Viewed from the **exterior**, the Parthenon rests on a marble stylobate and is surrounded by a peristyle of 46 fluted columns (8 at the ends and 17 down each side). The pediments were decorated with painted sculptures against a blue background. The east pediment showed the Birth of Athena, fully armed, from the head of Zeus in the presence of the Sun (Helios) and the Moon (Selene) who are driving their chariots. The west pediment represented the quarrel between Athena and Poseidon for possession of Attica; two very damaged pieces have survived. The Doric frieze consisted of the usual triglyphs alternating with 92 *metopes* showing sculpted battle scenes against a red ground. Only a few of the original *metopes* still exist: there are 15 in the British Museum, one in the Louvre in Paris and several others in the Acropolis Museum. The shields which were presented by Alexander the Great were attached to the architrave.

inside (o━ *closed to the public)*, the east portico *(prónaos)*, where the offerings were placed, led into the sanctuary through a door 10m/33ft high. The inner chamber *(naos)* contained a gigantic statue of Athena (12m/39ft high). Behind the *naos* there was another chamber housing the treasures of the Delian League which was under the leadership of Athens.

The wall enclosing the *naos* and the Parthenon was decorated on the outside with the **frieze of the Panathenaia**; this famous band of sculpture, which contained 400 human figures and 200 animals, depicted the Panathenaic procession. About 50 pieces, the best preserved, are displayed in the British Museum; a few others can be seen in the Acropolis Museum.

Casts of the majority of the Parthenon sculptures can be seen at the Acropolis Interpretation Centre.

◗ *Cross the area between the Parthenon and the Erechtheion: look for traces of the foundations of the earlier Temple of Athena Nike (Arhéos Naós Athinás) built in the early 6C BC and destroyed 100 years later to make room for the Erechtheion.*

Erechtheion★★★

This little Doric and Ionic temple, which was completed in 407 BC, incorporated several existing shrines, including those

"Elgin" Marbles

When **Lord Elgin** arrived in Constantinople as British Ambassador to the Porte (the central office of the Ottoman government in Constantinople) he obtained permission from the Sultan to make copies and models of ancient buildings and to remove any interesting pieces. Elgin's purpose in acquiring his collection of antiquities had been to improve artistic taste and design in Britain. His expenses, which he had hoped to recover from the government, made him bankrupt and he was finally forced to sell his collection to the British Museum at half the cost of obtaining it. The British Museum still displays this collection and there is today a great deal of debate about the return of the Marbles to Greece – thus far the Greek government has not been successful in calls for their return.

to Athena, Poseidon, Erechtheos and Cecrops, kings of Athens.

The famous southern portico faces the Parthenon. It is known as the Kariátides, the **Porch of the Caryatids**, because it is supported by six statues of young women. The figures are copies; one of the originals is in the British Museum; the others are on display in the Acropolis Museum. The eastern portico opens into the sanctuary that contained the oldest statue of Athena, which was made of olive wood.

From the viewpoint in the northeast corner of the site there are dramatic **views**★★ over the Roman town (east) (Hadrian's Arch, Temple of Zeus), down into the old district of Plaka (north) and over the suburbs to the northeast of Athens surrounded by the Parnes, Pentelikon and Hymettos ranges.

▷ *Walk along the southern edge of the Acropolis Hill: interesting views down over the theatres of Dionysos and Herodes Atticus).*

Naós Athinás Níkis★★★ (Temple of Athena Nike)

The **Temple of Athena Nike**, which was formerly known as the **Temple of Nike Apteros** (Wingless Victory), stands on a projecting bastion west of the Propylaia. A small but graceful Ionic temple (late 5C BC), it consisted of a chamber (naos) between two porticoes supported on monolithic columns. The badly damaged exterior frieze comprises a few original pieces (east and south sides); the rest are copies.

▷ *Leave the Acropolis by the Beulé Gate and bear right to the Areopagos.*

Ários Págos★ (Areopagos)

Theseus' enemies, the Amazons, camped on this limestone hill and consecrated it to Ares, god of war. Another legend says that **Orestes**, who was being pursued by the **Furies**, was judged here. **St Paul** is thought to have preached at Areopagos when he converted the senator who was to become **St Dionysius the Areopagite**, the first Bishop of Athens.

Fine **view** of the Acropolis and of the Greek agora and Roman forum below.

▷ *Return to Leofóros Dioníssou Areopagitou. Those braving the climb to Philopappos Hill and the Pnyx will be rewarded with stunning views.*

Lófos Filopápou★★★ (Philopappos Hill)

Paths start near the Dionysos restaurant.

In antiquity Philopappos Hill was dedicated to the Muses and bore the name **Mouseion**. The path climbs past ancient troglodyte cave-dwellings; one was long thought to be **Socrates' prison**. The hill is dominated by the **Philopappos monument** (AD 116) commemorating a benefactor of Athens.

There are spectacular **views**★★★, of the Acropolis, Athens, Hymettos and the Plain of Attica. The Philopappos Theatre on the west face of the hill presents performances of traditional dances.

Pníka★ (Pnyx)

The **Pnyx** forms a sort of amphitheatre, where the Assembly of the people *(Ecclisía)* met between the 6C and the 4C BC. Many famous orators, such as **Themistocles**, **Pericles** and **Demosthenes**, spoke here. From the terrace there is a splendid **view**★★★ of the Acropolis; sound and light shows are held here during the summer.

Lófos Nimfóna★

The **Nympheion**, the Hill of the Nymphs, is scattered with traces of dwellings and offers a view of the Parthenon. The hill is crowned by an observatory, a Neoclassical building completed in 1957 with the addition of a seismology station.

▷ *Return to the foot of the Acropolis and turn right onto Leofóros Dioníssou Areopagitou to arrive at the New Acropolis Museum.*

Acropolis Museum★★★

🕓*Open Tue–Sun 8am–8pm (Fri till 10pm).* ≈€5. *2–4 Makrigianni, Plaka,* ✆ *210 90 00 900. www. theacropolismuseum.gr.*

Designed by Swiss architect Bernard Tschumi, this long-awaited, multi-storey, ultra-modern museum finally opened in 2009. It contains the sculptures and other objects found during the excavation of the Acropolis, which were previously displayed in the old Acropolis Museum (now closed). Glass floors show a glimpse of an archaeological excavation below, and the upper floor levels afford great views onto the ancient temples of the Acropolis itself. Greeks hope that the opening of this sophisticated modern museum will encourage the return of the controversial Elgin Marbles, which for many years have been on display at the British Museum in London. Exhibits include a beautiful fragment of a marble *quadriga* (four-horse chariot); the Pediment of the Olive Tree or of Troilus; and above all the **Moscophoros**, a painted marble statue with eyes originally of glass paste, a votive statue of about 570 BC; and a headless *kore* in white marble, the oldest of those from

the Acropolis (between 580 and 570 BC). There's also an important collection of statues of young women (**kore** in the singular, **korai** in the plural) in coloured marble (6C BC). The *peplos kore* is attributed to Phaidimos, the earliest known Attic sculptor; also by him are an extraordinarily lifelike dog, a lion's head and a smiling horseman (a copy; the original, known as the Rampin Horseman, is in the Louvre).

Note also 8–7C BC ceramics in the geometric style, and four statues from the pediment (c.525 BC) of the old Temple of Athena; Athena is recognisable, brandishing a lance. Among other remarkable works are the *kore* by Antenor, of great refinement, from the end of 6C BC, the statue of Nike (Victory) in flight dating from about 500 BC, and the *kore* with the dove. Try not to miss the famous **Athena Mourning**, a 5C votive relief, and a young man's head in marble from Pheidias' studio.

Reconstructions of the **Parthenon pediments** include the birth of Athena, and the quarrel between Athena and Poseidon. Some sculptures were removed from the temples for preservation: the Panathenaic procession from the Parthenon, and items from the Temple of Athena Nike including the figure of **Nike** (Victory) undoing her sandal before offering a sacrifice. Several of the famous **caryatids** from the Erechtheion are displayed behind a protective glass screen.

▷ *Return to the foot of the Acropolis and follow Apostolou Pavlou, which skirts the base of the hill. Cross the railway tracks; a bridge over the tracks leads to the Agora.*

Arhéa Agorá★ (Agora)

🕓*Open Apr–Oct Tue–Sun 8.30am–7.30pm, Mon 11am–7.30pm, Nov–Mar 8am-3pm.* ≈€4 *(ticket also valid for museum entry).*
✆ *210 32 10 185.*

The agora, which is now a confused jumble of ruins, was originally a rectangular open space covering about 2.5ha/6 acres and divided diagonally

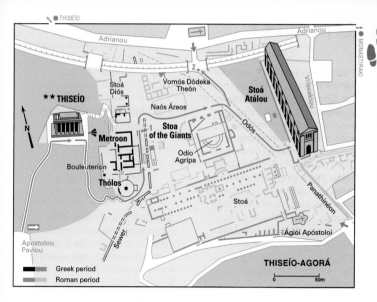

by the Panathenaic Way, which ran past the Altar of the Twelve Olympian Gods from which the distances to other Greek cities were measured. The space was enclosed within buildings, temples and shops arranged in a long portico (*stoa*) where citizens gathered.

The Romans encroached on the open space with buildings such as the Odeon of Agrippa and the Temple of Ares. Under the Byzantines a district grew up around **Ágioi Apóstoloi** (the Church of the Holy Apostles – late 10C AD).

The **thólos**, which dates from about 470 BC, was a round building where the 50 senators (*prytaneis*) met to take their meals; the standard weights and measures were also kept here. To the north of the *thólos* stood the **Metroon** (Mitróo), the Temple of the Mother of the Gods, behind which stood the Bouleuterion, the Senate House; beyond the Metroon stood the Temple of Apollo Patroos and the Stoa of Zeus. Only the foundations of these buildings remain, but there are also traces of a great drain which passed to the east of them and of pedestals for statues: one of them bears the likeness of the Emperor Hadrian (**1**).

The **Stoá Atálou**, built in the 2C BC by **Attalos**, King of Pergamon, has been reconstructed. It is a long two-storey building which displays the articles found during the excavations in the agora. The external gallery displays the Apollo Patroos (4C BC), while the interior one contains objects from everyday life in antiquity. Near Odós Adrianóu's entrance there is a mosaic reconstruction showing the agora as it was in antiquity.

Thisío★★ (Theseio)

This 5C BC Doric temple, one of the best preserved in the Greek world, stands on a mound dominating the agora, the centre of Athenian public life in antiquity. Known since the Middle Ages as the **Theseio**, it is the **Hephaisteion** mentioned by Pausanias, the Temple of Hephaïstos, god of smiths and metalworkers.

In the Byzantine period the temple was converted into a church; under the Turks it became the burial place of Englishmen and other Protestants. The last service was held in 1834; it then housed the first collections of the National Museum. The stone Hephaisteion, older and smaller than the Parthenon, was originally painted. The deteriorated sculptures of the external frieze recall the exploits of Herakles (Hercules) and Theseus. The east portico with its marble coffered ceiling still in place leads into the *naós* (5C AD). The temple terrace offers fine views of the agora, the Monastiráki district and the Acropolis.

1 Pláka★★

Pláka – Πλάκα

Pláka's picturesque and peaceful narrow streets and alleys open out into tiny squares and terraces linked by steps and Byzantine churches peeking out from rows of old houses. Here and there one catches a glimpse of the rest of the city or the Acropolis. The broader streets below the slope are thronged with shops and inexpensive guesthouses. After dark Pláka comes alive with tavernas, some with live music. Crowds tarry late into the night, savouring the Greek cuisine with glasses of *retsina*, listening to the music and dancing the modern *sirtáki*.

✑ WALKING TOUR
Circuit from Sindagma Square. 1 day.

This route takes you through Plaka's narrow streets, many of which are closed to traffic, to discover Ancient Greek and Roman monuments, Byzantine churches and a handful of small museums. All in the shadow of the Acropolis.

▸ *From the southwest corner of Síndagma Square take Odós Mitropóleos.*

On the left under the arcade of a modern building is the tiny Chapel of **Agía Dínami** (17C). The street opens into a square, Platía Mitropóleos: the Orthodox cathedral is known as the **Megáli Mitrópoli** (Great Metropolis) and dates from the 19C.

Mikrí Mitrópoli★★
The **Little Metropolis**, dedicated to the Virgin who answers prayers swiftly (Panagía Gorgoepíkoos), is a charming 12C Byzantine church built on the Greek cross plan with a dome.
Incorporated into the external walls are many decorative pieces from an earlier age: between the two Corinthian capitals flanking the façade stretches an unusual ancient frieze (4C BC) showing

Info: www.breathtaking athens.com.

▸ **Location:** Pláka lies immediately below the Acropolis, to the east.

👪 **Kids:** Museum of Greek Popular Musical Instruments.

◉ **Don't Miss:** Temple of Olympian Zeus and Small Metropolitan Church.

the months and the signs of the zodiac. The cross with a double bar and the arms of the La Roche and De Villehardouin families *(pediment)* were added in the Frankish period (13C).

▸ *Take Odós Erehthéos and Odós Kirístou.*

Hammam Abid Effendi
No. 8. ⏱ *Open Wed–Sun 9am–2.30pm.* Exhibitions of contemporary art are presented in the shadowy light and echoing acoustics of these restored Turkish baths.

▸ *Walk around the Tower of the Winds and continue down Odós Diogénous.*

Mikrí Mitrópoli

© ЛВ/Photoshot

👥 Museum of Popular Musical Instruments

1–3 Odós Diogenous. ⏰ *Open Tue–Sun 10am–2pm (Wed 12–6pm).* 🎫 *No charge.* ☎ *21032 501 98.*

Look and listen (headphones at each display) to a fascinating collection of some 600 traditional musical instruments from the 18C to the present day.

Romaikí Agorá (Roman Forum)

Pelopida & Eolou. ⏰ *Open Apr–Oct 8am-7.30pm (Mon 11am-7.30pm), Nov–Mar 8am-5pm.* 🎫 *€2.* ☎ *210 3245220. http://odysseus.culture.gr.*

Walk round in an anti-clockwise direction *(Odós Diogénous and Odós Pelopida)* passing an old 16C mosque, the **Feti-hie Cami**, with domes and an attractive columned porch. On your left you'll see the **Tower of the Winds★ (Aerides)**, an octagonal tower of white marble dating from the 1C BC. It was built to house a hydraulic clock, supplied by the Klepsidra spring on the north slop of the Acropolis hill.

On the west side stands the monumental **Forum gateway** (AD 2), which gave access to the forum proper; the interior court has been excavated.

⏵ *Walk around the agora by Odós Epaminónda, then Dioskouron, and finally left on Odós Polignótou. Follow Odós Pános to the right as it begins the steep climb up the north flank of the Acropolis; turn left on Odós Theorías.*

Housed in a fine 19C residence, the **Moussío Kanelopoúlou★** *(corner of Odós Theorias and Odós Panos;* ⏰ *temporarily closed at the time of writing;* 🎫 *€2;* ☎ *210 32123 13)* is a fine collection of ancient ceramics, Tanágra figurines, busts of Sophocles and Alexander, jewellery, Byzantine icons and popular works of art.

A little way along on the right stands the small **Church of the Transfiguration** (Metamórfossis) which dates from the 12C–14C; it rises above the semi-rural district of Anafiótika, founded by refugees from Anaphe in the Cyclades.

Below and to the north of the church lies the **"Old University" (Palió Pane-pistímio)** (19C) which was originally the house of the architect **Kleánthes**.

⏵ *Turn right and continue for 100m/328ft up an alleyway which climbs above the Anafiótika quarter.*

A fine **view★★**, especially beautiful at sunset, unfolds over the roofs of the old quarters, beyond to the town centre, southeast to Hymettos, south to the columns of the Olympieion at the far end of the National Garden (Ethnikós Kípos), and north, to the slope of Pentelikon; to the east the town stretches to the foot of Mount Parnes.

Continuing along Odós Pritaniou, the **Church of Ágii Anárgirii** (17C) is on the left, in the courtyard of the Convent of the Holy Sepulchre. Farther on stands the 12C **Chapel of St John the Evangelist** (Ágios Ioánnis o Theológos). Bear south to join **Odós Tripódon** linking the Theatre of Dionysos to the Agorá.

Mnimío Lissikrátous★ (Lysicrates' Monument)

The only survivor of the votive monuments in Odós Tripódon was erected in 334 BC. The monument was used as a library and was known as the **Lantern of Demosthenes** since tradition wrongly asserted that the great orator had worked there. The rotunda-like structure escaped the turmoil of the War of Independence and was restored in 1845. Farther east on the far side of a shady square stands **St Catherine's Church** (Agía Ekateríni); it was built in the 13C but has been altered several times since.

⏵ *Proceed along Odós Lissikrátous to Leofóros Amalías.*

Píli Adrianoú★ (Hadrian's Arch)

The arch dates from c.131 BC, and bears an inscription in the frieze indicating that it divided the Greek city from Hadrian's new Roman city (Hadrianopolis), which extended from the present-day Leofóros Amalias as far as the River

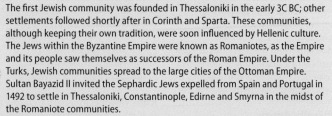

The Story of a Community

The first Jewish community was founded in Thessaloniki in the early 3C BC; other settlements followed shortly after in Corinth and Sparta. These communities, although keeping their own tradition, were soon influenced by Hellenic culture. The Jews within the Byzantine Empire were known as Romaniotes, as the Empire and its people saw themselves as successors of the Roman Empire. Under the Turks, Jewish communities spread to the large cities of the Ottoman Empire. Sultan Bayazid II invited the Sephardic Jews expelled from Spain and Portugal in 1492 to settle in Thessaloniki, Constantinople, Edirne and Smyrna in the midst of the Romaniote communities.

At the beginning of the Second World War, the Jews fought with great heroism at the Battle of Epiros. During the German occupation, 87 percent of the Jewish population was murdered, thus virtually wiping out a 2,000 year-old tradition. Today the Jewish community of Greece numbers about 5,000.

Ilissós. A short distance from the gate stands a monument to Lord Byron.

Naós Olímbiou Diós★★ (Olympieion)

Entrance at the top of Avenue Vassillis Olgas. ◷*Open daily Apr–Oct 8am–7.30pm (Mon 11am-7.30pm), Nov–Mar 8.30am–3pm.* ☞€4. ✆*21092 26 330. http://odysseus.culture.gr.* There are only a few traces beyond Hadrian's Arch of the temple to Zeus, which was one of the largest in the Greek world. As early as the 6C BC this site was chosen for a colossal temple, not completed until AD 132 under the Emperor Hadrian. Of the 84 original marble columns only 15 remain. Even today the Corinthian columns are impressive because of their width and height.

▷ *Make for Odós Kidathinéon; turn left to reach Odós A. Hatzimiháli.*

At no. 6, the **Centre for Popular Art and Traditions** (◷ *Tue-Fri 9am-1pm, 5-9pm, Sat-Sun 9am-1pm;* ☞*no charge;* ✆*210 3243987*) presents collections of weaving and embroidery, along with costumes, musical instruments and agricultural implements.

▷ *Return to Odós Kidathinéon and turn right on Odós Monis Asteriou.*

At no. 3, the **Frissiras Museum**★ (◷*open Wed–Fri 10am–5pm, Sat–Sun 11am–5pm;* ☞€6; ✆*210 32 346 78*)

mounts rotating displays of works from its collection of some 3,500 paintings of the human figure by well-known Greek and international artists.

▷ *Return to Odós Kidathinéon.*

The **Museum of Greek Folk Art**★ (no. 17; ◷ *open Tue–Sun 9am–2pm;* ☞€2, Sunday free, ✆*210 3213018*) features traditional costumes, household objects and objects related to cultural traditions such as shadow theatre and Dionysian rituals.

Be sure to see the life-size reconstruction of a room frescoed wall-to-wall by 19C folk artist Theofilos Hadjimichael.

▷ *Turn left into Odós Nikis.*

The **Jewish Museum of Greece**★ (no. 39, on the right; ◷*open Mon–Fri 9am–2.30pm, Sun 10am–2pm; ring bell for access;* ☞€6; ✆*21032 255 82; www. jewishmuseum.gr*) traces the 2,000-year history of the Jewish presence in Greece. Exhibits include religious artefacts, traditional costumes, jewellery, books and household objects, and there is an entire section devoted to the holocaust. It also hosts occasional temporary exhibitions. Turn north into Odós Filelínon to visit the **Russian Church of St Nicodemus** (Ágios Nikódimos), an 11C building with a dome, which was altered in the last century.

2 Monastiráki

Monastiráki – Μοναστηράκι

This was the centre of the Turkish town with the bazaar and the souks as well as the main mosques and administrative buildings. Now it is a popular commercial district incorporating the Athens Flea Market.

> **Info:** www.breathtaking athens.com.
> **Location:** Monastiraki lies north of the Acropolis and west of Síntagma Square, to which it is joined by Ermou street.
> **Don't Miss:** Keramikós Cemetery.

WALKING TOUR

This route follows a series of pedestrian-only streets, so you'll see little traffic, despite being in the city centre. If you do this walk on a Sunday, the streets will be very crowded, thanks to the Monastiraki Flea Market, which draws visitors from all over the city.

> *From Síndagma Square, head down Odós Ermoú, a busy shopping street.*

Kapnikaréa

The church, which is attached to the University of Athens, consists of two adjoining chapels: the one on the right dates from the 11C; the other dates from the 13C.

> *Walk south down Odós Kapnikaréas and turn right into Odós Pandróssou.*

Odós Pandróssou★

Thronged with busy crowds, this street resembles a market, complete with awnings and pavement stalls. There is an amazing range of articles for sale. On the left was the entrance to the bazaar, set up in the ruins of Hadrian's Library.

Platía Monastiráki★

This square, with its metro station and nearby attractions ranging from shops to tavernas and archaeological sites, is the heart of the old Turkish district and one of the most popular meeting points in Athens. The church, **Pandánassa** (17C) originally belonged to the convent from which the square takes its name.

Dzistaráki Mosque

○*Open Wed–Mon 9am–2.30pm.*
☞*€2.* ℘*210 32 42 066.*

At the junction of Odós Pandróssou with Odós Áreos stands the former **Dzistaráki Mosque** (1759); it has lost its minaret but it was skilfully restored in 1975 to house the **Museum of Traditional Greek Ceramics** (○*open Wed–Mon 9am–2.30pm;* ☞*€2*). Pottery and porcelain from the different regions are

Monastiraki flea market

© R. Mattes/MICHELIN

pleasantly displayed in the setting of a Muslim place of worship with its *mihrab* and its galleries.

Vivliothíki Adrianoú (Hadrian's Library)

Odós Áreos. The destruction by fire of the bazaar in 1885 made it possible to investigate the remains of **Hadrian's Library** built in 132 BC. It was an impressive rectangular building with a peristyle of 100 columns, restored in the 5C AD. The entrance façade on Odós Áreos is quite well preserved, particularly the Corinthian colonnade. It is about half the length of the original façade.

▶ *Return to Monastiráki Square and continue westwards along Odós Iféstou, running on from Odós Pandróssou. As in antiquity, it is occupied by metalworkers and takes its name from Hephaïstos, god of the forge. At the end, take Odós Astingos to Odós Ermou and continue to Odós Agiion Asenaton.*

At no. 22 you'll find the **Benaki Museum of Islamic Art** (⊙*open Tue–Sun 9am–3pm; 9am–9pm Wed;* ∞€5; *no charge Thu;* ℘ 210 3225550; www.benaki.gr), an annex of the main Benaki Museum. The terrace offers nice views of the Keramikós Cemetery. Inside there are ceramics, jewellery, decorative arts and arms originating mainly from Egypt, Iran and Turkey, arranged in chronological order on four floors. Retrace your steps to Odós Melidoni to nos. 4–6, location of the **Museum of Contemporary Ceramics** (⊙*open Mon–Fri 10am–3pm;* ∞€3; ℘ 210 3318491) dedicated to the study of traditional and modern ceramics.

▶ *Retrace your steps to Odós Ermou.*

Ierá Píli ke Dípiloa★

The **Sacred Gate** was built at the same time as Themistocles' wall (5C BC) and marks the beginning of the Sacred Way to Eleusis. The **Dipylon**, from the same period, was the main entrance to Athens. The Panathenaic processions started here.

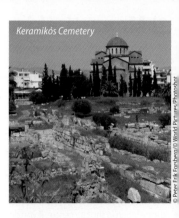

Keramikós Cemetery

© Peter Erik Forsberg/© World Pictures/Photoshot

Keramikós Cemetery★

148 Odós Ermou. ⊙*Open Apr–Oct daily 8am–7.30pm (Mon 11am-7.30pm), Nov–Mar 8.30am–3pm.* ∞€2 *(ticket also valid for museum entry).* ℘21034 635 52.

The **Keramikós**, the largest **cemetery** in Athens, was situated outside the wall of the ancient city. From the 6C BC the graves were marked with gravestones and statues. The site has yielded some handsome finds now displayed in the National Archaeological Museum; a few statues and stones have been left in place.

There is also a small museum on the site, close to the entrance, exhibiting finds such as grave stele, sculptures, vases and terra-cotta figurines, displayed in chronological order. Leaving the **museum** on the left descend the path (South Way) that leads to the best-preserved part of the cemetery: tombs dating from the 4C BC to the 1C AD. Turn left into the West Way, lined by tombs erected in the 4C BC. On the corner there is a tomb with a low relief (moulding) of a cavalryman fighting: this is Dexileos, who was killed in 393 BC in the war against the Corinthians. Look for the tomb of Dionysos, the treasurer (bull standing on a pillar); the monument to Lysimachides; the archon (a dog). On the other side of the West Way stands the famous gravestone of Hegeso (moulding); the original is in the National Museum. On the south side are the gravestone of Antidosis, which was painted, and the vase *(lekythos)* of Aristomachos.

3 Síndagma Square and Omónia Square

Platía Sindágmatos kai Platía Omónias –
Πλατεία Συντάγματος και Πλατεία Ομόνοιας

Síndagma Square was created in 1834 when the city centre was redesigned. It is overlooked by the former Royal Palace (today the parliament) and some of Athens' grandest hotels, and is joined to Omónia Square by two parallel roads, Stadiou and Panepistimiou.

- **Info:** www.breathtaking athens.com.
- **Location:** Síndagma Square lies halfway between the Acropolis and Mount Lycabettus, Athens' two highest peaks.
- **Kids:** The changing of the guard at Sindagma Square.
- **Don't Miss:** Shopping at the National Market.

🐾 WALKING TOUR

This route follows busy central thoroughfares with lots of traffic. It reflects the image of the city as most Athenians live it, with the Parliament, the Univeristy and the vast National Market.

Platía Sindágmatos★

Síndagma Square (Constitution Square) is in the elegant part of Athens that attracts many tourists. The east side is filled by the former Royal Palace, built for Otto I of Bavaria, which became the **Parliament (Voulí)** in 1935.

In front, before the monument to the Unknown Soldier, stand two **soldiers** (*évzoni*), dressed in the distinctive kilt and pompom shoes. At appointed times they emerge from their boxes to perform a sort of military ballet. Try to visit on Sundays at 11am when the ceremony is conducted with additional military personnel.

Panepistimíou★

Return to Síndagma Square, north side.
This is University Avenue, which is lined with luxury hotels, large terraced cafés, restaurants and smart boutiques. **Schliemann's House** is a large private house known as the "palace of Troy" (Iliou Mélanthron) which the brilliant German archaeologist had built in 1879; it now houses the **Numismatic Museum** (*no. 12;* ⏰ *open Tue–Sun*

8am–3pm; 💶*€3;* 📞*21036 437 74; www. nma.gr)* with a noteworthy collection of 600,000 coins and medals, including some of the earliest ever made). A little further on stands the Roman Catholic Cathedral of **St Dionysius the Areopagite** (Ágios Dionisis Areopagitis).

Panepistímio, Akadimía, Ethnikí Vivliothíki★
(The University, Academy and National Library)

These three 19C buildings in white Pentelic marble form an architectural group in the Neoclassical style. The **University** in the centre is the oldest; it was designed by Christian von Hansen, the Danish architect, and built between 1837 and 1864. To the right, the **Academy** was designed by von Hansen's brother Theophilos in the style of an Ionic temple. On the left, the **National Library**, which contains 500,000 volumes and 3,000 manuscripts.

Continue on to **Platía Omónia** (Concord Square) with its noise, crowds and hawkers, particularly in the evening. From here go left along Odós Athinas to **Platía Kodziá**, the centre of Athens in the second half of the 19C.

The National Bank of Greece (Ethnikí Trápeza tis Eládos) on the east side was founded in 1842. About 500 ancient tombs have been found in the centre of the square, just outside the city walls.

▷ *Follow Odós Eolou (pedestrian street) to the market.*

Ethniki Agorá★

Athens' **National Market** (🕐 *closed Sun*) is a spectacular sight with its vendors, goldsmiths and money changers on the north side (Odós Sofokléous), and a series of vast halls filled with stalls selling meat, fish and fresh fruit and vegetables (Odós Athinas). From the south side of the market go west along Odós Evripídou to no. 72 where stands the **Chapel of St John of the Column** (Ágios Ioánnis stin Kólon), much sought-after for curing fevers.

Odós Stadíou

Street parallel to Panepistimíou.
At its start this is a shopping street; half-way along on the south side is **Platía Klafthmónos** (Wailing Square). In the west corner stands the 11C **Church of the Sts Theodore** (Ágii Theódori), the oldest in Athens. The small Neoclassical mansion (1834) southeast of the square was the residence of the Greek royal family from 1836 to 1842; it now houses the **City of Athens Museum** (🕐 *open Mon & Wed–Fri 9am–4pm, Sat–Sun 10am–3pm, closed Tue;* ✆€3; *☎210 3246164*) highlighting daily life in Athens during the reign of King Otto. At no. 13 stands the **National Historical Museum**★ (🕐 *open Tue–Sun 9am–2pm;* ✆€3 *(Sun free);* ☎*210 3237617*) housed in the former Parliament building and highlighting the history of modern Greece from the fall of Byzantium in 1453 right to the end of the Second World War.

4 Mount Lycabettus★

Vounó Likavittoú – Βουνό Λυκαβηττού

The rocky slopes of Mount Lycabettus, Athens' highest point, rise directly behind Kolonaki, the capital's most expensive residential quarter and home to chic boutiques and smart designer stores.

- 🛈 **Info:** www.breathtaking athens.com.
- ▶ **Location:** Mount Lycabettus lies northeast of the Acropolis.
- 👫 **Kids:** The small zoo in the National Gardens.
- ☺ **Don't Miss:** The panorama from the top of Mount Lycabettus.

🐾 WALKING TOUR

This route involves a lot of green spaces, offering respite from city-centre traffic. Note that the peak of Mount Lycabettus can be reached by funicular or on foot – a lovely winding path leads to the summit, but you will need to wear decent walking shoes and carry a bottle of water.

▶ *Leave Sindagma Square by Vassilissis Sofias, left of the Parliament.*

Grand avenue Vassilissis Sofias, beside the National Garden, is lined with embassies, bank headquarters and several important museums, notably the Benáki Museum, the Museum of Cycladic Art and the Museum of Byzantine Art (ⓘ *see descriptions below*).

Platía Koloniakíou

Kolonáki Square, ringed with luxury shops, cafés and restaurants, is at the centre of the elegant Kolonáki district. The streets are lined with the smartest shops in Athens.

Likavitós★★★ (Lycabettus)

Access by funicular (at junction of Aristipou and Ploutarchou; bus no. 60 stops in Odós Kleomenous below the funicular): departs every 30min from 9am–3am. Return ticket ✆€4.
According to legend, Athena dropped Mount Lycabettus (Wolves' Hill) from

St George chapel on Likavitós hill

© Vladimir Alexeev/Bigstockphoto.com

the heavens to provide the setting for the Acropolis. The summit is crowned by a chapel dedicated to St George; the adjacent terraces offer an admirable **panorama** of the city of Athens, the Acropolis, the sea coast at Piraeus and the major mountain peaks.

▷ *Descend back to Vassilissis Sofias.*

Near the Byzantine Museum (⌂ *see below*) stands the **War Museum** *(Avenue Vassilissis Sophia and 2 Odós Rizari;* ⏱*Tue–Fri 9am–2pm, Sat-Sun 9.30am–2pm;* ♿€2; ℘*210 7252975; www.war-museum.gr).* Its fine collection of models (Byzantine and Frankish fortresses), arms and military gear illustrate Greek military history from antiquity onwards.

▷ *Continue to Leofóros Vassilissis Konstantinou.*

Ethnikí Pinakothíki – Moussío Alexándrou Soútsou★
No. 50, Leofóros Vas Konstantinou. ⏱*Open Thu-Mon 9am–3.30pm, Wed 2-9pm.* ⏱*Closed Tue.* ♿€6.50. ℘*210 72 359 37. www.nationalgallery.gr.* This excellent museum presents a comprehensive panorama of Greek painting. The first level, devoted to the different periods in Hellenic art since its inception, presents 18C works from the Ionian Islands and 19C canvases of the Munich School; pride of place goes to the

remarkable works by Domenico Theotocopoulos **(El Greco)**. The upper floor is devoted to contemporary Hellenic painting. You'll see works by **Konstantinos Parthenis**, influential in the development of 20C Hellenic art, and by **Nikos Engonopoulos** (surrealism) and **Nikos Chazikyriados-Ghika** (Cubism).

Stádio
Avenue Konstandinou.
The **stadium** stands on the site of its ancient predecessor laid out in the 4C BC and rebuilt by Herodes Atticus in AD 144. In 1896 it was rebuilt on its original plan for the modern Olympic Games. From the top of the white marble terraces, which can accommodate 70,000 spectators, there is a view of the National Garden and the Acropolis. Today, the annual Athens Marathon *(www.athens classicmarathon.gr)* finishes here.

♁♁ National Garden★ (Ethnikós Kípos)
⏱*Open 8am–sunset.*
The former royal garden was remodelled in 1840 and is a pleasant stroll. There are some 500 species of trees and plants, a **botanical museum** and a small zoo. Adjoining the National Garden to the south is the **Zappeion Park (Zápio)**, very popular with Athenians, particularly in the evenings. The **Zappeion Hall** is a pleasant Neoclassical building (1888) now used for exhibitions.

Major Museums★★★

A must-see, the National Archaeological Museum is one of the most important museums in the world devoted to Ancient Greek art. The Benaki Museum traces Greek culture from the Stone Age up until 1922, while the Museum of Cycladic Art displays a private collection of prehistoric art, and the Byzantine Museum examines the development and influence of the Byzantine Empire.

🛈 **Info:** www.breathtaking athens.com.

▶ **Location:** The National Archaeological Museum lies near Omónia Square. The Museum of Cycladic Art and the Byzantine and Christian Museum lie near one another, southeast of Mount Lycabettus.

👪 **Kids:** The Museum of Cycladic Art has special tours arranged for kids.

◉ **Don't Miss:**
The Mycenaean antiquities in the National Archaeological Museum.

ETHNIKÓ ARHEOLOGIKÓ MOUSSÍO★★★ (NATIONAL ARCHAEOLOGICAL MUSEUM)

Plan II, C1. 44 Patission St. Metro stop Omónia (green line), or bus nos. 224, 226 ⏱*Open May–Oct Tue–Sun 8am–8pm, Mon 1.30pm–8pm; Nov–Apr Tue–Sun 8am–3pm, Mon 1.30pm–8pm.* ⊚*7€.* ✆*210 82 177 24.*
www.namuseum.gr.
The National Archaeological Museum, one of the richest of its kind in the world, is devoted to ancient art from the Neolithic period to the Roman era and displays the major works of art from the Greek archaeological sites, except for Macedonia, Delphi, Olympia and Crete.

Neolithic and Cycladic Antiquities

Idols, notably the idol of the Goddess with Child *(Kourotrophos)* and a seated male idol, ceramics originating in Thessaly in particular, and jewellery (earrings) from Polióhni similar in style to finds from Troy. Vases and stylised marble idols with rounded contours originating in the Cyclades. The shape and decoration of the vases, especially the examples from Filakopí (Melos), recall the Santorini ceramics.

Mycenaean Antiquities (16C–11C BC)

Finds from the excavations conducted at Mycenae since 1876 by Schliemann and his successors. Notable among the exhibits are the **"mask of Agamemnon"**, the famous funerary mask of an Achaean king discovered by Schliemann in the Mycenae acropolis (fifth tomb in the first circle) and believed by him to be the mask of Agamemnon; bronze daggers with blades encrusted with gold, silver and enamel (Mycenae, same tomb); and a hexagonal wooden box covered with embossed gold plate showing lions pursuing deer (same tomb).

Also from Mycenae are: a **flask** *(rhyton)* used for libations in the shape of a **bull's head**, in silver with gold horns and muzzle and a gold rosette; a shallow vessel, like a sauceboat, in the shape of a duck made of rock crystal; and a woman's or sphinx's head in limestone painted to pick out the features in vivid colours. In addition there are two admirable **gold cups** discovered at Vafió near Sparta, and a seal ring depicting spirits offering libations to a goddess holding a cup (Tiryns Treasury).

Geometric and Archaic Art (10C–6C BC)

The main attraction is the huge geometric *amphora* dating from the mid-8C. The **"Dipylon Head"** belonged to a funerary *kouros* standing on a tomb. The huge votive *kouros* from Sounion once stood in front of the first temple to Poseidon.

*Part of the sculpture collection
National Archaeological Museum, Athens*

© Hellenic Ministry of Culture and Tourism /
Archaeological Receipts Fund

Kouroi or *korai* from the Cyclades and Attica, include the crowned *kore* Phrasikleia, and the statue of Winged Victory from Delos. Note also the very fine *kouros* found at Volomandra in Attica. Other artefacts of the same period include the funerary *stele* of Aristion, the **"warrior of Marathon"**, sculpted by Aristokles. An unusual tombstone shows a "running hoplite" or a Pyrrhic dancer.

In addition there is a superb funerary *kouros* from Anávissos in Attica (520 BC). The statue of Aristodikos, one of the later *kouroi*, shows the transition from Archaic to Classical art. Two bases of statues discovered in Themistocles' wall are decorated with low reliefs showing youths *(ephebes)* practising physical exercises.

Among the tombstones and votive tablets there is a votive relief in honour of a girl named Amphotto holding an apple (c.440 BC); also the Attic relief of the *ephebe* crowning himself, found at Cape Sounion.

Classical Art (5C–4C–3C BC)

Masterpieces include the extraordinary bronze **Artemision Poseidon** c.460–450 BC; and the **Eleusinian Relief** (c.440–430 BC).

Among the numerous funerary *steles* stands the great Myrrhine *lekythos*. Note also the Classical sculptures and votive reliefs; worth seeing are the relief dedicated to Hermes and the Nymphs, a second dedicated to Dionysos, and the copies of the original Classical 5C and 4C BC statues, in particular the Parthenon Athena, a lost work by Pheidias. The astonishing **Horse and Jockey of Artemision** is a 2C BC Hellenistic bronze.

The Karapános Collection consists of figurines and various small bronze items from 8C BC to 3C BC. The most remarkable are those from the Sanctuary of Zeus at Dodona (Epiros). Note the little statue of Zeus, a horse and a statuette of an armed man. Also worthy of note is the interesting series of 4C BC sculptures from the Temple of Asklepios (Aesculapius) at Epidaurus (attractive *acroteria*). Finally, four remarkable works attract attention. A high relief of a horse held by a slave comes from a 2C BC funerary monument found in Athens in 1948 near Lárissa Station; this realistic work shows the transition from Classical to Hellenistic art. The **Ephebe of Antikythera**, a statue in bronze of 4C BC, shows Paris offering the apple *(missing)* to Aphrodite. A stone head of Hygeia is attributed to Skopas. The bronze Ephebe of Marathon (4C) may have come from the School of Praxiteles.

It is impossible to miss the colossal and dramatic statue of **Poseidon** of Melos (2C BC); also worthy of note are two bronze portraits: a philosopher's head (3C BC), and a man's head (c.100 BC) excavated on Delos.

The "little refugee" statue of a child wearing a cape and holding a dog was found at Smyrna in 1922 and brought back to Athens when refugees from Asia Minor were arriving in Greece. Note the group with Aphrodite, Eros and Pan (c.100 BC) and a marble statue of the goddess Artemis, both found on Delos.

Roman Art

The period is represented by works from various Greek schools from the 1C BC to the 3C AD, the heyday of the Roman Empire. Portraits of the emperors include a bronze statue of Octavion Augustus, and a bust of Hadrian.

Bronzes

Works in bronze include smaller sculptures dating from as early as the 8C BC; jewellery, vases, figurines and votive offerings.

Egyptian antiquities (5000 BC to 1C BC)

Dating from the pre-Dynastic to the Ptolemaic period, the collection comprises 7,000 items and is the fourth most important of its kind in Europe.

Santorini Frescoes and Ceramics

These magnificent frescoes discovered in the 1970s on Santorini depict life on the island in the 16C BC. Note the one showing a naval battle framed in a frieze containing numerous figures, various types of vessel, and a villa.

Ceramics

Among the most precious pieces are the funerary *krater* of the Dipylon type found near the Keramikós Cemetery, the Nessos Amphora and the four *kraters* from Melos, a *krater* showing Herakles (Hercules) struggling with Nereus and white-ground funerary *lekithoi*.

MOUSSÍO BENÁKI★★ (BENÁKI MUSEUM)

Plan II, D3. Kolonáki district. 1 Odós Koumbari, via Vassilissis Sofias Avenue. Metro stop Syntagma. ☏ *21036 710 00. www.benaki.gr.* ⏰ *Open daily 9am–5pm (until midnight Thu); Sun 9am–3pm.* ⏰ *Closed Tue.* 🚭 €*7, free on Thu.*

This museum, devoted mainly to Greek and oriental art, houses the collection of **Antonis Benáki** (1873–1954), a wealthy patron of the arts. Further enriched by later bequests, the museum has been expanded and remodelled.

The collections of ancient art, which reveal aspects of cultural life, are displayed in chronological order, from prehistoric times to the present, and highlight the continuity of Greek civilisation and traditions.

First Floor (Rooms 1 to 12)

This covers the period from prehistory to the post-Byzantine era, includes a fine series of **gold objects** (3200–2800 BC), Hellenistic jewellery, and vases and idols from Alexandria. Examples of Coptic art include two **portraits from Fayyum** (2C–3C AD); there is a remarkable series of **icons** on subjects such as *The Hospitality of Abraham* which is of superb quality (late 14C), *St Demetrios* (15C), a fine *Transfiguration* (or Evangelismos tis Theotokou, 16C); also on display are a superb icon depicting St John and two youthful works by El Greco: the *Adoration of the Magi* (1560–65) and *St Luke* (1560).

Second Floor (Rooms 13 to 27)

This focuses on the development of Hellenism under foreign domination, and contains a large collection of regional **costumes**, traditional jewellery and embroidery, and some beautiful pieces of **gold work** from islands in northern Greece. Don't miss the two 18C reception rooms from Siátista and Kozáni in Macedonia. Works of religious art bear witness to the unifying role of the Orthodox Church during the occupation. On display are some beautiful **icons** *(Room 25)*, including an extraordinary composition by Th. Poulakis (Crete, 17C), a pictorial synthesis of the Hymn to the Virgin and the Last Judgment.

Third Floor (Rooms 29 to 32)

Here the spotlight is on pre-War of Independence economy and society as well as the Age of Enlightenment in Greece. Fine musical instruments, vessels and tools.

Fourth Floor (Rooms 33 to 36)

Greece during the 20C is the focus, with objects such as the Constitution signed in 1844 by King Otto, personal items (including a gold seal) belonging to the poet Dionysios Solomós, and copies of the first printed works of the poets Geórgios Seféris, Odysséus Elýtis, Ángelos Sikelianós and Andréas Embiricos. There are also works by Konstandínos Parthénis, Níkos Engonópoulos, and the composer Nikos Skalkotas.

MOUSSÍO KIKLADIKÍS TÉHNIS★★ (MUSEUM OF CYCLADIC ART)

Plan II, D3. Kolonáki district, 4 Odós Neofytou Douka. ◑*Open Mon, Wed, Fri–Sat, 10am–5pm; Thu 10am–8pm; Sun 11am–5pm.* ◑*Closed Tue.* ✆€7. ✆*21072 283 21/3. www.cycladic.gr.*
The private collection of **NP Goulandris** provides the major part of the exhibits in the Museum of Cycladic Art, which illustrates the development of Greek art over a period of 3,000 years.

First Floor
The first floor Is devoted to Cycladic Art and displays a total of 230 objects produced by the Cycladic Island civilisation – Ancient Cycladic I (3300–2700 BC), Ancient Cycladic II (2800–2300 BC) and Ancient Cycladic III (2400–2200 BC) including marble and pottery vessels, and marble **idols**.

Second Floor
The second floor focuses on Ancient Greek art, with 300 works including: Minoan and Mycenaean artefacts; a fine collection of vases with red and black figure decoration, in particular an Attic bell *krater* (430 BC) and a *lekythos* (560–550 BC); the Lambros Evtaxias Collection of **bronze vessels** (8C BC–1C AD) including a *kados* from Thessaly; jewellery and clay vases from Skíros (1000–700 BC); south Italian fish plates (4C BC); glass perfume flasks; a fine collection of Boeotian terracotta and female idols with bird faces from the same area (590–550 BC); marble sculpture and funerary reliefs.

Third Floor
The third floor examines Cypriot Culture, with some 800 exhibits illustrating the history of the island and its relations with the rest of the east Mediterranean from 4000 BC to 600 AD. Of special note are the stone figurines and clay flasks.

Fourth Floor
The fourth floor houses a permanent exhibition entitled "Daily Life in Antiquity". A virtual tour takes visitors through

© J. Malburet/MICHELIN

Seated figurine, "The Cup Bearer", Early Cycladic II period (2800–2300 BC), Museum of Cycladic Art

the world of Ancient Greek mythology, examining the role of gods and heroes in everyday public and private life. It also looks at attitudes towards death and the afterlife.

New Wing
Accessed through the garden. Built in the Neoclassical style in 1895, this building hosts temporary exhibitions.

VIZANDINÓ MOUSSÍO★★ (BYZANTINE AND CHRISTIAN MUSEUM)

Kolonáki district, 22 Vassilis Sofias Avenue. ◑*Open May–Oct Tue–Sun 8am–8pm, Mon 1.30–8pm; Nov–Apr Tue–Sun, 8am–3pm.* ✆€4. ✆*213 213 9572. www.byzantinemuseum.gr.*
This engaging museum offers a look at artistic development from the end the 3C AD to the 20C. The exhibition is divided into four sections: From the Ancient World to Byzantium; The Byzantine World; From Byzantium to the Modern Era; and Byzantium and Modern Art. Of particular note are the reconstructions of two early churches and a remarkable collection of **icons**; also frescoes and illuminated manuscripts.

Outskirts★★

Athens' port since the 5C BC, today industrial Piraeus is a hub for container ships and ferries to the Greek islands. In contrast, Kifissia is a smart, green suburb of tree-lined avenues, expensive villas and chic modern apartment blocks.

SOUTHWEST OF ATHENS
Pireás (Piraeus)

▷ *10km/6mi southwest of the centre of Athens. Access by metro (Peiraias, line 1) see p138, or by car along Odós Piréos or Leofóros Singroú (the latter is less direct but quicker).*

Lively and cosmopolitan, Piraeus (pop. 476,304) is the principal port of Greece; it was chosen in ancient times as the port of Athens because of its exceptional situation. It was **Themistocles** in c.493 BC who decided to move Athens' harbour to Piraeus. The new town was linked to Athens by the Long Wall, which formed a fortified corridor. In the Age of Pericles the town was rebuilt according to a grid plan. In 85 BC the Romans sacked Piraeus and set it on fire. The designation of Athens as the capital, however, and the opening of the Corinth Canal in 1893 brought a commercial revival. The modern **port** consists of Piraeus Harbour, Herakles Harbour, the Eleusinian Gulf and the two small harbours, Zéa and Mikrolímano. From Piraeus to Eleusis the coast is lined with commercial installations; it is Greece's largest industrial complex.

Zéa★

In antiquity this round bay was a large port for triremes; traces of boat-sheds are visible today. Today the waterfront is lined with busy cafés and the harbour is packed with expensive motorboats and yachts.
The fine **Archaeological Museum**★ *(31 Odós Kariloau Trikoupi; currently closed for restoration. €3; 210 45 215 98)* features well-known works including the Piraeus **Apollo**, a splendid Archaic *kouros* (c.525 BC), probably the oldest known Greek statue; the Piraeus

- **Info:** www.breathtaking athens.com.
- **Location:** Pireas lies 10km/ 6.2mi southwest of Athens city centre; Kifissia lies 14km/8.7mi northeast of the city centre. Pireas and Kifissia are connected by the metro line 1 (green line).
- **Kids:** The 20C Design Museum has a special area where children can learn and play.
- **Don't Miss:** Mikrolímano in Pireas.

Athena, c.340 BC; two bronze statues representing **Artemis**; a reconstruction of a sanctuary from the classical period; and the **Kallithéa Monument**★, an impressive 7m/23ft-high tomb.

The **Hellenic Maritime Museum** *(Akti Themistokleous; open Tue–Sat 9am–2pm, Sun 9.30am–2pm; closed Mon; €3; 210 4516264)* illustrates the history of navigation in Greece from antiquity to the Second World War.

Mikrolímano★★

Like Zéa, Mikrolímano was an ancient harbour, and today is lined by fish tavernas and filled with sailing boats. The harbour lies at the foot of **Mounychia Hill** (Kastéla), 87m/285ft high.

Mikrolímano

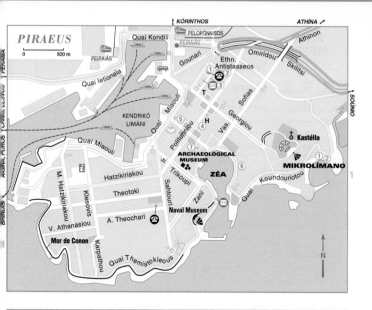

PIRAEUS

From the neighbourhood of the open-air theatre there is a fine view of Piraeus, the coast and the Saronic Gulf.

Aktí

The **coast road** round the peninsula gives attractive views of the port and the coast. There are traces of the sea wall (Tíhos Kónonos) built by Konon in the 4C BC.

Near the public garden at the western end of the peninsula stands the tomb of **Andreas Miaoúlis**, a famous Hydriot admiral.

NORTHEAST AND EAST OF ATHENS

Kifisiá★

▶ 14km/8.75mi northeast of Athens. Metro stop Kifisiá (line 1), 🖢 see p138.
Kifissiá is an elegant residential town at the foot of Mount Pendeli, pleasantly cool and fresh in summer because of its altitude, its water and its trees.

The lower town features relaxed tavernas and the public park; the elegant upper town boasts avenues of trees, 19C villas and luxury hotels and restaurants.

Goulandris Museum of Natural History★

13 Odós Levidou. ◷Open Mon–Sat 9am –2.30pm, Sun 10am–2.30pm. ☞€5. 𝄞210 8015870. www.gnhm.gr.
Housed in an elegant 19C villa, the museum is dedicated to the study, conservation and protection of the natural environment. The **herbarium** contains 80,000 plant varieties from the Balkan peninsula. There are also sections focusing on Terrestrial Zoology, Marine Biology and Geology-Palaeontology.

20C Design Museum

▶ 12km/7mi northeast of Athens, in Maroússi. Metro Maroussi (line 1) 🖢 see p138. 4–10 Odós Patmou. ◷Open Tue & Thu–Fri 10am–8pm, Mon and Wed 9am–6pm, Sat 10am–3pm, Sun closed. ☞Entry is free. 𝄞210 6850611. www.designmuseum.gr. This little-known museum is part of the Design Plaza complex and houses excellent displays of furniture and works by renowned contemporary designers Hoffmann, Mies Van der Rohe, Le Corbusier, Mackintosh, Dalí, etc. There's a special area for children too.

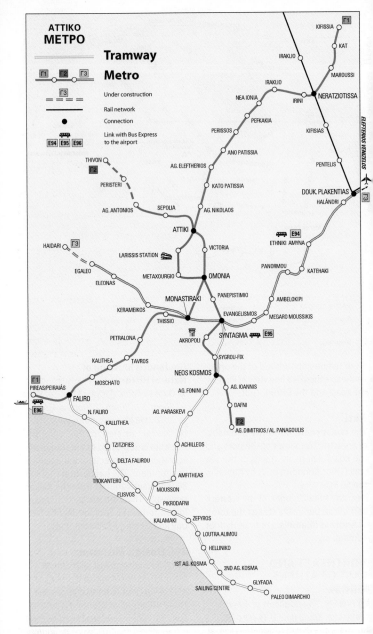

ATTIKO ΜΕΤΡΟ

Tramway

Metro

Under construction

Rail network

Connection

Link with Bus Express
to the airport

On the Flanks of Mount Hymettos★★

▶ 9km/5.5mi east of Athens. Beyond Kessarianí (bus terminus) the road climbs up the verdant slope. After 3km/2mi the Kessarianí Monastery appears on the right.

Kessarianí Monastery★★

🕘 Tue-Sun 8.30am-3pm. 🚌€2.
📞21072 36 619.

The silent, serene monastery (11C) was dedicated to the Presentation of the Virgin; it is now deconsecrated. A recess in the outer wall of the monastery on the

Murals in Kessarianí Monastery

© Independent Picture Service/Alamy

east side of the first courtyard contains the famous **Ram's Head Fountain**, a sacred spring in antiquity that was celebrated by the Latin poet Ovid in his *Ars Amatoria*.

Ancient fragments dot the inner **courtyard**. In the Middle Ages the 11C building *(left)* was the monks' bathhouse. The adjoining wing has a gallery at first-floor level serving the monks' cells.

The **church** (11C; the narthex and the side chapel were added in the 17C) is decorated with **murals**: those in the narthex date from 1682; those in the church itself are probably 18C. Opposite the church are the **convent buildings**.

▶ Leave the monastery on this side and take the path up through the trees (15min on foot there and back) to a sanctuary southeast of the monastery.

Here there are traces of a 10C church built on the foundations of a palaeo-Christian basilica; a 13C vaulted Frankish church; and a chapel dedicated to the Archangels. Fine **views** of Athens, Attica and the Saronic Gulf.

Mount Hymettos★★

Continue up the road past the 11C **Asteri Monastery**. There are views of Athens and the Saronic Gulf as far as the Peloponnese to the west, and of the Attic peninsula (Mesógia), its eastern shore and Euboea to the east. The summit is prohibited *(military zone)*, but in antiquity it was crowned by a statue of Zeus. The Hymettos range, which rises to 1,026m/3,366ft, extends north–south for about 20km/12.5mi.

▶ From Kessarianí head straight on past the monastery to rejoin the main road, then head in the direction of Lavrio/Sounion.

Vorres Museum

In Peania, Odós Diadochou Konstantinou. ◯*Open Sat–Sun 10am–2pm.* ⊚€5. ℘210 6642520.
An old estate not far from Athens Airport is now a museum with two main collections. Two traditional village houses and a building once used for wine pressing have been carefully restored and decorated to display examples of village traditions and folk art from different regions of Greece. Pottery, paintings, rugs and antique furniture, as well as examples of objects of everyday use, are on show. The other collection has works of modern art – paintings and sculptures – by Greek artists, mostly from the period after the Second World War.

Peaches performing at Synch Festival

© Vangelis Patsialos/Synch Festival

Summer Festivals

Each summer, from July till September, Athens hosts the Athens and Epidaurus Festival (www.greekfestival.gr). The Odeon of Herodes Atticus (👣 see p119), the main venue, is a 2C AD open-air theatre, carved into the rocks of the southern slopes of the Acropolis, which can accommodate 6,000 spectators. Previous performers include the St Petersburg Philharmonic Orchestra, the Vienna Boys' Choir, the New York City Ballet, and contemporary musicians such as Laurie Andersona and Demis Roussos. Simultaneously, the 1C BC Epidaurus Ancient Theatre (👣 see p249), near Argolida on the Peloponnese, hosts comedies and tragedies based on works by renowned ancient Greek writers such as of Sophocles.

Tickets can be bought online, by telephone (☎210 3272000; daily 9am–9pm), in person at the box office in Central Athens (39 Panepistimiou, Athens; Mon–Fri, 8.30am–4pm, Sat 9am–2.30pm), or at the box offices in front of the respective venues.

On a more contemporary note, each summer Athens also hosts the two-day Synch Festival (www.synch.gr), featuring electronic, experimental and indie bands, and held at Technopolis in early June. Past line-ups have seen names such as Florence and the Machine, the Friendly Fires and Peaches.

Likewise, the three-day Rockwave Festival (www.rockwavefestival.gr) brings alternative rock to Greece, with international bands such as Placebo, Massive Attack and Gogol Bordello drawing the crowds. Rockwave takes place each year in early July, and as of 2004, Terravibe, near Malakassa (37km/23mi north of Athens), has been the fixed venue. Tickets for both the Synch and Rockwave festivals can also be bought from the box office in central Athens (👣 see above).

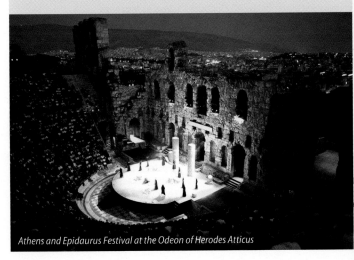

Athens and Epidaurus Festival at the Odeon of Herodes Atticus

ADDRESSES

🏨 STAY

Hotel options can be rather expensive in Athens, especially during the high season *(April–October)*. Prices can nearly double during holidays *(Easter)* or special events. Internet reservations generally result in the best prices.

KOLONÁKI

More popular with Greek visitors than foreign tourists, smart Kolonáki is backed by Mount Lycabettus. You'll find foreign embassies, smart shops and some of Athens' best museums here.

🛏 **Athinea** – *9 Odós Vilara, pedestrian street off Agios Konstantinou.* 📞*210 524 2315. www.athineahotel.gr. 45 rooms.* Very simple, comfortable hotel; excellent value.

🛏🛏🛏 **Pythagorion** – *28 Odós Agio Konstandinou.* 📞*210 5242811. www.pythagorion-hotel.gr. 56 rooms.* Well-kept rooms, some with balconies.

🛏🛏🛏 **Periscope** – *Haritos 22.* 📞*210 7297200. www.yeshotels.gr. 22 rooms and suites.* Sleek minimalist design hotel. All rooms have wooden floors and luxurious bathrooms.

🛏🛏🛏 **Xenos Lycabettus** – *Valaoritou 6 & Voukourestiou.* 📞*210 3600600, www.athenslycabettus.gr. 25 rooms.* On the edge of Kolonáki, this hotel has smart, comfortable rooms and suites plus a ground-floor café-restaurant.

🛏🛏🛏🛏 **St George Lycabettus** – *Kleomenous 2.* 📞*210 7290711. www.sglycabettus.gr. 154 rooms.* At the foot of Mount Lycabettus, overlooking Kolonaki, this smart hotel has two restaurants, a rooftop pool and a spa in the basement.

MONASTIRÁKI

A popular base for tourists due to its proximity to the Acropolis, the nightlife area of Psirri, and Monastiráki metro station, with trains running directly to Piraeus port.

🛏🛏 **Tempi** – *29 Odós Eolou.* 📞*210 32 131 75. www.tempihotel.gr. 24 rooms.* Very well situated in a pedestrianised street near the Agia Irini church. Simple, but with a welcoming air. No breakfast but kitchen for guests' use.

🛏🛏 **Cecil** – *39 Odós Athinas.* 📞*/Fax 210 32 170 79. www.cecil.gr. 40 rooms.* Set in a beautiful, Neoclassical building, recently renovated. Some of the charming guest rooms are noisier than others (ask for a room on the little back street). Welcoming atmosphere.

🛏🛏 **Attalos** – *29 Odós Athinas.* 📞*210 32 12801. www.attalos.gr. 80 rooms.* Beautiful roof terrace; clean and comfortable rooms. View of the Acropolis from the balconies.

🛏🛏🛏 **Athens Center Square Hotel** – *Aristogitonos 15, Psirri.* 📞*210 3222706. www.athenscentersquarehotel.gr. 54 rooms.* Opened June 2009. Located near the National Market, halfway between Monastiraki and Omónia Square. Colourful modern rooms, excellent value for money.

🛏🛏🛏 **Fresh** – *Sophocleous 26 & Klisthenous, Psirri.* 📞*210 5248511. www.freshhotel.gr. 113 rooms and suites.* Modern, cool and fun, this chic design hotel has a minimalist interior. There is a restaurant, and a roof with a small pool and an Acropolis view.

PLÁKA

Athens' most touristy area Is also one of its prettiest, with Neoclassical buildings and pedestrian-only cobbled streets in the shadow of the Acropolis. It does, however, get very busy in high season.

🛏 **Kimon** – *27 Odós Apollonos.* 📞*210 33 146 58. www.kimonhotelathens.com. 14 rooms.* Satisfactory rooms, all individually decorated; good views of the Acropolis from the pretty terrace.

🛏🛏 **Adonis** – *3 Odós Kodrou.* 📞*210 32 497 37. www.hotel-adonis.gr. 26 rooms.* Situated in the heart of Plaka, this comfortable hotel has superb views of the Acropolis from its terrace bar. Rooms without air-conditioning cost less.

🛏🛏 **Acropolis House** – *6–8 Odós Kodrou.* 📞*210 32 223 44. www.acropolishouse.gr. 19 rooms.* This Neoclassical hotel has every modern comfort. All **non-smoking**. Rooms without air-conditioning cost less.

Metropolis – *46 Odós Mitropoleos. 210 32 174 69/178 71. www.hotelmetropolis.gr. 22 rooms.* Clean, comfortable hotel in a pink building with flower-filled balconies. No breakfast. Rooms without en-suite cost less.

Omiros – *15 Odós Apollonos. 210 32 354 86. www.omiroshotel.gr. 40 rooms.* Modern, comfortable hotel. Enjoy views of the Acropolis over breakfast on the pleasant terrace.

Niki – *27 Odós Nikis. 210 32 209 13. www.nikihotel.gr. 23 rooms.* Discreet, quiet hotel in a narrow street off Sindagma Square.

Adrian – *74 Odós Adrianóu. 210 3221553. www.douros-hotels.com. 22 rooms.* A comfortable little hotel in the heart of Plaka . Beautiful, shady terrace with views of the Erechtheion.

Plaka – *7 Odós Kapnikareas. 210 32 227 06. www.plakahotel.gr. 67 rooms.* Recently renovated, with comfortable rooms (ask for one with a view of the Acropolis). Beautiful terrace with wonderful views.

Byron – *19 Odós Vironos. 210 32 303 27. www.hotel-byron.gr. 22 rooms.* Modernised and comfortable hotel, well-situated and with a welcoming ambience. Acropolis view, free Wi-Fi.

Central – *Apolonos 21, Pláka. 210 3234357. www.centralhotel.gr.* A smart modern hotel, within easy walking distance of the Acropolis and Síndagma Square.

Art Gallery Hotel – *Erechthiou 5, Koukaki. 210 9231933. www.artgallery hotel.gr. 21 rooms.* Just a few minutes' walk from the Acropolis, this hotel has discreetly furnished rooms with antiques.

Electra Palace – *Nikodimou 18–20, Pláka. 210 3370000. www.electra hotels.gr. 135 rooms and 20 suites.* The smartest hotel in Pláka. It has a rooftop pool and restaurant, plus a spa. Expensive but worth it.

Hermes – *19 Odós Apollonos. 210 32 35 514. www.hermeshotel.gr. 45 rooms.* Each spacious guest room has a balcony. Comfortable, well-designed and equipped; in-house travel agent; games room for kids.

SÍNDAGMA SQUARE & OMÓNIA SQUARE

Some of Athens' most luxurious and expensive hotels stand on Síndagma Square. Slightly less smart, Omónia Square is popular with business travellers.

Arethousa – *Mitropoleos 6–8. 210 3229431. www.arethusahotel.gr. 87 rooms.* Mid-range hotel with simple but comfortable rooms, a café and rooftop restaurant with an Acropolis view.

Art Hotel – *Marni 27, Omónia. 210 5240501. www.arthotelathens.gr. 30 rooms and suites.* Friendly boutique hotel with individually decorated rooms and suites with free Wi-Fi. Close to the National Archaeological Museum.

Baby Grand Hotel – *Athinas 65 & Lycourgou, Omónia. 210 3250900. www.classicalhotels.com. 76 rooms and suites.* Amusing and quirky, this hotel's rooms and suites are each individually decorated by a graffiti artist.

Grande Bretagne – *Platía Síndagma. 210 3330000. www. grandebretagne.gr. 262 rooms and 59 suites.* Athens' most prestigious hotel, the Grande Bretagne stands opposite the parliament. Its rooms and suites are adorned with antiques, and there's a summer rooftop restaurant and pool, plus a spa in the basement.

THISSÍO

Thissío makes a fine base due to its proximity to the Acropolis and the alternative nightlife area of Gazi. As several of the main streets are now pedestrian-only, it's also a pleasant area to explore on foot.

Erechthion – *8 Odós Flamarion on the corner with Odós Agias Marinas. 210 34 596 06. www.hotelerechthion.gr. 22 rooms.* Near the Observatory in a quiet street, this hotel dates from the 1960s. Clean, quiet, comfortable rooms.

Phidias – *39 Odós Apostolou Pavlou. 210 3459511. www.phidias.gr. 15 rooms.* Clean and comfortable though interior decor slightly dated. Great location, just a 10min walk from the Acropolis. Good value.

Jason Inn – *12 Odós Agion Assomaton. ☎210 32 511 06. www.douros-hotels.com. 57 rooms.* Every comfort, situated in a residential street near the Benaki Museum of Islamic Art.

PIRAEUS

Piraeus may not be pretty, but its proximity to the port makes it a good overnight base if you have an early-morning ferry to catch.

Eva – *2 Odós Notará. ☎210 41 701 10. w ww.hotel-eva.gr. 20 rooms.* Pleasant hotel with small but comfortable rooms (the quietest on the sixth floor). No breakfast.

Anita-Argo – *23–25 Odós Notará. ☎210 41 21 795. 55 rooms.* Modern hotel behind the metro station. Ask for a room on one of the upper floors overlooking the street. Minibus service to the harbour. Free parking.

Phidias – *189 Odós Kontouriotou. ☎210 42 964 80. www.hotelphidias.gr. 26 rooms.* Comfortable hotel off Zéa Marina. Charming welcome.

Lília – *Marina Zea (Passalimani) – 131 Odós Zeas. ☎210 41 79 108. www.liliahotel.gr. 20 rooms.* Small, quiet hotel in an attractive street overlooking the marina. Recently renovated. Ask for a room overlooking the street (the others face a blank wall). Ideal base from which to explore Piraeus. Free shuttle service to the harbour.

Poseidonio – *3 Odós Charilaou Trikoupi. ☎210 42 866 51. www.hotel poseidonio.com. 91 rooms.* Recently renovated hotel with comfortable rooms. No restaurant, but room service is available.

Noufara – *45 Odós Iroon Politehniou. ☎210 41 155 41. www.noufarahotel.eu. 56 rooms.* Same proprietor as the Poseidonio, but located along the main avenue of Piraeus, near the square.

ⵏ/EAT

KOLONÁKI

Upmarket Kolonáki, frequented mainly by rich Athenians, is home to some excellent Greek restaurants as well as a few eateries serving foreign cuisine.

To Kioupi – *4 Platía Kolonakíou. Open Sun–Fri 11am–7pm.* A local institution since 1929. Family-style dishes served up quickly; friendly atmosphere.

Athinaïkon – *2 Odós Themistokléous (near Omónia Square). ☎210 38 384 85. www.athinaikon.gr.* Open for lunch; closed Sun. Traditional marble tables; aura of Athens during the 1930s. Spend the hottest part of the day sampling *mezes* in air-conditioned comfort.

Peros Cafe – *Platia Kolonaki 7. ☎210 3645068.* This see-and-be seen café has a large terrace with outdoor tables – ideal for a drink, a snack, and people-watching.

Altamira – *Tsakalof 36, Kolonaki. ☎210 3614695. www.altamira.com. gr. Closed Sun.* On the first floor of a Neoclassical building, Altamira's menu covers four cuisines – Asian, Indian, Arabic and Mexican – making a change from the omnipresent Greek fare.

Dimokritos – *Dimokritou 23, Kolonaki. ☎210 3613588. Closed Aug.* Quality Greek taverna fare served in a rustic interior in smart Kolonaki. A sound and reliable choice.

Orizontes – *Mt Lycabettus. ☎210 7227065. www.orizonteslycabettus.gr. Open daily lunch and dinner.* On the summit of Mount Lycabettus, Orizontes affords stunning city views and a creative Mediterranean menu to match.

MONASTIRÁKI

Known for its traditional Greek fast food eateries serving kebabs, Monastiráki also has some good restaurants, the best of which have Acropolis views.

Thanasis – *Mitropoleos 69, Monastiráki. ☎210 3244705.* Popular with locals and visitors alike, this is the place to stop for kebabs served with pitta bread and chips. Tables indoors and out, takeaway also available.

Dioskouroi – *Dioskouri 13. ☎210 3253323.* Below the Acropolis, next to the ancient Agora, this is a great place to drink ouzo with platters of light snacks.

⊝⊜🍽 **Café Avissinia** – *Platia Avissinias.* ✆*210 3217047.* This tiny café serves delicious snacks overlooking a square where craftsmen restore antique furniture.

⊝⊜🍽 **To Kouti** – *Adrianou 23, Monastiráki.* ✆*210 3213229.* Just off Monastiráki, with a view of the Acropolis rising behind the ancient Agora. Serves creative Mediterranean cuisine in an informal atmosphere.

PLÁKA

Pláka is filled with old-fashioned tavernas décorated in rustic style and serving traditional Greek food. Some also have live music, geared primarily for tourists.

⊝ **Platanos** – *4 Odós Diogenous. Closed Sunday evenings.* Eat in the shade of eucalyptus and plane trees. Classic Pláka taverna; a local haunt.

⊝ **Sholarhio to Geraini** – *14 Odós Tripodon. Open for lunch.* Large assortment of delicious *mezes* served under a vine-covered pergola.

⊝⊜ **Zorbas** – *Lissiou & Erehtheos.* ✆*210 3226188. www.zorbasrestaurant-plaka.gr.* Traditional Greek dishes and barrel wine, plus live music at weekends.

⊝⊜ **O Glikis** – *Odós A. Gerondas.* A local institution; note the grand wooden bar. Excellent *mezes*.

⊝⊜ **Tou Psara** – *16 Odós Erehtheos.* ✆*210 3218733. www.psaras-taverna.gr. Open for lunch.* Charming and unique setting and delicious cuisine. One of the best restaurants in Plaka.

⊝⊜🍽 **Hermion** – *15 Odós Pandróssou.* ✆*210 32 471 48. www.hermion.gr.* Elegant atmosphere, refined cuisine and service. Try the swordfish (lemon and olive sauce) and baklava.

⊝⊜ **Diogenes** – *Platía Lysikrátous.* ✆*210 32 248 45. www.diogenes.gr.* Calm, pleasant atmosphere in which to sample a drink or a variety of house specialities.

⊝⊜🍽🍽 **Daphne's** – *Lysikrátous 4, Pláka.* ✆*210 3227971. www.daphnes restaurant.gr. Dinner only.* High-class traditional Greek cuisine served in a Neoclassical building with frescoed walls and occasional live music.

SÍNDAGMA SQUARE & OMÓNIA SQUARE

Athenian business people and office workers eat lunch out in the area between Síndagma and Omónia.

⊝⊜ **Petrino** – *Themistokleous & Akadimias.* ✆*210 3804100.* Serves a wide choice of Greek meat and fish dishes, in a pseudo-rustic dining room.

⊝⊜🍽 **Cellier Le Bistrot** – *10 Panepistimiou, Síndagma.* ✆*210 3638525. www.cellier.gr.* In an arcade close to Síndagma, this French bistrot-style eatery dates back to 1938. Mediterranean menu, extensive wine list and occasional live music.

⊝⊜🍽 **Tzitzikas kai Mermigas** – *Mitropoleos 12, Síndagma.* ✆*210 3247607.* Behind Síndagma Square, on the edge of Pláka, this cheerful place serves modern Greek taverna fare. Very popular with locals and visitors alike.

THISSÍO

Thissío has some good restaurants and tavernas, the most memorable of which have Acropolis views.

⊝⊜🍽 **Dionysos** – *43 Odós Rovertou Gali, intersection of Apostolou Pavlou and Dionissiou Areopagitou.* ✆*210 9233182. www.dionysoszonars.gr.* Solid reputation for fine Greek and international cuisine. The place to sample authentic *dolmades* or the excellent *baklava*.

PIRAEUS

Thanks to its location on the coast, Piraeus is known for its seafood tavernas, the best of which ring the pretty harbour of Mikrolímano.

⊝⊜🍽 **Jimmy and the Fish** – *Akti Koumoundourou 46, Mikrolímano.* ✆*210 4124417. www.jimmyandthefish.gr. Open daily for lunch and dinner.* Classic old-fashioned seafood restaurant with outdoor tables overlooking the fishing harbour.

⊝⊜🍽 **Plous Podilato** – *Akti Koumoundourou 42, Mikrolímano.* ✆*210 4137910. www.plous-podilatou.gr. Open daily for lunch and dinner.* Modern creative seafood dishes served in a smart minimalist interior with several tables out front overlooking the water.

⊜⊜ Tony Bonanno –
63 Panapastasiou. 📞*210 4111901.*
The best Italian restaurant in Piraeus;
excellent Italian food and large portions.

🚄 TAKING A BREAK

Nikis – *Odós Nikis. From Síndagma
Square, take the first right off Odós Ermou.*
Close to the shops of Odós Ermou, this
calm street café is the perfect place for
a coffee break.

Aiolis Cafe – *Eolou 23.* 📞*210 3312839.*
Fashionable café in a restored
Neoclassical building, on a pedestrian-
only street. Serves drinks and snacks,
indoors and out.

Nefeli – *24 Odós Panos and Odós
Aretousas.* Charming views of the palm
trees of the Agora from the little tables
of this café set along Odós Dioskouron,
particularly at dusk when the sun sets
on the Hephaïsteion.

Metropol – *Platia Mitropoleos.*
Old-fashioned café; tempting pastries.
A great place to stop for a mid-day treat.

🛒 SHOPPING AND STROLLING

For tourists the centre of Athens is
Síndagma Square with its large hotels,
travel agencies, banks and cafés. Bars
and nightclubs crowd the side streets.
Women's dress shops line **Odós Ermoú**.

Southwest of Síndagma Square lies
Plaka; in the evenings tourists throng
the souvenir shops in **Odós Adrianoú**
and **Odós Pandrássou** and the tavernas
blare *bouzoúki* music.

Plaka merges into **Monastiráki**, an old
Turkish bazaar, now a sort of flea market,
particularly on Sunday mornings.

Northeast of Síndagma Square lies
Kolonáki, a wealthy, elegant district
with **luxury shops**: fashion, antiques,
jewellery, galleries and gourmet foods.

Síndagma Square is joined to Omónia
Square *(northwest)* by two busy
shopping streets, **Odós Stadíou** and
Odós Venizélou.

Lively **Omónia Square** bustles with
the shops of tradesmen and artisans.
Running south, Odós Athinas passes
through the **Kendrikí Agorá**, a huge

> ## 🎭 Useful Tips 🎭
>
> **Odós Adrianoú** – Pedestrian
> streets lined with cafés and
> restaurants; views of the Acropolis,
> popular the day through.
>
> **Odós Apostolou Pavlou** – Lively
> evening scene in the cafés along
> this pedestrian street near the
> Acropolis.

covered market which sells a fascinating
and astonishing variety of foodstuffs.

On fine evenings Athenians stroll in
Síndagma or Omónia Squares, in the
Kolonáki district or in the Zapio Garden,
where they dine or attend the popular
musical entertainment. **Lycabettos**
(café-restaurant) has a magnificent view
south over Athens, and Pedío Áreos is
known for its **open-air cinemas**.

SOUVENIRS

Browse the shops along Odós
Kidathinaion and Adrianoú for leather,
statuettes, ouzo and honey.

🎫 EVENTS AND FESTIVALS

Athens Festival – *23 Hatzihristou
& Makrigianni.* 📞*210 9282900.
www.greekfestival.gr.* The festival is held
from May to September at the foot of
the Acropolis in the **Odeon of Herodes
Atticus** and the **Lycabettus Theatre**.
International and national companies
perform plays, operas, concerts, ballets,
contemporary and traditional dancing,
and Classical tragedies; also concerts
of jazz, rock and Greek music. Tickets
available at the office *(above)* or at the
door just before the performance.

Traditional dance – *Dora Stratou
Theatre. 8 Odós Scholiou, in Plaka.* 📞*210
32 443 95 (9am–4pm); www.grdance.org;*
⊜*€15.* Performances take place May–
September Wed-Fri at 9.30pm (Sat-Sun,
8.15pm) on Philopappos Hill.

NORTH OF ATHENS

Vória tis Athínas – Βόρεια της Αθήνας

Delphi aside, the area north of Athens is undervisited and underexplored. Its tourist economy is based on local rather than foreign visitors who are usually bussed from Athens to Delphi and back in a day. Many of them, stunned by the beauty of Mount Parnassus, regret the speed of it all and wish they had allowed more time. Being close to Athens, criss-crossed by excellent roads and offering a range of ancient, Byzantine and Frankish monuments – including the two UNESCO world heritage sites of Delphi and Óssios Loukás – it is worth renting a car and spending at least two or three days in the area.

Highlights

1 The Archaeological Museum in **Thebes** (p147)
2 The UNESCO Heritage site of **Óssios Loukás** (p148)
3 A visit to the cave of **Koríkio Ándro** (p151)
4 A climb up **Mt Parnassos** (p152)
5 A day in **Delphi** (p154)

A Bit of History

In the ancient world the area north of Athens was dominated by Thebes, a city that competed with Athens and Sparta for the dominance of Greece. The alliances and battles between these three cities shaped the history of antiquity for more than 100 years until their unification under Macedonian dominance. On the island of Euboea, ancient Erétria was another prosperous urban hub, whereas in the west, the oracle at Delphi was what we would now call the world's biggest tourist attraction for centuries – until the advent of Christianity.

During the Byzantine era, the area was invaded by Slavs and Albanians; until recently, an Albanian dialect (Arvanitika) was still spoken in Thebes and Aráhova. Later, the outstanding monastery of Óssios Loukás became a focal point of local pilgrimage. Most of the area fell to the Franks (Venetians, French and Catalans) before succumbing to the Ottoman Turks in the 15C. Today the landscape of the area alternates between the amorphous commercial cities of Thebes and Chalkis, dramatic mountain landscapes like Parnassus and the Eagles' Road in Euboea, and picturesque towns like Nafpaktos and Aráhova. It is worth noting that the strategic importance of the area around Athens was such that its surrounding seas have been the setting of arguably the three most important sea battles in pre-modern history: the Battle of Salamis (480 BC) between the Greeks and Persians, the Battle of Aktion (31 BC) when Octavius beat Mark Antony and Cleopatra, and the Battle of Lepanto (AD 1571) between an alliance of Catholic powers headed by Spain and the Ottoman Empire.

Temple of Apollo, Delphi

Thebes

Thíva – Θήβα

Of the legendary Thebes, home of Oedipus, virtually nothing remains; the ancient city was razed to the ground by Alexander the Great and devastated by earthquakes; only a few vestiges remain and Thebes today is a modern commercial centre. To get an idea of the past glories of this, the capital of Boeotia, the visitor must spend some time in the Archaeological Museum.

▶ **Population:** 24,443.
Michelin Map: 737 H 8 – Boeotia – Central Greece.
Location: Thebes is located 69km/43mi northwest of Athens (84km/53mi by motorway) and 97km/61mi west of Delphi. Thebes is served by the E 75 motorway and the E 962.
Don't Miss: The Archaeological Museum for a reminder of what Thebes once was.
Timing: An hour or two will be more than sufficient.

A BIT OF HISTORY

Ill-Fated Oedipus – The most famous Theban is legendary **Oedipus**, son of Laios, King of Thebes, and Jocasta. An oracle foretold that Oedipus would kill his father and marry his mother so he was abandoned on Mount Kitherónas (Kithairon); rescued by shepherds, he was raised by the King of Corinth in ignorance of his true parentage.

On reaching manhood Oedipus left Corinth; near Thebes he quarrelled with a man and killed him; it was Laios.

At that time the countryside was being terrorised by the **Sphinx**, a winged monster with a lion's body and a woman's head, which devoured passersby who couldn't answer the riddles it posed. Jocasta's brother, **Creon**, offered the throne of Thebes and Jocasta's hand to anyone who would rid the country of the Sphinx. Oedipus did so and became King of Thebes and married his mother, thus fulfilling the oracle's prediction.

When Oedipus discovered the truth, he destroyed his own eyes and Jocasta hanged herself. Blind, Oedipus left Thebes accompanied by his daughter Antigone to lead a wandering life until his death at Colonus (Kolonós) near Athens. After his death, his two sons fought over the kingdom and killed each other. Antigone returned to Thebes and insisted, to the point of her own death, on burying her brother Polyneices (who had been declared a traitor). The tragic legends of Oedipus and Antigone inspired the trilogy of **Sophocles**: *Oedipus Rex, Oedipus at Colonus* and *Antigone*.

Decline and Renewal – Thebes' moment of glory came in the 4C BC when the city headed the Boeotian Confederacy and defeated Sparta at Leuctra in 371 BC, initiating a period of Theban hegemony over Greece that only lasted for 10 years. After defeat by Sparta at the Battle of Mantineia in 362 BC, Thebes declined and in 336 BC the city was eventually destroyed by Alexander except for the house of the poet **Pindar**.

MUSEUM

Arhaeological Museum★

⚊*Temporarily closed, new museum opening 2013.* ☎22620 279 13. ⊕*The museum is being reorganised so the sequence below may have changed.*

In the room on the right of the entrance, Archaic sculptures including *(centre)* a superb 6C BC **kouros**★★; in the third room funerary *steles* in black stone (5C BC) showing representations of warriors; in the fourth room a series of sarcophagi from the Mycenaean period (13C BC).

Other treasures of this important museum include a Statue of Hecate and a statue of Artemis from the Sanctuary of Artemis at Avlis and clay tablets with the earliest evidence of Greek writing, Linear B, (13C BCE).

EXCURSION
Glá Fortress

▶ *27km/17mi northwest of Thebes by E 75 towards Thessaloniki. In Kástro take the road east to Lárimna; turn right into a stony track which circles the fortress.*

The fortress of Glá, which was originally surrounded by the dull waters of Lake Copaïs (Kopaïda), is composed of a rocky plateau enclosed by a perimeter wall built in the 14C–13C BC following the contours of the rock.

Enter by the northeast gate, which is flanked by square towers. There are also traces of a Mycenaean-type palace with two *megarons*.

Óssios Loukás★★★

Ósios Loukás – Όσιος Λουκάς

Deep in beautiful countryside, this Byzantine monastery ranks among the finest in Greece and is a UNESCO heritage site. Its principal church is decorated with a wealth of 11C mosaics, and is a masterpiece of Byzantine art.

A BIT OF HISTORY

The monastery was founded by a hermit, Luke (Loukás), who was born in AD 896. He entered a monastery at the age of 14. He lived an ascetic life in Athens and Corinth and various islands before settling in Phocis in 946 CE.

Loukás built his cell in the beautiful spot where the monastery lies now and his reputation as a healer led other holy men to join him. After attracting sponsorship from his followers and state

- ⚜ **Michelin Map:** 737 G 8 – Boeotia – Central Greece.
- ▶ **Location:** 36km/23mi southeast of Delphi, and 24km/15mi from Aráhova, off the main road network; follow the road from Aspra Spitia (19km/12mi).
- Ⓟ **Parking:** There is a large car park at the entrance.
- 👁 **Don't Miss:** The church, with its extraordinary decoration and murals.
- 🕐 **Timing:** Allow for about an hour inside the church.

functionaries, a first church, initially dedicated to St Barbara and subsequently to the Virgin, was built. When Luke died in 953, the monastic community became a

Katholikon (left) and Theotókos (right)

place of pilgrimage, and a second church was erected in his honour. Prophesies of his abound and it is said that he had foreseen both his death and the Bulgarian raids which started after his death. His reliquary is inside the church.

The monastery suffered during the Fourth Crusade (1204) when Catholic knights sacked it and carried off many of its treasures. Like the abbeys at Daphne and Orchomenos, the convent was occupied in the 13C and the 14C by Cistercians who preferred an isolated site. The monastery was damaged by earthquakes in the 16C and the 17C and leter restored in the mid-20C; Orthodox monks still reside here.

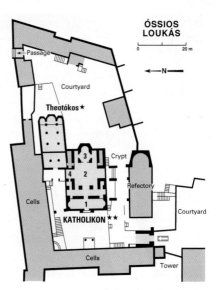

ÓSSIOS LOUKÁS

0   20 m

← N

VISIT

🕐 Open daily May–mid Sept 8am–2pm, 4–6pm; winter 8am–6pm. ☏ 22670 22228/21305. http://osiosloukas.gr. ✆ Entry to the churches is free, entry to museum €3. Modest attire required.

The monastery is set in glorious **countryside**★★ surrounded by mountains. The precinct is shaped like an irregular pentagon with two churches in the centre. The peripheral buildings comprise the monks' cells (north and west sides) and a refectory (south side), now housing a museum (small collection of religious artefacts).

Visitors pass through the main entrance under a clock tower into the precinct to arrive in front of the pilgrims' church (Katholikon); set back on the left is the conventual church (Theotókos).

Katholikon★★

The huge pilgrimage church (11C) rises over the tomb of Luke the Hermit. From the **exterior** the building is typically Greek; built on the Greek-cross plan beneath a central dome with an apse, and faced with brick and stone.

The **interior** decor is mostly 11C; the murals, which replaced damaged or lost mosaics, are later (16C–17C). The visitor will marvel at the multi-coloured marbles facing the walls and pillars, the

jasper and porphyry in the floor, the delicate sculptures decorating the iconostasis and the extraordinary **mosaics**★★ on the ceiling, pediments and pilasters. To examine the interior decoration start at the main door. The mosaics are set against a gold background, a typical example of the 11C hieratic style, sober and expressive, which was executed by artists from Thessaloniki and Constantinople.

Begin with the fine mosaics in the **narthex** (1). In the **dome** (2) the origi-

"Óssios and Agios"

Why "Óssios" Lukás but "Agios" Georgios, since both are translated as "saints"? Is there a difference? Indeed, the early Orthodox church used to differentiate between saints who went through a "baptism of blood" – namely who were subject to martyrdom and died for their faith – who were called "Agios", and saints who led an exemplary Christian life – usually monks and hermits – who were called "Óssios". Later the two were merged and the "Óssios" now only remains in toponyms and early Christian references.

Mosaics inside Katholikon

Brick and stone decoration of the exterior of Katholikon

nal mosaics were replaced by frescoes in the 16C and the 17C. The **iconostasis** is made of white marble and was formerly hung with four great icons (1571), the work of the famous Cretan artist, Mihális Damaskinós, who taught El Greco *(stolen; replaced with copies)*.

Chancel and Apse (3)
The two mosaics facing one another in the little apse *(right)* are among the most admired in the church: *Daniel in the Lions' Den* and *Shadrach, Meshach and Abednego in the Fiery Furnace.*

North transept (4)
Fine mosaic of Luke the Hermit.

Crypt
Access from south side outside the church.
The crypt containing the Tomb of Blessed Luke dates from the 10C; murals 11C.

Theotókos★

A doorway beneath a double arch leads into the monastic enclosure and the open court in front of the church.
This church is very different from its neighbour; some experts think it is contemporary with Luke the Hermit, 10C; others think it is 11C. In fact, even if Luke's oratory did stand on this spot, the present church was likely built or rebuilt in the 13C for the Cistercians.
On leaving go round the south side of both churches into the eastern courtyard to compare the east elevations: the Byzantine pilgrims' church is massive and crowned by an imposing round dome; the conventual church soars up to an elegant octagonal lantern. Conventual buildings range the east side of the courtyard.

Aráhova★

Aráhova – Αράχωβα

This small mountain town on the southern flanks of Mount Parnassus above the Pleistos Ravine is a popular winter resort for skiers, and makes a good base from which to explore the surrounding area. The narrow main street abounds with cafés, restaurants and shops; a lovely **view**★ extends from the terrace of the Agios Georgios church.

EXCURSIONS
Koríkio Ándro★★

Koríkio Ándro (the Corycian Cave) and Óros Parnassós (Mount Parnassus) are about 45km/27mi (about 2hrs 30min) from Aráhova. Take the road towards Delphi; turn right towards Lílea. After 11km/7mi, just beyond Kalívia, turn left (sign "Chat Tours") into a narrow stony track which winds uphill for 5km/3mi. It's best to turn off after the first 2km/1.25mi onto the side road leading to a car park; 5min on foot to the cave.

The cave is high above the sea and very extensive. In antiquity it was devoted to **Pan**, the shepherd god, a horned and bearded deity. The cave was already in use in the Neolithic and Mycenaean periods. One can penetrate right into the cave which has good natural light and interesting stalactites and stalagmite

> **Population:** 3,236.
>
> **Michelin Map:** 737 G 8 – Boeotia – Central Greece.
>
> **Information:** Plateia Xenias. ℰ 22670 31630.
>
> **Location:** To the northwest of Athens; once over the Aráhova Pass on the traditional road from Livadiá (44km/28mi) to Delphi (10km/6mi), you'll be enchanted by the lovely view down into the town.
>
> **Parking:** Locals are fond of double-parking on the main road but it is not recommended.
>
> **Don't Miss:** An excursion to Livadiá and a climb up Mount Parnassus.
>
> **Timing:** To take in all the sights more than one day is needed.

formations that resemble "Korykes", namely a boxer's punchbags, after which it got its ancient name. The cave has drawn visitors from ancient times; Pausanias himself was very impressed. The cave has been used as a refuge from invaders: from the Persians in 5C BCE to the Germans in the Second World War. Subsequently it was used as a refuge from Persian invaders.

Aráhova in spring

© Georgios Alexandris/Dreamstime.com

The Muses

Parnassus, which is often under snow or enveloped in clouds, was thought to be the home of **Apollo** whose main sanctuary was nearby, and of the nine **Muses**: Clio (History), Euterpe (Music), Melpomene (Tragedy), Thaleia (Comedy), Terpsichore (Dancing), Urania (Astronomy), Erato (Love poetry), Polymnia (Hymns) and Calliope (Epic poetry).

Óros Parnassós★★ (Mount Parnassos)

The road follows the hanging valley of Kalívia where sheep are pastured. After about 15km/9mi turn right into a good road which climbs through a mountain landscape of pine trees to a chalet belonging to the Athens Ski Club and continues to Liákoura (2,457m/8, 061ft), the highest peak of Parnassus.

🚶 *Climbing this peak takes about 1hr 30min on foot there and back.*

The Mount Parnassus massif is a National Park, established in 1938, and it is the second largest in the country after that of Mount Olympus, spanning an area of 3,600ha/9,000 acres. It contains some of the rarest European ecosystems; it is home to wolves, jackals and foxes and to endangered creatures such as griffon vultures, golden eagles or the Parnas-

Snow-capped Mount Parnassos

© Georgios Alexandris/Dreamstime.com

sian butterfly; and it is covered with rare plants such as the Parnassian thyme and the red lily. On rare clear days, there is a superb panorama of a large part of Greece from the Peloponnese to Mount Athos. Four-wheel drive vehicle trips are also available.

The impenetrable Parnassus massif is still home to wolves; it was the base of the local *klephtes* during the **Greek War of Independence** and served again after the Second World War as the stronghold of the ELAS resistance movement which survived there until 1949. There is also extensive **bauxite** mining.

Livadiá★

▶ *34km/22mi east of Aráhova.*

Livadiá, the capital of Boeotia, lies at the mouth of the gloomy Erkínas (Hercyna) Gorge, thought in antiquity to be the entrance to the Underworld. During the Turkish occupation it became Greece's second most important city after Thessaloniki.

It is a lively town, and an industrial centre. The **upper town** is graced by white houses dating from the 18C and the 19C, little shops shaded by broad awnings and tavernas where *souvláki* and cherry conserve, the local specialities, are served.

▶ *Park the car in the square in the centre of the modern lower town and take one of the streets leading to the upper town.*

Erkínas Gorge★★

🚶 *Walk upstream, leaving the great square tower to the right. An old humpbacked stone bridge spans the river.*

On the east bank the spring of **Mnemosyne** (Remembrance) flows into a pool where niches for votive offerings have been carved out of the cliff face. A passage not far away leads to what is thought to be the spring of **Lethe** (Oblivion). Continue up the gorge, deep into the rocky mountain. Return to the square tower, which is at one end of the fortress's outer wall, and turn left into a path that follows the line of the wall past a beautiful Byzantine church with an apse and a dome. From the Kástro★ crowning Mount Agios Ilias, there is a spectacular **view**★★ over gorge, mountains and town.

Herónia

◯ *14km/9mi north of Livadiá.*
The village is home to a grand marble **lion** commemorating those who died in the Battle of Heronía in 336 BC. There is also a small **Archaeological Museum** (𝒫*26100 952 70*).

Orchomenós

◯ *14km/9mi northeast of Livadiá.*
Orchomenós, which had been the capital of the Minyans in the prehistoric era, was the rival of Thebes in antiquity. It is now a small country town on the edge of what was formerly a huge marsh known as **Lake Copaïs (Kopaïda)**. The ruins of ancient Orchomenós and the Church of the Dormition of the Virgin face each other on the Kástro road at the eastern outskirts of the modern town.

Ancient Ruins

On the left of the theatre is the path leading into the **Treasury of Minyas**★, a huge Mycenaean *thólos* tomb similar to the Treasury of Atreus at Mycenae. The roof has fallen in but the huge blue marble lintel is still in place over the door, and the inner chamber has retained part of its original ceiling decoration.

The acropolis *(1hr on foot there and back)* gives a fine **panorama**★ over Orchomenós and the Copaïc region. Remains of old walls and temples are visible.

Kimísseos Theotókou★

The Byzantine **Church of the Dormition of the Virgin**, which dates from the 9C, belonged to a monastery built on the site of a temple dedicated to the Graces *(charities)*. In the 13C the monastery passed to the Cistercians, who altered the church and the conventual buildings. Inside the church is an unusual Byzantine paved floor. There are Greek inscriptions and many Byzantine stones sculpted with symbolic motifs along the exterior wall.

ADDRESSES

🛏STAY

⊖ **Nostos** – *In the town centre.* 𝒫*22670 31 385. nostos@otenet.gr. 15 rooms.* ⌸ The proprietor offers a minibus to take guests sightseeing in the area. Excellent value.

⊖ **Lykoreía** – *145 Delphi St. Turn right 300m/984ft out of town on the Delphi road.* 𝒫*22670 31 180/321 32. 28 rooms.* Comfortable, discreet little hotel; terrace overlooking the valley. Closed Jul–Aug.

⊖⊖ **Villa Filoxenia** – *Follow signs to the right along the road to Delphi.* 𝒫*22670 310 46. www.villafiloxenia.gr. 16 studios.* Welcoming traditional house; spacious rooms all with wooden balconies.

⊖⊖💰 **Skamnos Boutique Hotel** – *Close to the National Park, 10mi/16km outside Aráhova.* 𝒫*22670 29109. www.skamnos.com. 22 rooms.* This boutique hotel has a fitness room, an indoor pool and superb views.

🍴EAT

Aráhova is well known for its culinary specialities: sample the *loukanika* (sausages), *formaeia* (cheese) and honey. *Syros Formaela*, the cheese used to make *saganaki*, can be found in the excellent shop in the centre of town.

⊖ **Parnassos** – *Next to Hotel Santa Marina.* A small, simple local restaurant, good quality, a bit off the tourist trail.

⊖⊖ **Taberna Karaouli** – *Next to Hotel Lykoreia.* Traditional cuisine in a vast dining room with bay windows overlooking the valley.

⊖⊖ **Gerontovrahos** – *In the centre of Aráhova.* 𝒫*22670 32550.* Greek meat barbecue specialities like *kokoretsi* and *kontosouvli*, and the local *Tripa Gemisti*: a kind of rustic Cordon Bleu.

🎭 EVENTS AND FESTIVALS

For three days starting on the evening of 22 April, the town holds a festival in honour of St George, including a procession, feasts, dances and sports.

Delphi★★★

Delfí – Δελφοί

In antiquity Delphi was one of the most important religious centres; the Sanctuary of Apollo, situated above the River Pleistos gorge against the backdrop of Mount Parnassus, attracted hordes of pilgrims who came to consult the oracle. Now it is tourists who come here in droves to explore these mysterious ruins.

A BIT OF HISTORY

Gaia, Earth Goddess – Mythology relates that Delphi was founded by Zeus. By the second millennium BC Delphi was already a place of worship dedicated to the earth goddess (Gaia) and her daughter Themis, who was said to reside at the bottom of a fault, guarded by her son, the snake Python.

The Oracle – A hymn attributed to Homer tells how the god Apollo in 750 BC killed the Python and took his place, giving oracles through a priestess known as the Pythia (later called the Delphic Sibyl).

The priestess (always a woman over 50 whose life was beyond reproach) would go into the temple and enter a trance, delivering ambiguous replies in hexameter verse in response to questions put by pilgrims. The Pythia seems to have been well informed in politics; in turn she favoured Xerxes during the Persian invasions, then Athens, Sparta and Thebes in the 4C BC, then Philip of Macedon and Alexander the Great, whom she proclaimed invincible, and finally Rome.

The sanctuary itself was served by two high priests, a steward, a treasurer, five priests, of whom Plutarch was once one, and several acolytes, who attended the Pythia.

Enduring Importance – During its heyday as a Panhellenic sanctuary, Delphi attracted pilgrims from all over the Greek world, from Spain to the Black Sea. Despite fire, earthquakes and pillaging, Delphi was still thriving under the Emperor Hadrian in the 2C AD. It was

- ▶ **Population:** 2,435.
- **Michelin Map:** 737 G 8 – Fokída – central Greece.
- **Info:** 11 Odós Apollonos and 12 Odós Pávlou & Frideríkis *(at the top of a flight of steps)*. Open daily except Sun and bank holidays, 8.30am–3pm. ℘22650 829 00.
- **Location:** Perched high on the mountainside, Dephi lies 160km/99mi northwest of Athens via Thebes and Livadía. The archaeological site is near the road, about 1km/.6mi before the modern village. Hotels line the two principal streets which run one-way in each direction.
- **Parking:** Car parks near the site and at the village entrance.
- **Don't Miss:** The theatre, the museum and the Thólos.
- **Timing:** The site is steep; plan at least one (tiring!) day.

finally closed in 394 CE by the Byzantine Emperor Theodosius the Great. Delphi then became a Christian site. In the early 6C it was laid waste by the Slavs.

SANCTUARY OF APOLLO★★

A pedestrian path links the village with the sanctuary of Apollo, situated along the road to Aráhova. Above the museum, cross the road and follow the path to the entrance.

Open Apr–Oct, daily 8am–7pm; Nov–Mar, daily 8.30am–3pm. €6 (site and museum €9; museum only €3; 8.30am–3pm). No charge Sun from 1 Nov to 31 Mar and the first Sun of the month except Jul–Sept, 6 Mar, 18 Apr, 18 May, 5 Jun and last weekend in Sept. ℘22650 823 12.

The ancient ruins range down the mountainside below two roseate rock faces,

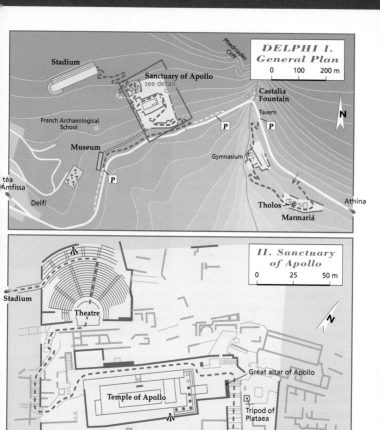

the Phaidriades. Between them is a deep cleft from which emerges the Kastalian Spring. The view to the south overlooks the River Pleistos winding round the foot of Mount Kírphis towards the coastal basin and the bay of Itéa.

▷ *It is a short walk uphill to the agora, which precedes the Sanctuary of Apollo.*

Agora

Traces of brick houses and baths from the Roman period are visible above the agora. Down one side ran an Ionic portico with shops for pilgrims; a few of the columns survive. Fragments from a palaeo-Christian church are displayed (**1**) in the far corner.

Four steps lead to the main entrance to the **sacred precinct** (téménos). The wall encloses a trapezoidal area of which the lower part contains votive offerings and the **Treasuries**, small temples erected by the Greek city states to receive the offerings made by their citizens.

Sacred Way

The Sacred Way leads up to the Temple of Apollo; the paving dates from the Roman period. It is lined with **votive offerings**; on the right stands the base of the bull of Corcyra (**2**). Again on the right is the votive monument of the Arcadians (**3**) next to that of the Lakedaimonians; on the left the votive monument of Marathon, followed by the monument of the Argives. These monuments, what little is left of them, testify to the rivalry between the Greek cities.

The Sacred Way then passes between the foundations of two semicircular structures erected by the Argives; to the right was the monument of the King of Árgos (**4**), built in 369 BC; it was decorated with 20 statues of the kings and queens of Árgos.

The first **treasury** is that of Sikyon (**5**); the bases remain (6C BC).

Beyond stands the wall of the **Treasury of Siphnos** (**6**), built of marble in about 525 BC. In the southwest corner stood the **Treasury of Thebes** (**7**); the tufa foundations are visible. Nearby are the foundations of the Treasury of the Boeotians and a limestone version of the omphalos (**8**).

The **Treasury of the Athenians**★ (Thissavros Athinéon) is a Doric building (490–480 BC) in white Parian marble, decorated with sculptures illustrating the battle between the Greeks and the Amazons (in the museum). Inscriptions on the walls, base and terrace are in honour of the Athenian victory at Marathon.

After the Treasury come the sparse ruins of the **Bouleuterion** (**9**) (the Senate of Delphi), followed by a pile of rocks (**10**) marking the site of the early Delphic oracle; behind the rocks stood the Sanctuary of the Earth goddess, Ge or Gaia. Farther on are the fallen drums of

Treasury of the Athenians

an Ionic marble column (**11**), a gift from the Naxiots in about 570 BC.

The polygonal wall (6C BC) retaining the terrace on which the Temple of Apollo is built is inscribed with more than 800 Acts granting slaves their freedom during the Hellenistic and Roman periods. Three columns of Pentelic marble mark the Stoa of the Athenians (**12**) which dates from about 480 BC

At this point the Sacred Way crosses a circular area (halos) where processions to the temple formed; note the handsome Ionic capital (**13**) and the curved seat (exedra) for the priests. On the edge of this area stood the Treasury of the Corinthians; nearby under the Sacred Way a cache of precious objects (in the museum) was discovered in 1939.

The Sacred Way rises steeply; the circular pedestal (right) bore the **Tripod of Plataia** (**14**), now in Constantinople. On the left are the foundations of the great **Altar to Apollo** (**15**) which dates from the 5C BC.

The huge stone pillar (**16**), to the right of the temple façade, bore an equestrian statue of Prusias (2C BC), King of Bithynia in Asia Minor.

Temple of Apollo★★

The existing ruins date from the 4C BC. It was a Doric building with a peristyle; a half dozen of the columns have been re-erected. A statue of Homer stood in the portico. The *naós* at the centre of the temple was furnished with altars and statues; beyond was the crypt *(adyton)* where the Pythia sat near the *omphalos* and the tomb of Dionysos.

The views from here are magnificent. To the south the temple columns stand out against the backdrop of the Pleistos Valley. To the northwest rise the perfect curves of the theatre.

Parallel with the uphill side of the temple runs a retaining wall, or **"Iskégaon"**, built in the 4C BC; at the western end, on the site of the votive offering of Polyzalos (**17**), was found the famous Charioteer of Delphi *(in the museum)*.

The rectangular base of a votive offering (**18**) has preserved the dedicatory stone on the back wall on the left.

Theatre★★

Dating from the 4C BC, the theatre could seat 5 000 spectators. From the top row there is a marvellous **view**★★★ down over the sanctuary ruins, across the Pleistos Valley to Mount K'rphis.

The gangway *(diázoma)* running round the theatre halfway up continues westwards as a path winding up the hillside to the Stadium; very fine views of the site of Delphi (⏱*30min on foot there and back).*

▷ *To reach the stadium, take the path to the left of the theatre (steep climb).*

Stadium★

Before the first stone seating was built in the 3C BC the stadium was surrounded by earth terraces buttressed by a polygonal wall. In the 2C AD it was altered by Herodes Atticus, who built the present terraces to seat 6 500 people and erected a monumental **gateway**. The starting and finishing lines are still in place.

Museum★★★

🕐*Open daily 8.30am–3pm.* ✆*€3, no charge on Sun from 1 Nov to 31 Mar and the first Sun of the month except Jul–Sept, 6 Mar, 18 Apr, 18 May, 5 Jun and last weekend in Sept.* 🕐*Closed on national holidays.* ✆*22650 823 12.*

This museum displays to good effect the works of art excavated at Delphi.

At the top of the steps stands a conical block of marble, a Hellenistic copy of the famous **omphalos**★ (navel) which was kept in the Temple of Apollo and was supposed to mark the centre of the world.

The **Hall of the Siphnian Treasury** is devoted to Archaic sculpture (6C BC). In the middle stands the winged Sphinx of the Naxiots flanked by two caryatids from the Treasuries of Knidos and Siphnos. Around the walls are pieces of the marble frieze from the **Siphnian Treasury**★; the sculpted decoration was brightly painted.

View of the theatre

© dave tonkin/Bigstockphoto.com

Charioteer of Delphi

ç Greek National Tourism Organisation

In the next room are two huge **kouroi**★, (6C BC) depicting twins from Árgos who died of exhaustion after pulling their mother's chariot for 45 *stadia* (just under 5 miles).

In the **Hall of the Bull** you'll find cult objects discovered beneath the Sacred Way. The principal item is an Archaic **bull**★ dating from the 6C BC; also several gold panels from a statue, and a statuette in ivory of a god taming a fawn. Bronzes include an incense burner held by a young girl dressed in a *peplos* (5C BC).

In the **Hall of the Athenian Treasury** there are sculpted *metopes (damaged)*, which date from the Archaic period; the head of Theseus *(left)* is very fine.

A magnificent group of **three dancers**★★ in Pentelic marble stands on an acanthus column; the dancers are *bacchantes* or Thyiades, priestesses of Dionysos. Against the wall are the statues from the Monument (4C BC) of Daochos II. Note the figure of the athlete Agias; it is probably a copy of a bronze by Lysippos.

The **Charioteer of Delphi**★★★, the jewel of this museum's collection, is one of the most beautiful Greek statues from the late Archaic period (478 BC). The figure was part of a bronze votive offering representing the winning *quadriga* (four-horse chariot) in the Olympic Games of 473 and 474. The noble, life-size figure wears the victor's headband. A showcase in the same room displays a white **libation cup** (5C BC) showing Apollo seated, wearing a crown of laurel and holding a tortoiseshell lyre. Note also the marble **statue of Antinous** (2C AD), a favourite of Hadrian.

KASTALÍA KRÍNI★

The **Kastalian Spring** wells up at the end of the wild ravine dividing the Phaidriades Rocks. Here Pythia, the priests and the pilgrims who requested an oracle performed ritual ablutions

---

Pythian Prophecies

We can never be 100 percent certain of the exact wording of the prophecies received by the pilgrims and it may be that only the sensational ones have survived the centuries, but it seems that their success lay in their ambiguity. Some were transparent: that "wooden walls will save Athens against Xerxes" which the Athenians correctly interpreted as ships (and won the Salamis naval battle); or that Philip of Macedon would conquer the world with "silver spears" upon which he captured the silver mines in Thrace.

The prediction of Lysander's death in the Peloponnesian War was trickier: he should "beware the earthborn dragon following behind" – he was slain in his back by Neochorus whose shield had a serpent design. It was certainly suicidal to confront Emperor Nero after he had killed his mother with "Your presence here outrages the god you seek, matricide. Number 73 marks your downfall." Nero had Pythia buried alive and, though he thought he'd die at 73, the prophecy actually referred to Servius Galba, a 73-year old Roman consul, who acted as his nemesis.

It appears that only once did Pythia give a straight answer. When asked if there was a man alive wiser than Socrates, she answered "No."

Thólos

© Greek National Tourism Organisation

to purify themselves before entering Apollo's Sanctuary.

There are two springs: the first, near the highway is dated to c.590 BC and was only discovered in 1960. The later one, dated 1C BC and about 50m/110ft higher up was the one described by Pausanias and was discovered in 1878. It include a huge Archaic paved basin, a longer basin hewn out of the rock with steps leading down into it, and above it part of the side of the reservoir that supplied the basin below through openings that are still visible.

It is from the top of the Phaidriades Rocks *(Fedriádes)* that **Aesop** (6C BC), author of fables, is supposed to have been hurled for mocking the Delphians.

MARMARIÁ★★

▶ *South of the road to Aráhova.*
Main entrance to the east (sign "Temple of Athena Pronaia").

Occupying a beautiful site, Marmariá is the site of the **Sanctuary of Athena Pronaia**, which pilgrims visited before going on to the Sanctuary of Apollo.

Old Temple of Athena

All that remains of this Archaic Doric temple (6C BC) are the bases of some columns and some sections of wall. Abandoned in the 4C BC, the building

incorporated elements of an earlier 7C BC temple.

Between this temple and the rotunda *(thólos)* are the remains of two treasuries; the second probably belonged to Massalia, present-day Marseilles.

Thólos★★

This elegant marble peristyle rotunda (4C BC) was probably built as a shrine of the earth goddess (Ge or Gaia). Remains include drums of fluted columns, lower courses of a circular wall and three Doric columns (re-erected) supporting an entablature.

New Temple of Athena

Visible are the foundations of a small limestone temple (4C BC).

A steep path leads to the upper terraces where a **gymnasium**, built in the 4C BC and remodelled by the Romans, extended over two levels.

OUTSKIRTS
Itéa

▶ *17km/11mi to the southwest.*

The road descends the slopes of the Pleistos Valley into the coastal plain, which belonged to the Sanctuary of Apollo and was the setting of the ancient racecourse.

The famous olive groves here are aptly referred to as a **sea of olives**★. Together with recent plantations on the slopes of the Pleistos Valley they number some 400 000 olive trees; harvesting begins in September. The olive mills are powered by the waters of the Pleistos. Itéa is a bathing resort and port at the head of Itéa Bay. It was chosen by the Allies in 1917 as the base town on the supply route which ran to the eastern front. To the east of Itéa lay the ancient port of Delphi, Kirra; there are traces of an ancient jetty.

Galaxídi★

▶ *33km/21mi southwest via Itéa.*
Fine view of the Bay of Itéa. Galaxídi is a charming old town with a sheltered harbour, which until early this century rivalled Syros *(see SÊROS)*.

The fine stone houses with their balconies suggest former days of wealth; in the 19C Galaxídi traded throughout the Mediterranean. A small **Maritime Museum** evokes the port's past glories. The **cathedral** at the top of the town contains a beautiful 19C carved-wood iconostasis.

Ámfissa

▶ *20km/12mi northwest.*
The rival of Delphi in antiquity, Ámfissa is built against the curved slope at the head of the valley. Known as Salona in the 13C, it was the seat of a Frankish domain taken by the Turks in 1397. Its fortress, formerly called Château de la Sole, was erected on the site of the old acropolis that can still be traced; there are remains of the keep, the living quarters and a 13C round tower. Fine views of the town and of the valley.

ADDRESSES

Aráhova, a mountain village 13km/8mi to the east of Delphi, offers options for accommodation and food.

🏠STAY

🛏 **Thólos** – *31 Odós Apóllonos. ✆/Fax 22650 822 68. www.tholoshotel.com. 17 rooms.* Clean rooms, near the church. Breakfast served on the terrace next door (magnificent view). Open mid-Mar to end of Oct, Fri–Sun only in winter, (closed Nov).

🛏 **Pan** and **Artemis** – *Loutraki – Odós Pávlou & Frideríkis, between the bus station and the Post Office. ✆22650 822 94. www.panartemis.gr. 25 rooms.* Two traditional establishments; modest, attractive rooms.

🛏🛏 **Argo** – *Galaxídi, on a street perpendicular to the harbour. ✆22650 419 96/421 00. 16 rooms.* Recently built, all-white building with marble floors. Small, pleasant rooms. Home-made cakes and jams at breakfast.

🛏🛏 **Galaxa** – *Galaxídi, Odós Eleftherías & Kennedy, near the sea. ✆22650 41 620; in Athens ✆21065 220 92. 10 rooms.* Small hotel in a former sea captain's house. Serene, family atmosphere and immaculate rooms.

🛏🛏 **Iníohos** – *19 Odós Pávlou & Frideríkis. ✆22650 82701/2. www.delphi-hotels.gr. 60 rooms.* This reliable hotel has clean, stylish rooms with balconies.

🍴EAT

🛏🛏 **Lekaria** – *Odós Appollonos.* Delicious dishes (try the lamb or the saganaki sausage) served on a terrace overlooking the gulf.

🛒SHOPPING

Crafts – Carpets, cushions and curtains made of woven cotton; a good selection at Níkos Giannópoulos in the upper part of the town.
Antiques – *Odós Apóllonos 56.* Superb selection of traditional objects (pottery, old signs, fabrics), albeit at high prices.

🎭EVENTS AND FESTIVALS

The inhabitants of Delphi hold an **Easter parade** for which they dress in traditional costume, and cook mutton kebabs.

Performances (drama, poetry) in fine weather) in the sanctuary stadium.

Nafpaktos
Náfpaktos – Ναύπακτος

A charming city which can serve as a base for exploring the surrounding area. During the Peloponnesian war between Athens and Sparta, the Athenians made Naupaktos their chief naval station in western Greece. It is better known by its medieval name of Lepanto, recalling the naval battle that took place in 1571 and which marked the end of Turkish expansion.

HARBOUR
The entrance to the oval basin is protected by two towers fortified with crenellations and merlons. Views of the town and the citadel from the parapet walk.

CITADEL
Access from the west of the town by a narrow road that climbs through the pine trees.
The Venetian fortress dates from the Middle Ages; its walls extend downhill to link it with the harbour; other walls built laterally divide the town into compartments, each one forming one keep. The castle was so strongly fortified that in 1477 it successfully resisted a four-month-siege by a Turkish army of some 30,000 strong.
In 1687, the town was recaptured by the Venetians, but only until 1699 when it reverted to the Turks.

▶ **Population:** 18,259.
◉ **Michelin Map:** 737 F 8 – Akarnanía – Central Greece.
▦ **Info:** At the port, 1 Noti. Botsaris. ℰ 26340 385 33. Open daily.
◉ **Location:** Náfpaktos is 100km/63mi west of Delphi.
◕ **Timing:** The town itself can be explored in under an hour.
▲▲ **Kids:** A healthy climb up the hill to the castle.

ADDRESSES

🏠 STAY / 🍴 EAT

⊜ **Akti** – *East of the town.* ℰ 26340 284 64 *www.akti.gr. 59 rooms.* Very near the beach. Pleasant decor with all modern comforts. All rooms have balconies.

⊜ **Diethnes** – *3 Athinas Nova, near the port.* ℰ 26340 273 42. *www.diethnes nafpaktos.gr.* Pleasant, colourful interior; good value hotel.

⊜ **Lepando Beach** – *Odós Gribova.* ℰ 926340 239 31. *www.lepantobeach.gr .* *48 rooms.* Large, comfortable hotel.

⊜ **Spitikó** – A traditional taverna on the beach, popular with locals.

⊜ **Tsaras Taverna** – *Odós Ioan, Kanavou.* ℰ 26340 278 09. Tasty traditional dishes, views from the terrace.

🏃 SPORTS AND LEISURE
Kayaking, hiking, mountain biking with **Club Metavasi**, ℰ 26340 245 56; *info@metavasi.com.*

Fishing port of Náfpaktos

© Panagiotis Karapanagiotis/Dreamstime.com

Euboia is the second largest Greek Island after Crete and a favorite resort for people from Athens, Thebes and Attica. Its landscapes are beautiful and varied: wooded mountains and fast-flowing rivers in the north, wild, rocky inlets on the east coast, and sandy beaches and plains on the west coast. It is divided from the mainland at Halkída by the Evripean Strait, 39m/128ft wide, 40m/131ft long and 8.4m/27.5ft deep, subject to a unique tidal phenomenon that confounded the Ancient Greeks. The sea across the channel runs north to south for six hours and then changes direction for about 22–23 days per month. The rest of the days – corresponding to the quarter phases of the moon – it is erratic and can change up to 14 times a day. The phenomenon, now explained via the tidal currents across the Aegean, can be easily observed from the bridge at Halkída.

Highlights

1 The tidal phenomenon in **Halkída** (p163)
2 The **Eagles' Road drive** (p164)
3 The port of **Kárystos** (p164)
4 The ancient city of **Erétria** (p165)
5 The **beaches** of the wild north (p166)

A Bit of History

The island was densely populated during antiquity and around the 9C BC it was settled by Ionians in Erétria, Halkída and Kárystos. Erétria was the richest town and suffered during the Persian Wars (490 BC) when it was burned down and its inhabitants taken as slaves. The cities recovered and the island was one of the war theatres during the Peloponnesian War. When the Romans invaded they destroyed Erétria for the second time in its history (198 BC) from which it never recovered.

Ever since, Halkída has been the de facto capital of the island. The island was conquered by Venice in 1205 and by the Turks in 1470. Under the Turks Halkída was developed into a fortified town and the capital of an area that included Thebes and Athens.

As a result, the island was quite impregnable during the Greek War of Independence and was only surrendered to the new Greek state in 1833, long after the war had ended and the new frontiers agreed.

▷ **Population:** 207,305.
◔ **Michelin Map:** 737 H I7, I-J 8, J-K 9 – Évia central Greece.
ℹ **Info:** ET-kosmos, 7 Karistos Square, Karistos, western side of the main esplanade. ☎ 22240 262 00/257 00.
▷ **Location:** The largest of the Greek islands after Crete, Euboea lies off the coast to the east of Boeotia and Attica, 1hr from Athens. A bridge at Halkída spans the Evrípos Channel from the mainland.
◉ **Don't Miss:** For scenic beauty, the road between Stíra and Káristos.
🕐 **Timing:** At least one day to see parts of the island; a longer sojourn is tempting.
👪 **Kids:** The car journey notwithstanding, there are beaches to explore and places for swimming.

Excursions

Maybe because it is near Athens, maybe because it does not attract many foreign tourists, Euboia has been spared the mass developments of the other islands. A holiday here feels more like experiencing Greece as it was 20 years ago. Though there is nothing spectacular to see, the pellucid Greek landscapes

GETTING THERE

BY SEA - Ferries serve **Marmari** from **Rafína** *(6–8/day)*; **Erétria** from **Skala Oropou** *(every 30min from 5am–10pm in summer)*. From **Arkitsa** to **Loutra Aidipsou**: *(every 30min from 7am–8.30pm)*. Other ferries also connect the mainland to numerous ports on the west coast: Glyfá to Agiokambos, Agia Marina to Néa Stira. A hydrofoil operates from **Kími** to **Skyros** *(1–2/day; ℰ 22220 220 22)*.

BY CAR - **Halkída** is about one hour north of Athens easily reached via a new modern highway.

---

have been preserved here better than most. In a few days' drive around the island you will learn more about Greece than in a fortnight on an island resort.

🚗 DRIVING TOURS

THE SOUTH OF THE ISLAND ▶

625km/391mi departing from Halkída.

Euboia's south is more developed and populated than the north and contains its major cities and sites.

Halkída (Chalkída)

The capital of Euboia and very popular with tourists, Halkída is a port, an agricultural market and industrial centre. The modern seafront sports hotels and cafés.

Halkída was one of the most dynamic cities of ancient Greece. Her powerful fleet allowed her to establish colonies in Thrace and Macedonia in the 8C BC. The colonists there named the region Chalcidice and went on to found other settlements in Italy and Sicily.

The Church of **Agía Paraskeví** is in the second street on the left coming from the bridge. The church is Byzantine in origin and rests on ancient columns of Cipolin marble. It has fine mosaics and a marble iconostasis. Not far away in the small square *(Platía Kóskou)* there is a disused mosque and a Turkish fountain; the small alleyways are lined by traditional houses with wooden balconies.

The **Archaeological Museum**★ contains fine pieces from the prehistoric, Hellenistic and Roman periods. Note the funerary *stele* (4C BC) depicting a young athlete and his dog *(13 Venizelou; ⏱ open daily 8.30am–3pm; ▨ €2; ℰ 22210 761 31)*.

Returning towards the bridge, note the ruined **Karababá Fort** (1686) across the water. From the west bastion, there is a fine **view**★ of Halkída, the Evrípos and the Bay of Aulis *(south)*.

▷ *Leave Halkída and head towards Néa Artaki and Psachna, where the route bears right in the direction of Attali and Steni, and climbs the slopes of Mount Dyrfis.*

Stení★

32km southeast of Halkída.

Steni is a cool and shady mountain resort; its chalets are built on either side of a mountain torrent. There are many walks in the forests of which cover the slopes of Mount Dírfis *(allow 2hrs 30min if planning to climb to the summit).*

▷ *Follow the road to Metochi 21km/13mi away. From there, a well-surfaced road leads to Kími (another 20km/12mi away) via Vitala.*

Kími

The little town of Kími developed from the ancient town of Kyme, whose inhabitants founded Cumae near Naples in Italy. The town stands on a rocky plateau overlooking the Aegean Sea towards the island of Skíros.

A fine old house has been turned into a **Museum of Folk Art** (Laografikó Moussío), featuring crafts, costumes and furniture *(between the village and the port; ⏱ open 10am–1pm and 5–7.30pm).*

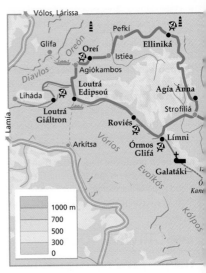

▶ *From Kími head back towards Lepoura (35km/22mi), passing through Koniastres and Monodryio.*

Beyond **Lepoura**, the south of the island unfurls; the route becomes steeper as it winds around arid mountains; white windmills dot the landscape.

Styra

41km/25mi from Lepoura.
The village on the slopes of Mount Klióssi is known for its marble quarries and its beach at **Néa Stíra** down below on the coast; to the east stood the mighty Frankish Castle of Lármena.

"Drómos ton Aetón"★★★

Between Stíra and Káristos (about 30km/18.5mi) the **Eagles' Road** runs along a ledge on the southwest coast of Euboia. Birds of prey hover over the hillsides, which offer splendid views down over Marmári and across the bay to the Petalií Islands.

Kárystos★

At the bottom of Mount Ochi (1,400m/4,724ft), the port of Kárystos is one of those resorts, rare in Greece, that combine the pleasures of the sea with those of the mountain. Although mostly a summer resort with a port for fishing boats and ferries (from Rafína), there are good hikes on Mount Ochi with a rest cabin on top. To the east of the quay are the remains of a 14C Venetian fortress, the Bourtzi. Opposite is a small **Archaeological Museum** (◷open Tue–Sun 8.30am–3pm; ✆€2; ✆22240 256 61). By the small village of Myloi, just outside Kárystos, and the ruins of a Venetian castle built in 1030, called **Castel Rosso** (Red Castle) because of the colour of the stone.

From Kárystos the coast road leads to the southeast tip of the island (Platanistos, Komito), taking in some beautiful inlets and wild beaches.

Castel Rosso

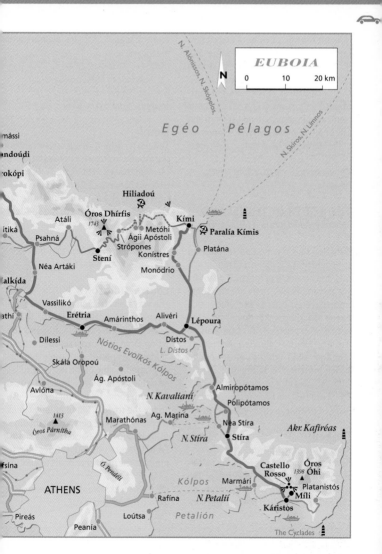

Head back on the same road as far as Lepoura, then follow directions to Velos. From there, take the minor road to the ruins of Dístos.

Dístos (Ruins)

Isolated on flat, open ground by a little lake lie the ruins of ancient Dístos. The 5C BC walls are of polygonal construction with strengthened square towers.

Return to Velos, then take the coast road (heavily developed) to Aliveri and Amarynthos. Continue to Erétria.

Erétria★

There are several traces of the **ancient city**, which was extensive and prosperous. The main ruins lie to the north, including vestiges of a **gymnasium** and a fairly well-preserved **theatre** (3C BC) at the foot of the acropolis with the foundations of a **Shrine to Dionysos** nearby.

A little to the east is the **House of the Mosaics**, a 4C BC villa centred on an open courtyard surrounded by a peristyle. The reception rooms on the north side were decorated with magnificent mosaic pavements depicting mythological scenes (⊙*open Tue–Sun 8.30am–3pm;* ✆*€2.)* Be sure to stop in at the Archaeological Museum to see 6C BC **sculptures of Theseus and Antiope** from the ruins of Erétria, and items from neighbouring sites at Lefkandi and Chiropolis (⊙*open same hours as House of the Mosaics; ticket admits to both sites).*

▷ *Return to Halkída, 22km/14mi to the west.*

THE NORTH OF THE ISLAND
350km/219mi departing from Halkída.

Between Halkída and Loutra Aidipsou the countryside is green and mountainous, and has some of the most beautiful scenery in Greece. There are also some undiscovered beaches to enjoy such as the sparkling-clean Roviés near the eponymous village (1.5hrs from Halkída towards Aidipsos, turn left at Strofiliá), and Agía Anna, Euboia's most popular beach (turn right at Strofiliá).

▷ *Leave Halkída heading towards Néa Artaki. Continue north beyond Kastella.*

Prokópi
52km/33mi from Halkída.
South of Mandoúdi, deep in the picturesque **Klissoúra Valley** lies Prokópi. The banks of the stream which runs through the valley are covered by luxuriant vegetation: planes, poplars, walnuts and oleanders.

▷ *Continue to Mandoúdi and Strofylia, where the route bears left towards Limni, 19km/12mi away.*

Limni
This pretty fishing village is perched on the mountainside with houses hanging out over the sea. From here, walk to the isolated convent of **Galataki** (fine 16C frescoes in the catholicon) at the far end of the promontory to the south of the village.

▷ *Returning from Limni take the coast road leading to Loutrá Edipsoú.*

Loutrá Aidipsoú★
This was a very fashionable spa in antiquity; Sulla, Augustus and Hadrian came here to take the waters. Beyond the pump room on the east side of the town are the hot springs with their sulphurous vapour; some of the water tumbles into the sea by a little beach, **Loutrá Gialton**, some 15km/9mi to the west. Today the town is full of elderly Greek couples who come here to cure rheumatism, arthritis and backache problems. From Loutrá Aidipsoú it is possible to return to the mainland (boats to Arkitsa).

▷ *Head back towards Agiokambos (ferry to Glyfá) and Oreoí.*

Old fortification by Oreoí

Shortly before Oreí is a pleasant beach overlooked by a tower on an islet, which is the perfect spot for a swim.

Oreoí

From the port (numerous cafés and restaurants) there are fine views across the Oreoí Channel to Mount Óthris on the mainland and the entrance to the Vólos Gulf. The north and northeast of the island are its most inaccessible areas. From Oreoí take the main road back to Pefki and Ellinika (fine beaches) and Agía Anna, the most popular one.

▶ *Head back towards Halkída via Strofilia.*

ADDRESSES

🛏️STAY

NORTH

🍽️ **Límni Hotel** – *Límni, south of the quayside.* 🗲22270 313 16/317 48. *27 rooms.* Comfortable, good-value hotel, away from the bustle of the harbour. Most rooms have sea views.

CENTRAL

🍽️🍽️ **Sunrise** – *Erétria.* 🗲22290 60004/60647. *www.hotelsunrise.gr. 17 studios, 15 villas.* Modern, boutique villa complex 150m/492ft from the sea.

🍽️🍽️ **Hotel Stení** – *Stení.* 🗲22280 512 21. *www.hotelsteni.gr. 35 rooms.* Comfortable rooms which are well-kept, quiet and spacious, with attractive wood panelling and fine views of the valley. Swimming pool.

🍽️🍽️ **Corali Hotel** – *Kími, 300m/984ft south of the harbour, 150m/492ft up and to the right.* 🗲22220 222 12/220 02. *www.coralihotel.gr. 22 rooms.* Quiet, spacious and comfortable rooms with balconies.

SOUTH

🍽️🍽️ **Galaxy** – Kárystos, Omirou & Odysseus Street by the quayside. 🗲22240 22600. *72 rooms.* Spacious hotel with views towards the sea.

🍽️🍽️ **Karystion Hotel** – *Kárystos, 3 Kriezótou, at the eastern end of the quay, after the "Bourtzi".* 🗲22240 2291/2291. *karistio@otenet.gr.* 🛏️ *39 rooms.* Modern, tasteful, comfortable hotel; professional service. Ask for a west-facing room so you can enjoy the sunset from your terrace. Excellent breakfast served on the garden terrace.

🍷/EAT

NORTH

🍽️🍽️ **Ageri Beer restaurant** – *Loutrá Aidipsoú (1km out towards Halkída).* 🗲22260 23530. *www.ageriedipsos.com.* A *meze* and grilled meat restaurant with 65 different beers on offer from all over the world – bottled and draught.

🍽️🍽️ **To Ástro (Ioánnou Brothers' Taverna)** – *3.5km/2.2mi south of Límni in a hamlet on the water.* 🗲22270 314 87/324 26. The place for a romantic dinner; meals are served on the large terrace in a charming setting. Classic dishes offering variety and quality.

🍽️ **O Plátanos** – *Límni, under the only plane tree on the quayside.* Pleasant shaded terrace, popular with locals. Specialities include grilled and fried fish. Efficient family management. Open weekends only, out of season.

SOUTH

🍽️🍽️ **To Kalámia** – *At the start of the beach, Kárystos.* Nice taverna close to the water and off the tourist trail. Traditional cuisine, tasty and inexpensive.

🍽️🍽️ **Cavo d'Oro** – *Kárystos, Párados Sahtóuri (an alleyway at right angles to the quayside beyond the esplanade).* Traditional taverna serving copious meat dishes in sauces. Menu only in Greek.

CENTRAL

🍽️ **Kissos** – *Stení, on the left hand side of the road.* 🗲22280 512 26/5127. A large restaurant; several terraces and a wide range of reasonably priced dishes.

The southernmost tip of continental Greece, Attica juts out into the Aegean Sea. Of the timeless landscapes described by poets and travellers, there remains woefully little. The mainland section, covering 2,600sq km/1,000sq mi, makes up about one-fortieth of Greece, but is home to nearly half the population. The ceaseless expansion of Athens has made most of the peninsula an urban and industrial area but, as the cradle of Greek civilisation, it boasts some of the most interesting museums and sites in Greece.

Highlights

1 **Cape Sounion** drive (p169)
2 A visit to the memorial at the **Battle of Marathon** (p173)
3 The **Dafní Monastery** (p175)
4 A meal in one of the fish **tavernas** on the coast (p178)
5 **Aigósthena** (p179)

A Bit of History

"Granary of the Ancients", and covered with olive groves, the region also had lead mining and marble quarries. Today's industry (refineries, metalworks, chemical plants, textile manufacturers and so on) produces two-thirds of the nation's wealth, but at considerable cost to the environment of the area.

Although Attica has always been dominated by Athens, two cities also played an important role in antiquity. The first is Megara, one of the most important cities in Ancient Greece, which has been continuously settled since 11 BC. It was powerful enough to spread in the Mediterranean, one of its colonies

▶ **Population:** 3,894,573.

⚲ **Michelin Map:** 737 H-J 9-10.

Info: In Athens: 26 Odós Amalias, by Síndagma Square. ☎210 331 0392.

▶ **Location:** Attica is composed of the peninsula up to its border with Boeotia, the islands of the Saronic Gulf, Hydra, Spetsae, and Kythera. The E 75 motorway runs through it, starting from Athens.

Don't Miss: Cape Sounion at sunset.

Timing: Factoring in some beach time, you can explore the coast in two days (overnight at Cape Sounion). If time is limited, a day or less for excursions from Athens.

Kids: Swimming and playing on the beach.

Temple of Poseidon, Soúnio

© Bryan Busovicki/Dreamstime.com

being Byzantium. The other is Eleusis where the famous "mysteries" were held and which today is notable as the place with the highest recorded temperature in Europe (48°C/118.4°F in 1977).

During Byzantine times, its importance declined and the economic centre of gravity moved north to Thebes. After the Fourth Crusade in 1204 and until the Ottoman occupation in 1456, the area was governed by Boniface of Monferrat but it eventually came in the possession of the Burgundian de la Roche family based in Thebes.

An invasion by the Catalan company in 1311 brought it under the crown of Aragon but in 1387 a Florentine adventurer, Nerio Acciauoli, claimed the city for Florence and kept it until 1456 when the Turks occupied it until the War of Greek Independence.

As a result, Attica has the greatest concentration of historical sights in Greece apart from Athens itself: Marathon and Plataia commemorate the battles fought during the Persian Wars; the archaeological sites in Eleusis, Sounion and Braurona are all must-sees; and the Byzantine Monastery at Dafní is a UNESCO Heritage Site.

Beaches

During the summer Athenians flock to the region's 100-plus beaches every weekend. As a rule, the further out, the better the beach. The best ones near Athens are Lagonisi Anavyssos and Saronida, next to each other (between 40km/25mi and 48 km/29mi south of Athens). They are best reached via the Attiki Odos Avenue that passes by the new Eleftherios Venizelos airport.

Further out the sandy and protected Panormos by Lavrion (63km /39mi southeast of Athens) and Vravróna Beach by the archaeological site are both protected from the northern summer winds.

On the west tip of Attica, Porto Germeno, Psatha and Alepohori are all fine beaches facing the bay of Corinth, (60 km/37mi west of Athens).

🚗 DRIVING TOURS

1 APOLLO COAST TO CAPE SOUNION★★

69km/41mi one way.

This is the most popular drive for Athenians so best avoid weekends especially Sundays when roads tend to gridlock.

▷ *From Athens, take the fast Mesogeion road to Ellinikó (old) airport which then goes on to the coast.*

Glifáda

This sizeable resort just 14km/9mi from Athens comprises a beach, a marina and an 18-hole golf course.
The road passes through **Voúla** *(beach) and* **Kavoúri***, skirting small bays.*

Vouliagméni★

An elegant resort pleasantly situated at the head of a deep inlet, Vouliagméni offers beaches, safe moorings and several hotels. From the southern headland beyond the harbour there is a fine **view** of the coast extending south towards Cape Sounion.

The road continues to **Várkiza** and then to **Lagoníssi**, another summer resort. The dramatic coastline features views of the Saronic Gulf and the **Isle of Patroclos**.

Soúnion

A small seaside resort on the site of the ancient town and port of Sounion. In an inlet near the headland, dry-dock facilities for two triremes have been found. **View★** of Cape Sounion, crowned by the columns of an ancient temple.

Temple of Poseidon at Soúnion★★

🕐 *Open every day from 10am–dusk.* 🎟️€4. 📞22920 393 63.

The "sacred headland" (Homer) is the outpost of Attica, occupying a commanding position facing the Aegean Sea and the Cyclades at the entrance to the Saronic Gulf. Famed ruins of a temple to the god of the sea crown the precipitous headland.

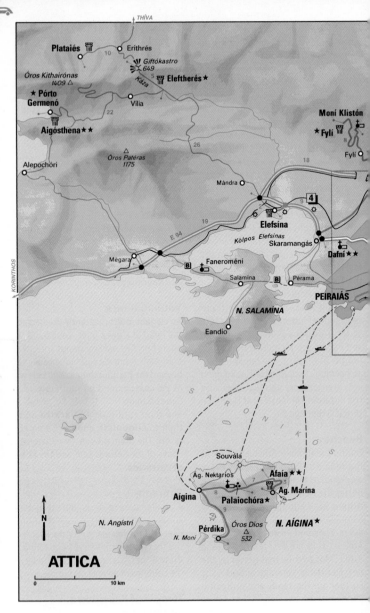

ATTICA

N

0   10 km

The marble **Temple of Poseidon** (440 BC) was a Doric building with a peristyle. The path leading up to it crosses the wall, which enclosed the ancient acropolis, and then enters the sacred precinct at the point where the original gate stood, flanked by a large portico where the pilgrims assembled. The entrance façade *(facing east)* con-sisted of a portico leading into the *naós,* of which the corner pillars have been preserved. Of the original 34 columns of the peristyle, 16 remain.

Abandoned for many years, the temple was restored in the 19C.

Excavations uncovered two colossal Archaic *kouroi,* which are now in the Athens Museum.

THESSALONÍKI ▷

Amfiaraeio ★

Ramnoús ★ 🏛

★ Ag. Marina

E 75

21

os Párnitha
413 △

*Límni
Marathóna*

Marathónas ★

★ Schiniás

**Eladikó
Nekrotafío**

Týmvos Plataiéon

Týmvos Marathóna

Agriliki

*Akti
Marathóna* ★

★ Néa Mákri

1109 △
Óros Pentéli

K Ó L P O S

Kifisiá ★

Rafína ●

DOUK. PLAKENTIAS

ATHÍNA ★★★
➡

P E T A L I Ó N

1 3 4

★★ **Kaisarianí** ✝

Paianía ●

★★ **Vravróna**
🏛

1026 △
★★ **Óros Ymittós**

M e s s ó g i a
✈

Koropi ●

2

★ Markópoulo ● Pórto Ráfti

Glifáda

Voúla
Vari

A p ó l l o n a ★★

Kavoúri

Vouliagméni ★

Várkiza

1

636 △

Keratéa ●

30

Lagoníssi ●

L a v r e o t í k i

Thorikó ★
🏛

Anávissos ●

Lávrio ●

N. Makroníssi

N. Patróklou

2 ➡

Soúnio ◉
🏛

AKR. SOÚNIO ★★★

② THE EAST COAST

160km/100mi from Sounion to Ramnoús.

From Sounion to Lávrio the road winds its way along the east coast of Cape Sounion.

The landscape is more verdant than on the western side; villas and hotels are dispersed among the pine and olive trees above little beaches nestling in the bays.

Lávrio

This small industrial town and mineral port lies at the foot of Mount Lavreotíki. Recent excavations suggest mining activity here as early as the third millennium BC.

Sanctuary of Artemis, Vravróna

© Greek National Tourism Organisation

It was early in the 5C BC that the deposits of silver-bearing sulphides began to be exploited, bringing wealth and power to Athens. Extraction ceased in the 2C BC, but in 1864 a new process for treating the mineral restored production of silver and zinc.

Thorikó

Inhabited from 2000 BC until the Roman period, Thorikó was a large fortified city where wood was imported for the foundries in Lávrio. The site comprises a 5 000-seat **theatre** with elliptical terraces, and a residential district below an acropolis.

▷ *Return to Lávrio to rejoin the Athens road. Beyond Keratéa it enters the Messógia, a sparsely inhabited plain. At Markópoulo, join the road towards Vravróna and Pórto Ráfti and continue 8km/5mi to the entrance to the archaeological site of Brauron.*

Vravróna★

In ancient times the **Brauron** sanctuary was a place of pilgrimage dedicated to Artemis Brauronia. According to Pausanias, Agamemnon's daughter Iphigenia, who had escaped being sacrificed, returned with the sacred statue of Artemis to found the sanctuary. It was served by young priestesses, called "bears" in

honor of Artemis' mascot and dedicated to the goddess at the age of seven.

Sanctuary

🕒*Open Tue–Sun 8.30am–3pm.* ✆*€3.* 📞*22990 270 20.*
Beyond a 6C AD basilica *(left)* is the sacred fountain that flowed into a stream spanned by a 5C BC bridge.
On the right, below St George's Chapel (15C), are the foundations of the Temple of Artemis (5C BC); behind in a crack in the rock is the "Tomb of Iphigenia". Opposite was the grand peristyle courtyard, which was flanked on three sides by the "parthenon"; part of the colonnade has been re-erected.

Museum

500m/1,640ft from the sanctuary.
🕒*Open Tue–Sun 8.30am–3pm.* ✆*€3.*
This displays geometric vases (9C–8C BC), a low-relief votive sculpture showing the figures of Zeus (seated), Leto, Apollo and Artemis (5C BC) and particularly a series of ravishing statuettes or marble heads of little "bears" (4C BC): the *Bear with a Bird* and the *Bear with a Hare* are masterpieces.

▷ *Return to Markópoulo via Pórto Ráfti, a seaside resort, and the port of the Messógia (Limáni Messogéas).*

At the mouth of the bay there is an island crowned by a colossal Roman marble figure of a man sitting cross-legged; it is popularly called the tailor *(ráftis)* and was probably used as a leading mark.

MARATHON COAST★

Rafína
Ferries for Euboea and the eastern Cyclades leave from Rafína, a commercial and fishing harbour. Fish tavernas line the waterfront and the beach.

◗ *Take the coast road which passes a series of beaches, then rejoin the main road at Néa Makri; after 5km/3mi turn right onto the road to Marathon.*

Marathon Battlefield
◷*Open Tue–Sun and public holidays 8.30am–3pm. ☞€3 (site and museum). ℘22940 551 55.*
The stretch of coastal plain south of Marathónas was the scene of the famous battle (490 BC) described by Herodotus. Isolated in the plain is the **Marathon Barrow** commemorating the defenders who died in battle. At the foot is a reproduction of the gravestone of the Soldier of Marathon (original in the National Museum in Athens). From the top there is a fine view of the plain, and the surrounding mountains.

◗ *Return to the main road and 1km/0.5mi farther north turn left to the Barrow of the Plataians. Immediately on the right stands a hangar covering a cemetery.*

The **Helladic cemetery** is proof of ancient human occupation of the plain of Marathon. The tombs (2000 BC) contain perfectly preserved skeletons. The **Barrow of the Plataians** covers the graves of Plataians who died at Marathon.
The **museum** contains an interesting collection of primitive objects from the Helladic and Mycenaean periods: funerary urns; statuettes; helmets and weapons.
Near the museum is a Helladic and Mycenaean cemetery.

◗ *Return to the main road continuing north; just before Marathon turn right to the pleasant beach at Shiniás (beautiful pine grove) and Ramnoús.*

Ramnoús★
◷*Open daily 8.30am–3pm.*
☞*€2. ℘22940 634 77.*
The ruins of ancient Ramnoús lie in a remote valley running down to the sea. Here lie the foundations of two Doric temples. One is dedicated to Themis (6C BC). The other temple (5C BC) con-

---

The Battle of Marathon

In 490 BC a Persian fleet sent from Asia Minor to quell the Greek rebellion anchored in the Gulf of Marathon and prepared to march on Athens. Camped on the lower slopes of Mount Agriliki, some 8,000 Greek defenders faced 20,000 Persians.

Under General Miltiades the Athenians surrounded the Persians, inflicting heavy casualties and forcing them to retreat. It is traditionally believed that the Persians lost 6,400 men, against Greek casualties of just 192.

Legend has it that, victory assured, Miltiades dispatched Pheidippides, a messenger, to Athens with the news. Pheidippides ran to Athens where, after announcing the victory, he collapsed from exhaustion and died.

The "marathon" of the first modern Olympics in 1896 was run over 40km/25mi, the distance between Marathon and Athens. The official distance for marathons is now set at 42km/26mi as laid down at the 1908 London Olympics; this corresponds to the distance between Windsor Great Park and White City Stadium, the start and finish points for the event on that occasion.

Ruins at Ramnoús, with a view to the Gulf of Euboea

tained a famous effigy of Nemesis, goddess of Punishment and Divine Retribution (now displayed in the British Museum in London).

Continue down the path to the site of the ruined acropolis (4C BC). There are traces of the enclosing wall, a small theatre, buildings and a citadel. Fine views extend over the wild and rocky coast; the position of the ancient lower town can be surmised.

▷ *Rejoin the E 75 motorway and head north towards Chalkida. Turn off at Malakasa and follow the signs for Skala Oropou/Amfiaraío.*

Amfiaraío

⏱*Open Tue–Sun 8.30am–3pm.*
☞*€3.* ☎*22950 621 44.*

In a narrow peaceful valley lie the ruins of a sanctuary (4C BC) dedicated to **Amphiaraos**, King of Árgos; he was also a seer and healer whose cult developed in these remote parts as did the cult of Asklepios in Epidaurus.

To the right of the path was the temple, with the base of the cult statue and the offering table in the centre; in front of the temple was a huge altar. On the other side of the path is the "Statue Terrace"; the pedestals date from the Roman period.

Beyond was the portico *(abaton)* where the sick lay down to sleep. Note the feet of the supports for the marble bench which ran the whole length of the portico. Farther on was the theatre (3 000 seats) where the votive festival (Amphiaréa) took place.

3 NORTH OF ATHENS, TOWARDS FILÍ★

56km/35mi there and back.

This is a plasant drive to Mount Parnes, again very popular with Athenian families, so avoid travelling there on a Sunday.

▷ *Leave Athens by Odós Liossíon, which follows the railway to Néa Lióssia and then Áno Lióssia. Beyond the village of Phyle the road starts to climb Mount Parnes. Turn right at one of the bends into a road (sign "Moní Klistón").*

Moní Klistón

This convent takes its name from its spectacular **position**★ 600m/1968ft above a deep gorge riddled with caves, some of which were occupied by hermits. It is not known exactly when the convent was established, but the current structure dates from the 16C or 17C. The entrance bears a date of 1204.

▷ *The road continues upwards past the track (right) to the Plátani Kriopigí taverna; soon after turn left to reach Phyle Fortress.*

Filí★

In an empty landscape the ruins of **Phyle Fortress** command one of the passes between Attica and Boeotia. Considerable sections of the enclosing wall are still standing; it was built in the 4C BC of huge rectangular blocks up to 2.7m/8ft thick and reinforced with several towers.

WEST OF ATHENS

Around 90km/56mi.

This drive takes in the Byzantine UNESCO site of Dafní monastery, the sacred site of Elefsína to the large beach of Porto Germeno.

Leave Athens by E94.
See Athens map.

Dafní★★
(Daphne Monastery)

Open Tue–Sun 8am-8pm.
𝒫 210 5811558.

Just at the motorway to Corinth, at the foot of a wooded hill, stands Dafní Monastery, renowned for its church and mosaics, which are some of the finest in Greece.

Climb the slopes to the west for a fine view of the whole complex: the primitive gateway, the walls including a section dating from the 5–6C, the cloisters and the church.

Mosaic of Christ Pantocrator, Dafni Monastery

© Tony Gervis/Robert Harding

In the dome, Christ Pantocrator, surrounded by the 16 Prophets; in the squinches, the Annunciation (**1**), the Nativity (**2**), the Baptism (**3**) and the Ascension (**4**) of Christ.

In the apse, the Virgin Mary (**5**) flanked by the Archangels Michael (**6**) and Gabriel (**7**). In the transept arms, gospel scenes including the Birth of the Virgin, the Entry of Christ into Jerusalem (**8**) and the Crucifixion (**9**) (north transept), the Adoration of the Magi, Christ rising from the dead (**10**), Doubting Thomas (**11**) (south transept). In the

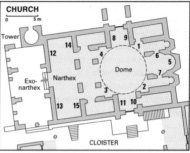

narthex, the Betrayal by Judas (**12**) and a scene from the legend of Joachim and Anne (**13**) are opposite the Last Supper (**14**) and the Presentation of the Virgin in the Temple (**15**).

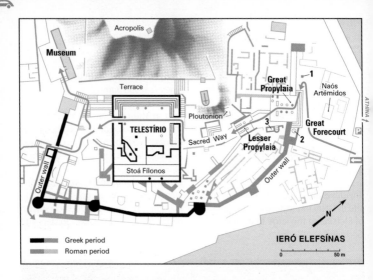

IERÓ ELEFSÍNAS

Greek period
Roman period

0   50 m

The peaceful paved **cloisters** are flanked on the east side by a typically Cistercian arcade. Under the western arcade are ducal sarcophagi. Fragments of stonework were discovered in the crypt.

The domed **Byzantine church** was built over the crypt in the 11C and enlarged in the 13C by the Cistercians.

There is a fine view from the cloisters of the south front of the church. The narthex, which is crenellated, must have been built on the model of Citeaux; the tombs of the Dukes of Athens were placed here. The pointed arches of the west front and traces of a groined vault suggest the inspiration of Burgundian architecture.

On the north side of the church beyond the square tower are the remains of the 11C refectory. The elevation of the church and the dome can be admired; the small windows date from the 11C; the others are probably 13C.

Inside, the church is magnificently decorated with late-11C **mosaics**★★ against a gold background, which are remarkable for their delicacy of line and colouring. The scenes, are arranged according to the theological concepts of the period.

Elefsína (Eleusis)

🕐*Open Tue–Sun 8.30am–3pm.* ✒€3 *(site and museum).* ☏*21055 434 70.*
The sanctuary at Eleusis, where the fertility cult of the "great goddesses" Demeter and Persephone was celebrated, was one of the great shrines of antiquity. It was linked to Athens by the Sacred Way. The sanctuary lies against a low hill topped by an acropolis overlooking Eleusis Bay and Salamis Island. Part Greek and part Roman, the ruins convey a great sense of history, despite modern-day pollution.

The Eleusinian Mysteries

In mythology, it was at Eleusis that Demeter found her daughter, Persephone, who had been abducted by Hades, King of the Underworld, near Lake Pergusa in Sicily. Keleos, King of Eleusis, gave the goddess hospitality and in return she gave the king's son the first grain of wheat and showed him how to make it bear fruit. .

The secret rites of the fertility cult, known as the "Eleusinian mysteries", were celebrated until the 4C BC, and took place during a great festival in the autumn. Themes included the union of Zeus and Demeter – a sign of fertility; the legend of Persephone detained in the world of the dead for six months –

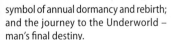

symbol of annual dormancy and rebirth; and the journey to the Underworld – man's final destiny.

The dramatist Aeschylus was born at Eleusis c.525 BC.

Great Forecourt

2C AD. The square, which is paved with marble, was laid out in the Roman era. Near the site of a Temple to Artemis *(Naós Artémidos)* is the colossal medallion bust of the Roman Emperor Antoninus Pius (**1**) from the pediment of the **Great Propylaia**.

To the left of the entrance is the **Kallichoron Well** (**2**) (6C BC). Inside are traces of the Roman sewer *(cloaca)* (**3**). To the right are parts of the architrave of the **Lesser Propylaia** (1C BC) decorated with symbolic ears of corn.

The Sacred Way, which was paved by the Romans, leads past caves on the right hollowed out of the hillside to symbolise the entrance to the underworld; at the base on a triangular terrace stands a little temple, the **Ploutonion**, which was dedicated to Hades.

Telestírio

The Telesterion at the heart of the sanctuary was a majestic building. It has been refashioned many times and retains traces of every period. The ground floor consisted of a huge room that could accommodate about 3,000 people. A paved portico, the Portico of Philo (Stoá Fílonos), runs along the southeast front. From the terrace, climb the steps to reach the museum overlooking the Bay of Eleusis and Salamis Island.

Museum

Sculptures from the site are on view in the museum. There is also a reconstruction of the sanctuary in its heyday. The courtyard contains a horse's head dating from the Hellenistic period, and a sarcophagus from the Roman era.

⊳ *On leaving Elefsína (Eleusis) bear right into the Thebes (Thíva) road, which climbs gently towards the Kithairon mountain range forming the border between Attica and Boeotia. Continue past the turning (left) to Vília; the ruins of Eleutherai (Eleftherés) are soon visible on a rock spur to the right.*

Eleftherés★ (Eleutherai)

Park near a disused petrol station and taverna and return to the path (left) which leads up to the fortress (30min on foot there and back).

Eleutherai Fortress stands on a desolate site, exposed to the wind, commanding the way over the Kithairon range at the southern end of the Káza Pass.

The walls were built by the Athenians in the 4C BC. The parapet walk is quite well preserved, particularly on the north side; views of Attica.

⊳ *Continue by car to the* ***Giftókastro Pass*** *(649m/2,129ft), where there is a magnificent view westwards over Mount Kithairon and northwards over the fertile Boeotian plain. A short distance away are the ruins of Plataia.*

Plateés (Plataia)

Only a few traces remain of the ancient city of **Plataia**; they lie on a sloping terrace at the foot of the north face of Mount Kithairon (Kitherónas). There is a fine view of the Boeotian plain. Northeast of the site by the River Assopós, the **Battle of Plataia** took place in 479 BC and ended the Persian Wars.

On the right of the road from Erithrés, just outside the modern town, are the ancient ruins, in particular traces of the 5C–4C BC circular walls.

⊳ *Return downhill to the turning (right) to Vília.*

The road runs through the pleasant little town of **Vília** *(hotels, restaurants)* – past the military road *(right)* leading to the summit of **Mount Kithairon** (1,409m/4,623ft) – and winds down through stands of Aleppo pines to the bay of Pórto Germenó.

Savatiano grapes

© Georgas Family Organic Grape Products

Attica Wines

According to legend it was Dionysus himself who introduce vine cultivation to Attica and Aristotle believed that tragedy started with the dithyramb, a spontaneous hymn in honour of Bacchus. Wine production in Attica has been going on for thousands of years and the most famous wine of Greece, retsina – broadly based on the taste imparted by the resin used to line the ancient *amphoreis* (clay bottles) – comes from a variety native to Attica called Savatiano. Today cultivation in the region comprises around 6,000ha/15,000 acres, mostly in the central Mesogaian Plain around Markópoulo and Spata near the Eleftherios Venizelos airport, which makes a wine tour very easy and compact.

Some wineries that offer tastings in the area (call before arriving) are:

Markou Vineyards 1st km Peanias – Markópoulou Ave., ℰ210 6644711, www.markouwines.gr.

Kellari Papachristou 16th km Athens–Spata Ave., ℰ210 6032510, www.kellari.gr.

Allagianni 27th km Peanias – Markopoulou Ave., ℰ22990 25562, www.allagiannis.gr.

Kontogianni 16 Petoura & Dragonea St., Markópoulo, ℰ22990 25418, www.kontwines.gr.

Domain Fragou 21 K. Palama St. Spata, ℰ210-6632087, www.fragou.com.gr.

Georgas 12 G. Georga St. Spata, ℰ 210-6633345, www.geowines.gr.

A full list and more information from the Attica Wine Growers' Association at www.enoaa.gr.

Georgas Family vineyards

Pórto Germenó★

This quiet seaside resort (the beach is huge) is pleasantly sited in a bay at the eastern end of the Gulf of Corinth. It is a resort much beloved by Athenian families because of the shade it provides with its abundance of pine trees. It has recently started to attract surfers.

Aigósthena★★

Access by the narrow coast road.
Above the olive groves stands a well-preserved fortress, a good example of Greek military architecture. It has been dated to 343 BC. The enclosing wall is strengthened with posterns, huge lintels and high towers.

Because of its strategic site, it changed hands between Athens, Megara and Thebes and it was subsequently occupied and used by the Byzantines.

In the 13C it was restored by the Franks – there are traces of a monastery – and linked to the seashore by two fortified walls enclosing the lower town; part of the northern wall survives.

ADDRESSES

🛏 STAY

EAST COAST

⊖⊖ **Kyani Akti** – *Pórto Raftí, 40 Agias Marinas.* &22990 864 00. www.kianiakti.com. *25 rooms.* Small hotel at a reasonable price; open all year. A charming spot.

⊖⊖⊖⊖ **Mare Nostrum** – *Vravróna, Club Med, on the seafront.* &22940 710 00. www.mare-nostrum.gr. *300 rooms.* Recently renovated and one of the few hotels on the east coast. It offers games, activities and shops, as well as a nearby thalassotherapy centre.

SOUNION

⊖⊖⊖ **Aegon** – *Below the Temple of Poseidon, at Sounion.* &22920 392 00. www.aegeon-hotel.com. *89 rooms.* This hotel is the closest to the temple at Sounion. Rooms overlook the beach.

MOUNT PARNITHA

⊖⊖⊖ **Mont Parnes** – *Aharnés.* &21024 691 11, Fax 21024 6068.

www.regencycasinos.gr. *39 rooms, 6 suites.* Mountain hotel exudes bygone splendour. Spacious rooms with marble bathrooms, spectacular views. Casino.

WEST COAST

⊖⊖ **Hotel Calypso Beach** – *Anavysos. 49th km Athens–Sounion Ave.* &22910 601 70. *66 rooms.* Rooms in the main building and in 28 bungalows (with air-conditioning) next to a calm bay.

⊖⊖⊖ **Xenia Ilios** – *Anavysos.* &22910 370 24. *103 rooms.* A hotel-management school open Jun–Sept. Good service; comfortable rooms overlook the sea. Full- or half-board options.

🍽 EAT

Tavernas and fresh fish restaurants abound in villages all along the Attica coast. On the east coast, look for restaurants in Rafína and Pórto Ráfti.

WEST COAST

⊖⊖ **Kyra Popi** – *(40th km Athens Sounion Avenue opposite the Lagonisi resort).* &22910 26388. Fresh fish imaginatively cooked.

⊖⊖⊖ **Eating Marina** – *(Athens–Sounion Ave, at Legraina, 5km before Sounion).* &22920 51221. Has been in the same family for two generations: specialities octopus, swordfish, and yogurt with quince jelly.

⊖⊖⊖ **Artemis** – *(60th km Athens–Sounion Ave, well signposted).* &22920 48473. An institution in seafood and fish in an excellent position. Always busy. Do not go without a reservation.

EAST COAST

⊖⊖ **Oceanis** – *Rafína, Nireos Ave., and Thaleias 3.* &22940-24292/25712. By the sea. Although specialising in fish, it also offers a large selection of meat dishes.

⊖⊖ **Psaropoula** – *Porto Rafti 118, Avlakiou Avenue.* &22990 71292. Fish mezedes followed by fish on the barbecue.

⊖⊖⊖ **Patitiria** – *Marathon. Marathonos Ave 285.* &22940-55261. Excellent rustic decor. Traditional meat dishes on the barbecue and in the oven. Live music Fri–Sat evenings. Reservations recommended.

EPIRUS AND THESSALY

Thessalía kai Ípiros – Θεσσαλία και Ήπειρος

These two neighbouring regions spread across the north of Greece from the remote and mountainous border with Albania in the northwest to the popular Óros Pílio Peninsula and the Aegean Sea in the east. On the west coast the busy holiday resort of Párga is the only face of this region that many visitors see, but inland from here is a fascinating area that includes lesser-known archaeological remains, mountains where wolves and bears still roam, the second-longest gorge in Europe, huge lakes which have a timeless beauty, historical towns like Ioánnina and Métsovo which are off the usual tourist trail, and magical archaeological sites like Dodóni, where fewer visitors make it easier for you to connect with the past. In short, here there is a genuine feeling of discovering that elusive destination, the "real Greece".

Highlights

1. Marvel at the construction of the **Meteora** monasteries (p183)
2. Explore the dramatic coastline of **Óros Pílio** (p188)
3. Check out the Venetian fortress in the resort town of **Párga** (p193)
4. Enjoy a stay in the bustling, modern city of **Ioánnina** (p196)
5. Experience the charm of the mountain town of **Métsovo** (p198)

Rising from the Sea

Also here is one of Greece's most spectacular sights, the monasteries of Meteora. These buildings sit on top of – or are set into – the sides of enormous rock columns which jut out of the surrounding plain like lighthouses thrusting up out of the sea. This gives an indication of the geological origins of this part of Thessaly, which was indeed once the bed of an enormous inland sea. The rock columns of Meteora were formed some 30 million years ago, beneath that inland sea, carved by the pounding of waves against limestone. When the land

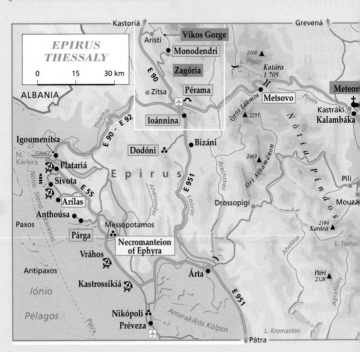

shapes shifted and the sea poured out into the Aegean, these rocks were left standing in all their weird wondrousness.

Compared to this, the presence of the Romans from 146 BC onwards is comparatively recent history. The Via Egnatia, that majestic Roman road which linked Rome with Constantinople ran in an almost straight line through Thessaly and into Thessaloniki, the capital of Macedonia, of which Thessaly was then a part. Before the Romans the first settlers in the region were Neolithic peoples in about 2500 BC, and after the Romans left the area became part of the Byzantine Empire. At various times it was under the rule of the Bulgarians, the Serbs, and most significantly (as for most of modern Greece) the Turks. The fascination of cities l ike Ioánnina is that they show all these various influences while remaining recognisably Greek.

Even when the two regions of Thessaly and Epirus became part of modern Greece in the late 19C, it wasn't the end of foreign invasions as Germany occupied the area and there was bitter fight-

View of Vikos Gorge

© Antonis Nikolopoulos/Greek National Tourism Organisation

ing in the mountains during the Second World War. Further fierce fighting took place between the Greeks themselves during the subsequent Civil War, and anyone visiting the region today, especially if driving through the mountains, can see what a rugged terrain it is, and can feel in the towns and cities the resonance of this history all around.

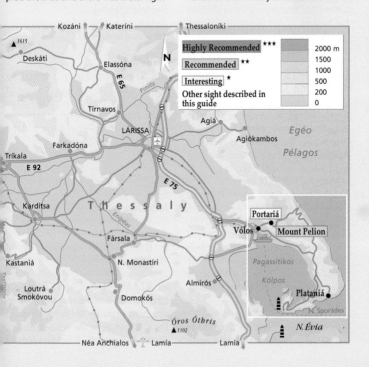

Larissa

Lárissa – Λάρισα

Lárissa is the capital of Thessaly and an important junction on the south bank of the River Piniós. Occupied by Turks for five centuries, it is today a market for produce and a food-processing centre, and the ideal base from which to explore the archaeological and natural attractions of the area.

VISIT

In **Odós Venizélou**, the main street in the old part of town, the low houses with awnings and the open-air street stalls are reminders of the Turkish occupation. The ruins of a Hellenistic **theatre** are visible from the corner of Odós Papanastasiou. The street climbs up to the site of an ancient acropolis where a **medieval castle** stands. Excavations in front of the castle have revealed an early-Christian basilica; the painted tomb may be that of St Achileos. Visit the **Archaeological Museum** (*Odós 31–Avgoustou 2; ⊙closed 2012 for refurbishment; ⊜no charge; ℘24102 88515*) to see Hellenistic and Roman sculptures, Neolithic vases, and mosaics, all housed in a 19C mosque.

OUTSKIRTS
Kiláda Ton Témbon★
▶ *22km/14mi northeast of Lárissa.*
On the northern border of Thessaly stretches the valley of the River Piniós. In antiquity this region was sacred to **Apollo**, son of Zeus and Leto. After killing Python at Delphi Apollo came to wash in the waters of the Piniós. There he fell in love with the nymph **Daphne**, who was changed into a laurel tree (*dáphni*) to escape his advances. Disappointed, Apollo gathered a sprig of the laurel and planted it at Delphi near the Kastalian Spring. Tour the valley by travelling upstream; most of the sights lie on the north (right) side of the road.

Agía Paraskevi
This important place of pilgrimage dedicated to the Virgin is on the north

- **Population:** 140,000.
- **Michelin Map:** 737 G 5 – Thessaly.
- **Info:** Odós Epirou 58. ℘24106 18189. Open Mon–Fri 7.30am–2.30pm.
- **Location:** Lárissa is situated 151km/94mi southwest of Thessaloniki and around 360km/225mi northwest of Athens.
- **Parking:** There is ample parking space in the town centre.
- **Don't Miss:** A picnic by the Piniós.
- **Timing:** A day could be spent visiting the valley of the Piniós and the castle.
- **Kids:** The medieval castle.

bank of the River Piniós at the foot of an impressive cliff of rock. From the footbridge over the river there is a beautiful **view**★ of the Vale of Temple.

Daphne's Spring
Also known as Apollo's Spring, this shady site is cool and restful.

Ambelákia
This pleasant small town is splendidly situated on the northwest slope of Mount Óssa, at the opening of the gorge in the Vale of Tempe, with an extensive view of the River Piniós basin and the heights of Mount Olympus.
In the 17C and 18C Ambelákia bustled with workshops producing fabrics dyed scarlet with madder from the neighbouring plain. The richly decorated **residence**★ of George Schwarz, head of a sales and production cooperative for the fabrics (the first of its type, founded in 1780), is a superb example of a typical 18C Thessalian house.

PLATAMÓNAS CASTLE★
▶ *55km/34mi northeast of Lárissa. Access by a footpath road in Néa Pandeleimónas.*
On a hill between the sea and Mount Olympus stands the Frankish castle of

Platamónas Castle

© J.-P. Nail/MICHELIN

Platamónas. Begun in 1204, it occupies a commanding position at the seaward end of the Vale of Tempe. The **fortress**★ is an excellent example of medieval military architecture; note especially the entrance to the keep, which could only be reached by ladders.

Meteora★★★

Metéora – Μετέωρα

North of Kalampáka in the northwest corner of the Thessalian Plain, a group of precipitous grey rocks rise up out of the trees in the flat Piniós Valley. Perched on top are the coenobitic monasteries known as the Meteora, sacred sites of orthodox monasticism. The landscape and near-miraculous construction of these buildings draw many tourists, yet the monasteries do still maintain their magical, mystical air.

A BIT OF HISTORY

These towers of sandstone and tertiary conglomerate stand on the border between the Píndos massif and the Thessalian Plain at the lower end of the gorges carved by the Piniós River and its tributaries. There are some 60 of these columns of rock, and they rise up to 300m/984ft high.

In the 11C, hermits sought refuge in the solitary caves of the Meteora. When the Serbs invaded Thessaly in the 14C, the

- ◔ **Michelin Map:** 737 E 5 – Thessaly.
- ▥ **Info:** Town Hall Square in Kalampáka. ℰ 24320 779 00. Open Mon–Fri 8am–9pm, Sat–Sun 10am– 4pm in summer only.
- ▻ **Location:** 125km/78mi east of Ioánnina and 85km/53mi west of Lárissa. The town of Kalambáka makes a good base from which to explore the Meteora.
- ▣ **Parking:** Finding space should not be a problem.
- ☺ **Don't Miss:** The driving tour of monasteries but remember, photographing frescoes is not permitted, and visitors must be modestly dressed.
- ◔ **Timing:** See Megálo Metéoro and Varlaám in the morning, the rest in the afternoon. Avoid visiting at Christmas and Easter if possible.

Roussánou Monastery

© Greek National Tourism Organisation

hermits began to establish monasteries. The first was founded by **St Athanasius** from Mount Athos, who founded the Great Meteoron. Others followed, despite the monumental task of transporting the building material to the top of the rock pillars.

During the 15C and 16C the number of monasteries grew to 24 and the buildings were decorated with frescoes and icons by the great artists of the day such as **Theophanes**. Today only five monasteries are inhabited by monks or nuns: St Nicholas, Roussánou, the Great Meteoron, Varlaám and St Stephen's. The Meteora draws many tourists, and some monks have now sought isolation at Mount Athos or other monasteries. Originally the only access was by means of very long ladders or by baskets suspended from winch-drawn ropes. Steps have now been cut in the rock face and there is a fine modern road serving the main monasteries.

🚗 DRIVING TOUR

17km/11mi. Begin at Kalambáka.

Note that the opening times of the monasteries do change from year to year so always check ahead as to which days and times the places are open.

Kalampáka

The 14C Mitrópoli (cathedral) stands on an earlier church's foundations. Inside, note the marble pulpit, canopy, and dark 16C frescoes in the Cretan style.

▷ *Drive west; after Kastráki, park the car and take the path on the left.*

Doúpiani

The **Chapel of the Virgin on the "Column"** was part of the Doúpiani hermitage to which, until the 14C, the scattered hermits were attached.

Ágios Nikólaos★

🕐*Open Sat–Thu, 9am–4pm (closed in winter).* 🎟️€2. ☎️24320 773 92.
Although the monastery dates from the 14C the church was built in the 16C and was decorated at that time by Theophanes the Cretan with remarkable frescoes. The monastery itself is small; it is composed of 10 cells and its katholicón is only large enough to accommodate three worshippers. It was abandoned in the late 19C.

Roussánou Monastery

🕐*Open Thu–Tue 9am–5.45pm (5pm in winter).* 🎟️€2. ☎️24320 225 19.
This monastery is also known as St Barbara; for many years the head of the saint was among the relics venerated here. Note the 16C frescoes in the *katholicón*. The road skirts the foot of the rock then reaches a T-junction. Bear left past the Varlaám Monastery to reach the Great Meteoron Monastery.

Megálo Metéoro★★

🕐*Open Wed–Mon 9am–5pm (summer); Thu-Mon, 9am–4pm (winter).* 🎟️€2. *Access by steps cut into the rock.*
The foremost of the Meteora monasteries was founded in 1356 by St Atha-

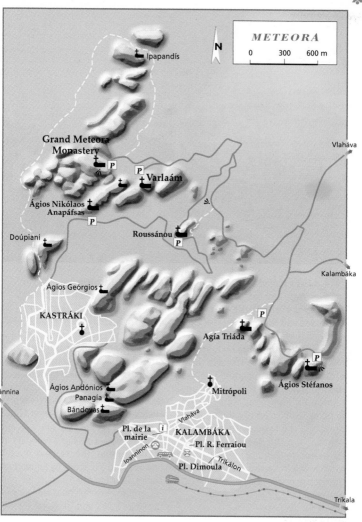

nasius and enriched with relics and works of art by his successor St Ioasaph (John Uros).

Church

The apse and the chancel (14C) are decorated with mid-15C frescoes; the rest of the building was rebuilt in the mid-16C according to the architectural style of Mt Athos (square-cross plan with lateral apses roofed by domes). St Ioasaph's tomb is in the narthex. The imposing 16C **refectory** now houses the Treasury: manuscripts, icons, liturgical ornaments, reliquaries and a carved

cross of St Daniel. From the southeast of the monastery there is an impressive view over the valley.

Varlaám Monastery★★

🕓 Open Wed–Mon 9am–4pm (summer), Thu–Mon 9am–4pm (winter). ☞ €2. 𝒫 24320 753 86.

A footbridge and a stairway lead up to this monastery (1518); in the 16C, visitors and provisions were hoisted up from the winch tower.

All Saints' Church, which incorporates the original 14C chapel dedicated to the Three Hierarchs, was completed in

Varlaám and Megálo Monasteries

1544. It has a remarkable collection of frescoes. Note also the 17C frescoes in the **Chapel of the Three Hierarchs**, the carved and gilded iconostasis (16C icon) and the inlaid furnishings.
Conventual buildings include the refectory housing the treasury (icon of the Virgin by Emmanuel Tzanés), the infirmary, the storerooms (containing an enormous water barrel holding 12,000 l/2,640 gal), the wine press and the tower with its winch.

◗ *Return to the junction across the river; bear left: spectacular view★★ of the Roussánou Monastery. Continue on, turning right at the second T-junction.*

Agía Triáda
◷*Open Fri–Wed, 9am–5pm (summer); Fri–Wed 10am–3.30pm (winter).* ✆€2. ☎24320 753 86.
The Monastery of the Holy Trinity (15C–17C) was richly endowed with precious artefacts and manuscripts, but its treasury was looted in the Second World War. The little chapel of St John the Baptist hewn into the rockface has some fine 17C frescoes, as does the *katholicón*, which dates to the 15C.

Ágios Stéfanos★
◷*Open Tue–Sun, 9am–1.30pm and 2–5.30pm (summer; 9.30am–1pm, 3–5pm (winter).* ✆€2. ☎24320 222 79.
St Stephen's Convent is reached by a bridge spanning the chasm that separates the rock pillar from the mountain mass. It is occupied by nuns, who maintain the traditions of icon painting (examples can be purchased by visitors). The older church of St Stephen's (15C) is closed to visitors; the more recent church (18C) is contains a reliquary of St Charalambos. The refectory houses fine 16C and 17C icons by Emmanuel Tzanés, 17C illuminated manuscripts and 16C embroidery. Splendid **views**★★ of the Piniós Valley and Thessaly.

EXCURSIONS
Tríkala
◗ *22km/14mi south of Kalambáka on the E 92.*
The town of Tríkala is on the river Lethíos, on the northwestern edge of the Thessalian Plain, 56km/35mi southwest of Larisa. Today an agricultural market – wheat, maize, tobacco, and cotton are grown in the region – Tríkala was famed in antiquity for its sanctuary to Asklepios, the oldest medical centre of its kind in Greece. The town was the Thessalonian capital during Turkish occupation. Containing the main

churches and a picturesque bazaar, the **Old Town** spreads over the lower slopes of Mt Ardáni below Fort Trikkis, a Byzantine restoration of a 4C BC original. Head for the top of the hill, a pleasant spot with a busy café. South of town enroute to Kardítsa stands a 16C **mosque** with an imposing dome.

Stená Pórtas★ (Pórta Defile)

▶ *2km/1.25mi from Tríkala. Take the road to Píli up the south bank of the Portaïkós.* Narrow and high, the **bridge**★ (16C) spans the river in one impressive arch at the entrance to the pass.

◐ *Return to Píli, cross the stream and climb up the north bank.*

Sanctuary of Pórta Panagía★

The isolated monastery dates from 1283, and comprises two buildings set in a beautiful landscape. In the eastern church (Latin style) note the dressed stone, the transept and the nave buttressed by side aisles. The entrance to the chancel is framed by mosaics. The western church (Orthodox), reveals the Greek-cross plan beneath a dome (15C); the façade and the stone walls seem to date from the 13C. The chuches are built on the site of a sanctuary of Athena or Apollo and its ancient masonry was used in the construction of the monastery.

ADDRESSES

🛏 STAY

🛏 **Aeolic Star** – *Kalambáka, 4 Odós A. Diákou, up from the Town Hall square.* ✆*24320 223 25. 21 rooms.* Simple accommodation; some rooms have balconies, all have TVs and private bathrooms. It includes generous breakfast.

🛏 **France** – *Kastráki, outskirts.* ✆*24320 241 86. 26 rooms.* Faultless rooms, some with views of the Meteora.

🛏 **Odysseion** – *Kalambáka, 30 Odós P. Dimitriou.* ✆*24320 223 20. 22 rooms.* ☕ Modern hotel with great views; breakfast on the terrace. Charming welcome.

🛏 **Hotel Tsikéli** – *Kalambáka, from the main road for the Meteora, take the street diagonally left.* ✆*24320 22 438, www.hotelskalambaka.gr. 18 rooms.* ☕ Welcoming place; breakfast served overlooking the garden. Some rooms have a view of the Meteora.

🛏 **Vasilikí & Gregóry Ziógas** – *Kastráki, main street.* ✆*24320 240 37. 10 rooms.* Friendly welcome, comfortable rooms with views over the Meteora.

🛏🛏 **Doupiani House** – *Kastráki outskirts, turn left.* ✆*24320 753 26. www.doupianihouse.com. 11 rooms.* Quiet, secluded hotel with some of the best Meteora views. Breakfast on the terrace. Walking routes and maps provided.

🛏🛏 **Kastráki** – *Kastráki, outskirts of the village in the direction of the Meteora.* ✆*24320 753 36. 27 rooms.* A modern, comfortable hotel; some rooms have views of the Meteora.

🛏🛏🛏 **Meteora** – *Kalambáka, 13 Odós Ploútarchou.* ✆*24320 781 80. www.meteorahotels.com. 63 rooms.* A smart, 5-star hotel catering to the active type.

🍴 EAT

🍴 **Taverna Gardenia** – *Kastráki, below the church.* Fresh, family-style dishes served on the pretty terrace.

🍴 **Filoxenia Taverna** – *Kastráki, road leading to the Meteora.* A pleasant spot to sample brochettes or *souvlaki*.

🍴 **Taverna Kosmiki** – *Kastráki, main street.* Lovely terrace with views of the Meteora; vegetable specialities.

🍴 **Panellínion** – *Kalambáka, Platía Dimarheíou.* Great for a drink or good, plain Greek food.

🎭 EVENTS AND FESTIVALS

Traditional folk dances are held in **Kalambáka** and **Kastráki** on Easter Sunday. In May, dances and sporting events take place in **Tríkala**.

🛒 SHOPPING

Korákis Bros, *Kalambáka, Platía R. Feréou.* An Ali Baba's cave with wood and copper crafts, plus icons and jewellery.

Mount Pelion★

Óros Pílio – Όρος Πήλιο

Mount Pelion forms a promontory jutting out into the sea. Its western side forms a tranquil coastline along Vólos Bay (Pagassitikós Kólpos) and to the east its cliffs plunge into the Aegean Sea. In summer the area is a pleasant respite from the heat, and popular with the people of Vólos and Athens as a holiday destination. In winter, its snowbound slopes attract many skiers.

A BIT OF HISTORY

The schist mountain range culminates in **Mount Pelion** at 1,551m/5,089ft, extends north towards Mount Óssa (1,978m/6,488ft) and also south, curving west to form the Magnissía Peninsula. Mediterranean plants thrive on the lower slopes and mountain plants at altitude. The famous Vólos olive is grown here, along with citrus and other fruit and various types of nuts. Higher up there are forests of beech, oak and chestnut.

Villages here in this quiet corner of Greece are full of charm. Most feature a shaded central square **(platía)** and traditional-style houses. The local churches diverge from the usual Orthodox style, being instead rectangular, wide and low, and with detached bell-towers.

VÓLOS

Vólos stands at the head of a vast bay. According to legend, this was the port from which **Jason and the Argonauts** set sail in search of the Golden Fleece. Earthquakes are frequent here and the rebuilt city is laid out on a grid pattern, quite modern in appearance. Vólos is an important industrial city and port, transporting goods by ship to the Middle East.

The **Archaeological Museum**★★ *(Odós Athanassaki; ○open Tue–Sun 8am–8pm, Mon 1.30–8pm; ⊚€2; ℘24210 252 85)* displays 300 painted or sculpted Hellenistic funerary *stelae*, Neolithic objects, Mycenaean vases and jewellery, and Hellenistic and Roman ceramics.

- **Michelin Map:** 737 H 6 – Magnissía – Thessaly.
- **Info:** Vólos, corner of Odós Lambraki and Sekeri. ℘24210 309 30/30940. www.travel-pelion.gr. Open daily 8am–10pm (summer), Mon–Fri 8am–8pm, Sat–Sun 8am–3.30pm (winter).
- **Location:** Vólos is 62km/39mi southwest of Lárissa and its airport, 216km/135mi south of Thessaloniki and 325km/203mi north of Athens. Train service to Athens and Thessaloniki; ferry links to Skiathos, Skopelos, Alonissos.
- **Don't Miss:** The beaches and the traditional mountain villages; Vólos Archaeological Museum.
- **Timing:** Plan a three-day visit by car; be ready for the narrow, twisting roads.
- **Kids:** Beaches with organised activities.
- **Also See:** Lárisa, Óros Ólimbos, The Sporades.

🚗 DRIVING TOUR

162km/101mi. From Vólos take Odós Venizélou towards Portariá (east).

This tour around the Pelion Peninsula combines some of the traditional villages with great views.

Anakassiá

🅿 *Park the car next to the church and walk to Odós Moussíou Theóphilou.*

The **Theophilos Museum** *(○open Mon–Fri 8am–2.30pm; ℘24210 473 40)* occupies the House of Kondós, a beautiful building decorated with frescoes by the great primitive painter, **Theophilos** (1873–1934), who spent part of his life in Vólos.

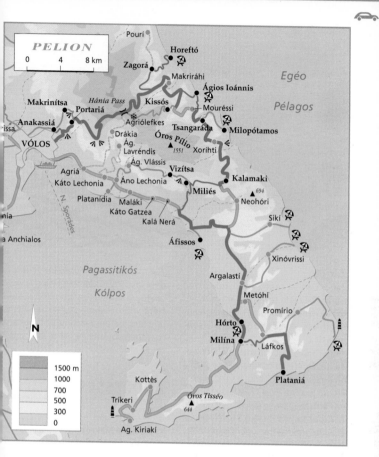

The road continues to climb towards Portariá with a view over Vólos Bay; it passes close to **Episkopí**, a hill crowned with a historic church.

Portariá★

This pleasant resort provides a cool spot in summer and the view extends up to Makrinítsa and down over Vólos Bay.

▷ *From Portariá take the road (panoramic view) to Makrinítsa (3km/2mi).*

Makrinítsa★★

Makrinítsa occupies a magnificent **site**★★ on a verdant slope facing Vólos Bay; it is pleasant to stroll through the steep and narrow streets.
The main **square**★★ *(platía)* is especially attractive with its fountain and

tiny church (18C); beautiful icons inside. Higher up is the former convent, now the **Church of the Virgin** (18C).

▷ *Return to Portariá and continue to climb.*

Marvellous **views**★★★ across Vólos Bay to Mount Óthris, northwards into Thessaly and south to Euboia.

Agrioléfkes (Hánia Pass)

Winter sports resort, set in beech and chestnut woods; there is a road from here to the summit of Mount Pelion.
The road descends towards the Aegean through beech and chestnut woods before reaching the level of the orchards. 13km/8mi from the pass bear left to Zagorá.

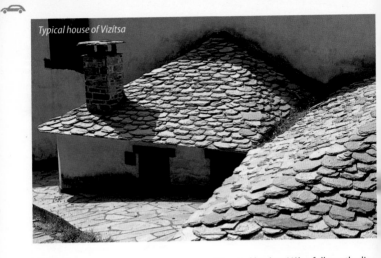

Typical house of Vizítsa

Zagorá

Zagorá was a centre for hand-woven cloth. The main **square** is at the top of the town near St George's Church (Ágios Geórgios); carved and gilded 18C **iconostasis**★.

From Zagorá a side road plunges downhill to Horeftó, a fishing village with a long beach of fine sand.

Return towards Hánia Pass; take the narrow but picturesque road to Tsangaráda. At **Ágios Ioánis** there is a lovely beach of white sand at the foot of green hills.

Tsangaráda

The peaceful resort village boasts one of the oldest and largest plane trees (15m/49ft circumference) in Greece. Nearby is **Milopótamos**, which has two beaches.

Beyond Xoríhti a splendid sea **view**★★ extends to Skiathos and Skopelos.

▷ *At the next junction, where the road continues south to Argalastí and Plataniá (36km/22mi – beautiful sheltered beach), bear right uphill to Miliés.*

Miliés

This attractive village possesses a history **library** containing some 3 000 rare volumes (⊙*open Tue–Sat 8am–2pm;* ⊙*closed public holidays;* ℘*24230 862 60*). Nearby lies **Vizítsa**★, with many typical old houses.

The road back to Vólos follows the line once taken by the famous Pelion railway. There are several beaches; stop at **Kalá Nerá**, with a seafront promenade. At the junction, before reaching Kalá Nerá, a road *(left)* branches off to the small resort of Áfissos.

ADDRESSES

🏠 STAY

🍽 **Domátia Makrópoulo** – *Makrinítsa, above the village.* ℘*24280 990 16. 8 rooms. Jun–Oct.* This small, quiet guesthouse has simple, clean rooms. Terrace overlooks the village.

🍽🍽 **Admitos** – *Vólos, 5 Odós A. Diákou.* ℘*24210 211 17. www.admitos.gr. 33 rooms.* A quiet hotel with simple, spotlessly clean rooms, balconies. Breakfast €6.

🍽🍽 **Archontikó Repaná** – *Makrinítsa, main street.* ℘*24280 990 67. 7 rooms.* 🛏 Enchanting 19C house with a magnificent view; attractive rooms furnished with antiques.

🍽🍽 **Domátia Réna** – *Áfissos, quayside.* ℘*24230 334 39. 10 rooms.* A pleasant guesthouse offering spacious studio accommodation (a little noisy) with kitchen facilities. Good value for money.

🍽🍽 **Drosseró Akrogiáli** – *Plataniá, on the harbour.* ℘*24230 712 10. 30 rooms.* A long building with comfortable rooms but no sea views. The friendly owner, who speaks only Greek, runs the restaurant of the same name.

🍽🛏 **Maistráli** – *Áfissos, near Abovos Beach*. ☏24230 334 72. *www.maistralihotel.com*. 12 rooms. Comfortable, well-presented rooms and balconies with sea views.

🛏🛏 **Parádisos** – *Tsangaráda, main street*. ☏24260 492 09/49551. *www.paradisoshotel.gr*. 29 rooms. A comfortable, welcoming hotel; the rooms overlooking the street have good views but are a little noisier. The hotel also organises horse treks.

🛏🛏🛏 **Aegli Pallas** – *Vólos, 24–26 Odós Argonaftón*. ☏24210 24 471. *www.aegli.gr*. 87 rooms. 🖳 Recently renovated Neoclassical hotel style has pleasant rooms with views of the port.

🍽/EAT
VOLOS
Seafood restaurants abound on the quayside; cafés are grouped at the eastern end of Odós Dimitriados, along the waterfront esplanade.

ON THE MOUNTAIN
🍽 **Taverna Apaulosi** – *Makrinítsa, main street*. ☏24280 900 85. Roast meats, chicken and *spetsofáy* (sausages): all the local delicacies are served here. Get a table on the terrace: the view is superb.

🍽 **To Balconi** – *Kalamaki, entrance on the main square*. Excellent cuisine, and magnificent view from the terrace; a great place to eat.

🍽 **Kira Marías** – *Miliés, church square*. Simple cuisine (cheese tarts, salads) served in the shade of a plane tree.

🍽 **Café Óasis** – *Áfissos, near the square on the seafront*. The ideal spot for breakfast or an evening drink. Also has bicycles for hire.

🍽 **To Panórama** – *Miliés, opposite the museum*. Specialities here include chicken, pork in wine and spinach tart.

🍽 **Panthéon** – *Makrinítsa, village square*. ☏24280 99 143. Another place to try *spetsofáy* and bean soup. Lovely view.

🏃SPORTS AND LEISURE
Les Hirondelles – *Vólos, Odós Koumoundourou*. ☏24210 321 71. *Also in Agios Ioánnis (*☏24260 311 81, *Fax 24260 311 80) www.holidays-in-pelion.gr*. In addition to standard rentals, this agency organises a range of activities (walking, four-wheel drive treks, riding, diving and kayaking), and rents out caiques to allow visitors access to the more isolated beaches.

Arta★
Árta – Άρτα

A small town situated on a bend in the River Árahthos and dominated by a 13C citadel built on much earlier foundations, Árta was the former capital of the Despotate of Epiros; it has some fine examples of Byzantine architecture.

SIGHTS
Panagía Parigorítissa★★
Near Skoufá Square. ⊙*Open Tue–Sun 8.30am–3pm.* ⊛€2.
The great Church of the Virgin Comforter (13C), with its six domes, was inspired by the churches of Constantinople. The interior is surrounded by galleries for women *(gynaecea)*. The central dome is raised on three stages of projecting columns and the base is supported on

▶ **Population:** 23,863.
⛪ **Michelin Map:**
737 D 6 – Epiros.
▷ **Location:** Árta lies in the south of Epiros, 77km/48mi south of Ioánnina, 97km/61mi northeast of Préveza.
🅿 **Parking:** Finding space for a vehicle should not be a problem.
🏛 **Don't Miss:**
The photogenic bridge and the church are the main places of interest.
🕐 **Timing:** An hour will be sufficient time.
⛪ **Also See:** The site of ancient Dodoni★★ (Dodona) 🕐see Ioánnina.

17C bridge over the Árahthos

squinches of an unusual type, seen elsewhere only at St Theodore's Church in Mistrás. The oldest of the wall paintings dates from 1558, while later paintings were made in the 17C and 18C. There is an archaeological museum in the neighbouring building.

Bridge★

The 17C humpbacked bridge over the Árahthos on the edge of Árta (Ioánnina road) is celebrated for its elegant curve and its wide arches alternating with smaller ones, which ease the flow of water when the river is in spate.

Agía Theodóra★

Off the main street heading towards the citadel. ⏰*Open 7am–1pm; 5–8pm.*
The church houses the tomb of Theodora, wife of the despot Michel II and now the town's patron saint. Theodora was responsible in the late 13C for extensive restoration work on the church, which was first built on this site c.11C–12C.

OUTSKIRTS
Monastery of Vlahérna

▶*3km/1.9mi northeast of Árta.*
Ask for the key at the kiosk.
The monastery at Vlahérna is thought to have been first built in about the 10C, although much of what we see today was built in the 13C. There are some noteworthy frescoes inside the church,

which have unfortunately been damaged over time, although restoration work has revealed some of the ancient workmanship. Look for the murals on the floor, some dating back to the 13C.

Rogoús Fortress

▶*15km/9.5mi west of Árta, near the village of Néa Kerassoús on the Préveza road.*
Above a bend in the River Loúros stand the ruins of this ancient fortress (late 5C BC), impressive for its size and state of preservation. It has some fine polygonal stonework, although the frescoes in the little church are in poor condition.

ADDRESSES

🛏STAY

🍽🍽 **Cronos** – *Platia Kilkis.*
✆*26810 22 211, fax (26810) 73 795.*
www.hotelcronos.gr. 55 rooms.
Comfortable air-conditioned rooms; well placed for visiting Árta.
🍽🍽 **Byzantino** – *On the Préveza road, 47042 Filothei.* ✆*26810 52 205.*
www.byzadino.gr. 53 rooms.
Comfortable modern hotel with a swimming pool and tennis courts.

🛒 SHOPPING

The town is a centre for citrus-fruit farming, but there is also a craft market selling embroidery and *flokatia*.

Párga★★

Párga – Πάργα

Parga is a charming resort on a particularly attractive **site**, on the neck of a promontory flanked by two bays, screened from the open sea by rocky islets and a huge sandy beach. Its location on the Epirot Coast makes it an ideal base from which to visit sites of cultural interest, with the added benefits of beach and sea.

A BIT OF HISTORY

From the 15C to 1797 Párga belonged to the Venetians, who called it Le Gominezze, the anchorage. Much against the will of the inhabitants, in 1817 it was sold by the British to Ali Pasha (*see IOÁN-NINA*) and did not return to the Greeks until 1913.

The **Venetian fortress** (now in ruins but still impressive) was built late in the 16C. It stood on a now-overgrown rocky peninsula that offers **views**★★ of Párga, the bays and the islands.

 DRIVING TOUR

THE IONIAN COAST

108km/68mi from Párga to Vonitsa. At Párga join the E 55 heading south.

Ephyra Sanctuary★

Near the village of **Messopótamo**.
Open daily, 8.30am–3pm. €2.
26840 412 06.

Also known as the Nekromanteion of Acheron, here stood a sanctuary dedicated to the Oracle of the Dead (Nekromanteion) on the banks of the River Ahérondas (Acheron). The estuary was eventually filled and drained to form the fertile Fanári Plain. In antiquity the **Acheron** (Ahérondas) emerged from a wild ravine to form a mysterious lagoon, Lake Acheroussia, thought to lead to the mythological underworld realm of **Hades**, King of the Dead.

- ▶ **Population:** 4,000.
- **Michelin Map:** 737 C 6 – Préveza – Epiros.
- **Info:** There is no official tourist office but the town's website is a useful source of information: www.parga.gr.
- **Location:** 141km/88mi southwest of Ioánnina and 78km/49mi northwest of Árta.
- **Parking:** It is usually possible to find parking spaces.
- **Don't Miss:** Strolling in the village streets; a tour of the Ionian Coast.
- **Timing:** Plan two to three days here.
- **Kids:** The sandy beach.

Sanctuary★

A chapel on a hill near the site of the former Lake Acheroussia marks the position of the **Nekromanteion**, a sanctuary dedicated to Hades and his wife Persephone, where seekers came to consult the spirits of the dead.

The sanctuary existed in the Mycenaean period, but the traces of the building are Hellenistic (3C BC). A series of corridors led to the sanctuary, a huge chamber where priests wreathed in sulphurous vapours pronounced the oracle to the pilgrims, who had previously taken hallucinogenic drugs. The oracle was located in a crypt beneath the central chamber, which was thought to communicate with the abode of Hades.

Items found during the excavations are on display in the museum in Ioánnina.

▷ *Continue south along the coast road.*

A turning to the left climbs the lower slopes of **Mount Zálongo** and offers glimpses of the colossal sculpted effigies of the "Souliot Women". After about 6km/4mi a path, on a bend to the left, leads to the ruins of Kassópi.

Souliot Country

The Acheron river flows through a desolate mountainous region where, in the 15C, Christians took refuge from the Turks. Albanian in origin, these **Souliots** (named after their major settlement), were brave and indomitable. Protected by the inaccessibility of their mountain fortresses, they maintained their autonomy until 1803. Today only a few hundred people of Souliot origin remain.

Kassópi★

Open daily 8.30am–3pm. € 3. No phone. Founded in the 4C BC and later destroyed by the Romans, Kassópi stood on the slopes of Mount Zálongo on a terrace which offers extensive **views**★ south to Leukas and east over the Ambracian Gulf. Excavations have uncovered the agora and the remains of a portico, an odeon and the *prytaneion*, where the city magistrates met.

▷ *Continue north from Kassópi for 4km/2.5mi.*

Zálongo Monastery

In 1803 the **Souliots** (villagers from Souli) fleeing the troops of Ali Pasha hid in this monastery. To escape capture by the Turks, 63 women climbed the bluff above the convent, performed their national dance, and then threw themselves and their children over the precipice. The impressive cement figures recalling the event was sculpted by Zongolopoulos in 1954.

The song which the Souliotises sang in their final, fatal dance was based on a poem by the Greek national poet Dionysios Solomos (who also wrote what became the Greek national anthem):

> *Farewell miserable world,*
> *Farewell oh sweet life,*
> *And as for you ill-fated home*
> *Farewell for ever...*

A painting by Ary Scheffer (1795–1858), now in the Louvre, depicts the scene that led to the Dance of Zálongo.

▷ *Rejoin the E 55 and continue south.*

Ruins of Nikopolis★ (Nikópoli)

The Ioánnina road crosses the site.
🕐*Open daily 8.30am–3pm. €3.*
📞*26820 413 36.*

Nikopolis was an important Roman and Byzantine city founded in 31 BC by Octavian Augustus to commemorate his victory over Mark Antony and Cleopatra at the Battle of Actium.

St Paul is said to have visited the city in AD 64 and it developed into an active centre of Christianity. The city was largely destroyed in the 4C AD but rebuilt only to be finally destroyed by Bulgarians in the 11C.

Ruins of Nikopolis

The **city** consists of a ruined external wall dating from the time of Augustus and a huge internal Byzantine wall (6C). The main features are the museum (same hours as site, included in admission) (lion, Roman portraits), the remains of Doumetios' basilica (5C, mosaics) and Augustus' *odeon (restored)*, which from the top gives a good overview of the ruined site.

There are impressive traces of the 6C **Basilica of Alkyson** *(on the right of the road going towards the theatre)*: atrium, narthex, nave and four aisles, and mosaics. The **theatre** dates from 1C BC; note the stage and the rows of seats.

On a hill to the north of the theatre, beyond the village of **Smirtoúla**, are the remains of a monument commemorating the victory of Actium.

Préveza

Founded in the 3C BC by Pyrrhus, King of Epiros, Préveza guards the entrance to the **Ambracian Gulf** (Ambrakikós Kólpos) opposite Cape Áktio (Akteion) where a famous naval engagement, the **Battle of Actium**, took place in 31 BC. Octavian, the future Emperor Augustus, routed the fleet of his rival Antony, who was accompanied by Cleopatra, Queen of Egypt. The town is now a port and pleasant seaside resort.

Continue southeast by the ferry and the Gulf Coast road.

Vónitsa

From Cape Akteion the road leads to Vónitsa. This little old town was once defended by a 17C Venetian **fortress** and from here are glimpses of the coast and the Ambracian Gulf.

ADDRESSES

⌂ STAY

⌾ **Avra** – *Préveza, 9 Odós El. Venizélou.* ☎ *26820 212 30. www.hotelavra.net. 28 rooms.* A comfortable three-storey hotel opposite the landing stage for ferries to Áktio. Most rooms have beautiful views over the Bay of Árta. Breakfast €5.

⌾ **Minos** – *Préveza, 11 Odós 28 Oktovriou.* ☎ *26820 284 24. katda@otenet.gr. 23 rooms.* Simple, clean rooms with small balconies; a good value hotel. Breakfast €6.

⌾⌾ **Paradise** – *Párga, Odós Spírou Livadá.* ☎ *26840 31 229. www.paradise-palatino.com. 16 rooms.* An attractive two-storey hotel which has its own pool, sauna and Turkish bath.

⌾⌾⌾ **Achilleas** – *Párga, at the end of Krionéri Beach.* ☎ *26840 316 00. www.hotelachilleas.gr. 33 rooms. May–Oct.* Comfortable rooms set around an inner courtyard. The hotel has direct access onto Paleó Krionéri Bay and a pleasant bar at the top of the promontory.

⌾⌾⌾ **Acropol** – *Párga 4 Platia Agios Apostolon.* ☎ *26840 318 33. www.acropol.biz. 10 rooms.* The oldest hotel in town, opened in 1884, but today has jacuzzis in every room. Breakfast €5.

⌾⌾⌾ **San Nectarios** – *Párga, 2 Odós Marinas.* ☎ *26840 31 150. www.san-nectarios.gr. 20 rooms and one suite.* A two-storey hotel with simple, decent rooms; excellent value.

☕/ EAT

⌾ **Ambrosios** – *Préveza, Odós Grigoriou, at right angles to the quayside.* This popular taverna, one of the oldest in Préveza, serves good plain food. Try the fish in white wine, under the shade of the trellis: a moment of pure harmony.

⌾ **Castello** – *Párga, in the Hotel Acropol, May–Oct.* A very popular restaurant serving Greek, Italian and French cuisine. Good wine list.

⌾ **Dyonisos** – *Párga, on the quayside.* Unpretentious taverna serving delicious fresh fish; superb views.

⁂ SPORTS AND LEISURE

Shuttles offer service to the **beaches** at Sarakiniko and Lichnos; there are also boat excursions to the islands of **Paxos** and **Antipaxos**. You can also take a boat trip to the cave of Aphrodite.

Ioánnina★

Ioánnina – Ιωάννινα

Standing on the shore of Lake Pamvotis, the capital of Epiros is a dynamic modern city with a fascinating history. Ioánnina serves as a convenient base from which to explore the Pérama Cave, the site of Ancient Dodona, and a little farther away, the mountain village of Metsovo to the east and the extraordinary Zagória district to the north.

A BIT OF HISTORY

"The Lion of Ioánnina" – In the 15C, Ioánnina came under Turkish control. The city rose to prominence in the late 18C under the rule of **Ali Pasha**, who was appointed by the Turkish Sultan in 1788. An adroit political manoeuvrer, Ali formed alliances with Greek partisans and European nations, playing all sides against each other in an effort to become independent of the Sultan. For more than 30 years he exercised almost sovereign power over western Greece and Albania. Despite his reputation for cruelty, Ali Pasha exercised tolerance toward Christians, and Ioánnina developed into an important centre for Greek culture. Alarmed at his power, the Sultan in 1820 besieged the citadel of Ioánnina for 15 months. Ali Pasha was eventually killed by the Turks in 1822;

▶ **Population:** 70,203.
⚅ **Michelin Map:** 737 D 5 – Ioánnina – Epiros.
🔲 **Info:** 39 Odós Dodónis, ℘26510 41868. Open Mon–Sat, 9am–1pm, and 5.30–8.30pm in summer.
▷ **Location:** Three major roads provide access to the city: the E 92, E 90 and E 951.
🅿 **Parking:** There is a car park near the lake.
◈ **Don't Miss:** A trip to the site of ancient Dodóna.
🕐 **Timing:** At least one day is needed, and more if the area is to be explored in depth.
👥 **Kids:** The cave will appeal to children, as will a boat ride across the lake.
⚅ **Also See:** Meteora, Párga.

his head was put on display in Ioánnina and then sent as a trophy to the Sultan.

FROÚRIO★★

The huge fortress dominating the lake was originally constructed in the 11C but was restored in the early 19C during the reign of Ali Pasha, whose palace stood atop the rock.

Byzantine Museum and the mosque

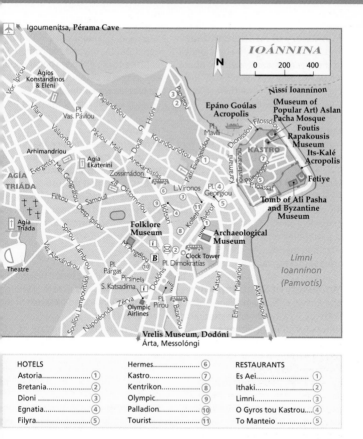

IOÁNNINA

N   0   200   400

Ágios Konstandínos & Eléni

Vor. Ipírou

Vílara

Valáontos

Arhimandríou

Evergetón

Mel. Georgíou

Pl. Vas. Pávlou

Papandréou

Pl. Hróni

Paléológou

Palaiou Melá

Agía Ekateríni

Zossimádon

28 Oktomvríou

Doúli

Koundouriótou

Anexartissías

Botsári

Patr. Evangelídou

Epáno Goúlas Acropolis

Pl. Mavíli

Dionisíou

Filosófou

Kalarí

Tousistnaríou

Karamanlí

Paleológou

Nissí Ioannínon (Museum of Popular Art) Aslan Pacha Mosque

Foutis Rapakousis Museum

Its-Kalé Acropolis

KASTRO

Fetiye

Tomb of Ali Pasha and Byzantine Museum

AGÍA TRIÁDA

Filítou

Spírou Lámbrou

Desp. Ipírou

Samouíl

L.Víronos

Pl. (4) Georgíou

Anéxor

Kólletí

Agía Triáda

Vas. Alexándrou

Soúli ou Lampovítidi

Napoleónda

Theatre

Pl. Párgas

Pirsinéla

S. Katsadíma

Zérva

M.Angelou

Dodónis

Pl. Pírou

Bizaníou

Olympic Airlines

Folklore Museum

Clock Tower

Pl. Dimokratías

Archaeological Museum

Katsarí

Ethn. Makaríou

Akti Miaoúli

Límni Ioannínon (Pamvotís)

Vrelis Museum, Dodóni
Árta, Messolóngi

HOTELS		Hermes	⑥	RESTAURANTS	
Astoria	①	Kastro	⑦	Es Aei	①
Bretania	②	Kentrikon	⑧	Ithaki	②
Dioni	③	Olympic	⑨	Limni	③
Egnatia	④	Palladion	⑩	O Gyros tou Kastrou	④
Filyra	⑤	Tourist	⑪	To Manteio	⑤

The northern end of the fortress, **Aslán Dzamí**★, includes the attractive Aslan Aga Mosque (1619) with its slim, pointed minaret. The building has been converted into a **municipal museum** displaying items illustrating the history of the town. The embroidered costumes and archaeological finds are remarkable. ◷*Open daily, 8am–8pm (summer), Mon–Fri 8am–3pm and Sat–Sun 9am–3pm (winter).* ☎*26510 263 56.* ∞€4.

From the terrace there are very fine **views**★★ of the lake and mountains. Below the mosque stands the former Turkish library roofed with several little domes; farther west is the **Old Synagogue**, a reminder that in the 19C there were nearly 6,000 Jews in Ioánnina. In the **Inner Citadel** there is another mosque, the Fetiye; in front of it is the tomb of Ali Pasha. To the right is the former *seraglio*, now home to the **Byzantine Museum** (◷*open daily 9am–3pm;*

∞€4), with early Christian and Byzantine sculpture, pottery, manuscripts, post-Byzantine icons and silverware.

IOÁNNINA LAKE★★ (LAKE PAMVOTIS)

◷*Boats to the island (10min) depart from Mavili Square every 30min 6.30am–11pm in summer, hourly 7am–10pm in winter.*

Still known as Lake Pamvótis, Ioánnina Lake has a remarkable island (**Nisi Ioannínon**★★), home to five Byzantine monasteries and a fishing village.

The lake collects the waters flowing down from Mount Mitsikéli to the north, and its level varies according to the seasons and the outflow of the swallowholes *(katavóthres)* worn through the soft limestone round the shore.

On disembarking, walk through the village to enjoy the houses, and in fact you can walk all the way around the island.

Monastery of Pandeleímonas

This 16C foundation is the best known of the island's monasteries: the house where Ali Pasha was killed by the Turks (now a museum) is located here (⏰*open daily, hours vary;* ⮾*€2*).

Beyond is the **Monastery of St John the Baptist** (Ágios Ioánnis Pródromos) with its 16C church and a cave that was once home to hermits.

Monastery of the Philanthropiní

Also known as Nikólaos Spanós, this monastery on the other side of the village was built on a hill in the 13C, but altered in the 16C. The church is decorated with remarkable 17C **frescoes**★.

Monastery of Stratigópoulos

Also known as Nikólaos Dílios, it dates from the 11C; the church is decorated with beautiful 16C **frescoes**★.

OUTSKIRTS

Pérama Cave★★★

▶*6km/3.75mi to the north.* ⏰*Open daily, 8am–8pm, 9am–5pm in winter.* ⮾*€6. Guided tours every 15min (45min) along a route of 800m/.5mi.*

This remarkable cave extends for about 1km/0.5mi and covers an area of 14,800sq km/5,714sq mi. Most of the caverns are lit to enhance the splendid colored limestone formations which include stalagmites and stalactites, excentrics, curtains, low walls and pools. The bones and teeth of cave bears have been discovered here. From the exit, superb **views**★★ extend over Ioánnina. From the cave, drive east along the road to Métsovo to see lovely **views**★★ down over the valley, the lake and the town of Ioánnina.

Dodóni★★ (Dodona)

▶*21km/13mi south. From Ioánnina take the road to Árta (E 951), after 8km/5mi turn right.* ⏰*Open every day, 8am–8pm, Mon–Sat 10am–3pm in winter.* ⮾*€3.* ✆*26510 822 87.*

Situated in a high, fertile valley, ancient Dodona grew out of a sanctuary initially dedicated to the goddess Dione, and later Zeus. A famous oracle flourished here from the second millennium BC until the 4C BC. Although not as important as that at Delphi, the Dodona oracle was renowned throughout Greece. Croesos and Alexander the Great both consulted it, and it was referred to in the *Odyssey*.

In response to an enquiry, the oracle's answer was conveyed in the rustling of nearby oak leaves and it was the task of priests to interpret the rustlings.

Along the road to the site, magnificent **views**★★ extend back over the Ioánnina basin; to the southwest Mount Tómaros rises to 1,974m/6,476ft.

Ruins

Part of the walls still exists. Beyond the entrance lie the remains of the **stadium** (late 3C BC) indicated by traces of the terraces of seats.

First constructed in the late 3C BC, the **theatre**★★ is one of the largest and best preserved of Ancient Greece. Under the Romans it was transformed into an arena for gladiatorial and animal combats.

Beyond the theatre are the foundation of an **assembly hall** (bouleuterion) and a little Temple to Aphrodite. Next come the remains of the Sanctuary to Zeus Naios which included the precinct of the oracle. Finally, look for traces of a Byzantine-period **basilica**.

Métsovo★★

▶*53km/33mi east of Ioánnina on the E 92.*

Métsovo is admirably situated in a mountain combe just below the highest road pass in Greece (Katára, altitude 1,705m/5,594ft), which marks the border between Epiros and Thessaly. In summer the little resort town offers bracing walks in the forest; sport opportunities abound in winter.

Architecture and tradition are a large part of Métsovo's charm. It's common to see old women in traditional costume and peasants riding mules. Métsovo cuisine is celebrated for its cheese, trout and wine. In the village centre there is a vast open space shaded by huge plane trees; nearby is the Church of **Agía Paraskeví**, which contains a flamboyant 18C **iconostasis**★.

▶ *Follow the main street and turn left into a narrow street near the petrol pump.*

This leads to the **Tosítsa Foundation Museum of Folk Art**★, housed in the Tosítsa family residence in the heart of the old quarter.

Note the carved woodwork interior; the rooms are furnished with fine carpets and embroidered textiles and decorated with gold ornaments, beaten copperwork and icons. The huge reception room is particularly impressive with its divans and its monumental samovar. ○*Open Fri–Wed 8.30am–1.30pm and 4–6pm in summer, 8.30am–1pm and 3–5pm in winter.* ●*Guided tour, 30min (door locked during tour).* ●€3. ☏026560 410 84.

▶ *Return to the main square and take the path on the right of the Bank of Greece.*

The **Avéroff Gallery** has an interesting collection of 19C and 20C Greek paintings (○*open Wed–Mon 10am–4pm and 10am–6.30pm 15 Jul–15 Sept.* ●€3. www.averoffmuseum.gr).

Ágios Nikólaos★

▶ *45min excursion from Métsovo.*

The restored Monastery of St Nicholas features a nice display of icons in the narthex. In the church, note the 16C–17C frescoes and the iconostasis. The conventual buildings contain the monks' cells and the school.

🚗 DRIVING TOUR

THE ZAGÓRIA★★

80km/49mi there and back. Allow one day.

The Zagorian region north of Ioánnina is a scenic and remote part of Greece, filled with small but characterful villages.

▶ *From Ioánnina take the road to the airport which follows a valley dominated to the east by Mount Mitsikéli. Turn right at Asfaka into a narrow tarred road, which climbs towards Vítsa.*

In the heart of a mountainous region including the Timfi massif (2,497m/8,190ft) and a small section of the northern Pindos, the Zagória seems to occupy something of a time warp. The natural habitat is undisturbed; the traditional architecture (greystone houses with projecting upper storeys, churches with painted interiors, old "Turkish bridges") survives, and residents adhere to a traditional way of life.

Part of the region falls within the Vikos-Aoos National Park, an area of forests and pasture where bears and wolves still roam. At this elevation, winter snowfall is heavy and frequent.

In these wild mountains, Greek troops defied the advancing Italian forces when they invaded from Albania in November 1940.

▶ *Before reaching Vítsa, 10km/6.25mi after turning off the main road, take the narrow tarred road to the right.*

The route leads to a very unusual **bridge** (*géfira*) with three arches (1814) downstream from Kípi, the administrative centre of the Zagória country.

▶ *Return to the Vítsa road.*

Vítsa★

The town is built on a picturesque site; most of the houses are in the traditional style. Excavations have discovered evidence of a settlement here from the 9C BC to the 4C AD.

▶ *Take the minor mountain road to Monodéndri, 3km/5mi away.*

Monodéndri★

This is a picturesque village of stone houses with shingle roofs and a fine

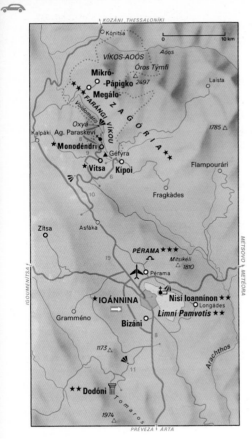

There is another magnificent **view**★★★ of the gorge from the hamlet of **Osía**, which can be reached by a narrow forest road *(7.3km/4.5mi)* from Monodéndri.

🚶 Víkos Gorge (listed as the deepest gorge in the world relative to its width by the Guinness Book of Records) is well known to hikers because of the interconnecting footpaths that link the villages tucked into the folds of mountains.

Monodéndri is a good place from which to start off on one of the trails. Cool winds blowing through the gorge make it a popular route for hikers in the summer months when the rest of Greece is baking in the sun.

For a short taste of the walking opportunities, follow the path near the square in Monodéndri that leads down to the bottom of the gorge (45min) and to the village of Víkou, which is a five-hour walk in the shadow of the cliffs.

○ *Head towards Kónitsa, take the Kalpaki road and after several miles turn right in the direction of Aristi.*

Megalo Papigko and Mikro Papigko

These are two beautiful and undiscovered villages which deserve a visit. **Megalo Papigko** has retained its character, tranquility and historic buildings. **Mikro Papigko**, a little further on, has an attractive church and produces good wine. Take a stroll through its streets; there are many pleasant walks in the vicinity. There are places to stay, should you be tempted into spending another day here, as well as rustic tavernas serving up traditional Greek food and drinks. *For more information, see www.papigo.gr.*

church with an external gallery typical of the Zagória region.

🚶 Take the narrow road (600m/1,970ft long) on the far side of the village, which leads to the Monastery of Agía Paraskeví and, on the way back to Monodéndri, the Víkos Gorge. *Allow a day if returning via Víkos.*

Farángi (or Harádra) Víkou★★★ (Víkos Gorge)

The greystone buildings of the Monastery of Agía Paraskeví cling to the rocks directly above a precipitous drop into the Voldomátis River gorge 1,000m/3,281ft below.

From the monastery, a path winds down the face of the cliff past terraces and caves that sheltered *klephts* and hermits. It reaches a platform overlooking the confluence of the Voidomátis and a neighbouring mountain stream.

ADDRESSES

🛏 STAY

🛏 **Hotel Tourist** – Ioánnina, Odós Kolleti 18. ☏26510 264 43. www.hotel tourist.gr. 29 rooms. Clean, bright rooms near the citadel; excellent value. No breakfast.

🛏🛏 **Philyra** – Odós Paleologou 18, in the citadel. ☏26510 835 60. http://hotel filyra.gr. 4 rooms. Renovated stone building; spacious, comfortable studios.

🛏🛏 **Astoria** – Ioánnina, Odós Paraskevopoúlou 2. ☏26510 207 55, Fax (26510) 784 10. http://hotelastoria.gr. 16 rooms. Renovated, comfortable rooms.

🛏🛏 **Palladion** – Ioánnina, 1 Odós Nóti Bótsari. ☏26510 258 56. www.palladion hotel.gr. 128 rooms. High standards of comfort and English-speaking management. The view of the lake from the upper floors is stunning. Prices negotiable out of season; good value.

🛏🛏 **Kastro** – Ioánnina, Odós Paleológou 57. ☏/Fax 26510 228 66. ritzan@otenet.gr. 7 rooms. In an old house, a charming hotel. Comfortable rooms.

🛏🛏🛏🛏 **Olympic** – Odós Melanidis 2. ☏26510 222 33. www.hotelolymp.gr. 54 rooms. Luxury hotel with charming rooms; lake views from the top floor.

🛏 **Egnatia** – Main street, Metsovo. ☏26560 412 63. www.hotel-egnatia.gr. 32 rooms. An attractive reception area and clean, comfortable rooms. The owner is an avid hiker and offers advice on treks.

🛏🛏 **Koukouli Guesthouse** – Koukouli, main square. ☏26530 710 70. 10 rooms. Pretty *pensione* in 3 traditional houses. Comfortable rooms, warm welcome, advice on area hikes.

🛏 **Monodendri Hotel** – Monodendri. ☏26530 71 300. www.monodendri hotel.com. 8 rooms. A magnificent 17C property with a fine restaurant. Plenty of charm, but not all bathrooms are en suite.

🛏🛏 **Nikos Tsoumanis** – Megalo Papingo. ☏226530 418 93. 6 rooms. Spacious rooms attached to the owner's excellent restaurant, some with kitchenettes; bikes available.

🛏🛏🛏🛏 **Hotel du Lac and Congress Centre** – Ioánnina, Leofóros Andréa Miaoúli. ☏26510 59100, Fax 26510 59200. 139 rooms. This lakeside hotel and conference center has all the latest amenities and two restaurants, but is a short walk from the centre of the town.

🍽 EAT

🍽🍽 **To Koumanio** – Ioánnina, Platía Georgíou. Simple, quality Greek cuisine such as grills and spit roasts.

🍽 **To Mánteio Psistariá** – Ioánnina, Platía Georgíou. Similar style and menu to the previous entry, but a bit livelier.

🍽 **Límni** – Odós Papágou. The last restaurant but one in this row; delicious *bekrí mezé* (beef in tomato sauce).

🍽🍽 **Es Aei** – Ioánnina, Odós Koundouriótou 50. ☏26510 345 71. In an old mansion, this restaurant is known for refined, creative cooking (try the signature *"Es Aei"*, a tasty plate of cheeses and kebabs).

🍽 **Gastra** – Kostáki 16a, Eleoúsa. ☏26510 61530, Fax 26510 61797. www.gastra.gr. Well worth making the drive towards the airport to dine at this exceptional restaurant which specialises in cooking in gastra, the local clay pots.

🛒 SHOPPING

Market – Odós Papafilou, mornings except Sun.

Antiques – Ioánnis Kariofilis – Odós Paleológou, in the citadel. ☏26510 36 047. Antique jewellery.

Crafts – Métsovo, main square and streets. Boutiques with wooden items, traditional fabrics.

🚋 TAKING A BREAK

Walking – Robinson Expeditions – Kípi, Ioánnina. ☏26530 71041, www.robinson.gr. This agency specialises in adventure tours in Zagória (hiking, mountain biking, climbing, canyoning).

WWF Centre – ☏26530 410 71, www.papigo.gr. 10am–5.30pm, Fri–Sat, 11am–6pm, closed Wed. Information on the flora and fauna of the region, and on the Voidomatis Coast, the cleanest stretch of coastline in Europe.

MACEDONIA *Makedonía – Μακεδονία*

Strictly speaking, Macedonia is a geographical region mostly spanning the countries of Greece, Bulgaria and FYROM (also confusingly called Macedonia). When it was part of the Roman, Byzantine or Ottoman Empires, its geography coincided with the political and administrative authority; it was only in the 20C with the collapse of the Ottoman Empire that the area and its people were divided.

Highlights

1 A hike or at least a drive around **Mount Olympus** (p204)

2 A stroll in the old centre and the promenade of **Thessaloníki** (p207)

3 A day in **Kastoriá** and its lake (p215)

4 The incredible riches of **Vergína** (p219)

5 An archaeological visit in **Philippi** (p230)

A Bit of History

Ancient Macedonians spoke Greek, were admitted in the Olympic games (where "barbarians" were banned) and were part of Greek creation myths: **Macedon** was the son of **Zeus** and **Thya**, daughter of **Deucalion** and sister to **Helen**, ancestor of Greeks.

In the 6C AD, Slavs and then Bulgarians started settling in, resulting in a mixture of ethnicities, with only the Orthodox religion as a unifying force. It is for good reason that a fruit or vegetable salad is called "Macedonia" in Italian and French. In 1904–08 a "dirty" war

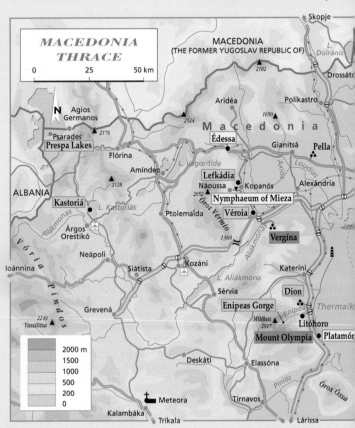

between Bulgaria and Greece took place in the still-Ottoman province when each party used commando forces to compel Christian villages to submit either to the Greek Patriarchate or the newly formed Bulgarian Exarchate. Soon after, Macedonia was carved on a conquer-keep basis between Greece, Bulgaria and Serbia during the Balkan Wars of 1912–13. Greece won the lion's share, its current province of Macedonia.

Although the Serbian part of Macedonia was considered Bulgarian by its Balkan neighbours, it nevertheless acquired a separate national consciousness under President Tito in post-Second World War Yugoslavia. In the 1990s it became a separate republic called the Former Yugoslav Republic of Macedonia (**FYROM**) and has been arguing with Greece over the name Macedonia – and the region's heritage – ever since.

Ruins of the pillared basilica, Fílipi

© Megdanis Nikos/iStockphoto.com

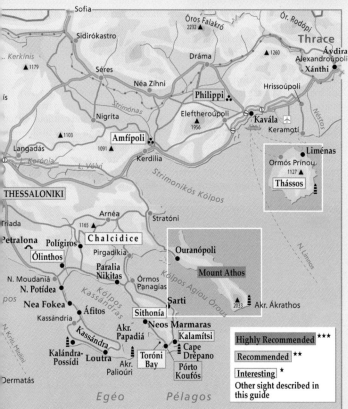

Mount Olympus★★★

Óros Ólimbos–
Όρος Όλυμπος

To the Ancient Greeks Olympus, the highest mountain in the country, was a mysterious presence, usually wreathed in clouds, the godly home of Zeus and the immortals. Today, walkers and hikers enjoy it for its earthly attributes and its remarkable views. On the northern flank of the mountain is Dion, the sacred city of Macedonian antiquity.

> ⏱ **Michelin Map:** 737 G 4 – Thessaly and Macedonia.
> ℹ **Info:** 16 Odós A. Nikolaou, in front of Hotel Mirto. ☎23520 83 100. Open 9am–9pm.
> 🅿 **Parking:** There are assorted places to park along the approaches to the mountain.
> ⊛ **Don't Miss:** Sunrise over the mountain.
> 🕐 **Timing:** Up to half a day walking Lower Olympus.
> 👪 **Kids:** A picnic after a rambling walk.

VISIT

Olympus is a huge and complex massif of crystalline schist. It is the highest mountain range in Greece, consisting of nine peaks (exceeding 2,600m/8,530ft). The southern section, Lower Olympus, is wooded and fairly easy to climb. Upper Olympus' precipices cleft by deep ravines pose more of a challenge. The first successful ascent of the mountain was only achieved in 1913.

Litóhoro is the main town on Olympus and the principal base for walking and climbing in the region.

The four major peaks form a rocky cirque including **Mítikas** or **Pantheon** (2,917m/9,580ft) and Zeus's Throne or Crown *(stepháni)* (2,909m/9,547ft). It is there that the gods – who lived in its impassable ravines – were supposed to congregate. The peaks can be viewed by car: from Litóhoro take the road to the monastery (Moní Ágios Dioníssios and continue along a track *(suitable for motor vehicles)* to the hamlet of Prióna (about 1,100m/3608ft).

THE ASCENT

Engage a guide before venturing to the summit.

🚶 Experienced walkers may park at junction before the monastery (Moní Ágios Dióníssios) and continue on foot to Petrostrounga *(3hrs)* to the right and along the bare Skoúrta Pass to the Muses Plateau (Oropédio Moussón *(5hrs)* to the refuge of the Hellenic Alpine Club of Thessaloníki (2,750m/9,022ft).

Mítikas peak, Mount Olympus

Clinging to the southern flank of the mountain, at an altitude of 300m/984ft, the large village of Litóhoro is an excellent starting point for exploring the mountains.

Before the climb, take the time to stroll among the greystone houses, from Agiou Nikolaou (main street), until the Kentrikí Platía (Central Square), the busiest spot of the village. However pretty the village though, tourism has greatly altered its authenticity.

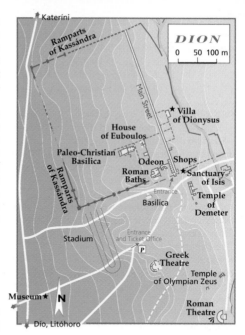

Taking on the Domain of the Gods

Two days min. ascent, with a night in a shelter.

Conducted for the first time in 1913, this climb is not particularly difficult technically, but it requires a good degree of fitness. Beware of sudden changes in weather and prepare to dress warmly. Remember to protect yourself against the sun.

From Litóhoro, several routes are possible, but that from Priona *(18km/11mi from Litóhoro by car or taxi, via a partly paved forest road)* is the one with an interesting detour. Two kilometres before the finish, a path on the left leads to the monastery of Ágios Dionysios (16C), rebuilt after its destruction by the Turks (1828), then by the Germans (1942) who suspected the presence of the Resistance.

The toughest will opt for the approach via the Enipéas Gorge, two sheer vertical walls bristling with fir trees *(4hrs walk from Litóhoro)*; the less brave can join by car at the starting point of the hike. After arriving at Priona perched at an altitude of 1,100m/3,280ft, on the edge of the National Park, you can enjoy a meal at the restaurant before beginning the ascent proper. Follow the trail to the refuge of Spilios Agapitos *(3hrs)* at 2,100m/6,890ft altitude. From there, join the Plateau of the Muses *(3hrs)*, where you will find refuge C and then that of the EOS. The last part of the climb to the summit is more challenging, as the terrain becomes steeper and rocky. But you will be richly rewarded for your efforts by the terrific panorama at the top.

DION★★

> *16km/10mi south of Kateríni.*

At the foot of Mount Olympus in the Pieriá Plain lies the sacred town of ancient Macedon. It was famous in the past for its athletic and dramatic festival known as the **Olympic Games of Dion**, instituted by Archelaos in the 5C BC.

At the height of its prosperity (the Roman period) the town numbered 15,000 inhabitants, and was served by a river port. The fortifications were built in the reign of Alexander the Great. Dion's demise came in the 4C when it was sacked by the Ostrogoths.

Old Town

> *Open every day, 8am–7pm (8am-3pm winter). www.ancientdion. org €4.*

Access to the site is from the south of the village. Within 4C BC ramparts, the town visible today dates from the Roman period. It had a complete network of streets with administrative buildings, warehouses, houses, baths and public latrines. The greatest discovery is the villa of Dionysos, which dates to around AD 200.

Outside the ramparts were numerous sanctuaries, the most important of which was dedicated to the Egyptian divinities Isis, Serapis and Anubis. The Temple of Demeter, the earliest-known Macedonian temple, dates from the 6C BC and remained in use until the 4C AD. Also worthy of note is the Temple of the Olympian Zeus, which Alexander the Great visited before conquering Asia.

Two **theatres**, one Hellenistic, one Roman, two Roman **odeons** and a **stadium** bear witness to the cultural activities that took place in Dion.

Museum★

Open Apr–Oct Tue-Sun 8am-7pm; Nov–Mar Tue–Sun 8.30am-3pm . 23510 53206. €3.

The museum displays riches from the various shrines and public buildings found during excavations at Dion and neighbouring sites. The large baths, in particular, yielded a rare series of statues representing the six children of Asclepius (Aesculapius).

The Temple of Demeter is showcased by several marble heads of the goddess and of Aphrodite, accompanied by terracotta figurines, jewellery and a sacred vessel made of glass. Many artefacts were also found in other sanctuaries of the site – statues of Hygeia, Nemesis and Medea – and in the cemeteries of Dion, in particular a *stele* of the 5C BC with a figure of a mother and her child.

Two other rooms are dedicated to the Paleo-Christian era. Do spend some time here, where you can see exhibits, besides bronzes, funerary *stelae*, statues of philosophers and ceramics, a rare bronze hydraulic organ of the 1C BC.

The visit ends in the basement, where the exhibits deals with the everyday life (coins, vases, furniture) and the examination of techniques of sculpture and of

mosaics, the latter being illustrated with impressive Roman examples.

ADDRESSES

STAY

Papanikolaou – *Litóhoro, Odós Kitrous on the left of the square.* 23520 81 236. www.xenonas-papanikolaou.gr. *16 rooms.* Rooms with kitchen facilities are split between two pleasant buildings surrounded by flowers and trees. A good place to stay.

Enipéas – *Litóhoro, Platía Kentrikí.* 23520 843 28. *25 rooms.* A small, quiet, well-run establishment with a lovely view of Olympus.

Mirto – *On the right of the main road, just before the main square.* 23520 813 98. www.hotelmirto.gr. *31 rooms.* Pleasant rooms with balconies; one of the best in town.

Villa Pantheon – *From Platía Kentrikí, take the street leading to the Mylos Restaurant, on the right, and follow the coast road.* 23520 839 31. www.villapantheon.gr. *12 rooms.* A white building visible from the village, this hotel has rooms with balconies, which are spotlessly clean and comfortable.

Refuge A – *Spílios Agapitós.* 23520 818 00. 110 beds. May–Oct 6am–10pm. Mountain refuge.

EAT

To Pazari – *Litóhoro, Odós 28 Oktomvríou.* Taverna, grilled meat and fish.

Erato – *Litóhoro, Platía Kentrikí.* Good atmosphere; mountain view.

SPORTS AND LEISURE

Litohoro Alpine Club – *2, Odós Ioannou Olymbiou.* 23520 845 44/81800. Jun–Sept. This association runs several refuges and has loads of information about Mount Olympus.

EVENTS AND FESTIVALS

During the Festival of Mount Olympus (July and August), plays and concerts are staged in Dío, Kateríni and at Platamónas Castle on the coast.

Thessaloníki★★

Thessaloníki – Θεσσαλονίκη

Second city of Greece and capital of Macedonia, Thessaloníki cultivates a reputation as a carefree Mediterranean seaside resort, with its wide avenues plunging towards the sea. It is a city of contrasts, cheerfully blending the trappings of a modern city with 23 centuries of continuous history.

A BIT OF HISTORY

Thessaloníki, an Imperial City – Founded in 315 BC on the site of the ancient town of Therme, the city was named after the half-sister of Alexander the Great. Under Roman rule it developed into an important port and staging post. In 148 BC it became the capital of the Roman province of Macedonia and was an important cultural centre. **St Paul** visited Thessaloníki twice during his journeys, in AD 50 and 56, and addressed several Epistles to the Thessalonian people.

Early in the 4C Thessaloníki became the residence of the **Emperor Galerius**, under whose edict Christians were persecuted; in 306 St Demetrios was martyred here. After **Theodosius the Great** (379–95) gave official recognition to the Christian religion, he became the patron saint of the city and was later also worshipped by Muslims. Under the return to order following the barbarian invasions in 527–65, Thessaloníki became the second city of the Eastern Empire after Byzantium. St Cyril, inventor of the Cyrillic alphabet, was born here in 827. After being captured in the Fourth Crusade, Thessaloníki was returned to Byzantium and fell prey to anarchy until it was captured by Sultan Mourad II in 1430, who gave it the name Salonika and sold its inhabitants to slavery. Mourad repopulated the city with Muslims and some 20,000 Jewish refugees from Spain. They formed a community of craftsmen and merchants who traded throughout Europe (by 1910 the Jewish community was 65,000 strong and made up nearly half the population).

▶ **Population:** 385,406 (1,084,001 metropolitan area).

⬡ **Michelin Map:** 737 H 3 – Macedonia.

▤ **Info:** 132 Odós Tsimiski. ℘23102 521 07.

◑ **Location:** Thessaloníki lies on a sloping site on the Thermaic Gulf, 530km/ 331mi north of Athens.

🅿 **Parking:** Use the designated car parks.

◈ **Don't Miss:** The Apsída Galeríou, and the Archaeological Museum.

◔ **Timing:** Allow two days.

👫 **Kids:** Enjoy an ice cream in Odós Iktinou.

Modern Era – Under the Turks the city's economy developed in the late 19C; in 1888 it was linked by railway to Central Europe and from 1897 to 1903 a new port was constructed. In 1912 the Greek army marched into Salonika during the Balkan Wars literally hours before the Bulgarian army and the city was returned to Greece.

During the First World War in 1918 Greek troops joined the Allies in advancing into Serbia and Bulgaria; those who fell in the campaign are buried in the Allied military cemetery at Diavatá *(north of Thessaloníki)*.

A large part of the city was destroyed by fire in 1917, and rebuilt according to plans by the French architect Hébrard. In the 1920s an exchange of populations with Turkey expelled all the Muslim residents and brought in hundreds of thousands of refugees from Asia Minor. In 1941 Thessaloníki was occupied by the Germans, who deported some 60,000 Jews; there is a monument at the beginning of Leofóros Langada *(in the direction of Kavála)*. An earthquake in 1978 grievously damaged the city.

Thessaloníki stands at the crossroads of the land and sea routes linking Western Europe with the Levant; it has long been a trading centre and since 1926 has organised an International Fair (Diethnís Ékthessi) each September. It is an active industrial centre (zone west of the city), and in 1997 was named the European Capital of Culture under the auspices of the European Union for its intellectual and cultural significance.

LOWER TOWN★★

The lower town is bordered by Odós Olimbiados to the north and by the seafront. Devastated by the 1917 fire, the city centre was completely rebuilt, but has retained numerous important monuments, museums and commercial enterprises. Under the Ottomans, the lower town was a squalid area confined behind fortifications that were only demolished in 1866. The main square, **Platía Aristotélous★**, is the termination of the central axis of the city overlooking the sea.

Galerius Complex★

A block of buildings encloses the ruins of what was the ancient centre of Thessaloníki by Galerius (AD 300). All together they form a UNESCO World Heritage site. *Start at Platía Navarínou.*

The Palace of Galerios is built around a courtyard with a peristyle, galleries paved with mosaics and marbles, which is open to the south by a monumental entrance leading to the port. The main palace building is the Octagon, within the semicircular niches. Its size

(30m/98ft diameter) and the remains of its decoration suggest a marble throne room. Nearby, archaeologists have uncovered rooms paved with splendid mosaics. Complete the visit of the palace by going to Platía Ipodromou where you can see the remains of the hippodrome, which extended over 100,000sq km/38,610sq mi.

The **triumphal Arch of Galerius**★ was part of a monument erected in the 4C AD; the pillars were faced with stone decorated with four rows of bas-reliefs celebrating Galerius' victories over the armies of Persia, Mesopotamia and Armenia. The south pillar is well preserved.

Byzantine Sights

Continue north of the Arch of Galerios.
Rotónda★★★
🕐 *Open Tue–Sun 8.30am–5pm.*
Generally known as the church of St George, this building was erected in the 4C AD as a mausoleum for the Emperor Galerius (he is not buried here). In the following century, the mausoleum was converted into a church, and then under the Turks it became a mosque while the saint was still specially venerated. The building now houses a **Lapidary Museum**. The interior was decorated with mosaics on a gold ground, of which a few survive, particularly at the base of the dome, where eight saintly martyrs can be seen in prayer.

Rotónda

Agía Sofía★★
🕐*Open daily, 8am–1pm and 5–7pm.*
The **Church of the Holy Wisdom** (8C), is remarkable for its huge dimensions and unusual design: the standard basilica plan of a nave and two aisles with galleries is combined with the Greek-cross plan beneath a dome. Note the base of a minaret (northwest corner) from the structure's incarnation as a mosque until 1912. The interior displays unusual **capitals**★ with acanthus-leaf decorations probably taken from a 5C building. The **mosaics**★★★ (9C–10C) depict the Ascension of Christ and form a particularly harmonious composition.

Close by is the church of **Agios Panteleimonas** (13C), a superb stone and brick building containing beautiful frescoes.

Panagía Achiropíitos★
56 Odós Agías Sofías. 🕐*Open daily 7am–noon and 4.30–6.30pm.*
☎*23102 728 20.*
The restored church dates from the 5C. Nearby stands a small baptistery chapel. The church was named after a miraculous icon of the Virgin (Panagía Ahiropíitos, "not made by human hand") *(to the left of the entrance).*

Ágios Dimítrios★★
🕐*Crypt opening hours: Mon 12.30–7pm; Thu–Sat 8am–8pm; Sun 10.30am–8pm.*
The impressive St Demetrios' Church marks the site of the martyrdom and tomb of St Demetrios, patron saint of Thessaloníki. After the fire in 1917 the church was restored to reproduce the 7C basilica; some of the old material (marbles, columns, mosaics) were reused. To the left are traces of Roman baths and of a minaret (the church became a mosque from 1491 to 1912).

The pillars on either side of the entrance to the apse are decorated with small 7C **mosaics**★★. The relics of St Demetrios are venerated before the iconostasis. A stairway descends from the apse *(right)* into a **crypt** (small **Lapidary Museum**) where, according to tradition, the miraculous oil that flowed from the saint's tomb was collected.

Mosaics in Ágios Dimítrios

© Greek National Tourism Organisation

Central Market Area
The picturesque central market **(Kendrikí Agorá)** *(open Mon–Sat)* exudes an easterly ambience along its alleys crowded with stalls of fish and various foodstuffs. It extends westwards to the beautifully restored old textiles market, the **Bedesten** (now shops).

The monument at the southwest corner of the market, a woman's head surrounded by outstretched arms, commemorates a politician assassinated here in 1963.

A little south of the market lies the **Yahudi Hamam** (16C), a Turkish bathhouse that is now a flower market. Nearby is the **Panagía Halkéon** (Our Lady of the Coppersmiths) 11C church. It was built on the Greek-cross plan with a central dome and a façade flanked by two towers over the narthex.

The city retains some beautiful remnants of the Ottoman period. Built in 1467 for Bey Hamza's daughter, **Hamza Bey Mosque** was restored in 1620 after a fire. The building has been converted into shops.

Jewish Museum
13 Agios Mina. 🕐*Open Tue, Fri and Sun 11am–2pm, Wed–Thu 11am–2pm and 5pm–8pm.* 🕐*Closed Jewish holidays.*
☎*2310 25 04 06. www.jmth.gr.*
This museum traces the history of the Jewish communities in Thessaloníki

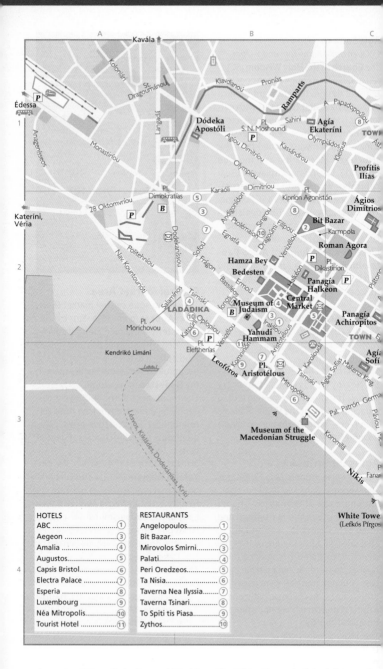

since the 15C until the Second World War. Most exhibits are historical photos of Jewish life and testimony to the Holocaust, in which 96.5 percent of the Jewish population of the city was wiped out.

Lefkós Pírgos★

The **White Tower**, built by Suleiman the Magnificent, was originally incorporated in the ramparts that surrounded the city; it stood in the southeast corner and was the main defensive element in the section fronting the sea. Site of a mas-

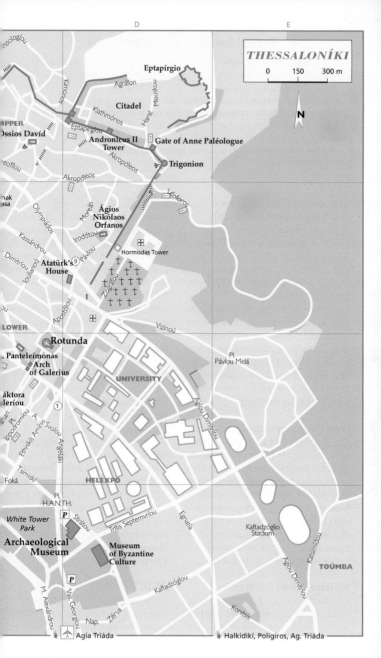

THESSALONÍKI

0   150   300 m

N

Eptapírgio

Agráfon

Kímonos

Citadel

Klathmónos

PPER

)ssios Davíd

Eptapírgiou

Andronicus II Tower

Akropóleos

Gate of Anne Paléologue

Trigonion

Akropóleos

Leofóros

Olympiádos

Ágios Nikólaos Orfanos

Kassándrou

Irodótou

Dimitriou

Ioulianoú

Atatürk's House

Pávlou

Hormisdas Tower

LOWER

Apostólou

Vizinoú

Rotunda

Pantéleímónas

Arch of Galerius

Pl. Pávlou Melá

áktora

leríou

Ippodromíou

Ethnikís Amínis

A... ns Svólou

Angeláki

UNIVERSITY

Agíou Dimitríou

Tsimiskí

Foká

HELEXPO

Pl. H.AN.TH.

White Tower Park

Strátou

Trítis Septemvríou

Egnatía

Kaftadzóglio Stadium

Archaeological Museum

Museum of Byzantine Culture

Kaftadzóglou

Agíou Dimitríou

Katsimídou

TOÚMBA

M. Alexándrou

Vas. Georgíou

Zéfxa

Nap.

Konítsis

Agía Triáda

Halkidikí, Polígiros, Ag. Triáda

sacre of rebellious Sultan guards, the building became known as the Bloody Tower, an unwelcome title which the Turks decided to suppress by painting the walls with whitewash and renaming it the White Tower. From the top there is a fine view over the city and the port. Beyond the White Tower on the seafront stands an equestrian statue of Alexander the Great.

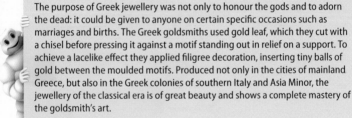

The Goldsmith's Art in Ancient Greece

The purpose of Greek jewellery was not only to honour the gods and to adorn the dead: it could be given to anyone on certain specific occasions such as marriages and births. The Greek goldsmiths used gold leaf, which they cut with a chisel before pressing it against a motif standing out in relief on a support. To achieve a lacelike effect they applied filigree decoration, inserting tiny balls of gold between the moulded motifs. Produced not only in the cities of mainland Greece, but also in the Greek colonies of southern Italy and Asia Minor, the jewellery of the classical era is of great beauty and shows a complete mastery of the goldsmith's art.

Arheologikó Moussío★★★ (Archaeological Museum)

6 Odós Andronikou. Open Apr-Oct Mon 1.30–8pm; Tue–Sun 8am–8pm, Nov–Mar Mon 10.30am–5pm, Tue–Sun 8.30am–3pm. *2310 830538; www. amth.gr* €6 (€8 combined ticket with the Byzantine museum).

In addition to objects excavated from sites in Macedonia and Thrace, is an outstanding collection of treasures of ancient Macedon. Recently discovered in various tombs in northern Greece, the objects bear witness to the splendour of Macedonian society at the time of Philip II and Alexander the Great.

From Prehistory to the Classical Era

The ground floor is devoted to prehistoric dwellings in Macedonia from the Neolithic to the Bronze Age. Finds from excavations on the west face of Mount Olympus are also on display, as well as funerary items (9C BC) from the cemetery at Toróni in Chalcidice. Arms, vases and jewellery in copper, gold and silver have been uncovered on the site of Agía Paraskeví southeast of Thessaloníki.

Sculpture, Glass and Mosaics

Sculptures include a *kouros* and a *kore*, Roman copies of Muses, and Roman portraits, including one of Emperor Alexander Severus (3C). The mosaics depicting Ariadne and Dionysios were found in Roman villas in Thessaloníki, and there is a fine Roman glass collection.

Treasures of Ancient Macedon

This stunning collection of precious metal objects, housed in a separate wing, consists of offerings found in tombs dating from the 4C BC and the Hellenistic period. The Dervéni Treasure comprises material discovered in 4C BC tombs at Dervéni: golden jewellery, vases and a huge cup in bronze gilt, and reliefs illustrating the life of Dionysos. And the **Treasury of Sindos** groups objects taken from the Sindos Cemetery (6C–5C BC) west of Thessaloníki.

Moussío Vizandinoú Politismoú (Museum of Byzantine Culture)

2 Odós Stratou. Open Apr–Oct Mon 1.30pm–8pm, Tue–Sun 8am–8pm, Nov–Mar Mon 10.30am–5pm, Tue–Sun 8.30am–3pm. €4.

The museum houses a collection of early-Christian art and icons formerly in the White Tower. It displays various aspects of Macedonian church decoration and funerary art, and has a fine reconstruction of an ecclesiastical interior. There are many fine icons, as well as embroidery, in particular the famous **Thessaloníki Epitáphios** (14C), used as a corporal cloth.

ADDITIONAL MUSEUMS

There are three further museums of interest in Thessaloníki: the **Photography Museum** (Apothiki A, Harbour; open Tue–Thu and Sun 11am–7pm, Fri–Sat 11am–9pm; €2; 23105 93 275; www.thmphoto.gr) which exhibits historical and artistic photographs of Greece; the **Contemporary Art Museum★** (21 Odós Kolokotroni; open Tue-Sun 10am-6pm; €3; 23105 891 40-41; www.greekstatemuseum.com)

with permanent collections by Russian modern artists such as Kandinsky, Rodchenko, Malevich, Popova and Rozanova; and the **Ataturk House Museum**★ *(75, Apostolou Pavlou;* ⏰*open daily 10am–5pm;* 🎫*free;* ✆*23102 48452).* This latter museum is the house where the founder of modern Turkey was born (on the second floor) containing authentic furniture and some of his personal effects.

UPPER TOWN
The oriental upper town stretches from Odós Olimdiados to the ramparts; it is a network of paved alleyways leading to the acropolis and the Byzantine citadel.

Ramparts★
The principal section of the ramparts were built late in the 4C on Hellenistic foundations and were altered in the 14C and again in the 15C. Following the ramparts entails a 4km/2.5mi walk. There are watchtowers at regular intervals; towards the northeast end is the great **Chain Tower** (Dingirlí Koulé) dating from the 15C. From near the large tower the **view**★ extends over the town and the bay. From this side the ramparts make a fine sight, linking the **towers of Manuel Palaiologos and Andronikos II** (14C).

Churches
Dódeka Apóstoli (⏰ *open daily 8.30am–noon and 5–7pm)* is an attractive 14C church, dedicated to the Twelve Apostles. This church features external **brickwork**★ ingeniously arranged to form decorative geometric motifs. The mosaics and frescoes are 14C (note the Dance of Salome).

Óssios David church (5C) (⏰*open Mon–Sat 8am–12pm & 6–8pm; Sun 8–10.30am)* contains a well-preserved **mosaic**★ representing the Vision of Ezekiel. There are also some rare 12C **frescoes**★★; **view** of the tower from the garden.

The **Church of St Catherine** (Agía Ekateríni) is a 13C church with mosaics and frescoes; the 14C **Prophet Elijah's Church** (Profítis Ilías) contains superb monolithic columns in the transept;

St Nicholas' Church (Ágios Nikólaos Orfanós) is a charming 14C church decorated with frescoes.

ADDRESSES

🛏️STAY
🛏️ **Augustos** – *4 Odós Svorónou.* ✆*23105 225 50. www.augustos.gr. 24 rooms.* Simple, well-done rooms situated in an alley set back from Odós Egnatía.

🛏️🛏️ **Aegeon** – *19 Odós Egnatía.* ✆*23105 229 21. www.aegeon-hotel.gr. 59 rooms.* Recently renovated with small, clean rooms. Those overlooking the courtyard are the quietest.

🛏️🛏️ **Amalia** – *33 Odós Ermoú.* ✆*23102 683 21. www.hotelamalia.gr. 66 rooms.* Centrally located by the market, this nine-storey hotel is very comfortable; good value.

🛏️🛏️ **Esperia** – *58 Odós Olímbou.* ✆*23102 693 21. www.hotelesperia.gr. 70 rooms.* Located in a quiet street, this hotel offers simple, comfortable accommodation. No breakfast or air-conditioning.

🛏️🛏️🛏️ **Capsis Bristol** – *2 Odós Oplopiou, corner of Katouni.* ✆*23 105 065 00. www.capsishotel.gr. 16 rooms and 4 suites.* At the heart of Ladádika. Rooms are classically furnished, spacious and very comfortable, named after Greek celebrities. Same chain as the grand Hotel Capsis next to the railway station.

🛏️🛏️ **Nea Metropolis** – *22 Odós Sigrou.* ✆*23105 255 40. www.neametropolis.gr. 35 rooms.* In a quiet street, this early-20C hotel is decorated with kitschy flair. Its spacious, high-ceilinged rooms are pleasant, and some have TV and air-conditioning.

🛏️🛏️🛏️ **ABC Hotel** – *41 Odós Angeláki.* ✆*23102 654 21. www.hotelabc.gr. 99 rooms.* Immaculately clean accommodation; management speaks English.

🛏️🛏️🛏️ **Electra Palace** – *9 Platía Aristotélous.* ✆*23102 940 00. www.electrahotels.gr. 135 rooms.* This hotel offers every imaginable comfort. English-speaking staff. Ask for a room on an upper storey, with a view of the square and the seafront.

Luxembourg – *6 Odós Komninón.* ℘*23102 526 00. www.hotelluxembourg.gr. 36 rooms.* A very comfortable hotel with pleasant, if small, rooms. One of the least expensive hotels in its class in this district.

Tourist Hotel – *21 Odós Mitropóleos.* ℘*23102 705 01. www.touristhotel.gr. 37 rooms.* Well located and welcoming, this hotel has spotlessly clean high-ceilinged rooms. Very popular and usually full.

ⓨ/EAT

Zithos – *5 Odós Katoúni, Ladádika. www.zithos.gr* Elegant brasserie-style restaurant. Its chic clientele use it for lunch, dinner, or just a drink.

Tsinari – *72 Odós Papadopoulou, corner of Kleious.* ℘*23 102 840 28.* In the upper city, a taverna painted all blue with a nice terrace in the shade of an acacia. A varied, tasty kitchen at reasonable prices.

Taverna Nea Ilyssia – *Corner Egnatia/Léondos Sofou.* Cheap Greek Cuisine. Open until late.

Mirovolos Smirni – *32 Odós Komninon.* ℘*23102 741 70.* In a busy covered market passage, a taverna that offers seafood, grilled meats and kebabs. The Greek clientele and the local music animates the atmosphere in the evenings.

Peri Oredzeos – *18–20 Odós Balanou, Central Market, East of Odós Aristotelous.* Among the taverns of the alley, this restaurant offers fresh and tasty Greek cuisine. The service is fast and the ambiance pleasant.

To Spiti Tou Pasa – *35 Odós Apostolou Pavlou.* ℘*23 102 082 95.* Housed in a pretty building located in an alley that rises behind the house of Atatürk towards the upper town, this restaurant offers Greek and international cuisine.

Palati – *3 Morichovou Square, Ladádika.* ℘*23105 508 88.* Another address in the chic neighbourhood with a vast room with brick walls and exposed beams, where music groups play Greek music. Varied menu of Greek and international cuisine, as well as a good selection of wines.

Bit Bazaar – *33 Odós Prosfigiki.* ℘*23102 780 97.* On the small square of Bit Bazaar, a restaurant offers a wide variety of dishes from all over Greece. Enjoy seafood, grilled meat or cheese on the lovely terrace. Often full in the evening by tourist groups.

Ta Nisia – *13 Odós Koromilas.* ℘*23102 859 91.* Modern and sophisticated decor, all in white and light blue, which serves Greek tasty cuisine. The wine list is extensive.

🚃TAKING A BREAK

Buzapio – *Corner of Odós Ermoú and Agía Sofia.* Enjoy a wonderful view of the church, while sampling from the wide selection of pastries or liqueurs.

Kiss Fisch – *On the port, Odós Fokeas Averof.* This large, modern bar is a haven of peace by day, and a techno-music hangout by night.

🛒SHOPPING

For **icons,** peruse the boutiques along Odós Egnatia near the Arch of Galerius. Head for Odós Tsimiski if you're shopping for **clothes** or **home decor**.

🎭EVENTS AND FESTIVALS

The **Thessaloníki International Fair** is held over two weeks in September and ends with a festival of Greek music. This is followed by an international film festival during October and November, which is part of **Demetriosa**, the feast of the city's patron saint.

Kastoriá★★

Kastoriá – Καστοριά

The history of Kastoriá is inextricably linked to that of the Balkans and Central Europe. Renowned for its furriers, it maintains much of its traditional charm; known as the "town of a hundred churches", it has many fine examples of Byzantine architecture. Kastoriá lies at the neck of a peninsula jutting out into the picturesque waters of a lake bearing the same name. Close by are the Prespa Lakes, a protected area of great natural beauty.

A BIT OF HISTORY

For some 600 years Kastoriá has been a centre of the fur industry. Exemption from import tax on the pelts, and particular skill in working with skins enabled local workshops to produce coats and wraps for export to Constantinople and to the capitals of Central Europe. The goods are now exported directly to Western cities. The local furriers buy pelts mainly from America and Scandinavia, but there are also mink and wolf farms on the outskirts of town. Workshops are dotted about the town, and skins stretched out on frames and drying in the sun are to be seen on the pavements.

BYZANTINE CHURCHES★★

About 50 survive, some dating from the 10C. The churches are beautifully decorated with frescoes and sculptures. To visit them, enquire at the **Byzantine Museum** (🕐 *open Tue–Sun 8.30am–3pm;* ✆*no charge;* 🖉*24670 267 81*), which offers a good introduction to the town's religious heritage; on view are fine icons and other artworks dating from the 12C–17C.

Panagía Koubelídiki★

Near the school. 🕐 *Open Tue–Sun 10am –3pm.* ✆*No charge.*

The emblem of Kastoriá. Built in the mid-9C and dedicated to the Virgin, it is the only domed church in the city with a tall drum, hence its name, from a Turk-

> ▶ **Population:** 17,038.
> ⛭ **Michelin Map:** 737 E 3 – Macedonia.
> ▯ **Info:** www.gokastoria.gr.
> ⊙ **Location:** Kastoriá is located 209km/131mi west of Thessaloníki and virtually on the frontier with Albania and Macedonia.
> P **Parking:** There is an official car park near the tourist office but everyone seems to park everywhere.
> ⊘ **Don't Miss:** Byzantine churches and traditional houses; the Prespa Lakes.
> 🕐 **Timing:** Plan a two-day visit.
> 👪 **Kids:** Boat rides and motor-launch trips on the lakes.

Panagía Koubelídiki

© J.-P. Nail/MICHELIN

ish word *(kouben)* meaning drum. The narthex vaulting bears the Holy Trinity, which is rarely represented in the Byzantine tradition.

Ágios Nikólaos Kasnídzis (St Nicholas of Kasnitsis)

Below Platía Omónia. The exterior of this small 12C church was partly decorated with frescoes; traces are visible above the apse. 12C frescoes in the nave.

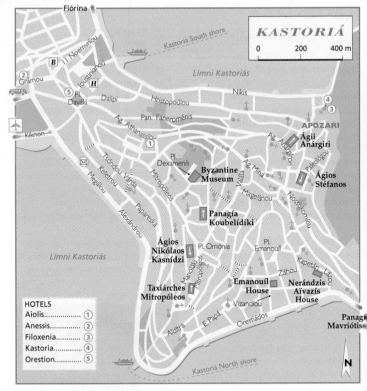

From Platía Omónia, go to Odós Manolaki and turn left into an alley.

Taxiárchis Mitropóleos
The 9C Metropolitan Church of the Taxiarchs (leaders of the heavenly host), the Archangels Michael and Gabriel, contains capitals from an early-Christian basilica that previously stood on the site. Inside, the east walls still bear traces of 9C frescoes.

Ágios Stéfanos★ (St Stephen's)
Northeast, Odós Paleológou.
The vaulting of the lofty nave (9C) is painted with 12C frescoes. In the rest of the church, the 9C frescoes have been preserved. A stairway leads to a women's gallery, a unique feature in Kastoriá (St Ann's Chapel).

Ágii Anárgiri Varlaám★
Odós Vitsiou, not far from Ágios Stéfanos.
High up above the lake, the church (10C) is among the largest in Kastoriá and is dedicated to the "holy penniless ones", the physicians who practised medicine without charging fees *(anárgiri)*. Inside most of the frescoes are 11C or 12C, but an earlier 10C layer is visible in some parts of the church.

OLD HOUSES★
A few handsome, tower-like houses *(arhondiká),* built in the main in the 17C and 18C in the typical Macedonian style using large stones for the rich local furriers, add to the charm of the quarters near the peninsula.
There are two of these old houses in the north Arozari quarter near the lake: the **Sapoundzís Mansion** (Odós Christopoulou) and **Tsiatsapás Mansion**. Most are situated in the Doltso district south of the town and, in particular, in Odós Vizandiou south of Platía A Emanouíl: the **Nadzis**, **Emanouil** and **Bassarás Mansions**. Farther along, near the peninsula, the restored Nerándzis Aïvázis mansion is now the **Museum of Folk**

Traditions★, giving a good picture of Macedonian family life in bygone days *(Odós Kapetan Lazou;* ⏱ *open daily 10am–6pm;* ✆*€0.80).*

EXCURSIONS

Límni Kastoriás★ (Kastoriá Lake)

▶ *Tour of the peninsula: 9.2km/5.5mi.*
At the start of the drive there are lovely views of the southern part of the town and of the traditional flat-bottomed boats with raised prows. Not far from the Monastery of the Virgin *(2.5km/1.5mi)* the road widens. Fine view of the lake.

Panagía Mavriótissa★★

Macedonian-style monastery building. The exterior south wall of the Church of the Virgin (Panagía), which dates from the 12C, is decorated with 13C frescoes *(under cover)*; there are 12C frescoes on the east and west walls of the nave.
Return to Kastoriá by the same route (⚠ *drive carefully as cars on the return journey do not have right of way)* or continue round the peninsula *(one-way road from the monastery)* to the north side of the town and the small harbour.

Límnes Préspes★★ (Préspa Lakes)

▶ *64km/40mi. From Kastoriá take the Flórina road north.*
Beyond the town *(about 5km/3mi)* a fine **view★★** unfolds. Beyond a pass the road skirts the wooded valley of the Ladopótamos River. After 35km/21.5mi turn off the Flórina road and bear left towards the lakes and Lemós. After a saddle (low ridge) the road affords a splendid **view★★** of the Little Préspa Lake. Both the Préspa Lakes are shared by the three republics of Macedonia, Albania and Greece. The area used to be underpopulated and was also militarily sensitive (requiring special permission for outsiders to visit) and so it was kept fairly unknown until the 1970s. Its promotion as a tourist destination has proved successful and with an abundance of rare fauna and flora it has a lot to offer. Little Préspa Lake in particular is recognised as an important wetland

ecosystem for rare waterbird species. The flora in the region – consisting of 1,249 plant species just on the Greek side which spans 277sq km/107sq mi – is especially rich and varied.

Mikrí Préspa★ (Little Préspa Lake)

The lake, which extends southwest into Albania, was designated as a national park in 1974 together with the Greek section of the Great Préspa Lake. It is one of the few places where one can encounter the Balkan lynx. Abundant birdlife also thrives in the reed beds around Little Préspa, including rare Dalmatian pelicans, pygmy cormorants, egrets, herons and cranes. There are two islands: on the larger, Ágios Achílios, are several Byzantine churches including the 11C Church of St Achilles. There are boat trips to the islands and to birdwatching posts from **Makrolímni** *(4km/2.5mi from the junction)*.
The main road skirts the little lake, and at the junction at the far end a road on the right leads to the village of **Ágios Germanós** with its 11C domed church and fine frescoes, at the foot of Mount Varnoús (Peristéri – 2,156m/7,074ft).

Megáli Préspa★ (Great Préspa Lake)

The lake lies in three nations: Albania, Macedonia and Greece.
The village of **Psarádes** with its traditional houses with wooden balconies *(hotel, guesthouses)* overlooks a deep bay on the other side of the peninsula *(9.5km/6mi farther on)*. On the Greek side

Megáli Préspa
© J.-P. Nail/MICHELIN

excursions by motor launch take visitors to the rugged cliffs and caves (in particular the cave of the Panagía Eleoússa) painted by hermits in the 14C and the 15C. Good **views**★ of the Albanian shore and mountains.

Siátista★

▶ *59km/36.75mi southeast of Kastoriá; 30km/18.5mi west of Kozáni.*

Formerly renowned for its wine and leather, Siástista *(www.siatista.gr)* joined the fur trade in the early 20C.

In the upper town, Hóra, most of the Macedonian-style 18C mansions *(arhondiká)* are in the care of the archaeological department housed in

the **Neranzópoulou Mansion**★, built in 1754, which has painted ceilings and stained-glass windows. Farther down the street are **Manoúsi Mansion** and **Poulkídi Mansion**, splendidly decorated with painted walls and ceilings. The building of Manoúsi Mansion began in 1747 for Georgios Manousis, an uncle of Theodoros Manousis who was the first Professor of History in the University of Athens. The town monument commemorates a battle that took place just outside the town. On 4–6 March 1943, Siatista's inhabitants joined the residents of nearby villages and fought under the leadership of the left-wing EAM and captured an Italian battalion.

ADDRESSES

🏠STAY

⊝ **Aiolis** – *Kastoriá, 30 Odós Agíou Athanassíou. ℘24670 210 70. www.aiolis.gr. 14 rooms.* Occupying a colonnaded corner building, this luxurious hotel is extremely comfortable, with first-class service.

⊝ **Europa** – *Kastoriá, 12 Odós Agíou Athanassíou. ℘24670 238 26. www.europahotelkastoria.gr. 36 rooms.* A good hotel near Platía Daváki; well-kept, clean, comfortable rooms.

⊝ **Pension Filoxenia** – *Kastoriá, in the Profitis Ilias area to the northeast of the centre (follow signposts). ℘24670 221 62. www.filoxeniakastoria.gr. 7 rooms.* Guesthouse on the lakeside to the north. All rooms are clean, pleasant and have balconies; fine views.

⊝⊝ **Ágios Achílios** – *Island of Ágios Achílios. ℘23850 466 01.* This guesthouse is a solid traditional-style building and has a pleasant lounge with fireplace.

⊝⊝ **Ágios Germanós** – *Ágios Germanós, right of the village square. ℘23850 513 97. www.prespa.com.gr. 11 rooms.* Two traditional buildings provide spacious and comfortable rooms with central heating. Diners eat in a room overlooking the courtyard; good breakfast.

⊝⊝ **Psarádes** – *Psarádes. ℘23850 460 15. 16 rooms.* A modern and comfortable hotel on the other side of the bay, facing the village. Breakfast not included.

♀/EAT

⊝ **Nostalgia** – *Kastoriá, 2 Odós Nikis, opposite the landing stage. ℘24670 226 30. www.tavernanostalgia.gr.* Grilled meat and fish dishes in a quiet setting facing the lake.

⊝ **Omonoia** – *Kastoriá, 97 Odós Mitropóleos, near Platia Omonoías.* Small restaurant, simple and inexpensive. A good spot to eat after visiting the nearby churches.

⊝ **Swan** – *Kastoriá, 1 Odós Thomaídos.* Excellent value; very good trout and grilled meats; the lake can smell rather unappetising though.

⊝ **Taverna Kostas** – *Psarádes, on entering the village.* A warm welcome and reasonably priced fish dishes.

🎭EVENTS AND FESTIVALS

From 6–8 January, a colourful carnival takes place during the **Ragoutsaria**. The first weekend in August, the village of Nestorio (20km/12mi from Kastoriá) has a series of concerts as part of the **River Festival**.

Veria and Vergina

Véria kai Vergína –
Βέροια and Βεργίνα

Veria is sited on a spur of Mount Vérmio overlooking the Macedonian Plain. Hidden in courtyards and blind alleys among the concrete buildings of the modern town are a few Macedonian houses, Byzantine and post-Byzantine churches and a mosque. Vergina/Aigai is one of Greece's most important UNESCO sites and has, among others, the tomb of Philip II of Macedon, Alexander the Great's father.

VERIA

At the centre of the town in the **Kiri-otissa Quarter**★★ stands the **Church of the Resurrection** (*Odós Mitropoléos;* ⏱*open Tue–Sat, 8.30am–3pm)*, a Byzantine brick building (recently restored). Step inside to see the remarkable collection of early-14C frescoes signed by the famous Salonika painter, Georgios Kaliergis. Walk a short distance to see two other churches: Ágios Kerikos with 13C frescoes (altered in the 16C); and Ágios Vlassios (Odós Perdika) dating from the 14C, with frescoes of the same date. The **Byzantine Museum** (*Odós Thomaidou*) contains ceramics, mosaics and a fine collection of icons. Also worth a peek is the **Archaeological Museum** (*Odós Mitropoléos*) with a colossal 2C AD head of Medusa.

VERGINA

▷ *15km/9.5mi southeast of Veria on the road to Melíki; after 12km/7.5mi turn right to the modern village of Vergina; at the end of the village turn left (sign to "Royal Tombs").*

The discovery in 1977 of the spectacular tomb of Philip II positively identified Vergina as the ancient capital of Macedonia, and site of the royal burial ground. The city was built on the slopes of a hill at the end of a valley separating the Pierian chain from the Vermio massif; the necropolis was down on the plain.

▶ **Population:** 47,677.
⏱ **Michelin Map:** 737 F 3 – Imathía – Macedonia.
▷ **Location:** Veria is located 73km/46mi southwest of Thessaloníki. Vergina is 13km/8mi southeast of Veria.
🅿 **Parking:** There is usually parking space available in Veria town.
🏛 **Don't Miss:** The Royal Tombs.

Ancient City (Aigai)

⏱*Open Apr–Oct Tue–Sun 8am– 7.30pm; Mon 12–7.30pm Nov–Mar 8.30am–3pm.* 📞*23310 92347.* 💳*€8, including museum admission.*

The **Palace** (4C BC), of which only the foundations remain, consisted of a large central courtyard accessed via a portico and a *thólos*. The royal apartments were in the east wing. In the south wing, there are splendid mosaics *(covered for preservation purposes)*. The west wing was composed of a series of huge vestibules, their floors paved in *opus sectile*. The north wing was an open veranda looking out over the plain and the town. Just below the palace lie the remains of the theatre where Philip II was assassinated.

Further down the site is the *agora*, dominated by the Temple of Eukliea (a Macedonian divinity), where several marble statues, includin g one thought to depict the mother of Philip II, have been discovered. *(To the left of the road.)* Dating to the 3C BC, the *hypogeum* has an Ionic façade.

In the funerary chamber, the marble throne has retained some of its original painted decoration.

The route comes to a small plateau from where a path leads to the remains of the little palace, the **Palatítsia**, which dates from the Hellenistic period.

Royal Tombs★★★

▷ *On the plain below the city.* ⏱*Same opening hours as the ancient city.*

The necropolis is a veritable mass of *tumuli* (300). The royal tumulus has been restored and now houses a superb **museum**★★★. The burial chambers cannot be accessed, but their façades and the stunning finds excavated from them are on display.

The façade of the great central **tomb**, identified as that of Philip II, is closed behind a door with two marble leaves, and adorned with a magnificent frieze. The interior, which consists of a vestibule and an inner chamber, has a magnificent collection of funerary objects.

A golden coffer *(larnax)* is decorated with a 12-pointed star, the emblem of the Macedonian kings; it contained the bones of a woman and a magnificent gold diadem forming a riot of leaves, twigs and flowers with bees gathering pollen. A larger and heavier solid **gold coffer**, is decorated with a 16-point star; it contained bones – probably those of Philip II, whose exquisite crown of golden oak leaves is displayed above. Objects thought to have belonged to Philip include a quiver covered in gold leaf embossed with scenes from the sack of Troy, an iron cuirass decorated with bands of gold, an iron sword with gold and ivory hilt and his magnificent bronze shield.

There are also some very expressive, delicately carved portraits made of ivory, probably representing the royal family of Macedon: Philip II with a beard, his wife Olympia and son Alexander.

Nearby there is a smaller tomb of the same type, thought to be the tomb of Alexander IV (son of Alexander the Great, assassinated at the age of 15). The frieze in the vestibule depicts a wonderful scene of harnessed horses racing.

Further off, a third **tomb** houses marvellous paintings (Persephone being carried off by Pluto), which according to Pliny were executed c.350 BC by Nikomachos, son of Aristides.

EXCURSIONS
Lefkadia★★

▶ *From Veria take the Édessa road to Kopanos, 12km/7.5mi away. From there, follow the signposts.* ⏱*Open Tue–Sat*
8.30am–3pm; Sun and public holidays, 9am–2pm.

The region of **Náoussa**, well known for its fruit and wine production, is also famous for three unusual Macedonian *hypogea* (3C–2C BC), huge temple-like underground tombs located near the little village of Lefkádia on the Veria to Édessa road.

The first tomb, called the Tomb of Judgment from the painting it depicts, was excavated in 1954, and is built of conchitic limestone. A flight of steps leads down to the two-storey façade; the lower section is Doric, the upper Ionic. It was decorated with paintings; those remaining show a warrior (probably Death), the god Hermes (leader of souls to the Underworld), Aiakos and Rhadamanthos (Judges of Hades) and battle scenes.

The interior has a vestibule and a chamber that still contains a sarcophagus.

Walk 150m/492ft beyond the Great Tomb, left of the path, to see majestic steps descending to the superb columned façade of a well-preserved *hypogeum.*

The second tomb is named Kinch's Tomb after the Danish archaeologist who discovered it in 1880. It is composed of an antechamber and main chamber which still show traces of the original painted decoration.

This final underground tomb (3C or 2C BC) is accessed by a ladder. It is a burial vault for three families furnished with 22 funerary recesses inscribed with the names of the dead Lyson and Kallikles, after whom the tomb itself is named; the ornamental paintings are in an excellent state of preservation.

Édessa

▶ *89km/55mi northwest of Thessaloníki.* Built on the edge of a plateau overlooking the Macedonian Plain, Édessa was in antiquity one of the main strongholds in Macedon. The town is known for the waters of the **River Vódas**. The soothing sound of running water, its mild climate and attractive old Ottoman quarter, make Édessa quite an agreeable summer resort.

Old Town

A stroll in the old town – below the modern town and north of the Thessaloníki road – is well worthwhile. Excavations in the Longos area have revealed the remains of a Macedonian fortress and its surrounding wall built in the 4C BC and restored by the Romans, as well as ruins of early-Christian basilicas. Further east a sign saying *"Waterfalls"* and *"Pros Kataráktes"* marks the beginning of a public garden shaded by huge plane trees *(restaurant)* and leads down to the point where the various streams flowing through the town meet in an impressive waterfall; the water tumbles down a rockface covered by luxuriant vegetation.

It is possible to continue to the foot of Mount Voras and the spa at Loutra Loutrakiou (Pozar), where bathers can luxuriate in the warm water (37°C/100°F!).

Péla

▶ *38km/24mi east of Édessa on the E 86 Thessaloníki road.*

The ancient city of Péla was situated in the heart of the fertile Macedonian Plain on the road from Édessa to Thessaloníki. Under Philip II and Alexander the Great it was the capital of Macedon. Péla is first mentioned by Herodotus (Book 7) in his account of Xerxes' campaign; the town is also mentioned by Thucydides (Book 2) in relation to Macedonian expansion and a local war against the Thracians. Xenophon, writing at the beginning of the 4C BC, notes it as the largest Macedonian city.

Late in the 5C BC King Archelaos abandoned Aigai (Vergina) and moved to Péla, where he built a splendid palace decorated with paintings by the famous Zeuxis. Here Archelaos maintained a sophisticated court, welcoming artists and men of letters, including **Euripides**, whose plays *Archelaos* and *Bacchae* were written there.

Both **Philip II of Macedon** and **Alexander the Great** were born in Péla. Alexander, the son of Philip and Princess Olympia, was educated in literature as well as the military arts; one of his tutors was **Aristotle**, a native of Chalcidice.

Péla grew to be the largest town in Macedon and was linked to the sea by a canal. The Roman Consul Aemilius Paulus laid waste to it in 168 BC, and the city never recovered.

Excavations begun in 1957 revealed its vast extent and its grid plan, which was recommended by the architect **Hippodamos of Miletus**. Remarkable Hellenistic mosaic pavements (4C–3C BC) have also been excavated. The extent of the complex indicated by the archaeology suggests that, unlike the palace at Vergina, this was not only a royal residence but also a place of government.

Ruins

🕐*Open Apr–Oct Tue–Sun 8am–8pm; Mon 1.30–8pm Nov–Mar Tue–Fri 8.30am–3pm.* 𝒫*23094 31160.* ⊗*€6.*

The excavations on the north side of the road have uncovered the foundations of the *agora*. To the right lay a huge complex of buildings erected round a courtyard and an Ionic peristyle; some of the columns have been re-erected. Certain rooms were paved with mosaics: some geometric *(in situ)*, others figurative *(in the museum)*.

To the left are the foundations of other buildings; the most distant are decorated with fine **mosaic pavements**★★ illustrating the Abduction of Helen and of Deïanira, the Battle of the Amazons and a deer hunt signed by Gnosis.

The Museum displays the finds from the excavations, including some superb **mosaic pavements**★ (4C–3C BC): the most beautiful show Dionysos seated on a panther (the god's favourite animal) and a lion hunt in which Krateros, a comrade in arms, is supposed to have saved the life of Alexander the Great. Among the other Hellenistic figures are a marble dog from a tomb, a head of Alexander, a small bronze statue of Poseidon and some attractive terra-cotta pieces.

At a distance of 3km/2mi away, on the Péla acropolis, near to the village of ancient Péla, recent excavations have discovered more ruins, including a royal residence, which could be Philip II's palace. ☺*Excavations in progress at the time of publication.*

ADDRESSES

🏠 STAY

☕ 🛏 **Villa Elia** – *Veria, 10 Odós Elias.* 📞 *23310 268 00. www.hotel-villaelia.gr. 27 rooms, 4 suites.* Good breakfast and sizeable rooms at this pleasant spot just steps from the old Kiriotissa quarter.

☕ 🛏 **Varosi** – *Édessa, 45–47, Odós Arh. Meletiou.* 📞 *23810 218 65. www.varosi-hotel.com. 8 rooms.* In a traditional house in the old Ottoman quarter, this charming hotel has small, but comfortable and attractively decorated rooms. Good breakfast.

☕ 🛏 **Xenia** – *Édessa, 35 Odós Filípou.* 📞 *23810 297 0607/08. www.xeniaedessa. gr. 36 rooms, 6 suites.* This is the most luxurious hotel in town, with a clifftop setting and a fine view over the plain.

Extremely comfortable, with very professional staff.

🍽 EAT

☕ **Katarraktes** – *Édessa, Dimotikós Kípos.* Pleasantly situated in the middle of the waterfall park, this large restaurant serves unsurprising cuisine.

☕ **Peskaoudritsa** – *Veroia. Odós Ioakem, Kiriotissa area.* Small family spot specialising in fish dishes; good *mezés*.

🚍 TAKING A BREAK

Odós Konstantinoupoloeos – *Edessa.* Bordered by a canal, a street of shady terraces invite strollers to take a break.
Erateinon – *Veroia, Odós Ioakem.* Stop for a meal or a drink in this romantic courtyard, located in the old quarter.

Chalcidice★

Halkidikí – Χαλκιδική

To the south, the Peninsula of Chalcidice extends outwards in three promontories: Kassándra, Sithonía and Mount Áthos. The last of these is dedicated to monasticism; the other two offer more earthly pleasures; their 500km/310mi of fine beaches are virtually deserted, especially the ones further away from Thessaloníki.

- ▶ **Population:** 104,894.
- 🗺 **Michelin Map:** 737 I-J 4, I 5 – Halkidikí – Macedonia.
- ℹ **Info:** www.halkidiki.com and www.halkidikinet.gr.
- ▶ **Location:** The Strymon Gulf and the Gulf of Thessaloníki, coupled with a depression forming two large lakes, delineate the northern boundary of the Peninsula of Chalcidice, located 60km/37mi southeast of Thessaloníki.
- 🅿 **Parking:** Trade fairs in Thessaloníki can make parking difficult.
- ⊘ **Don't Miss:** The Sithonía Peninsula.
- 🕐 **Timing:** Allow the best part of a day and consider an overnight stay.

🚗 DRIVING TOUR

SITHONÍA PENINSULA★★

Round-trip of 109km/68mi along attractive coastline.

Sithonía boasts many natural beauty spots: forests of sea and umbrella pines, fine sandy beaches, deep fjords with sheer rock walls. The coast road runs past many beautiful sites, becomes a corniche road along the cliffs and offers extensive views – particularly east to Mt Áthos, although the summit is often shrouded in clouds.
Starting the drive from the east coast, the first picturesque hamlet, set in a rocky bay, is Órmos Panagias. It takes

its name from the Byzantine church that dominates the village, which was reconstructed in 1970. Boats leave the small quay to Mt Áthos opposite. After a pleasant coastal drive you arrive at Sárti, the main east-side resort, set in a small cultivated coastal plain running down to a sandy bay. Although the site was visited by Xerxes' fleet and is mentioned by Herodotus, today's village is modern, having been founded by refugees from the Sea of Marmara during the 1920s population exchange. If you continue the drive, you reach the tip of the peninsula, **Cape Drépano**★, a rocky promontory indented with many inlets extending into fjords, particularly at **Koufó** and round **Kalamítsi**★. **Pórto Koufó**★ the port and 1.6km/1mi beach are magnificently located in a protected inlet.

Toróni Bay★

Going north, the long sandy beach of the idyllic **Toróni Bay**★ curves gently south into a tiny peninsula which bears the remains of an ancient fortress and palaeo-Christian basilicas. Beyond Toroni, the coast has many beautiful and unspoilt **beaches** until you reach the new development of **Porto Karrás**. Developed by the oil tycoon, John C Karras, this seaside resort centres on two imposing hotels, a charming seaside village with a harbour, a golf course, tennis courts, a casino, a riding stable etc.

◐ *From the Sithonía Peninsula, you can continue east along the coast to get to Mount Áthos .*

KASSANDRA PENINSULA

◐ *60km/37mi south of Thessaloníki, then a round trip of 118km/73mi to make a complete tour of the peninsula.*
This peninsula is less attractive than Sithonía, the next peninsula down, but it is more fertile and more densely populated. The isthmus has been breached by a canal at Néa Potídea, the site of ancient Poteidaia. There are pleasant beaches and a number of hotels especially at **Saní**, **Kalithéa**, **Agía Paraskeví** and (most notably) **Palioúri**, which lies at the southern end looking across a bay to the Sithonía Peninsula.

Olynthos★

◐ *5km/3mi to the east of Nea Moudania, turn left.* ◑ *Open Tue–Sun, 8.30am–3pm.* ◔€3.
This was an important and powerful city allied with Athens against Philip II

of Macedon who in 348 BC razed it to the ground and sold its citizens into slavery. The site has been abandoned for more than 20 centuries, but it is notable for the rare geometric layout laid down by Hippodamus of Miletus which is still visible, with main artery roads crossing at right angles. Some black and white mosaic work remains; don't miss the one depicting the hero Bellerophon.

Petrálona

◐ *12km/8mi to the east off the road from Thessaloníki to the peninsula; turn left towards Néa Silata and left again to Elaiochoria.* ◑ *Open daily 9am–3pm.* ◔€7. ✆22373 716 71. www.aee.gr.
The **cave of Kókines Pétres** (the Red Stones) is known to palaeontologists for the discovery of a Neanderthal skull and fossils of prehistoric animals. Only 2km/1.25mi may be visited. There is a museum with a selection of finds.

ADDRESSES

⌂ STAY

⊜⊟ **Marmarás** – *Sithonía, Néos Marmarás.* ✆23750 721 84. www.hotel marmaras.gr. 15 rooms. Breakfast not included. Comfortable hotel with balconies overlooking the sea.

⊜⊟ **Zeus** – *Kassándra, Afytos.* ✆23740 911 32. 24 apartments. Good decor, fully equipped; garden with pool.

⊜⊟⊟ **Pórto Koufó** – *Sithonía, Pórto Koufó.* ✆23750 512 07. www.porto koufohotel.gr. 26 rooms. Opposite the bay. Comfortable rooms with balconies.

⋔ EAT

⊜⊟⊟ **Chrístos Fish Tavern** – *Néos Marmarás, Sithonía.* ✆23750 712 11. On the left of the bay facing the sea (entrance difficult to see). A vast selection of fish and seafood served indoors or on the raised terrace.

⊜⊟⊟ **Filaktos** – *Porto Koufo, Sithonía.* ✆23750 512 80. Terrace dining; ideal spot to try grilled sardines. Rooms to let upstairs.

⊜⊟⊟ **Kyaní Aktí** – *Paralía Nikítas.* ✆23750 229 08. Pleasant restaurant by the beach serving fresh fish dishes.

Mount Áthos★★

Ágion Óros – Ἅγιον Ὄρος

Mount Áthos or Agion Oros (Holy Mountain) is covered with forests (oaks, chestnuts and pines) culminating at the southern tip in Mount Áthos, 2,033m/6,670ft high. Since the 5C the peninsula has been a centre of Orthodox monasticism. This forbidding place has many treasures, but opens its doors to few travellers.

A BIT OF HISTORY

The first community *(lávra)* of monks dates from AD 963 when **St Athanasius of Trebizond** was encouraged by the Emperor Nikeforos Focas to found the monastery of the Megisti Lavra. Other communities were established from the 13C onwards, and by the 16C there were 30 000 monks in about 30 monasteries.

Since the 10C, Mount Áthos has existed as a kind of Orthodox monastic republic, the capital of which is Kariés.

The major monasteries were usually arranged round a courtyard and fortified with towers. The walls of the churches and refectories are decorated with frescoes; the most beautiful were painted by artists such as M Panselinos (14C), **Theophanes the Cretan**, Tzortzios and Frango Kastellanos (16C). The

▶ **Population:** 1,961.
▤ **Info:** www.mountathos.gr and www.inathos.gr.
◐ **Location:** The mountain lies 36km/85mi southeast of Thessaloníki, 161km/ 101mi south of Kavála, on the easternmost peninsula of Chalcidice.
🅿 **Parking:** Spaces for vehicles are limited.
⊘ **Don't Miss:** The monastery of Megistis Lavras and its superb treasury.
◷ **Timing:** One-day boat tours around the Holy Mountain are available for those barred from visiting the mountain itself (⊘*see Getting There*).

libraries, which are often housed in the keep, contain upwards of 10 000 ancient manuscripts.

MOUNT ÁTHOS TODAY

Today there are around 1,472 monks in about 20 monasteries; the majority are Greek. The main Russian monastery is Agios Panteleímonas, while Moni Zografou has a Bulgarian history and tradition.

Símonos Pétras

GETTING THERE

Mount Áthos is closed to tourists and women. Only visitors able to demonstrate religious or academic motives are allowed; the minimum age for applicants is 21. Contact the **Pilgrim Office of Holy Mount Áthos**, *Odós Egnatia, Thessaloníki;* 🕐 *open Mon–Fri 8.30am–2pm, Sat 10am–12pm;* ℘ *2310 252578, Fax 2310 222424.* The daily limit for permits is 10 for foreigners so book well in advance; religious holidays are best avoided altogether. Once a permit is secured, book accommodation at the monastery where you wish to stay. Keep the acknowledgement of your reservation to show at the office in Ouranópoli, where you collect the entry permit (€30) which allows stays of up to four days. Access is by boat from Ouranópoli at 9am to Dáfni.

Boat excursions skirt the coast of Mount Áthos; **passengers must be appropriately dressed**.

During the season these excursions leave from Ouranópoli, Órmos Panagías on the Sithonía Peninsula, and Thássos.

WEST COAST MONASTERIES

The monasteries mentioned here are the most famous or the most easily visited. They all close at sunset. Depart by boat from Ouranópoli to Dáfni. Alight at Dáfni and then continue by bus or another boat.

Símonos Pétras★★★

The lofty 13C monastery with its row upon row of wooden balconies occupies a spectacular site on the western face of the mountain. Founded by St Simon (13C), it was extended in the 14C by a Serbian prince, and was extensively restored after an 1891 fire.

Ágiou Dionissíou★

This monastery was founded in 14C on a rocky site overlooking an inlet on the west coast. The church and refectory stem from the 16C and are decorated with remarkable frescoes dating from the 16C by Tzortzis the Cretan dating from the 1540s. Its treasury contains a 10C ivory relief of the Crucifixion and several relics including the right hand of John the Baptist.

Grigoriou★

🕐 *Closed daily 1pm–5pm.*

The elegant 14C Grigoriou Monastery overlooks the sea. The 18C *katholikón* is awash with frescoes and contains a magnificent iconostasis decorated with scenes from the Old Testament.

Docheiariou

Surrounded by wooded hills, Docheiariou Monastery (10C) looks like a castle with its crenellated tower and tall stone wall. Its 16C *katholikón* houses beautiful frescoes of the Cretan School of painting.

Xenofóndos

A small harbour precedes the Xenofóndos monastery (of Xenophon), also lying close to the shore. Founded in the 10C, it fell in decline following pirate raids and it was rebuilt in the early 19C. Its new *katholikón* is the largest on Mount Áthos. The former *katholikón* remains nevertheless more interesting with its beautiful 16C frescoes and a graceful iconostasis.

Ágios Panteleímonas

The imposing monastery of Ágios Panteleimonas is very distinctive with its green onion domes crowned with golden crosses. Founded by Russian monks in the 11C, it continues the tradition with Slavic ancient liturgical chants. At the foot of the tower, the dining hall can accommodate 800 guests.

The monastery also boasts one of the richest **libraries** of Mount Áthos.

EAST COAST MONASTERIES

The monasteries mentioned here are the most famous or the most easily visited. They all close at sunset.

Megístis Lávras★★★

This is the oldest and largest (around 320 monks) monastery of Mount Áthos, considered *primus inter pares* in the monastic hierarchy. Perched on the forested southeast of the peninsula, it overlooks a majestic panorama.

Founded by Athanasius the Athonite (963), it peaked with 700 monks in the 11C, before a long decline between the 14C and 17C. At first glance, the monastery is rather reminiscent of a large fortified village, guarded by a powerful square tower. Do not miss the large *katholikón*, dedicated to the monk Athanasius whose remains are buried inside. It houses 16C **frescoes**★ by **Theophanes the Cretan**, considered his masterpieces, as well as many remarkable icons. In the entrance stands a **baptistery** *(phial)*★ surrounded by a colonnade and lined with sculptures and frescoes. The nearby refectory also contains many frescoes such as the *Last Supper, Jacob's Ladder* and the *Life of Mary* accompanied by portraits of Greek philosophers.

The **treasury** has enough riches to rival the great museums of the world including the crown and the mantle of Emperor **Nikeforos Focas** (963–969). Its incomparable library★★★ keeps Mount Áthos' most important collection of manuscripts.

Ivíron★★

This monastery, which was founded in 980 by monks from Georgia (Iviría), is dedicated to the Dormition of the Virgin. It is hidden in a hanging valley overlooking the sea and surrounded by olive and pine trees. The church is 11C; a chapel contains the miraculous icon of the Mother of God of the Gate (Panagía Portaítissa) (10C). The library possesses many illuminated manuscripts (11C to 13C), and the **treasury** is among the finest on Mount Áthos.

Vatopedíou★★

This huge monastery, second in the monastic hierarchy, was established in 972, and was fortified early in the 15C.

The 15C bronze entrance doors came from Agía Sophía in Thessaloníki; the mosaic is a remarkable piece of 11C work. The treasury boasts some rare gold reliquaries and a 15C jasper cup on an enamelled silver base. The library is well stocked with 2,050 ancient manuscripts including a 12C copy of Ptolemy's *Geography*.

ADDRESSES

⌂ STAY

⊜⊜ **Akrogiali** – *Ouranópoli, 100m/328ft from the bus stop, on the left by the sea.* ℘*23770 71 201. www.ouranoupolis-akrogiali.gr. 13 rooms. No breakfast.* Comfortable rooms if a little monastic; ideal if preparing for life on Mount Áthos. Some rooms with sea view.

⊜⊜ **Makedonia** – *Ouranópoli, take the second street on the left after the Akrogiali (same management).* ℘*23770 71 085, Fax 23770 71 395. www.hotel-makedonia.gr. 18 rooms.* A comfortable, quiet hotel 100m/328ft from the sea.

⊜⊜ **Xenios Zeus** – *Ouranópoli, in the main street on the seaside.* ℘*23770 71 274, Fax 23770 71 185. www.ouranoupoli. com/zeus/index.html. 18 rooms.* This small hotel represents good value for money. Ask for a room with a sea view. Breakfast extra.

⊜⊜⊜ **Xenia** – *outskirts of the village.* ℘*23770 71 412. www.xeniaouranoupolis. com. 88 rooms.* A very pleasant, quiet and comfortable hotel with its own beach. The service is good, but prices are high (although heavily discounted out of season). Breakfast is included and half-board is available.

⦿ EAT

⊜ **Karidas** – *Ouranópoli.* ℘*23770 71 180.* A taverna on the harbour offering a wide selection of fish dishes.

⦿ SHOPPING

Icons – Painted by the monks, they can be bought in Ouranópoli and Kariés.

Kavála★

Kavála – Καβάλα

Dominated by the Turks from 1380 to 1913, Kavála still has an oriental air. It is a lively town built on the shores of a broad bay. In antiquity it was the port of Philippi; it retained its importance through the classical and Byzantine periods, as evinced by its majestic ruins.

A BIT OF HISTORY

First a colony founded by Thássos and later (called Neapolis) the main port of Philippi, Kavála was an important settlement throughout the classical period. St Paul passed through with Silas on his way from Asia Minor to Philippi.

In the Middle Ages the town was called Christoupolis. Raids on the city were undertaken first by Normans, and then the Ottomans, who conquered it in 1391. In the 16C it was called Bucephalos, after Alexander the Great's horse; this is probably the origin of its present name, Kavála. In 1913, the city was ceded to Greece and in 1922 it became home for 25,000 ethnic Greek refugees from Asia

▶ **Population:** 63,293.

⚲ **Michelin Map:** 737 K 2 – eastern Macedonia.

▯ **Info:** Eleftherias Square. ☏ 2510 231011. Open daily 10am–2pm, 6–9pm. Closed Sun. www.danek.gr or www.cityofkavala.gr.

◉ **Location:** Kavála is 175km/109mi northeast of Thessaloniki on the Aegean coast; airport 30km/19mi to the west on the Xanthi road.

🅿 **Parking:** There is precious little by way of official car parking but a space can usually be found.

⌖ **Don't Miss:** The Imaret, the view from Kastro.

🕐 **Timing:** Try to plan for an overnight stay and follow the Walking Tour to see the town sights.

⚲ **Also See:** Thássos (Eastern Aegean Islands).

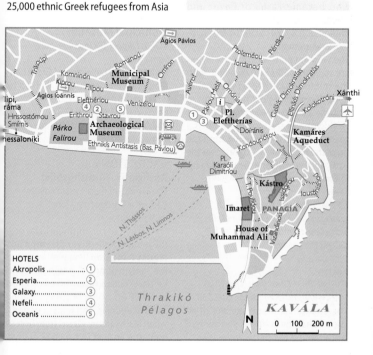

HOTELS

Akropolis	①
Esperia	②
Galaxy	③
Nefeli	④
Oceanis	⑤

Minor. Today it is an industrial centre and the hub of the Macedonian tobacco export business. The old district huddles on a rocky promontory crowned by a citadel, and the modern town extends westwards along the harbour.

OLD TOWN (PANAGIA)

Within the ramparts lies the picturesque old town; its narrow streets and steps wind between the Turkish houses with their tiny courtyards and flowering balconies.

Imarét

This is an unusual group of Muslim-style buildings founded by Mehmet Ali as an almshouse, run by Islamic monks (dervishes) for 300 poor men. The building work started in the early 19C and it serves nowadays as a classical example of Islamic architecture. Today it is also a luxury hotel.

Ikía Mehmét Áli

This 18C house was the birthplace of Mehmet Ali (1769–1849), son of a wealthy Albanian tobacco merchant, who became Pasha of Egypt and founded a royal dynasty which lasted until 1952. It is now owned by the Egyptian Government.

The wooden partitions and the layout are typical of a Turkish dwelling, with the stable and kitchen on the ground floor. The second-floor harem is fitted with *moucharabies*, wooden lattices that enable one to see out without being seen. An extensive **view**★★ from the tip of the promontory extends over the harbour, the town and the bay as far as Thássos Island.

▶ *Walk through the old Turkish quarter, Odós Vizandinóu and Odós Fidíou, past a mosque and up to the Kástro, the citadel.*

Kástro

◷*Open daily 8am–9pm (4pm Nov–Mar). www.castle-kavala.gr.* ⊜€2.50.
The citadel stands on the site of an ancient acropolis and is surrounded by Byzantine ramparts, with views of

Kavála. Prisons and a cistern lie within the ramparts. What you see was built in the first quarter of the 15C on the foundation of far earlier settlements. Its open-air theatre is used occasionally for shows.

Kamáres Aqueduct★★

Spanning the depression between the modern town and the old town, the aqueduct was built in 1530 by Suleiman the Magnificent to supply Kástro with water from local springs.

MUSEUMS
Archaeological Museum

Odós Ethnikis Antistasis. ◷*Open Tue–Sun 8am–8pm Mon 1–8pm.* ⊜€2.
𝄞 25102 223 35.
This modern museum covers eastern Macedonia from the Neolithic period to the Roman Empire. On display are finds from the Neolithic Age, such as objects of stone and clay, as well as colossal Ionic capitals from the Sanctuary of Athena Parthenos, and fine examples of gold **Hellenistic jewellery**. Separate rooms are devoted to finds from Neapolis and ancient Amphipolis.

Municipal Museum

4 Odós Filipou. ◷*Open Tue–Sun 9am–1pm.*
An interesting collection of Greek contemporary and folk art, highlighted by works of the painter and sculptor Polygnotos Vagis (1894–1965). The museum building itself is a good example of 19C vernacular architecture.

EXCURSIONS
Amfípoli★ (Amphipolis)

▶ *88km/55mi southwest of Kavála.*
◷*Open every day 8am–7pm.*
⊜*No charge.*
The ancient city of **Amphipolis** lay near the mouth of the **River Strymon** and **Mount Pangaion** (Pangéo), known as the "holy mountain". Amphipolis was officially founded as an Athenian colony in the 5C BC, and it prospered during the Macedonian and Roman periods, when Mark Antony set sail from here to do battle against Octavian at Actium.

St Paul passed through around AD 50, marking the beginning of the city's palaeo-Christian era, and it was still an important centre in Byzantine times.

The Lion
On the left of the road from Thessaloníki, just before the bridge over the Strymon, stands a huge marble lion. It resembles the lion of Chaironeia, although it is later, dating from the end of the 4C BC.

▶ *After crossing the bridge over the Strymon, take the road to Sérres (left); after 1.5km/1mi turn left to the modern village of Amfípoli and then left again towards the church; after .5km/.3mi a path to the right leads to the ruins.*

Ruins
The prosperity of the city is evident from the monumental buildings decorated with mosaic floors and wall paintings. The recently-discovered Hellenistic **walls** are 7m/23ft high in places; they stretched for 7km/4.5mi and included towers, gateways and bastions. The northern section gives visitors a good picture of how things looked. The most surprising feature is the **bridge** constructed from wooden beams, parts of which show posts standing out from the structure as a result of having dried out. On the plateau, not far from what was probably the *agora*, are traces of palaeo-Christian basilicas: **mosaics** of birds.

Archaeological Museum★
🕒*Open Mon–Sun 8.30am–3pm (closed Mon in winter).* 🎟€2. 📞23220 324 74. Finds from the site include gold **Hellenistic jewellery**, Roman sculpture, a silver ossuary and gold-leaf **diadem**.

Xanthi
Gateway to Thrace, Xanthi reveals an unfamiliar feature of Greece, the one before the great upheavals of the interwar years, when the north of the country was the abode of a large population of Turkish-speaking Muslims. This aspect of its old character is mainly evident in the old Ottoman quarter, one of the few to have survived the earthquakes of 1870

and 1910 where Greece's small Turkish minority still lives. Elsewhere, the modern but pleasant city unfolds an extraordinary tapestry of large avenues, which are crowded with shops and cafés.

ADDRESSES

🛏 STAY
🛏 **Nefeli** – *50 Odós Erithroú Stavroú.* 📞25102 274 41. www.nefeli.com.gr. *94 rooms.* A comfortable hotel, but the most expensive in its category.

🛏 **Espería** – *44 Odós Stavroú.* 📞25102 274 41. www.esperiakavala.gr. *105 rooms.* Large hotel with very comfortable, but impersonal rooms. Those facing the inner court are quiet.

🛏🛏 **Akropolis** – *29 Odós Venizelou.* 📞25102 23543. *14 rooms.* This renovated hotel has rooms with coffee-makers and refrigerators. The bigger rooms have large balconies with superb views to the port. No breakfast.

🛏🛏 **Oceanis** – *32 Odós Erithroú Stavroú.* 📞25102 219 81. www.oceaniskavala.gr. *168 rooms.* This luxury hotel has a rooftop pool with stunning views. A haven of peace amid the hustle and bustle.

🛏🛏🛏 **Galaxy** – *27 Odós Venizelou.* 📞25102 24521. www.airotel.gr. *150 rooms.* A grand hotel with spacious rooms, some with balconies overlooking the harbour.

🍴 EAT
🍴 **Antonia** – *Odós T Poulídou.* Popular with the locals for its fish dishes.

🍴 **Apiko** – *29 Odós T Poulídou (in the citadel).* Good-value grilled fish dishes.

☕ TAKING A BREAK
Café Nikitoros *(42 Platia Karaoli)*, engaging, traditional café; **Café Imaret** *(Odós T Poulídou)*, good for a coffee, or a salad; **Flyboat** *(Odós Ethnikis)*, intriguing café aboard a yacht.

🎭 EVENTS AND FESTIVALS
The **Macedonian Festival of Philippi-Thássos** *(Jul–Aug at the theatre at Philippi)*. Bookings: Kavál a Tourist Office, 📞25102 31011, or at the theatre, 📞25105 164 70, 6–9pm.

Ruins of Philippi★★

O Arhaiologikós Hóros ton Filíppon – Ο Αρχαιολογικός Χώρος των Φιλίππων

Sitting in the fertile Macedonian plain is the site of the ancient city of Philippi. Founded in 360 BC by the Thassians, it was renamed four years later in honour of King Philip II of Macedon, who protected the inhabitants from the Thracians. It is the most important archaeological site in eastern Macedonia.

⊟ **Info:** ℰ 2510 622 810.
◐ **Location:** 15km/9mi northwest of Kavála near the village of Krinides, the ancient city is bisected by the Kavála–Drama road, which takes the route of the old Via Egnatia. Open daily Jun–Oct 8am–7pm, Apr–May and Oct 8am–6pm, Nov–Mar 8am–5pm. €3.
⚮ **Kids:** They will be impressed with the ancient latrines.

A BIT OF HISTORY

In AD 42, two historic battles were fought just west of Philippi: **Mark Antony** and **Octavian** twice faced Julius Caesar's assassins, **Brutus** and **Cassius**, whom they narrowly defeated. First Cassius and then Brutus committed suicide on the spot. The whole of Act V of **Shakespeare**'s *Julius Caesar* takes place "on the plains of Philippi" following the fates of the protagonists.

In 49 AD, **St Paul** began preaching in the town, the first in Europe to hear the gospel; he was denounced and imprisoned. However, Christianity spread rapidly and St Paul's Epistle to the Philippians was sent from Rome in AD 64. The ruins now visible date mostly from the Roman and early Christian eras; the main vestiges of the Macedonian city are the theatre by the Acropolis, and the walls. The Romans modified the layout, and the original heart of the settlement (forum, temples, market, *palaestra*) did not revive until the 6C and 7C.

NORTH SECTION★

Foundations from Philip II's era are still visible, especially the Neapolis Gate (4C BC); however, most of the remains date from Emperor Justinian's time (6C). Immediately on the right, leaning against the wall and the slope of the hill, the **theatre**★ unfolds its white-bleached seats. Built by Philip II (4C BC), it was later modified to accommodate

Roman gladiatorial combat and wild animals. Today, it hosts the more peaceful annual festival of Philippi (*Jul–Sep*).

In the Roman era, cave temples dedicated to various deities were arranged on the hillside path to the Acropolis, in small niches carved into the rock. Just before Basilica A is the **Sanctuary of Artemis**, with a bas-relief showing the goddess hunting a deer. The three neighbouring niches probably formed the Shrine of Silvanus, which historians associate with Latin inscriptions carved into the rock on the right (2C–3C AD).

Little remains of **Basilica A**, whose levelled walls still evoke the magnitude of the three aisles, the narthex and the location of the atrium. Only two columns break the sight of the scattered marble blocks and beautiful capitals. It was probably destroyed by an earthquake soon after it was built (late 5C AD). There are still traces of the steps that descended into the confessional, which housed the relics beneath the high altar. In the western extension are the massive foundations of a building that may have been a Hellenistic **Heróon** (monument to heroes). Down below, near the road, is a Roman cistern later transformed into a place of pilgrimage. According to tradition this was the **Prison of St Paul**. Before crossing the road, walk a few metres towards the northwest to **Basilica C** "Outside The Walls" (late 5C), which contains a beautiful marble floor. The nearby

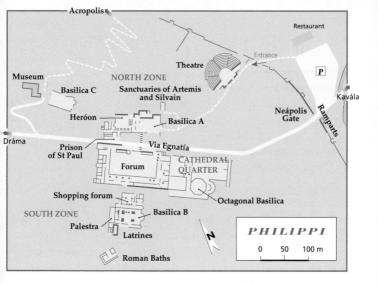

museum (⚿ *closed for renovation,* 📞 *25 105 162 51*) presents the Philippi findings of the École Française of Athens. From there, you can take the path to the Acropolis and view the site from between two Byzantine square towers.

SOUTH SECTION

As you descend to the bottom of the steps, you can still distinguish the pavement of the ancient **Via Egnatia**, which runs along the **forum** of Roman Philippi. The ancient heart of the city, this vast square paved with marble (100m x 50m) is enclosed on three sides by steps and porticoes. Built under Marcus Aurelius (2C AD), it was the centre of public life. Beside the Via Egnatia, you can see the fountains and the platform from which orators once addressed the crowds. On the south side some columns indicate the site of the **shopping forum**, partly covered by Basilica B. This vast market had a central courtyard and a peristyle that led to the shops. **Basilica B**★★ the "Pillared Basilica" (550 AD), is an impressive, but unfinished, palaeo-Christian monument dominating the site. Ruined walls outline three aisles and the apse, preceded by the narthex and the atrium. The dome seems to have collapsed and the narthex was then converted into the main sanctuary. What remain today are the marble arch in the wall separating the narthex from the nave, and the four huge pillars that supported the dome. Some give an idea of the building's splendour: made out of green marble from Thessaly, they are topped with Byzantine Corinthian capitals with acanthus leaves. Next to the market plaza, the church is also close to the Roman *palaestra*, a vast athletic training ground (2C). Situated below the southwest corner is a huge **public latrine**★, which still has most of the original marble seats and water ducts. Further south, the ruins of Roman baths (3C) have some beautiful mosaics.

The Episcopal Quarter

Next to the forum in the east, the **Episcopal district**★ is one of the best preserved among the ancient cities of the Balkans. To the right of the Via Egnatia, a majestic *stoa* leads to the narthex of an octagonal basilica, the former cathedral of Philippi. Built c.400 on the original Basilica of St Paul, it was destroyed in the 7C and you can now only see the base of the walls. The plan was an octagon inscribed in a square topped by a dome. The basilica has kept some floor mosaics and marble paving. The Macedonian tomb beside it, and the residential area just to the east remain closed to the public.

THE PELOPONNESE

I Pelopónnisos – Η Πελοπόννησος

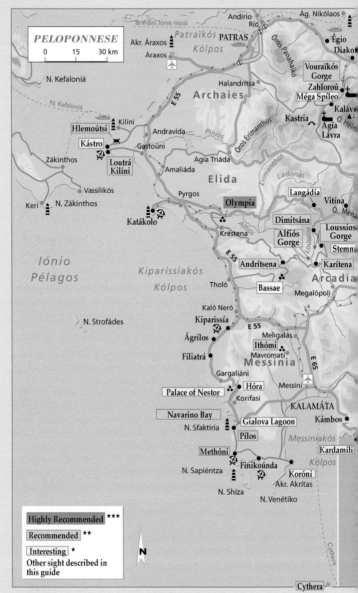

The Peloponnese contains some of the most familiar and least familiar sights in Greece. Familiar from photographs or by reputation will be places like the Corinth Canal and the original Olympic Games stadium at Olympia. Less familiar, perhaps, will be the thrilling ride on the Kalavryta Railway, the rugged Máni Peninsula in the far south, or the ruined hilltop city of Mistras. The name Peloponnese means "the island of Pelops", Pelops being one of the Greek Gods. The region wasn't technically an island until the completion of the Corinth Canal in the 1890s, which severed the Peloponnese from the rest of the Greek mainland, but it still feels very much a part of mainland Greece.

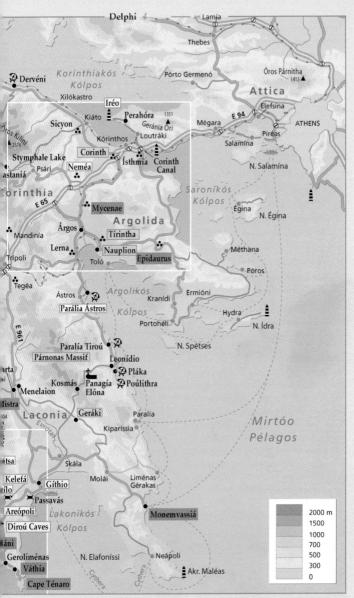

Its attractions include a mountainous interior with unspoilt villages, beach resorts that are less busy than those on the islands, and some of the country's major archaeological sites. Even with a brief visit to the northern Peloponnese from Athens you could see the royal tombs at Mycenae, the ancient Epidaurus theatre, and the even more ancient site of Tiryns, dating back to the 13C BC. Near all these is one of the mainland's most beautiful waterside towns: Nafplion. Further south, the highlights include the monumental and totally isolated Temple of Bassae, and the unusual medieval fortified town of Monemvassia, which is linked to the mainland by a causeway.

CORINTH AND THE ARGOLIS

Kórinthos kai Argolída – Κόρινθος και Αργολίδα

"Not anyone can sail to Corinth", the Ancient Greeks used to say – a reference to the town's notoriously high cost of living. Corinth and its hinterland were something akin to the Las Vegas of the ancient world, complete with a plethora of high-class *hetairai* – modern prostitutes – fine artists, gourmet food and an *agora* for luxury shopping. It would be a miracle had such a rich town survived so many cumulative centuries of jealousy, so it is not a surprise that modern-era Corinth is but a dim shadow of its former self. However, the town is still the gateway to the Peloponnese and the start of many a driving tour around this astounding region.

Highlights

1 Cross the bridge over the **Corinth Canal** (p236)

2 Climb the **Acrocorinth** for views across the Corinthian Gulf (p238)

3 Swim at the beach of **Portohéli** and try some seafood (p245)

4 See a play at the open-air **Epidaurus** theatre (p248)

5 Visit the spectacular **Mycenaean** civilisation ruins (p260)

Evening play, Epidauros theatre

The Argolis

The Argolis region, including the Argolid plain, is where everyone is heading first. This is a mythical place where **Perseus** was king and **Herakles** (Hercules) was born. This is where a Neolithic people built some of the largest standing fortified towns in **Mycenae** and **Tiryns**; where the best example of an ancient Greek theatre – still in operation – remains at **Epidaurus**; and, finally, this is

where modern Greece was born, when **Nauplion** became the country's first post-Independence capital.

But this is not all. This is prime beach country too. Whether shaded by pines or groves of citrus trees, the eastern part of the Argolis Peninsula has a coastline that has only recently been discovered by the tourists who would normally flock to the islands. Whether in a spa in Methena, in a high-class resort in Portohéli or at a fishing taverna in Ermioni, there is something for everyone in this region of Greece.

First Circle of Royal Tombs, Mycenae

Corinth★★

Kórinthos – Κόρινθος

Extensive remains, an impressive acropolis and the port of Lechaion all recall the golden age of "wealthy Corinth". Cosmopolitan and dissolute, it was one of the busiest trading cities in antiquity. Corinth is well placed for trips along the coast of the Gulf of Corinth, and for exploring other Classical sites further inland.

A BIT OF HISTORY

According to legend, the founder and first king of Corinth was **Sisyphus**, a mortal whose cunning ways drew the ire of Zeus. Jealous, the god condemned Sisyphus to carry a rock up a steep slope in Hades, only to have it tumble back to the bottom over and over again, for all eternity. Corinth occupies an eminently favourable position at the crossroads of the land and sea routes linking Attica and the Peloponnese, and the Ionian and the Aegean Seas. High on a hill, its almost impregnable acropolis controlled movement in all directions on the Isthmus of Corinth in ancient times.
A Strategic Site – Only 6km/3.75mi wide, the isthmus was the site of fortification works as early as the Mycenaean period, and plans were laid to dig a shipping canal across the isthmus. Nero began such a project in AD 67, but left it unfinished.

> ▶ **Population:** 29,787.
> ⚲ **Michelin Map:** 737 G-H 9 – Korinthía – Peloponnese.
> ◐ **Location:** Located 85km/53mi west of Athens along the E 94 motorway, Corinth lies at the end of the isthmus separating the Gulf of Corinth and the Saronic Gulf. The ancient city is 8km/5mi away by the E 65 motorway. Near the entrance, a road to the left leads to Acrocorinth.
> 🅿 **Parking:** There is parking space in the modern town and a car park for visitors to the ancient site.
> ⊛ **Don't Miss:** The ancient city; Acrocorinth; the view from the Heraion Headland.
> ◷ **Timing:** The ancient city takes a least a day to visit. An overnight stay at Loutraki is recommended.

In those days the isthmus was more densely inhabited than it is now, and there were three ports on its coastline. From 582 BC the Isthmian Games, second only to the Olympic Games, were held here every two years in honour of Poseidon.
An Opulent City – In the Archaic era Corinth prospered and became a major

Heraion Headland with the sanctuary of Hera

© gabriela insuratelu/Bigstockphoto.com

trading centre dealing in wheat from Sicily, papyrus from Egypt, ivory from Libya, leather from Cyrenaica, incense from Arabia, dates from Phoenicia, apples and pears from Euboea, carpets from Carthage and slaves from Phrygia. A famous saying used to be: "not any-one can sail to Corinth", a reference to its high cost of living.

The **Corinthian capital** (an architect-ural feature) is thought to have been invented here in the 5C BC by the sculptor **Kallimachos**. The Corinthians produced pottery for export as well as bronze, glass and purple-dyed cloth; their naval shipyards launched the first *triremes*. In the 4C BC the city led Greece in the **League of Corinth** under Mac-edonian rule.

Corinth also gained renown for its courtesans *(hetairai)* and priestesses *(hierodules)* engaged in sacred prosti-tution in the precincts of the Temple of Aphrodite.

Corinth, a Roman Colony – Corinth was sacked by the Romans in 146 BC in the same year as Carthage; the precious metals on the city's statues eventually ended up on the baldaquin in St. Peter's basilica in Rome.

In 44 BC Julius Caesar founded a town on the ruins of ancient Corinth. It became the capital of Roman Greece and a desti-nation for commerce and tourism.

Beginning in AD 51 **St Paul** spent 18 months here; in his first Epistle to the Corinthians, written in Ephesus, he cas-tigated the shameless behaviour of the citizens. The Jewish priests had Paul tried in the *agora*, but he was acquit-ted. Paul returned to Corinth for a sec-ond time, where he wrote his Epistle to Romans.

Following the rule of Hadrian, who erected many buildings and an aque-duct to bring water from **Lake Stym-phalia**, Corinth declined thanks to earthquakes and invasions. Only the acropolis retained a certain importance as a military stronghold.

Excavations and the Opening of the Canal – During the Turkish occupation ancient Corinth disappeared under urban development. Excavations began in 1896 and uncovered a jumble of ruins, mostly Roman.

Around this time the project to create a canal was resurrected. Work began in 1882, and was completed in 1893. The **Corinth Canal**★★ permanently altered the shipping routes, and ena-bled Piraeus to become the major port of Greece.

CORINTH TODAY

The modern town grew up after two earthquakes decimated the area, the second one in 1928. Laid out on a linear grid plan, the city offers little of inter-est but is a useful base from which to explore the area.

Worth a stop is the **Historical and Folk Museum** *(close to Elefterio Venizelou Square;* ◷*open daily 8.30am–1.30pm;* ◉*€1.50)*, to see its fine collection of traditional costumes, embroidery and finely worked silver jewellery.

ARCHAIA KÓRINTHOS★★ (Ancient Corinth)

▷ *7km/4.5mi southwest of the modern town. Take the motorway towards Tripoli; after 6km/4mi follow the signs for the ancient site. Park in the car park; the main entrance is on the west side of the archaeological site. It is also possible to reach the site from the Lechaion road. Allow 2hrs.* ◷*Open 1 Apr–30 Oct, daily 8am–7.30pm; 1 Nov–31 Mar, daily 8.30am–3pm (9pm on Wed).* ◉*€6 (Sun no charge).* ☎*27410 312 07.*

Inhabited since Neolithic times, Corinth has a vast array of archaeological mate-rial, although the visible remains date from the Roman period.

Start from the **Naós Oktavías**, the Tem-ple of Octavian, a Roman building from which three fine Corinthian capitals have been re-erected.

Archaeological Museum

The collections include most of the objects discovered from excavations on the site, including fine **Archaic ceram-ics** with oriental decoration, and exam-ples of Roman mosaics.

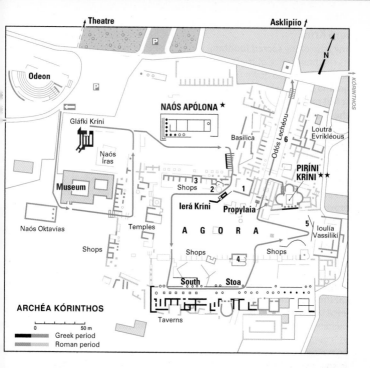

Make for the upper level of the *agora* and then bear left round **Naós Íras**, an old sanctuary to Hera, to reach the adjoining **Gláfki Fountain**.

Naós Apólona (Temple of Apollo)★

The highest point of ancient Corinth is marked by remains of the Temple of Apollo: seven out of 38 monolithic Doric columns, that were originally covered with stucco. The site affords spectacular views of the Gulf of Corinth and of Acrocorinth.

A grand flight of steps built in the 5C BC leads down to the lower level of the *agora*. The façade (**1**) of a Roman **basilica**, which stood in the centre of the north side, was adorned with four huge statues (two are displayed in the museum).

View to the Temple of Apollo, Ancient Corinth

© Greek National Tourism Organisation

Ierá Kríni

The base of the **sacred fountain**, with its rhythmic frieze of triglyphs, is still visible. Steps lead down to the underground spring, which was linked by a secret passage with the **Sanctuary of the Oracle** (**2**). A priest hidden beneath an altar answered the petitioners, who thought they were in direct communication with the god.

Agora

This huge, rectangular open space provides remarkable views up to Acrocorinth. Along the north side, below the terrace supporting the great temple, are the remains of 15 Roman shops; the one in the centre (**3**) is still roofed.

South Stoa

On the south side of the *agora (upper level)*, stood the South Stoa, an immense building which was used by the Greeks as a guesthouse and converted by the Romans into an administrative centre. At the west end you can still trace the arrangement of each "compartment" with its courtyard and well.

In front of the stoa stood **Bema** (**4**), the platform from which the governor Gallio passed judgment on **St Paul** (there was a church on the site in the Middle Ages).

To the east lie the remains of the **Julian Basilica** (Ioulía Vassilikí) dating from the Roman era. Excavations in front of

it have revealed earlier Greek paving with the starting line of a racetrack (**5**).

Propílea

The base of the monumental entrance *(propylaia)* to the *agora* remains. In the Roman era it was surmounted by gold chariots for the god Helios and his son Phaeton.

Piríni Kríni★★

Many times remodelled, the **Peirene Fountain** dates from the 6C BC. The original Greek part is at the back of the atrium *(south side)*: six stone arches stand in front of a row of underground reservoirs.

Leave the ancient city by the **Lechaion Way** (Odós Lechéou), the beginning of a road running from the *agora* to the harbour at Lechaion. In the Roman period it became a ceremonial way leading to the Propylaia and bordered by porticoes housing the **Baths of Eurykles** (Loutrá Evrikléous) with their public latrines (**6**), which are well preserved.

Odeon

Excavations have revealed a small, semicircular Roman theatre dating from the 1C AD. The banks of seats could accommodate about 3,000 spectators.

Theatre

Begun in the 5C BC it was remodelled several times; the stage was enlarged to accommodate gladiatorial combats and nautical spectacles. It held about 18,000 people.

Asklipiío

The plan of the temple dedicated to Asklepios, the god of medicine, can be clearly traced on the ground. Near the entrance *(east)* is an unusual stone offertory. West of the temple is the Fountain of Lerna, for hydrotherapy.

AKROKÓRINTHOS★★ (Acrocorinth)

❯ *Take the signposted road on the left going uphill (7km/4.5mi there and back) which passes the old potters' district on the right, bears left in front of a Turkish*

A Redoubtable Magician

Medea, a charming sorceress, fell in love with Jason during his quest for the Golden Fleece and gave him a magic balm to protect him in his adventures. Upon the Argonauts' triumphant return, Jason married Medea. One day King Creon offered his daughter Glauce to Jason, who abandoned Medea. The sorceress killed her children to spite her husband and gave her rival a poisoned wedding dress, which ignited, causing Jason's bride to throw herself into the fountain.

Acrocorinth

fountain not far from the excavated remains of a temple to Demeter, and then climbs in a succession of bends up to the citadel entrance. ○*Open 1 Apr –30 Oct, daily 8am–7pm; 1 Nov–31 Mar, Tue–Sun 8.30am–3pm.* ◎*No charge.* ℘*27410 312 66.*

Poised between heaven and earth and almost indistinguishable from the rock, the ruins of Acrocorinth are some of the most impressive in the world because of their extent, the desolate grandeur of their elevated site and the immense panorama which they command. Acrocorinth was first a Greek acropolis, then a Roman citadel and then a Byzantine fortress. Frankish, Turkish, Florentine and Venetian occupiers possessed it in turns, adding to it over the centuries.

The access ramp from the car park to the fortress offers spectacular views of the three lines of defence and the three gates that protect the citadel on the western approach.

Monumental Gateways

The first gateway (14C) is defended by a moat; a tower flanks the second (also 14C). The third is flanked by two powerful rectangular towers: the one on the right is mainly ancient (4C BC).

A steep path leads up the slope among the ruins (note the fine views of the Gulf of Corinth), through the old Turkish district (remains of mosque – *left*) to the rampart and the northern postern. Return to the decapitated minaret and pass a fine brick-vaulted cistern to reach the medieval keep.

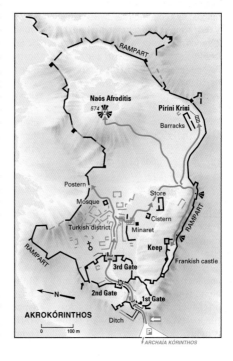

239

Keep

The keep dominates the remains of the Frankish castle of the De Villehardouins, princes of Morea in the 13C and the 14C. Fine view of the Byzantine ramparts with their rectangular towers, the surrounding heights and the Gulf of Corinth. From the keep, return along the south ramparts and continue eastwards (view of the mountains of the Peloponnese) to the Upper Peirene Spring, which is to be found near a bend in the wall next to a ruined Turkish barracks.

Ano Piríni Kríni (Upper Peirene Spring)

Steps lead down into a Hellenistic underground chamber (ancient graffiti), thence to another chamber, which has since flooded with water. According to legend the Upper Peirini Spring was created by the winged horse Pegasus stamping its foot; Pegasus was then captured by Bellerophon while drinking at the spring.

Naós Afrodítis (Temple of Aphrodite)

The site of the famous temple is now marked by a column. There is a splendid **panorama**★★★ extending beyond the Isthmus of Corinth to Mount Parnassus (*north*), across Attica (*east*) and to the Peloponnese (*south*). To the southwest, perched on a rocky peak, are the medieval ruins of the Frankish Castle of Montesquieu.

OUTSKIRTS

◐ *From the canal, turn right to the Possidonía Bridge (2km/1.25mi) at the west end of the canal.*

Diolkós

The central section of the bridge sinks onto the canal bed to let boats pass. Near the bridge on either side of the modern road one can see the *diolkós*, an ancient portage way paved with stone along which the ships were dragged on chariots or on wooden rollers across the lowest and narrowest part of the isthmus.

On the side near the Gulf of Corinth the paving stones are marked with letters of the Corinthian alphabet; on the other side the ruts worn by the chariots can be seen. This stone slipway was probably built in the 6C BC and was still in use in the 12C AD.

Isthmía (Isthmian Sanctuary)

◐ *From Athens, exit the expressway at the interchange just after the Corinth Canal and proceed as for ancient Epidaurus; on leaving the village of Kirá Vrissi turn right at the junction, then immediately left into the first uphill road.* The museum is at the entrance to the site. ◑Open Tue–Sun 8.30am–3pm. ◉No charge (site); €2 (museum). ℘27410 372 44.

The **museum** presents objects found during the excavations of the Isthmian Sanctuary and the port of Kenchreai. There are some unusual glass mosaics (decorated with plant and bird motifs, human figures and landscapes) found in submerged packing cases at Kenchreai; they were probably imported from Egypt. Amphoras, gymnastic apparatus and ceramics are also on view.

The **excavations** have revealed the foundations of a Temple to Poseidon (5C BC) and the stadium that from 582 BC hosted the biannual Isthmian Games; note the 16 grooves made in the stone which diverge near the starting line. Fine mosaics include one depicting a dancing Dionysos surrounded by dolphins; this was originally the floor of a Roman swimming pool. At the southern end of the stadium, traces remain of the Palémonion (1C BC). Beyond are the ruins of a Roman theatre, a defensive wall and the Roman fortress.

Port of Kenchreai

◐ *7km/4mi S of Isthmia on coast road.* In antiquity, this was the port for Corinth on the Saronic Gulf. Traces of harbour installations extend beneath the water. To the south lie the foundations of a Christian basilica (4C) which replaced a temple to Isis. St Paul disembarked here in AD 51 to begin his sojourn among the Corinthians.

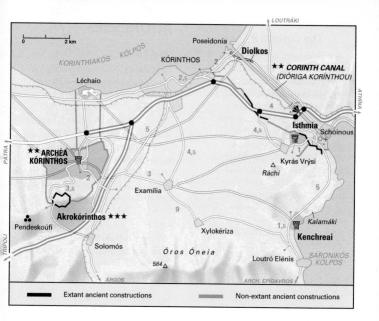

| Extant ancient constructions | Non-extant ancient constructions |

Loutráki★

Combining the charm of a traditional spa with the modern attractions of a seaside resort, Loutráki lies in the crook of the Bay of Corinth at the foot of the **Mount Geránia** chain. Luxury hotels, a casino, a palm-tree walk and a luxuriant public garden bordering a little harbour all add to the visitor's pleasure.

Loutráki is the largest spa in Greece; its radioactive warm water is used to treat various ailments. Bottled Loutráki **mineral water** is sold throughout the country.

Akrotírio Iréo★★★ (Heraion Headland)

▶ *46km/29mi return trip to Loutráki.*

The corniche road runs north, offering admirable views of the coast and the Bay of Corinth; then it bears right inland by a taverna (view north towards the headland crowned by a lighthouse).

On the outskirts of **Perahóra** (small archaeological museum) turn left into a narrow road *(sign "Limni Heraion")* which passes through olive groves and then skirts **Lake Vouliagméni**.

At the junction marked by a chapel bear right. The **Heraion** (a sanctuary dedicated to **Hera**) occupies the rocky slopes of the headland separating the Bay of Corinth from the Gulf. Its remote and wild **site**★ is hidden in the bottom of a narrow valley below an acropolis. From the car park walk down into the valley. Near a house are the ruins of a Hellenistic cistern. Above are the remains of temples to Hera Limenia (6C BC) and Hera Akraia (8C BC).

The path from the car park to the lighthouse *(30min on foot there and back)* provides a splendid **panorama**★★★, particularly at sunset, of the ancient site, the coast and mountains of the Peloponnese *(southwest)*, the Gulf of Corinth stretching northwest, the Halcyonic Gulf *(Kólpos Alkionídon)* on the north side of the headland and on the skyline to the north the Parnassos massif towering over Delphi.

Sikyón

▶ *25km/16mi west of Corinth. Follow the coastline; from Kiáto take the small road (sign "ancient Sikyon") through the modern village of Sikióna to the ancient site.* ⏱ *Open daily 8.30am–3pm.* 🚫 *No charge.* ☏ *27410 312 07.*

The ruins of Sikyon recall an earlier ancient city that flourished in the Archaic period. That city stood in the

The Corinth Project

A million years ago, the Peloponnese formed part of the mainland, but Greece, and especially the Gulf of Corinth, is subject to a great deal of seismic activity. The movement of tectonic plates pulls the peninsula 1.5cm/.5in further away from the mainland every year and has created the Gulf of Corinth. All this activity has meant the development of a major programme of research: The Corinth Project. The establishment of a permanent observation station will allow information to be gathered which will permit scientists to better understand seismic faults.

plain, but it was razed in 305 BC, and rebuilt on the plateau. It became famous for its school of painting on wax, which produced among others Pamphilos, the Master of Apelles.

The **ruins** date from the Hellenistic and the Roman periods. Beyond the museum, which stands on the site of the old Roman baths, is a large theatre (3C BC) (restored) on the right built against the flank of the former acropolis. Below to the left are the foundations of a huge gymnasiu m on two levels bordered by porticoes and linked by a central staircase between two fountains that are clearly identifiable. The ground also shows traces of a temple, presumably dedicated to Apollo, and a senate house *(bouleuterion)*.

ADDRESSES

STAY

⊖ **Marínos** – *Old Corinth, in the first street on the right after the Tássos taverna.* ☏27410 312 09. www.marinos-rooms.com *22 rooms.* ⌸ A large house, not luxurious, but with a friendly welcome. Quiet rooms in the pavilion.

⊖⊖ **Le Petit France** – *Loutraki, 3 Odós Botsari, to the right of the main road.* ☏27440 224 01. lepetitfrance@yahoo.com. *15 rooms.* Centrally located but shielded from the noise, this hotel is run by a Franco-Greek couple and offers a warm welcome and clean, spacious rooms.

⊖⊖⊖ **Loutraki Palace** – *Loutraki, 19 G. Lekka St, towards the northern end.* ☏27440 266 95. www.hotelpalace.gr. *43 rooms.* This 1920s palace is in a class of its own. Huge rooms, some with balconies.

⊖⊖⊖ **Kalamaki Beach** – *Isthmia.* ☏27410 37653/6. www.kalamakibeach.gr. *76 rooms.* Large international hotel on the beach. Spacious rooms with terraces. Half-board.

EAT

⊖ **Tássos** – *Old Corinth, centre of the village.* A typical taverna with great ambience: *souvláki* being grilled, friendly staff and local music.

⊖ **Marínos** – *Old Corinth, at the guesthouse of the same name.* An excellent taverna with tables laid out beneath the trees. Set menu (wine included).

⊖⊖ **Ta Kioupiá** – *Kalámia, near Corinth.* ☏27410 81818. Taverna on the beach serving Greek mezedes and barbecued fish.

TAKING A BREAK

At Posidonia, to the left of the bridge on the west side of the canal, the **café-taverna Diolkós** offers fine views of the canal. The bar, Posidonio, on the right, is the ideal place to watch the sunset.

Neméa★

Neméa – Νεμέα

The ruins of Neméa, legendary site of Herakles' (Hercules) first "labour", lie in a peaceful valley between Mount Kilíni to the west and the slopes of the Argolid and Arcadian ranges to the south. The ancient site is near the head of the valley of the River Elissos, in the northeast of the Peloponnese.

A BIT OF HISTORY

Herakles' (Hercules) first labour or task was to kill a ferocious lion that lived in a nearby cave; the mythological hero strangled the beast and wore its skin as a trophy. Lions did, in fact, roam the region in the Mycenaean period (there are lion hunts depicted on items found at Mycenae).

In the archaic and classical periods the Nemean Games were one of the four great competitions of the Greek world. Nowadays modern Neméa's reputation rests on its red wine, which is strong and sweet and known locally as "the blood of Herakles".

RUINS★

🕐 *Open Tue–Sun 8am–7pm; Mon 8am–12pm.* ∞€3 *(combined ticket with stadium €4).*

The largest set of ruins here were part of the huge Doric **Temple of Zeus** (4C BC).

Remnants of the Temple of Zeus

© Greek National Tourism Organisation

- ⚬ **Michelin Map:** 737 G 10 – Korinthía – Peloponnese.
- ▶ **Location:** Neméa is 35km/22mi southwest of Corinth, and about the same distance northwest of Nauplion, with easy access by the E 65 Corinth–Tripoli motorway.
- 🅿 **Parking:** There is a car park at the site.
- ⊚ **Don't Miss:** A stroll around Lake Stymphalia.
- 🕐 **Timing:** An hour at the very least; longer if a picnic suggests itself.

Three columns are still standing, and other displaced drums lie about. A ramp marks the centre of the façade; in front stood an immense sacrificial altar.

Formerly a grove of sacred cypress trees ringed the sanctuary, which was surrounded by buildings including nine houses *(oikoi)* built for participants in the Nemean Games. To the north were potters' ovens *(now reburied)*. The thermal baths from the same period *(recently laid bare and roofed over for protection)* consisted of two covered underground rooms, reached by stairs lined with columns.

MUSEUM★

The museum displays engravings, drawings, photographs and visitors' notes relating to the site. Among the objects in the collection are architectural elements and inscriptions unearthed during the excavations, most notably 312 items from the **Mycenaean Cemetery of Aidonia**. The treasure is many objects of precious stone and metal: rings, seals, ornaments, necklaces and pendants.

STADIUM★

▶ *Turn left when exiting the ruins, then left again at the next junction; the stadium is 100m/328ft further on the right, before a bend.* 🕐*Same opening hours as the ruins.*

The Stymphalian Birds

According to the legend the gloomy waters of Lake Stymphalia were haunted by nauseating birds with huge wings who seized on passersby, suffocating them and killing them with their beaks before eating them. **Herakles** rid the region of them as the sixth of his Twelve Labours by killing them with his arrows and then offering them to Athena.

In the hillside southeast of the Temple of Zeus lie the remnants of the stadium (4C BC) where the Nemean Games took place on the third year of every Olympiad. It held 40,000 spectators. South of the arena, earthenware pipes supplied the stadium with spring water, purified in a system of basins and stone gutters around the arena. The starting line, marked with stones, is well preserved; it supported the wooden mechanism which gave the starting signal. The competitors, trainers and judges entered the

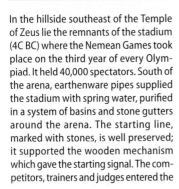

Herakles and the Hydra of Lerna

In this labour Herakles had to confront the multi-headed monster Hydra, daughter of the viper Echidna, whose putrid breath had the power to kill. The Hydra was protected by the Goddess Hera, who hated Herakles (her husband Zeus' illegitimate son). While he was doing battle with the monster, she sent a giant sea creature who attacked Herakles, injuring his heel before being killed by him.

Herakles could not kill the Hydra single-handedly (the heads grew back as soon as they were cut off); his nephew Iolaos came to his aide by setting the nearby woods alight and applying flame to the severed necks of the monster. Thus cauterised, the Hydra was unable to regenerate its heads.

stadium through a building whose interior was decorated with colonnades on three of its sides. It was here, too, that the athletes got ready for the competition, before entering the arena through a vaulted passage. The names of some of the winners and young athletes are clearly legible on the walls.

EXCURSIONS
Límni Stimfalía★
(Lake Stymphalia)

▶ *30km/19mi west of Neméa. Take the road to Kalianoi; follow signs to Karteri.* The route crosses the coastal plain and then climbs the eastern foothills of Mount Kilíni overlooking the Gulf of Corinth. The road then descends into the huge and barren depression at the bottom of which lies Lake Stymphalia. *Park in the car park and take the path up the hill overlooking the lake.*

Lake★

Below the acropolis of the city of Stymphalos extends an immense reed-covered marsh surrounded by a ring of dark peaks. This vast tract of land is inhabited only by herds of cows or flocks of sheep grazing in the custody of herdsmen.

Old Abbey of Zaraká

On the east side of the road from Kiáto lie the ruins of a Cistercian monastery (13C). The church was Gothic: the pillars in the nave were formed of engaged columns and the chancel was square, a Cistercian hallmark. A single tower marks the entrance to the precinct.

Remains of the City

▶ *500m/1,640ft beyond the town and old abbey, take the path through the fields that leads to the foot of the rock.* Here lie traces of the Temple of Athena Polias, a *palaestra*, and stairs carved into the rock. Make a detour to the small town of Kartéri *(it has good tavernas)* and at the church turn left towards Lafka: here, at the entrance to the village, a road on the left leads to the opposite side of the lake.

Argolída★

Argolída – Αργολίδα

This peninsula, which separates the Saronic and Argolic Gulfs, is composed of limestone hills, some forested; the coastal plains are planted with citrus orchards. The little ports and sheltered creeks for bathing which are dotted along the shore were formerly accessible only by sea, but now there is a coast road serving the modern hotels and resorts offering attractive views of the islands of Póros, Hydra, Dokós and Spetsae.

DRIVING TOUR

PENINSULA CIRCUIT

Starting from Portohéli at the southern end of the peninsula, this 216km/135mi circuit leads back to Kósta, looking out towards Spetsae. Allow one day.

Portohéli

Well sheltered in its attractive bay, Portohéli (the name means "eel port") is a fishing village and port for Spetsae. To the north, where Halieisonce stood *(signposted)*, traces of the base of an acropolis (dating from 700 BC) can be seen.

Kranídi

This beautiful village of stone houses is set in pleasant surroundings. The Church of Agía Triáda boasts some magnificent 13C frescoes, and nearby stand the monasteries of St Anne, Panagias tis Pantanassas and Agion Anargiron, all from the 11C.

▶ *Turn left just after Kranídi.*

Koilada

This little fishing village occupies a lovely setting with some very inviting beaches nearby, particularly the one at **Korakia**. A footpath in the mountains to the north leads to Fraghti Cave, which was inhabited as early as the 8th millennium BC.

▶ **Population:** 105,770.

Michelin Map: 737 G 10, H 10-11 – Peloponnese.

Location: To get to the peninsula, take the E94 motorway from Athens; exit at Corinth and follow signs for Spétses.

Parking: No official car parks but roadside spaces are plentiful.

Don't Miss: Trizína and the surroundings.

Timing: Give yourself a day to complete the driving tour.

Kids: A boat ride to Méthana if coming from Piraeus and a swim in the sulphurous waters.

▶ *Head back towards Kranídi and turn left onto the road to Ligourió.*

Beyond **Foúrni**, a dirt track on the right *(signposted)* leads past the Church of Agion Anargiron to the northern entrance to the wild and secluded **Katafýgi Gorge**.

Craters of Dídima

Just past the village of Dídima lies a vast crater on the mountainside to the

Crater of Dídima

left. According to local tradition it was formed by a meteorite and dates from the 19C. A dirt road suitable for cars (*sign "pros spilia"*) leads to a larger crater which is not visible from the road. Steps lead down a tunnel to a little chapel.

▷ *Continue towards Ligourió. Just before Trahiá turn right to Fanári.*

Beyond **Fanári**, clinging to the steep hillside, a corniche road descends the cliff face providing spectacular **views**★ of the Saronic shoreline and the **Méthana Peninsula** which ends to Mount Helóni (743m/2,438ft), an extinct volcano.

▷ *7km/4.5mi beyond Kaloní turn left towards Méthana.*

The road crosses the neck of land leading to the former volcanic island of Méthana. Just before Méthana there is a great view of the town and harbour.

Méthana
There is a boat service from Piraeus to Méthana, where traces of a 4C BC fortress have been found. It is a seaside resort and spa featuring warm sulphurous waters.

Vathí
This fishing village is tucked away in a small bay. Further north along the coast road, a footpath heads off through the forest to the remains of the surrounding wall of the ancient acropolis of Méthana (*300m/984ft from the road*). Continuing northwards, the road provides bird's-eye **views**★ of the sea before plunging into the forest on the way to **Kaïméni Hora**. This deserted village stands at the foot of a volcanic cone, whose summit (*access by footpath in poor condition*) affords magnificent views of the wild and beautiful countryside.

▷ *Return to Méthana by the same road, and at the crossroads on the mainland turn left towards Galatás; after 2km/1.25mi turn right (sign) into a minor road leading to Trizína (formerly Damalas).*

▷ *Go through the village and follow the signs "Acropolis of Trizína"; turn right into a minor road (signs "Diavologéfira" and "Antiquities"). At a junction near a Roman bridge bear right and continue for 1.5km/1mi along a track past two churches (after the second church the track is in poor condition for 700m/2,300ft). Signs "Sanctuary of Hippolytos, Asklepieion, Episkopi".*

Trizína★
On the left of the road are the scanty remains of the shrine of Hippolytus and, on the right, those of an asklepieion, a sanctuary to **Asklepios**, the god of healing. A short distance away stand

Ruins of a Byzantine church and a bishop's palace

View towards the island of Hydra from Ermióni

© R. Mattes/MICHELIN

the ruins of a Byzantine church and a bishop's palace. Return to the junction and turn right at the Roman bridge, continuing to a Hellenistic tower, part of an Ancient fortress; the upper section dates from the Middle Ages.

Continue to the end of the road. A 5min walk leads to the lower end of the **Devil's Gorge**★ and to the Devil's Bridge, "**Diavologéfira**", a natural rock formation linking both sides of the gorge. The path runs west to the top of the cliffs where an ancient acropolis, a sanctuary to Pan, and the 13C fort of Damalet stood.

▷ *Return to the road to Galatàs.*

Galatàs
Magnificent **views**★★ of the straits and Póros Island.

▷ *Head for Ermióni.*

Lemonodássos★
On the coast opposite Póros Island there is a huge lemon grove of about 30,000 trees covering a slope above **Alíki** beach. *Park the car beside the road near the sign by a chapel.* From there walk up the hill *(30min on foot there and back)* through the scented lemon grove. The path *(sign "Pros Kéntron Cardássi" or "Restaurant Cardássi")* soon reaches the Cardássi taverna; attractive view of Póros Island. The coast road to Ermióni affords many fine

views of Hydra and Dokós through the ubiquitous olive groves. Pass **Plépi**★, an attractive resort with a small harbour.

Ermióni
Seat of a Byzantine bishopric, the town is now a resort and sheltered fishing port. *Regular services to Hydra.*

▷ *Continue along the coast road bearing left at the fork to Kósta, an attractive modern resort. Ferry to Spetsae and coastal vessels to Hydra.*

ADDRESSES

🛏 STAY
🍴🍴🍴 **AKS Porto Heli** – *Portohéli.* ℘*27540 98073. www.akshotels.com/en/porto-heli-hotel.html. 204 rooms, 10 suites.* Four-star hotel and resort, the only one open all year round. In the summer it organises excursions to most of the places in this section.

🍴 EAT
🍴🍴 **Delfini** – *Portohéli on the road to Kósta.* ℘*27540 52455. http://fish-tavern-restaurant-delfini-portoheli.focusgreece.gr/index.htm.* Taverna that offers Greek traditional dishes such as aubergine stew and fried courgette balls, as well as cheese pies and *dolmades.* Best known for its daily fresh fish catch.

Ancient Epidaurus★★★

Arhéa Epídavros –
Αρχαία Επίδαυρος

The elegance, perfection of design and quality of conservation at the Theatre of Epidaurus cannot be overstated and were already acknowledged in antiquity. It was the jewel in the crown of the Sanctuary of Aesculapius (Asklepios), the god of medicine; from all over Greece people came to consult the oracle here. Its ruins occupy an isolated site of gently rolling hills carpeted with pine trees and oleanders.

A BIT OF HISTORY

The Power to Heal – According to legend, **Asklepios**, a son of Apollo, was trained by the centaur Cheiron in the healing arts, becoming so proficient that he was able to resuscitate the dead, drawing the ire of Zeus and Hades. Jealous of a power reserved for the gods, Zeus sent a thunderbolt to strike Asklepios dead and his body was buried at Epidaurus. From the 6C BC Asklepios became the object of a cult of healing, which reached its greatest intensity in the 4C BC. The great Greek doctors, even the famous **Hippocrates** of Kos, claimed authority from him.

- **Michelin Map:** 737 H 10 – Argolída – Peloponnese.
- **Location:** 68km/43mi south of Corinth, 30km/19mi east of Nauplion. Note that there are three places named "Epidaurus": the villages of Néa Epidaurus and Paleá Epidaurus (near the sea), and Arhéa Epidaurus, the ancient site, also known as Askilipió.
- **Parking:** Large car park next to the road from Nauplion (signs from Ligourio).
- **Don't Miss:** The theatre.
- **Timing:** At least two hours to visit the site.

Asklepios is generally represented as a bearded figure leaning on an augur's wand accompanied by the magic serpent; these elements later came to be included in the rod of Asklepios, the doctor's emblem.

The Epidaurus Treatment – Supplicants would proceed through stages of sacrifice and purification before sleeping in a sacred dormitory *(abator)*. They might be cured instantly or Asklepios might appear to them in dreams, which the priests would translate into treatment, accompanied by exercises, relaxa-

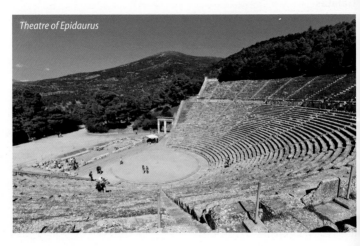
Theatre of Epidaurus

tion, baths or intellectual pursuits. This explains the importance given to the theatre and the sports facilities and to the Asklepian Games, held every four years. The people expressed their gratitude with the sacrifices and votive offerings. Under the Romans, thaumaturgy gradually yielded its place to a more scientific form of medicine. Late in the 5C AD a Christian basilica was built on the site of the ancient sanctuary.

Epidaurus languished until the beginning of the 19C. In 1822 the independence of Greece was proclaimed in the theatre. In 1881 Greek archaeologists, assisted by the French School in Athens, began to work on the site.

SIGHTS

From the car park a path leads through the trees to the archaeological site.
Open Apr–Oct daily 7.45am–6.45pm; Nov–Mar 8am–5pm. €6. 27530 2309 or 27530 226 66.

Theatre★★★

Outstanding for the beauty of its setting, its magnificent lines and harmonious proportions, the theatre is set underneath the shadows of Mounts Arachnaion, Koryfaion and Tithion facing the valley sacred to Asklepios who according to legend was born on Tithion. The theatre, designed by Polykleitos the Younger in the 4C BC, originally had 34 rows but an extension in Roman times added another 21 rows. In 1954 it was restored to accommodate modern productions of the ancient repertory as well as musical recitals.

The theatre, which can accommodate 14,000 spectators, consists of 55 rows divided by a promenade *(diázoma)* into upper and lower sections. The circular orchestra, where the chorus performed, is marked at the centre by the base of the altar to Dionysos. On the north side of the orchestra are the foundations of the stage and the proscenium incorporating an arch that supported the scenery.

It is worth climbing the steps between the rows of seats to appreciate the structure's contours and proportions. The view from the top is great, particularly in the early evening when the sacred valley of Asklepios lies peacefully in the shelter of the surrounding hills.

In the **museum** *(closed Mon morning)* you'll find *stelae* bearing inscriptions, a collection of Roman medical instruments and a partial reconstruction of the rotunda using authentic elements).

Asklipiío★ (Sanctuary of Asklepios)

From the theatre, pass the museum to reach the **gymnasium***; the central part of it was converted into an odeon by the Romans. Descend the ramp, which led up to the main entrance to the gymnasium, passing the remains of the* **palaestra***.*

To the northwest are the foundations of the Temple of Artemis, Naós Artémidos (late 4C BC), which has been partially reconstructed in the museum. In the Sanctuary of Asklepios, the main monuments are surrounded by a wall that confined the sacred serpents. An outline of rectangular foundations marks the site of the **Naós Asklipioú**, a small Doric temple with a raised peristyle. It contained a statue of Asklepios seated on a throne, a baton in his right hand and his left resting on the head of a serpent. South of the temple are the remains of the sacrificial altar. More foundations belong to the famous rotunda *(thólos)* built in the 4C BC by the theatre's

Perfect Acoustics

The performance at the Theatre of Epidaurus could be heard and seen perfectly from every seat. Sit at the topmost row and have someone whisper, strike a match or rustle a piece of paper in the centre of the orchestra to demonstrate. It is not known for certain if the perfect acoustics are the result of design or accident but the rows of limestone seats filter out low-frequency sounds while amplifying high-frequency ones from actors on the stage.

Sanctuary of Asklepios

architect, **Polykleitos the Younger**, as a mausoleum for Asklepios. The rotunda was sumptuously decorated with different-coloured marbles, paintings and finely sculpted motifs, some of which are on display in the National Archaeological Museum in Athens.

To the north of the rotunda and the temple are the foundations of the dormitory where the sick slept in the hope that Asklepios would appear to them in a dream. On the north side are traces of a huge 4C BC hotel (katagógeion) comprising 160 rooms arranged round four courtyards.

Stadium

This was built in the 5C BC in a hollow in the ground. Look for the starting and finishing lines, 181m/594ft apart (distance of "one stadium"). Seating was provided for important people only.

Sanctuary of Apollo Maleatas

3km/2mi from the theatre (30min on foot). Take the road above the theatre, behind the Hotel Xenia. ⚬━ *The sanctuary is often closed to the public, as excavations are in progress.*

Discovered in 1928, the building dates from the 6C BC; there are ruins of a supporting wall and some 2C AD Roman structures including a cistern and baths. There is a fine view of the surrounding area.

OUTSKIRTS
Ligourió

▷ *5km/3mi to the north of the archaeological site.*

This small town, renowned for its good tavernas, also boasts a beautiful 11C **Church of St John** (Ágios Ioannis o Eleïmon), built with material from the Epidaurus Theatre and Sanctuary of Asklepios. The Byzantine **Kimissis tis Theotokou** Church (16C) contains some splendid frescoes. There is also a private **Natural History Museum Leoforos Asklipiou 27** (○ *open May–Sep Tue–Sat 9am–7.30pm Sun 10am–4pm; Oct–Apr Tue–Sat 9am–5pm, Sun 10am–4pm;* ⊛ *€4;* ℘ *27530 22587/22588).* Mostly contains fossils, mainly ammonites from 530 million to 3 million years ago.

Agnountos Monastery

▷ *7km/4.5mi northeast, before the village of Néa Epidaurus (on the right when coming from Arhéa Epidaurus).*

A fortified building of the 6C and 8C with an interior courtyard and an 11C church, remodelled in the 14C. The Byzantine form with a plan in the shape of the Greek cross is here combined with a basilica plan with an octagonal dome. Inside there are 13C frescoes, icons dating from 1759, and an iconostasis in decorated carved wood of 1713 (a copy, for security reasons). The monastery has been reoccupied since 1980 and the nuns are restoring it stage by stage.

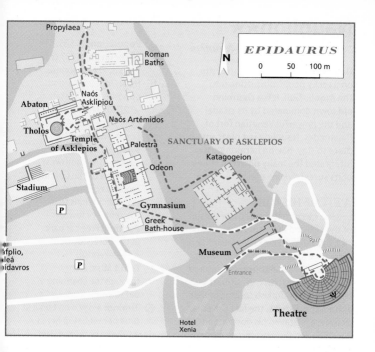

Paleá Epidaurus

▶ *9km/5.5mi northeast of the ancient site.*

Small fishing village and resort with several fish tavernas at the end of a picturesque valley. At the end of the road running along the seashore, a path through a citrus orchard leads to a recently discovered small theatre from the time of Alexander the Great *(10min on foot, turn right at the junction).*

ADDRESSES

STAY

⊖ **Staying Angelica Vilas** – *Giálasi, 10km/6mi from the site.* ☏*27530 41818. www.epidaurushotels.com.* Large rooms arranged in a villa complex, only 100m/328ft from the sea.

⊖⊖⊖ **Eleni** – *Giálasi, 10km/6mi from the site.* ☏*27530 41364/41864. 15 rooms.* More upmarket option with bar, roof garden and restaurant.

EAT

⊖⊖ **Eating Leonidas** – *Ligourio* ☏*27530 22115.* Fifty years and still going strong. Eating here is quite an experience. Every star who has participated in the Epidaurus Festival from Maria Callas downwards has eaten here as the photos on the walls remind you. Book well in advance in the summer as the stars still come over after the performances.

⊖⊖ **Mouria** – *Palea Epidaurus by the port. Mar–Oct only.* ☏*27530 41218/ 42101/42103.* Less crowded than Leonidas, but as cosmopolitan, with excellent pork and fish dishes.

EVENTS AND FESTIVALS

Epidaurus Festival – Held in July and August; the great plays of classical Greece are performed at 9pm on Fridays and Saturdays; be sure to book well in advance. Tickets may be purchased here three hours before performances, ☏*27530 2226*; or at the tourist office in Nauplion, *Odós 25 Martiou,* ☏*27520 244 44*; also in Athens from the **Athens Festival Box Office**, *4 Odós Stadiou,* ☏*210 32 21459.*

Nauplion★★

Náfplio – Ναύπλιο

Nauplion occupies a delightful site on a rocky peninsula jutting into the Argolic Gulf. It is a charming old town dominated by its citadel and the powerful Venetian fort of Palamedes. Nauplion is a pleasant place to stay, having harmoniously integrated the many different styles of its successive invaders.

A BIT OF HISTORY

Legend has it that Nauplios, grandson of the sea-god Poseidon, founded the city. Byzantines, Franks, Venetians and Turks have fought over it. On 20 November 1822, when **Staïkópoulos** captured the Palamedes Fort, Nauplion was wrenched from Turkish control. In 1828 **John Kapodístrias**, the first Governor of Greece, installed his government in Nauplion and the city officially became the capital of Greece in the following year. But bitter dissension developed and on 27 September 1831 Kapodístrias was assassinated on the steps of St Spiridon's Church by his political opponents. The Great Powers – England, France and Russia – turned to **Otto of Bavaria**, then 17 years old; his accession to the throne was ratified in 1832 by a National Assembly held at **Prónia**.

Otto's reign was marked by the construction of Neoclassical buildings; their sober lines lend the city its aristocratic

- ▶ **Population:** 16 885.
- **Michelin Map:** 737 G 10 – Argolis – Peloponnese.
- **Info:** Odós 25 Martiou opposite the bus station. ✆ 27520 24 444. Open daily 9am–1pm, 4–8pm.
- **Location:** 64km/40mi south of Corinth and 132km/85mi southwest of Athens by the Corinth motorway. From the exit, follow signs to the centre of town.
- **Parking:** Free car park at the port (crowded on weekends!).
- **Don't Miss:** A stroll through the charming old town.
- **Timing:** A day won't do it; if time permits, stop here for a sojourn of several days.
- **Kids:** Kombolóï Museum, Stathmos Children's Museum.

character. A colossal carved lion on the road from Nauplion to Toló commemorates the death of Bavarian soldiers who died in an epidemic in Tiryns in 1833–34. There are other monuments and inscriptions recalling the days of newly won independence.

View of Nauplion

Palamedes Fort

© Vangelis Thomaidis/iStockphoto.com

PALAMÍDI★★

Access by Leofóros 25 Martíou and the road leading to the east entrance or by 999 steps (20min climb) from Platía Arvanitiás. ⏰*Open daily 8am–6.45pm.* ⊛€4. ✆27520 280 36.

The **Palamedes Fort** dates from the second Venetian occupation (1686–1715) and is a powerful complex of eight bastions linked by defilades, vaults, corridors and secret passages. St Andrew's Bastion enclosed a courtyard overlooked by the quarters of the Governor of the Fort and by St Andrew's Chapel, near the cell in which Kolokotrónis was detained.

The parapet walk provides magnificent views of Nauplion, the bay, the Argolid Plain and the Peloponnese coastline.

⏺WALKING TOURS
OLD TOWN★★
Platía Síndagmatos

Centre of Nauplion, the square served as the political forum during the struggle for independence. At the west end of the square stands a naval warehouse (1713) now converted into a museum; the cinema opposite was once a mosque. In the southwest corner of the square, a flight of steps leads to another former mosque, which was the site of the first meeting of the Greek National Assembly in 1822.

The **Archaeological Museum** (⏰*open 8am–7.30pm;* ⊛€2; ✆27520 275 02) housed in a 1713 Venetian mansion is of interest for its rare Neolithic pottery, a magnificent fresco known as *"The Lady*

of Mycenae", and Archaic art found during excavations in the Argolid.

▷ *From the centre of the east side of the square take Odós Konstandínou, a busy shopping street; turn right and then left into Odós Plapoúta.*

Ágios Geórgios

St George's Cathedral was built in the 16C in a mixture of Byzantine and Venetian architectural styles. The interior contains the throne of King Otto.

▷ *Turn right into Leofóros Singroú and return to the old town by Odós Papanikoláou, a narrow street crossed by steep lanes leading up to the Acronauplia. One of these lanes on the left (Odós Potamianou) leads to the Frankish Church.*

Frangoklissiá

A flight of steps and an attractive 13C porch lead up to the **Frankish Church**. Inside stands a **Memorial to the Philhellenes** who fell in the Greek War of Independence. Behind the high altar is the Muslim prayer recess *(mihrab)*.

▷ *Return down Odós Potamianou to St Spiridon's Church near a Turkish fountain.*

Ágios Spirídonas

St Spiridon's is a tiny Orthodox church built in 1702. Here on the threshold two members of the Mavromichalis family from the Máni assassinated Kapodístrias, who had imprisoned one of them, **Petrobey Mavromihális** (picture inside the church).

▷ *Continue along Odós Kapodistríou past another Turkish fountain and turn right on Odós Kokkinou to Odós Staikopoulou, a shopping street.*

At no. 25 Odós Staikopoulou, stop in at the intriguing ♦♦**Komboló ̈ı Museum** (⏰*open Wed–Mon 9.30am–8.30pm, weekends 10am–8pm)* with over 200 *komboló ̈ı* made of amber, stone, glass beads, ivory and shells.

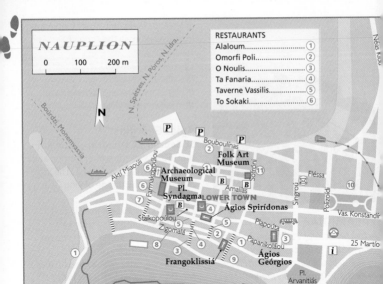

SEAFRONT★★

About 2hrs on foot.

▶ *Starting from Platía Nikitará (northwest corner), take Leofóros Amalías and turn right on Odós Sofroni.*

Well worth a stop, the charming ▲▲**Folk Art Museum** (🕐*open 9am–1.30pm, 6–9pm; ⊙€4)* presents daily life of centuries past via a remarkable collection of costumes from the Peloponnese, tools, jewellery and traditional embroidery.

Harbour

This extends on both sides of Platía Iatroú, a square containing the Town Hall, St Nicholas' Church for sailors (early 18C) and the French Philhellene Monument. Just short of the southern tip of the promontory a path *(left)* leads up to the **Chapel of the Little Virgin** (Panagítsa), clinging precariously to the rocky slope.

▶ *Follow the coast (magnificent views of the sea and Palamedes Fort) to Arvanitiá, Nauplion's beach; then make for Platía Nikitará.*

Isle of Boúrdzi★

Ask at the harbour for the times of the shuttle boats.

The island was first fortified in 1471 by the Venetians to protect the harbour entrance and was reinforced early in the 18C; view of the city and its citadels.

Acronáfplia★★
(Citadel of Acronauplia)

Access on foot by one of the steep lanes leading off Odós Potamianou; by car by the road from Arvanitiá.

First a Greek and then a Frankish fortress were built on Acronáfplia. The final structure, which until recently housed a hospital, barracks and prison, consists of

HOTELS	
Acronafplia	①
Byron	②
Guesthouse Dimitri Becas	③
Ilion	④
Kapodistrias	⑤
King Othon I	⑥
King Othon II	⑦
Leto	⑧
Marianna	⑨
Nafsimedon	⑩
Omorfi Poli	⑪

View to Isle of Boúrdzi

© Georgios Alexandris/iStockphoto.com

several wards with the lion of St Mark over the gates.

OUTSKIRTS
Karathóna Bay and Beach★★

▶ *3km/2mi south. Access by car by the road marked Palamídi from which a secondary road branches off to the bay.*

A gently curving bay protected by an island encloses a huge sandy beach.

Kazarma Acropolis

▶ *14km/8.75mi east, near the small town of Arkadiko: take the path (signposted) which leads to the top of the mountain (20min walk).*

Remains of the fortress built by the Argives (5C BC) can be seen on the hillside.

Lerní

▶ *On the northwest shore of the Argolic Gulf near the modern village of **Míli** lies the site of ancient Lerna.*

The narrow tract of land between the road and the seashore contains the Hydra Springs and the Lerna Marshes, now much reduced in size but still the source of many springs.

House of the Tiles

▶ *On leaving Míli going south, bear left after a church into a path leading to the site (200m/656ft).*
🕐 *Open every day, 8.30am–2.30pm.*
🎫 *€2.*

The **House of the Tiles** takes its name from the great quantities of tiles that were found among the foundations. This ancient palace (2200 BC) is the best-preserved large building from the early Bronze Age.

THE ROAD TO TOLÓ
Agía Moní

▶ *12km/7.5mi southeast. From Nauplion take the Epidaurus road; after 1.5km/1mi turn right into a narrow road (sign "Agía Moní").*

The monastery was founded in 1144 near the Kánathos Spring *(on the right below the convent)* which in mythology was supposed to return Hera to a state

The Battle of Lepanto (7 October 1571)

The last and greatest battle to engage oar-propelled vessels took place in the Bay of Pátra to the leeward of Oxiá Island, where the Christian fleet from Kefalonía met the Turkish fleet from Lepanto. The fleet of the Holy League was commanded by **Don John of Austria** (1547–78), then 23 years old. The Turkish fleet, led by Ali Pasha, consisted of 200 galleys.

The 12 Venetian galleys – huge ships carrying 750 men, of whom half manned the oars – wrought havoc among the Turkish fleet, most of which was destroyed. It was a severe blow to Turkish sea power.

The battle was the subject of many paintings by celebrated artists such as Titian, Tintoretto and Veronese; it also inspired some well-known works of poetry.

of virginity once a year. There is a guided tour by the monks of the 12C Byzantine church.

▶ *Return to the Epidaurus road and continue for 2km/1.25mi. Turn right into the road to Toló; before reaching the coast, turn left into the road to Drépano, which passes a chapel near the Assíni acropolis.*

Assíni (Asine)

The remains of the ramparts are part Mycenaean and Archaic and part Hellenistic. Huge beehive tombs have yielded Mycenaean objects. From the top, fine **views**★★ of Toló.

Toló★

Toló is a popular and pleasant seaside resort sheltered by the Assíni promontory at the end of a long sandy beach with the islands of Rómvi and Platía offshore.

NORTH TO AGÍA TRÍADA
Agía Triáda

▶ *8km/5mi north. Take the Árgos road; immediately after the site of Tiryns (Tírintha) turn right into a minor road which runs through orange groves in the direction of Midéa.*

On the left just before the village is the 12C **Church of the Virgin** (Kimisseos tis Theotókou). The village was previously known as Mérbaka after Wilhelm van Moerbeke, a Fleming who was Archbishop of Corinth in 1280.

Dendra

▶ *3km/2mi northeast of Agía Triáda.* 1km/0.6mi from the village *(signposted)* is the burial chamber where the oldest known cuirass, a leather breastplate, (15C BC) – was found (now in the Archaeological Museum of Nauplion).

ADDRESSES

🛏 STAY

🛏 **Pension Dimitri Becas** – *Odós Efthimiopoulou.* ℘27520 275 49. *8 rooms.* This modest guesthouse has some rooms with showers and WCs. Fine views over the town; good value.

🛏🛏 **Omorphi Poli** – *5 Odós Sofróni.* ℘27520 215 65. *www.omorfipoli-pension. com. 7 rooms, 2 suites.* Creatively decorated hotel feels like a traditional Greek house. Breakfast on the ground floor. Good value.

🛏🛏 **Akronafplia** – *34 Odós Papanikolaou (corner of Odos Terzaki).* ℘27520 24486. The hotel's decor mixes wood, metal and colourful weavings. Several houses scattered in the old city add up to 35 rooms of comfort and size. They are quite variable, but all have that distinctive decor. Taverna on the ground floor of the parent hotel.

🛏🛏 **King Othon I** – *4 Odós Farmakopoúlou.* ℘27520 275 85. *www. kingothon.gr. 11 rooms.* Ideally located, this hotel is a refurbished Neoclassical house in front of the sea near Platía Sintagmatos. Small but comfortable and tastefully decorated rooms. Breakfast served in a charming garden. The best recommendation in Nauplion.

🛏 **Marianna** – *9 Odós Potamianoú.* 🕿*27520 242 56. www.hotelmarianna.gr. 12 rooms.* Bright and clean, in the street leading to Acronáfplion, all rooms look out onto the harbour and town. Best views from the rooms on the top floor. Laundry service and good breakfast.

🛏 **Leto** – *28 Odós Zigomala.* 🕿*27520 28093. 12 rooms.* Overlooking the old town on the slopes of Acronáfplion, this unpretentious property allows one to stay in Nauplion at affordable prices. Prefer the top floor rooms that benefit from a view. Good value for money.

🛏🛏 **Kapodistrias** – *28 Odós Kokiknou.* 🕿*27520 29366 www.hotelkapodistrias.gr. 12 rooms.* Hotel occupying a traditional house with old furnishings and high ceilings. Each room has its own personality (and size). Some have balconies overlooking the alley in front. A real charmer.

🛏🛏🛏 **Nausimedon** – *9 Odós Merarhías, near the old railway station.* 🕿*27520 250 60. www.nafsimedon.gr. 13 rooms, 3 bungalows.* Magnificent mansion with high-ceilinged rooms and antique furnishings. Cocktails served under the palm trees in the garden.

🛏🛏🛏 **King Othon II** – *5 Odós Spiliadou, near the old railway station.* 🕿*27520 97790.* The Greeks only had one King Othon; the Latin numeral in this hotel refers not to a royal dynasty but to a dynasty of hoteliers. In the same spirit as the parent King Othon I: the charm is still there.

🛏🛏🛏 **Byron** – *2 Odós Platonos, near the church of St Spyridon.* 🕿*2752022351. www.byronhotel.gr. 18 rooms.* Recognisable by its elegant ochre façade, this charming hotel has a very good reputation in the town. Too bad the beds are steep and that sometimes rooms are overbooked.

🛏🛏🛏 **Ilion** – *4 Odós Efthymiopoulou, just behind Odós Kapodistriou.* 🕿*27520 25114. www.ilionhotel.gr. 10 rooms and 5 studios.* This luxury hotel is housed in an old townhouse and boasts beautiful common areas. Its murals and decoration are not without a kitschy charm. Its studios located in the heights of the city, at the corner of Odós Zigomala, are more sober and can accommodate up to four people.

⍾⁄ EAT

🛏 **To Sokáki** – *Between Sýndagma Square and the King Othon Hotel.* Excellent full breakfasts, giant crepes and enormous mixed ice creams.

🛏 **O Noulis** – *22 Odós Moutsourídou, an alley on the right at the bottom of Odós Papanikolaou.* Traditional, popular with locals. The tray with 10 different types of *meze* is a meal in itself.

🛏🛏 **Ta Fanaria** – *Odós Stoikopoulou.* Excellent cooking (the chef has been here for 25 years) and streetside tables.

🛏🛏 **Alaloum** – *In the lower city in front of the church of Agios Nikolaos.* 🕿*27520 29883.* Traditional setting with a touch of elegance. Sit in the main restaurant room or roof terrace for a good conventional cuisine.

🛏🛏🛏 **Nautikos Omilos Náfplio** – *Nauplion Sailing Club, seafront road at the foot of the walls.* Fine views over the Gulf of Argolis, traditional cuisine and quality service. Book ahead.

🛏🛏🛏 **Aiolos** – *30 Vasilissis Olgas St.* 🕿*27520 26828.* A long six-page menu offering extensive mezedes, main courses, large portions and an enormous selection of Greek wines.

🛏🛏🛏 **Kakaranakis** – *18 Vasilissis Olgas.* 🕿*27520 25371. www.kakanarakis.gr.* Family restaurant in business since 1986, offering imaginative versions of traditional dishes.

🚃 TAKING A BREAK

Stathmós – Located in the warehouses of the old railway station, this is the first children's museum in Greece, founded in 1989. 🕘*Open Mon–Fri 5.30pm–7.30pm Sat 11am–1pm.* 🎟 *Varies.* 🕿*27520-23792/28947.*

Antica Gelateria di Roma – *Odós Farmakopoúlou, in front of King Othon I Hotel.* Serving artisanal ice cream since 1870.

🛍 SHOPPING

Don't leave Nauplion without worry beads (*komboloï*); great selection at the **House of Amber** *(12 Odós Konstantinou).* Food of the gods, all honey-based delicacies can be sampled at **Nectar and Ambrosia** *(Odos Farmakopoulo).*

Tiryns★★

Tírintha – Τίρυνθα

Set amid a fertile plain, the Mycenaean fortress of Tiryns is a Cyclopean structure (13C BC), a well-preserved masterpiece of ancient military architecture. Comparable in size to Mycenae itself, it appears in the epic poems of Homer.

A BIT OF HISTORY

The Legend of Herakles – The mythological demi-god and hero Herakles was born of the union between Zeus and Alkmene, Queen of Tiryns. Brave and strong, Herakles as a baby strangled the serpents sent to kill him by Hera, the jealous wife of Zeus.

Later, in a fit of madness, Herakles killed his own children, and the Pythia at Delphi ordered him to enter the service of Eurystheus, King of Árgos, who set him the **Twelve Labours** as a penance: to strangle the Nemean lion, to execute the many-headed hydra of Lerna, to run down the hind of Ceryneia, to capture the Erymanthian boar, to cleanse the Augean stables, to destroy the Stymphalian birds, to tame the Cretan bull, to capture the man-eating horses of King Diomedes, to obtain the girdle of the Amazon queen, to carry off the cattle of Geryon (a three-headed monster), to fetch the golden apples from the Garden of the Hesperides and finally to bring back Cerberus from Hades.

Michelin Map: 737 G 10 – Argolis – Peloponnese.

Location: 55km/34mi south of Corinth, on the road from Nauplion to Argos.

Parking: Car park on the left, just after the "Tiryntha" sign, 4km/2.5mi north of Nauplion.

Timing: Plan 2hrs; the site is a good excursion from Nauplion.

Kids: The legend of Herakles should stimulate an interest in the rocky ruins.

Trojan War – In the Achaean period (13C BC) Tiryns was subject to Mycenae and took part in the Trojan War under Agamemnon. During the Dorian invasion (12C BC) it was an independent kingdom with about 15,000 inhabitants; it was frequently in conflict with its neighbour Árgos. In 468 BC the Argives captured the city and laid it waste.

ACROPOLIS★★

Open daily 8am–7pm (summer); 8.30am–3pm (winter). €3.

The ruins now visible date mostly from the late 13C BC. They comprise the palace on the upper level, and on the lower an elliptical precinct enclosing buildings for military, religious and economic use.

Remains of Acropolis

Fine views of Árgos and the Argolis, Mycenae, Nauplion and the bay. Frescoes, ceramics and terracottas from the acropolis may be seen in museums in Athens and Nauplion.

Ramparts★★

Impressive in size and strength, the ramparts were compared by Pausanias to the ancient pyramids. The ramp (broad enough for a chariot) leads up to the main entrance to the acropolis, leaving would-be attackers exposed from the right. The gateway was reinforced by two flanking towers. On passing through the gateway, turn left into the passage (**1**) between the outer wall and the palace. It was a real death-trap; if the attackers managed to force the gate they could easily be annihilated by projectiles hurled from every side.

Palace★

The door to the palace is marked by a stone threshold, and by one of the jambs containing the socket for the wooden bar that held the doors shut. Inside is the forecourt; steps *(left)* lead down to the east casemates.

East Casemates★★ – A narrow gallery with a vaulted roof was built in the thickness of the ramparts; it had six casemates which were used as stores or barrack rooms.

Great Propylaia – The Great Propylaia on the Acropolis in Athens was designed to the same plan as the one here: an inner and outer porch covering a central passage. The Great Propylaia leads into the palace's great court from which a staircase descends to the **South Casemates**. A bit further, the **Smaller Propylaia** (**2**) links the Great Court to the Inner or Megaron Court.

Inner Court – Originally covered with white cement; it was enclosed on three

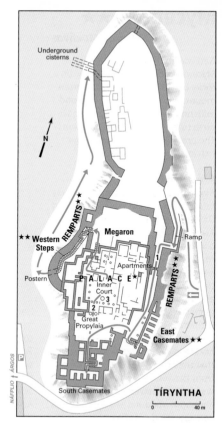

Undergound cisterns

N

REMPARTS★★

★★ Western Steps

Megaron

Ramp

Postern

Apartments

P A L A C E★

Inner Court

3

REMPARTS★★

2

Great Propylaia

East Casemates★★

South Casemates

TÍRYNTHA

0   40 m

NAFPLIO   ÁRGOS

sides by porticoes of which traces remain; at the far end rose the façade of the *megaron*. On the right, within the entrance, stood the royal altar (**3**).

Megaron – As at Mycenae the *megaron* had a porch, a vestibule, and a central hearth; the king's throne stood on the right.

Steps and Western Ramparts★★

A flight of steps winds down inside the crescent-shaped wall to a postern gate, an effective defence. If attackers succeeded to breach the gate, it was assailed on all sides by the defenders, and even if some of the attackers managed to climb the steps they fell into a sort of trap at the top. There was, moreover, an additional bastion protecting the heart of the acropolis. At the foot of the steps at the end of the ramparts are the vaulted **cisterns**.

Mycenae★★★

Mikínai – Μυκήναι

Gateway to the rich Argolis region, Mycenae occupies a wild site★★ on a rocky hillside surrounded by barren mountains. Dating from the second millennium BC, the settlement gave birth to the Mycenaean civilisation. The proud ruins are beautiful and rich in archaeological finds.

A BIT OF HISTORY

According to legend, Mycenae was founded by Perseus, son of Zeus and Danaë, who raised the city walls with the help of the Cyclops, giants who had one eye in the middle of their forehead. After the Perseids came the Atreids, an accursed clan whose members and their exploits of fratricidal vengeance are recounted in the *Iliad* by Homer and other plays by Aeschylus, Sophocles and Euripides. For many years the story was thought to be the stuff of legend, but historians and archaeologists now think that the Atreids did exist. Regardless, from the 16C to the 12C BC, Mycenae was the most powerful state in the Mediterranean world and had close relations with Crete and even Egypt.

By the 2C AD Mycenae was reduced to a few overgrown ruins. Enter **Heinrich Schliemann**, a wealthy German businessman with an obsession for the

- ◐ **Michelin Map:** 737 G 10 – Argolid – Peloponnese.
- ▷ **Location:** On the old national route, about 40km/26mi southwest of Corinth and about 120km/75mi west of Athens. The road passes through the modern village of Mycenae, before heading up to a car park on the left.
- ℙ **Parking:** There is a car park at the site.
- ⊚ **Don't Miss:** The treasures in the museum, the Royal Tombs, the Lion Gate.
- ◕ **Timing:** Plan two hours; visit in the cool of the morning.

Homeric heroes. This brilliant amateur had discovered the site of Troy on the coast of Asia Minor in 1874.

Two years later he began to dig on the site of Mycenae in the hope of finding the Tomb of Agamemnon. Guided by a sentence in Pausanias which said that Agamemnon had been buried within the city walls, Schliemann discovered, just inside the Lion Gate, a circle of royal tombs containing 19 corpses, which he thought to be those of Agamemnon, Cassandra and their companions. Within

Lion Gate

a month a large collection of jewellery, vases and precious items was recorded. Today they can be seen on display in the Mycenaean Room in the Athens Museum.

Extensive excavations and restoration of the site have continued in this century, including the discovery in 1951 of a second circle of royal tombs near the Tomb of Clytemnestra. Excavations continue today on the site within the western wall.

ANCIENT CITY★★★
ACROPOLIS

🕐 *Open daily 8am (midday on Mon)– 7.30pm (summer), 8.30am–3.30pm (winter). Museum: Mon noon–3pm; Tue–Sun 8.30am–3pm.* ✆*€8 combined ticket for the site, museum and treasury.* ✆*27510 76 585. A torch is useful for visiting the tombs and cistern.*

The **acropolis** hill is fringed to the north and south by two deep ravines. Triangular in shape and surrounded by ramparts, the acropolis housed the king, the royal family, the nobles and the palace guard. The town lay at the foot of the fortification.

Ramparts★★

Built of stone, the Cyclopean fortifications date mostly from the 14C–13C BC.

Píli ton Leónton★★★ (Lion Gate)

The main entrance to the acropolis takes its name from the two headless wild animals (probably lionesses) sculpted on the huge **monolithic pediment**. A symbol of Mycenaean power, the animals stand on either side of a central column, their front paws resting on a double altar which also supports the pillar and an entablature.

The gateway proper is flanked by two protective walls. Note the enormous stone blocks used in the construction; the lintel weighs over 20 tonnes. The wooden doors were reinforced by a bar, which slotted into holes that are visible in the uprights. Just over the threshold lay the porter's lodge *(left)* and the remains of a **grain store** (1) *(right)*

where carbonised grains of cereal were discovered in large jars.

First Circle of Royal Tombs★★

On the right within the Lion Gate is the famous cemetery where Schliemann thought Agamemnon and his suite were buried. It is, in fact, much older (16C BC). A double row of stones marks the circular outline. Within, six shaft graves contained the bodies of eight men, nine women and two children, accompanied by precious burial items (now displayed in the Athens Museum). The deceased bore gold **funerary masks** moulded onto their faces after death.

From the First Circle of Tombs take the paved ramp, "the Royal Way", which leads up to the palace past an area of houses and depositories *(southwest)*. Discovered here were terracotta idols (on display at the Archaeological Museum of Nauplion) and numerous tablets (used for bookkeeping) in the Archaic **Linear B** script.

Palace★

Only foundations are visible of the royal palace (15C BC). The main western block contains the **megaron,** (fairly well preserved), and the **main stairs** (**2**).

The *propylaia* opened into the **great courtyard** (**3**). Beyond was a portico, a vestibule and the *megaron* itself, a royal chamber with a round hearth in the centre surrounded by four pillars (the bases are extant); the throne probably stood on the right.

The upper terrace of the palace has been altered by the later construction of a **Temple to Athena** (**4**); only a few traces remain but there is a beautiful view of the site.

The visit to the acropolis is quite tiring; visitors can either return to the Lion Gate or the more energetic can continue to the eastern spur of the site.

Eastern Spur★

The remains of a later set of **fortifications** (**5**), dating from the 12C BC, can be seen at this end of the fortress, as well as an open **cistern** (**6**) from the Hellenistic period.

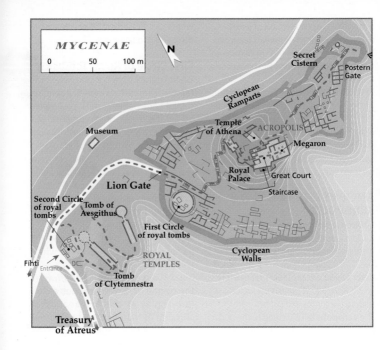

On the right a postern *(no access)* opens to the southeast. On the left is the entrance to an underground stairway; its 99 steps bend round beneath the walls to a secret **cistern** below.

Follow the inside of the north rampart to the **North Gate**; walk out through the gate for a few yards to get an overall view of the impressive ramparts.

Museum★

Opened to the public in 2003, the museum presents the finest objects excavated from the site, with the exception of the funerary items from the tomb of Agamemnon, now on display in the Athens Museum (copies on view here). There's a helpful model representing the city during its heyday, and items illustrating ancient Mycenaean culture of (terra-cotta idols, frescoes, etc.).

Tombs

As you exit from the Lion Gate, paths lead to the Tomb of the Lions *(right)* and the Aigisthos Tomb *(left)*.

Táfos Klitemnistras★

This communal royal tomb dates to the 14C BC. The huge round funeral chamber is roofed with a dome 12.96m/42.52ft above the floor.

Second Circle of Royal Tombs

Dating to the 17C BC, the second circle enclosed 24 graves; excavations have uncovered important archaeological material now on view in the Athens Museum.

⟢ *Drive down the road to the Treasury of Atreus (right).*

Treasury of Atreus or Tomb of Agamemnon★★

This tomb (mid-13C BC and four centuries before the likely time of the Trojan War) is the largest and the most beautiful of the nine communal beehive tombs which have been discovered near the Acropolis of Mycenae. Partially hewn out of the hillside, it features remarkable stone construction including a majestic **funerary chamber**, the *thólos*, which is roofed with a conical corbel vault that

The Tragedy of the Atreids

The Atreids' complicated history is well known thanks to the works of the Greek poets. The best known of this accursed family are:

Atreus, son of Pelops, who killed the sons of his brother Thyestes and served them to him during a banquet.

Menelaus, son of Atreus and King of Sparta, whose wife **Helen** was seduced by Paris, son of Priam, King of Troy, thus provoking the Trojan War.

Agamemnon, Menelaus' brother, King of Mycenae and husband of **Clytemnestra**, Helen's sister; he was the leader of the Achaeans in the expedition against Troy, and ordered the sacrifice of his daughter Iphigenia at Aulis to obtain a favourable wind.

Aigisthos, younger son of Thyestes who killed his uncle Atreus to avenge his father's death and became Clytemnestra's lover; she asked him to get rid of Agamemnon, just returned from Troy, and his captive **Cassandra**, Priam's daughter, known for her gloomy predictions which all refused to believe.

Orestes, son of Agamemnon and Clytemnestra, who was persuaded by his sister **Electra** to kill Clytemnestra and her lover Aigisthos; he was pursued by the **Furies** but acquitted on the Areopagos in Athens by a jury presided over by Athena and then purified by Apollo on the *omphalos* in Delphi before ascending the throne of Mycenae; he gave his sister Electra in marriage to his faithful friend **Pylades**.

gives it the appearance of a beehive. The *thólos* is built up from 33 rings of conglomerate ashlar blocks, each perfectly fitted so as to ensure a slight projection beyond the edge of the one below it. A passage leads into a smaller rectangular chamber hollowed out of the rock; some think it was the funeral chamber of the head of the family, others that it was the treasury itself.

The tomb was visible and had already been plundered when Pausanias mentioned it in his travel guide of the 2C AD. It was used for some time by shepherds and their fires blackened the walls. Fragments of the relief decoration, taken by Lord Silgo and Lord Elgin, have ended up in museums outside of Greece.

ADDRESSES

☆ STAY

⊜⊜ **Belle Hélène** – *In the middle of the village on the left as you descend from Mycenae.* ☎27510 76179. *Open Mar–Nov.* **8 rooms.** This old hotel (1862) offers plenty of character, antique furniture, etc. Schliemann himself stayed here. Bathrooms at the end of the corridor. Restaurant on ground floor.

⊜⊜ **Petite Planète** – *On Tsounta Ave. between the village and the archaeological site.* ☎27510 762 40. **30 rooms.** Modern hotel, comfortable rooms with terraces. The view over the Argolid from the restaurant is magnificent. Rates vary depending on the season.

☆ EAT

Modern Mycenae is well developed for tourism with a plethora of restaurants and cafés, but most of these close evenings in the off-season. In the centre of the village, you'll find a few spots favoured by locals, including:

⊜ **Spiros** – Small family restaurant with modest but excellent grilled dishes (try the lamb).

⊜ **Mykaïnos** – A local favourite; stop in for a drink or the daily special.

Árgos

Árgos – Άργος

Árgos, the oldest city in Greece according to the ancients, is today an unremarkable modern city. The population of the capital of the Argolis of classical times was as large as that of Athens. However, there are many important reminders of its great past, including its striking theatre, its Roman baths and fine archaeological museum.

A BIT OF HISTORY

Perseus, Hero of the Argolis – Árgos was founded by an Egyptian, Danaos, father of the famous Danaids. Later the city came under Perseus and his descendants.

Perseus' origins are mired in myth. As the story goes, the nymph Danaë was imprisoned by her father, King Acrisius, in order to thwart a prophecy that her son would kill his grandfather. But the god Zeus visited her in a shower of gold, fathered **Perseus**, and brought mother and son to safety on the island of Serifos. After heroic feats including the slaying of the Gorgon Medusa (a mythical creature with snakes for hair and the power to turn onlookers to stone), Perseus arrived in Árgos.

The grim prophecy was fulfilled when Perseus, competing in the ceremonial games, threw the discus, hitting the king on the head and killing him. Refusing to accede to Acrisius' throne, Perseus became king of Tyrins instead.

Changing Fortunes – Throughout the Archaic period the city dominated the northeast of the Peloponnese in rivalry with Sparta. During the classical period it supported a brilliant civilisation which produced a school of sculptors in bronze including **Polykleitos,** second only to Pheidias. Argos was supplanted in importance by Nauplion under the Franks. The town was burned during the War of Independence and rebuilt on a grid plan. Today it is a communications centre and a market for the agricultural produce of the coastal plain.

▸ **Population:** 29,228.
⌖ **Michelin Map:** 737 G 10 – Argolid – Peloponnese.
▷ **Location:** Árgos is south of Mycenae, 135km/84mi SW of Athens and 48km/30mi SW of Corinth. The city is dominated by a rocky peak upon which the citadel sits; the settlement fans out beneath it and on a lesser hill, the Aspis. Seek accommodation in Nauplion or along the coast, where the choice of hotels and restaurants is better.
🅿 **Parking:** The town centre has; you may have to park on the outskirts and walk in.
⊛ **Don't Miss:** Iréo, the sanctuary to Hera.
🕐 **Timing:** Half a day.

ARCHAIÓTITES★ (ANCIENT RUINS)

▷ *Southwest along the road to Trípolis.* 🕐*Open Tue–Sun 8.30am–3pm.* ✆*27510 68 819.* ⊜*€2 (joint ticket with museum: €3).* ⊶*The Agora is usually closed to the public.*

Excavations reveal evidence of activity on this site going back 5,000 years.

By the western entrance to the site is an ancient road leading to a theatre, to the left of which are the remains of a large building. Roman **baths** were built here in the 2C; there are traces of mural paintings and mosaics (partly covered up).

The **theatre** (late 4C BC), was one of the largest in Greece; the terraces could accommodate 20,000 spectators more than Epidaurus. To the left of it are the remains of an odeon (AD 2C–3C). Further south are the ruins of the Sanctuary of Aphrodite and the foundations of a 5C BC temple. On the opposite side of the road are the remains of the **agora** (4C BC). Finds from the site and from Lerní are handsomely displayed in the **Archaeological Museum** (🕐open Tue–Sun 8.30am–3pm; ⊜€2).

OUTSKIRTS

Árgos is so close to Mycenae, Tiryns and the town of Nauplion that most travellers pass it by without stopping. However, as with most places in Greece, it is worth spending an extra few hours driving around and visiting the local sights before heading to the majors. Certainly Iréo is worth a small diversion.

▷ *From Agios Petros Square take the Mycenae (Mikínes) road and head up the road which winds up to the citadel.*

Lárissa Citadel★

⏱*Open Jul–Oct Tue–Sun 8.30am–3pm.*
The Deirás Gap separates Aspís Hill (traces of a sanctuary to Apollo and a fortress; fine view of the citadel) from Lárissa Hill. The citadel on this wild, isolated but very beautiful site was completed by the Franks (13C–14C) on the foundations of an ancient acropolis. The building now consists of an outer wall with towers and the castle itself. The water cisterns are impressive. There is a fine **view**★★ of the plain of Argolis stretching from the mountains to the Gulf of Nauplion.

▷ *8km/5mi NE of Árgos. From the centre take the road to Corinth; bear right after the river bed (sign "Inahos", "Prósimna"). In Inahos continue straight ahead (sign "Ireon"); in Hónikas (11C Byzantine church) take the road to Mycenae (Mikínes) and continue for 2km/1.5mi along a minor road (sign "Ancient Ireo").*

Iréo★

The ruins of the sanctuary of Hera occupy a magnificent solitary **site**★★ above the plain of Árgos. On the first terrace stand the bases of the columns which formed a 5C BC portico *(stoa);* at the back, built of limestone blocks, is the retaining wall of the second terrace, which was the platform for a Classical temple (late 5C BC). The sculptures are on display in the Athens Museum. On the upper terrace are the massive lower courses of an Archaic Doric temple (early 7C BC), which burned down in 423 BC.

▷ *9km/5.5mi SW of Árgos. Take the road to Trípoli. After 5km/3mi turn right into a track leading to Erássinos Spring.*

Kefalári

The water here gushes from a cave consecrated in antiquity to **Pan** and **Dionysos**. Strabo, the ancient geographer, believed this to be the outflow of the Stymphalian Lake. A former sanctuary on the terrace above is now an Orthodox chapel to the Virgin as the Zoodohos Pigi (Spring of Life). Next to it there is an ancient fort, called "the Pyramid", erroneously interpreted as a Roman mausoleum. In summer the cool shade of the huge plane trees and the tall poplars is particularly welcome *(open-air cafés).*

Lárissa Citadel

© Olivier Meerson/Dreamstime.com

Lakonía kai i Aktí Arkadías – Λακονία και η Ακτή Αρκαδίας

Sparta is the obvious attraction in this region with a a reputation second to none. From the two still-surving adjectives "laconic" (short and to the point) to "spartan" (hardy and frugal) the inhabitants of this, the most successful of Greece's classical city states with a reputation second to none, have left us with a description of their behaviour that hardly needs any further explanation. What they have not left behind is art, however – the preoccupation of those effete Athenians – which is why the two main monumental towns in the area, Mistra and Monemvasia, date from the middle ages.

Highlights

1 Have a stroll around the town of **Monemvasia** (p269)

2 Spend a day among the UNESCO site of **Mistrás** (p273)

3 Admire the bust of King Leonidas in the museum in **Sparta** (p280)

4 Meet the extraordinary people of **Máni** (p282)

5 Enjoy the coastal drive from **Gíthio** to **Cape Matapan** (p283)

On the road to Leonídio

© J. Malburet/MICHELIN

The Rugged Coast

The coast from **Lerna** in **Argolis** to Kalamáta in Messinia over which once Sparta ruled triumphant is one of the most varied in Greece. It starts pleasantly enough with sandy beaches, picturesque coves and small family resorts on the Arcadian Coast and ends in the remote, almost inaccessible peninsulas formed by Mts Parnon and Taygetos straddling the Laconian Gulf. Yet, these are also lands of lore: **Máni**, the central peninsula is as exotic in its landscapes and attitudes as anyone would expect to find in a modern EU state. It peaks at **Cape Matapan,** continental Europe's southernmost tip where the British navy won one of its epic sea battles when it destroyed the Italian fleet over two days from 27 March to 29 March 1941.

14C murals, Moní Perivléptou, Mistras

Arcadian Coast★★

Aktí Arkadías – Ακτή Αρκαδίας

The isolated east coast of the Peloponnese, forming the foothills of the **Mount Párnonas** (Parnon) range, has long been overlooked by tourists. The area has become more accessible thanks to a new road along the winding coastline of the Argolic Gulf. It offers a succession of views across the gulf to the Argolid Peninsula and the island of Spetsae.

- ♿ **Michelin Map:** G-H 11 – Argolid – Peloponnese.
- ▶ **Location:** On the east coast of the Peloponnese below Argos and Nauplion.
- 🅿 **Parking:** Beware of road traffic when parking your vehicle.
- 🚶 **Don't Miss:** Leonídio for its peaceful atmosphere.
- 🕐 **Timing:** The drive takes about two hours.
- 👫 **Kids:** Swimming in the Argolic Gulf!

A BIT OF HISTORY

A Literary and Pictorial Myth – Inhabited by followers of Pan, god of shepherds, Arcadia represented a pastoral idyll to the ancients, affording its people a life of ease in stark contrast to the toil that was the lot of most Greeks.

From the 1C BC it became fashionable in Rome to aspire to the simple pleasures of Arcadian life. Against this backdrop Virgil wrote the *Bucolics* (42–39 BC); later, during the Renaissance, the same inspiration was to produce *Arcadia* by Jacoppo Sannazzaro (1455–1530). Painters were equally captivated, including Guercino and most famously Nicolas Poussin (*The Shepherds of Arcadia*, c.1640).

🚗 DRIVING TOUR

50km/31mi. Allow 2hrs.

Ástros

Ástros is an agricultural centre specialising in the cultivation of fruit trees.

The Archaeological Museum displays finds from excavations at the site of the Villa of Herodes Atticus (🕐*see below*). On view are some beautiful Greek and Roman sculptures, marble heads, Roman ceramics, inscriptions and architectural elements. 🕐*Open Tue–Sun 8.30am–3pm.* ⌖€2. 🕿*27550 22 201.*

Villa of Herodes Atticus

Visit on request at the Archaeological Museum. Located 4km/2.5mi from

GETTING THERE

From **Árgos**, take the **Lerna road** 32km/20mi south to **Ástros**. 50km/31mi separate Ástros from **Leonídio**. There are few service stations, so fill your tank before you leave.

Ástros on the road to Tegéa and Trípoli (at Eva Dolianon Kynourias), near the Loukoús Monastery.

The excavations at the site of the magnificent residence have unearthed remains that are now on display in the museums of Ástros and Trípoli.

Monastery of Metamorphoseos tou Sotiros Loukoús

4km/2.5mi east of Ástros (signposted). 🕿*27550 41260.*

Built in the 12C, the monastery's Byzantine church is decorated with beautiful 17C frescoes. Further on to the left of the same path lie the ruins of a Roman aqueduct (2C) built to supply Herodes Atticus' villa. It is still currently a convent.

Parálio Ástros

This small seaside resort has the longest sandy beach along this coast; it is situated on a promontory below the remains of an ancient citadel refurbished by the Franks. Return to Ástros and take the road south to Leonídi; beyond Ágios Andréas it passes above pebble beach inlets suitable for bathing.

Leonídi

Tirós★

28 km/17mi below Ástros.

This old town, which spreads out like a fan among terraced olive groves, is bypassed by the new road running along the coast below through the little resort of **Paralía Tiroú** *(several hotels).*

Sambatikí★

The narrow road that winds down to the car park requires great caution.

Attractive site in a curving bay protected by a watchtower; lovely pebble beach with crystal-clear water and fishing boats. The road runs high up above Leonídio Bay and the fertile coastal strip. The river mouth is flanked by two small beaches: Lékos and **Pláka** *(tavernas; guesthouses)*. Nearby is the peaceful seaside resort of **Poúlithra**; a lovely place for walks and a starting point for trips out to the mountain villages.

Leonídi★★

Timeless and peaceful (at least out of season), the little town of Leonídi extends from the bank of its river to a high red cliff. It has a certain old-world charm: a 12C fortified house and old rough-cast houses with balconies and Saracen chimneys.

Walk to the far end of the town for a view (near the ruined tower) over the site and the coastal basin down to the sea.

Further inland *(32km/20mi there and back)* along the road to Géraki lies the 15C **Elóna Monastery** huddled against the rocks on a wild **site**★ overlooking a narrow valley; it safeguards a miraculous icon of the Virgin, supposedly the work of Saint Luke.

The road beyond the monastery is magnificent, but very rough in places, as it continues to **Kosmás**, a charming mountain village with a beautiful church over a main square shaded by enormous 100-year-old plane trees and lined with cafés and tavernas; and **Geráki** (*see SPÁRTI)*, from where one can reach **Monemvasia** and **Gíthio**.

ADDRESSES

🏨 STAY

🛏 **Hotel Apollon** – *Paralía Tiroú, by the sea to the south of the village.* ☎27550 41 393. *12 rooms.* A clean hotel of recent construction. Kitchen facilities available. The most pleasant rooms overlook the sea.

🛏 **Hotel Dionysos** – *Pláka Port, Leonídio.* ☎27570 23455. *16 rooms.* A quiet and well-maintained hotel. Very popular and thus advisable to book well in advance.

Monemvasia★★

Monemvasía –Μονεμβασία

Invisible from the coast, this silent, partially ruined medieval fortified town sits in a slight depression on the southern face of a steep rocky peninsula. The peninsula, linked to the mainland by a narrow causeway and a bridge, takes its name from the Greek words *móni emvassía* meaning "only entrance".

A BIT OF HISTORY

Monemvasia dates back to the 6C when inhabitants of ancient Laconia settled on a rock that had become separated from the mainland by an earthquake some two centuries earlier. The location offered the prospect of a safe retreat from the Slavic invaders who dominated much of Greece from about 500 to 700 AD.

The town's strategic site was only appreciated by the various powers that tried to wrest control from each other. Monemvasia was fortified by the Byzantines against the Slav invasions, but in 1248, after a three-year blockade, it fell into the hands of **William of Ville-hardouin**. The Franks repaired the castle, but in 1263 William was obliged to return it to Michael VIII Palaiologos as part of his ransom.

Venetians took control of the town in 1464 and quickly set about building

▶ **Population:** 4,660.

Michelin Map: 737 H 12 – Laconia – Peloponnese.

Info: www.monemvasia-online.com.

Location: 350km/217mi from Athens, 202km/126mi south of Nauplion and 110km/69mi southeast of Sparta. Monemvassía is difficult to access by road. A dyke connects Monemvassía to the town of Gefyra; shuttles operate from there (every 15min).

P Parking: Vehicles are banned from the medieval centre.

Don't Miss: The view from the citadel, at dawn and at dusk.

Timing: The best light is in the morning.

Kids: The climb up to the ruins of the citadel.

Also See: Máni, Sparta, Kíthira.

the massive fortress that still dominates the landscape. The Turks laid siege and seized the town in 1540 and, despite a 1554 siege by the Knights of St John, they held it until 1690. That was the year when the Venetians once again

Aerial view of Monemvasia

© Greek National Tourism Organisation

Rock of Monemvassia

© Greek National Tourism Organisation

took over after their fifth attempt in as many decades.

Under the Despotate of Morea *(see MISTRÁS)* and during the subsequent Turkish and Venetian occupations, Monemvasia was an active trading port. The town was protected by a fortified bridge, by the Venetian castle on the top of the rock and by a circuit wall that enclosed the town on three sides.

In 1715, possession reverted to the Turks, but in 1770 a rebellion in the Peloponnese aided by the Russians was brutally suppressed and signalled the decline of the town. By 1804 the town was almost deserted: only six Greek households out of 350 remained.

During the Greek War of Independence Monemvasia was liberated from Ottoman rule on 23 July 1821. The Greek force was led by Tzannetakis Grigorakis who financed his own army.

The city has undergone a major restoration programme and all construction is strictly controlled. Since the 1970s it has become a popular location for holiday homes and the grand old mansions and some 40 Byzantine churches – reflecting the prosperity which Monemvasia enjoyed under her various rulers – continue to draw in a steady stream of annual visitors. Some of the old mansions have been restored and converted into neat little boutique hotels. The popularity of Monemvasia

has brought in its wake a stream of tourist shops retailing predictable schlock; the shop next to the Byzantion Hotel, selling Greek glassware and jewellery, is an honourable exception.

WALKING TOUR
KÁSTRO★★

This forms the **old** or **lower town**. Begin at the causeway and proceed through the West Gate; both it and the walls date from the Despotate.

▷ *Walk up the main street between the ancient houses to the main square.*

Platía Dzamíou

This charming square extends south into a terrace graced by an 18C cannon and the observation hole of an underground cistern. On the east side stands the **Church of Christ in Chains** (Chrístos Elkomenós), a former cathedral (12C; rebuilt 17C); note the detached Italianate bell tower, and the symbolic peacocks carved in low relief on a piece of Byzantine sculpture that has been reused in the façade.

Inside are some beautiful Byzantine icons, including one of the Crucifixion (14C). The church's most precious artwork was a depiction of Christ Elkomenós, which was removed and transported to Constantinople. In the place of the old picture is one with the same subject from 1700, painted in the Ionian Islands.

In a 16C mosque, there is a fine **archaeological collection** highlighting everyday life in Monemvasia; it's a good introduction to the visit *(open Apr–Oct Tue–Sun 8am–7.30pm (11pm every Wed); Nov–Mar 8.30am–3pm; no charge).*

▷ *Walk down to the ramparts along the seafront and follow them eastwards.*

Southern Rampart

There are extensive views of the sea and the Peloponnese coast south towards Cape Malea. The landing at Portello is a great spot for a swim as are nearby **beaches** Géfyra and, further north, Xifias *(6km/3.75mi)* and Pori *(4km/2.5mi).*

Panagía Chrissafítissa

The façade of this 16C church looks very Venetian with its framed doorway surmounted by an oculus; the open space in front was used as a parade ground. Near the ramparts stands a tiny chapel built over the "sacred spring"; it contains an icon from Chrysapha (Chríssafa) near Sparta.

Stroll the sentry walk to the corner bastion; return and descend to visit **St Nicholas'** (Ágios Nikólaos) which has a 16C Venetian doorway. The churches of St Demetrios (Ágios Dimítrios), St Anthony (Ágios Antónios), St Andrew (Ágios Andréas) and St Anne (Agía Anna), a 14C basilica, can also be visited. Nearby are several Venetian houses; note the door and window mouldings, flamboyant recesses and broad-mouthed chimneys.

▷ *Return to Dzamiou Square; an alley leads to the Church of Panagía Mirtidiótissa.*

Panagía Mirtidiótissa or Kritikia

⊶ *Closed for restoration at time of publication.*

This little church dates from the Frankish period (13C); It has a beautiful iconostasis carved in wood. It was once a command post belonging to the Templars and then to the Knights of St John of Jerusalem.

AKRÓPOLI★★

Originally the citadel covered a wide area; the ruined fortifications are mostly Venetian (16C). Visitors who cannot climb all the way to the citadel *(15min)* are advised to go halfway up, if possible, for a very fine **view**★★★ of the lower town. A vaulted passage in the fortified entrance emerges into an open space; take the path leading north up the hill to the Church of St Sophia.

Agía Sofía★

Principal church of the citadel, this large Byzantine church on the cliff's edge offers a vertiginous **view**★★★ of the sea below. Built at the end of the 12C by the emperor Andronicos, Agía Sofía became a Catholic cathedral during the Venetian occupation and a mosque during Turkish rule. Only a few wall paintings survive. The recently restored building may have been occupied by Cistercians during the Frankish period; it was refurbished during the 14C–15C. There are some unusual early-Byzantine capitals in shallow relief, Byzantine marble carvings over the doors in the narthex and traces of murals.

A rough path leads to the **highest point** on the rock overlooking the isthmus and the mountains to the west. From there, return to the main gate and follow the sentry walk westwards to reach the highest point along the circuit wall: splendid **views**★★ of the old town and the coast.

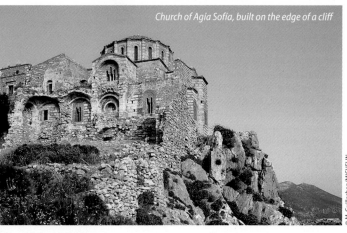
Church of Agía Sofía, built on the edge of a cliff

© M. Guillochon/MICHELIN

Greece's Voice of Conscience

On 1 May 1909 the poet **Yánnis Rítsos** was born in Monemvasia. He published his first poem collection in 1934, and in 1936 he published his masterpiece, **Epitáphios**, later set to music by **Mikis Theodorakis** and sung by **Nana Mouskouri**. In that decade he also joined the Communist Party to which he remained faithful until his death in 1990. He fought with the Resistance in the Second World War but, following the Greek Civil War, he was imprisoned by the Greek anti-communist governments in 1948–52. During 1967–74 he was also persecuted by the junta for his political beliefs. After the return of democracy in 1974, he became a leading proponent for human rights in Greece and was respected by all parties for his principled stance.

EXCURSIONS

Liménas Géraka

▶ *16km/10mi north of Monemvasia on the coast road. Hydrofoil landing stage.*
A charming fishing village tucked away in an impressive little rocky bay.

Molái

▶ *24km/15mi northwest of Monemvasia on the road to Sparta.*
A few remains, a palaeo-Christian Byzantine church and the ruins of a medieval fort are visible here; mosaic paving of three 6C BC temples can be seen in Halasmata.

Neápoli

▶ *61km/38mi south of Monemvasia.*
This small town stands opposite the wonderful little island of Elafónissos. There are only a few remains here, since the ancient city is now beneath the waves. The bays with their crystal-clear water and golden beaches are perfect for swimming.

ADDRESSES

⌂ STAY

⊜⊜⊜ **Villa Doúka** – *Géfira, 3km/2mi north of the town.* ☎*27320 61 181, Fax (27320) 61 751. 25 studios and apts.* Activities include table tennis and basketball; long sandy beach. Good base for families with cars.

⊜⊜ **Beléssis** – *Géfira, to the right of the main road.* ☎*/Fax (27320) 61 217. 10 rooms and 5 apts.* Traditional old house, close to the road; more modern rooms set back a little off a quiet patio.

⊜⊜ **Villa Diamantí** – *Topalti district, just before Géfira.* ☎*27320 61 534. 9 rooms and 12 bungalows.* Decent rooms and communal kitchen in the hotel. Well-equipped bungalows with terraces.

⊜⊜ **Malvasia** – *Monemvassía, Kástro.* ☎*27320 630 07. www.malvasia-hotel.gr. 28 rooms.* Occupying three historic properties, Malvasia has magnificent rooms with traditional decor. Below one of these houses (Ritsou) there is a permanent bathing platform.

♈ EAT

⊜ **Fótis** – *Géfira, beginning of the seafront road.* Unpretentious bistro offering *souvláki* and *pita* dishes.

⊜ **Limanáki** – *Géfira, just before the bridge.* Traditional taverna where dishes are selected from the kitchen.

⊜ **Matoúla** – *Monemvassía, Kástro, below the main street.* Fine dishes such as *saganáki* and delicious *arnáki*.

⊜ **To Kanóni** – *Monemvassía, off the main street.* The *pikilía* (appetisers) are especially good.

⊜⊜ **Le Castellano** – *On the dyke.* ☎*27320 199 94. Breakfast and dinner.* Traditional Greek specialities along with classics of French and Italian cuisine. Excellent wine list.

🚄 TAKING A BREAK

Traditional cake shop in Géfira below the Minoa Hotel, on the main street.

📅 EVENTS AND FESTIVALS

Local festivals – For five days around 23 July the town celebrates its liberation from the Turks.

Mistrás★★★

Mistrás – Μυστράς

Occupying an exceptional **site**★★★ on a steep spur of Mount Taygetos overlooking Sparta and the Evrótas Valley, Mistrás was known as the "pearl of Morea" during the Frankish and Byzantine periods. Today the churches, monasteries, ruined palaces and houses are largely deserted, yet retain their architectural grandeur; the churches especially are outstanding examples of Byzantine religious art and architecture.

A BIT OF HISTORY

Franco-Byzantine Conflicts – The famed fortress of Mistrás was built in 1249 when **William de Villehardouin**, Frankish Prince of Morea and Duke of Achaia, began to construct an impregnable stronghold to control the region of Laconía. The Franks did not hold the site, set on a high bluff commanding the Eurotas Valley, for long. In 1259 **de Villehardouin** was captured in Macedonia and held prisoner for three years. He regained his freedom by ceding three fortresses (Monemvassía, the Great Maina and Mistrás) to his captor, Michael VIII Palaiologos, Emperor of Byzantium. **Florence of the Orient** – In the 14C and 15C Mistrás became the capital of the **Despotate of Morea**, a province of the Byzantine empire covered almost the

- ♿ **Michelin Map:** 737 G 11 – Laconía – Peloponnese.
- **Info:** No local office. For information: ✆ 27310 262 43/258 98.
- **Location:** 144km/90mi southwest of Corinth and 5km/3mi west of Sparta. The ruins of ancient Mistrás lie above the modern village; there are separate entrances for the Upper and Lower Towns.
- **Parking:** Car parks at the entrance of the modern village and near the Lower Town.
- **Don't Miss:** The murals inside Odigítria.
- **Timing:** Allow a full day; stick to the Lower Town if you're pressed for time.
- **Kids:** The castle.

whole of the Peloponnese and was ruled by the heir (despot) to the emperor. The despots made Mistrás a centre of Hellenic politics and culture, building a palace and arranging for the construction of many churches that combined Eastern and Western influences.

The intellectual life of Mistrás flourished under cultivated emperors such as John VI Kantakouzenos and particularly Manuel II Palaiologos.

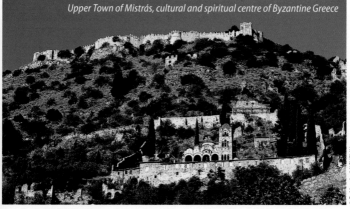

Upper Town of Mistrás, cultural and spiritual centre of Byzantine Greece

© R. Mattès/MICHELIN

Neo-Platonic philosophy was espoused by **Manuel Chrysolorás**, "the sage of Byzantium", who had taught in Florence in 1397 where he influenced the architect Brunelleschi.

A Long Decline – When Mistrás was surrendered to Turkey in 1460 its churches were converted into mosques, the despot's palace became the residence of the Pasha, and the town continued to thrive.

During the centuries following the Venetian occupation, however, it declined as a result of invasions by Russians, Albanians and the Egyptian troops of Ibrahim Pasha. In the 19C it was abandoned in favour of the new town of Sparta.

VISIT

🕐 *Open every day in summer 8am–7pm (site closes at 7.30pm); winter 8.30am–3pm.* €5. 📞27310 833 77. *Bring water and comfortable shoes; modest dress required to visit the churches.*

The road from Sparta presents a lovely **view**★★ of Mistrás, a patch of white on the dark bulk of Mount Taígetos. Beyond Néa Mistrás, a pleasant flower-bedecked village, rise the ruins of old Mistrás widely scattered on a stunning hillside **site**★★★.

The ancient city consisted of three distinct sections: the castle *(kástro)* built by the De Villehardouins, the Upper Town for the aristocracy, and the Lower Town where the citizens lived. There are two entrances: to the Lower Town through the main gate; and to the Upper Town, via the road that skirts the site.

1 LOWER TOWN★★

The 14C defensive wall enclosed the cathedral, several churches and monasteries, elegant houses and craftsmen's workshops.

Enter through the little **fort** that marks the site of the old town gate and turn right towards the cathedral.

Mitrópoli★★

The Metropolitan Orthodox Cathedral of St Demetrios (1270) stands below street level. The narthex was added in 1291 by Nikephoros (named as the founder of the church in an inscription on the wall of the stairway).

In the precinct there is a court with steps descending to the parvis of the cathedral. The paving continues round the northeast side of the church into an 18C arcaded court overlooking the Evrótas Valley; the Roman sarcophagus decorated with a carving of a Bacchanalian revel and winged sphinxes was used as a basin for the Mármara Fountain.

Church

Built in the late 13C as a basilica with a central nave and two vaulted side aisles, the church was reconstructed (15C) on a cruciform plan with domes: in the nave the join between the 13C and 15C work is clearly visible. The columns in the nave bear engraved inscriptions listing the privileges bestowed on the cathedral by the emperors.

Note on the floor in front of the iconostasis a stone bearing the crowned Byzantine eagle showing the place where Constantine Palaiologos is said to have been consecrated Emperor of Byzantium in 1449. There are a few low-relief sculptures (9C–11C) taken from the ruins of ancient Sparta. Note also the 13C–14C **frescoes**★ throughout the interior (Last Judgment in the narthex; Martyrdom of St Demetrios in the north aisle; Virgin and Child in the central apse).

Museum

🕐 *Same opening hours as site.*
🕐 *Closed Mon.*

The collection, founded by Gabriel Millet, is displayed in the old bishop's palace. Among the Byzantine sculptures are an Eagle seizing its Prey (11C) and a Christ in Majesty (15C). Further west along the street is the mortuary chapel of the Evangelístria (14C–15C); the well-proportioned cruciform distyle structure stands in a little cemetery not far from the Brontocheion Monastery.

Moní Vrondohíou★★

Within the walls of the Brontocheion Monastery are two great churches.

Ágii Theódori★
St Theodore's Church was built on the cruciform plan late in the 13C; it has been heavily restored. The dome, resting on a 16-sided tall drum, is the most imposing feature. The angles of the cruciform plan contain four funerary chapels.

Odigítria★★
Dedicated to the Virgin, this church is also known as the *Afendikó* (belonging to the Master) because it was built in the 14C by Pachomios, an important ecclesiastic in the Orthodox Church. Its architecture is a combination of the basilical plan with a nave and side aisles on the ground floor and the cruciform plan topped by domes in the upper storey, according to a design found only in Mistrás. The approach provides a spectacular view of the apse with triple windows, blind arches and the different roof levels. Both the church and the belfry have been restored.

The interior is decorated with remarkable **murals★★** (14C) by several different artists. Those in the narthex reveal flowing composition, harmony of colours and introspective expressions suggesting the hand of a great artist, perhaps the equal of Duccio and Giotto. The funerary chapel at the far end of the narthex *(left)* contains the tombs of Pachomios, shown offering his church to the Virgin, and Theodore I Palaiologos, shown both as despot and as the monk he became at the end of his life; among the other paintings is a very well-preserved Procession of Martyrs in red raiment.

The walls of a second chapel at the other end of the narthex are covered with inscriptions copied from *chrysobulls*, the imperial decrees granting goods and privileges to the monastery.

The paintings on the ground floor are mostly effigies of saints; in the central apse are the saintly hieratic prelates. The brilliantly coloured paintings in the galleries evoke the Resurrection and the Flight into Egypt; saints are portrayed on the walls *(access through the Chrysobulls Chapel)*.

From the monastery precinct take the path leading uphill towards the Pandánassa Monastery.

Moní Pandánassas★★
Dedicated in 1428, the **monastery** is today inhabited by a few nuns who do very fine embroidery work. The main entrance leads into a narrow courtyard; on the left are the conventual cells; straight ahead are steps ascending to the church.

Moní Perivléptou

© M. Guillochon/MICHELIN

Church

The elegant east portico of this beautiful 15C structure is a charming spot to pause and enjoy the magnificent **view**★★ of the Evrótas Valley. The narthex contains the tomb of Manuel Katzikis, who died in 1445 and is shown in effigy on the wall. The church itself is decorated with **paintings**★ from various periods.

Beyond the church, the path descends past the **House of Phrangopoulos** (Ikia Frangópoulou), which dates from the 15C; note the machicolated balcony.

Moní Perivléptou★★

This tiny **monastery** dates from the Frankish period (13C) but was altered in the 14C when the murals were executed. The entrance to the precinct is an attractive arched gateway; over the arch is a low relief showing a row of fleurs-de-lis surmounted by the lions of Flanders flanking a circle containing the word *"perívleptos"* (which means "attracting attention from every side") in the form of a cross; this heraldic device and motto indicate the founder of the monastery, who was one of the first two Latin emperors of Constantinople, Baldwin of Flanders or his brother Henry.

Church

From the gateway there is a picturesque view of the church with its two external funerary chapels beyond which rises a 13C tower. A door to the right of the chevet leads into the interior, which is decorated with an exceptional series of 14C **murals**★★★ illustrating the New Testament and the Life of the Virgin. The church is linked to the old monolithic **hermitage,** which consists of a single chamber converted into a chapel and to St Catherine's Chapel, an early sanctuary surmounted by a belfry on the clifftop.

On leaving the Perívleptos Monastery take the path which passes **Ágios Geórgios**, a baronial funerary chapel dedicated to St George, the entrance *(right)* to the **Kríni Marmáras**, which takes its name from a marble fountain, and Ágios

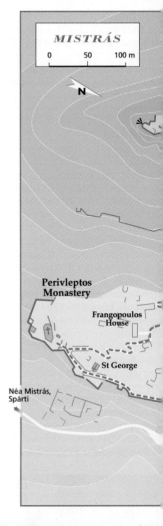

Hristoóforos *(left)*, a funerary chapel dedicated to St Christopher.

Íkos Láskari

The Lascaris House is a fine example of a 14C patrician house. It is thought to have belonged to the famous Láscaris family, related to the emperors of Byzantium and family of the humanists, Constantine and **John Láscaris** (1445–1534). The vaulted chamber on the ground floor was probably the stable; a balcony decorated with machicolations looks out over the Eurotas Plain.

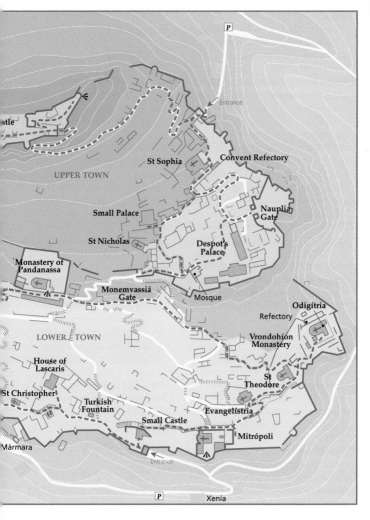

Return to the main entrance and drive up the hill to the Upper Town. Visitors on foot should walk up through the Monemvassia Gate and start at the Despot's Palace.

2 UPPER TOWN★★

The Upper Town, site of the castle (kástro), is enclosed within 13C ramparts; there were two entrances: the Monemvassía Gate (Píli Monemvassías – east) and the Nauplion Gate (Píli Nafplíou – west). Near the modern entrance from the upper car park stands Agía Sofía.

Agía Sofía★

St Sophia was the palace church, founded in the 14C by the despot Manuel Kantakouzenos, where the ceremonies of the Despotate were conducted and where Theodora Tocchi and Cleophas Malatesta, the Italian wives of Constantine and Theodore Palaiologos, are buried.

The church is distinguished by its tall narrow proportions and by its spacious narthex, roofed by a dome. Western influence is evident in the three-sided apses and in the detached bell-tower. Traces of an internal spiral staircase suggest that the tower was used as a minaret during the Turkish occupation. In the interior beneath the dome there are fragments of the original multi-coloured marble floor. The most interesting murals are in the apse (Christ in Majesty) and in the chapel to the right (fine narrative scene of the Nativity of the Virgin).

▷ *Head down to the Little Palace by the path that weaves through the ruins.*

Mikró Anáktoro (Little Palace)

This is a huge house incorporating a corner keep with a balcony. For defensive reasons only the upper floors had windows; the vaulted ground floor was lit by loopholes. After passing the 17C Church of St Nicholas (Ágios Nikólaos), the path reaches the **Monemvassía Gate** (Píli Monemvassías). Turn back uphill past the ruins of a mosque into the open square in front of the Despot's Palace, where the market was held during the Turkish occupation.

Despotikó Anáktoro★★

⌐ *Closed to the public for restoration.*
The Despot's Palace consists of two wings: a northeast wing (13C–14C) and a northwest wing (15C). The building at the east end of the **northeast wing** (**1**) dates from the 13C and was probably built either by the Franks or the first Byzantine governors. Under the despots it was probably used as a guardroom. Next come two smaller buildings; the more northerly contained kitchens. The last building in this group is a great structure with several storeys (late 14C). It was designed as the residence of the despot Manuel Kantakouzenos. The north façade sports an elegant porch supporting a balcony overlooking the Lakonian Plain.
The **northwest wing** (**2**) wing consists of an imposing three-storey building constructed by the Palaiologi (early 15C). The lowest floor (partially underground) is faced on the courtyard side by a row of round-headed arches supporting a terrace on the middle floor. The top floor consisted of an immense hall for receptions and entertainment. The throne

stood in the centre of the east wall in a shallow alcove.

③ KÁSTRO★

A steep and winding path (steps) leads up from the modern entrance to the Kástro (45min on foot there and back).
Built in the 13C by De Villehardouin, the structure was much altered by the Byzantines, the Venetians and the Turks. William II de Villehardouin and his wife Anna Comnena held court there in grand style, surrounded by knights from Champagne, Burgundy and Flanders.
The fortress consists of two baileys. The entrance to the first is guarded by a vaulted gateway flanked by a stout square tower; the southeast corner of the bailey is marked by an underground cistern and a huge round tower (**3**) which gives impressive **views**★★ of the ravine facing Mt Taygetos. The inner bailey *(northwest)* contained the baronial apartments (**4**) *(left on entering)*, another cistern and the castle chapel (**5**) of which only traces remain. The ruined tower (**6**) on the highest point provides spectacular **views**★★ down into the many gullies in the wild slopes of Mt Taígetos; in the other direction lie the ruins of Mistrás, modern Sparta and the Evrótas Plain.

ADDRESSES

🏠STAY / 🍴 EAT

🍽 **O Palaiológos** – ☎27310 83 373. Convivial atmosphere and traditional dishes; popular with families from nearby Sparta.

🍽 **Xenia** – *Above the village.* ☎27310 205 00. xenia@galaxynet.gr. Overlooking the Sparta Plain. Traditional Greek cuisine and a pleasant rosé wine. Reserve in advance on weekends.

🍽 **Byzantion** – *Village centre.* ☎27310 833 09. www.byzantionhotel.gr. 6 rooms. Spacious rooms and bathrooms. There is also a swimming pool.

🎉EVENTS AND FESTIVALS

Exhibitions and concerts at the site start in July and run into the autumn.
Local festival – 26–31 August, market and traditional music concerts.

Sparta

Spárti – Σπάρτη

Courage, austerity, physical prowess and patriotism are synonymous with the name of Sparta. Modern Sparta, however, has little in common with the warlike city of classical times. Today, Sparta is a modern provincial capital and a tourist centre, well placed for visiting the ruins of Mistrás and the medieval village of Geráki.

A BIT OF HISTORY

An Aristocratic and Military State – Remains from the Mycenaean period, when Sparta formed part of the King-dom of Menelaeus, have been found at the Menelaion itself **(Geráki road)** and at Amíkles (7km/4.25mi south). Sparta was most influential, however, from the 9C to the 4C BC, in the Pelopon-nese and throughout Greece. The Spartans' oligarchic constitution was created in about 900 BC by the lawgiver **Lycurgus**. The state was led by two kings assisted by a council of 28 elders and five *ephors* who had executive power.

- 🗓 **Info:** www.e-sparta.gr (in Greek); 52 Gortsologiou (4th floor), near the main square; English spoken. 𝄆27310 24852. Open Mon–Fri 7.30am–2.30pm.
- ▶ **Location:** Located 61km/38mi east of Kalamáta (airport), 43km/27mi north of Gíthio and 141km/87mi southwest of Corinth, Sparta is served by the E 961.
- 🅿 **Parking:** There are no big car parks but plenty of street parking.
- 🚫 **Don't Miss:** The view of Mount Taygetos from the Tomb of Menelaus.
- 🕐 **Timing:** An overnight stay could be convenient.

There were three distinct classes: the **Spartiates**, the warrior class, who were also landowners; the **Perioikoi**, who were traders and artisans or farm-ers; and the **Helots**, or serfs.

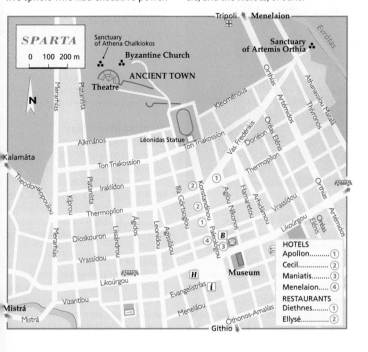

Spartan Way of Life – Forbidden to work, the Spartiates trained continually in combat. They ate communally, living mainly on herbs and wild roots, with a rare feast of black broth (pork stewed in blood). At age 7 boys were drafted into youth troops inured to physical exercise. On reaching age 20, the young Spartiates faced a series of initiation tests, the *krypteia*; they were flogged, sometimes to death, abandoned in the countryside and instructed to kill any Helots who tarried outdoors after dark. The girls were also given to strenuous exercise, and married women were not expected to be faithful to their husbands. The Spartan soldiers gave their lives without hesitation in combat, as did **Leonidas** and his warriors at Thermopylae in 480 BC. The Spartiates' numbers over the centuries, and their defeat in 371 BC at Leuktra, began the city's decline. Eventually it was supplanted by Mistrás, and ancient Sparta was abandoned.

Statue of Leonidas

© B. Chabrol/MICHELIN

MUSEUM
Archeologikó Moussío★
71 Ossiou Nikonos St. ○*Open Jul–Oct, daily 8.30am–5pm; rest of year, Tue–Sat 8.30am–3pm.* ◉€2. ℘27310 285 75.
The **Archaeological Museum** displays the finds from local excavations, particularly Sparta and Amyklai; sculptures from the Archaic period; terra-cotta masks from the Sanctuary of Artemis Orthia;

and objects from Mycenaean tombs. Note the **bust of King Leonidas**, who along with 300 Spartans held back the Persians at the Battle of Thermopylae, and the bas-relief of a couple bearing gifts and framed by a snake (540 BC).

RUINS
Ancient Ruins
◈*No charge.* Most date from the Hellenistic or Roman periods. The **Kenotáfio Leonída** (Leonidas' Tomb) was on the Acropolis and is, in fact, the base of a small Hellenistic temple. The remains of the **Acropolis** buildings are half-hidden in an olive grove north of the modern town *(sign: "ancient Sparta")*. Go through the Byzantine wall and bear left to reach the theatre (1C BC). Above it are the foundations of a Temple to Athena and a Byzantine monastery (10C AD).

Naós Orthías Artémidos (Sanctuary of Artemis Orthia)
The ruins of a temple (7C–6C) and an amphitheatre mark the site where ritual endurance tests of young Spartans took place (flogging and athletic dances).

EXCURSIONS
Tomb of Menelaus
▶*8km/5mi south by the road to Gíthio, then a narrow road on the left.*
After turning, continue on foot up to Prophitis Ilias Hill, site of the ruins of a 5C BC sanctuary to Menelaus and Helen. Marvellous **view**★ of Mount Taygetos.

Zerbítsa Monastery
▶*12km/7.5mi to the south. Take the Gíthio road, then turn right on the road passing through Xirokámbia and follow the signs.* ℘27310 35091.
The monastery has a beautiful 17C Byzantine church with frescoes, and a small museum (**Epitáphios** of 1539, icons, early Christian architectural fragments).

Geráki★★
▶*31km/19mi southeast of Sparta.*
The little medieval town of Geráki has no fewer than 30 Byzantine churches (12–15C) many decorated with murals. The ruins of Geráki Castle and of a medi-

eval town (kástro) lie on an outlying spur of Mount Parnon, on the northern edge of the Laconian Plain.

Kástro

🕐 Open Tue–Sun 8.30am–3pm. Take the road below the village towards Ágios Dimítrios past a school and a cemetery near several Byzantine churches. Turn left after the cemetery and continue for 2.5km/1.5mi to the car park.

The **castle**, built in 1254 in imitation of the one in Mistrás, is shaped like an irregular quadrilateral; huge cisterns enabled it to withstand long sieges. The tour includes several Gothic and Byzantine chapels decorated with painted murals, notably **Agía Paraskevi Church** (15C frescoes), and **St George's Church** (14C). Nearby stands the **Zoodóhou Pigi Church**, a basilica decorated with vivid 15C Byzantine frescoes. The parapet walk offers extensive **views★★** of Mt Parnon (north), the Eurotas Valley running south to the sea and Mt Taygetos (west).

Byzantine Churches

Down in the village, by the road to the castle, the early-13C church of **Ágios Athanássios** stands near the cemetery. Nearby, a byroad on the other side of the main road leads to the domed **Ágios Sózon** (12C) and to **Ágios Nikólaos** (13C). The tiny church of **Ágii Theodori** stands in the middle of a field near the road. Also worth a visit is the **Ágios Ioánnis Chrysostomos Church**, a 12C basilica with early-14C frescoes relating to the Life of Christ and the Virgin. Above the cemetery, walk up in the village to the 12C church of the **Evangelístria**; the well-preserved frescoes were probably painted by an artist from Constantinople during the period of the Comnenos.

Chríssafa

▶ 18km/11mi east of Sparta.
The village has several churches, including the 13C Chryssaphiotissa Church, the 18C Church of the Dormition and the 13C Church of St John. To visit, contact the priest at the Church of the Dormition (Kimisseos tis Theotokou).

ADDRESSES

🛏️ STAY

🛌 **Cecil** – 125 Leofóros K. Paleológou. 🕾 27310 249 80. 23 rooms. 🄳 Modest but clean, this friendly hotel occupies a pre-war building. Good value.

🛌 **Apollon** – 84 Thermopylon St. 🕾 27310 22491. 47 rooms. 🄳 Simple but well-maintained, occupying an ancient battlement. Excellent value for money.

🛌🛌 **Maniatis** – 72–76 Leofóros K. Paleológou. 🕾 27310 226 65. www.maniatishotel.gr. 80 rooms. 🄳 A pleasant hotel; some rooms have balconies and views. Good restaurant.

🛌🛌🛌 **Menelaion** – 91 Leofóros K. Paleológou. 🕾 27310 221 61/5. www.menelaion.com. 48 rooms. Well-located hotel, offering spacious rooms, double-glazed windows and a swimming pool.

🍴 EAT

🍴 **Diethnes** – 105 Leofóros K. Paleológou. 🕾 27310 28636. Nice family restaurant with a shaded garden where customers choose the dishes from the kitchen.

🍴 **Elysé** – 113 Leofóros K. Paleológou. Small restaurant serving traditional dishes as well as unusual ones, such as orange-flavoured Greek sausages.

🍴 **Maniatis** – 72–76 Leofóros K. Paleológou. This hotel/restaurant has neo-Spartan decor. The Greek menu also includes international dishes.

🍴 **Menelaion** – 91 Leofóros K. Paleológou. One of Sparta's most elegant establishments, with tables on a cool poolside patio. Greek and French cuisine.

🤾 SPORTS AND LEISURE

Hiking and refuge information: **Sparti Alpine Club** (97 Odós Górtsoglou; 🕾 27310 225 74) or from the photographer who is a member of the climbing club (36 Odós Likourgou). There are information offices in the villages of Paleopanagia, Socha, Anavriti and Koumousta.

🎎 EVENTS AND FESTIVALS

On 26 November, the city celebrates the feast of its patron saint.

Máni★★

Máni – Μάνη

The southern spur of Mount Taýgetos, (2,407m/7,896ft) extends south between the Messenian and Laconian Gulfs to form a promontory which ends in Cape Matapan (Akrotíri Taínaro), the southernmost point of continental Greece. This is the Máni Peninsula, a barren windswept landscape. Today it is largely depopulated; the villages with their abandoned towers and Byzantine chapels and churches appear frozen in time.

A BIT OF HISTORY

Originally from the north of Laconia, the defiant Maniot people maintained their autonomy from Greece's many occupiers, particularly the Turks. Introspective and bellicose, the Maniots lived in tribal villages under the rule of the local chiefs, sometimes confronting one another in vendettas. These disputes explain why the houses and even the fields were fortified.

There are about 800 **Maniot towers**, some dating from the 17C. Made of stone and square in shape, they comprised three or four rooms linked by ladders and trapdoors. Many towers may be found in **Kíta** and **Váthia** in the south. Small **churches** and chapels in this region date from the 11C and the 12C; their interiors are often decorated with

▸ **Population:** 23,887.
✦ **Michelin Map:** 737 G 12–13 – Lakonía – Peloponnese.
▯ **Info:** At Gíthio, 20 Odós V Georgiou. ✆276330 244 84. Open Mon–Fri 11am–3pm.
◐ **Location:** 43km/27mi south of Sparta, in a wild and rocky region. Access is easiest by road from Sparta; also from Kalamáta by the coast road.
▣ **Parking:** Plenty of space for parking vehicles throughout the year.
⊛ **Don't Miss:** The isolated region between Areópoli and Cape Matapan.
◷ **Timing:** Plan three days, alternating between sight visits and beach time.
▲▴ **Kids:** The spectacular Dirós Caves (Spílea Diroú).

charming 12C–13C and 14C frescoes. *The sites of interesting Byzantine churches are underlined in red on the map of Máni.* Few in number, the Maniots live in their steep villages, preserving the tradition of honour and hospitality. Women still wear the long black dress and veil of mourners in antiquity and perpetuate their tradition of singing funeral dirges *(mirológia).*

View of Váthia

Spílea Diroú

© Sergio Bertino/Dreamstime.com

🚗 DRIVING TOUR

FROM GÍTHIO TO CAPE MATAPAN★★★

Starting from Gíthio 160km/100mi

▷ *Plan two days for this driving tour; progress will be slow along the narrow, winding roads. Summer heat is intense, but villages along the way provide opportunities to stop and refresh. Check the Address Book for overnight accommodations en route.*

Gíthio

Situated just west of the mouth of the **River Evrótas** (Eurotas) overlooking the Laconian Gulf, Gíthio is a quiet seaside resort and a port.

Dominated by a medieval castle, the harbour area consists of picturesque alleys; the street parallel to the quayside is lined by attractive Turkish houses with balconies. There is a small ancient theatre next to the barracks northwest of the town. On the island of Marathónissi stands one of the typical towers of Máni. The **Historical and Ethnological Museum** (in the Tzanetáki Tower), traces the history of Maní.

▷ *Take the Areópoli road; 3km/ 2mi from Gíthio is the village of* **Mavrovoúni**.

The road climbs into the mountains through a gorge *(11km/7mi from Gíthio)*, guarded at its northern end by Passavant Castle (**Pasavás**), a Frankish fortress.

Continue on the Areópoli road across the mountain chain; the western approach is guarded by Kelefá Castle *(3km/2mi on)*, a huge Turkish fortress (16C–17C).

Areópoli★

Capital of the Maní region, this is a large, typically Maniot village with services for tourists. It was here on 17 March 1821 that the Maniots rose up against the Turks. The **Taxiarchs' Church** (18C), is unusual for its sculpted decoration; **St John's Church** (Ágios Ioánis), in a neighbouring street, is decorated with naive frescoes (18C).

▷ *At the junction with the road to Kótronas (left), bear right to the Dirós Caves.*

👥🧍 Spílea Diroú★★

🕐*Open Jun–Sept daily 8.30am–5.30pm; Oct–May daily 8.30am–5.30pm.* 💶*€12.* 📞*27330 522 22.*
Partway down the west coast of Máni, are two caves; the largest, Glifáda, is one of the most spectacular natural sights in Europe; the other, Alepótripa, shows traces of prehistoric occupation *(🔒closed to the public).*

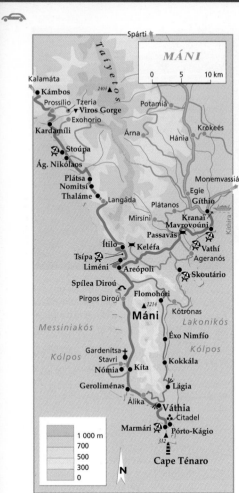

collection of weapons, tools made of stone and bone, earthenware jars and other vessels, utensils and other domestic items (such as needles), as well as human skulls and skeletons. The cave was abandoned when an earthquake blocked the entrance.

Return to the Geroliménas road, which runs along a sort of limestone terrace between the mountain and the sea, dotted with villages of tower houses, such as Dríalos. At the village of **Haroúda**, the Taxiarch's Church (12C) features interesting frescoes.

Gardenítsa

1km/0.5mi west of the road (sign).

St Saviour's Church (Ágios Sotírios), (12C), has a porch and an interesting apse with a sculpted decoration in Kufic script; inside are 13C–14C frescoes.

Nómia

Nómia lies on the west side of the road with **views**★★ of the towers of Kíta. Along the road stands the white Taxiarchs' Church (fine series of frescoes, 13C–14C).

Glifáda Cave

The cave consists of chambers and a gallery created by an underground river forcing its way through the limestone of Máni to reach the sea below the actual entrance. Guided boat tours *(about 2km/1.25mi)* explore both arms of the river. All along the route are white or coloured concretions: pillars, curtains, stalactites and stalagmites named for their appearance (the Dragon's Cave, the Cathedral, the Pavilion).

Moussío (Neolithic Museum)

🕔*Open daily 8.30am–3pm.* ✆€2. 📞*27330 522 233.*

Items from the Neolithic period found in Alepótripa Cave are on display: a fine

Koíta

The village appears abandoned, despite its many towers. In the hamlet of Tourlotí, St Sergius' Church (12C) is well proportioned. Northwest of Kipoúla rises a rocky bluff on which the famous **Castle of the Great Maina** (Kástro tis Oriás, *difficult access*) was built in 1248.

Geroliménas★

This is a simple resort and fishing village tucked into a rocky inlet in remote and wild **surroundings**★.

Váthia★★

Forsaken by almost all its inhabitants, Váthia is the most impressive o

Pórto Kágio with a view to Cape Matapan

© Dbdella/Dreamstime.com

the Máni's tower communities. Stony paths wind between the silent towers and empty houses. From Váthia the road continues south to **Pórto Kágio** (Quail Port), situated on the neck of a precipitous peninsula, and ends in **Cape Matapan**.

Cape Matapan★★
Akrotírio Taínaro, the southernmost tip of the Peloponnese, was once crowned by a temple to Poseidon, which was replaced by the **Church ton Assomatón**, of which traces remain. In March 1941, off the coast of Cape Matapan, a naval battle occurred between ships of the British and Italian navies. An easy victory by the British drastically curtailed the prospect of future Italian naval activity in the Eastern Mediterranean. Return to Álika and bear right into the road to Lágia over the ridge of the Máni. Beyond Lágia (towers) it descends, offering magnificent **views**★★ of the Maniot Coast. Beyond **Ágios Kiprianós** it skirts the east coast of the Máni. The corniche road provides spectacular views of the coastline and of the occasional villages and feudal ruins on the mountain slopes. Worth exploring are the villages of **Kokkála**, in an attractive sheltered inlet; and **Flomochóri**, with tall towers and cypress trees. A mile beyond the latter, turn right to **Kótronas**, a small seaside resort and fishing port.

FROM AREÓPOLI TO KALAMÁTA★★
80km/50mi one way.

The magnificent road between Areópoli and Kalamáta climbs high into the western foothills of the Taýgetos chain, providing views of the indented eastern shoreline of the gulf (many quiet inlets ideal for bathing).

Areópoli
See p283.

Liméni
Built very prettily around a bay, this is the birthplace of the most famous family in Máni, the Mavromichalis, who played an important role in the War of Greek Independence and later in the governance of the new Greek state. Despite the abundance of yachts in the marina during the summer, this is sadly a village with an ever-diminishing population.

Oítylo
The ancient capital of the Máni, now a wine-producing centre, stands on a hill facing the Turkish castle of Kelefá (16C and 17C) inland and a sheltered bay on the coast at Néo Oítilo, where Napoleon's fleet anchored in 1798 en route for Egypt. Néo Oítilo has a beautiful sandy beach.

On the slope below the road lies the Dekoúlou Monastery (18C); the church is decorated with frescoes and wood carvings (iconostasis, baldaquin).

◯ Leave the car in the village and climb a steep street and steps (out of season it is possible to go by car as far as the small square in front of the Byzantine monastery in the citadel).

Citadel
The entrance to the very extensive citadel is an imposing Gothic gate built by the Venetians. Views of Korone and the Messenian Gulf. The citadel encloses a few houses, former storehouses, the Byzantine Monastery of St John the Baptist (Timiou Prodromou) and the remains of the Basilica of St Sophia; part of the apse has been converted into a chapel.

Thalámes
13C Church of St Sophia. At **Langáda**, with its church and towers, there are great views looking down over the gulf.

Nomitsí
Beside the road through the village stands the Anárgiri Chapel, a rare example of a cruciform plan within a square, decorated with frescoes.
In an enclosure on the left side of the road between Nomitsí and Thalámas stands the Church of the Transfiguration (Metamórfossis) which dates from the 11C; unusual capitals carved with Byzantine motifs (peacocks, cockerels etc); traces of frescoes.

Ágios Nikolaos Kampinari★
About 1km/.5mi after Nomitsí on the left.
This little chapel (10C) stands among the olives and cypresses on the terraced hillside facing Koróni across the Messenian Gulf.

Plátsa
Several Byzantine churches worth visiting, superb view of the gulf.
Just after a cluster of pine trees an admirable **view**★★★ opens out over the whole of the Messenian Gulf.

Ágios Nikólaos
Little fishing village with small tavernas by the sea.

Stoúpa
Fine, pink-pebbled beach, good for swimming.

Kardamíli★
Kardamíli is an unpretentious resort and fishing port protected by a fortified islet; its old houses and churches cluster on the banks of a mountain stream. The best-known church is St Spiridon (13C) in the old quarter of Kardamíli (Ano-Kardamíli). The land behind Kardamíli, now planted with olive trees, was once

Towers in the village of Langáda

guarded by **Beaufort Castle** which was
built by the Franks on an isolated site.

◯ *From Kardamíli it is possible to
make a detour on foot to the Viros
Gorge. Allow 6hrs extra and take good
shoes and a supply of water.*

Harádra tou Viroú
(Viros Gorge)

▷ *The hike is easier starting from Tséria
(6km/4mi northeast of Kardamíli),
taking a track on the right from there.*
The splendid hike involves first descending to the bottom of the gorge and then
climbing out again up a track leading
to Exohóri. Continue along the same
path, and after reaching the monasteries of Sotíras and Likaki return to Ano-
Kardomíli.

◯ *Resume the itinerary from
Kardamíli.*

Koskarás Defile★

The river has created a gorge spanned
by a bold, modern bridge. Park the car
and climb down a short way to admire
the design and the site.
Leaving the Kámbos Basin, presided
over by the medieval ruins of **Zarnáta
Castle**, the road climbs then drops to
Kardamíli, giving bird's-eye **views**★★
over the Kardamíli Basin and the coast.

ADDRESSES

⚛ STAY

◯◯ **Akrotiri** – *Porto Kagio.* ☏ *27330 520
13. 9 rooms.* Large, clean, simple rooms
with fridges and balconies overlooking
the sea. Peace and quiet, especially out
of the August high season.

◯◯ **Aktaion** – *Gíthio, 39 Odós V. Pávlou.*
☏ *27330 29114. www.aktaionhotel.gr.
20 rooms and two suites.* On the harbour
along a noisy street, this large hotel has
rooms with balconies overlooking the
port. Prices rise in summer.

◯◯ **Marmari** – *Marmári (south, end
of the point).* ☏ *27330 52 111. 24 rooms.*
Overlooking the beach, this is the
more attractive of the two hotels here.

Simple rooms with fresco decoration;
good restaurant (◯◯). Magnificent
sunset views.

◯◯ **Skoutari Beach Resort** – *Skoutari.*
☏ *27330 936 84. 20 rooms. ⌦. Open end
May–Oct.* Very good hotel above quiet
Skoutari Beach. Vehicle a must. Rooms
all with kitchenettes.

◯◯ **Tsimova** – *Areópoli, behind the
church.* ☏ *27330 513 01. 7 rooms. ⌦.*
A guesthouse in a real Maniot tower.
Kitsch decor with war souvenirs of the
grandfather, a former resistance fighter.

◯◯🛏 **Kastro Maïni** – *Areópoli.*
☏ *27330 512 38, www.kastromaini.gr.
29 rooms, 3 suites.* Only 3km/2mi from
the sea, a charming hotel, beautifully
decorated with a swimming pool.

◯◯🛏🛏 **Porto Vitilo** – *Itylo.* ☏ *27330
592 10/20 www.portovitilo.gr. 33 rooms.*
Luxurious hotel (priced according to
the view), with elegant furnishings.
Excellent breakfast.

⊻ EAT

◯ **To Nissi** – *Gíthio, islet of Kranai.*
One of Gíthio's best and quietest
spots: salads and grilled fish, excellent
espresso.

◯ **O Bárba Pétros** – *Areópoli.* ☏ *27330
512 05.* The best place in town, set in a
flowered courtyard. Well-prepared Greek
dishes, and local wine served chilled.

◯ **Theodorákis** – *Geroliménas, far end
of the harbour.* This taverna serves fresh
grilled fish and good traditional Greek
cuisine. A warm welcome and mainly
Greek clientele.

🛒 SHOPPING

Hassanakos Art Gallery – *Githio, facing
the port.* Excellent newsstand (maps
available) and gallery with old photos
of the town, books and paintings.

🎭 EVENTS AND FESTIVALS

The **Marathonissia Festival** takes
place between 15 July and 15 August
in Gíthio and features concerts and
theatrical performances.

WEST PELOPONNESE

Thitikí Pelopónnisos – Δυτική Πελοπόννησος

Looking at the map, someone might expect that this region – far as it is from the hub of Athens and the Cyclades – is less frequented by tourists. There could be nothing further from the truth, with three factors operating in its favour. It is a short hop from the Ionian Islands, it is connected – via **Pátra** – by ferries to Italy and it contains one of Greece's top sites, **Olympia** (as well as one of its best preserved castles at **Hlemoútsi**). Such is Olympia's allure that even cruise boats regularly anchor at the small fishing village of **Katákolo** for a day trip to the scared ancient site.

Highlights

1 Watch the sunset over the beautiful **Pílos** harbour (p292)
2 Stop by the many monasteries along the **Loússios Gorge** (p298)
3 Visit **Olympia**, one of the world's top archaeological sites (p300)
4 Explore the Temple of Apollo at **Bassae**, a UNESCO site (p307)
5 Go to see the famous Frankish castle of **Hlemoútsi** (p308)

Philippeion, Olympia

The Pelopennese

Any day trippers would be advised to stay longer here. The district of Messenia in the southwest offers a wealth of sights, beaches and several towns with many reminders of Venetian rule in **Kalamáta**, **Pílos**, **Methóni** and **Koróni**, as well as the **Mycenaean Palace of Nektor**, better than anything on offer in Mycenae or Tiryns.

On the other hand, the centre of the Peloponnese – wild, mountainous and never unbearably hot – is where one can delve deeper into the Greek soul, this is after all where independence was forged in the early 19C. The picturesque villages of **Karítena**, **Andritsena** and **Stemnitsa** not only offer a base for hiking and rafting, but they are also a taxi ride away from the remote and stunning UNESCO World Heritage site of **Bassae**. Finally, if around Pátra at all, one should not miss the hour-long trip on Europe's narrowest gauge railway from **Diakofto** to **Kalávryta**.

Village of Dimitsána, Loussios Gorge

Kalamáta

Kalamáta – Καλαμάτα

This Frankish city, capital of
Messenia under the Venetians,
was the first to be liberated during
the Greek War of Independence
in 1821. It paid dearly for that,
being completely destroyed by
Ibrahim Pasha in 1825, and now
offers little in the way of sights.
It remains a busy town, however,
with a thriving daily produce
market, and is an ideal base from
which to explore the area.
This is the place where the
Kalamatianós dance originated,
the de facto Greek national dance,
which is watched by thousands of
tourists in folk nights offered by
resorts throughout the summer.

▶ **Population:** 57,620.

Michelin Map: 737 F 11 –
Messinía – Peloponnese.

Info: Two offices; one at 6
Odós Polyvriou, 1st floor.
℘27210 86868.
Open Mon–Fri 8am–
2.30pm; another at the
airport (closed Sun).

Location: Kalamáta is
located 169km/106mi
southwest of Corinth and
61km/38mi west of Sparta,
on the Gulf of Messinía.

Parking: It may take a
while, but there are spaces
to be found on side streets.

Don't Miss: Try to find
time to explore the west
coast of the Messenian
Gulf (see Máni).

Timing: Too much to see
all in one day.

Kids: Beaches and
swimming spots along
the coast.

ᴗ WALKING TOUR
OLD TOWN

*Proceed via Odós Faron, passing through
Ipapandis Square with its church, and
continue as far as the entrance on Odós
de Villeardouin.*

Kástro

The Frankish castle (13C) stands on a
rocky eminence overlooking the coastal
plain on the site of the ancient acropolis.
All that remain are traces of the 13C keep
and the circuit walls. From the terrace
there is a view of Kalamáta and the Gulf
of Messinía.

Bazaar

Shops surround a teeming daily produce
market in the old town between the
Benaki Museum and the double Church
of the **Holy Apostles** (chancel originally
a 10C Byzantine chapel).

Coastline of the Messenian Gulf near Kalamáta

© World Pictures/Photoshot

Stadium, Messene

Kalamáta is not only the capital of the fertile region of Messenia (Messinía) but also an agricultural market celebrated for its black olives, dried figs, honey and sesame cakes, and *raki*.

Benakeion Archaeological Museum

6 Odós Papazoglou. ⓒ*Open Tue–Sun 8am–3pm.* ⊜€*2.* ℘*27210 63100.*
Housed in a handsome two-storey Venetian mansion, the museum presents artefacts from the Bronze Age to the Roman period from various sites in Messinía.

Stop in also at the **Folklore and History Museum** (*Odós Kiriakou;* ⓒ*open Tue–Sun 9am–1pm.* ⊜€*2.* ℘*27210 284 49).*

EXCURSIONS
Messene★★

▶ *25km/15mi northwest of Kalamáta. Once through modern Messinía, follow the Mavromáti road. The site of Ithómi (signposted "Ancient Messene") is on the left on leaving the village. Turn onto the unpaved road which heads down to the ruins.* ⓒ*Open daily 8.30am–6.30pm.* ⊜*No charge.* ℘*27240 51 201.*

The ruins of Ancient Messene lie against a majestic backdrop of mountains dominated by **Mount Ithómi**; at the centre stands the modern village of Mavromáti. Destroyed by Spartans, Messene was rebuilt by **Epaminóndas**, who defeated the Spartans at Leuktra (371 BC). Excavations are in progress on the site at the time of publication and new finds are constantly being made.

Circuit Wall★★

The circuit wall (over 9km/5.5mi long), which dates from the 4C BC and was well known in antiquity, turned the town into a sort of fortress. The best-preserved section is on the north side around the Arkadia Gate. Follow the ancient road (wheel ruts) out beyond the gate for a view of the ramparts; several tombs have been found in this area.

Asklepieion★

A path leading off the road northwest of Mavromáti descends to the remains of a small theatre, the Fountain of Arsinoë and a sanctuary dedicated to the god Asklepios (Aesculapius) *(sign "Ithómi, Archaeological site"; about 30min on foot there and back)*. The excavations have uncovered the foundations of a temple to Asklepios from the Hellenistic period. As at Epidaurus, next to the sanctuary there is a theatre *(ecclesiasterion)*; adjoining this are the council chamber *(bouleuterion)* and the *propylaia*.

Between the theatre and the agora there are the remnants of an old fountain in honour of Arsinoë, legendary mother of Asklepios.

To the south of the Asklepieion lay the Hellenistic public baths (included a swimming bath fed by terra-cotta pipes) and the *hierothysion* (temple).

Further south are the remains of a stadium and its *palaestra*, as well as vestiges of a large Doric funerary monument.

Lakonía Gate

From Mavromáti drive up to the Lakonía Gate to see a fine view of Mount Éva; below lies the new Voulkáno Convent.

Archaeological Museum

🕐 *Open daily 8.00am–2.00pm.* 🚫 €2. 📞 *27240 512 01. Between the Arkadia Gate and the village of Mavromáti.*

Worth a stop to see architectural elements, sculptures, including the Hermes of Andros, and a model of the Asklepieion.

Mount Ithómi

🚶 *798m/2 618ft. From the Lakonia Gate a steep path (1hr 30min on foot there and back) climbs up past the remains of a temple to Artemis to the ancient citadel of Ithómi.*

At the summit is the old Voulkáno Convent (8C). Magnificent **views**★★ of Messene, the region of Messenia and the southern Peloponnese.

Koróni

▶ *52km/33mi southwest of Kalamáta, on the west coast of the Messenian Gulf.*

The white houses of Koróni (called Coron by the Franks) are scattered over the slope of a promontory that protects a charming little port. A castle surmounts the high point at the end of the promontory and a long beach skirts the southern shore.

ADDRESSES

🏨 STAY

😊😊🛏🛏 **Messinia Bay Hotel** – *Verga Beach, 5km/3mi from Kalamáta.* 📞 *27210 41001. www.messinianbay.gr. 71 rooms, 2 suites.* Luxury hotel on a beach under the shadow of Mount Taýgetos.

😊😊🛏🛏 **Elite** – *Kalamáta, on the jetty, corner of Odós Vérga and Leofóros 2 Navarínou.* 📞 *27210 224 34. www.elite. com.gr. 57 rooms, 87 bungalows.* Pleasant new hotel; bright, clean, comfortable rooms with balconies overlooking the beach. English-speaking staff.

😊😊🛏🛏 **Rex** – *Kalamáta, 26 Odós Aristoumenous.* 📞 *27210 944 40. www.rexhotel.gr. 42 rooms and two suites.* Illustrious hotel with an air of bygone splendour.

¶/EAT

😊 **I Psaropoœla** – *Kalamáta, Leofóros Navarínou 14.* Taverna on the water overlooking a small fishing port. Excellent grilled fish and *kokorétsi* (kebabs).

😊 **Symposium** – *Koróni, main street.* 📞 *27250 223 85.* Popular hangout with good fish and grilled meat. Rooms available upstairs (😊).

😊😊 **Mangiona** – *Kalamáta. Chiou and Salaminos St.* 📞 *27210 98988.* Italian-Mediterranean restaurant with superb decor on the marina. Open daily for dinner and on weekends for lunch as well.

🚌 TAKING A BREAK

Igloo – *Kalamáta, Leofóros Navarínou, opposite the Bank of Greece.* One of the best ice-cream parlours in town.

🛒 SHOPPING

Household linen made of **cotton** or **silk**, woven, embroidered or dyed by the nuns at the Monastery of St Constantine and St Helen.

🎭 EVENTS AND FESTIVALS

International dance festival, held from late-June to mid-July in the theatre at the foot of the fortress.

Pílos★★

Pílos – Πύλος

Pílos, also known as Navarino, lies on the southern shore of a majestic bay bounded on the seaward side by the rocky ridge of the island of Sphakteria (Sfaktiría). It is endowed with a good harbour and an excellent anchorage. The modern town, which boasts a superb beach, was built in 1829 by the French military expedition to Greece and is a good base for making excursions into the southern Peloponnese.

▶ **Population:** 5,402.

Michelin Map: 737 E 12 – Messinía – Peloponnese.

Info: www.pylos.net.

Location: 217km/136mi southwest of Corinth and 48km/30mi southwest of Kalamáta, Pílos is located in the southwest Peloponnese on the Ionian Sea.

Parking: There is usually space for plenty of cars.

Don't Miss: Sunset over the bay.

Timing: Visit on foot; Pílos is a pleasant small village.

Kids: Birdwatching at Giálova Lagoon.

Also See: Kalamáta.

A BIT OF HISTORY

Bronze-Age Pílos was excavated in the 1950s and the remains of a large Mycenaean palace were excavated and named after the character Nestor who ruled this region, according to Homer. The site was abandoned sometime after the 8C BC. The ruins of a stone fortress on nearby Sphacteria Island, also thought to be Mycenaean, were used by the Spartans during a famous incident during the Peloponnesian War. In 425 BC the Athenians captured some 400 Spartan soldiers on the island and concern over the return of the prisoners contributed to their acceptance of the Peace of Nicias in 421 BC.

The strategic importance of Navarino Bay was recognised both in antiquity and the Middle Ages from the 6C to 9C. In those days the town lay at the north-ern end of the bay beneath an acropolis, later a medieval castle (Paliókastro). Later, the Turks built a fortress (Niókastro) to guard the southern approach. The focal point of the town is Three Admirals Square (Platía Trion Návarhon), named for the commanders of the victorious fleet at the Battle of Navarino. Stop in at the **Antonopoulos Archaeological Museum** (*Odós Philéllinon, off the square;* open Tue–Sun 8.30am–3pm; €2) to take in a collection of art, arms, tools and other objects from the Neolithic to the Roman periods.

Battle of Navarino

This was the decisive naval engagement which took place on 20 October 1827 between the allied fleet, made up of English, French and Russians, and the Turks during the War of Greek Independence.

The presence of the allied fleet was intended to intimidate **Ibrahim Pasha**, and to force the Porte to agree to an armistice with the Greeks. The allied force, commanded by Admirals Codrington (Britain), De Rigny (France) and Heyden (Russia), consisted of 26 ships with a total of 1,270 cannon. The 82 Turkish and Egyptian ships were caught in a trap without room to manoeuvre and were annihilated, despite their superior firepower (2,400 cannon) and the support of the artillery at Niókastro.

The Battle of Navarino forced the Sultan to negotiate and paved the way for Greek independence.

Beach at Voidokilia

© Greek National Tourism Organisation

SIGHTS
Niókastro★
Access from the Methóni road.
🕐 *Open Tue–Sun 8.30am–3pm.* ✎€3.
📞 *27230 22897.*
This citadel was built by the Turks in the 16C. A large building near the entrance houses a **museum** dedicated to the French philhellene **René Puaux**: lithographs, engravings and objects recalling the struggle for Greek independence. From the southwest redoubt there are remarkable **views**★ over the bay; the tiny islet (south of the island of Sfaktiría bears a monument to the French who fell in the War of Independence.

Navarino Bay★
In the summer season boats operate from Pílos to Sphakteria and Paliókastro. Information available at the harbour.

Paliókastro★
Accessible by car from Petrohóri taking a bad road that goes to Voidokilia (follow signs for the archaeological site).
On a spur of rock near the northern approach rise the crenellated walls and towers of the **Castle of Port de Junch** (1278). The circuit wall and keep command the lagoon and the ancient port of Pílos. At the foot of the cliff there is a cave with stalactites, named after King Nestor. There is a beautiful beach further on, at Voidokilia.

Sfaktiría (Sphakteria)
The uninhabited island of Sphakteria is the site of several monuments commemorating those who died in the cause of Greek independence. On the summit there are traces of an ancient fortress where 420 Spartans made a heroic stand against the Athenians during the Peloponnesian War (425 BC).

OUTSKIRTS
Methóni★★
▶ *12km/7.5mi south of Pílos.*
Methóni, the watchtower of the eastern Mediterranean, stands on a pleasant **site**★ overlooking a bay protected by two islands, Sapiéntza and Schíza, which provide good inshore fishing grounds. A beach adjoining the quiet fishing harbour, with several hotels and tavernas, makes it a pleasant place to stay.
From the early 13C to the 19C, Methoni passed back and forth between Venetian and Turkish control. Ultimately, during the War of Independence, French troops took it from Ibrahim Pasha; the French troops then rebuilt parts of the town.

Citadel★★
🕐*Open daily 8.30am–7pm.* ✎*No charge.*
The citadel was begun in the 13C , but most of the construction occurred during the Venetian period, evidenced

Legendary King

Nestor, youngest son of Neleus and Chloris, attributed his longevity to Apollo's remorse after killing Nestor's siblings. Despite his great age, King Nestor commanded a large fleet of ships at the Siege of Troy; Homer praised him for his wisdom. After Troy fell, he returned to Pílos. Here in his palace Nestor received **Telemachos**, when he came to ask for news of his father Odysseus.

by the lions of St Mark and the carved escutcheons.

Beyond the counterscarp a bridge spans the moat, which was covered by crossfire from the **Bembo Bastion** (15C) *(right)* and the **Loredan Bastion** (1714) *(left)*.

An outer gate (early 18C) opens into a passage against the northern rampart (13C); a vaulted approach precedes the **Land Gate** (13C), which has Gothic arches and gives access to the open space once occupied by the medieval town. Follow the eastern rampart (16C–18C); on the left lies the port, on the right the remains of a Turkish bath, some cisterns, a powder magazine and the old Latin cathedral.

The **Sea Gate** on the south side of the citadel gives access to the picturesque **Boúrdzi Tower**★ (16C) on an island of rock linked to the citadel by a bridge;

Boúrdzi Tower, Methóni

climb to the platform for a splendid **view**★★ of the citadel, the harbour and the islands. The western rampart leads back to the keep; most of its fortifications date from the 15C but it was modernised in the 18C (firing steps for artillery).

EXCURSIONS

The Messenian Coast – 79km/49mi round trip from Pílos.

Giálova Lagoon

▶ *3km/1.8mi north of Pílos.*
℘ *2108 279 37.*

The peaceful lagoon is an important resting spot for nearly 270 species of migratory birds, 79 of which are endangered, and other wildlife. Best time to visit: May–Sept.

Anáktora Néstoros★

▶ *18km/11mi north of Pílos (bus service €1.80).* ◷ *Open Jul–Oct daily 8am–7.30pm; rest of the year daily 8.30am–3pm.* ▩ *€3.* ℘ *27630 314 37.*

The buildings comprising the **Palace of Nestor** (destroyed about 12C BC) date from the Mycenaean era. They contained clay tablets bearing inscriptions in **Linear B**, which have contributed to our understanding of the Mycenaeans' language, the earliest known form of Greek. The ruins reveal that the palace was similar to those in Crete or the Argolis (Mycenae, Tiryns). The entrance *(propylon)* is flanked by two archive rooms where about 1,000 clay tablets were found. On the far side of the courtyard stood the *megaron*, the royal residence; at the centre was a round hearth, the throne was to the right. On the east side of the court are the queen's apartments, which include a bathroom containing a **bath**, the only one known to have survived from this period. Also excavated at the site were murals depicting lyrists and griffins and floors with decorative drawings.

Hóra

This town has an interesting **Archaeological Museum** (◷ *open Jul–Oct daily 8am–5pm; rest of the year Tue–Sun, 8.30am–3pm;* ▩ *€2; €4 combined ticket* with the Palace of Nestor) which displays the objects excavated in the palace and the region, especially at Peristéria: fine golden cups and jewellery from the Mycenaean period; fragments of frescoes and mosaics; and mouldings of inscribed tablets.

Kiparissía

Kiparissía, the town of cypresses, is set just back from the coastline; in the Middle Ages it was called **Arkadia**, Destroyed in 1825 by Ibrahim Pasha, it is today a modern city, dominated by the ruins of a Frankish castle. From the top there is a fine **view**★ across the Ionian Sea to Zakynthos (northwest). Due west lie the **Strofádes Islands**, Kiparissía was the legendary home of the **Harpies** (also called the **Furies**), tempestuous divinities represented as birds with women's faces.

Peristéria Tombs

▶ 10km/5mi northeast; take the Pírgos road for 5km/3mi; turn right (sign) and continue for 5.5km/3.25mi (⌚very poor road).

Among the green hills looking down into the narrow valley of the Peristéria, excavations have revealed some domed royal tombs (thólos), dating from the Mycenaean period. A fine collection of jewellery, seals and vases found in one of the tombs is currently on display in Hóra Museum. Note especially in the museum the fine cups with spiral decorations and the sheet gold used to represent leaves and flowers (some so small that a magnifying glass comes in useful).

The construction of domed tombs dates back to the 2nd millennium BC and are considered to have originated in Messinia and from that area spread to the rest of mainland Greece and to Mycenae. The thólos tombs of Peristéria, some of the best-preserved to be found anywhere in mainland Greece, consist of a circular, subterranean burial chamber, roofed by a corbelled vault and approached by a entrance passage that narrows abruptly at the doorway opening into the tomb chamber. They are built of stone, not simply hewn out of bedrock.

ADDRESSES

▨STAY

😑😑 **Karalís** – Pílos, 26 Odós Kalamáta. ✆27230 22 960. www.hotel-karalis.com. 35 rooms. Charming hotel in a historic house on the coast road. Small but comfortable rooms with balconies. Generous breakfast.

😑😑 **Karalís Beach** – Pílos, between the fortress and the beach. ✆27230 23 021. 14 rooms. Very well situated among pine trees below the fortress, 20m/66ft from the sea. Comfortable rooms with large bathrooms; balconies for those overlooking the sea. Pleasant terrace bar.

😑😑 **Kstéllo** – Methóni, near the citadel and the sea. ✆27230 31 300. www.castello.gr. 15 rooms. ⌛. This modern hotel with garden has clean, simple rooms. Animals allowed.

😑😑 **Zoé** – Giálova, by the beach. ✆27230 22 025. 32 rooms. (♿wheelchair accessible). A row of native trees separates the beach from this modest, friendly hotel.

😑😑😑😑 **Methoni Beach Hotel** – ✆27230 287 20. www.methonibeach hotel.gr. 12 rooms. Renovated, contemporary styling, comfortable hotel. Restaurant overlooks the beach.

▨EAT

😑 **O Grigóris** – Pílos, above the main square. ✆27230 22621. A garden taverna, with several flower-decked terraces, serving good Greek food to the sound of local music.

😑 **Klimataria** – Methóni. ✆27230 315 44. Good family-style cooking, vegetarian dishes and live music.

▨SHOPPING

Kellari – Facing the harbour en route to Kalamáta. Family-owned boutique specialising in olive oil and local products (honey, wine, ouzo, etc.)

▨ EVENTS AND FESTIVALS

On 20 October, Pílos commemorates the Battle of Navarino Bay.

Central Peloponnese

Kentrikí Pelopónnisos –
Κεντρική Πελοπόννησος

The central Peloponnese is often neglected by tourists and is recommended to those who prefer their holidays off the beaten track. It is a mountainous area with a cool and sunny climate in the summer, many beautiful stone villages, excellent hikes and some superb archaeological sites and monasteries.

KARÍTENA

Start with Karítena, a picturesque medieval town built into the curve of a hillside and dominated by an imposing Frankish castle. The villages in this isolated area, composed of the beautiful landscapes of the Alfiós and Loússios Gorges, retain their traditional building styles (stone roofs, wooden balconies). From the modern bridge there is a spectacular **view**★★ of the site of Karítena. The **medieval bridge**, built by the Franks in the 13C and subsequently restored in the 15C, has four of its six original arches. One of the pillars of the structure houses a small chapel.

In the **village** is the 17C Church of Our Lady (Panagía) with a square stone belfry and, on the way up to the castle, Ágios Nikólaos, a small village church. The feudal **castle**★ (1254) was the stronghold of a powerful Frankish barony. During the War of Independence Kolokotrónis defied Ibrahim Pasha from here. Only the ruins of the residence of the lord of the castle remain against the south wall, but several cisterns have been preserved *(beware of falling)*.

From the top there are extensive **views**★★ of the gorge *(west)*, the Megalópolis basin *(east)* and Mount Líkeo (Lykaion) *(south)*.

The Frankish **bridge**★★ below Karítena over the river Alfiós next to the small church of the Dormition is one of the most picturesque in Greece and it was used as the background to the 5,000 drachma note before the advent of the euro.

ANDRÍTSENA

▶ *29km/18mi west of Karítena.*

Andrítsena is a charming market town, with old wooden houses and craft workshops lining the streets where goats, donkeys and pigs roam at will. The charming main square has a café and a fountain shaded by a plane tree. Among the peaks bordering Elis to the east is Mount Líkeo (Lykaion); it was a primitive sanctuary to Zeus, involving human sacrifice and ritual cannibalism, before the establishment of the magnificent **Temple of Bassae**★★.

Near the Trani Fountain (18C), you'll find the **Folk Museum** *www.andritsainamuseum.gr* (◷open Tue–Sun 10am–1.30pm), with displays of fabrics and costumes. Andritsena also boasts a magnificent historical **library** of 25,000 volumes.

- ⚅ **Michelin Map:** 737 F 10 – Arcadia – Peloponnese.
- ▷ **Location:** Karítena is located 56km/35mi west of Trípolis by the Megalópolis road and 107km/69mi southeast of Olympia. Tripolis is 82km/51mi southeast of Corinth, 175km/109 mi south of Pátra and 131km/81mi west of Olympia.
- 🅿 **Parking:** Not usually a problem.
- ◉ **Don't Miss:** Views from the ramparts of the castle in Karítena.
- ◔ **Timing:** From a couple of hours to a couple of days, depending on the time available to you.
- 🏃 **Kids:** The castle in Karítena.
- ⚅ **Also See:** The Temple of Bassae.

RUINS OF MEGALÓPOLIS

◐ *15km/9mi southeast of Karítena.*
1km before Megalópolis on the right.
◷ *Open Mon–Sun 8.30–3pm.*
✺ *No charge.*

The ancient city of Megalópolis was built between 371 and 368 BC by Epaminóndas as part of his plan to contain Sparta. It was the native city of Philopoimen (253–183 BC), the "last of the Greeks", who sought to maintain Greek unity in the face of the Roman expansion, and of the historian Polybius (204–122 BC).

Thersilion

The huge assembly hall was designed to hold the "Ten Thousand", the representatives of the Arcadian League. The 67 pillars were placed so that almost all those present could see the speaker.

Theatre

The theatre, the largest in Greece, could accommodate about 20,000 spectators; the acoustics were excellent. The lower rows are well preserved.

TRÍPOLIS

◐ *Tripolis is located 85km/53mi southwest of Corinth, 60km/38mi north of Sparta and 87km/54mi northeast of Kalamáta.*

Trípolis is the capital of Arcadia (Arkadía) and the central point in the road network of the Peloponnese. The town is built in the centre of a high, flat plain in the limestone massif formed by erosion and surrounded by mountains of up to 2,000m/6,560ft. Because of the altitude, the climate is cool, even in summer. Modern Tripolis ("three cities") was created in 1770 near the ruins of the ancient cities of Pallantron, Tegéa, and Mantínia. During the Greek War of Independence, Tripolis was the first major city to be taken by the Greeks; Ibrahim Pasha retook the city in June 22, 1825, killing the Christian population and burning the city. After it was retaken by the Greeks in 1829, Tripolis became a major centre of the independent Greek state. The city was rebuilt. Today, the central square is bordered by the metal awnings typical in the mountains, whereas Areos Square is open and planted with gardens; the bazaar lies to the south on the Kalamáta road.

Panarcadic Archaeological Museum

6–8, Evangelistrias Street.
Take Odós Georgiou right of the church, then the third street on the right, then immediately left towards Odós Evangelistrias. ◷ *Open Tue–Sun 8.30am–3pm.* ✺ *€2.* ✆ *27102 421 48.*

This museum is located in a fine Neoclassical former hospital and contains items from Arkadía dating from the Neolithic and Bronze Age to the Roman period).

VYTINA

◐ *40km/25mi northwest of Tripolis.*

Dead in the centre of the Peloponnese and at an altitude of 1,036m/3,390ft, lies **Vytina**, spread under the peak of **Mount Mainalon**. Not a town with tons of character, but famed in Greece for its healthy climate; a sanatorium used to operate in the area until recently. It is also the place that offers the best hotel in the region, Menalon Art Hotel, which can serve as a base for exploring. A year-round resort, it is a short drive away from the **Mainalon Ski Centre** www.mainalo-ski.gr.

TEGÉA

◐ *10km/6.25mi southeast of Tripolis.*
Follow the road to Sparta for 8km/5mi; in Kerassítsa turn left (sign "ancient Tegéa").

Tegéa was the most important city in Arcadia in antiquity; it came under Spartan domination in the 6C BC, was destroyed by barbarians in the 5C AD, but resurrected later by the Byzantines. Great verbena fairs were held a few miles to the south. Some ancient vestiges can be seen around the modern **Paléa Episkopi**; nearby is a small warehouse with a mosaic from an early 5C church.

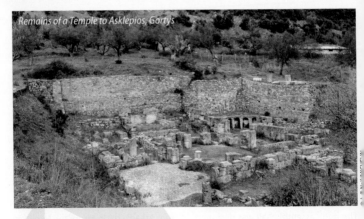

Remains of a Temple to Asklepios, Gortys

🚗 DRIVING TOUR

VILLAGES AND MONASTERIES OF THE LOÚSSIOS GORGE★★

The Loússios, a tributary of the Alfiós, is a spectacular geographical feature forming the backdrop for numerous monasteries and villages.

The gorge itself is 15km/9mi long and approximately 2km/1.2mi wide; very popular with hikers. It is girdled by the Karítena road to Dimitsána which is spectacular, but narrow and dangerous in wet weather when the whole road may be closed for safety reasons.

Gortys

12km/7.5mi north of Karítena; signposted from the junction near Ellinikó.

On this beautiful, remote **site**★ at the bottom of the gorge lie the remains of a Temple to Asklepios and its surrounding wall, and the bases of some buildings and baths. It is in this Asklepieion that Pausanias was impressed when he saw Alexander the Great's breastplate and spear, who Alexander himself had dedicated to the god.

Stemnitsa

This attractive mountain village on the slopes of Mount Menalon was an important metalworking centre in Byzantine times and the tradition is still alive today. Being the seat of the famous Kolokotronis clan, the village became the capital

of the Greek rebellion for 15 days in 1821 and the first National Assembly sat in the 15C Zoodohou Pigis Church. There are 18 churches here, the most important ones being the Three Hierarchs (17C), St Nicholas (14C with 16C frescoes) and Panagía Baféro (12C). A beautiful carved stone bell-tower adorns the main square. You can also visit the local **Folk Art Museum** *(opposite the Three Hierarchs church)*, with icons, traditional costumes, ceramics and wood carvings.

▷ *Before entering Dimitsána, turn left and follow the winding road 8km/5mi down into Loússios Gorge.*

Agiou Ioánnou Prodrómou Monastery

A few monks still live in this 11C monastery built next to a vertical rockface in a beautiful, isolated **setting**★. The tiny church houses some frescoes.

Philosóphou Monastery

Opposite the Agiou Ioánnou Prodrómou Monastery.

The old monastery has been abandoned in favour of a new building, situated on the west bank next to the Byzantine Church of Naos Panagias and its 17C frescoes.

Dimitsána

25km/15mi north of Karítena on the road to Trípoli.

Buried at the heart of the Peloponnese is the old medieval city of Dimitsána, which is built on a spectacular **site**★★ overlooking the Loússios Valley.

In the 18C it was a centre of the independence movement; its secret schools were attended by patriots such as Germanós. You can visit the **Ecclesiastical Museum**, with its collection of religious art; also the House of the Patriarch. Its rise after 1830 in the new Greek state caused the decline of Karítena.

Aimyálon Monastery

Beautiful 16C monastery, built beneath the rock; 17C frescoes in the church.

Ipethrió Moussío Hydrokinissis★

4km/2.5mi south of Dimitsána. ◷*Open Wed–Mon, Apr–Oct 10am–2pm and 5–7pm; winter 10am–4pm.* ◉*€1.50.* ✆*27950 316 30.*

The **Open-Air Water-Power Museum** shows how the forces of the local rivers have been harnessed in the region, and demonstrates various manufacturing processes.

ADDRESSES

🛏STAY

🍽🍽 **Artemis** – *Tripolis, 1 Dimitrakopoulou St.* ✆*2710 225221/3. 69 rooms.* ⌂. Good location, large rooms.

🍽🍽 **Epicurios Apollo** – *Andrítsena, main square.* ✆*26220 22 840. 6 rooms.* Large comfortable rooms; a good place to stay. Book in advance.

🍽🍽 **Maria** – *300m/984ft from the station, in a pedestrian street to the right of the main square.* ✆*26920 22 296. 11 rooms.* A quiet, small hotel offering simple, though clean and pleasant, accommodation.

🍽🍽🍽 **Dimitsána** – *Dimitsána.* ✆*27950 315 18. 30 rooms.* ⌂. Outskirts of the village, this refurbished hotel has pleasant heated rooms overlooking the valley. Dining either on the terrace or indoors. Prices rise by a third in winter.

🍽🍽🍽 **Menalon Art** – *Vitína, on a quiet square not far from the town centre.* ✆*27950 222 00. 46 rooms.* ⛶⌂. This relatively recent establishment is one of

the best hotels in the area and certainly the friendliest.

🍽🍽🍽 **Mainalon Resort** – *Tripolis, Areos Sq.* ✆*2710 230300. www.mainalon hotel.gr. 31 rooms.* ⌂. Overlooking Tripolis' large square, this is a 1930s building renovated in 2004 that combines atmosphere with luxury and service.

🍴EAT

🍽 **Taverna 1821** – *Stemnitsa, near the main square.* ✆*27950 815 18.* Traditional Greek dishes at good value, served in a large dining room.

🍽–🍽🍽 **Ta Aidónia** – *Vitína.* ✆*27950 222 24. www.taidonia.gr.* The best restaurant in town. Enjoy goat ("*katsíki*") with oregano and lightly resinated white wine while sitting in the shady garden.

🍽🍽 **Refené** – *In the north part of Tripoli off the Kalavryta Road next to Alsos Agíou Georgiou.* ✆*2710 235475. www.refene. gr.* Specialises in local specialities such as salted beef, salted pork, country sausages and mezedes.

🍽🍽🍽 **Sideris** – *Tripolis. 113 Agíou Konstantinou St.* ✆*27102 25452. www.taverna-sideris.gr.* Family-run with Kyria Roula, the cook, taking personal pride in her traditional dishes.

🍷TAKING A BREAK

Tsigouri – *Andritsaina, up the steps leading to the main square.* An old-fashioned taverna with blackened "*briki*" (coffee pots), oilcloths and a friendly landlady who also keeps the keys to the Ethnographic Museum.

🏃SPORT AND LEISURE

Outdoor pursuits – This is prime country for adventure holidays, primarily trekking, canyoning and rafting. Contact Trekking Hellas ✆*21033 10323/6* or *27102 21912* for gorge descents, gorge crossings and rafting on the Alfíos. The company is based at the village of Blachorraptis, 220km/137mi from Athens between Megalópolis and Gortyna. Another company is No Limits, ✆ *26550 23777*, which offers longer rafting and trekking packages and is based in Gortyna.

Olympia★★★

Olimbía – Ολυμπία

Here at the heart of the idyllic Alfiós Valley, the ruins of Olympia bear witness to the grandeur of the ancient Sanctuary of Zeus which, through the Olympic Games, was a symbol of Greek unity. Physical and intellectual prowess, a spirit of concord and peace; such were the aspirations which in antiquity drew Greeks from all states to the Games at Olympia some 2,800 years ago.

A BIT OF HISTORY

The Site★★ – Below the wooded slopes of Mount Kronion (125m/410ft) to the north, the Sanctuary of Zeus shelters under the trees between the River Alfiós (Alpheios) and its tributary, the Kládeos. Upstream, the valley of the Alfiós narrows between the foothills of the mountains of Arcadia; downstream, it widens out towards the Elian Plain in a fertile basin surrounded by gently rolling hills.

Originally a Sacred Grove – The original place of worship at Olympia seems to have been a sacred grove, the Áltis, which was succeeded by a sanctuary on Mount Kronion dedicated to Kronos, the god of Time. Kronos was the son of Ouranos (the Sky) and Gaia (the Earth). He was later supplanted by

- **Michelin Map:** 737 E 10 – Ilia – Peloponnese.
- **Info:** In the middle of the main street. ☏26240 231 00. Open daily June–September 9am–9pm.
- **Location:** The ruins of Olympia lie in the western Peloponnese, 110km/69mi south of Pátra, 17km/11mi east of Pírgos and 215km/134mi southwest of Corinth. The modern village extends past the ruins.
- **Parking:** There is a car park outside the site.
- **Don't Miss:** The ancient ruins and the Archaeological Museum.
- **Timing:** Allow a day; see the museum in the heat of the day.
- **Also See:** Hlemoútsi, Kalamáta, Pátras.

his son Zeus, however, as worship of the king of the gods began to attract pilgrims to the site. Several legends relate to these distant times, the best known of which is the story of Pelops, the first prince of the Peloponnese. The local ruler, King Oenomaos, is said

Ruins of the Temple of Zeus

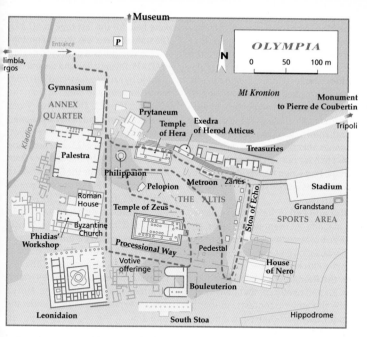

to have been warned by an oracle that he would lose his throne to his son-in-law. To prevent this from happening, he decreed that any suitor wishing to marry his daughter Hippodamia must compete against him in a chariot race, in which the loser would be put to death. The catch was that Oenomaos had a team of invincible winged horses. So, it seemed that Hippodamia was destined to remain unmarried, until Pelops, the son of the Phrygian King Tantalos and the father of Atreus (🔲 *see Mycenae*), was able to bribe Myrtilos, the royal charioteer. Thanks to Myrtilos' sabotage, the king's chariot lost a wheel, costing him the race. Pelops killed Oenomaos, married Hippodamia and became king of the region that bears his name.

The Olympic Games – According to legend, Herakles, the son of Zeus, had the sacred enclosure of the Áltis built around the shrines dedicated to Pelops, Zeus and Hera after he had cleaned Augean Stables by diverting the waters of the river Alfiós. He then re-established the gymnastics and athletics contests in honour of Peplos, the hero who had defeated Oenomaos.

The institution of the games actually appears to dates back to the 8C BC, when King Iphitos of Pisa, and Lycurgus, the famous law-giver of Sparta, decided to organise sporting contests between the people of Greece. These games, during which a month-long sacred truce was observed, were held every four years and reached their peak in the 5C BC, when even the far-flung colonies took part.

The festivities took place in summertime and included religious ceremonies as well as a great fair. The athletic events themselves only lasted five days, but competitors had to perform lengthy training under the watchful eyes of the jury. It is thought that the games attracted 150,000 to 200,000 people.

The events held in the stadium were the foot race, boxing, wrestling, *pankration* (a combination of wrestling and boxing) and the pentathlon (consisting of discus and javelin throwing, a foot race, the long jump and wrestling). The hippodrome was the venue for horse racing and chariot racing, for which the owner would be represented by a charioteer. For each of these disciplines, the victors were crowned with an olive wreath cut from the sacred olive tree with a golden sickle and attended a banquet; they were honoured in verse by poets such as Pindar and immortalised by sculptors in statues. Finally, their native cities often marked their achievements by building votive monuments or treasuries to contain offerings to the gods. The best-known champion was the six-time winner Milo of Croton (6C BC), who is said to have out-run horses, but met a tragic end when he was devoured by wild beasts with his hand trapped in a tree trunk.

Rise and Fall – The games remained a magnificent event for centuries, and Philip II of Macedon even added a monument bearing his name, the Philippeion, to the Áltis enclosure.

In the Roman Era – Nero introduced music and poetry competitions alongside the athletic contests, so that he could take part himself, winning no fewer than seven prizes! Like other Greek sanctuaries, Olympia also gained new additions under the Romans: in the 2C AD, Hadrian and Herodes Atticus added houses, baths, aqueducts and a monumental fountain.

Things had changed, however: spectators were watching events that no longer had the same religious significance, and when the Emperor Theodosius outlawed pagan worship, the games were held for the last time in AD 393. The statue of Zeus was sent to Constantinople, where it was destroyed in a fire in AD 475. Dilapidation and destruction assisted by earthquakes, landslips from Mount Kronion and flooding from the Alfiós did the rest. The sanctuary was used as a quarry and finally laid buried under a layer of earth 3-4 metres thick.

Rediscovery – In 1723, a Benedictine monk from Paris by the name of Dom Montfaucon became the first person to take an interest in the site of Olympia, which was then identified in 1766 by the Englishman Richard Chandler. In 1786, the German "antiquarian" Winckelmann requested permission to carry out research from the Turks, but was assassinated soon afterwards. The first excavations were carried out by French scholars accompanying the Morea military expedition. In 1829, under the direction of the architect A. Blouet, they explored the Temple of Zeus, taking back mosaics and three metopes to the Louvre. Systematic excavation of the sanctuary, however, was carried out by German archaeologists from 1875 to 1885 and from 1936 to 1941.

RUINS★★

🕒 Open daily, 8am–7.30pm (sunset in winter). ✆€6 (joint ticket for site and museum: €9). ✆26240 22 517.

The Revival of the Olympic Games

It was a Frenchman, **Pierre de Fredy, Baron de Coubertin** (1863–1937), who revived the famous Games of Antiquity, the last of which took place in AD 393. A **monument** to the baron stands outside the ruins, along the road to Tripoli.

Rejecting the military path of his family, Baron de Coubertin devoted all his energy to promoting the importance of physical activity in education. He wrote articles, pestered authorities, undertook missions and set up sporting bodies. In June 1894 a conference was held at the Sorbonne "with the aim of the restoration of the Olympic Games"; by the end, Coubertin's cause was won. The stadium in Athens was restored and on 5 April 1896, before 60,000 spectators, George I, King of Greece, uttered: "I declare open the first international Olympic Games."

Since then they have been held every four years, except in time of war, and seek to promote the universal brotherhood of mankind. The first Winter Games took place until 1924 in Chamonix, France, with skiing and skating as their main focus. Athens hosted the Olympic Games again in 2004.

Palaestra

© Greek National Tourism Organisation

As you enter, note the archaeological traces on the right. The **gymnasium** was built in the Hellenistic era (3C BC) and surrounded by covered porticoes; only the foundations of the eastern and southern porticoes remain.

Palaestra★

The double colonnade of the porticoes makes it possible to envisage the Hellenistic *palaestra*, a sports arena. The athletes trained in the courtyard and bathed or anointed themselves with oil in the surrounding rooms.

South of the *palaestra* lies the **Hérôon** (6C BC), a single circular room, where there was an altar dedicated to an unknown hero. Adjacent to this is the **Théokoleon**, residence of the priests *(théokoloi)* of Olympia, which dates from the 4C BC.

Egastírio Fidía (Pheidias' Studio)

The studio was specially built for the sculptor Pheidias to work on the great statue of Zeus. Farther south are the remains of a Roman villa and a Byzantine church constructed in the ruins of the studio.

Leonidaion

The ground plan of this huge hostelry is reasonably clear. It was built in the 4C BC and consists of four rows of rooms set round an atrium, with a circular pool in the centre.

Follow the Roman processional way that skirts the south side of the sacred precinct enclosing the sanctuary. Next come traces of a **bouleuterion** (6C BC), two long chambers where the members of the sanctuary's administrative council met.

▷ *Continue into the sanctuary.*

Áltis (Sanctuary)

In the classical period the sanctuary covered an area about 200sq m/2,152 sq ft and was slightly enlarged by the Romans. Temples, altars and votive monuments were added over the centuries. On the right within the entrance stands a triangular pedestal which supported a Victory *(in the museum)* by the sculptor Paionios.

Naós Íras★ (Heraion)

A few columns have been re-erected among the remains of the imposing foundations of the temple of Hera.

Built about 600 BC in the Archaic Doric Order, the temple had six columns at either end and 16 down the sides; these columns, originally of wood, were soon replaced by others of tufa, short and stout, to support the typical Archaic capitals shaped like round cushions. The footings of the *naós* were of tufa, the walls of brick.

Inside stood an effigy of Hera (the colossal head has been found), and one of Zeus, as well as many other statues including the famous *Hermes* by Praxiteles.

Exédra of Iródou Atikoú★

This unusual, semicircular Roman monument was built in AD 160 by **Herodes Atticus** as a conduit head supplying drinking water. A basin, architraves and columns are still extant. The *exédra* formed a sort of *nymphaeum* with niches containing effigies of the Emperor Hadrian and the imperial family and also of Herodes Atticus and his family.

Ándiron Thissavrón (Terrace of the Treasuries)

Steps lead up to the terrace which bore an altar consecrated to Herakles and some dozen treasuries. These small Doric temples were built by the cities of Greek colonies (Mégara in Attica, Gela and Selinus in Sicily, Cyrene in Africa, Byzantium, etc.) to receive offerings made to the gods. At the foot of the terrace is a row of pedestals on which stood the bronze statues of Zeus erected out of the proceeds of the fines which were imposed on those who broke the code of the Olympic Games.

Below the Terrace of the Treasuries was the **Métrôon**, a peripteral temple built in the 4C BC in the Doric Order, and first dedicated to the goddess Rhéa.

Stadium★

In the 3C BC a passage was built beneath the terraces to link the sanctuary to the stadium; a small section of the vaulting remains. The starting and finishing lines are still visible; the distance between them was a *stadion* (about 177m/581ft). The spectators, men only, occupied removable wooden stands mounted on the bank surrounding the stadium. It

Entrance to the stadium with the remains of the vaulting

was enlarged several times until it could accommodate 20,000 people.

Parallel with the south side of the stadium was the **racecourse**; it was destroyed in the Alfiós floods.

Eptaéchos (Poikilí)

The Echo Portico, erected in the 4C BC with a façade of 44 Doric columns, separated the stadium from the sanctuary. Its name was due to the resonant acoustic (a voice echoed seven times) and also to the various frescoes decorating the interior walls.

Archaeological Museum★★

🕐 Open Tue–Sun 8am–7.30pm (Mon 12.30–7.30pm). ☞€6 (joint ticket for site and museum: €9). ✆26240 225 29, www.olympia-greece.org/museum.html.

A model of the archaeological site is on view in the vestibule. Objects uncovered at Olympia are organised in chronological order around the central hall.

Among the items from the Archaic and Geometric era there is a colossal **head of Hera**★ which was excavated in the temple of the goddess; and bronze armour. Also on display is a reconstruction of the pediments of the Treasury of Mégara, and of the Treasury of Géla in painted terracotta. Note also the battering ram, a war machine made of bronze (mid-5C BC). Among the museum's finest exhibits is a remarkable terra-cotta group showing **Zeus abducting Ganymede**★★ (c.470 BC).

The sculptures of the two **pediments**★★ from the Temple of Zeus have been largely reconstructed with pieces found on the site. The originals were carved in Parian marble (470–456 BC) in a striking and monumental style. The sculpture from the west pediment shows the battle of the Lapiths and Centaurs and the figure of Apollo. The east pediment depicts Zeus observing a chariot race between Oinomaos, the king of Pisa, and Pelops, the legendary figure who secured Oinomaos' daughter by loosening the chariot pins in his rivals' vehicles. The central hall also displays

Head of Apollo, Archaeological Museum

© S. Chevreuse/MICHELIN

the **metopes**★ from the temple frieze illustrating the Labours of Hercules. Another item of particular interest is the **Victory**★ (5C BC) by the sculptor Paionios, at the moment of landing on earth to announce the triumph of the Messenians and the Naupaktians over the Spartans. Also on view are the helmet consecrated to Zeus by Miltiades

Zeus abducting Ganymede, Archaeological Museum

© Panagiotis Karapanagiotis/Bigstockphoto.com

before the Battle of Marathon, ceramic items from the studio of Pheidias (440–430 BC).

Among the exhibits from the late classical and Hellenistic periods is a fine head of Aphrodite attributed to Praxiteles.

Hermes Room

The famous statue of **Hermes by Praxiteles**★★★, a masterpiece of Classical art in polished Parian marble dated to 330 BC, was found in the Temple of Hera near a pedestal bearing an inscription relating to the famous sculptor Praxiteles.

Hermes, the messenger of the gods, is depicted carrying the infant Dionysos, son of Zeus and Semele, to the care of the nymphs out of reach of Hera's jealousy. The perfection of the modelling and the harmony of the proportions are remarkable.

The last rooms display works from the Hellenistic and Roman eras including a statue of **Antinoús** (Hadrian's favourite) and a **marble bull**★.

Museum of the History of the Ancient Olympic Games

Access via the stairs above the parking lot. ○*Open Mon 12.30–7.30pm, Tue–Fri 8am–7.30pm.* ○*No charge.* ℘*26420 291 07.*

Displays here tell the fascinating story of the ancient Games, from prehistory on. Artefacts of an athletic kind include stone and bronze weights used by jumpers and the bronze and stone discuses. Note the oversized stone with an inscription bragging that a weight lifter had raised it over his head with only one hand.

Museum of the Modern Olympic Games★

In the modern town, Odós Kapsali, just off the main street. ○*Open daily 8.30am–7.30pm.* ℘*26240 225 44.*

Artefacts and documents relating to the modern Olympic Games, especially those held in Athens in 1896.

EXCURSIONS

Kaïafa Lake

⊙*22km/13.5mi south via Kréstena.*

Stretching between two fertile plains, the lake is home to a wealth of waterfowl. A hot sulphur spring deep in the caves is used by the nearby spa. The coast is lined with lovely beaches.

Katákolo

⊙*3km/2mi west via Pírgos.*

This charming port with its quayside crowded with café terraces is very popular. A walk along the coast to the north skirts golden sandy beaches, particularly those of Ágios Andréas and Skifadiá.

ADDRESSES

⌂ STAY

▱ **Poseidon** – *Karamanli.* ℘*26240 225 67. 10 rooms.* ⊑. Simple, quiet and clean; attractive price.

▱▱ **Krónio** – *1 Tsoureka St.* ℘*26240 221 88. www.hotelkronio.gr. 23 rooms.* ⊑. Recently refurbished; comfortable rooms with balconies and bathrooms.

▱▱▱ **Europa** – *On the hill over-looking Olympia.* ℘*26240 226 50/23650. www.hoteleuropa.gr. 78 rooms.* A Best Western hotel situated in the middle of wooded parkland; taverna under the trees, swimming pool.

▱▱▱▱ **Antonios** – *Near the cemetery.* ℘*26240 22547. www.olympiahotels.gr. 65 rooms.* A large, modern establishment surrounded by pine trees. Very comfortable rooms.

⊙ EAT

▱▱ **Bacchus** – *Mirakas, 3km/2mi from Olympia* ℘*26240 22298. www.bacchustavern.gr.* This village taverna serves inventive and enjoyable local dishes. Try the aubergine fritters, sausage *(loukániko)* or kebabs. Six rooms offered upstairs (▱).

Temple of Apollo Epicurius at Bassae★★★

O Naós tou Epikouríou Apóllonos Vassón – Ο Ναός του Επικουρίου Απόλλωνος Βασσών

Sitting majestically in an isolated site, the Temple of Bassae is thought to be the work of Iktínos, one of the designers of the Parthenon in Athens. The imposing building, a UNESCO Heritage site, is the subject of an extensive restoration programme.

- Ⓖ **Michelin Map:** 737 F 11 – Ilia – Peloponnese.
- Ⓞ **Location:** Some 200km/ 125mi south of Pátra and 14km/9mi south of Andrítsena.
- Ⓟ **Parking:** There is a car parking area at the site.
- Ⓐ **Don't Miss:** The views from the temple site.
- Ⓣ **Timing:** Allow for an hour; longer if you bring a picnic.

VISIT

Ⓞ*Open daily Apr–Oct 8.30am–8.30pm, Nov–Mar 8.30am–3pm. ⏣€3. ☏26240 22 529. Taxis serve the temple from the centre of the village of Andritsaina.*

The **Temple of Apollo Epicurius** at Bassae is on a lofty forbidding **site**★★ on the southern face of Mt Paliovlátiza (Kotìlion) surrounded by ravines *(bassai)*; on the horizon rise the mountains of Laconía and Messinía. Built of greyish limestone in the Doric style, it was erected in the mid-5C BC by the ancient Phigaleians in honour of Apollo Epikurius (Helper). The internal frieze and other fragments were acquired by the **British Museum** where they are now displayed. It is one of the best preserved Greek temples but, due to its remoteness, it has been the subject of extensive conservation efforts since 1965. Among other unusual characteristics, the building faces north (Greek temples traditionally face eastwest). At the southern end stands a Corinthian column, the first known in this style; the base is extant but the capital, which was decorated with acanthus leaves, is missing; the two flanking columns may also have been Corinthian. The architrave was surmounted by a frieze of sculpted metopes and the walls of the *naós* were decorated on the inside with another frieze of low reliefs representing the battles between the **Greeks and Amazons** on the one hand and the **Centaurs and Lapiths** on the other. This is the earliest example of a sculptured frieze decorating the interior of a Greek building, and these remarkable works can now be seen in the British Museum in London. There is an overall view of the site from above the keeper's house.

Temple of Apollo

© Bettmann/Corbis

Hlemoútsi★★

Hlemoútsi – Χλεμούτσι

The largest and best preserved citadel in the Peloponnese, the famous castle of Hlemoútsi is a masterpiece of medieval defensive architecture. It lies in the west-facing region between Kyllini and Andravida, which was the base of the Franks in Morea from the 13C to the 15C. The area bears many monuments and other reminders from this time.

A BIT OF HISTORY

Completed in 1223, the Clermont (Hlemoútsi) fortress was the most imposing in Morea. It bears the modifications made by its various possessors over the centuries: the Angevins of Naples (late 13C); the despotic Palaiologi (1427); and the Turks (1460). It was significantly damaged in 1827 by the forces of Ibrahim Pasha.

CASTLE

6km/4mi from Kástro. ⏱*Open Apr–Nov Tue–Sun 8am–7pm, Mon 12pm–7pm, Dec–Mar Tue–Sun 8.30am–3pm.* ⊚ *€3.* ☏ *22610 950 33.*
The fortress consists of an outer court and the castle proper, which is built on a polygonal plan. The **outer court** was the domain of the servants. There

- ♿ **Michelin Map:** 737 D 9 – Ilía – Peloponnese.
- ▷ **Location:** The fortress lies 75km/47mi southwest of Pátra and 60km/38mi northwest of Olympia, on the Kilíni Peninsula overlooking the islands of Cephallonia and Zákinthos.
- ⊜ **Don't Miss:** The fortress and its wonderful panoramic view.
- ⏱ **Timing:** Plan an hour for the visit.
- 👪 **Kids:** Children of all ages should enjoy exploring the castle.

is a fine view of the walls of the castle; originally the round towers were some 6m/20ft higher than the walls.

A plaque placed at the entrance to the **castle** recalls that **Constantine XII Palaiologos**, the last Byzantine emperor, lived here for five years and died in the Battle for Constantinople, which was taken by the Turks on 29 May 1453.

The impressively large vaulted entrance is flanked *(left)* by the two-storey chapel, and *(right)* by a vast structure also with two storeys.

Hlemoútsi's castle walls

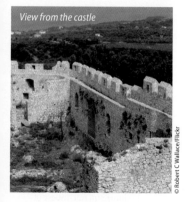

View from the castle

© Robert C Wallace/Flickr

At the centre of the castle is a hexagonal court where jousts and other kinds of entertainment were held. Surrounding it are vast halls built against the outer curtain wall, which is up to 8m/26ft thick in places.

From the terraces atop the curtain wall there is a splendid **panorama**★★ of Zakynthos *(west)* and the other Ionian Islands *(northwest)*; the coast by Missolonghi *(north)*; the Plain of Elis *(east)*, which is bordered to the north by Mount Skólis and Sandoméri; the valley of the River Piniós *(east)*, the mountains of Arcadia *(southeast)* and Cape Katákolo *(south)*.

OUTSKIRTS
Kilíni (Kyllene)
▶ *6km/4mi north of Hlemoútsi.*
A seaside resort (Olympic Beach) and a sheltered harbour make up the modern town of Kilíni. The **Ruins of Clarence**, famed in the Middle Ages, include a few traces of the Clarence citadel; there is a fine view of the coast and the islands *(1.5km/1mi by car along the coast to the northwest then 10min on foot from a farm up to a bluff marked by a concrete post).*

Moní Vlahernón
▶ *On leaving Kilíni heading eastwards, turn right in the hamlet of Káto Panagía into a narrow road (sign); follow for 2km/1.25mi.*
The road enters a verdant but deserted valley containing the **Vlacherna Monastery,** named for a famous church in Constantinople dedicated to the Virgin.

The monastery was built in the Byzantine period (12C), it may at one time have served as a Cistercian community and bears the hallmarks of French Gothic architecture.

Loutrá Kilínis
▶ *7km/4mi south of Hlemoútsi.*
This spa, set in a beautiful eucalyptus forest, uses the waters of several springs to treat respiratory ailments, and has developed into a seaside resort best known for the long stretch of sand called **Golden Beach**.

ADDRESSES

STAY
⊜⊜ **Catherine Lepida** – *Kástro, in the town centre 9, Loutropoleos St.* ℘*26230 95 224, in winter.* ℘*26230 95 444.* Renovated in 1998, these five large studios are quiet, cheerful and well equipped (good kitchens).

⊜⊜ **Paradise** – *On a minor road between Kástro and Kilíni.* ℘*26230 95 209.* A pleasant modern establishment; garden with trees. Waterskiing and parascending can be arranged. Swimming pool.

⊜⊜ **Arcoudi** – *Arkoudi, slightly out of the way by woodland.* ℘*26230 96 350/51. www.arcoudi-hotel.gr.* Pleasant, comfortable spot near the beach. Play-area for kids. Swimming pool.

EAT
⊜⊜ **Castello** – *Kástro, in the town centre.* A shady terrace and good-quality cuisine: beef in filo pastry, grilled meats that melt in the mouth, home-made *taramosaláta*, all washed down with a pleasant, slightly smoky white wine.

EVENTS AND FESTIVALS
Festival of theatre, dance and music; held in the castle *(July and August).*

SHOPPING
In Kástro there is a shop called **Camara**, in a street which descends on the left from the town centre, which sells attractive pottery.

Pátra

Pátra – Πάτρα

Pátra, the modern capital of the Peloponnese and Achaïa, is the third largest city in Greece and a major port, commercial and industrial centre. The city, whose combined history spans four millennia, lies in the foothills of Mount Panachaikon overlooking the gulf of Pátra. Its arcaded streets, shady squares and harbour breakwater, where people gather in the evening, provide a pleasant stroll. The local Carnival is the most spectacular in Greece.

A BIT OF HISTORY

Tradition has it that Pátra was converted to Christianity during the reign of Nero by **St Andrew**, the Apostle, who was crucified there on an X-shaped cross (henceforth known as the St Andrew's cross). In the 4C some of his relics were removed to Constantinople; others were carried off by St Regulus (or Rule) who was shipwrecked off the coast of Fife and founded St Andrews in Scotland. The head remained in Pátra, where in 805 a miraculous apparition of the Apostle put to flight the bands of Slavs who were attacking the city. When the city was captured by the Turks, St Andrew's head was removed to Rome where it was kept in St Peter's Basilica until 1964, when it was returned to Pátra.

The Turks set fire to the old city in 1821 and destroyed it; it was rebuilt later under Kapodístrias.

SIGHTS
Acrópolis

🕐*Open Tue–Sun 8am–7.30pm.*

The Byzantine fortress (9C), on the site of the ancient acropolis, was enlarged and remodelled by the Franks, Venetians and Turks. On the highest point rises the medieval **castle**, defended by towers and a square keep.

The lower ward is reinforced by towers and a round 17C bastion; beautiful **view**★ of Pátra and the Gulf of Pátra as far as Kefalonía and Zakynthos.

▶ **Population:** 163 446

⌖ **Michelin Map:** 737 E 9 – Achaïa – Peloponnese.

ℹ **Info:** Main office: Othonos Amalias 6. Open year-round 8am–10pm. ☏26104 617 40-1. www.infocenter patras.gr. Branch offices also operate from April to September at the entrance to the port and in Trion Simachon Square.

◔ **Location:** Pátra lies 133km/83mi northwest of Corinth and 22km/14mi south of Naupaktos, served by the E 65 motorway and by ferries from Italy.

🅿 **Parking:** Difficult to park in the centre of town.

🕐 **Timing:** Allow for an hour or so in town; the best part of a day if undertaking some of the excursions.

👫 **Kids:** The beaches at Cape Áraxos.

Ágios Andréas

The modern neo-Byzantine **St Andrew's New Church** (1979) receives a great pilgrimage which occurs on St Andrew's Day (30 November).

The great icons of St Andrew and of the Virgin, the "Source of Life", are to be found at the end of the nave.

St Andrew's relics are displayed at the end of the side aisle: a chased gold casket containing the saint's head, which was venerated in St Peter's, Rome from 1462 until 1964, when it was returned to Pátra by Pope Paul VI; and a reliquary with remnants of St Andrew's cross.

Archeo Odío

🕐*Open Tue–Sun 8am–7.30pm.*

👓*No charge.*

The Roman *odeon* (2C AD) was restored in 1963; today it accommodates 2 500 spectators at the cultural events organised in summer. As part of a programme to renovate the **old warehouses** at the port, the building at no. 6 Odós Otho-

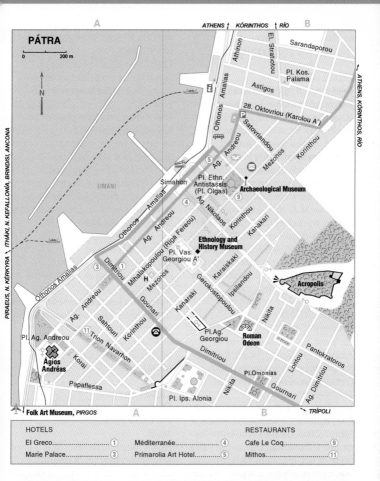

PÁTRA

0   200 m

N

PIRAEUS, N. KÉRKYRA \ ITHÁKI, N. KEFALLONÍA, BRÍNDISI, ANCONA

ATHENS ↑ KÓRINTHOS ↑ RÍO

ATHENS, KÓRINTHOS, RÍO

LIMÁNI

Sarandaporou

Pl. Kos.
Palama

Athinon

El. Stratiotou

Astigos

28. Oktovriou (Karolou A')

Satovriandou

Korinthou

Othonos Amalías

Ag. Andreou

Simahon

Pl. Ethn.
Antistassis
(Pl. Olgas)

Mezonos

Archaeological Museum

Othonos Amalías

Ag. Andreou

Ag. Nikolaos

Korinthou

Kanakari

Ethnology and
History Museum

Mihalakopoulou (Riga Fereou)

Pl. Vas.
Georgiou A'

Karaiskaki

Gerokostopoulou

Ipsilandou

Acropolis

Othonos Amalías

Dimitriou

Ag. Andreou

Sahtouri

Korinthou

Gournari

Mezonos

Kanaraki

Nikita

Korai

Trion Navarhon

Pl. Ag. Andreou

Ágios
Andréas

Papaflessa

Pl.Ag.
Georgiou

Dimitriou

Roman
Ódeon

Nikita

Pantokratoros

Lontou

Ag. Dimitriou

Pl.Omonias

Gournari

Pl. Ips. Alonia

Nikita

Folk Art Museum, PIRGOS

TRÍPOLI

HOTELS

El Greco.............................①
Marie Palace....................③

Méditerranée....................④
Primarolia Art Hotel............⑤

RESTAURANTS

Cafe Le Coq.....................⑨
Mithos.............................⑪

Pátra port

© Mauritius-images/Photoshot

nos Amalias is now a venue for painting, sculpture and photo **exhibitions**.

MUSEUMS

The **Archaeological Museum** (17 Odós Mezonos; ⏰open Tue–Sun 8.30am–3pm; ∞no charge) presents objects excavated locally: ceramic vases, arms, goldware, sculpture and Roman mosaics. The **Ethnology and History Museum** (King George Square; ⏰open daily Tue–Thu and Sat–Sun, 11am–1pm; ∞no charge) displays items representing the period from the 1821 revolution up to the Balkan Wars of 1913. In the **Folk Art Museum** (Moussío Laikís Téhnis; 110 Korytsas and Mavrokordatou; ⏰open Mon–Fri 10.30am–1pm; ∞no charge) you can peruse an interesting collection of costumes, icons, arms, etc.

EXCURSIONS
Río
▶ 7km/4.25mi northeast of Pátra.
Access via Charilaos Trikoupis, for the bridge linking the Peloponnese with Central Greece (∞€10.50 to cross). Many beaches nearby.
The **Castle of Morea** (18C; Venetian) commands the narrow passage (2km/1.25mi) known as the Little Dardanelles separating the Gulf of Pátra from the Gulf of Corinth. Today a prison, the castle is triangular in plan and surrounded by a moat; it has vast casemates and a bastion (north); fine view over the straits.

Achaïa Klauss Vineyards in Petroto
▶ 8km/5mi southeast of Pátra via Mavromandila. ⏰Cellars open until 10pm. 🚶Guided tours every hour 11am–4pm; call ahead. ✆26103 681 00.
These vineyards were planted by the Bavarian Gustave Klauss and have belonged to the Antonopoulos family since 1920. The beautiful dressed stone buildings are traditional in style. The guided tour takes in cellars and old warehouses; on display in the "imperial cellar" are carved wooden barrels containing wine produced in 1873.

Halandrítsa
▶ 25km/15mi south of Pátra by the road to Agía Triáda then left towards Kalávrita.
Halandrítsa lies deep in the hills above the coastal plain. Reminders of the Frankish period, when it was the seat of a barony, include a huge square tower and several Gothic churches (St Athanasius').

Cape Áraxos
▶ 45km/28mi. Head south out of Pátra and follow the coast road via Kato Ahaïa.
Beyond Kato Ahaïa, the coast is lined with golden beaches (**Kalogriá**).
After Áraxos, near the village of Kalogriá, the remains of the **Dymean Wall**, or Kástro tis Kalogrias, stand out on the hillside (signposted). This Cyclopean con-

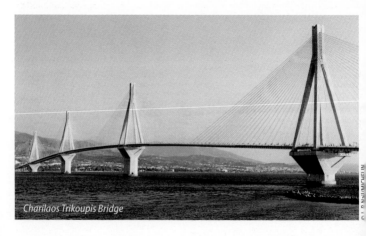
Charilaos Trikoupis Bridge

Odontotós running through Vouraïkoú gorge

© Nigel Reed QEDimages/Alamy

struction from the Mycenaean period formed part of the fortifications of the ancient city of Dyme during the Hellenistic period.

Aigio

Those who find the hustle and bustle of Pátra too tiresome might want to consider Aigio as an alternative centre from which to explore the region.

This pleasant town, on the south bank of the Gulf of Corinth, makes a good base from which to visit the spectacular Vouraïkós Gorge. Nowadays the town's activity mainly centres around the port, which is linked to Ágios Nikólaos on the opposite side of the gulf by a daily ferry service.

While in the village, stop by the **Archaeological Museum** (◯open Tue –Sun 8.30am–3pm (Wed until 9pm in winter, 11pm in summer); ☏26910 215 17) to see objects excavated from digs in the region, which are pleasingly displayed in chronological order. Note especially the handsome terracotta vases, tools and jewellery. Also worth a stop is the **Museum of Folklore and History** (☏26910 621 06/233 77) where objects of daily life offer glimpses of days gone by.

Vouraïkoú★★

The gorge can be reached either by train from Diakoftó to the southeast of Aigio, or by a scenic road from Trapeza (19km/12mi southeast of Aigio) which leads to Kalávrita (30km/19mi).

From the heights of Mount Aroánia, which rises to 2,340m/7,677ft, the River Vouraïkós flows down into the Corinthian Gulf some 50km/30mi to the north. Along the way it has worn a deep channel through the limestone rock, creating a fantastic gorge.

The **narrow-gauge railway (Odontotós)**, which was built late in the last century between **Diakoftó** on the coast and **Kalávryta**, is a particularly bold feat of engineering. Having the narrowest gauge in Europe, it runs for 22km/nearly 14mi along a vertiginous route, through tunnels, along overhangs, across bridges and viaducts and on a rack in certain sections where the incline is steeper than 7 percent. The railway was reopened in 2009 after a long period of modernisation. (◯Departures from Diakofto Mon– Fri at 8.10am, 11.15am, 14.12pm Sat–Sun 8.10, 11.15, 12.33, 14.12 and 15.32, duration 1hr 9mi, ☎€3).

On leaving Diakoftó station the train crosses the foothills of Aroánia, passing through vineyards and orchards before entering the gorge between high sheer cliffs which are riddled with caves. The railway line crosses from one side to the other high above the racing torrent.

Zahloroú (26km/16mi from Diakoftó) lies on a natural terrace overlooking a narrow basin. The charming little station is half hidden in the trees between

313

the rockface and the stream *(tavernas, small hotel)*.  From there it is up a winding path *(2hrs there and back)* to the monastery of Méga Spíleo *(also reachable by road)*.

The train continues to the terminus at Kalávryta (&see Kalávryta).

Méga Spíleo★

▶ *22km/13mi from Diakoftó.*

The monastery of Méga Spíleo ("great cave"), which attracts many pilgrims, appears at the foot of a bare rockface on a wild **site**★★ deep in the magnificent landscape of the Vouraïkós Valley, at an altitude of 924m/3,030ft.

It was founded in the 8C by two hermits, Simeon and Theodore. The monastery reached its apogee in the Middle Ages under the Palaeologi, the despots of Mistrás. The rock church (17C) occupies the great cave from which the monastery takes its name. There is a beautiful door of embossed copper (early 19C). A recess harbours the miraculous image of the Virgin, attributed to St Luke.

A small **museum** houses a collection of liturgical ornaments and objects, carved crosses, manuscripts, old books and icons. The treasury is full of reliquaries, icons and Byzantine manuscripts, some of which date from the 9C.

The guests' refectory and the household rooms (bakery, cellar) are also open.

ADDRESSES

🛏STAY

⊜ **Méditerranée** – *Pátra, 18 Odós Agíou Nikoláou.* ✆*26102 796 02. www.mediterranee.gr. 96 rooms.* This hotel is somewhat noisy, overlooking a busy pedestrian street, and has no character, but is clean and central. Have your breakfast outside where it is more lively.

⊜ **El Greco** – *145 Agíou Andreou.* ✆*26102 72931.* Clean but dull. Still, it provides some kind of alternative.

⊜ **Marie Palace** – *6 Gounari.* ✆*26103 31302, Fax 26103 31346. www.marie palace.gr.* Atmospheric and furnished with good taste. The breakfast room is full of light and the buffet is of high quality. A good choice.

⊜⊜💰 **Primarolia Art Hotel** – *33 Othonos Amalia (at the port).* ✆*26106 24900, Fax 26106 23559. www.arthotel.gr. 14 rooms and theme suites.* The only luxury hotel in the city, cleverly decorated with works by Greek artists and designers. Offers many services and an excellent restaurant.

🍴EAT

⊜ **Mithos** – *181 Riga Ferreou & TrionNavaron.* ✆*26103 29984. Closed 3–20 August.* This restaurant is housed in a 19C mansion and freshly cut flowers, music and photos make up the ambience. The kitchen dishes are skilfully presented by Eleftheria, the owner and her staff. A warm welcome. In the shade of the trees surrounding the 25 March Square, there are two places to stop for a bite: Cinema Café, near the old *odeon* (down the steps), and **Cafe Le Coq** on Olga Azzarga Square.

From mid-January to Ash Wednesday, the **Karnavali** at Pátra is one of Greece's most famous festivals.

Méga Spíleo

© World Pictures/Photoshot

Kalávryta
Kalávrita – Καλάβρυτα

This attractive town is situated in the heart of a mountainous wooded district. It is linked to the Achaïan Coast by a narrow-gauge railway which follows a spectacular route.

SIGHTS
Kástro tis Orias
Just beyond the village on the road to the Agía Lávra Monastery, turn left onto a dirt track (signposted) and walk up to the fortress (15min).

Remains of the Frankish fortress can be seen on the hill. Beautiful view of the surrounding area.

▷ *From the road to Pátras, take the first turn to the left.*

Monastery of Agía Lávra
7km/4.5mi southwest of Kalávryta.
🕐 *Open daily 10am–1pm and 3–4pm.*
📞 *29620 223 63.*

This 17C church has earned a place in history: here, on 25 March 1821, **Germanós**, Archbishop of Pátra, raised the standard of revolt against the Turks in the War of Independence.

Outside is a tree-shaded terrace where Germanós stood when addressing the crowd. The monastery buildings now house a **museum** containing manuscripts, icons, gold and silver ware, and souvenirs of the War of Independence. On a hill opposite, a monument stands to the heroes of the Revolution of 1821. Above the monastery a path *(sign "Paleón Monastírion"; 30min on foot there and back)* leads to the original hermitage where the monks lived until 1689.

EXCURSION
Head east out of Kalávryta, towards the ski resort. After 7km/4.25mi, turn right towards Klitoría.

"Cave of the Lakes"★★
An underground river has carved 1,980m/6,496ft of galleries out of the limestone, forming caverns that contain 13 lakes on three levels.

▷ **Population:** 1,747.
⬡ **Michelin Map:** 737 F 9 – Achaia – Peloponnese.
▷ **Location:** Kalávryta is located 72km/45mi southeast of Pátra by mountain road and 47km/29mi south of Aigio small ski resort on the northern slopes of Mount Helmos.
▷ **Don't Miss:** The scenic views on the road to Klitoría.
▷ **Kids:** The cave and its bat population.

Entrance to the cave is via a man-made tunnel that leads to the second level and the so-called "Room of the Bats". In summer, the drop in the water level reveals basins that are separated by sawtooth barrages up to 4m/13ft high, and cave walls blanketed in stalactites and stalagmites.

The temperature remains a constant 13–15°C/55–59°F. In the Neolithic period (4200–3000 BC), the cave served as a dwelling and storage area, place of worship and burial ground. Excavations have uncovered animal bones and human skeletons, as well as scales dating from the Neolithic and Protohelladic periods.

The road to Klitoría passes through a magnificent **region**★★ covered with forests of plane trees and crystal-clear streams brimming with trout: a wonderful place for a walk.

Kalávryta Ski Resort
The ski resort, with 7 lifts and 12 ski runs, has been operating since 1988. There is plenty of free parking, a cafeteria and a restaurant plus, of course, a ski rental shop. The resort is 14km/8.5mi from Kalávryta and is open daily throughout the ski season (December to April) from 9am to 4pm. For further information, including accommodation in the area and photographs of the skiing, see www.kalavrita-ski.gr.

View of Oia, Santorini, the Cyclades
BlueOrange Studio/Fotolia.com

DISCOVERING THE ISLANDS

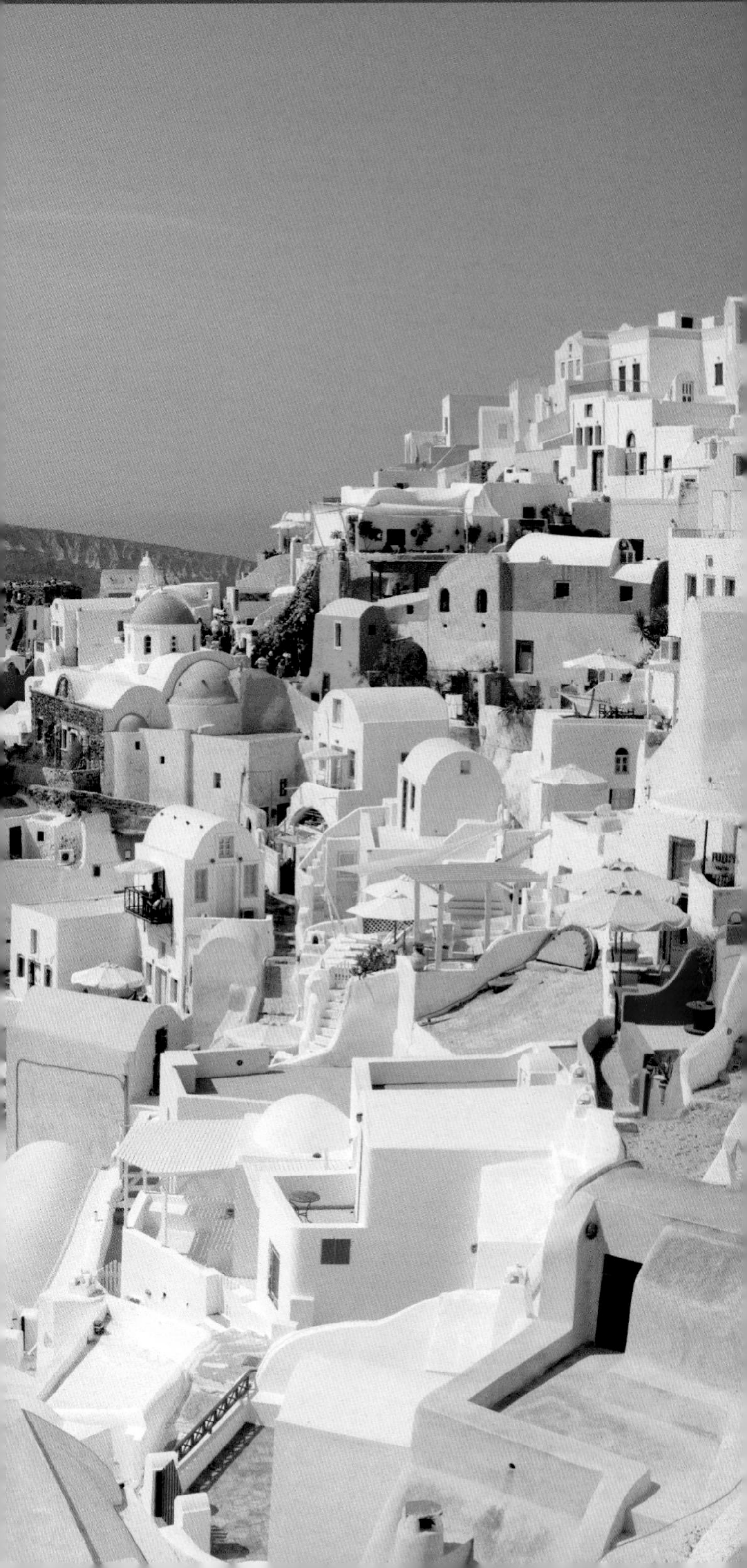

The Islands

CRETE★★★ *Kríti – Κρήτη*

A visit to Crete offers a unique opportunity to explore some of the most fascinating stories of antiquity, both mythological and historical. The brilliant Minoan civilisation, one of the very first in Europe, flourished here, leaving a legacy of richly decorated palaces. While development has overtaken the north coast, the rest of the island reveals extraordinary gorges, mountainous landscapes and rocky coastal outcrops.

▶ **Population:** 623,666.

Info: Xanthoudidou 1, Herákleion. ☎2810 246296.

Location: 100km/63mi from the Peloponnese coast, Crete is the largest and southernmost of the Greek Islands. Fifth-largest island in the Mediterranean, Crete measures 260km/163mi long from east to west. There are three major mountain peaks. It is a distinct administrative region consisting of the districts of Hania, Rethymnon, Herákleion (the capital) and Lassíthi. Crete has air links with all the major cities in Europe. The main airports are Herákleion and Hania. Flights also link Rhodes and Herákleion. There are frequent ferry services from Piraeus to the main ports on the island: Herákleion, Hania, Rethymnon, Ágios Nikólaos and Sitía.

Don't Miss: The Samariá Gorge, the palm groves of Váï and Mirambelou Bay; the Minoan palaces of Knossós, Phaistos, Mália and Zákros.

Timing: A three-week stay will allow you to visit all the sights of Crete in a leisurely fashion. If your time is limited (10 days or less), stick to one region .

Kids: The beaches.

Highlights

1 Visit the Palace of **Knossós** (p327)

2 Enjoy the beaches and palm groves of **Váï** (p334)

3 Admire the ruins of **Phaístós** (p341)

4 Relax by **Hania**'s Venetian harbour (p345)

5 Walk the **Samariá Gorge** (p347)

Crete Today

Crete has some wonderful beaches. The best lie to the west of the island (around Kastelli, for example Balos Peninsula and the Island of Gramvousa, Falasarna on the west coast, also Elafonisi on the southwest tip) and to the east (notably Váï palm beach). Those on the south coast are usually pebbly, backed by steep cliffs and often difficult to get to (some are nudist-friendly). The beaches on the north coast are the busiest and most commercial. There are watersports centres across the island (more so on the north coast): waterskiing, paragliding, windsurfing, pedaloes, and more. Head for the south coast for scuba diving.

Local crafts include leather (Hania), rugs, quilts, ceramics, jewellery and embroidery. The island's gastronomic specialities include thyme honey, wine (Minos, Lato, Angelo, Gortys, Sitía) and especially the excellent olive oil.

The markets usually offer the best choice and the lowest prices. The covered market in Hania is one of the best in Crete.

A Bit of History

The first people to come to Crete were Neolithic-age settlers who arrived around 8000 BC. Trade developed with neighbouring islands, Egypt

GETTING ABOUT

BY BUS – The buses are frequent and the timetables reliable for the two main lines (Herákleion–Sitía via Ágios Nikólaos and Herákleion–Hania via Rethymnon). Be sure to confirm times for the smaller lines to the interior of the island. Service is spotty on Sundays and public holidays. See www.bus-service-crete-ktel.com.

BY SEA – Boats link certain towns with surrounding beaches and islands, particularly in the southwest: Kastelli, Paleohóra, Sougia, Agia Roumelli, Loutro, Sfakiá.

BY CAR OR TWO WHEELS – Numerous rental car agencies, particularly in Herákleion. Plenty of petrol stations (often closed Sundays and public holidays). The car is best for long journeys; certain places are not accessible by bus. You can rent bicycles, scooters and motorbikes in all the main towns.

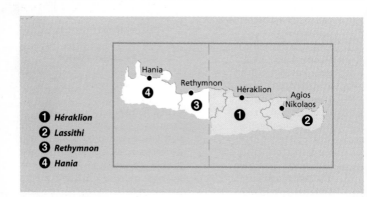

1 *Héraklion*
2 *Lassithi*
3 *Rethymnon*
4 *Hania*

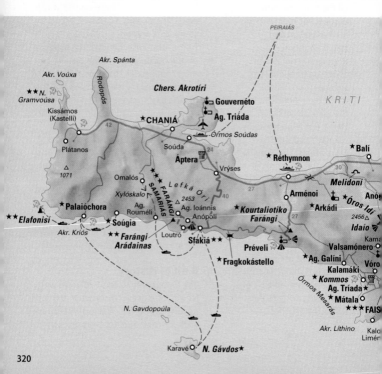

and parts of the Middle East. In this way bronze was brought to Crete and precipitated the first Minoan period.

Minoan Civilisation – History and mythology combine in the story of Crete, legendary birthplace of **Minos**, son of the god Zeus and the nymph **Europa**. A wise and powerful king, Minos and his heirs presided over the Minoan civilisation, a sophisticated culture that endured from 2800 BC to 1000 BC.

Pre-Palace Period (c.2800–c.2000 BC) marked by domed circular tombs which have yielded jewellery, seals, Cycladic statuettes and pottery.

Old Palace Period (c.2000–c.1700 BC) named for the first palaces built round a central courtyard bordered by the public rooms and the private apartments. The pottery, known as Kamáres ware, is decorated with exuberant polychrome patterns. During this period, Crete was the centre of a maritime empire, trading with Egypt and the Middle East. Flagstoned-paved roads were built to connect the island's settlements and writing took the form of ideograms. A devastating earthquake about 1700 BC brought an end to this period.

New Palace Period (c.1700–c.1400 BC), so-called for the new palaces built at Knossós, Phaistos, Mália and Zákros. The new palaces were larger and incorporated light wells, networks of stairs and piped water. Wood and stone were used in combination in an attempt to make the buildings more earthquake-proof. The walls are covered with low-relief sculptures or clean-lined paintings often depicting ritual scenes. The script current during this period, known as **Linear A**, has not yet been deciphered. Trade was developed and extended, with colonies set up on Santorinì and Rhodes. Art flourished and gave confident expression to a prosperous culture.

Post-Palace Period (c.1400–1100 BC) is marked by the arrival of the Mycenaeans to settle definitively in Crete, where they introduced their less-refined customs, of which traces remain (tombs of warriors buried with their weapons, palaces with a *megaron*). The Mycenaeans had already been subjected to the influence of Minoan civilisation, but Minoan culture gradually gave way.

The Minoan civilisation extended beyond Crete particularly to Santorini

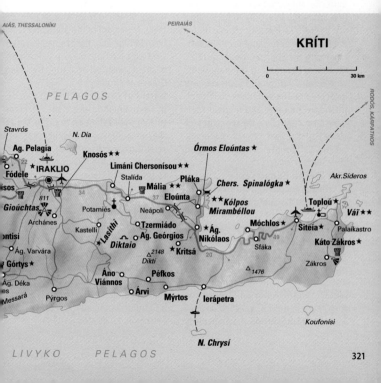

321

(👆see Thíra) but in about 1530 BC an earthquake, probably connected with the volcanic eruption on Santorini, seems to have produced a tidal wave which destroyed most of the (new) palaces. Numerous tablets bearing inscriptions in **Linear B** – a transcription of the Mycenaean dialect considered to be the oldest form of the Greek language – have been found at Knossós.

The palace at Knossós was the only one to be rebuilt but around 1380 BC it was burned down again. Over the next two centuries the Minoan–Mycenaean civilization gradually disappeared as Crete was invaded by a new wave of Greek-speaking settlers known as the Dorians. By the Archaic period (700–500 BC) Crete once again had a recognisable art but it did not flourish during the Classical period. The island lost its artistic and political clout and pirates roamed its coastlines.

Rome, Byzantium, Venice – In 67 BC the Romans took over Crete. In AD 59 St Paul landed at Kalí Liménes; his disciple **Titus** was later sent to convert the island to Christianity. From 395 to 1204, except for a brief Arab intervention, Crete was under Byzantine rule. The Saracens had first arrived in 823, only to be pushed out in 961 by a Byzantine force under the future emperor Ikephóros Phokás.

Following the Fourth Crusade in 1204, Crete was assigned to the Venetians, who retained it for 400 years despite local revolts. The Venetians built many fortresses on Crete and made it their main base, controlling the sea routes for trade with the East. Churches, loggias, houses and fountains in the Venetian style remain today.

The Cretan Renaissance – The fall of Constantinople to the Turks in 1453 brought artists and men of letters to the island. Churches and monasteries were enriched with frescoes and icons by painters of the **Cretan School** in which the traditional Byzantine formality was softened by Italian influence. This school, which migrated to Metéora and Mt Athos with Théophane the Cretan in the 16C, reached its apogee with **Damaskinós** and particularly

Domenico Theotokópoulos, known as **El Greco** (1541–1614), a painter of icons who emigrated first to Venice, then to Rome and finally to Spain. Later in the 17C other artists such as Emmanuel **Tzanés** settled in the Ionian Islands.

Crete Under the Turks – The Ottomans declared war on Malta in 1645 and Sultan Ibrahim dispatched a large fleet to capture the island. On its way there, the decision was made to attack Crete as well and most of the island was taken. The city of Heraklion, though, was able to hold out with the aid of its massive walls and port facilities. It was not until 1669 that the city finally fell.

The Turkish occupation of Crete following the capture of Herákleion in 1669 was very harsh, and entailed forced conversions to Islam. Colonists from Turkey were invited to the island and given some of the best land. Revolts erupted, particularly in 1770 under the leadership of the Sfakiot **Daskaloyánnis**. Works of the Cretan writers, Kazantzákis and Prevelákis, recall this conflict. Finally in 1878 Crete acquired a certain measure of autonomy under the aegis of the Great Powers and the regency of Prince George of Greece. Crete was finally attached to Greece in 1913. By 1900, 11 percent of the population had been Muslim and those remaining after 1913 were forced to leave in 1924 as part of the population exchange between Greece and Turkey.

Battle of Crete (1941) – After occupying mainland Greece the Germans turned their attention to Crete. On 21 May, in what was the world's first successful invasion from the air, 3,000 parachutists captured Máleme aerodrome to the west of Hania which served the Germans as a base for their penetration along the north coast of the island. The British, Australian and New Zealand troops were obliged to retreat over the White Mountains to embark at Sfakiá. It took the Germans 10 days to capture the whole island. There were acts of resistance during the occupation of the island; the most noted being the abduction of a German commander by Patrick Leigh Fermor and Billy Moss in 1943.

1 Herákleion and the Region

Iráklion – Ηράκλειον

Presided over by the busy industrial port of Herákleion, central Crete is home to the island's most important archaeological site, Knossós, plus its highest peak, Mount Idi, which rises a dramatic 2,456m/8,058ft. The region also produces some of the island's best wines.

HERÁKLEION★

Crete's biggest city combines an elegant Venetian-era old town with a bustling port and high-rise suburbs. According to legend, Herákleion takes its name from **Herakles** (Hercules) who landed on Crete to master the Cretan bull that was ravaging the Kingdom of Minos; the task was one of his Twelve Labours (♿ *see Tírintha*).

Known as Candia under the Venetians, the city became a commercial and military centre, the key to the rest of Crete. The Cretans, however, hated the Venetians, who oppressed them with heavy taxes.

The year 1648 began the **Great Siege**, a 20-year battle between the Turks and the Venetians for control of Candia (and thereby Crete). The Venetians surrendered in 1669, marking the end of Venetian sway in the eastern Mediterranean. Under the Turks Candia gradually lost its importance to Hania, which

became the capital of Crete until 1971. Since 1971, the capital has been Herákleion, a modern town buzzing with life, its grand avenues lined with shops. It is often an obligatory point of reference for many travellers as its airport is the largest on the island. Favourite meeting places include Platía Eleftherías and Platía El Venizélou with their pavement cafés, bookshops and newspaper kiosks; and Odós Dedálou with its souvenir shops, local crafts, restaurants and tavernas.

Although the old town has largely been rebuilt since The Second World War, many old buildings have been preserved. There is also a very good archaeological museum devoted to the Minoan civilisation.

Historical and Ethnographical Museum – (Istoriko Moussio)

🕐 *Sofokli Venizelou 27. Open Apr–Oct Mon–Sat 9am–5pm, Nov–Mar Mon–Sat 9am-3.30pm.* 👓 *€5.* 📞 *2810 2 832 19. www.historical-museum.gr*

In an elegant Neoclassical building, insight into the history and traditions of Crete from the Byzantine period to today; two El Greco paintings.

🐾 WALKING TOUR

This walk takes you through Herákleion's pedestrian-only old town, to discover the outstanding archaeological museum, Venetian-era monuments, the old port and the colourful open-air market.

Portico at the north entrance, Palace of Knossós

© P. de Franqueville/MICHELIN

GETTING THERE

BY AIR – In high season (Jun–Sept), the airport (4km/2.5mi east) is served by daily charter flights from major European cities. Out of season, daily connecting flights from Athens. Bus shuttle to Odós Eleftherias on the outskirts of town.

BY SEA – Ferry services between Herákleion and **Piraeus** *(2/day, 8hr)*; **Santorini** *(1/day in season)*; **Paros** *(1/day summer)*; **Mykonos** *(1/day summer)*, Ios *(1/day summer)*, Rhodes *(1/week summer)*

Archaeological Museum★★

🕐*Open Apr–Oct, Tue–Sun 8am– 7.30pm, Mon 1pm–7.30pm; Nov–Mar, daily 8.30am–3pm.* ☞ €4. ✆28102 26092. Allow 1hr.

The **National Archaeological Museum** *(✆see sidebar opposite)* is devoted to the Minoan civilisation discovered at the end of the last century. Until the completion of the long-awaited new museum building, there is a small temporary exhibition on show.

▶ *Opposite the museum stands the useful city tourist information centre. From here, proceed along pedestrian-only Odós Dedálou Street to arrive on Platiá Eleftherias.*

Platiá Eleftherias

Futuristic sculptures and fashionable cafés lend this large, bright square an air of modernity.

Stroll south beyond the public gardens to begin a walking tour, starting with the Venetian fortifications.

Market★ (Odós 1866)

In the morning the street is the scene of a lively **market** for local products: yogurt and honey, herbs, ornamental bread, fruits, cheeses, fish and meat. At the end of the street, in **Odós Kornarou**, note the Bembo Fountain, erected by the Venetians in 1588, and a Turkish fountain converted into a street stall.

▶ *Walk the length of Odós 1866 , retrace your tracks then turn left onto Kosmon Street to arrive at Agía Ekateríni Church.*

Agía Ekateríni

The little church, with two centres of worship, which was built in 1555 by the Venetians, contains six remarkable **icons**★ by **Mihális Damaskinós**.

Platía El. Venizélou

Pleasant pedestrian square; note the basin of the 17C **Morosini Fountain**, decorated with sea creatures. Odós Dedálou, leading out of the southeast corner of the square, is a pleasant shopping street lined with boutiques and tavernas.

Ágios Márkos

Italianate **St Mark's Church** (14C) was the cathedral of Candia during the Venetian occupation. The building is now used for exhibitions and concerts.

▶ *Also on 25th Avgoustou Street, a few doors down, stands the Venetian Loggia.*

Venetian Loggia

The reconstruction has been carried out in the style of the 17C original, which was inspired by the Venetian architect Palladio. It was here that the money changers set up their stalls and the merchants met to discuss business. Nearby is the El Greco Park.

Ágios Títos

St Titus' Church was built by the Venetians in the 16C; the Turks transformed it into a mosque; it is now the Metropolitan Church. The little streets (pedestrians only) around here come alive at night.

Oldport

Flanked by a busy highway, **Paleo Limani** (the old Venetian port) now berths fishing boats.

At the far end you can see parts of the **Venetian Arsenal**.

At the Archaelogical Museum★★

(Please note when the New Archaeological Museum opens (date uncertain), exhibits will be rearranged.

NOT IN CASE
Relief fresco of Prince of the Lilies, from Knossós.

NEOLITHIC PERIOD
Case 1: Pottery, tools and figurines from central and eastern Crete.

PRE-PALATIAL PERIOD
Case 2: Vases and figurines from settlements and cemeteries in central and eastern Crete.

Case 3: Jewellery and daggers from central and eastern Crete.

Case 4: Figurines, models and seals from sanctuaries and tombs in central and eastern Crete.

OLD-PALACE PERIOD
Cases 5&6: Kamáres-style pottery from Knossós and Phaistos.

Case 7: Luxurious swords and jewellery from central Crete, including a golden pendant ★★ composed of two foraging bees.

Case 8: Clay model of a Minoan house from Archanes, and the town mosaic from Knossós.

NEW-PALACE PERIOD
Case 9: Vases and vessels from palaces and settlements in central and eastern Crete.

Case 10: Raw materials, tools and inscribed tablets from central and eastern Crete.

Case 11: The "chessboard" from Knossós; a luxurious gaming board with inlays of ivory, crystal and glass, covered with gold and silver leaf.

Case 12: Ritual vessels from the Palace of Zakros.

Case 13: Soapstone vase ★★, in the shape of a bull's head, from Knossós.

Case 14: Snake Goddess ★★, figurines and religious symbols from Knossós and other sites.

Case 15: Libation vase in the shape of a lioness's head, from Knossós.

Case 16: Stone libation vases from Zakros and Agía Triada.

Case 17: Bull-lepear, from Knossós.

Case 18: The Phaistos Disk (aa, 2 stars); the hieroglyphs inscribed in a spiral on the clay are suggestive of the labyrinth of the Minotaur.

NOT IN CASE
Frescoes from Knossós: Bull-leaping, Ryhton-bearer, Dancing Lady, La Parisienne ★★, Saffron Gatherer-Monkey, Blue Bird.

NEW-PALACE CEMETERIES
Case 19: Agía Triada sarcophagus ★★.

Cases 20 & 21: Vases, vessels, jewellery and seals from cemeteries at Knossós and tombs at Poros-Katsambas.

Case 22: Jewellery, plaques and a mirrors from the cemetery at Phourni, Archanes.

Case 23: Vases and vessels, models, jewellery and seals from cemeteries at Phaistos.

Case 24: Armour and vessels from tombs at Knossós and Phourni, Archanes.

POST-PALATIAL PERIOD
Case 25: Figurines of deities with upraised arms and a model of a cart, from Gazi, Karphi and Gortyn.

Case 26: Anthropomorphic and zoomorphic figurines, models, vessels and jewellery from sanctuaries and cemeteries in central and east Crete.

GEOMATRIC-ARCHAIC PERIOD
Case 27: Vases, vessels, figurines and jewellery from sanctuaries in from central Crete.

Case 28: Statuettes, figurines and cut-outs from Symi and Dreros.

Case 29: Vases from cemeteries in central and eastern Crete.

HELLENISTIC–ROMAN PERIOD
Case 30: Vases, vessels, figurines, coins and jewellery from central and eastern Crete.

NOT IN CASE
Grave *stele* of Kounavoi (early classical period) and statues and portraits (Roman period) from central and eastern Crete.

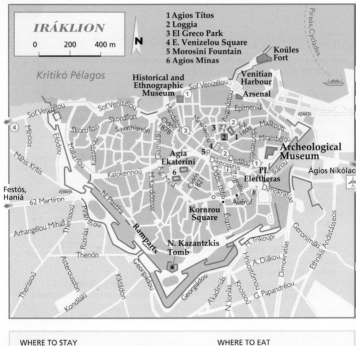

IRÁKLION

0   200   400 m

N

1 Agios Títos
2 Loggia
3 El Greco Park
4 E. Venizélou Square
5 Morosini Fountain
6 Agios Minas

Pireás Cyclades

Koúles Fort

Kritikó Pélagos

Historical and
Ethnographic
Museum

Venitian Harbour

Arsenal

Sof.Venizélou

Epiménidi

Sof.Venizélou

Sof.Venizélou

Skordílon

Savathianón

Skordílon

Kissámou

Makaríou

Minoos

Eródou

Máhis Krítis

Ag. Títou

Malikoúti

Mirambélou

Archeological
Museum

Ágios Nikólac

Agia
Ekateríni

Kalokerinoú

M.Karditotsa

M.Kardítsas

Ag. Mína

Odós 1866

Odós

Dikeossínis

Dedálou

Pl.
Eleftheras

Dimokratías

Averof

Evans

Kornrou
Square

N. Plastíra

N. Kazantzkis
Tomb

Ramparts

Festós,
Haniá

62 Martíron

Arhangélou Mihaíl

Thenón

Rizínias

Priam inou

Asteroussión

Kikládon

Kondiláki

Thenón

Thenisoú

Georgíadou

Akadimías

N. Ionías

H. Trikoúpi

A. Diákou

Geronimáki

Ethnikís Andistásseos

Hrisostómou

G. Papandréou

WHERE TO STAY
Astoria...............① Kastro....................③
Lena....................② Mourtzanakis..........④

WHERE TO EAT
Lounies....................................①
Pagopion (Ice Factory)............②

The entrance to the harbour is commanded by the Koúles, the 16C **Venetian Fortress**★ still bearing the lion of St Mark. From the terrace (now an open-air theatre) there is a fine **panorama**★ over the port and town. Be careful, as there is no parapet around the tower. (○open Tue–Sun 8.30am–3pm; ◉ €2).

Venetian Walls (Venetiká Tíhi)

The **Venetian town walls** (5km/3mi long) were the work of **Michele Sanmicheli** (1484–1559), architect of the fortifications of Padua and Verona.
The road running along under the walls leads to the **Martinengo Bastion** (Promahónas Martinéngo); on the top is the tomb of the great Cretan writer **Nikos Kazantzákis** (1883–1957).

KNOSSÓS★★

▶ 5km/3mi southeast of Herákleion.
○ Open Apr–Oct, daily 8am–7.30pm; Nov–Mar, daily 8.30am–3pm. ◉ €6.

☏ 2810 2 31940. ○── During ongoing renovations, the Royal Apartments are visible from the outside only.
One of Crete's most important sights, the Palace of Knossós was the first and oldest of the Minoan palaces to be discovered. According to legend, the palace and its **Labyrinth** were designed by the cunning **Daidalos** to confine the **Minotaur**, a monster with a man's body and a bull's head.
The site of Knossós was already inhabited in the Neolithic period; in about 2000 BC a palace was built which was destroyed in 1700 BC. It was replaced by a new palace, of which traces can be seen today. At this point Knossós was one of the greatest cities in the whole of the Mediterranean, with some 50, 000 inhabitants.
In c.1530 BC (or possibly 1630 BC) an earthquake and a tidal wave, provoked, it seems, by the eruption of the volcano on Thíra (Santorini), laid waste the new palace. Later it was sacked and occu-

The Legend of Daidalos and Theseus

Every nine years the Athenians, in retribution for the death of King Minos' son at the hands of their King Aegeus, had to deliver a human sacrifice of seven youths and seven maidens to be fed to the **Minotaur**. It was as part of this tribute that **Theseus** arrived from Athens and seduced **Ariadne**, King Minos' daughter. The princess gave her lover a thread which Theseus unwound as he penetrated the **Labyrinth**. He was thus able to find his way out after killing the Minotaur, and escaped with Ariadne.

To punish Daidalos for revealing the secret of the Labyrinth, Minos had him imprisoned within the palace, but Daidalos constructed wings using birds' feathers and wax and escaped from the palace with his son **Icarus**. Alas, Icarus flew too close to the sun, which melted the wax, and the unfortunate young man fell into the sea near to the present island of Icarus (Ikaría, west of Sámos in the Aegean).

pied by the Mycenaeans. It was finally destroyed by fire between 1375 and 1250 BC.

Palace Ruins★★

Beyond the entrance gate pass through the trees into the West Court, which was probably an *agora*. On the left are three disposal pits. Behind the base of an **altar** (**1**) lie the foundations of the pal-ace. Pass the West Entrance and follow the **Corridor of the Procession** (**2**); the walls were decorated with frescoes (Herákleion Museum). Then turn left to reach the partly-reconstructed *propylaia* (**3**), a pillared porch at the foot of the grand staircase.

The upper floor comprised a number of pillared rooms, some of which have been restored and decorated with

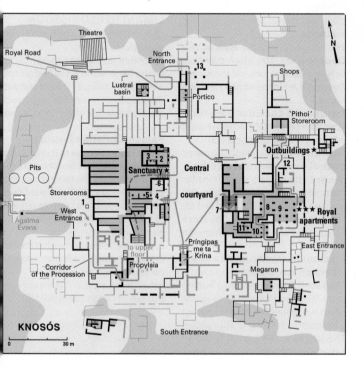

copies of frescoes; the famous *Parisienne* (Herákleion Museum) may have formed part of the decoration. To the east another staircase leads down into the **central courtyard**. It (or the theatre) was probably the site of the perilous, acrobatic, ritual bull-leaping. Down the west side of the courtyard lie the rooms of the sanctuary★.

On the right a **vestibule** (**4**) leads into the **Throne Room** (**5**), which contains a bench and the alabaster throne on which the High Priestess of the Labyrinth may have sat; the griffin frescoes are reconstructions.

On the left another vestibule (**6**) leads into the two **pillar crypts** (**7**), site of ritual ceremonies (double axeheads carved on the pillars) and into the **treasury** (**8**) *(right);* the famous *Snake Goddesses* (Herákleion Museum) were found here.

On the east side of the courtyard, accessed by a flight of steps (**9**) are the **royal apartments**★★★, occupying four floors of rooms built into the slope of the hill above the river. Here, as in other parts of the palace, there are shafts (light wells) providing light and ventilation.

The first rooms are the **Hall of the Double Axes** (**10**), which may have been the Guard Room, and the **King's Room** (**11**), which contained a wooden throne.

The **Queen's Chamber** (**12**) is decorated with a copy of the Dolphin Fresco; adjoining is a tiny bathroom (**13**).

From the royal apartments a covered portico *(views),* leads to the **outbuildings**★; there were workshops for craftsmen, stone polishers, potters (**14**) (remains of kilns), tailors, gold and silversmiths, and storerooms. The **store** containing the *pithoi* dates from the first palace.

Return to the central courtyard and bear right down a passage.

This lane is lined by a portico leading to the "Customs House" (**14**); its square pillars are thought to have supported a banqueting hall on the floor above. The **Royal Road** probably led to Katsámbas and Amnisós, the harbours

to the east of Herákleion. On the right of the road stands a set of terraces, which are thought to belong to a sort of theatre, mentioned by Homer as the setting for ritual dances.

MOUNT GIOÚTHAS★

◗ *15km/9mi south of Herákleion.*

It is in this mountain (811m/2 661ft) that the god Zeus is supposed to be entombed. From the pilgrimage church at the top on the edge of a steep cliff there is a vast **panorama**★ over Herákleion and the sea (north), Mount Díkti (east) and Mount Ídi (west), the highest peak on Crete.

Thalassocosmos★★

◗ *Gournes (13km/9mi east of Heraklion).* ℘ *2810 337788, www.cretaquarium.gr.* ◷ *May–Sep daily 9.30am–9pm, Oct– Apr 9.30am–5pm.* €*8.*

This vast aquarium introduces visitors to plant and animal life found along Crete's turquoise-blue coast. Thirty-two tanks display everything from sharks and jellyfish to lobsters and sea horses.

LIMÁNI HERSONÍSSOU★

◗ *30km/19mi east of Herákleion by the old road after Goúmes.*

A sizeable resort and fishing village, Limáni Hersoníssou is situated around a little bay. In antiquity it was a port and the ancient city retained its importance into the beginning of the Christian era.

Palaeo-Christian Basilica

On the rocky peninsula that shelters the bay to the north, on a fine site overlooking the port, are the foundations of a Christian basilica (6C). The ground-floor plan can be deduced from the remains of the floor, partially decorated with wavy mosaics.

Beyond and below the church at the end of the promontory are Roman fishtanks cut into the rock at sea level.

Before departing stop in at the open-air Museum of Cretan Traditional Life.

MÁLIA RUINS★★

▶ *12km/8mi to the east of Limáni Hersoníssou.* ⏰*Open Tue–Sun, 8.30am–3pm.* ✎*€4.*

Extending east of the village of the same name, the ruins of Mália are of particular interest since the site ceased to be inhabited at the end of the second millennium BC and is not therefore compounded with later construction. Most of the finds made here are displayed in the Archaeological Museum at Herákleion.

Anáktora Malíon★★

This Minoan **palace**, which was destroyed in c.1500 BC, was smaller and less luxurious than Knossós.

The paved **outer courtyard** is bordered on the east by the foundations of the palace. Walk up the east side of the court towards the sea as far as the Minoan paved road, which leads to the north entrance to the palace; the enormous terracotta vessel *(pithos)* (**1**) could hold over 1, 000 litres/220 gallons of oil or wine.

North Entrance

Pass through the vestibule (**2**) then a portico. On the left near a row of storerooms was another *pithos* (**3**).

Buildings west of the **central courtyard** were used, as at Knossós, for religious and official activities. At the centre of the courtyard is a shallow pit for sacrifices.

The sanctuary was in the northwest corner. The royal lodge or **throne room** (**4**) is marked by a terrace and a Byzantine cannonball (**5**). Next are the steps of a staircase (**6**), and then a cult room (**7**).

Beyond the four monumental steps (**8**) in the southwest corner is a circular stone table *(kérnos)* (**9**) thought to be either an offering site or a gaming table. The buildings east of the courtyard comprise the **royal treasury** followed by a range of storerooms *(not open)* and the kitchens. The north side of the court is taken up with a hall (**10**) flanked by a vestibule (**11**).

▶ *From the precinct drive northeast.*

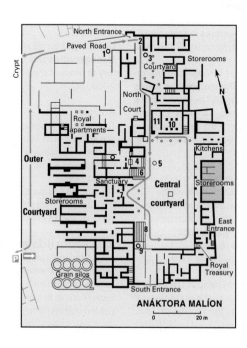

ANÁKTORA MALÍON

0   20 m

The Town★

Follow the Minoan paved track, heading west.

This leads to the Hypostyle Crypt. The steps at the end led to meeting rooms, still partially furnished with benches, which were probably part of the Prytaneion.

Other buildings have been discovered on the outskirts of the town.

The **Krysólakos** (gold pit) necropolis on the north side near the sea was a royal graveyard; it contained the famous **bee pendant** now in the Herákleion Museum.

Nearby is one of the loveliest beaches on the coast.

LASSÍTHI PLATEAU★

▶ 30km/19mi southeast of Limáni Hersoníssou.

Lying in the **Díkti Mountains**, the Lassíthi Plateau is an enormous hanging basin of rich alluvial soil, perfect for the cultivation of crops. Artisans producing honey, pottery and embroidery also ply their crafts here.

The road from Limáni Hersoníssou winds its way up through hairpin bends offering spectacular **views**★ down into the deep, narrow Avdoú Valley. At the entrance to **Potamiés** is a tiny church *(left)* built in the Venetian Gothic style (14C frescoes).

The road passes through the charming villages of **Dzermiádo** and **Ágios Geórgios** where there is a **Folk Museum** housed in an early-19C farm which reconstructs the life of the period (⊙ *open Apr–Oct, daily 10am–4pm.* ⊛€2).

👤👤 Diktéo Ándro

A small track leads from the village of Psihró as far as the car park (charge). Then proceed on foot down a steep and sometimes slippery slope.
⊙*Open Tue–Sun 8.30am–7pm in summer; 8.30am–3pm in winter.* ⊛€4. 𝒫 28410 22462.

The deep and mysterious **Diktean** or **Psihró Cave** was the mythological refuge of Rhea, the mother of Zeus. The goddess was forced to hide from her husband Kronos, to keep him from devouring her children. Thus Zeus, the king of the gods, was born in a cave, suckled by the goat Amalthea and fed by the bee Melissa.

The Diktean Cave was a shrine from the Minoan period to the Archaic period and it has yielded many cult objects. The path descends past enormous rocks to a little lake. The lower section of the cave contains a variety of stalagmites and stalactites.

🚗 DRIVING TOURS

IDAIAN MASSIF★

110km/69mi round-trip to the southwest.

This drive takes you into the dramatic north-facing slopes of Mount Ida, culminating at the Idaian Cave, where, according to Greek mythology, Zeus was hidden by his mother as a baby, to save him from the wrath of his father.

▶ Head west out of Herákleion.

Tylisos ruins

Bear left on entering the village.
⊙*Open daily, 8.30am–3pm.* ⊛€2.
𝒫 2810 226470.

On the top of the hill are traces of **three Minoan villas** which are contemporary to those of the palace at Knossós (c.1800 BC).

Anógia

This mountain town occupies a majestic site at the foot of Mount Ida *(Óros Ídi)*, also known as Mount Psilorítis; the summit (2 456m/8 058ft) is snow-capped almost all year.

On entering Anógia, the road to the left leads up to the Nída plateau and the Idaian Cave. **Views**★.

Idéo Ándro **(Idaian Cave)**

22km/14mi south of Anógia, 🚶then 30min on foot (there and back). ⊙*Open daily in summer 9am–2pm.* ⊛€3.

Excavations at the end of the 19C here yielded objects dating from the 9C BC, including objects made of gold, silver, pottery and rock crystal as well as small ivory pieces, now displayed in the museum in Herákleion.

NORTH COAST TOWARDS RETHYMNON

Rethymnon is 71km/44mi west of Herákleion.

At the end of the bay the road passes Paleókástro, a Venetian fortress.

Agía Pelagía

This fishing village flanks a pleasant beach which is popular with tourists.

Fódele★

Surrounded by olive and carob trees and orange and lemon groves, the village is thought to be the birthplace of the painter Domenico Theotokópoulos, known as **El Greco** (1541–1614). Wonderful beach.

Balí★

The village *(tavernas)* in a little creek offers good fishing and walking along the spectacular and rugged coast.

ADDRESSES

🏠 STAY

Due to the proximity of the airport, planes fly overhead day and night. So choose a room with double glazing and air-conditioning.

Mourtzanakis Residence Achlada – ℘2810 812096. www.ecotourism greece.com. In the mountains, 18km/1mi west of Herákleion, this friendly eco-hotel offers self-catering apartments, a pool, and activities such as hiking, caving and Cretan cookery lessons.

Hotel Lena – *Odós Lahana 10.* ℘2810 2 23280. www.lena-hotel.gr. *16 rooms.* Some rooms with en suite facilities, some with shared baths. Warm welcome.

Kastro Hotel – *Odós Theotokopoulou 22.* ℘2810 284185. www.kastro-hotel.gr. *38 rooms.* Modern, tasteful hotel, a good choice in this price range.

Astoria – *Platía Eleftherías 11.* ℘2810 343080. www.astoriacapsis.gr. *131 rooms.* Once of only three luxury international hotels in town. Spacious, impeccable rooms. Roof terrace with a tiny swimming pool and a bar.

🍴 EAT

Kounies – *Sofokli Venizelou 19.* ℘2810 301448. Next to the Historic Museum, this smart modern taverna is popular for its delicious charcoal grilled meats, creative salads and irresistible deserts.

Pagopion (Ice Factory) – *Platía Ágios Títos, just behind the town hall.* ℘2810 346028. This ultra-trendy bar-restaurant is perfect for a change from kebabs and moussáka. Copious portions of elaborate international fare.

🚃 TAKING A BREAK

Fix – *Odós Pardiari, on the left coming from Odós Dedálou.* Relaxing atmosphere with gentle jazz in the background. It can get crowded here. Concerts in winter.

Vicenzo – *Corner of Odós Vanou and Platía Kornarou.* Pleasant refreshment stall where you can take a break with a salad or a sandwich.

🛒 SHOPPING

Market – The town's main market has been named after the street in which it is located, Odós 1866. Look out for olive oil, pistachio nuts (delicious), thyme honey and other Mediterranean specialities.

🎭 EVENTS AND FESTIVALS

Herákleion Summer Festival – *Information* ℘28103 99399. In August the town organises concerts, exhibitions, plays (particularly in Fort Koúles), singing and dancing.

2 Saint Nicholas, Lassíthi Region

Ágios Nikólaos kai Nomos Lassithíou – Άγιος Νικόλαος και Νομός Λασιθίου

The landscapes of eastern Crete are more wild and arid, and the towns and villages less refined than those of the west, with fewer traces of Ventian-era architecture. The main settlements, Ágios Nikólaos, Sitía and Ierápetra, are relatively bland and modern. But to compensate, you'll find some of Crete's most luxurious hotel resorts and most spectacular beaches in this region.

▸ **Population:** 19, 462.
- **Michelin Map:** 737 M 16 – Lasithi.
- **Info:** Koundourou 21, Ágios Nikólaos: north of the canal linking the lake with the sea. ℘28410 22357, www.aghios nikolaos.eu. Open Tue–Sat 8am–4pm.
- **Location:** The easternmost region of Crete. Its capital is Ágios Nikólaos – other major towns are Ierápetra and Sitía.
- **Don't Miss:** The Driving Tours, which could take anything from a couple of hours to a couple of days. A walk on the Spinalónga Peninsula.
- **Kids:** Sandy spots in Mirambélou Bay.

ÁGIOS NIKÓLAOS★

▶ *70km/44mi east of Herákleion.*

Ágios Nikólaos (St Nicholas) is a lively resort on a small lake linked to the sparkling waters of Mirambélou Bay – a former fishing village, it now lives primarily from tourism. On the waterfront, cafés, tavernas and restaurants spill out onto the pavement in typical Mediterranean style. The resort of Ágios Nikólaos is ideal for lingering over a glass of *soumáda*, a refreshing almond drink. Ágios Nikólaos makes a good centre from which to explore the eastern end of the island.

Lake Voulisméni★

Steep slopes riddled with caves encircle this pretty lake. The lake was formerly known as "Artemis' Pool" and believed to be bottomless. In fact it is 64m/210ft deep; the channel to the sea was dug in 1870.

Fishing Harbour

Extending behind the quayside, the harbour is a lively spot lined with restaurants. Boats to the island of Spinalónga depart from here. At the end of the quay there is a fine **view**★ taking in island, mountains and bay.

Ágios Nikólaos

Kitroplatía Beach

East of the resort, 3min on foot from the lake.

Bordered by restaurant terraces, this sandy beach is overlooked by mountains. Stroll the north promenade to the port, or along the south **promenade**★ along the parapet; both offer lovely views. Farther to the south are the yachting marina and long, sandy Amnos Beach.

Archaeological Museum

North of the town, in Odós Konstandínou Paleológou.
⊙—*Currently closed for renovations.*
𝒫 28410 24943.

A wealth of objects found at Agía Fotia (near Sitía), the largest ancient necropolis unearthed on Crete, illustrate the daily life and religious practices of the Early Minoan period.

Amongst the museum's showpieces are the Goddess of Mírto, an extraordinary libations vase in the shape of a woman (7C BC) and the head of a young athlete with a laurel crown in gold (1C BC).

IERÁPETRA

◑ *31km/19.2mi south of Ágios Nikólaos. The town is connected by roads heading east and west and by one that connects with the north coast. www.ierapetra.net.*

Situated on the southeast coast of Crete, Ierápetra is the most southern town in Europe and enjoys a mild winter climate. It is a market for the agricultural products of the coastal plain and is also a popular resort with a long sandy beach bordered by a taverna-lined promenade. Although devoted to fishing and coastal traffic, the **port** is not unattractive; the entrance is commanded by a 13C **fortress** with square bastions.

A labyrinth of alleyways and little houses, the **old town** has a tranquil feel. Bearing traces of Turkish occupation, Odós Anagnostaki leads to the **Ottoman Fountain** and a minaret. Heading towards the seafront, look out for the house where Napoleon is supposed to have spent the night on his return from Egypt (1799).

Ierápetra port
© Martina Misar/Dreamstime.com

The small **Archaeological Museum** (⊙*open Tue–Sun 8.30am–3.30pm;* ss€2; 𝒫 28420 28721) features a fantastic Minoan sarcophagus in terracotta.

Hrissí Island

Boat trip (allow 1 day) departs from Ierápetra.

A wild and beautiful island, also called Donkey Island (Gaidouronisi) or Golden Island, with pretty beaches, clear blue water and cedar forests. There are no inhabitants but a taverna materialises in the summer and sunbeds are available. The beach, covered with millions of variously coloured seashells, is attractive.

West of Ierápetra

The coast has been largely developed for tourism, sometimes to the detriment of aesthetics. After 20km/13mi the road reaches the verdant **Mírtos Valley** (oranges, bananas, vines) and the resort of **Mýrtos** where rooms and restaurants cater to visitors. The beach here is shingly but still inviting. Beyond the village of **Péfkos** a track bears left, past an imposing monument dedicated to the victims of German execution squads, down to **Árvi**, a fishing village overlooked by a monastery of unusual construction. Farther along the road is **Áno Viános** (43km/27mi), which stands on a spectacular mountainous site overlooking a great sweep of olive trees.

A little way west of Ierápetra look for a signpost to **Fournou Korifi** (also called Néa Mýrtos), the site of excavated Minoan villas dated to around 2500 BC. Finds from the site, mainly of an agricultural kind, are exhibited in a small museum (⏱ *open Apr–Oct, daily 9am–1pm;* ⊜*€2*).

SITÍA★

📍 *70km/44mi east of Ágios Nikólaos.*
The town has a small airport, 11km/7mi to the north, which offers flights (5/wk) to Athens (no bus service to the airport).
The charming town of Sitía nestles deep in a bay at the far east of Crete; its white and ochre houses give it a slightly African appearance. The Sitía white wine is some of the best in Crete.

In the past, the town has been subjected to destructive earthquakes (1508), pirates (1538) and even the Venetians (c.1650), who destroyed their own fortress so that it would not fall into the hands of the Ottomans.

For a look to the past, stop in at the **Archaeological Museum** (*Odós Eleftheriou Venizeliou;* ⏱ *open Tue–Sun 8.30am–3pm;* ⊜*€2;* ✆ *28430 23917*), which holds a good collection of Minoan finds from the area.

It is pleasant to stroll about the **port**★ and under the shade of the enormous tamarisk trees where the promenade has been pedestrianised. Cafés and tavernas along the quayside serve Cretan specialities al fresco.

Venetian Fort

⏱ *Open Tue–Sun 8.30am–2pm.*
⊜*No charge.*
The hillside leading up to the fort is crossed by alleyways and flights of steps flanked with little houses. The pace of life is very relaxed here, far from the crowds in the holiday resorts. Nowadays the fortress houses an open-air theatre. From the keep there is a splendid view of the fort.

Beaches★★

In summer, sun-worshippers and their paraphernalia all but cover the large beach. There is a watersports centre where you can hire pedaloes. If it is solitude you seek, head farther south to the bay nestling behind the hill. It takes about 15min (*follow the red markers*) to a very quiet stretch of beach at the foot of some cliffs. Another beach lies to the north and is only accessible by boat.

Beaches and Palm Groves of Váï★★

📍 *28km/18mi east of Sitía.*
Bus service from Sitía (3/day; 1hr).
Situated to the far west of Crete, at the edge of a desertlike landscape, the beaches of Váï are renowned for their natural palm grove – the only one in Europe. There is no development on this part of the coast – a rare thing indeed. Now a protected area, the **palm grove**★★ is closed to the public but there

Beach of Váï

...re two observation points. One of them *(north of the beach)* is set back from the coast. The other *(to the south, above the restaurant)* offers spectacular **views**★★, over the thousands of palm trees, the coast and out to sea.

Kato Zakros Ruins★

⤵ *45km/28mi east of Sitía via Palaiokástro.* ⏱*Open Tue–Sun 8.30am–3pm.* ✒€3.

In an isolated **setting**★★, deep in the little bay *(beach)*, excavations have unearthed vestiges of a fourth Minoan palace which rivals those at Knossós, Phaistos and Mália. The site was first excavated by a group of British archaeologists and 12 houses were unearthed before the site was abandoned; it was 12 years later, in 1961, that Nikolaos Platon resumed the excavation and discovered the palace ruins. This site has yieled several clay tablets with Linear A inscriptions. An ancient labyrinth has also been discovered at this site similar to the Minoan sites of Knossós and Phaistos.

The oldest palace was built around 1900 BC. It was replaced around 1600 BC, but the buildings were destroyed around 1450 BC by earthquakes following the eruption of the volcano on Santorini. Like the other Minoan palaces the buildings are arranged around a central courtyard.

To the north is the large kitchen, the only one of its kind that can be identified as such; to the west are the reception rooms and places of worship; to the east, the royal apartments feature a round basin, probably used as a cistern; to the south are the workshops and warehouses near which is the well.

⚑ There is a lovely **walk**★★ between the village of Zakros and Kato Zakros *(2hr round-trip)* through the Valley of Death.

Monastery of Toploú★

⤵ *15km/9mi to the east.* ⏱*Open 8am–5pm.* ✒€3. ✆*28430 61172. Modest dress required.*

The **road**★ follows the coast at the foot of the arid hills. After a large holiday village which resembles an oriental town,

turn left. The road then climbs to a barren plateau. The fortresslike monastery was founded in the 14C as Our Lady of the Cape. The present buildings largely date to the 17C and the 18C. In 1821, following a slaughter of the monks by Turks, the monastery was deserted for 7 years. In 1866 the monastery was once again the victim of Turkish misrule and monks were executed in the grounds of the monastery.

A handsome Gothic door opens into the entrance court, which leads into an inner court surrounded by arcades and the stairs up to the cells. The Venetian-style church contains two very rich **icons**★ by an 18C Creto-Venetian master, Ioánnis Kornáros (Cornaro). The **museum** features a collection of icons from the 15C to the 19C, as well as precious ecclesiastical items, rare documents, ancient editions of the gospels and parchment manuscripts. A permanent exhibition traces the history of Orthodox Christianity, with particular reference to Mount Áthos and Toploú Monastery.

🚗 DRIVING TOURS

BAY OF ELOUNTA★

43km/27mi round-trip from Ágios Nikólaos. Allow 1 day including Spinalónga Island.

Follow the coastal road around this dramatic bay, with time for a swim and a seafood lunch. From Ágios Nikólaos take Odós Koundoúrou, which turns into a very beautiful corniche road providing frequent **views**★ over Mirambélou Bay.

Elounta

Situated at the end of the bay of the same name, the fishing port of Elounta has become a busy holiday resort known for its luxurious modern hotels.

Spinalónga Peninsula★

Protected area, access only on foot.
East of Elounta, the peninsula lies on the far side of the salt pans created by the Venetians. **Oloús**, a settlement

View to Spinalónga Island

dating back to Minoan times, rises near two windmills. Most of the ruins now lie underwater but are visible in calm weather. Lovely little bays provide good swimming opportunities, but be careful of the waves. There is a fine **view**★★ of Spinalónga Island and the coast.

▷ *Proceed to Elounde harbour to take a boat trip to Spinalónga Island.*

Spinalónga Island
Access by boat from Ágios Nikólaos or Elounta. ⏰*Daily departures 9.30am–4.30pm.*
Off the northern end of the peninsula lies a rocky islet on which the Venetians built a fortress in the 16C. From 1904 to 1958, the island housed a leper colony; today it is uninhabited. The historical novel *The Island* by Victoria Hislop is set on Spinalónga.

Pláka
The little village is a popular resort with a fishing harbour and pebble beach.

MIRAMBÉLOU BAY★★
100km/63mi round-trip. Head east out of Ágios Nikólaos.

The road follows the magnificent rocky coast of Mirambélou Bay, passing many attractive inlets, some of them suitable for swimming and scuba diving. Fine **views**★★ down over the headlands and islands and up to the inland mountains.

Ruins of Gourniá
20km/12.5mi east of Ágios Nikólaos.
⏰*Open Tue–Sun 8.30am–3pm.*
⊜€2. ℘28420 93028.
On a hill above Mirambélou Bay lie the ruins of a Minoan city dating from 1500–1450 BC. The town plan is clearly visible; it's easy to make out streets, squares, buildings and houses.

Pahía Ámos
This fishing village flanks a rather windswept beach. From here the road turns inland but continues to run parallel to the coast, affording fine sea views.

Móhlos★
In Sfakiá the road descends to this little quay which is hidden in an inlet opposite a tiny island where a mass of Minoan material was discovered. Terrace restaurants and cafés make the harbour a pleasant stop. ⬛Wonderful **walks**★★ along the bay departing from Móhlos. *Botanic tours* ℘08430 94725.

HINTERLAND★
25km/15mi round-trip. Head southwest out of Ágios Nikólaos.

Church of Panagía Kerá★
1km/0.5mi from Kritsá. ⏰*Apr–Oct Tue–Sun 8.30am–3pm.* ⊜€3. ℘28410 515 25
A clump of cypress trees conceals a charming white church built in the 13C at the beginning of the Venetian occupation.

The church contains a vivid series of 14C and 15C **frescoes**★★, both sophisticated and naïve, in vivid colours.

Kritsá★

This is a picturesque little town: its streets, arches and steps cling to the mountain slope among almond orchards overlooking Mirambélou Bay. In the summer season traditional folklore festivals (*enactment of a Cretan wedding*) are held.

▶ *Return in the direction of Ágios Nikólaos. Take the first left out of Kritsá.*

Ruins of Lató★

4km/2.5mi northeast of Kritsá.
This isolated and awesome **site**★★ reveals traces of an ancient town scattered over the slopes in a sort of suspended amphitheatre.
Lató was founded in the 8C BC on a saddle between two crags, each crowned by an acropolis; the position of the *agora* is indicated by the rectangular open space at the centre of the site; there are traces of a small shrine and a cistern at its centre. It was Dorian Greeks who developed the city and, along with a number of other late Bronze Age sites on eastern Crete, Lató was one of the first non-Minoan cities of the island.
The steps on the left of the *agora* led up to a **Prytaneion** (3C BC) where the magistrates met in a small court surrounded by a peristyle. From the northern acropolis there is an extensive view down to Mirambélou Bay.
From the other side a path leads to a polygonal retaining wall below a little **Temple of Apollo** (4C–3C BC). Beyond, a series of steps indicates the site of a theatre.

ADDRESSES

🏠 STAY

⊖ **Victoria** – *34 Aktí Koundoúrou.* ℘*28410 22731. www.victoria-hotel.gr. 18 rooms.* Simple but comfortable, overlooking the sea. Prices are reasonable.

⊖⊖ **Lato Hotel** – *Ammoudi,* ℘*28410 24581. www.lato-hotel.com.gr.* Friendly little hotel with 37 simple but comfortable rooms, garden and pool.

⊖⊖ **Du Lac** – *17 Odós 28-Oktomvriou.* ℘*24810 22711. www.dulachotel.gr. 24 rooms.* Best location in town; ask for a room with lake view.

⊖⊖ **Miramare** – *Gargadoros.* ℘*28410 86030. www.miramarecrete.gr. 223 rooms.* South of the town centre, handsome group of rooms and bungalows overlooking Mirambélou Bay. Swimming pool.

⊖⊖⊖ **Minos Palace** – *on the Eloúnta road, running on from Aktí Koundoúrou.* ℘*28410 23801/9. http://www.lux-hotels. com/gr/minos-palace/. 148 rooms.* A huge extravagance! Antique furniture, reception area with flagstone flooring, magnificent terrace shaded by olive trees overlooking the sea. The rooms are also luxurious.

⊖⊖⊖ **Elounda Gulf Villas & Suites** – *Elounta Road.* ℘*2810 227721. www.eloundavillas.com.* The ultimate escape, this modern complex offers 18 luxurious villas, each with a private pool, 10 upmarket suites, two gourmet restaurants and a spa. The service is impeccable.

IERÁPETRA

⊖ **Cretan Villa** – *16 Odós Lakerda.* ℘*28420 28552. www.cretan-villa.com. 9 rooms.* Ierápetra's most charming address. Old stone building with large rooms around a pleasant patio. Warm welcome.

⊖⊖ **Villa Mala** – *Malles.* ℘*28420 91382. www.villamala.gr.* In the mountains west of Ierápetra, these five luxurious self-catering apartments each accommodate 4-5 people, making them ideal for a family escape.

⊖⊖ **Porto Belissario** – *Ferma, 12km/8mi east of Ierápetra.* ℘*28420 61360. www.belissario.com. 33 rooms.* Modern establishment between the sea and the mountains. Large rooms with balconies and sea views. A pleasant base for a holiday.

SITÍA

⊖ **El Greco** – *13 Odós Arkadíou,* ℘*28430 23133. http://www.elgreco-sitia.gr/index.php. 20 rooms.* A simple, friendly little hotel. Traditional decor, warm welcome, and clean comfortable rooms with enormous private balconies.

Flisvos Hotel – *K Karamanlí 4.* ℘*28430 27135. www.flisvos-sitia.com.* This mid-range hotel offers basic but comfortable rooms. Great location, close to Sitía's cafés and beach.

🛏️🍽️ **Itanos** – *4 Odós Karamanlí.* ℘*28430 22900. www.itanoshotel.com. 72 rooms.* Marble in the bathrooms, very pleasant roof terrace. Every modern comfort and the decor of an international hotel.

🍽️EAT

🍽️ **Avli** – *12 Odós Príngipa Georgíou.* ℘*28410 82479.* Welcoming tables in a gravel courtyard shaded by a huge fig tree. Good food, and very friendly service.

🍽️ **Pelagos** – *10 Odós Keteháki, set back from the lake.* ℘*28410 25737.* Excellent fish, including swordfish fillets, crayfish, sea-urchin soup and mussels with cheese. The setting is delightful. Booking essential for dinner.

🍽️🍷 **Barko** – *on Kitroplatia Beach.* ℘*28410 24610. www.barko-palazzo.gr.* Creative Cretan cuisine is served in a slick modern interior overlooking the beach.

IERÁPETRA

🍽️ **Babi's** – *68 Odós Samouíl.* ℘*28420 24 048.* Mainly frequented by locals. Go for the fish and seafood specialities.

🍽️ **Levante** – *Odós Samouíl, heading towards the centre from the Hotel Kástro.* ℘*28420 80585.* For a good introduction to Cretan cuisine, try the speciality platter. Overlooking the beach, family-run, since 1936.

SITÍA

🍽️ **Kritiko Spiti** – *Odós Karamanlí 10.* ℘*28430 25133.* Try some authentic island specialities: *omatiés* (little sausages made with rice, liver, onions and almonds), *kochlis boumbouristi* (fried snails with olive oil, vinegar and tomatoes). Friendly service.

🍽️🍷 **The Balcony** – *On the corner of Odós Kazantzáki and Odós Foudalidou 19.* ℘*28430 25084. www.balcony-restaurant. com.* This rather chic restaurant on the top floor of an old house prides itself on its creative Cretan cooking. Vegetarian *moussáka* for a change, or

kléftiko (a lamb dish with potatoes, cheese and herbs).

🍷🍷 **Taverna Zorbas** – *On Sitía's seafront promenade.* ℘*28430 22689.* Friendly service and authentic Cretan cooking at this long-standing taverna overlooking the harbour.

🍴TAKING A BREAK

Café du Lac – *17 Odós 28-Oktomvríou. Open late, every day year-round.* Popular hangout for locals. Quietly trendy atmosphere; subdued lighting. Excellent choice of international music.

Café Candia – *12 Odós Iossif Koundoúrou.* One of the town's busiest bars. Popular for music and atmosphere.

IERÁPETRA

Cafétéria Veterano – *On the corner of Odós M. Kothri and Koundourou.* Popular snack spot, morning and night.

SITÍA

Drosoulites Platia Brasserie – *Platía Iróon Politehníou.* This large central café, the oldest in town, is an institution. Great for people-watching, with ouzo and pistachios in the evening, when the birds gather in the enormous palm tree that dominates the square.

🎭EVENTS AND FESTIVALS

In 1999, the town inaugurated its first **Nationalities Festival**: every day a different European nationality is honoured through its dances and culinary specialities. The festivities, like a sort of village fair, are held at the open-air theatre near the lake in early October. There are also various other musical and theatrical events held over the summer.

🛒SHOPPING

On Odós 28 Oktomvríou there is a **delicatessen** with a vast and appetising range of island products, including honey, oil, fine spirits and preserves.

🏃SPORTS AND LEISURE

Boat trip to Spinalónga Island – fees and departure times, enquire at the Tourism Office.

Scuba Diving – *Pelagos* – ℘*28410 24376, www.divecrete.com.* Arrange diving trips as well as a Discover Diving beginners course.

③ Rethymnon and the Region

Réthimnon – Ρέθυμνον

Lying on the north coast, between Hania and Herákleion, Rethymnon makes a perfect base for exploring both west and central Crete. Nearby, there are some fascinating monasteries, plus some excellent unspoilt beaches less than a 1-hour drive away, on the south coast.

RETHYMNON ★ *(RÉTHIMNO)*

Despite its small size, this pretty port town remains animated the year through thanks to its sizeable student population.

Rethymnon offers a variety of attractions including fine beaches, charming squares and a magnificent fort overlooking the sea. Despite its sprawling suburbs, it preserves the oriental charm characteristic of many Cretan towns.

A modest Minoan town, Rethymnon experienced its first golden age under the Mycenaeans.

During the Venetian period it was the third-largest administrative centre on Crete, and became a gem of Italian architecture.

After a late 16C attack by the pirate Barbarossa, the Venetians strengthened the city's protective system by building ramparts and a fortress. Nevertheless, Rethymnon fell to the Turks in 1645. The Ottoman occupation left the interesting examples of oriental architecture visible today.

WALKING TOUR

A stroll through the pedestrianised streets is a great way to explore the old part of town, where there are numerous working artisans.

▷ *You can complete this walk in a couple of hours – wear comfortable shoes and bring a camera.*

Venetian Harbour★★

Framing the semicircular port are pastel-coloured houses converted into cafés

▶ **Population:** 41, 687.
Michelin Map: 737 K 15 – Rethymnon.
Info: Odós Sofokli Venizelou. Open Mon–Fri 8.30am–2.30pm. ℘28310 29148.
Location: Located between Hania and Herákleion, Rethymnon, the capital of the region, is on the north coast.
Kids: Rethymnon Fortress and the nearby beaches.
Don't Miss: A trip to the monastery of Arkadi.
Timing: You can easily stay 1 week, using Rethymnon as your base, to explore the city, and the beaches and mountains of western and central Crete.

and tavernas. Colourful fishing boats and coasters bob in the peaceful water. Just south of the port rises a Venetian **loggia** (17C) that was converted into a mosque. It now houses reproductions of artworks displayed in local museums.

Arimondi Fountain

Three Corinthian columns mark this monumental fountain (1629). Nearby, along **Odós Thessaloniki**, several 16C–17C Venetian houses with elegant doorways decorated with coats of arms stand next to 18C–19C Turkish houses with balconies and wooden projections. From here look left to see a slim **minaret**★ set back from the street marking the position of the **Nerandzé Mosque**, which replaced a 17C Venetian convent.

Fortétza (or Froúrio)★★

Northwest of the old town.
Open Tue–Sun 8am–6pm. €3.
The impressive **Venetian "Fortress"** (1582) is reinforced with seven curious bastions that have an orillion (rounded projection) on one side. On entering follow the ramparts round to the left to take in **views**★ of the town and the

harbour. There is a small **Archaeo-logical Museum** (🕐*Open Tue–Sun 8.30am–3pm;* 💶€3; 📞28310 54668), in the former prison just outside the fortress walls.

▶ *From the fortress, take Odós Nikiforou Foka, then cross the busy road of Gavril Igoumenou to arrive at the public garden.*

Public Garden★

Located south of the old town, this is a cool haven of peace and tranquillity, complete with refreshment stall and fountains. The central point, in the shape of a star, leads off in eight directions.

Beaches★

Two popular **beaches**★ extend east of the old town. The first, with tall break-waters, is very safe; the second (choppy waters, tidal currents) is dangerous for swimming.

MONASTERY OF ARKADI★

▶ *24km/15mi southeast of Rethymnon. Follow the coast in the direction of Herákleion, and take the road for Platanès.* 🕐*Open daily: Apr–May Oct–Nov 9am–7pm, Jun–Sep 9am–8pm; Dec–Mar 9am–4pm. Museum* 💶€2.50. 📞28310 83076. www.arkadimonastery.gr.

In 1866 some 1, 000 Cretans, includ-ing many women and children, took refuge here against an army of 12, 000 Turkish solders. After holding out for 2 days, they blew themselves up with the powder magazine rather than yield to the invaders.

The monastery (11C) enjoys a glorious **site**★ on the edge of a plateau over-looking a wild gorge. A few monks still live here.

The church **façade**★ (1587) is built of golden stone. The Corinthian columns, the arcading and the Italian-style *oculi* give it a Renaissance look; the curves and counter-curves of the pediments add a touch of the Baroque. The con-vent buildings (17C) comprise cellars, the kitchen, the huge refectory, the powder magazine and a small **museum** dedi-cated to the tragic struggle of 1866 From the monastery, continue to the **Melidoni Cave** (after Arkadi, access by one of the mountain roads to Margarites and then Melidoni; 🕐open daily 8am–8pm, 💶no charge), scene of another massacre of the Cretans by the Turks There are lovely **views**★ of Mount Ida.

NECROPOLIS OF ARMENI

▶ *South of Rethymnon.* 🕐*Open Mon–Fri 8.30am–3pm.* 💶*No charge.*

Next to the road, in a forest of oaks, lie nearly 200 Minoan tombs; it is the most important such site of the period.

PRÉVELI MONASTERY

▶ *To the south.* 🕐*Open Apr–Oct 9am–1.30pm and 3.30pm–7pm.* 💶€2.50. 📞28320 31246. www.preveli.org.

Situated on the far side of the impressive **Kourtaliotiko Gorge**★, the beautiful Préveli Monastery maintains a revered place in the long and heroic Cretan resistance against the Turkish and Ger-man invaders. Built in the late 16C and destroyed several times, the current monastery comprises two complexes 3km/1.6mi apart.

The first one, Káto Monastíri (⛔*entrance prohibited*) was abandoned after the First World War. The second one **Písso Monastíri**, is still inhabited The religious festival of the True Cross (named for the monastery's precious relic, reputed to have miraculous pow-ers) takes place on 14 September and is celebrated by pilgrims who come from all corners of Crete. The monas-tery's small **museum** (🕐open Apr–Oct 9am–1.30pm, 3.30pm–7pm, 💶 €2.50, houses a collection including beautiful icons dating from the 13–19C.

There is a superb **view**★★ of the Libyan Sea from the vast shaded terrace, where one can contemplate the site. A small trail cuts through the wild and rocky pass leading to a lovely **beach**★ with palm trees (30min walk).

MÁTALA★

▶ *70km/44mi south of Herákleion. The village lies in a peaceful bay of the Libya Sea.*

According to the myth, it was at this little fishing village and holiday resort that Zeus swam ashore in the shape of a bull, bearing Europa on his back. These days Mátala is better known for its white sandy beach and its caves, which are to be found in the parallel strata of tufa on the north side of the beach.

RUINS OF PHAISTOS★★★

🕑*11km/7mi east of Mátala.* 🕒*Open May -Sept, daily 8am–8pm; Oct–Apr, daily 8.30am–3pm.* 🎟€4. 🕾*28920 42315.*

On a spur of Mount Ida – a magnificent **site**★★ with a view of the Messará Plain – stand the ruins of the Minoan Palace of Phaistos. For 17 centuries this extraordinary city was a powerful force

in Crete. Start in the North Court (traces of Hellenistic and Roman structures) (**1**); then go down the steps (**2**) which lead to the base of the *propylaia* and the theatre.

The **theatre** is composed, like the one at Knossós, of straight terraces facing the West Court. There was a little shrine (**3**) in the northeast corner.

A flight of steps leads up to the *propylaia* (**4**). Beyond and to the left is a huge peristyle (**5**) surrounded by the royal apartment. East of these extend domestic buildings where the famous "Phaistos Disk" (now in the Archaeological Museum in Herákleion) was discovered. On the north side lies the **King's Megaron** consisting of a recep-

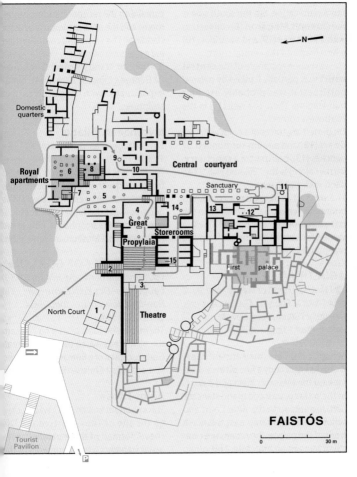

FAISTÓS

Ruins of Phaistos

tion room (**6**) and a "lustral bath" (**7**) for ritual purification. On the south side is the **Queen's Megaron** (**8**) connecting with a small court (**9**) and a corridor (**10**) which lead into the central court.

The vast open rectangle of the **central court** was partially flanked by pillared porticoes; it was probably used for bull-leaping. There is a well (**11**) in the southwest corner.

On the left are traces of a crypt with two pillars (**12**) and a room surrounded by benches (**13**), both part of a **sanctuary**. Farther along is the "Pillared Hall" (**14**), lined with alabaster.

The rows of **storerooms** contained enormous terracotta jars *(pithoi)*; in the last storeroom on the right (**15**) was a device for collecting the oil from the receptacles.

AGÍA TRIADA★

▷ *14km/9mi north of Mátala, and 3km/ 1.6mi west of Phaistos.* ◷*Open Apr– Oct, daily 7.30am–7pm; Nov–Mar, daily 8.30am–3pm.* ◉€3. ℘*28920 91564.*

Minoan ruins here (their ancient name is unknown) occupy a fine **site**★★ overlooking the Messarás Plain and Bay.

In the **palace**, pass the grand staircase *(left)* leading up to the Altar Court and follow the paved ramp past the north front of the palace; the redans are typical of Minoan architecture. This group of buildings comprised a central block containing the reception rooms, storerooms and the royal *megaron* (alabaster cladding). The west wing comprised living accommodations.

Further on stands **Ágios Georgios** (St George's Church), a small 14C building decorated with delicate Byzantine sculptures.

Mycenaean Village

The village was built later (1375–1100 BC) on the north side of the palace. The east side of the agora was bordered by a portico with shops. A large number of artefacts have been unearthed at the necropolis on the hillside, including a famed painted sarcophagus, now in the Archaeological Museum in Herákleion.

ANCIENT CITY OF GORTYN★

▷ *28km/18mi northeast of Mátala.* ◷*Open Apr–Oct, daily 8am–8pm; Nov–Mar, daily 10am–3pm.* ◉€4. ℘*28920 31 144.*

The impressive ruins straggling beneath the olive trees evoke the past glory of Gortyn, capital of a Roman province and seat of the first Christian Bishop of Crete.

Ágios Titos★

This important building (7C) was erected on the site of Titus' martyrdom. The chevet formed of three parallel apses is still standing; a few fragments of the carved decoration are on display in the Herákleion Museum.

Odeon★

The little theatre (restored) was built early in the 2C AD on the site of – and with materials taken from – an earlier rotunda *(thólos)*. Here and there lie damaged statues.

At the rear of the Odeon, under the vaulting of the outer corridor, are several blocks of stone bearing the text of the **Twelve Tables of Gortyn**.

The Dorian letters were inscribed in about 480 BC and the lines are written alternately from left to right and right to left; the text deals with individual liberty, property, inheritance, adultery, violence, etc.

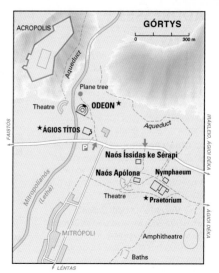

GÓRTYS

▶ *Retrace your steps, taking the Herákleion road for around 300m/330yds and the path off to the right.*

Naós Íssidas ke Sérapi (Temple of Isis and Serapis)

The remains of a cellar and a purification basin mark the site of the **Temple of Isis and Serapis** (1C–2C), which was dedicated to two Egyptian gods whose worship was widespread in the Roman world.

There are also traces of the **Temple of Pythian Apollo** which dates from the Archaic period (7C BC). Excavations have uncovered the impressive ruins of the enormous **praetorium**★; first built of brick in the 2C, it was reconstructed in the 4C following an earthquake.

Opposite the praetorium is a **nymphaeum**, which was built in the 2C and converted into a fountain in the Byzantine era.

BEACHES★

The ruins of the Minoan city of **Kommos**★ (3km/1.9mi), probably one of the two ports of Phaistos, rise above the sea. Stone buildings lining a wide street are visible from the fence enclosing the area *(closed to the public)*.

Further down is a magnificent, undeveloped **beach**★, very popular in summer. **Kalamaki** (7km/4mi north of Mátala), a small seaside resort with an excellent **beach**★ sits on the wide bay of Messarás. Another good possibility is **Agía Galíni**★ (28km/17mi north of Mátala), a charming and very popular resort, with a picturesque harbour and many tavernas serving fish. There are boat trips to the sea caves along the coast.

VÓROI

▶ *8km east of Mátala.*

In this village, the **Cretan Museum of Ethnology**★ *(◷open daily 10am–6pm; ◔€3)* displays its very fine collection of objects recalling everyday life in Crete in the 18C and 19C.

VORIZIA

▶ *30km/19mi north of Mátala/3.5km east of Kamáres.*

In the village of Vorizia visit the **Valsamonero Monastery**; Italian-style architecture and wonderful **frescoes**★ from the 14C and 15C. The **Vrondisi Monastery** (4km/2.5mi east of Vorizia) offers a magnificent **view**★ of the surrounding area. Note the 15C Venetian fountain, and, in the double-aisled church (one aisle for Catholics, the other for Orthodox), fine frescoes and icons.

ADDRESSES

STAY

Castello Pension – *10 Platía Karaolí Dimitríou, near the cathedral.* 🖉 *28310 23570. www.castello-rethymno.gr. 8 rooms.* An extraordinary calm reigns in this restored old house. Simple decor, all in white. Lovely cool garden with a little fountain. Quiet, spotlessly clean rooms.

Olga's Pension – *57 Odós Soulíou.* 🖉 *28310 53206. 22 rooms.* Pleasant and charming, for small budgets. Sometimes small but very comfortable, rooms have attractive tiled bathrooms.

Vecchio – *4 Odós Daliani.* 🖉 *28310 54985. www.vecchio.gr. 27 rooms.* Attractive hotel verging on the luxurious, but affordable. Large rooms decorated in pastels. Swimming pool.

Mythos Suites – *12 Platía Karaolí, on the cathedral square.* 🖉 *28310 53917. www. mythos-crete.gr. 14 rooms.* Suites and cottages of all sizes on the grounds of a 16C manor house. Rooms combine modern comfort with old-world charm. Swimming pool.

MÁTALA

Hotel Nikos – *In the street left of the Hotel Zafiria, entrance of the village.* 🖉 *28920 45375. www.matala-nikos.com. 20 rooms.* An attractive low building with terraces and small gardens. Tropical plants, natural colours, baked clay flooring... altogether very effective. The welcome is just as good, and the clean spacious rooms all have big showers. Excellent breakfast with freshly squeezed fruit juice.

Eleonas – *In Zaros (20km/12mi northeast of Mátala).* 🖉 *28940 31238. www.eleonas.gr.* Set amid olive groves and backed by dramatic mountains, this agritourism complex makes a welcome escape from the touristy coastal resorts. An ideal base for hiking as well as visiting Mátala and Gortys, it offers accommodation in traditional rooms plus a excellent taverna.

EAT

Pigadi – *Xanthoudidou 27.* 🖉 *28310 27522. www.pigadi-crete.com.* Pigadi means „well" and indeed there is one this 16thC stone courtyard. Serves delicous Mediterranean cuisine.

Veneto – *4 Odós Epimenídou.* 🖉 *28310 56634. www.veneto.gr.* Magnificent setting in a courtyard garden. Excellent Cretan fare, and superior service.

Avli – *Xanthoudidou 22 & Radamanthios.* 🖉 *28310 28250. www.avli.gr.* Superb decor, excellent service and refined, varied dishes: the best spot in town; one of the best on the island.

MÁTALA

Sirtaki Taverna – *Mátala.* 🖉 *28920 45001.* Classic taverna fare at affordable prices, with occcassional live music, overlooking the beach.

🛒 SHOPPING

Market – beside the public gardens. A big open-air food market is held on Thursday and Saturday mornings.

Art reproductions – these are sold in the Venetian loggia (*Odós Paleologou*).

Nikos Siragas – *Petalioti 2. www.siragas.gr.* Come here to buy bowls and vases made by artistic woodturner and carver, Nikos Siragas.

Aperitton – *Kallergi 1.* 🖉 *28310 28504.* You'll find this jewellery shop behind the Town Hall. Besides gold and silver Greek necklaces, earings and rings, it also specialises in precious stones. It stays open both summer and winter.

🚣 SPORTS AND LEISURE

Scuba diving – Paradise Dive Center – *Odós Eleftheríou Venizélou.* 🖉 *28310 26 317.* The club takes people to the south of the island, near Lefkogia.

Scuba diving – *Kalypso Rock's Palace Diving Centre. Sof Venizelou 42 (New Beach Road).* 🖉 *28310 20990. www.kalypsodivingcenter.com.* This scuba diving centre arranges transfers from Rethymno to their base at Plakias on the south coast. Besides organised diving trips, they also offer a half-day course for beginners.

Hiking – Ellotia Tours – *Arkadiou 155.,* 🖉 *28310 51981. www.rethymnoatcrete.com.* Organise 1-day trips from Rethymnon to walk the length of the Samariá Gorge.

Hiking – Happy Walker – *Tobazi 56.* 🖉 *28310 52920. www.happywalker.nl.* Organise many hiking trips in the Rethymnon area.

4 Hania and the Region

Haniá – Χανιά

West Crete is home to some of the island's most stunning beaches, mountains and gorges. The main city, the elegant Venetian-era port town of Hania, lies on the north coast, with daily overnight ferries connecting it to Athens.

HANIA★★★ (HANIÁ)

Crete's capital until 1971, when Herákleion took over, Hania is considered by many to be Greece's most beautful city.

Above a fishing port, the old town is criss-crossed with alleyways. Beyond the ramparts of the old Venetian and Ottoman settlement, however, extends a modern industrial area laid out on a grid pattern.

Hania Bay was particularly prosperous during the Minoan period and the Palace of Kydonia rivalled Knossós and Gortyn, especially in the 2C BC.

Renamed Canea, the city was redesigned in the Italian manner during the Venetian period (1252), but took on some oriental trappings during the Turkish occupation. In 1851, the Turks set up the Cretan headquarters for their Ottoman administration in Canea. The

▶ **Population:** 55, 838.
◔ **Michelin Map:** 737 J 15.
▯ **Info:** Hania: Kriari 40.
  ☏ 28210 929 43. Open
  Mon–Fri, 9am–2pm.
◑ **Location:** This is the westernmost part of Crete. The region capital, Hania, lies at the foot of the peak of Lefká Óri in the northwest.
🧑 **Kids:** Beaches for younger children and Samariá Gorge for older ones.
⊛ **Don't Miss:** Samariá Gorge.
◷ **Timing:** Use Hania as a base and explore the city, beaches and mountains of western Crete for a week.

GETTING THERE

BY AIR – The airport is 13km/8mi east of the town (bus service to Hania). In summer, there are numerous charter flights from the main cities in Europe. For the rest of the year the main air link (daily flights) is Athens; also Thessaloníki (2/wk).
BY SEA – Ferry service between **Piraeus** and the Hania port of *Souda*, 7km/4mi east of the town (bus links).

Port of Hania

© Phototravellers/MICHELIN

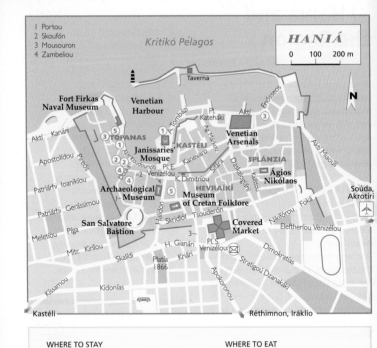

1 Portou	
2 Skoufón	
3 Mousouron	
4 Zambelíou	

Kritikó Pélagos

HANIÁ

0 100 200 m

N

Fort Firkas
Naval Museum

Venetian
Harbour

Venetian
Arsenals

SPLÁNZIA

Ágios
Nikólaos

Janissaries'
Mosque

KASTÉLI

TOPANAS

Archaeological
Museum

Museum
of Cretan Folklore

HEVRAIKI

San Salvatore
Bastion

Covered
Market

Platía
1866

Soúda,
Akrotíri

Kastéli

Réthimnon, Iráklio

town kept its status as capital of Crete until 1971.

Stroll through Hania's old town to explore its elegant buildings and harbour, bequethed by former occupiers, the Venetians and the Ottoman Turks.

Venetian Harbour★★

The old districts of Hania radiate from this superb crescent-shaped quayside, which forms a wide promenade lined with bars and restaurants that attract crowds in the evening. It's charming, and the noble Venetian façades are always a pleasure to look at.

The Topanas District★★

Northwest of the Venetian port.

At the end of Koundourioti Quay is the Firkas Fort (1629), housing the **Naval Museum of Crete** (Naftiko Moussio). The museum relates the naval history

of the island through a fine collection of model ships and other seafaring equipment (③open daily 9am-4pm; ⊙ €3; ☏28210 918 75. www.mar-mus-crete.gr). Heading back towards the port, the alleyways are lined with old **Venetian mansions**, their walls a yellow ochre. Look out for the ornate stone entrances with their coats of arms and carvings. There are also old Ottoman houses, their upper floors made of wood.

The Hevraiki District

South of the Venetian port.

Wedged between the buildings in the heart of the old Jewish quarter is the Venetian Church of Ágios Frangíscos, a majestic 4C basilica.

It was later transformed into a mosque by the Turks and now houses a fine **Archaeological Museum**★★ displaying stone sarcophagi, Minoan ceramics and Roman mosaics. (○open Apr-Oct Tue–Sun 8am– 8pm, Mon 1.30pm–8pm; Nov-Mar Tue–Sun 8am–3pm, Mon closed. ✆€2 (including entrance to the Byzantine Collection: €3); ✆28210 903 34).

In the Cathedral Square is the old Catholic church which now houses the **Museum of Cretan Folklore** (○open Easter–Oct, Mon–Fri 9am–9pm, Sat 9am–4pm, Sun 11am-4pm; rest of the year, Mon–Fri 9am–2pm, 6pm–9pm, Sat–Sun closed. ✆€2; ✆28210 908 16), where you can see lovely embroidery work as well as reconstructions of scenes from daily life on Crete.

Around the Covered Market★

Platía E. Venizélou.

Don't miss a late-morning stop at this bustling market hall purveying all kinds of foodstuffs including fish, seafood, meat, cheese, spices and cakes.

The Kastelli District

East of the Venetian port.

The district lies along the quayside towards the **Janissaries' Mosque** (Kioutsouk Hassan) (17C). Just behind it rises the site of Ancient **Kydonia**.

The Splánzia District

Continue east; the quayside is lined with the impressive arches of the Venetian arsenals (16C). Farther along, in the direction of the new town, take a look at the 14C Church of **Ágios Nikólaos**, flanked by both a campanile and a minaret.

AKROTIRI PENINSULA

East of Hania.

The arid Akrotiri Peninsula separates the Bay of Souda from the Bay of Hania. Although most of it is a military zone (*many of the roads are closed to civilians*) the island's traditional village and quiet beaches make for a pleasant trip.

Worth a stop is the **Tafos Venizé-lou★** (Venizelos' Tomb), *at the summit of the Profitis Ilias Hills,* tomb of Greek statesman **Elefthérious Venizélos** (1864–1936).

There's a grand **view**★★ over Hania, the bay and the White Mountains.

AGÍA TRIADA MONASTERY★

▶ *17km/11mi east of Hania, near the village of Koumares. Head for the airport. Where the runways end take the road for Mouzouras, and then left again.* ○*Open Tue–Sun 8am–sunset (winter closed 2pm-4pm).* ✆€2. ✆28210 635 72. www.agiatriada-chania.gr.

The church (1631) has a beautiful pink façade in the Italian Renaissance style and a campanile with three bells. There's also a small shop where the monks sell their own organic wine and olive oil.

APTERA RUINS

▶ *17km/11mi east of Hania in the direction of Rethymnon. Take the turning to the right (signposted).* ✆*No charge.*

At the foot of the mountain are the ruins of a town that flourished from the 5C BC to the Byzantine period. Within the fine outer walls are the remains of temples, a Roman theatre and a fine underground Roman cistern with three aisles.

From the fort at the far end of the promontory there is a very fine **view**★★ of the mountain and of **Soúda Bay**.

GONIA MONASTERY

▶ *26km/16mi west of Hania, on the Rodopos Peninsula, by the coast road to Kissamos.* ○*Open Sun–Fri 8am–12.30pm and 4–8pm, Sat closed.* ✆*No charge.* ✆28240 222 81.

The church and adjacent chapels of this Venetian monastery (1618) house an interesting **icon collection**★. From the rear terrace, there's a lovely view over the bay.

SAMARIÁ GORGE★★★

▧ *South of Hania – 41km/26mi from the car park to Xilóskalo where the walk starts.* ○*Open 1 May–15 Oct, daily 7am–3pm.* ✆€4. www.samariagorge.eu.

The awesome Samariá Gorge pierces the heart of the **White Mountains** (Lefká Óri), where surface water has worn away a huge ravine (18km/11.25mi long)

Samariá Gorge

© Greek National Tourism Organisation

Walking the Gorge

The simplest way of visiting the Samará gorge, classified as a National Park, is to join an organised all-day excursion starting from Hania; reservations can be made at hotels, a tourist agency or the EOT. Walkers are transported to the top of the gorge by coach. They are collected at the lower end in Agía Rouméli by boat, which docks about 1hr 30min later in Sfakiá (return coach to Hania).

The walk through the gorge takes 6–7hrs and makes a 1, 250m/4, 100ft descent. Be sure to carry water and wear stout shoes and a hat.

Those who do not wish to walk the entire gorge may go down as far as the viewing platform *(1hr 30min round-trip)*.

extending from the Omalós Plateau down to the Libyan Sea.

From the trailhead at Xilóskalo, a twisting path makes the steep descent to a platform where there is an impressive **view**★★ of the ravine between sheer rock walls. From there the path descends precipitously to the bottom of the gorge. Farther on sits the village of Samariá, its handful of houses now deserted.

Beyond are the **Iron Gates**★★★, where the distance between the vertical walls is not more than 2–3m/7–10ft. Walkers pick their way over stones and rocks, with precipices and wooded slopes to each side, as the gorge descends gradually towards the coast. Eventually the stream bed widens out and reaches **Agía Rouméli** (known in Antiquity as Tarrhia) with a black sand beach on the edge of the Libyan Sea. From here boats make the trip to Sfakiá.

SFAKIÁ★★

On the Cretan south coast, 70km/44mi from Hania. Boats carrying hikers from the Samaria gorge disembark here. Home to the Sfakiots, as the local sheep farmers are called, this peaceful seaside resort ranges around a little bay. Tavernas and cafés often bustle with hikers from the Samariá Gorge.

Samariá Gorge★★★

Allow one day, leaving early in the morning. See also p347.
Several times a day, the boats make the journey between Sfakiá and Agia Roumeli, the little port at the foot of the gorge. Usually visitors descend the gorge from Hania (*see p347*) but those in search of a challenge can climb it, departing from Agía Rouméli. The **boat trip**★★ between Sfakiá and Agía Rouméli, with a stop off at Loutro, is a joy in itself.
If you intend on hiking the gorge, be sure to wear good walking boots, and bring water and some food for a picnic lunch (no refeshments are available in the gorge).

Ágios Ioannis★★

▶ *20km/13mi west of Sfakiá, via Anopoli.*
On the drive to this small, traditional village, near the abandoned village of Arádena *(after 4km/2.5mi)* just before the metal bridge which crosses the Arádena Gorge, there is a particularly **stunning view**★★.

Arádena Gorge★★

Allow 1 day; take water, a hat and sturdy shoes.
Part of this spectacular gorge can be undertaken by any experienced walker, but the complete descent is only for the more adventurous: it includes negotiating a sheer rockface with steps and a rope. Allow 6hrs to get to **Loutro**. From here, take a boat back to Sfakiá, or take the path along the beach *(2hrs 30min)*.

Vryses★★

▶ *40km/25mi to the north.*
The road climbs through some of the highest mountains on the island. There are spectacular **views**★★ of the wild and scarcely inhabited south coast. **Vryses** is a pleasant well-shaded village by a stream.

Frangokástelo

▶ *15km/9mi east of Sfakiá.*
The coast road cuts between the mountains and the sea, leading to the ruins of the **Frangokástelo Citadel**★ (1371). It is rectangular in plan with crenellated walls and a square tower at each corner; nearby, a fine sandy **beach**★.

PALEOHÓRA★ (PALAIÓCHORA)

▶ *70km/44mi from Hania, on the Bay of Libya. ☎28230 424 38. www. paleochora.com.*
Such are the many attractions of this charming fishing village – beautiful beach of white sand, white houses with flowering terraces, little winding streets and alleyways – that it has developed as a holiday resort.
From the seafront there is a wonderful **view**★ of the sea and the mountains. In the evening the main street becomes a pedestrianised area brimming with life. A litte farther to the south is a Venetian **citadel** (13C) up on the rocks.
Paleohóra's excellent **beach**★ is one of the largest on the island, and boasts white sand and turquoise water.

Island of Elafonisos★★

Allow 1 day. Boat departs at 10am in summer. Reserve the evening before at the agencies in the village.
This lovely little island, which you can actually reach from mainland Crete by wading through a shallow lagoon of knee-high water, is edged with magnificent pink sandy **beaches**★★. Whales and dolphins sometimes appear alongside the boat. The island itself is a nature reserve popular with birdwatchers, as it's the last stop between Europe to Africa for migrating birds.

Sougia★

Boat trip. Allow 1 day. Departure at 9.30am in summer. Book the evening before at the agencies in the village.

East of Paleohóra is the delightful village of Sougia. Set up for low-key tourism, with just a handful of pensions and tavernas, its backed by mountains and gives onto a long pebble beach flanked by tamarisk trees. A boat trip is a great way to see the mountainous coastline in the south of Crete.

🥾 The village is also accessible by a beautiful hiking **trail**★★ from Paleohóra (5hrs; difficult).

Island of Gavdos

Boat trip – allow 1 day. The island is also accessible from Sfakiá.

50km/31mi from the coast, this island of 70 inhabitants is an amazing place, but is difficult to get to. The coastline is a mass of magnificent rocky outcrops. It is the southernmost point in Europe, just 300km/186.4mi from Tobrouk (Libya) and the Gulf of Soloum (Egypt), at the same latitude as Biskra (Algeria) and Sfax (Tunisia).

ADDRESSES

🛏️STAY

🛏️ **Stella Apartments** – *10 Odós Agélou.* 📞*28210 73756. 8 rooms.* A good place with affordable rates. Ask at the craft shop next door. Very clean medium-sized rooms with new bathrooms. Four rooms have little balconies.

🛏️🛏️ **Palazzo Hotel** – *54 Odós Theotokopoúlou.* 📞*28210 93227. www.palazzohotel.gr. Open Apr–Oct.* Warm welcome at this hotel with its wonderful old façade and antique furnishings. Spacious rooms (safes and fridges) named after Greek gods and goddesses (Athena, Apollo, etc); six have balconies and some have baths. Breakfast on the roof garden with lovely views of town and sea.

🛏️🛏️ **Porto del Colombo** – *On the corner of Odós Theofánous and Odós Moshón.* 📞*28210 98466. www.portodel colombo.com. 10 rooms.* One of the town's oldest Turkish houses; it may have served as a prison. However, don't be put off: though dark, the rooms are charming.

🛏️🛏️🛏️ **Hotel Amphora** – *2nd passage of Odós Theotokopoálou.* 📞*28210 93224. www.amphora.gr.* In a 14C building overlooking the old harbour, Amphora has 20 rooms furnished in traditional style, plus a breakfast room.

🛏️🛏️🛏️🛏️ **Casa Delfino Suites** – *9 Odós Theofánous.* 📞*28210 87400/93098. www.casadelfino.com.* Quite simply magnificent! Enormous, elegant, luxury suites. Immaculate marble bathrooms, large mezzanines preceding the bedrooms and sumptuous floor tiles. Wood and copper details – this old Venetian mansion has been superbly renovated. Booking recommended.

SFAKIA

🛏️ **Xenia** – *At the end of the seafront, Sfakia.* 📞*28250 91202. www.xeniacrete. com. 19 rooms.* A very attractive place. Large, cool rooms with blue doors and marble-effect flooring.

PALEÓHORA

There are numerous guesthouses in the village but be aware that in high season it'll be hard to find a room without a reservation.

🛏️ **Rea** – *In a street at right angles to the main street, heading towards the beach.* 📞*28230 41307. apap@cha.forthnet.gr. 14 rooms.* Attractive little hotel, hidden behind a wall of greenery. Warm welcome from the kindly owner. The quiet rooms have attractive, simple décor. Breakfast served on the terrace.

🍽️EAT

🍽️ **Monastiri** – *12 Aktí Tombázi.* 📞*28210 55527. www.monastiri-taverna.gr.* In the liveliest part of the harbour. Try 'the nun's mistake', grilled pork with a variety of fried vegetables.

🍽️ **Taverna Dinos** – *Odós Aktí Enósseos, after Vassiliko.* 📞*28210 41865.* Very good place in the quieter part of the harbour. Stellar service. Aubergine salads, fresh sea urchins and grilled fish.

🍽️ **Taverna Semiramis** – *Passageway to the right of Odós Skoufón, as you come from the harbour.* 📞*28210 98650. www.semiramis-restaurant-chania.gr.* Live, traditional music, diligent service. Try the succulent Cretan lamb slow-cooked in olive oil and white wine.

🍽 **Tholos** – *36 Odós Agíon Déka, behind the cathedral.* 📞28210 467 25. Housed in an old Venetian mansion. A smart restaurant; menu mixes traditional Cretan dishes with house creations.

🍽🍷🍴 **Tamam** – *49 Zambeliou.* 📞28210 96080. http://tamamrestaurant.com. In a pretty street one block back from the harbour, Tamam serves Cretan dishes with an eastern twist in the former Turkish bathhouse.

SFAKIA
🍽 **Three Brothers** – *Vrisi Beach, Sfakia,* 📞28250 91040. www.three-brothers-sfakia-crete.com. Delightful view over the bay. The food is also good, with generous portions. Warm welcome.

PALEÓHORA
Every evening, the main street is transformed into a terrace, with tables and chairs spilling out onto the pavements.

🍽🍷 **Third Eye** – *Paleóhora.* 📞28230 41234. www.thethirdeye-paleochora.com. In the old town, one block back from the main beach, this restaurant serves organic vegetarian dishes in a lovely leafy garden.

🍽🍷🍴 **Caravella** – *Main street, near the harbour, Paleóhora.* 📞28230423 54. www.caravella.gr. A great place to try authentic Cretan cuisine, with an emphasis on fresh fish. Guests are welcome to enter the kitchen to watch the cook at work.

🍴 TAKING A BREAK
Café Candia – *Aktí Tombázi, 30m/33yds before you reach the mosque.* A traditional old café where Greek couples come at dusk to enjoy the harbour air and a drink. Ouzo served with little snacks of olives, tomatoes, feta and prawns.

Kronos – *23 Odós Mousouron, behind the market.* A smart place in the heart of the shopping area. A little expensive, but the cakes are delicious.

Sinagogi – *Parodos Kondilaki.* 📞28210 95242. A trendy open-air lounge-bar in the ruins of the old Jewish synagogue, with relaxing chill-out music, popular through the day and into the early hours. Open May–Oct.

PALEÓHORA
Jetty Cocktail Bar – *On the main beach, Paleóhora. Open all day for drinks and snacks.* Great location, right on the sand, overlooking the sea.

🏖 BEACHES
There are several beaches to the east of the town. **Agia Marina**, about 10km/6mi, is the prettiest and the busiest: it can get very crowded in summer. If you have a car, drive to Falasarna (on the west coast) or Elafonisis (on the southwest coast), to enjoy some of Crete's most remote unspoilt sand beaches.

🛒 SHOPPING
PALEÓHORA
Jewellery Opal – *On the corner of the street which leads to the beach and the road that runs parallel to the main street, Paleóhora.* 📞28230 41522. The shop sells the work of a Greek silversmith – very creative jewellery – hence the prices.

Kihli – *25 Kondikali, Hania.* 📞28210 87927. Come here to shop for shop for brightly-coloured boho-chic silk skirts, tops and dresses, plus ethnic jewellery, perfect for a summer evening.

Miden Agan – *70 Daskalogianni, Hania.* 📞28210 27068. www.traditional-products.com. This delicatessen stocks a vast selection of Greek and foreign wines, to taste before buying.

🤸 SPORTS AND LEISURE
PALEÓHORA
Hiking – **Trekking Hellas** – *99 Apokoronou, Hania.* 📞28210 58952. www.trekking.gr. Arrange guided walking tours, including a 1-day visit to the monasteries of Akrotiri, and more strenuous hiking in the White Mountains.

Sailing – **Pentarakis** – *Hania.* 📞694 7181990 (mobile). www.notos-sailing.com. Charter a yacht and skipper for a 1-day private sailing trip, departing from Hania harbour.

Scuba Diving – **Blue Adventures** – *69 Daskalogianni, Hania.* 📞28210 40403. www.blueadventuresdiving.gr. Organise diving trips departing from Hania's old harbour, plus a 1-day Discover Diving course for beginners.

Situated at the heart of the southern Aegean Sea, the Cyclades present a strikingly beautiful landscape of volcanic peaks, barren plains and spectacular beaches bathed in bright sunshine. Historically very poor, the islands have become a major tourist destination in the last three decades.

Highlights

1 The **boat trips** offered to secluded beaches on every island (p353)
2 The unique atmosphere of the Apollo sanctuary on **Delos**. (p363)
3 The daytime charm and nightlife of **Mýkonos** (p379)
4 The caldera and volcanic beaches of **Santorini** (p399)
5 The Orthodox tradition of the Panagía Evangelístria on **Tinos** and Hozoviótissa on **Amorgós**. (p404, p356)

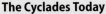

▶ **Population:** 119, 549.
Info: www.kykladesnews.gr.
◖ **Location:** Many of the capital towns on the islands carry the name of the island itself but are referred to locally as "Hóra" (meaning "main city").
ℙ **Parking:** At the height of the season parking can be a headache: too many vehicles on small roads.
◉ **Don't Miss:** Santorini boasts the archipelago's most impressive landscape; Mýkonos and Folégandros have the loveliest villages.
◷ **Timing:** During high season (15 Jun–15 Sept), tourists swarm the islands and prices rise into the stratosphere. Try to visit in May or June. In July and August, there is a refreshing north wind *(meltémi)*. If you have only a few days, stick to the islands nearest the mainland (Andros, Kea, Kýthnos). Stay a full week to visit the can't-miss islands: Mýkonos, Delos or Naxos, then Santorini. A visit of 10 days can include Ios and Folégandros.
👪 **Kids:** The Greek islands make for fantastic family holidays. For example, Naxos' safe beaches are perfect for young children.

The Cyclades Today

Apart from the coastal plains, the Cyclades are largely arid, and farming and fishing are limited. The tourism industry continues to grow. New development honours the local architectural tradition (whitewashed cuboid houses). There are thousands of beaches, from tiny coves to vast expanses of sand. The sea is warm and clear but often rough; between July and September the *meltémi* blows steadily and it is not unusual for ferries to be cancelled. Bear this in mind when planning your trip back to Athens for the flight home.

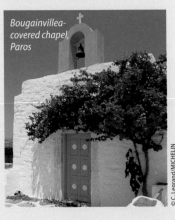

Bougainvillea-covered chapel, Paros

© C. Legrand/MICHELIN

The advent of tourism has changed some of the islands in ways that could never have been imagined. Mýkonos (Míkonos), once too poor to support a farmer's existence, has emerged as the most sophisticated of all the Greek islands. Santorini (Thíra) comes a close second, popular with cruise ships and honeymoon couples, and Ios completes the trio of islands whose prosperity and identity is inextricably tied to tourism. Naxos and Paros are more democratic in their appeal – their stunning beaches, see to that – while Delos has the strongest appeal for visitors with a historical imagination and a fascination with the world of ancient Greece.

Some of the islands are favourites with mainland Greeks, and Athenians flock to Amorgós and Folégandros. The islands of Andros, Kéa, Kýthnos and Serifos are best avoided on summer weekends because they are so east to reach from the mainland. At the height of the summer season it is impossible to escape the crowds. Kimolos, Tinos and Sýros – in their different ways – offer an alternative view of the Cyclades from the iconic one that most visitors experience. Day trip Island-hops are all in a days work here.

A Bit of History

Cycladic Art and Civilisation – The Cyclades are so named because they are the 'circling' islands around the sacred island of Delos. Some of the Cyclades Islands were inhabited in prehistoric times and the earliest settlers arrived around 6000 BC. Around 3200 BC, the Cycladic culture began to emerge, recognised in three phases; Cycladic I (3200–2800 BC), Cycladic II (2800–2300 BC) and Cycladic III (2300–2000 BC). The myth of King Minos of Crete delegating his brother Rhadamanthys to rule the islands reflects the period of Minoan influence that characterises Cycladic II. It is no coincidence that Cycladic III marks the fall of Crete and the rise of Mycenean influence. The culture fell into decline after 2300 BC, and was obliterated by the Santorini volcanic eruption in about 1500 BC. Islands like Paros and Naxos came under Ionian influence in the 8C BC and as formal allies of Persia fought against Athens at the Battles of Marathon and Salamis in the 5C BC. This led to many of the Cycladic Islands joining what became the Athenian Empire but they were always looking for a way out and some looked to Sparta during the Peloponnesian War.

Later, for the same reason, the islands would turn towards Macedon and Alexander the Great. Under Roman rule, the islands managed reasonably well but with the fall of Rome the islands were forgotten and lapsed into obscurity and piracy.

During the Venetian period (13C), the Cyclades served as ports of call on the sea route to Constantinople. Roman Catholic parishes that endure today were founded on the islands of Sýros, Naxos, Tenos and Santorini.

After the Greek War of Independence, Sýros became the main port of the new Greek kingdom. The focus eventually shifted to Piraeus, however, and the islands went into a decline until the advent of tourism in the 1960s.

The first archaeological excavations of the islands began towards the end of the 19C and the concept of a Cycladic civilization began to emerge. It was not until after the Second World War than archaeologists once more began to investigate and by then a market was developing for Cycladic art, whose simple forms were echoed by modern artists like Brâncuşi.

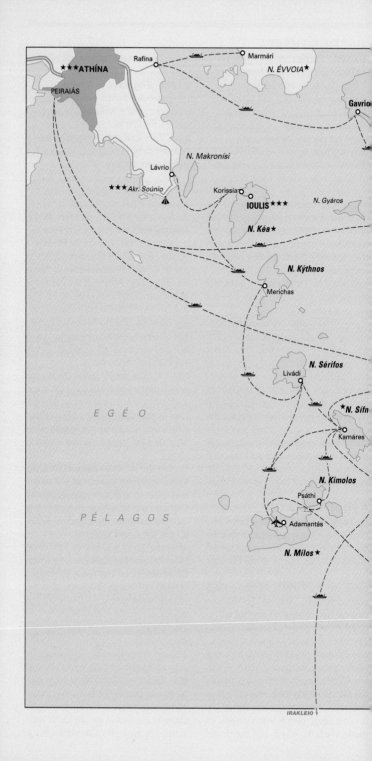

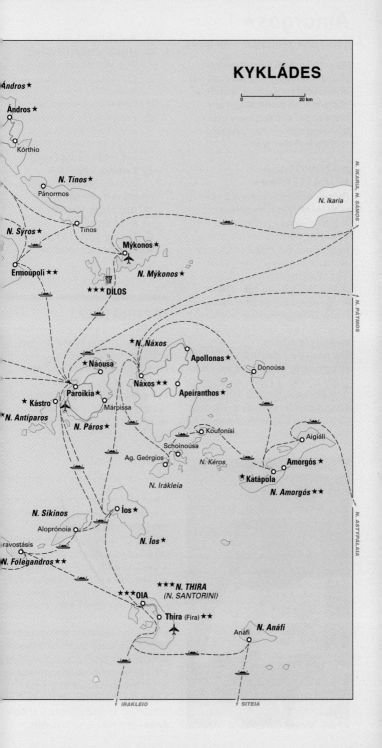

KYKLÁDES

0   20 km

Ándros ★

Ándros ★

Kórthio

N. Tínos ★

Pánormos

N. Ikaría

N. Sýros ★

Tínos

Mýkonos ★

Ermoúpoli ★★

N. Mýkonos ★

★★★ DÍLOS

N. Náxos ★

Náousa ★

Apollonas ★

Donoúsa

Paroikia ★

Náxos ★★

Apeíranthos ★

★ Kástro

Márpissa

★ N. Antíparos

N. Páros ★

Koufonísi

Aigiáli

Schoinoúsa

N. Kéros

Amorgós ★

Ag. Geórgios

★ Katápola

N. Irákleia

N. Amorgós ★★

N. Síkinos

Íos ★

Aloprónoia

ravostásis

N. Íos ★

N. Folégandros ★★

★★★ N. THIRA

★★★OIA

(N. SANTORINI)

Thíra (Fira) ★★

N. Anáfi

Anáfi

IRAKLEIO

SITEIA

N. IKARÍA, N. SÁMOS

N. PÁTMOS

N. ASTYPÁLAIA

Amorgós★

Amorgós – Αμοργός

Way off the main ferry route from Piraeus, this long, narrow island was little visited for decades, despite its fascinating monastery, many beaches and extraordinary beauty. New development has increased tourism in recent years.

HOZOVIÓTISSA MONASTERY★★★

🕐 *Open daily 8am–1pm and 5–7pm.* 🎟️ *No charge. Visitors must be attired so that arms and legs are covered; if dressed in trousers, women must also wear a pareo. For those without a car, access the monastery either on foot from Hóra (mountainous path, allow at least 1hr); or by bus from Hóra or Katápola, which drops off at the parking area below the monastery, from where it is a 15min walk (arrive early to avoid the heat of the day).*

This monastery, dating from 1017 and recognised by Emperor Alexios I Komnenos in 1088, occupies an extraordinary **site★★★**, perched halfway up a 500m/1 640ft high vertical cliff. Occupied virtually without interruption for over a thousand years, the monastery

- ▶ **Population:** 1, 859.
- ⚲ **Michelin Map:** 121sq km/ 48sq mi – Michelin Map 737 M-N 12 – Cyclades – Aegean.
- 🛈 **Info:** www.Amorgos.net
- ◉ **Location:** The easternmost of the Cyclades with good ferry connections to Athens and neighbouring islands.
- 🅿 **Parking:** A car is not essential because the island is so small.
- ⊘ **Don't Miss:** Hozoviótissa Monastery.
- 🕐 **Timing:** 1 day is a rush.
- 👥 **Kids:** A sandy beach at Egiáli.

GETTING THERE

BY SEA – There are one or two **ferry** services a day from Piraeus *(5–8hrs depending on the vessel)*.
From here there are links to **Naxos** *(daily)*, **Paros** *(daily)*, **Santorini** *(3/wk)*, **Folégandros** *(2/wk)*, and **Sýros** *(2/wk)*. In the high season, there is a local ferry link from Amorgós to the islands of Naxos, Paros and the lesser Cyclades (Iráklia, Schinoússa, Koufoníssi, Donoússa).

Hozoviótissa Monastery
© B. Chabrol/MICHELIN

is one of the great sacred sites of the Aegean. It consists of two churches, around 50 rooms and a library.
Visiting this holy place is an entrancing experience. Past the entrance gate, a staircase leads up through a tunnel in the mountain to the reception hall. The main church features some fine icons and the library has a collection of embroidered vestments, liturgical objects and important **manuscripts**★ (10C–18C). In keeping with the Orthodox tradition of hospitality, the monks (there are only three of them) offer visitors tea, lemon liqueur and Turkish Delight.
Below the monastery at the foot of the cliff lies the pebble beach of **Agía Ánna**★. It is popular with nudists.

HÓRA

▶ 5.5km/4mi east of Katápola.
Buses from Katápola (every hour) and Aigiáli (3–5 a day).
The **site**★ of this typical Cycladic village, dominated by a rocky outcrop, is extraordinary. Its alleys and little squares are best explored on foot.
The small **Archaeological Museum** (◷open daily except Mon and public holidays 9am–1pm and 6–8.30pm; ⊘no charge) displays statues, capitals, stelae and, in a wood-ceilinged room, a selection of ceramics.
The tiny **cathedral** (17C) is in an elegant square. A passageway leads to the citadel (1290), from where there is a **view**★ over the village.

KATÁPOLA★

This appealing town incorporates three villages strung out along the coast of a deep bay: **Katápola**, with its harbour for ferries and pleasure craft; **Rahídi**, still undeveloped; and **Xilokeratídi**, an attractive fishermen's quarter.
Some of the churches, like **Panagía Katapolianí** (centre of Katápola) are constructed of stone taken from the site at Minóa. Attractive beaches nearby.

Ruins of Minóa

Accessible on foot or by car (2.5km/1.25mi south of Katápola).
On foot: take the road that heads from the harbour up the hill overlooking the

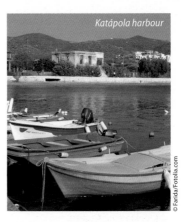
Katápola harbour

© Farida/Fotolia.com

bay (45min walk). By car: take the Hóra road, then the first right-hand turn.
The site, currently closed because of ongoing excavations, can be observed from the perimeter.
The settlement was inhabited from the 10C BC until the 4C AD. Archaeologists have excavated defensive walls, the walls of a gymnasium (4C BC) and the foundations of a Hellenistic temple dedicated to Dionysos. There are fine **views**★ over the bay and mountains.

NORTH OF THE ISLAND★

Narrow and steep, Mount Kríkelos (827m/2 710ft) is accessed by the road linking Egiáli to Katápola; the route threads between the sea and the arid peaks where herds of goats graze. The islet of **Nikoúria** (fine beaches) is acces-

---

🚶 Walks on Amorgós

From Hóra to Hozoviótissa Monastery★★   1hr along a raised pathway.
From the capital to the monastery on its cliff face; beautiful scenery.

From Hozoviótissa Monastery to Potamós★★   Signposted at the monastery exit. 5hrs along a ridge track. Views over the sea and mountain are impressive.
From Potamós it is easy to walk to Aigiáli (buses to Katápola).

From Aigiáli to Megáli Glyfáda★   3hr there and back by a good path. Climb as far as the attractive village of Tholária. From there head north to Megáli Glyfáda, a beautiful cove with a fine sandy beach.

Ruins of Arkessíni★   2hrs there and back from Vroútsi, south of Katápola.
A paved track, then a path, lead down to the sea, through an arid and desolate, yet magnificent, landscape. A rocky outcrop is the site of a city founded in the 4C BC. There are the ruins of an acropolis, ancient tombs and a defensive tower. The return journey may be made via the northern coast road (allow 1hr extra).

sible by boat from the beach of Ágios Pávlos, 2km/1.25mi southwest of Aigiáli, below a ruined Hellenistic tower.

Aigiáli evolved into a resort; this village is increasingly popular with visitors who enjoy its fine sandy beaches (the quieter ones are only accessible by boat). From Aigiáli you can take a pleasant walk to three mountain villages.

Mountain Villages★

Three whitewashed villages built on the mountainside dominate the bay of Aigiáli. **Potamós**, standing among thousands of boulders, stands balcony-like overlooking the Aegean.

Tholária has a pleasant square with a church and café, where visitors can try the local specialities: *rakomelo* (honey *raki*, a strong alcoholic spirit with cloves) and *psimeni raki* (honey *raki* with cinnamon). **Langáda**★, a maze of steep alleys, is the most charming of the three. From here paths lead to old churches, the most interesting being an 8C monastery.

SOUTH OF THE ISLAND★

The villages of the south (Kato Meriá) are reached by a single road which crosses the island's agricultural region. This is the most traditional area of Amorgós and is not as busy as other parts of the island. From Katápola, climb towards Hóra and then head down towards the sea; take the first turn to the right.

A little farther along, on the right-hand side *(not signposted)* is the monastery of **Ágios Geórgios Valsamítis** (16C), a stark white group of buildings in a terraced valley. The monastery has 17C frescoes and is renowned for its miraculous spring.

Beaches

Not far from the village of Vroútsi, **Moúros** is located in a wide bay. Farther south lie three popular beaches: **Kalotarítissa**, **Paradísia** and **Gramvoússa**★ (on the eponymous islet, accessed by boat from Paradísia Beach), a breeding ground for indigenous and migratory birds.

EXCURSION
The Lesser Cyclades
Daily (usually) ferry services from Amorgós and Naxos; boats leave from Katápola.

This tiny archipelago is made up of four small islands (Iráklia, Schinoússa, Koufoníssi and Donoússa) and hundreds of islets popular for their magnificent beaches.

ADDRESSES

🛏STAY
In August it is essential to reserve accommodation in advance.

🛏 **Pagali** – *Langáda, down from the main road.* ✆22850 733 10. *www.pagali hotel-amorgos.com. 19 rooms and studios.* Above the Níkos bar; pleasant, quiet rooms, some with kitchenettes. Bus stop nearby. Management will come to meet guests from the ferries. Breakfast €6.50.

🛏 **Voula Beach** – *Katápola, at the end of an alley running off from the landing stage.* ✆22850 740 52. *15 rooms and studios.* Very clean rooms of all sizes off a planted courtyard. Very friendly welcome. No breakfast.

🛏🛏 **Villa Katapoliani** – *Katápola* ✆22850 710 54. *www.villakatapoliani. gr. 13 rooms and studios.* A charming establishment centred around a planted courtyard near the harbour. Modest rooms, with balconies, fridges, safes and hairdryers; no breakfast, but communal kitchen facilities.

🛏🛏🛏 **Aigialis** – ✆22850 733 93. *www.amorgos-aegialis.com. 50 rooms.* 1km-0.5mi from the port but served by buses, this is the most comfortable hotel in Egiáli. The rooms overlook the bay. Swimming pool (open to the public), billiards room and nightclub. Transport to ports available (fee).

🍴EAT
🍴 **Liotrív** – *Hóra, in a narrow street to the right of the bus station.* Traditional dishes (*moussáka*) or more original cuisine (rabbit casserole). Arrive early.

🍴 **Mouráyo** – *Katápola, opposite the landing stage.* Superb fish and seafood

taverna which is deservedly popular.
Try the fried squid and the aubergines.

🦑 **Níkos** – *Langada, lower end of the
village, below the Hotel Pagali.* A great
place to eat, overlooking the boules
players. Considered one of the best
restaurants on the island; don't miss the
"Nikos Special" eggplant.

🦑 **Panorama** – *Tholaria, middle of the
village.* One of the most sought-after
dining spots on Amorgós. Delicious
kokoretsi (meat skewers) and goat's-
cheese dishes. In summer, local
musicians perform traditional tunes;
arrive before 9pm.

🚂 **TAKING A BREAK**
Frou-Frou – *Egiáli, in the alley leading
to the harbour.* A good cake shop with
a sea view. Breakfast, cakes, crêpes and
ice cream round the clock.

🎭 EVENTS AND FESTIVALS
Church of Panagía Epanohorianí –
North of Langáda. On 14 and 15 August
there are church services followed by a
banquet, vegetables only on the 14th
and goat on the 15th. This is free to all
comers, but it is customary to leave a
donation in the church collection box.
The evenings see traditional dancing in
all Langáda's tavernas.
**Feast of the Presentation of the
Virgin** – *Hozoviótissa Monastery.*
On 21 November; this is the only
opportunity to dine with the locals in
the monastery's refectory.

Andros★

Andros – Άνδρος

The northernmost Cycladic Island,
Andros, is lush and wooded.
Its many beaches are rarely
busy, except in August, and its
gently sloping mountain paths
are ideal for walkers. To top it
all, its picturesque capital is a
perfect example of that graceful
mixture of Venetian and Cycladic
architectural styles.

A BIT OF HISTORY
Neolithic village sites bear testimony
to prehistoric life on the island and the
first Ionian settlers arrived around 1000
BC. After the defeat of the Persians at
Salamis by Athens in the 5C, the people
of Andros were punished for their support of the invaders by having a large
fine imposed on them. As they were
unwilling to accept the punishment,
the Athenian general Themistocles lay
siege to the island but was not able to
compel their submission.
This led to long-term enmity between
the two states and, not surprisingly,
Andros joined forces with Sparta when
the Peloponnesian War broke out. This

▶ **Population:** 10, 009.
Michelin Map: 374sq km/
150sq mi – Michelin
map 737 K-L 9-10 –
Cyclades – Aegean.
Info: Tourist office
(June–September) near
the landing stage in
Gávrio. www.andros.gr.
▶ **Location:** Andros is the
most northerly of the
Cyclades and the second-
largest of the islands.
🅿 **Parking:** Car hire
companies are numerous
and the number of vehicles
on the road makes parking
difficult at times.
Don't Miss: A walk
through the medieval
quarter of Hóra.
Timing: At least a couple
of days are needed.

led to a period of harsh rule by the Spartans (and later by the Romans) and the
island never attained independence in
the ancient world.

GETTING THERE AND GETTING AROUND

BY SEA – **Ferries** to Andros leave mainly from Rafína *(daily, 2hrs)*. On Andros, Gávrio is the only ferry port; from here, there are also boats to Mýkonos *(daily)*, Tenos *(daily)*, Sýros *(3/wk)*, Paros *(6/wk)*, Naxos *(2/wk)*, Kýthnos *(1/wk)* and Kea *(1/wk)*.
BY ROAD – **Jeeps** are the best way to tour the island; agencies will deliver vehicles to your hotel. Try **Euro Car** ℘22820-71312, www.rentacareuro.com. **Mopeds** may be rented from **George Rentabike** *(Gávrio, at the port)*, **Dinos** *(Batsí ℘22820 41003)*, and **Aris** *(Hóra ℘22820 243 81)*.

BEACHES
Around Gávrio★

The beaches at **Vitáli** and **Gídes** on the west coast are at the end of a 4km/2.5mi track, and are pleasant as long as the *meltemi* wind is not blowing strongly. There is a beach taverna at **Vitáli** but that is as far as comforts go. Just south of Gávrio, **Ágios Kiprianos**, **Psilí Ámos** and **Kiprí** are three attractive, if busy beaches. **Felós**, to the north of Gávrio, has a small and peaceful resort nearby. **Batsí** *(27km/17mi west of Hóra)* is the island's principal resort where the village alleys have retained their Cycladic charm. More fine beaches lie to the southeast. **Limanáki**, an isolated beach with magnificent scenery at the end of

a track on the northeastern coast, will appeal to lovers of solitude as it is hardly frequented except during the high season.

Around Hóra

North of Hóra, **Paraporti, Nimborió** and **Giália** offer fine views of the island's capital. Located in a narrow inlet, south of Hóra, **Sinetí** is an attractive beach readily accessible from the village of the same name. Further out, **Órmos** *(10km/6mi south of Hóra)* is a rather charmless resort that is reached beyond the lighthouse to the north and Griás Pídima Beach. **Achaia**★★★ offers crystal waters and untouched natural beauty.

HÓRA★

Situated on the east coast and seat of shipbuilding and seafaring families, Hóra has remained off the main tourist trail. This highly picturesque town retains an unusual charm with its narrow alleyways, small stone-paved squares and the odd Venetian bridge and castle.

The Medieval District★

A vaulted archway (the old town gate) leads into the mediaeval district's alleyways lined with medieval houses, some neoclassical, some dating from the Ottoman period and many graced with loggias, which bear witness to the Venetian presence here from the 13C to the mid-16C. Overlooking Paraporti Beach, the **Church of Ágios Geórgios** (17C) is on a little shaded marble-paved

Beach of Achaia near Gávrio

square leading to a stone bridge to an islet where you can find the impressive ruins of a Venetian fortress.

The island's **Archaeological Museum** is on the main town square, Théofilos Kaïris. (○ *Open daily 8.30am–3pm.* €3. 22820 236 64). Displays include the wonderful statue of **Hermes of Andros**★ and other finds from the Cycladic, Classical, Hellenistic, Roman and Byzantine periods. On the same square, you can find the **Museum of Contemporary Art**. (○ *Open 1 Nov– 31 Mar, Sat–Mon, 10am–2pm; 1 Apr–31 May and 20 Sept–31 Oct Wed–Mon, 10am–2pm.* €6. 22820 22444. www. moca-andros.gr.) The museum is worth checking out, because its excellent summer exhibitions of Greek and international artists are generally noteworthy. The **House of Théofilos Kaïris** (1784– 1853) is a mansion belonging to one of the Greek heroes of the Enlightenment and subsequent War of Independence. He was a free spirit and, post-Independence, he clashed with the Orthodox Church which accused him of blasphemy. He was jailed for two years but, old and infirm, he died after a few days in prison. Eight days after his death, the Greek Supreme Court revoked the judgement.

GÁVRIO AND AROUND

In a narrow-mouthed bay, the harbour of Gávrio is lined by tavernas, cafés, hotels and guesthouses. It's a good base for exploring the north and west of the island. The village of Amólohos *6km/4mi north of Gávrio,* lies in an arid landscape surrounded by low walls. There is a pleasant fountain at the entrance to the village and, lower down the valley, three emblematic watermills.

The winding road to *Kalokeriní* heads upwards; in an olive grove to the right *3km/1.9mi northwest of Gávrio* stands the Tower Of Aghios Pétros, a round tower that dates from the Hellenistic; period (4C–3C BC) and the white Chapel of Ágios Pétros. This five-storey tower has served over the centuries as a signal- and watchtower, as well as a forge for the nearby iron ore mines.

A track off the coastal road 10km/6mi east of Gávrio leads up to the monastery of **Zoödóhos Pigí** (○ *open mornings only;* 22820 72459). Legend has it that it was established in AD842 at the end of the iconclastic conflict, but it is first recorded in a documented dated 1400. The monastery has a valuable collection of icons (14C–16C) – one of which is dated 1325 – frescoes and medieval manuscripts. Further south on the coastal road, 12km/8mi southeast of Gávrio, lies the village of **Paleópoli**★ (the name means "Old City") which was the island's capital in classical times, but was destroyed by an earthquake in the 4C BC. Today it is a modest mountain village; the archaeological site lies on the coast.

THE MESSARIÁ VALLEY★
Messariá

The village has a fine example of 12C Byzantine architecture, the **Church of Taxiárhis**★, decorated with marble sculpture and frescoes (18C). The Church of **Ágios Nikólaos** (1734), with its blue cupola, has an interesting iconostasis in carved wood. The huge **Monastery of Panahrándou** *(3km/1.9mi south of Messariá, beyond the village of Fálika;* ○*opening hours vary)* monastery, dating from the 10C and still active, resembles a white fortress clinging to the mountainside.

The village of Messariá itself has one particularly fine example of 12C Byzantine architecture, the **Church of Taxiárhis**★, decorated with marble sculpture and frescoes (18C). The Church of **Ágios Nikólaos** (1734), with its blue cupola, has an interesting iconostasis in carved wood which has been recently restored.

The huge **Monastery of Panahrándou** *(3km/1.9mi south of Messariá, beyond the village of Fálika;* ○*opening hours vary),* dating from the 10C and still active, resembles a white fortress clinging to the mountainside. *West of Messariá,* the village of **Menítes**★ is renowned for its springs, which gush from marble lions' heads. From the terrace outside the deserted Byzantine

Dovecote in Andros countryside

church there is a fine panorama of the village. North of Ménites, there is the village of Strapouriés where several *archontika*, grand mansions, and a richly decorated church testify to the wealth of the early island shipowners.

5km/3mi on the northwestern side of Hóra lies the charming village of Apoikía where the local Sáriza mineral spring gushes from a marble lion's head. This is Greece's own Evian, water bottled and sold for consumption within the country; it is supposed to cure kidney and liver disorders. Nearby the still-active 16C monastery of **Ágios Nikólaos** (*22820 22190*) is perched above the cultivated terraces of the Ahla Valley. In the courtyard behind the defensive wall, there is a colourful church where the icon of St Nicholas was woven from the hair of a pious nun.

THE SOUTH OF THE ISLAND

Take the Sinetí road south of Hóra.
South of the resort of Órmos Kórthi, built on a hillside in a sheltered bay, is Kórthi, with many old houses. Farther still are three of the island's most characteristic villages: **Aidonia, Moussiónas** and, **Amonakliós**★, where the traditional architecture blends into a beautiful mountain landscape.

ADDRESSES

🏠 STAY

🛏 **Meltemi** – *Batsí, above the Agios Philippos church.* *22820 41016. 11 studios.* Large studios with balconies in a lovely house.

🛏 **Villa Nora** – *Batsí, end of the coast road.* *22820 41651. 13 studios, 1 apt.* Ravishing studios; large garden with beach view. No breakfast.

🛏 **Riva** – *Hóra, on the beach.* *22820 24412. www.androsrooms.gr. 5 rooms, 3 apt.* Well-equipped, one of Andros' best lodgings. Scooter rental, touring information warmly offered.

🛏🛏🛏 **Pighi Sariza** – *Apikia.* *22820 23799. www.pighisarizahotel.gr. 42 rooms.* Very comfortable hotel near the Sarizia spring and its healing waters.

🍴 EAT

🍽 **Giakoumissi** – *Batsí.* Select your fish, then enjoy it while taking in the sea view. Generous portions.

🍽 **Konaki** – *Gávrio, by the port.* Decorated with ancient photos. Family-run with a simple local cuisine.

🏃 SPORTS AND LEISURE

Lovers of the open air should check with **Andrina Tours** (*Batsí,* *22820 410 64; www.batsiandros.com*) for organised excursions and other information.

🛒 SHOPPING

Andros is an island of beekeepers; take home some delicious thyme honey (*boutique near the post office in Gávrio*).

Delos★★★

Dílos – Δήλος

Today windswept and desolate, Delos was home to one of the most important sanctuaries in the Greek world and site of the greatest city in the Aegean during the classical period. In antiquity it played a leading role both commercially and in religious terms, and the Greek world was in awe of its riches.

A BIT OF HISTORY

Apollo's Sacred Island – Delos was the mythological birthplace of Apollo, god of light, and by the end of the 8C BC the sanctuary here was one of the most important in the Greek world. Even the Persian king Darius respected its status when invading Greece in 490 BC and assured its inhabitants they would not be harmed.

In 478 BC Athens formed the confederation known as the **League of Delos**; its treasury was first kept in the Apollo Sanctuary before being transferred in 454 BC to Athens (effectively turning the League into an Athenian empire).

Delos looked to Sparta for help and this incurred the wrath of Athens. In 422 BC, the whole population of the island was exiled by Athens to what is now the west coast of Turkey. This measure was rescinded during the Peloponnesian War and the islanders returned home. The Athenians built a new temple to Apollo and organised the **Delian Festival,** which took place every 4 years in May until the 1C AD.

Thanks to its central location, Delos gradually became the main port in the Aegean Sea. Its sacred standing preserved it from attack, and the island flourished. Early in the 1C BC the prosperity of Delos reached its zenith and the town numbered 25 000 inhabitants. The decline of Delos began in 88 BC when it was sacked by Mithridates, King of Pontus. In 69 BC it was sacked again by the pirate Athenodoros. Pilgrimages became less popular, depredations by pirates grew and the main shipping

routes moved elsewhere. The island was finally abandoned in the 6C–7C.

IERÓ★★
(Sanctuary of Apollo)

The whole island of Delos is a huge archaeological site centred upon the sanctuary of Apollo, legendary place of his birth.

Agora Kombetaliatón

Entry is through a paved open space called the Agora of the Competaliasts in honour of the Roman gods of the crossroads. Note the remains of a monumental altar.

- **Michelin Map:** 3.6sq km/1.4sq mi – Michelin map 737 L 11 – Cyclades – Aegean.
- **Info:** www.mykonos.gr. Open Tue–Sun 8.30am–3pm.
- **Location:** Delos is accessible year-round by boat from Mýkonos (30min; €10 round trip); several companies operate guided trips (approx. €32 including boat and entrance fees).
- **Don't Miss:** The Terrace of the Lions; the Theatre District.
- **Timing:** Timetables are displayed at the port and are subject to change. There is no accommodation on the island, and it's best to arrive early in the day. Bring sturdy shoes, water and a snack; there is a small café. Boats from other islands stop here, but may not leave much time for sightseeing.
- **Kids:** Delos is an unforgettable visit for young fans of archaeology and mythology.

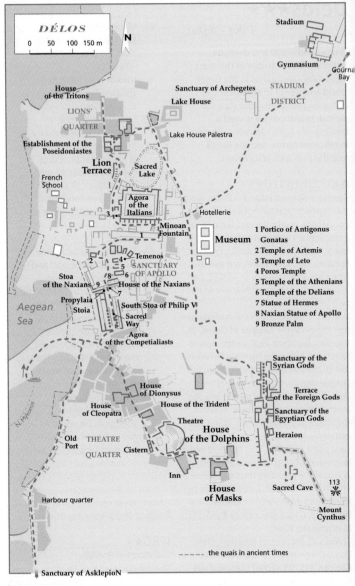

DÉLOS

0 50 100 150 m

N

House of the Tritons

LIONS' QUARTER

Establishment of the Poseidoniastes

Lion Terrace

French School

Sacred Lake

Agora of the Italians

Sanctuary of Archegetes

Lake House

Lake House Palestra

STADIUM DISTRICT

Stadium

Gymnasium

Gourna Bay

Hotellerie

Minoan Fountain

Museum

Temenos

SANCTUARY OF APOLLO

Stoa of the Naxians

House of the Naxians

Propylaia

Stoïa

South Stoa of Philip V

Sacred Way

Agora of the Competialists

Aegean Sea

N Mykonos

1 Portico of Antigonus Gonatas
2 Temple of Artemis
3 Temple of Leto
4 Poros Temple
5 Temple of the Athenians
6 Temple of the Delians
7 Statue of Hermes
8 Naxian Statue of Apollo
9 Bronze Palm

House of Dionysus

House of the Trident

House of Cleopatra

Theatre

House of the Dolphins

Old Port

THEATRE QUARTER

Cistern

Inn

House of Masks

Harbour quarter

Sanctuary of the Syrian Gods

Terrace of the Foreign Gods

Sanctuary of the Egyptian Gods

Heraion

Sacred Cave

113

Mount Cynthus

- - - the quais in ancient times

Sanctuary of AsklepioN

Sacred Way★

This processional road was lined by votive monuments; some of the bases are still visible. On either side stretched two porticoes; the portico on the left, Stoá Fílipou, was built by Philip of Macedon in the 3C BC; the one on the right, Stoá Pergámou, was built in the same period by the kings of Pergamon, a city in Asia Minor.

Propylaia

Little is left of this monumental entrance (propylaia), but the numbers of pilgrims who crossed the threshold in antiquity can be judged by how much the three steps are worn away. On the right stands a marble statue of a bearded Hermes (4C BC).

Íkos Naxíon
(House of the Naxiots)

On the right beyond the Propylaia lie the foundations of a rectangular building from the Archaic period. Against the north wall stands an enormous block of marble that was the base of a Statue of Apollo (6C BC), a colossal votive offering erected by the Naxiots; some parts of it can be seen near the Sanctuary of Artemis.

Stoá Naxíon★
(Stoa of the Naxiots)

On the left beyond the Propylaia are traces of this 6C BC portico; look for the circular granite base (**9**) on which stood a colossal bronze palm tree representing the tree beneath which Leto gave birth to Apollo and Artemis.

Témenos Apóllona★★

Lying south to north in the precinct are traces of three successive Temples of Apollo.

The **Temple of Delian Apollo** (**6**), is a Doric building begun in the 5C BC. The **Athenian Temple** (c.420 BC) was also Doric (**5**); the naós contained seven statues. The smallest and oldest was the **Porinos Temple**, built of hard limestone tufa, which contained an Archaic statue of Apollo and the treasure of the Delian League.

Near the Porinos Temple stand two pedestals; one is decorated with a Doric frieze of alternating roses and *bucranes* (ox heads) and the other in blue marble is inscribed in honour of Philetairos, first King of Pergamon.

Témenos Artémidos★
(Artemision)

Set back from the Sacred Way, on the site of an ancient Mycenaean palace, are the truncated columns of the façade of the Temple of Artemis, an Ionic building (2C BC) that succeeded two others.

Behind the Temple of Artemis lie the torso and the pelvis pieces of the colossal **Statue of Apollo★★** which was hauled this far by the Venetians in 1422.

Stoá Andigónou Gonatá★

Bordering the sanctuary on the north side, the *stoa* was built in the 3C BC. Two rows of statues lined the façade; their bases still exist. Behind the eastern end of the portico stands the **Minoë Fountain** (Minóa Kríni) which dates from the 6C BC.

Nearby are the remains of the precinct wall and of a Temple to Dionysos. There is also evidence of subterranean corridors in the theatre (3C BC), which allowed the actors to pass from the front of the stage to the orchestra.

PERIOHÍ LEÓNDON★★
(Lion District)

This urban district was built in the Hellenistic period. The path out of the sanctuary passes between the impressive remains of a granite building *(left)* and the walls of the **Temple of Leto** (6C BC) (**3**).

East of the temple extends the **Agora of the Italians** (Agorá Italón) (2C BC) surrounded by a portico into which opened the cells of the Italian merchants who settled on Delos *(several mosaics)*.

Ándiro Leóndon★★★
(Terrace of the Lions)

Facing the Sacred Lake is the row of famous Archaic lions sculpted in grainy Naxian marble. Originally there were at least nine; only five remain (a sixth was removed to Venice in the 17C). The stone animals, with long bodies and scarcely perceptible manes, sit on their haunches and give an impression of restrained power.

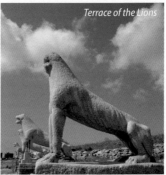

Terrace of the Lions

© Greek National Tourism Organisation

At the Centre of the Greek World

According to legend, **Leto**, whom Zeus had seduced and then abandoned, wandered about the world pursued by the anger of Hera, who had forbidden anyone to receive the pregnant goddess. Poseidon eventually took pity on her and hit the water with his trident, upon which a new island emerged (Delos – "she who has emerged"), which had not been part of the Earth when Hera uttered her curse. The island thus served as a safe haven for Leto, who, after nine days and nights, gave birth to twins, Apollo and Artemis.

Ierí Límni (Sacred Lake) was filled in 1924 to prevent malarial mosquitoes. The **Lion Terrace** leads to the **Ídrima Possidoniastón,** the Establishment of Possidoniasts of Bertyos (present-day Beirut) who were Syrian merchants and ship owners worshipping under the aegis of Poseidon. A group of Aphrodite and Pan statues was discovered in the peristyled court (now in the Athens Museum). Further out, the private **Ikía Límnis**★ (Lake House) is a well preserved villa with stucco work and mosaics comprising a charming pillared court and the cistern that gave it its name.

STADIUM DISTRICT

Beyond the ruins of the Sanctuary of Archegetes are the remains of the gymnasium (3C BC) and of the stadium (3C BC) with its track and starting line. In its heyday, the stadium could accommodate an audience of 5 500 people.

Museum★★

This is the best museum in the Cyclades, whose nine rooms provide excellent examples of Archaic Cycladic art such as the votive statues of the kouros and kore type, mostly from the Temple of Artemis; statues from the classical and Hellenistic periods such as the marble statue of Apollo attributed to Praxiteles, the bronze mask of Dionysos and the ivory plaques; plus Mycenaean jewellery. There are also some interesting items used in everyday life excavated from the private houses of the island, as well as rare wall frescoes, unique finds from that period.

ÓROS KÝNTHOS★★★
(Mount Kýnthos)

Mountain is a rather grandiose word to use for an easily accessible, 113m-high hillock which, nevertheless, commands excellent views over the island. **Ikía Ermi**★★, the two-storey **House of Hermes** (2C BC) is named after a fine head of Hermes (in the museum) found there. The ground floor includes a vestibule, an inner courtyard bordered on three sides by a portico and a nymphaeum.

Ándiro Xénon Theón★★

The **Terrace of the Foreign Gods** was built in the 2C BC for shrines to the non-Greek divinities worshipped by Delos' many immigrants. On either side of the path lie traces of semicircular shrines and rooms; one of the porticoes enclosed a theatre where orgiastic mysteries were celebrated in honour of Atargatis, the Syrian Aphrodite.

The **Shrine of the Egyptian Gods** contains the remains of a temple to Serapis and a temple to Isis; its náos sheltered a **statue** of the goddess. Nearby, foundations mark the site of a little Doric temple built of marble and dedicated to Hera (6C BC).

Ascent of Mount Kýnthos★★★

(45min on foot there and back). The **Sacred Cave** in the rock was covered with enormous slabs of granite in the Hellenistic era to form a shrine to Herakles. **The summit** (113m/370ft) has traces of a sanctuary to Zeus and Athena (3C BC) and a magnificent **panorama**★★★ over Delos and the Cyclades.

SINIKÍA THEÁTROU★★★ (THEATRE DISTRICT)

The Theatre District was built from the 2C BC onwards to house the many foreigners who came to live on Delos. It comprised many luxurious houses built round courtyards and decorated with superb mosaic floors in lively colours.

Coming from the harbour towards the Theatre, the first houses are Ikía Dionysou (**House of Dionysos★**) on the left and Ikía Kleopátras (**House of Kleopatra★**) opposite on the right. The first is named after the central motif of the mosaic in the peristyled courtyard that shows Dionysos on a panther. The House of Kleopatra was inhabited in the 2C by a woman named Kleopatra and her husband Dioskourides, whose damaged effigies can be seen on the north side of the peristyled courtyard.

The well still provides excellent drinking water. Further in on the left just before the theatre, Ikía Tríenas (**House of the Trident**) has mosaics decorated with a trident, a dolphin entwined round an anchor and geometric motifs. The majestic construction of the **Theatre★** itself dates from the Hellenistic era; is fairly well preserved, with marble walls and 43 rows of seats for 5 500 spectators. Past the theatre, there is Ikía Delfinión (**House of the Dolphins★**) paved with a mosaic signed by Asclepiades of Arados and the best villa of them all, the two-storey Ikía Prossopíon (**House of the Masks★★**), complete with a central courtyard surrounded with a peristyle and rooms decorated with magnificent mosaics showing figures wearing theatre masks.

Folégandros★★

Folégandros – Φολέγανδρος

Despite its popularity, Folégandros remains a haven of tranquility. It is typically Cycladic in character, with whitewashed houses, mountain churches, terraces planted with olive trees, and a little fishing port. Lapped by clear blue water, the beaches are particularly fine.

A BIT OF HISTORY

Folégandros was the son of King Minos of Crete but very little is known about the early history of the island other than it came under the influence of Athens during the classical period. It was conquered in the 13C AD by the Venetian Marco Sanudo and remained under the control of Venice until the middle of the 16C. The Ottoman Turks took the island off the Venetians and ruled the island uninterruptedly until challenged by the Greeks in the 19C. In the 20C it became an island of forced exile for political opponents of the military government and the left-wing George Papandreou was one such "guest".

- ▶ **Population:** 676.
- **Michelin Map:** 32sq km/ 13sq mi – Michelin Map 737 K-L 12 – Cyclades – Aegean.
- **Info:** Northern outskirts of Hóra. ✆22860 41158. www.folegandros.com.
- **Location:** Of volcanic origin, this small island is between Melos and Síkinos. Folégandros is linked to Piraeus along two routes.
- **Don't Miss:** Hóra, or a swim at Katergo Beach.
- **Parking:** Hiring a scooter rather than a car makes parking a lot easier on the small roads of this tiny island. No vehicles allowed in Hóra.
- **Timing:** Plan a 3-day visit including a day's boat trip.
- **Kids:** Safe beaches.

GETTING THERE AND AROUND

BY SEA – There are daily ferries from Piraeus *(fast: 4hrs, slow:10–11hrs)* and Santorini plus service from Ios *(5/wk)*, Naxos *(5/wk)*, Paros *(5/wk)*, Melos *(4/wk)*, Sífnos *(4/wk)*, Kýthnos *(3/wk)*, Amorgós *(2/wk)* and Serifos *(2/wk)*.
Buses meet all ferries, and depart from Hóra 1hr before ferry departures. Buses link Hóra Pano Meria, and Hóra Karavostássis; see schedules posted at stops.

KARAVOSTÁSSIS

The island's port Karavostássis ("ferry stop") is clustered around the Church of Ágios Artémios and along a pebble beach bordered by fish restaurants. The best beach is at Várdia to the north, accessible by a long flight of steps *(10min walk)*. To the south there are narrow beaches and it takes about 20 minutes to reach the nearest of these, called Livádi. The island's best beach **Kátergo**★★ can be reached by boat or on foot *(2hr there and back)* via a track behind the campsite at Livádi, south of Karavostássis. A note of warning though: the track is hard-going in places. Another delightful excursion is a **boat trip around the island**★★ along the rocky coastline, passing below Hóra before making its way around the bays. *(Book at the tourist office. €20; including lunch €25.)*

View of Karavostássis

© Vassilis/Dreamstime.com

HÓRA★★★

▶ *3.3km/2mi northwest of Karavostássis.*
The island's capital is on a fine **site**★★ at the top of a cliff some 200m/650ft above the sea. Built around its citadel, it is a charming maze of alleys and squares. Given that vehicular traffic is not allowed in the centre of the village, the setting is ideal for an al fresco meal (there is a surprisingly good range of places to choose from) or just a drink. From the end of Platía Pounda there is an impressive **view**★★ of the cliff.

Built in 1204, the **kástro**★★ (citadel) has houses making up its ramparts, transforming the citadel into a pleasant residential quarter that is often deserted. The Church of **Panagía Pantánassa** (17C) is built on the cliff edge and can be reached by a path from the village square where buses arrive; fine icons.
The rest of the town is composed of paved alleys centred around shaded squares, each with a little white church. The oldest is Platía Piátsa. Bar and restaurant tables are laid out all over the place, creating a festive feel.
On the outskirts of town, lie three attractive chapels: Ágios Vassílios, Ágios Sávas (west of town) and Panagía Plakianí (to the northwest, beyond the citadel wall).

Church of Panagía Kímissis★★

1hr there and back. Reached by a path which zigzags up from Hóra, this large church is built at the top of a cliff. From the top of the path, the views down over Hóra, the cultivated terraces, the coast and its cliffs are remarkable.

Monastery of Ágios Nikólaos

1hr south of Hóra, not far from the heliport.
This beautiful, partially ruined monastery in an austere landscape will appeal to lovers of solitude.

THE NORTH OF THE ISLAND★★

The extraordinary village of Áno Meriá is a scattered settlement of hamlets and outlying farms within a magnificent, desolate landscape. There is a small folk museum (*daily 8am–5pm)*

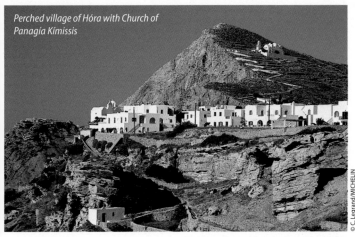

Perched village of Hóra with Church of Panagía Kímissis

© C. Legrand/MICHELIN

in one of the farms as you approach the village and this provides some information on the history of the locality and its people. From the village there are various winding footpaths that lead to sheltered coves, the most accommodating of which is **Angáli** due to the tavernas that open up here in the summer months. Rooms are also available at scattered intervals, should you choose to stay another day. Before the village of **Merovígli** (the last settlement on this road) is the Church of Ágios Ioánnis Pródromos, one of the island's oldest. Beyond the village, a track (20min) leads to the Church of Ágios Pandeleímon, sitting in a beautiful landscape. Accessible by tracks from Merovígli, the best beaches are **Livadáki, Ambéli**, surrounded by greenery and **Serfiótiko** with clear views of the seabed.

ADDRESSES

STAY

Do not arrive on Folégandros in the month of August without having your accommodation arranged in advance; there is limited availability.

Cástro – Hóra. ☎22860 41230. www.hotel-castro.com. 12 rooms. Impressive vaulted ceilings on the ground floor, roof terrace with sea views and nice rooms. Breakfast €11.

Ampelos – Hóra. ☎22860 41544. www.ampelosresort.com. 10 rooms. Traditional decor and style in this handsome structure. Classes offered in watercolour painting and cooking.

Kallisti – Hóra. ☎22860 41555. www.kallisti.net.gr. 14 rooms. Lovely Cycladic building; pool. Breakfast €8.

EAT

Local specialities – Mátsata (fresh pasta served in a rabbit and tomato sauce), liókafta (dried fish) and kalasouna (pastry with cheese).

Chic – Hóra. Spinach balls, mezes, carrot soup... delicious.

Kritikós – Hóra, Platía Piátsa. Specialising in grilled local meats.

Mimis – Pano Meriá, near the museum. Excellent mátsata and meats.

Pounta – Hóra. Excellent local specialities and breakfasts.

TAKING A BREAK

Astárti for Greek music, **Patitiri** for ambiance or, for a more lively atmosphere, the **Greco Bar** with rock music.

EVENTS AND FESTIVALS

Mid July, excellent world music **concerts** at Hóra. www.mediadellarte.gr.

Ios★★

Ios – Ίος

This little island has wild coves, rocky peaks and isolated coasts, a youthful charm and an excellent nightlife which attracts the young from all over Europe. It is the top island destination for Greek teenagers and students whose coming-of-age ritual will include at least one trip to the island.

PORT

The sheltered port, the best natural harbour in the Cyclades, lies in the rocky **Bay of Gialós**★. The town has many hotels, shops and restaurants; the adjacent Gialós Beach is fringed by tamarisks.

HÓRA (IOS)★

Standing on a hill, 2km/1.5mi from the port, the island's capital is a beautiful town with white houses, churches with blue cupolas, narrow alleys, windmills and chapels perched near the summit. The **Archaeological Museum** (open *Tue–Sun 9am–1pm;* €2) displays Cycladic artefacts discovered near Stavros; interesting bas-reliefs.

Near the windmills, a walkway offers fine views over the town. The lower town becomes very lively later in the evening, with crowds of clubbers here to drink and dance the night away.

BEACHES★★

There are excellent beaches on the island, many of which are rather inaccessible.

South of Hóra – Against an impressive backdrop of barren mountains, **Milopótas**★ beach (part nudist) is a long ribbon of fine sand facing due west, acting as a magnet to the young.

2km/1.25mi east of Páno Kámbos.

The beach at **Agía Theódoti** is dominated by a 16C church and the ruins of the Byzantine fortress of Paleókastro. It is accessed by a path to the right of the beach *(2km/1.25mi)*.

▶ **Population:** 1 838.
Michelin Map: 109sq km – Michelin Map – Cyclades – Aegean.
Info: 22860 91343. www.iosgreece.com.
Location: Ios is one of the islands furthest from Piraeus on the line to Santorini along with which it is normally visited.
Kids: Not quite the island for a family with kids under 16.

GETTING THERE

BY SEA – Mainland **ferry** service to Piraeus *(3–9hrs, depending on the vessel)*. Daily ferry service to Naxos, Paros, Santorini, and Mýkonos. Ferries also run to Folégandros *(5/wk)*, Sýros *(4/wk)*, Melos *(4/wk)*, Sífnos *(2/wk)* and Serifos *(2/wk)*.
BY BUS – Frequent daily service between Milopotas, the port and Koumbara.
Vehicle Rental – Several agencies; try **Trohokinisi** *(Hóra)*, *www.trohokinisi. com or* **Vangelis** *(Hóra)* for mopeds.

Turtles visit the beach at Psáthi *(east coast)* to lay their eggs.

Southern end of the island – Bordered by bars and tavernas, the beaches at **Manganári**★★ are situated in a calm, deep bay where many yachts drop anchor.

WALK

It is worth trekking for the various deserted coves to the north of the port. Halfway up the road to Hóra, there is a left turn that leads to **Vigla** and down to the beaches of **Koumbára, Loretzína** and **Diamoúdia**.

Near Vigla, the path ends at **Homer's Grave**, the final resting place of the poet according to local folklore.

Kea★

Kéa – Kéa

Kéa has many villas and hotels on its west coast. The mountainous and fertile island is popular with Athenian families and yachting types. Remains of numerous settlements bear witness to Kéa's long history.

A BIT OF HISTORY

This small island was the birthplace of a number of noted personages from the classical era. The most famous are the poet Simonides (556–468 BC) and his nephew Bacchylides. Legend has it that the islanders took hemlock when they reached the age of 70 – possibly something that happened when food was scarce.

BEACHES

Popular Gialiskári Beach is the best near the port of Korissiá. If you want some rest, 7km/4mi to the south is the attractive and little frequented beach at Xíla Bay. To the northeast is Kéfala Beach, at the far end of the Kóka Peninsula. The long beach at Otziás Bay, 11km/4mi from the capital, is the best for tourist facilities and water sports. The island's best beaches, usually deserted and accessible by small paths, are to be found on the east coast: Spathí, Kalidoníhi, Psili Ámos, Sikamniá, Psathí and Orkós are all fine beaches to the north; the south has Ágios Fílipos, Órmos Póles (near the ruins at Karthéa) and Kaliskiá. The best on the west coast are Písses (near the village of the same name), Koúndouros (next to one of the island's biggest resorts), Ágios Emilianós and Liparós.

THE NORTHWEST OF THE ISLAND★

The island's main port is Korissía (Livádi) situated at the foot of a hill; at the top lie the ruins of a Temple of Apollo, all that remains of the classical city. The walk is worth it for the fine **view**★ over the bay and the port.

North of Korissía, the promontory of **Agía Iríni** (○*open Tue, Thu–Sun, 9am–*

▶ **Population:** 2, 417.
◔ **Michelin Map:** 131sq km/ 52sq mi – Michelin Map 737 J 10 – Cyclades – Aegean.
◪ **Info:** Opposite the landing stage. ✆22880 21500. www.kea.gr.
▷ **Location:** This is the westernmost of the Cyclades and the closest to Attica.
🅿 **Parking:** Park your wheels anywhere.
◉ **Don't Miss:** An evening stroll through Hóra.
◷ **Timing:** A day or two… or more, to fully explore.

GETTING THERE AND GETTING AROUND

BY SEA – Ferry service *(daily in summer, 1hr 15min)* from Lávrio in Attica. From there, service to Kýthnos *(3/wk)*, Sýros *(3/wk)*, Ándros *(1/wk)* and Paros *(1/wk)*.
Buses link Hóra, Korissia, Vourkari and Otzias.
Mopeds are available to rent in Hóra and Korissia.

2pm; ﹩€2; ✆22880 21264), has been inhabited from the late Neolithic period until around 1500 BC; the maze of ruins makes an interesting visit.

HÓRA (IOULÍDA)★★★

Kéa's capital is one of the most beautiful towns in Greece. Along its winding alleyways, houses with tiled roofs sit cheek by jowl with typically Cycladic cuboid buildings.

From the Rokoménos Fountain, climb up to the pleasant square and continue through the vaulted passageway. Odós Harálambos leads to the site of the ancient acropolis, where the Venetians built their **kástro** (13C). Fine **views**★.

In the lower town, the main square, dominated by the **Town Hall** (1902),

The Lion's Enigmatic Smile

According to the myth, Kéa, then called Hydroussa, with its springs and oak woods, was inhabited by nymphs who bathed in its waters. One day a lion came down from the mountains, terrifying the nymphs, who fled to Euboea. A drought occurred, and the people asked Aristéos, son of Apollo and the nymph Cyrene, to help them. He erected a temple dedicated to Zeus, who sent a cooling breeze and rain to save the island from catastrophe. After that Keos, the son of Apollo and the Nymph Rodóessa settled on the island and gave it its current name. The inhabitants carved an image of the lion out of the rock on the top of a hill; this strange sculpture (6C BC) has a strikingly enigmatic smile.

has shops and restaurants. Above the main street, Odós Ieromnímonos has some fine houses.

The small **Archaeological Museum** (⏱ *open Tue–Sun 8.30am–3pm;* ⊗ *no charge;* ☎ *228810 220 79; temporarily closed*) displays numerous objects from the temple of Athena at Karthéa.

Near Ágios Spirídon is the famous **Lion of Kéa** *(1.5km/1mi northeast of the town centre),* a monumental hillside sculpture.

Around Hóra

Walking for 1hr southeast from Hóra towards Kastaniés and Orkós, you can reach the springs of Messariá. Among the ruins of the nearby **Monastery of Panagía Episcopí** is a fine white church. From Mount Profítis Ilías (560m/1 835ft), the **view**★ is breathtaking. Northeast of Hóra, the Chapel of Ágios Dimítrios marks the beginning of the Spathí Valley★ which runs to the sea. About 2 hours *(8km/5mi)* down the coast from Hóra, the **Monastery of Panagía Kastrianí** is a veritable eyrie; there is a splendid view over the island and the Aegean. The original church, built in 1708 on the site of the miraculous discovery of an icon of the Virgin by shepherds, is enclosed within a later structure.

On the outskirts of Hóra *(6km/4mi to the southwest)* is the **Monastery of Agía Marína**★. The building incorporates a crumbling Hellenistic tower. From here a road leads to the resort of **Pisses** on the west coast and its fine sandy beach makes the journey there a worthwhile one. There are pleasant tavernas open in the summer and rooms to rent as well.

The road struggles on to **Koúndouros**, a quiet bay but its coves cannot match the beach at Pisses.

Also on the outskirts of Hóra are the partially submerged classical remains **Karthéa**★, 19km/12mi to the southeast and accessible by a 2km/1.25mi path from Stavroudáki.

ADDRESSES

🏠 STAY

⊜⊜ **Ágios Geórgios** – *Koúndourous.* ☎ *22880 31277. 20 rooms. Open Apr–Oct.* Pleasant rooms with terrace in a typical Cycladic-style building. The restaurant has a fine view over the bay and a good reputation for its cuisine.

⊜ **Korali** – *Korissía, on the Vourkári road.* ☎ *22880 21268. 8 studios.* Pleasant, well-equipped studios in a large house. Warm welcome; no breakfast.

🍽 EAT

⊜ **Cyclades** – *Otziás, right-hand side on entering the village.* The best place for home cooking.

⊜ **Strofí tou Mími** – *Vourkári, beginning of the Otziás road.* Fish and grilled dishes served in this attractive building with terrace on the waterfront.

🛍 SHOPPING

Kéa's **honey**, subtly flavoured with thyme, is an ingredient in **pastéli** (nougat with sesame seeds). The island also produces large quantities of almonds. Also worth a try is **mávro**, the wine made here.

Kýthnos

Kíthnos – Κύθνος

Though flat and arid with little habitation, peaceful Kýthnos has a certain charm. Its many beaches are usually deserted (except in August), its coastal paths feature lovely views, and its quiet villages and hot-spring spas offer rest and retreat.

BEACHES
West Coast
5min from the landing stage at Mérihas. By the steps to the left lies Martinákia, the only beach on the island that gets crowded in the summer. A better option is Episkopí, a west-facing beach fringed by tamarisk trees *(2km/1.25mi north of Mérihas).* The finest beaches of the island are, however, the stunning **Fikiáda**★ and the almost always empty **Kolóna**★ accessed via a 30-min walk on a footpath north from Apókrissi or by boat from Mérihas during the summer.

Southeast Coast
Beaches along the coastline here are little visited. From south to north: **Ágios Dimítrios** *(southern tip of the island),* **Skílou** *(4km/2.5mi south of Driopída, access by road),* **Megáli Ámos** and **Antonídes** *(near Panagía Kanála),* Zogáki, Kourí and Náoussa *(north of Léfkes)* and Ágios Stéfanos *(east of Hóra, access by a stony path).*

▶ **Population:** 1,608.
Michelin Map: 99sq km/ 38sq mi – Michelin Map 737 J-K 11 – Cyclades – Aegean.
Info: On the landing stage at the port.
Location: Close to Athens, the usual route here is by ferry from Mílos.
Parking: A vehicle is not necessary.
Don't Miss: The quaint village of Driopída.
Timing: A couple of days could easily pass by if you want to just relax and take walks.
Kids: Lots of lovely beaches.

MÉRIHAS
Kýthnos' main port is on the west coast. Only until recently it was still the abode of fishermen, but the subsequent tourist upsurge has not affected its picturesque appeal. Amphitheatrically built in a semicircle, the quaint old harbour manages to be both busy and serene even in high season.

Peaceful island of Kýthnos
© Antonis Nikolopoulos/Greek National Tourism Organisation

GETTING THERE AND GETTING AROUND

BY SEA – Mainland **ferry** service to Piraeus *(daily, 1–3hrs)* and Lávrio *(6/wk, 2hrs)*. Also links to Serifos *(daily)*, Sífnos *(daily)*, Mílos *(daily)*, Kéa *(3/wk)*, Folégandros *(3/wk)* and Santorini *(2/wk)*. **Buses** meet all ferries. Service to Hóra and Loutrá nearly every day.

Scooters and **car rentals** are available at **Adonis** ℘22810 32 104.

Around Mérihas

🔼 From Apókrissi, north of Mérihas at the far end of the bay, a path leads to the extensive remains of the island's former capital of Vriókastro *(allow 30min heading south)*. Three cisterns, the foundations of a tower and the remains of a wall are visible. The partially submerged site is also accessible by boat from Mérihas. Small houses with tiled roofs mark the island's most beautiful village of **Driópida★**, 5km/3mi east of Mérihas. The main church, **Agía Ánna**, has a blue dome and twin bell-towers.

The adjacent **Byzantine Museum** (🕐*no fixed opening hours; key available from the parish priest)* houses some of the finest icons on the island. **Views★** of the island extend from the terrace of Ágios Nektários. Continuing for another 2km/1.25mi from Driópida, you reach the very agreeable village of **Léfkes,** which comprises barely 30 houses next to a tamarisk-fringed beach (bring your own water). Further out from Driópida (7km/4mi) lies the village of **Panagía Kanála** named for its 19C basilica which stands among nearby pine trees.

A pilgrimage takes place here every 15 August. Underneath the church, there is the fine sandy beach of Megáli Ámos.

HÓRA★

▶ *7.5km/5mi northeast of Mérihas.*
Built atop a hill, Hóra is a charming town with quiet alleys and fine churches. The Church of **Ágios Sávas** (1613) was designed to accommodate both Orthodox *(to the right)* and Catholic *(to the left)* traditions.

AROUND HÓRA
Eolikó

▶ *2km/1.25mi east of Hóra.*
A wind farm and solar-energy park here allow Kýthnos to generate much of its electricity. South of Eolikó are two immaculately white religious foundations, the Church of **Panagía tou Níkous** (Our Lady of Victories) and the **Monastery of Pródromou** with a fine 16C wooden iconostasis.

Loutrá

▶ *4.5km/3mi north of Hóra.*
Loutrá is what passes as the principal spa resort on Kýthnos designed in the 19C by the German **Ernest Tschiller**.
It has two hot springs (38°C/100°F and 52°C/126°F respectively), rich in iron and mineral salts, which are supposed to help treat eczema and rheumatism. To the north are the small beaches of **Maroulás, Kavourohéri** (popular with naturists) and **Potámia**, all within easy walking distance.

🔼 A 2hr walk on a mule track *(there and back)* from Loutrá lie the ruins of Kefalókastro, the original capital of the island destroyed by the Turks in 1600. You can see the remains of the defensive wall, several houses and two churches. The **view★** of the sea and the coast is exceptional.

ADDRESSES

🏠STAY

🛏 **Panorama** – *Mérihas, up the steps behind the port.* ℘22810 32184. *7 studios.* Overlooking the whole bay, this white building in the Cycladic style has rooms opening onto a terrace shaded by a blue wooden pergola. The studios have the bare necessities, but at a competitive price.

🛏🛏🛏 **Meltemi** – *Loutrá* ℘22810 321271. www.meltemihotel-kythnos.gr. 100m/110yds from Loutra Beach, 27 rooms and apartments, all mod cons.

🛏🛏 **Porto Klaras** – *Loutrá, near the pier.* ℘22810 31 276. www.porto-klaras.gr. *11 rooms.* This pleasant two-storey construction in the Cycladic style is the smartest place in town. Fine views from the balconies.

¶/EAT

🦪 **Kantouni** – *Mérihas, other end of the beach from the landing stage*. Dine on the terrace or on the beach; grilled meat specialists, including *kontosoúvli* (kebabs), *kokorétsi* (tripe), *paidhakia* (lamb chops), all accompanied by *sfougáto* (little balls of cheese).

🦪 **Ostria** – *Mérihas, near the landing stage*. The varied menu offers grilled meats and home cooking. Don't miss the *astakomakaronádha* (spaghetti with lobster), a house speciality.

🏃SPORTS AND LEISURE

Undersea adventures await off the coast of Loutrá. For information and equipment rental, **AquaTeam** (*℘22810 322 42, www.aquakythnos.gr.*)

🎭EVENTS AND FESTIVALS

An enormous meal, music and dancing usually make up the island's village festivals. The biggest diary dates are Panagía Kanála (15 August and 8 September), Panagía tou Níkous (15 August), Panagía tis Flambouriás (24 August), Agía Triáda at Hóra (end of June) and Agiou Ilía (in the mountains, 20 July).

Mílos★

Mílos – Μήλος

The world-renowned Venus de Milo statue was discovered on Melos in the 19C. The island's picturesque landscape features sea caves, rocky outcrops, cliffs of extraordinary colours, ribbons of sand, boulder-strewn mountainsides, green valleys and bright, white villages.

A BIT OF HISTORY

The Mílos Aphrodite – Widely known as the Venus de Milo, this world-famous statue of Aphrodite, goddess of love, dates from the 2C BC and is considered one of the finest examples of Classical art. The broken sections of the statue were discovered on Mílos near an ancient theatre around 1820 by a peasant farmer, who hid the pieces for a time. Eventually they were confiscated by Turkish officials, who planned to present the statue to the Turkish governor of the Cyclades. Before they could deliver it the French ambassador to Turkey, alerted to the statue's artistic significance, arranged to purchase it. It was quickly shipped to France, presented to Louis XVIII and put on display in the Louvre.

ADÁMAS

On the Bay of Mílos, Adámas is the island's main port and the ferry terminal. It was founded in the early 19C by Cretan

▸ **Population:** 4, 771.
🏅 **Michelin Map:** 151sq km/ 60sq mi – Michelin Map 737 J-K 12 –Cyclades – Aegean.
🏠 **Info:** In the port. ℘22870 22445.
◗ **Location:** Mílos is the most southwesterly of the Cyclades.
🏞 **Don't Miss:** The natural phenomenon at Sarakinikó or the boat trip around the island.
🕐 **Timing:** At least 1 night's stay.
👫 **Kids:** A boat trip around the island.

refugees. Perched on top of the hill, the Cathedral of **Ágios Harálambos** offers good views of the surrounding area.

A **boat trip**★★ (🕐*departures from Adámas 9am, 1 day with stops and lunch break; ⊙approx. €25*) shows the island's amazing geological phenomena and delightful seascapes. The volcanic islet of **Glaoríssa**★★ has imposing basalt cliffs. In the **Sikía Cave**★★ the light shining through the collapsed vault turns the water lovely colours. To the southeast are the tall white cliffs of **Kléftiko**★★★.

GETTING AROUND

BY BOAT – Several **ferries** a day from Piraeus (3–7hrs); also fast service (5hrs, daily Jul–Aug, weekends off season). Lane Lines offers service to Piraeus (2/wk, 5hrs), www.lane.gr. Also daily links to **Sífnos, Serifos, and Kýthnos**; and links to Santorini (4/wk), Folégandros (4/wk), los (4/wk), Paros (3/wk), Naxos (1/wk), Síros (1/wk) and Lavrio (1/wk).

BY AIR – Olympic Airways, Adámas, ℘ 22870 22380. At least 1 flight/day to Athens.

Agía Tríada★

Open daily except Mon, 9.15am–1.15pm and 6.15–10.15pm. No charge. The church (13C) has an **Ecclesiastical Museum** with a fine icon of John the Baptist (1639), and an ornate iconostasis. Interesting temporary exhibitions of sacred art.

PLÁKA★★

4.5km/3mi northwest of Adámas. The island's capital is a charming hill town of narrow alleys winding among bright white houses bedecked with flowers. From the **kástro**★★ at the top of the hill, the views over the bay and the hillside villages are impressive. On the way down, note the attractive Church of **Ipapánti**★ (Thalassitra), which has some fine 17C icons.

Archaeological Museum

Open Tue–Sun, 8.30am–2.30pm. €3. ℘ 22870 21 620. This small museum has a fine replica of the famous Venus de Milo (the original, found by a farmer on the Island, is now in the Louvre in Paris). It also has various other archaeological findings from the Neolithic period onwards.

Museum of Folk Art

Open Tue–Sat, 10am–noon, 6pm–9pm; Sun 10am–2pm. €2. ℘ 22870 212 92. In a traditional two-storey house in the town, this museum illustrates the life of the islanders from the 17C. It displays historical local costumes, house utensils, embroidery and photographs.

AROUND PLÁKA

Klíma, the ancient capital of Mílos, (2km/1.25mi south of Pláka) is now a fishing village with colourful boathouses (sirmata) between the cliff face and the water's edge. The remains of the ancient city include a **Roman theatre**, its marble seating terraces looking out to sea. (Open Tue–Sun 8.30am–3pm; no charge.)

The little harbour of **Mantrákia**, (northeast of Pláka), also has colourful sirmata boathouses. Dwellings carved out of the rock are still used as holiday homes in summer. In the east side of Pláka, **Sarakinikó**★★ is an impressive natural site; the volcanic tufa is bright

Sarakinikó coastline

White cliffs of Kléftiko

© Marco Simoni/Robert Harding

white, sculpted by the winds into cones, domes and terraces by the sea. Swimming is possible in calm weather.
Further east, the approach to the village of **Mítakas** is one of the most memorable of the island with painted *sirmata* dug into the rock. Beyond that, at the hamlet of **Ágios Konstandínos**, you'll see *"pozzolana"* (fine volcanic ash) stacks and solidified lava flows.

BEACHES

Mílos Bay forms the pivot around which the island is formed. A road along the bay provides access to a number of sheltered beaches. The long beach at **Achivadolimni** is good for water sports. Northwest of Pláka at the mouth of the bay is **Plathiená**, one of the island's most attractive beaches.
On the north coast, near the village of Kápros is the delightful Bay of **Papafrága**★★, a narrow inlet divided from the open sea by a stone arch *(access by steps carved into the rock)*. Continuing on the road east, beyond Cape Pelekoúda and to the east of the fishing village of **Pollónia** are some fine sandy beaches, such as **Písso Thálassa**.
On the south coast is the huge pebble beach of **Paliohóri**★ arguably the finest on the island. It is surrounded by multi-coloured cliffs stretched out in a wide bay which also contains the beaches of **Spathí** and **Firlígos** to the east. To

the west of Paliohóri is **Agía Kyriakí**★, a beautiful beach of volcanic origin and further out, the more remote beaches of **Gérontas**★ and **Kléftiko**★★★ which are reached by boat. Kléftiko is the more dramatic, lying below imposing white cliffs, called "marine meteors" by the locals.

EXCURSIONS
Filakopí
▶ *North coast.*
🕐 *Open Tue–Sun 8.30am–3pm.*
Excavations in this cove have uncovered traces of three superimposed cities dating from the Bronze Age, the Minoan period (c.1600 BC) and the Mycenaean period (1200 BC). Their stone houses are the first indications of urbanism in the Cyclades and were decorated with frescoes (now in the National Archaeological Museum in Athens).

Kímolos
Kímolos is served by ferries from Piraeus and neighbouring islands; there is a link with the village of Pollonia on Mílos 14km/19mi from Hóra five times a day in high season.
Separated from Mílos by a narrow channel formed by an earthquake, this is one of the smallest islands in the Cyclades; it is also the hilliest. Kímolos is renowned for its volcanic rocks of extraordinary colours, its jagged coastline and its

white beaches. The ferries arrive at the fishing port of Psáthi, which has an easily accessible beach nearby.

The capital, surprisingly called Chorió, not Hóra as in the rest of the Cyclades, is 2km/1.25mi north of Psáthi.

The fortifications and three gateways of the castle (Kástro) (16C) have been preserved in excellent condition. The Archaeological Museum at the entrance to the village displays items from the Cycladic period. (◷*Open Tue–Sat 8am–12.30pm; ⊜€3*).

The village of Prassá *(5km/3mi northeast of Hóra)* is memorable not only for its beach, but also for the Church of Evangelístria dating from1608.

🅺 Facing the village of Elliniká *(to the southwest of Hóra, 2hrs on foot there and back)*, the small island is notable for the remains of a submerged city dating from around 1000 BC.

Beaches★

The finest are at **Aliki**, **Bonatsa**, **Klima**, **Limni** and **Prassá**. All may be reached by boat from Psáthi. Ask the fishermen in the port; some will be able to show you magnificent sea caves, take you to the sanctuaries of the rare Mediterranean monk seals and leave you to swim in the most isolated beaches.

ADDRESSES

🏠STAY

⊜⊜ **Apollon** – *Polónia, in the residential district.* ☎22870 41347. www.apollon-milos.com. 11 rooms. Clean and comfortable rooms, a family atmosphere and an attractive setting by the water's edge. Breakfast €6.

⊜⊜ **Delfini** – *Adámas, west of the landing stage and up from Lagáda Beach.* ☎22870 22001. www.delfini-milos.com. *22 rooms*. This peaceful hotel is near the beach. Clean rooms; breakfast served on the terrace.

⊜⊜⊜ **Villa Hélios** – *Adámas, above the port.* ☎22870 22258. 15 rooms. Quiet, charming, with a lovely terrace.

⊜⊜⊜ **Portiani** – *Adámas, at the port.* ☎22870 22940. www.hotelportiani.gr. *23 rooms*. Large hotel with views over the bay. Comfortable rooms, lavish breakfast.

🍴EAT

⊜ **Archondoula** – *Pláka, main passage of the upper town.* Attractive tavern in a historic building.

⊜ **Armenaki** – *Polónia, on the main street upon entering the village.* ☎2287041061. www.armenaki.gr. Popular for its delicious lobster pasta. Delicious cold dishes as well; attentive service.

⊜ **Barco** – *Adámas, main street.* Tasty, fresh dishes; try the *pitaraki*.

⊜ **Sirocco** – *Paleochori, on the beach.* The house speciality: fish cooked on the beach.

🚋TAKING A BREAK

Utopia – *Pláka, in the centre of the village.* ☎22870 23678. The ideal spot from which to watch the sun go down while having a drink.

🤸SPORTS AND LEISURE

Scuba diving – *Diving Centre Mílos, Polónia.* ☎22870 41296. www.milos diving.gr. Equipment hire, organised dives and disabled facilities.

Sea kayaking – *Brau Kat.* ☎2280 23597. www.seakayakgreece.com. The ideal way to discover Mílos' rock formations.

Mýkonos★★

Míkonos – Μύκονος

Since the 1960s, the granite island of Mýkonos has been attracting the trendy and the hip for its superb beaches and whirlwind of a nightlife. Although the celebrity count during the summer is high, in autumn and spring the island regains its traditional appeal.

A BIT OF HISTORY

In Greek mythology Mýkonos was the place where the Olympian Gods battled with the Giants for power. According to some, the island was named in honour of Apollo's grandson Mýkonos. More prosaically it was the Ionians, arriving in the early part of the 11C BC, who built the first settlements on the island but Mýkonos remained unimportant, second to Delos during the classical era. Later in history the island came under Roman rule, followed by the Byzantines who fortified the island against Arab incursions in the 7C. Byzantine rule continued until the 12C and then Venetians governed it until the early 18C. The Venetians built warehouses where the merchants of Venice and Marseilles came for supplies. Later it was a haven for pirates.

As early as the 1930s artists and a smattering of the wealthy began visiting the island. The renown of Mýkonos' gorgeous beaches has now grown so much that Hóra, once a fishing village, has become a destination for the Greek and international jet-set and the island as a whole has developed into the Saint Tropez of the Greek world. It is currently known as a gay resort, but trends change quickly here and Mýkonos is not easily categorised. Nevertheless, its reputation as a pleasure island remains strong.

BEACHES★★

Most of the beaches are accessible by boat from Hóra's fishing port (departing in the morning and returning in the evening). There are two beaches close enough to Hóra to be reached on foot or by bus. The nearest one is **Tourlos**

▶ **Population:** 9, 306.
⏱ **Michelin Map:** 86sq km/ 34sq mi – Michelin Map 737 L-M 10-11 – Cyclades – Aegean.
ℹ **Info:** At the old ferry port. www.mykonos.gr, www. mykonosgreece.com and www.mykonos-web.com.
▶ **Location:** Hóra, the main city, is the heart of the island. Seaside resorts dot the southern coast, while the northern coast is less developed. There are two ports: the old port at Hóra and the new port 2–3km/1.5–2mi away at Tourlos. In summer, organise a transfer to your hotel, as you are likely to have a long wait for a taxi.
🅿 **Parking:** At the height of the season, parking is a challenge.
👁 **Don't Miss:** Sunset from "Little Venice".
🕐 **Timing:** You'll need 3 days to enjoy Mýkonos.

GETTING THERE AND AROUND

BY AIR – Olympic and Aegean Airways fly to Mýkonos and the frequency is seasonal. Check their timetables at *www.olympicair.com* and *www.aegeanair.com*.

BY SEA – Several daily **ferries** from Piraeus *(3hrs 20min–6hrs 40min)*, Rafína *(2hrs 10min–5hrs 40min)* and Lavrio *(3hrs)*; Also daily links to Ándros, Tenos, Sýros, Paros, Naxos, Ios and Delos.

BY CAR – Rentals available near the port from;
Avis ℘22890 22960
Europcar ℘22890 27111
Hertz ℘22890 23791
Kosmos ℘22890 24013

How Many Chapels Does Mýkonos Have?

For centuries chapels have been built on the island. Why? In stormy weather, many sailors (and pirates too) vowed to erect one if God returned them safely home. Given the Aegean's volatile weather patterns, there are many chapels on Mýkonos. Indeed, they are almost as numerous as the island's surviving historic houses.

but far more attractive is **Ágios Stéfanos** and it has better facilities by way of tavernas and bars. The more popular beaches are horrendously crowded in July and August and you will have to arrive early to be sure of finding a nice spot to park your towel or rent a lounger under a straw umbrella.

In an enclosed rocky bay in the south of the island you will find **Platís Gialós**, the island's main resort. The beach, along with the nearby **Psaroú** is one of the longest on the island and from it small boats run regular day trips to

neighbouring bathing spots. Buses to and from Hóra operate until very late at night. Further out, **Paránga**★ is made up of two beaches separated by a minor headland and, relatively speaking, is one of the quieter places on the island. **Paradise**★, a nudist beach, is bordered by a campsite and has a loud open-air disco. Super Paradise *(accessible by boat from Paradise, Platís Gialós o Psaroú)*, long popular with naturists and gay tourists, has big speakers blasting out techno music, making it the island's liveliest beach.

Agrari★ may be less busy, but the rocky hills behind are rapidly disappearing under development. A little way east of Agrari is **Eliá**★, one of the longest and most pleasant beaches on Mýkonos which, from late August onwards, takes on a pronounced gay identity.

Further to the east, the three pleasant beaches of Agía Ana, **Kalafáti**★ and **Liá**★ are reached via walking tracks from Ano Merá. The beach at Agía Ána is shingly and visitors tend to prefer Kalafáti because of its white sand. The best of the three, though, is Liá as it rarely becomes too crowded.

HÓRA★★★

The main street, Matoyanni, runs perpendicular to the harbour and is packed with shops, cafés and bars. The other hub of activity is around the central harbour. The best way to discover Hóra is to leave these quarters, however, and meander the alleys, winding past vaulted passageways, chapels, tiny squares and walls topped by hibiscus and bougainvillea.

There are four small museums in the town. The **archaeological museum** (⏱open Tue–Sun 8.30am–3pm; ✍€2) is on the road north into Hóra and contains a modest but interesting collection of pottery and other finds from the Cyclades (7C BC amphorae, statue of Herakles, items from the site on the island of Rínia). There is also the **Aegean Maritime Museum** (⏱open daily 10.30am–1pm, 6.30pm–9pm; ✍€3) with exhibits relating to the seafaring history of the island: ancient anchors, ships' models and even a recreated lighthouse. **Lena's House**, a restored 19C- home, is next to the maritime museum and entrance is free (⏱open Mon–Sat 6pm–9pm; Sun 5–7pm). The

largest of the museums is the **Folklore Museum** (⏱open Mon–Sat 5.30pm–8.30pm; ✍no charge), situated in a large house by the jetty.

From the **Bóni Windmill** (16C) to the east, there is a fine **view★** of the village.

Limáni (Fishing Port)

The terraces of cafés and restaurants line the quayside; it's very lively in the evenings. Nearby is the arcaded 18C town hall, and a little chapel dedicated to St Nicholas, patron saint of navigators. At the beginning of **Odós Andrónikou**, lined with jewellers and souvenir shops, is the Church of Agía Kiriakí, which has some fine icons.

Next comes the **Platía Tría Pigádia**, bordered by arcades.

Head right towards the **Mitrópoli** (cathedral), an imposing edifice and elaborately decorated interior. Behind this is the **Catholic Church**, with a blue cupola.

To the left, the **five windmills★** (Káto Míli) stand in a row on a low hill above the harbour; one of them still works. Head back towards the Catholic Church and the water.

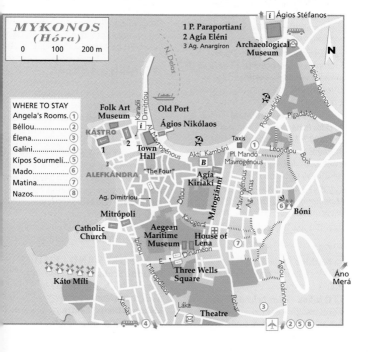

Alefkándra★★★

A number of the houses here have colourful loggias, giving the district the nickname **Little Venice**. Several waterfront cafés offer sunset views and there are numerous bars and discos squeezed into this part of town. There are also a number of art galleries to be found here.

Kástro★

The oldest part of the town began as a fortified stronghold. The much-photographed 16C church of **Panagía Paraportianí**★★ between the sea and the citadel gate is considered the jewel of the Aegean.

MONASTERIES

The 18C monastery of Paleókastro on a hill overlooking Áno Merá *(10km/6.25mi east of Hóra)* has a church of beautifully pure lines. The ruins of the Gyzi mediaeval castle and an ancient wall are nearby.

From here, there are panoramic views of the island and sea.

A further 1km/0.6mi east of Áno Merá is the **Monastery of Panagía Tourlianí**★, dominated by a bell-tower. Founded in 1542 by two monks from Paros, the monastery was renovated in 1767 to the structure you can see today. It has a gilded Baroque style iconostasis built in Florence (1775). In the yard outside, the bell-tower is one of the best examples of the traditional marble architecture of the Cyclades.

Monastery of Ágios Pandeleímon

Finally, on the way to Panormos *(4.5km /2.8mi from Hóra)*, near the charming village of Maráthi, there is the fortified monastery of **Ágios Pandeleímon**. It is a private monastery, rich in treasures, but open to the public only on the Saint's Day (27 July) and on the day before.

ADDRESSES

STAY

⌂⌂⌂⌂ **Karboni** – *Hóra, Odos Matogiani, in the old town.* ☏22890 22217. *40 rooms.* Well-located and comfortable, an ageing yet charming hostelry with balcony rooms.

⌂⌂⌂⌂ **Matina** – *Hóra, 3 Odós Fournákia, centre of town.* ☏22890 26433. *www.hotelmatina-mykonos.com. 19 rooms.* Balconied rooms overlooking a green garden. Breakfast €10.

⌂⌂⌂⌂ **Hotel Carbonaki** – *Hóra, 23 Odós Panachrantou, centre of town.* ☏22890 24124. *www.carbonaki.gr. 21 rooms.* Attractive, comfortable Cycladic-style hotel, with a small but refreshing pool. Breakfast €8.

⌂⌂⌂⌂ **Rochari** – *Hóra, Odós Matogiannis.* ☏22890 23107. *www.rochari.com. 60 rooms.* Views over the sea, the garden and town.

EAT

⌂ **Mathios** – *Tourlos.* Sample a wide variety of appetising Greek dishes while drinking in the bay views.

⌂ **O Níkos** – *Hóra, behind the town hall.* Good traditional Greek cuisine, fresh fish and very reasonable prices.

⌂⌂ **Vangelis** – *Áno Merá, main square.* One of the best tavernas on Mykonos; Freshly prepared authentic dishes such as grilled octopus or skewered meats.

⌂⌂ **Chez Maria** – *Hóra, Odos Kalogera.* Excellent-quality traditional dishes served in a lovely atmosphere (flowered garden in summer).

TAKING A BREAK

In the evenings, Hóra becomes one big nightclub. Start by having a drink in the Little Venice district (**Caprice** for sunsets, or **Kastro Bar** for classical music). After dinner, choose from a multitude of bars, bearing in mind that things don't heat up until midnight.

Montparnasse – *Little Venice.* Trendy mixed straight/gay bar for blues lovers.

Notte – *Near the port.* Greek music.

Astra Club – *Odós Matogiannis.* A 20-plus year-old institution.

Pierro's or **Manto** – both bars popular with gay clientele and open all night.

SPORTS AND LEISURE

Paradise Scuba Diving Club – *Paradise Beach.* ☏22890 265 39. *www.diveadventures.gr.*

Mýkonos Diving Centre – ☏22890 24808. *www.dive.gr.*

Naxos★★

Naxos – Νάξος

The largest of the Cyclades remains relatively unknown despite its magnificent beaches, dramatic coastline, fragrant valleys and imposing mountains. Hóra is renowned for its Ancient citadel; perched atop a hill, its alleys and ramparts have changed little since the Middle Ages.

A BIT OF HISTORY

After killing the Minotaur, Theseus stopped on Naxos with Ariadne, King Minos' daughter, on his way back to Athens. She was spotted there by Dionysus, who appeared in Theseus' dreams and persuaded him to abandon her there so that he could make her his own. Classical Naxos was a powerful ally of Athens, but in the Middle Ages was captured by the Venetians who have left their mark on the island's architecture.

BEACHES

Some of the best beaches of the island are close to the capital. The large beach of **Ágios Geórgios**, set in a shallow bay just 1km/0.6mi south of Hóra, is popular with surfers. From the far end of the beach there are good **views**★ of the capital, dominated by its **Kástro**. Further south, by the airport, is of **Ágios Prokópios**★, the most famous beach of the island. Next to it, **Agía Ánna** with its charming fishing port is a continuation of Ágios Prokópios. Not far away lies the vast expanse of sand at **Pláka**★. There are quieter beaches to the south: **Alikó**, **Pirgáki** and **Agiassós**, its sand a shimmering white.

WALK
Mount Zas

Walkers will enjoy climbing this island giant (1 001m/3 284ft), the highest peak in the Cyclades.
The walk (*1hr*) starts at the chapel of Agía Marína on the Danakos road. Descend along a steeper route to see the Grotto of Zeus. According to mythology, although Zeus was allegedly born on

- **Population:** 12, 089.
- **Michelin Map:** 430sq km/ 168sq mi – Michelin Map 737 L-M 10-11 – Cyclades – Aegean.
- **Info:** At the port, to the right of the landing stage. ℘22890 22490. www.naxosnet.com.
- **Location:** Naxos is a fertile island among its arid neighbours. The capital city Hóra has links to Piraeus and the main islands in the region.
- **Don't Miss:** The Kastro of Hóra; the climb up Mount Zas.
- **Timing:** The island merits a stay of at least 4 days.

GETTING THERE

BY AIR – Daily **Olympic Airways** flights from **Athens**.
BY SEA – Several daily **ferries** link Naxos to Piraeus (*5hrs 30min–7hrs 30min*), Rafina (*3hrs 30min–6hr*) and Lavrio (*2hrs 40min–3hrs*) on the mainland. Ferries run daily from Naxos to Amorgós, Ios, Paros, Mýkonos, Santorini, Sýros and Tinos; also Andros (*2/wk*), Folégandros and Mílos.
Vehicle Rentals – Car and scooter rental agencies near the port.

the island of Crete, he was raised in this cave on Naxos.

HÓRA★★★

Centred around its citadel, the island's capital is built on the site of an ancient city which was at its peak during the Archaic period.
The port **promenade**★, closed to vehicles in the evenings, is bordered by shops, cafés and restaurants. The area is very busy late into the night. In the square of the Orthodox Cathedral, in the Burgos quarter to the northeast of the port lies the unusual **Metrópolis Museum** which is located underground

View of Hóra

and allows visitors to examine the stratified archaeological layers beneath the town (*©open Tue–Sun 8.30am–3pm; no charge; 22850 24151*).

Visible from some distance, and accessed via a paved causeway on the islet of Palátia, the gate of the Temple of Apollo is all that remains of an Archaic Temple of Apollo (6C BC). The gate *(portara)* gives an idea of the monumental scale of the project. From here there are beautiful **views**★.

Kástro★★★

Take the alley to the right of the Old Captain's café.

This Venetian citadel (13C) is one of the finest in the Cyclades. To the right of the entrance gateway is a Venetian metre measurement used as an aid by merchants. Wander about this peaceful quarter to discover its alleys, vaulted passageways, flights of steps and hidden gardens.

To the rear of the Catholic cathedral is the Jesuit College built in the 17C; this houses the **Archaeological Museum**★, renowned for its collection of Cycladic idols (3200–2300 BC) found on Naxos and neighbouring islands. The ceramics collection, including items from the Mycenaean (late second millennium BC) and Geometric (9–8C BC) periods, is remarkable. (*©Open Tue–Sun 8.30am–3pm; €3; 22850 227 25*).

FLERIO KOÚROS★

▶ *12km/7.5mi east of Hóra. Take the Halkí road; turn left after 3km/1.9mi. Continue for 1km/0.6mi; turn right to join the Míli road. Beyond this village, follow the road along the Mélanes Valley (Flerió). A track descends to a stream; leave the car here and walk.*

Here, on a garden wall, lies a giganti kouros statue (6.5m/12ft in length which has remained there unfinishe and abandoned since the 6C BC.

A second, less-known *kouros* also lie near Flerió at the end of a purpose built track. There is also a third one, a 10m/33ft the largest, in the village c Apollona in the north.

🚗 DRIVING TOUR

THE TRAGÉA VALLEY★★

80km/50mi. Allow 1 day.

▶ *Head southeast from Hóra towards Halkí. Turn right 6km/3.5mi after Galanádc*

Belónia

This tower is a good example of th Venetian fortified houses built to repe pirate attacks.

Nearby is the double Church of Ágio Ioannis (13C), accommodating the Cath olic rite (on the left) and the Orthodo rite (on the right).

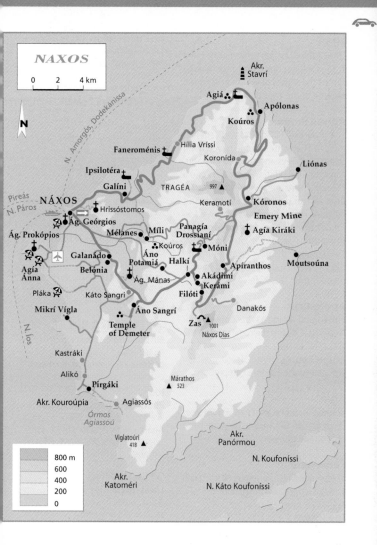

Potamiá Valley★

Continuing towards Halkí the itinerary reaches a valley planted with vineyards and orchards. Below the road is the Church of **Ágios Mánas**, seat of an Orthodox bishopric in Byzantine times *(reached by a path on the left 8km/5mi from Naxos)*. On the other side of the valley lie the ruins of Apáno Kástro, a 13C Venetian fortress.

Temple of Demeter
Head right towards Áno Sangrí.
This simple Doric building in the fields honours the island's protector-goddess.

▷ *Return to Áno Sangrí.*

Halkí
The old capital of the island is at the foot of a mountain; its Byzantine Church of **Panagía Protothrónos** dates from the 9C–12C and is decorated with frescoes. The **Barozzi Tower** has a marble doorway adorned with a coat of arms.

▷ *Turn left just before Akádimi.*

Panagía Drossianí
The simple church (9C) of this fine monastery has some impressive frescoes.

Filóti

One of the principal settlements in the Tragéa Valley; the road to the village climbs the slopes of Mount Zeus; good **views**★ of the west of the island.

Apíranthos★★

This mountain village has two Venetian towers. The white-marble paved main street has alleys and covered passage-ways running off it, watchtowers and a church. There are several small muse-ums (Natural History, Geology and Folklore; ⏱*opening hours vary;* ⊛*€1.50 for all three)*. The **Archaeological Museum** (⏱*open Tue–Sun 8am–2pm;* ⊛*no charge)* displays items found on the island, including engraved marble plaques from the 3C BC.

Apólonas★

This fishing village has become a popular resort. Close to the coast road on the way back to Hóra is an immense 7C BC marble **kouros** (10m/33ft long), which was abandoned before completion.

Agía

Below the ruined Venetian watchtower is an Orthodox monastery nestling among the greenery.

Faneroménis

This fortified 17C monastery has a chapel with an iconostasis and a library.

Ipsilotéra

Another fortified 17C monastery with loopholes, machicolations and crenelles.

ADDRESSES

⌂STAY

⊜ **Ánixis** – *Hóra, north of the kástro.* ℘*22850 26475, www.hotel-anixis.gr. 19 rooms*. A bright, charming hotel with a flowery garden terrace. Breakfast €5.

⊜ **Hotel Elizabeth** – *Ágios Georgios, along a lane parall to the beach.* ℘*22850 23505. www.hotel-elizabeth. com. 9 rooms, 3 studios*. Clean, quiet rooms with balconies; near the beach. Breakfast €4.

⊜⊜ **Hotel Spiros** – *Ágios Georgios, 15min walk from the port.* ℘*22850 24854. www.hotelspiros.com. 40 studios*. Modern, quiet, comfortable and well-run; rooms with balcony or terrace.

⊜⊜⊜ **Chateau Zevgoli** – *Hóra, foot of the kástro (follow signs).* ℘*22850 26123. www.apollonhotel-naxos.gr. 19 rooms*. Each room is unique; tester bed in no. 8, romantic balcony with no. 12 and harbour view from no. 10.

⊖/EAT

⊜ **Gorgóna** – *Agía Ánna, on the beach.* A large caféteria; place your order at the counter. Very popular with the locals.

⊜ **To Iriniss** – *Hóra, at the harbour.* Good traditional Greek cuisine; try the feta-stuffed peppers.

⊜ **Metaxy Mas** – *Hóra, in the kastro.* A tiny, smoky *ouzerie* serving tasty *mezes* and excellent *tarama*.

⋐TAKING A BREAK

Elli bar – *Hóra, street to the left of the tourist office.* Live *rembétiko* concerts.
Lefteris– *Aprianthos, main street.* A charming tearoom on a pretty terrace.

IOS

Phots – *Milpotas*. Large seaside terrace; live music, pleasant decor; a bit pricey.
Anaïs – *Hóra, near the church.* Vast selection of pastries made with almonds and other nuts.

⬓SHOPPING

Local specialities – Lemon liqueur *(kitro)*, wines (rosé) and cheeses (try *xenotiri* and *graviera*).

⬚EVENTS AND FESTIVALS

On **14 July** Hóra (Naxos) celebrates the Feast of St Nicodemus, patron saint of the town who was born there in 1749. On **15 August** the Dormition of the Virginis celebrated with processions in Sangrí, Apíranthos and Filóti (Naxos).

⫞SPORTS AND LEISURE

Wind and **water sports** abound; for information: *www.flisvos-sportclub.com,* or *www.naxos-windsurf.com.* For **horseback riding** (a superb means of seeing Naxos), contact *www.naxoshorseriding.com* (beginners welcome).

Paros★

Paros – Πάρος

Famed since classical times for its finely grained white marble, Paros is a large island rich in both natural beauty and monuments. It has excellent natural harbours, and its summer breezes make it a popular destination for windsurfers. All over the island there is evidence of the expanding tourist industry: holiday homes, hotels, guesthouses and restaurants. Náoussa has become one of the liveliest resorts in the Cyclades, with nightclubs, trendy bars and shops.

▶ **Population:** 12, 853.

Michelin Map: 196sq km/ 77sq mi – Michelin Map 737 L 11-12 – Cyclades – Aegean.

Info: On the quayside at the ferry port. www.parosweb.com.

Location: Paros is in the centre of the Cyclades and easy to reach from many of the islands around it.

Don't Miss: The annual festivals on July 6 and August 23.

Timing: Two days at least.

Kids: Beaches galore.

BEACHES
Náoussa Beaches

Naoussa lies facing north in a large, semicircular, sheltered bay perfect for swimming. The various beaches, running anticlockwise start with busy **Monastíri** (accessed by boat from the harbour) at the northwest of the bay. Just opposite (a 10min walk) is a virtually deserted beach, with white sand and clear water. Further south is **Kolibíthres**, lying below chaotic rock formations. In Naoussa itself are the family beaches of **Pipéri** and **Ághioi Anárgyroi** and about 30min walk further out, the gorgeous beach of **Lagéri★★**, one of the jewels of Paros.

On the east coast, **Mólos,** lying in a bay, is quite pleasant. The strip of coast between **Písso Livádi** and **Dryós** is a developed tourist area and includes **Hrissí Aktí** (Golden Coast), one of Paros' largest stretches of sandy coast, which hosts windsurfing competitions.

On the west coast, **Fáranga** is an isolated beach, set against a backdrop of arid hills. Near the village of **Alikí** which, although quiet, has a good tourist infrastructure, lies the eponymous beach, perfect for families with small children; farther north is exotic **Agía Iríni,** fringed by palm trees.

PARIKÍA★★ *(PAROS TOWN)*

The capital of the island has a busy port which teems day and night with ferries from all over the Aegean. Traffic, pedestrians and bars pumping out music add to the chaos. A short distance from the port, however, lie quiet white alleyways. The long, wide promenade at the foot of the Kástro Hill is pleasant in the evenings. Built on the site of an ancient city, Parikía is composed of two distinct districts: to the north lies

White houses of Náoussa

© R. Mattes/MICHELIN

GETTING THERE

BY SEA – Mainland **ferry** service daily to **Piraeus** *(3hrs 15min–4hrs 15min)*, Ráfina *(3hrs–5hrs 30min)* and Lávrio *(2hrs 30min)*. Also daily ferries to Amorgós, Naxos, Ios, Mýkonos, Santorini, Sýros and Tenos. Also service to Ándros *(6/wk)*, Folégandros *(5/wk)*, Mílos *(3/wk)*, Sífnos *(2/wk)* and Kéa *(1/wk)*.

BY AIR – There are two flights a day from Athens and, in summer, links to Rhodes and Herakleion (Crete).

Vehicle Rental – Numerous agencies in the vicinity of the port. For cars, **Sixt** 𝒫 *22840 510 37* or **Iria Rent a Car** 𝒫 *22840 212 32.*

the modern quarter of Livádia (hotels and restaurants) bordered by beaches; to the south is the old town, dominated by a small Venetian fortress.

Old Town★

This lower part of Parikía has long alleys, shaded squares, fountains, vaulted passageways and chapels.

In its blue-domed churches are some fine iconostases and, at the top of the hill where the acropolis once stood are the ruins of a 13C Venetian fortress *(kástro)*. Foundations of a temple can be seen near the Church of Ágios Konstantínos. Here there is also a terrace with fine views of the Gulf of Paros.

Panagía Ekatondapilianí★★★

🕐*Open daily, 8am–1pm and 4–9pm; 7am–10pm in summer.*

In a square to the east of the port, this church was founded by St Helen, mother of the Emperor Constantine (280–337). Also called the Church of the Hundred Doors, the existing structure dates from the 10C. Inside, the bright church combines a basilica layout with a Greek-cross plan. Note the fine icon of the Virgin (17C). A chapel on the right dedicated to St Nicholas has 6C **fonts**★ carved into the floor for total-immersion baptism.

A small **Byzantine Museum** *(to the left on exiting the church;* 🕐*open daily, 9.30am–1pm and 5–9pm, 9am–10pm in summer;* ⊛*€3)* has some fine icons and relics.

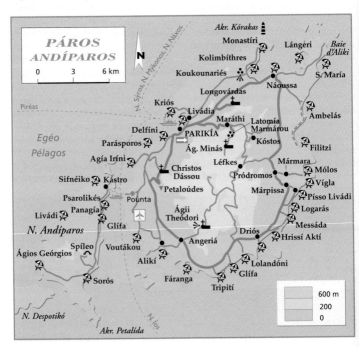

🚗 DRIVING TOURS

THE CENTRE OF THE ISLAND

This fairly mountainous area (Profítis Ilías, the highest peak stands at an altitude of 776m/2, 546ft) has numerous traditional villages. Head southeast from Hóra towards Halkí. Turn right 6km/3.5mi after Galanádo.

Léfkes★

Perched on the mountainside and surrounded by trees is the ancient capital of the island. Its steep alleys have seats, arcades and wells made from the famous local marble which is quarried nearby. The Church of **Agía Tríada** (19C) has two fine marble bell-towers. Inside, the pulpit, bishop's throne and iconostasis are also marble.

There is a small museum of local crafts in the Hotel Léfkes Village.

Marble Quarries

East of Maráthi, a rough track leads to the now-defunct marble quarries. The approach is marked by abandoned buildings; walk 100m/110yd beyond a chapel before climbing over the low wall and following the track to the site. There are three pits, their steep galleries extending down quite deep to reach the best-quality marble.

An ancient bas-relief stands at the entrance to one of them. Beyond the quarries lies the **monastery of Ágios Minás**, fortified in the 17C.

ISLAND CIRCUIT★

Allow 1 day.

Paros has a good road that runs all around the island, so it is worth a drive around rather than taking a boat trip by sea.

▷ *Head NE on the Náoussa road.*

Monastery of Longovárdas

Down a small road on the right, halfway between Parikía and Náoussa.
🕐*Open daily 9.30am–noon. Women not admitted; men must wear long trousers.*

The shaded courtyard is surrounded by buildings where the monks live and pray. Visitors can view cells, communal areas, an icon workshop and the interesting library. The church's façade is typically Cycladic in style; good **view** of the coast.

Náoussa★

This charming little fishing port lies in a bay, its white houses huddled around the imposing parish church.

The newly opened **Archaeological Museum** *(by the post office;* 🕐 *open daily 10am–1pm, 6–8pm;* ☞€2) displays finds from the area, including artefacts from **Koukounariés**, a Mycenaean and Archaic site to the southwest. Náoussa's narrow alleys throb with music from trendy nightclubs and discos. Things are quieter down by the port. Enjoy a meal on the shady terraces by the waterfront, looking up at the ruins of the fortress. Two big annual festivals attract thousands of visitors: July 6 sees the **Festival of Wine and Fish;** on August 23 the bay fills with illuminated ships and folk groups dance on the quayside in commemoration of their forebears' heroic resistance against raiders in 1537.

From Náoussa, head down the east coast, which faces the island of Naxos and has numerous beaches and resorts.

Monastery of Ágii Theódori

At Angeriá in the southwest; take a minor road to the right.
There is a fine **view**★ of the nearby islands from this spot.

Petaloúdes

At the junction where Poúnda is to the left, turn right along a minor road to the **Valley of the Butterflies** where cypresses, plane trees, laurels and carob trees provide an ideal habitat for breeding butterflies. 🕐*Open daily in summer, 9am–8pm.* ☞€1.50.

Convent of Hristoú Dássous

North of Petaloúdes. Women only admitted to convent areas.
Dedicated to "Christ of the Forest", this convent stands on top of a hill (fine

views) and houses the tomb of St Arsénios, the island's patron saint.

Musee Scorpios★★

Enroute to the main road, towards the airport. 🕐*Open daily 10am–12pm, 5–6pm,* ✺€2.

Astonishing scale model representations of scenes from Cycladic history.

EXCURSION
AntíParos★

Accessible by boat from Parikía (6/day, 40min, €3 round trip) or by car ferry from Poúnda (every 15min; €10 round trip for cars, €1.50 for pedestrians).

Once a stronghold of French and Maltese pirates, this peaceful island is a haven of tranquility.

The **boat trip**★ from Parikía is very pleasant; the vessel follows the rocky coast of Paros before picking its way between several islets.

ADDRESSES

🏠**STAY**

☞ **Ártemis** – *AntíParos, near the harbour on the right.* ✆22840 61460. *www. artemisantiparos.com. 30 rooms.* Set in gardens by the sea; good value for money. Breakfast 5€.

☞ **Pension Rena** – *Parikia, near the landing.* ✆22840 22220. *www.cyclades net.gr/rena. 12 rooms.* Simple yet charming, excellent value. No breakfast.

☞ **Stergía** – *Parikía, left of the landing, on the lane running up from Restaurant Katerina.* ✆22840 21745. *www.stergia hotel.com. 15 rooms.* An attractive hotel with plenty of flowers and comfortable rooms.

☞☞ **Argonauta Hotel** – *Parikía, behind the market to the right of the landing.* ✆22840 21440. *www.argonauta.gr. 15 rooms.* Tastefully renovated rooms with balconies. Great service and warm welcome. Breakfast €5.

☞☞☞ **Petres** – *3km/1.9mi before Náoussa.* ✆22840 52467. *www.petres.gr. 16 rooms.* A delightful hotel decorated with antiquities. Shuttle service to Náoussa.

The arrival in the colourful, boat-filled port of **Kástro**★ is delightful. Restaurant terraces line the quayside.

Grotto of Stalactites

▶ *6km/3.75mi south of Kástro.* 🕐*Open daily 10 May–10 Sept 10.45am –3pm.* ✺€3.

Tour buses run on an hourly basis from the port in high season. They take you to the top of 411 easy steps that lead to a huge cave with a wealth of stalactites and stalagmites, one of which bears the signature of Modern Greece's first King, Otto I.

Beaches

The best beach, **Livádi**★, lies to the west and is only accessible on foot. South of Kástro, an attractive coastal path leads past narrow beaches fringed by tamarisk trees such as Psaralykés, Panagía and, the furthest and often deserted, Sorós.

🍴**EAT**

🍽 **Christos** – *Parikía, along the quay to the right of the port.* A tiny room open to the kitchen; simple, copious and good. Try the *imam* (stuffed eggplant).

🍽 **Happy Green Cows** – *Parikía, behind the National Bank.* Generous portions of inventive vegetarian cuisine.

🍽 **Sigi Inthios** – *Náoussa, by the small harbour.* Tasty Greek food with a modern flair and summer terrace.

🍽🍽 **Le Sud** – *Náoussa, in an alley by the big church.* A sophisticated menu along Mediterranean lines.

🚌**TAKING A BREAK**

In Parikía the **Pirate Bar** *(Market Street)* offers a welcoming jazz-blues ambience and decor. Nearby, **The Balcony** has a great terrace overlooking the street. Or stop at Micro Café; Old Greece revisited with low tables and straw chairs.

Stop at **Sulla Luna** for a refreshing dose of fine artisanal ice cream.

🎭**EVENTS AND FESTIVALS**

Wine and Fish Festival in Náoussa on **July 6.** On **23 August**, commemoration of the island's resistance to Barbarossa.

Serifos

Serifos – Σέριφος

Although relatively close to Piraeus, Serifos is little visited, thanks to its industrial mining past. Its mining deposits petered out between the wars, and it is only recently that Serifos has opened up to tourism. Its strikingly white main town is one of the most attractive in the Cyclades.

LIVÁDI

Located in a sheltered bay on the east coast, Livádi is the island's port, and a resort which extends from Pounti (where the ferries dock) to Avlomó-nas Beach. Modern architecture here respects the Cycladic style.

BEACHES

There are four beaches around Livádi itself: from east to west: **Avolomó-nas** (best for watersports), **Livádi**, **Livadákia** and **Karávi** (nudist). North-east of Livádi, it is a good 30min walk to the shaded **Lia**★ Beach, then to the sheltered **Ágios Sóstis** beach and the more popular **Psilí Ámos**★. Beyond both is the quieter **Ágios Ioánnis** beach.

On the south coast **Ambeli Bay**★ is reached by taking the first path on the left after the village of **Rámos** above Livádi. An easier bay to reach by car from Hóra is **Koutalás Bay**★ where three good large beaches, **Koutalás**, **Gánema** and **Vayá** are situated next to each other.

On the north **coast**★, below the end of the road from Hóra to the village of Panagía, a 500m footpath leads from the village of Galaní to the pleasant Bay of **Sikamiás**★ and a shaded, pebble beach. Continuing from Panagía to Kendarhos and north of the monastery of Taxiárhes lies another footpath to attractive **Platís Gialós** Beach.

HÓRA★★

Accessed by bus from the port or on foot up a wide flight of steps.
Commanding a spectacular **view-point**★, the island's capital is typically Cycladic in style with its single-storey

---

- ▶ **Population:** 1, 414.
- ⚲ **Michelin Map:** 75sq km/ 30sq mi – Michelin Map 737 K 11 – Cyclades – Aegean.
- 🗋 **Info:** www.e-serifos.com
- ◗ **Location:** East of Paros and south of Kýthnos.
- ☺ **Don't Miss:** An evening stroll through Hóra.
- ◷ **Timing:** Allow for more than just a day trip.
- ⚌ **Kids:** A sandy beach at Panagía on the north coast.

GETTING THERE

BY SEA – Daily **ferry** service to Piraeus *(2hrs 20min–5hrs 10min)*; also to Paros by speedboat, Kýthnos, Sífnos and Mílos. Less frequent service to Sýros *(3/wk)*, Folégandros *(2/wk)*, Ios *(2/wk)*, Santorini *(2/wk)* and Tenos *(1/wk)*.
BY BUS – Frequent runs between Livadi and Hóra.
Vehicle Rental – **Krinas Travel** 📞22810 51488. www.serifos-travel.gr or **Blue Bird** 📞22810 51511; www.rentacar-bluebird.gr.

White houses in Serifos

© J.-P. Naíl/MICHELIN

white houses clinging to the hillside. It is a village of steep vertical alleys, flights of steps and small, inviting shaded streets. The town is divided into the Upper (Ano) and Lower (Kato) Hóra. Because of its structure, there are few open spaces, the biggest of which is Platía Dimarchíou where the Town Hall with its late-19C Neoclassical façade looks onto a pretty square with tavernas. The other focus of town life is Platía ton Mílon where two restored windmills provide the backdrop to the island's small nightlife.

At the top of the hill, little remains of the old Venetian citadel (Kástro) built in 1434. On the site stands the Church of Ágios Constantínos and Heléni, which commands a fine **view**★ of the bay and the nearby islands of Kimolos, Mílos and Sífnos.

NORTH OF HÓRA
Panagía

The pretty Cycladic village of Panagía, *4km/2.5mi north of Hóra,* stands on the slopes of **Mount Troúlos** and offers fine views over the island. Its **church of Xylopanagía**★ is the oldest on Sérifos (AD950–1000) and has some rare 13C frescoes.

ADDRESSES

⌂ STAY

⌒⌒ **Aretí** – *Livádi, up the steps from the landing stage.* ☏22810 51479. *13 rooms, 5 studios.* A well renovated hotel above the harbour. Comfortable rooms with balcony or terrace overlooking a garden. Breakfast €5.

⌒⌒ **Maïstrali** – *Livadi, end of the harbour on the right.* ☏22810 51220. *www.hotelmaistrali.com. 20 rooms.* Peaceful rooms, a bit away from the nightlife noise; lovely sea views. Breakfast €5.

⋔/EAT

⌒ **Margaríta** – *Livádi, end of the road along the beach, along the dirt track to the left.* ☏22810 51321. A traditional restaurant offering good food and authentic ambience.

Monastery of the Taxiarchs★

🚶 *8km/5mi north of Hóra. Beyond the hamlet of Galaní, follow the path to the left for 2km/1.25mi.* Built on a cliff, the Monastery of the Taxiarchs★ is the island's largest structure (1572). It looks like a white fortress, which it was, as the monks had to defend their riches against pirates. Inside there are many incomparable treasures that can be visited by appointment. ☏22810 51027.

Kéndarhos

▶ *10km/6.25mi north of Hóra.*
This very pretty village is built on a lush hill overlooking a fertile valley. Nearby there are the remains of the domed grave (**thólos**) of a Roman centurion.

South of Hóra

Situated in a narrow-mouthed bay, **Megálo Livádi port** (*13km/8mi southwest of Hóra*) was used for shipping bauxite from around 1880 and was the headquarters of the mining company. There is a grim reminder of the past in the monument commemorating the workers killed in a strike in 1916. The beach is now a popular destination for bathers; tavernas aplenty.

⌒ **Takis** – *Livadi, by the port.* ☏22810 51159. Typical but quality Greek food. Good *moussáka.*

⌒ **Zorbas** – *Hóra, on the town hall square.* Check out the interior decoration, handiwork of the proud owner. A good place to sample *mezes.*

⇎ TAKING A BREAK

There is plenty of choice along Livádi Beach. **Alter Ego** and **Captain Hook** will appeal to those who like Greek music. Alternatively **Bar Karnágio** has rock music and tables on the beach. There's a disco on the left, **Edem Club**, heading toward Hóra.

⌗ EVENTS AND FESTIVALS

Numerous processions on saints' days; The Feast of St Irene in Koutalás on 5 May, the Festival of Our Saviour at Pyrgos on 6 August and the festival of Ágios Sóstis on 7 September.

Sífnos★

Sífnos – Σίφνος

Formerly an active mining area, Sífnos is today an attractive island sporting fine sandy beaches, cultivated hillsides and ancient olive groves. The white cuboid houses, windmills, dovecots, and more than 300 chapels, churches and monasteries all add to its air of authenticity.

A BIT OF HISTORY

The earliest mines in Europe are said to be the gold and silver ones found on Sífnos and dating back to 3000 BC. The precious metals help explain why the Minoans, Phoenicians and then Ionians all came here. The story goes that the islanders sent gold to Apollo's temple at Delphi in the form of a golden egg but one year greed prevailed and they dispatched one that was filled with lead. Apollo took his revenge by causing the gold to run out and the island's mines became empty (*sifnós* in the local dialect).

BEACHES

The fishing port of **Chersónissos** is hidden in a rocky cove on the northernmost tip of Sífnos, *15km/9.5mi north of Apolonía*. The sandy beach, tavernas, quays, fishing nets and boats make up a very attractive image. On the south of the island, the pleasant, sheltered

Fisherman drying his nets in the port

© C. Legrand/MICHELIN

- ▶ **Population:** 2, 442.
- ⚲ **Michelin Map:** 74sq km/ 29sq mi – Michelin Map 737 K 12 – Cyclades – Aegean.
- 🛈 **Info:** www.e-sifnos.com. At Kamáres, opposite the landing stage. ℘22840 31997.
- ▶ **Location:** In the west of the Cyclades, north of Mílos.
- ⊘ **Don't Miss:** The magnificent seascapes visible from Kástro.
- 🕐 **Timing:** For a walking holiday, stay at least 2 days.

GETTING THERE

BY SEA – Daily **ferry** service from the Piraeus *(2hrs 40min–6hrs 20min)*, as well as Kýthnos, Serifos, and Mílos. Also links to Folégandros *(4/wk)*, Sýros *(3/wk)*, Paros *(2/wk)*, Ios *(3–4/wk)* and Santorini *(2–3/wk)*.

---

beach of **Vathí★★** and its little fishing port lie in a pretty bay *9km/5.6mi southwest from Apolonía*. The twindomed Monastery of Taxiárhis (16C) stands along the shoreline. On the other side, the fine sandy beach of **Platís Gialós**, *6km/3.75mi from Apolonía*, is Sífnos' main resort. To the north, overlooking the beach, is the white Monastery of **Panagía Vounoú** (1813) with an impressive view. About 1km/0.6mi to its north lies **Fáros**, the island's former port, where fishing boats still dock. Along the path to the lighthouse is the little beach of **Fassolou**. To the left is the sandy **Apokofto** Beach.

KAMÁRES

This port and family resort in the rocky Bay of Kamáres boasts a pleasant blue-flag beach. Tavernas, cafés and bars border the harbour and alleyways. It is worth visiting the churches of St Barbara (1785). On the other side of the bay is Agía Marína, which has two potteries still in operation and where it is usual to end the day watching the sunset.

Kástro cemetery

APOLONÍA

◯ *Centre of the island.*

Nestling in a natural bowl surrounded by terraced hillsides, Apolonía, the capital, converges with several other villages to form a broad settlement. The main square, **Platía Heróön,** has a small **Folk Museum** (◯ *open daily except Sun morning, 15 Jun–15 Oct 10am–2pm and 7pm–11pm; ⊛ €1)* displaying tools, textiles and ceramics. Nearby, a little alley of cafés, tavernas and shops, Stylianou Prokou, leads to the Cathedral of Ágios Spirídon with its attached museum. Also worth visiting is the **Old School of Agios Artemios** (est. 1832). In the upper town, towards Páno Petáli, reigns Apolonía's finest church, Panagía Ouraniofóra (Sky-Bearing)★ (18C); don't miss its fine iconostasis. Other churches worth visiting in town are Ágios Athanássios, Ágios Sostis and Tímios Stavrós, all of which have frescoes and impressive iconostases.

Profítis Ilías★

🚶 *West of Apolonía, at the island's highest point. The path begins 3km/ 1.9mi from Apolonía, to the right of the Vathí road. Walk fof 2hrs there and back.*

Sífnos' most important Byzantine building looks like an imposing fortress. Parts of the structure date from the 12C.

Areas of the monastery, including the cells, may be visited. On a clear day, the **view**★★ over the Cyclades is breathtaking, taking in Serifos, Sýros, AntíParos, Ios, Síkonos, Folégandros, Políegos and Kímolos.

Kástro★★

Northeast of Apolonía.

🚶 *Accessible on foot (45min) or by bus.*

The former capital of the island, Kástro is an attractive example of a fortified town. As at Folégandros, the ramparts are attached to local dwellings. Today the town is punctuated by flights of steps and narrow alleys.

The **Archaeological Museum** (◯ *open Tue–Sun 8.30pm–3pm; ⊛ no charge)* displays Archaic and classical statuary, antique and Byzantine ceramics.

North of Kástro, the typically Cycladic monastery of Panagía Pouláti (1871) with a blue dome and imposing steeples occupies a site with a dramatic view **west**★ over the sea. It explodes into life on 15 August on the feast of the Dormition.

ÁNO PETÁLI★

Stop here to visit the Italianate church of Ágios Ioánnis for the best view towards the eastern sea and and the church of Panagía ta Gourná near the bridge, decorated with frescoes and a fine wooden iconostasis. Another must-see is the church of Ágios Antypas (1636) famous for its role in the Greek War of Independence in 1821.

ARTEMÓNAS★

Once home to Sífnos' rich and powerful, this village was named for Artemis; a temple to the goddess once stood on the site now occupied by the Church of Kohis. Grand homes from the 18C and 19C rub shoulders with traditional village houses.

In the centre, the Church of **Panagía tis Ámou** has a fine giltwood iconostasis. The Church of **Ágios Konstandínos** (1462) is a magnificent example of Cycladic architecture. Above the church of Ágios Merkoúrios, there is a splendid **view**★.

Panagía Vríssis

Behind its fortified walls, this monastery, dating from the 17C, has a courtyard in the centre of which stands its Katholikón (Byzantine Museum) containing remarkable sacred artefacts.

Panagía Pouláti

© J.-P. Nail/MICHELIN

Panagía Hrissopigí★★

Turn left at the last junction on the road to Platís Gialós.

Dedicated to the island's patron saint since 1650, this monastery stands on a rocky promontory. It is the symbol of Sífnos and a popular place of pilgrimage.

ADDRESSES

🛏 STAY

🍴 **Kalypso** – *Vathi, by the sea.* ℘22840 71127. **5 rooms.** Idyllic location, perfect for a morning dip in the sea.

🍴🛏 **Villa Maria** – *Faros, near the beach.* ℘22840 71421. www.sifnosvilla maria.gr. **5 studios, 2 apts.** Very well-kept rooms around a flowered garden.

🍴🛏🛏 **Pétali** – *Livádi, on the pedestrian street leading between Apolonía and Artemónas.* ℘22840 33024. www.hotelpetali.gr. **23 rooms.** Magnificent view, pleasant swimming pool and efficient service. Tasteful decoration.

🍴 EAT

🍴 **Liotrivi** – *Livádi, in front of the church.* Small wooden tables in a charming setting; local cuisine (try the chickpea soup).

🍴 **The Star** – *Kastro, main street.* Sample the tasty dishes including *moussáka* and chickpea patties; lovely terrace.

🍴 TAKING A BREAK

Nightlife is concentrated along the main street called „Entertainment Alley" in Apolonía. Greek music at **Aloni**, and **Argo** offers cocktails and dancing. **Gerontopoulos** serves Greek pastries, plus home-made ice cream.

🛍 SHOPPING

Ceramics and **jewellery** are the specialities on Sífnos.

🎭 EVENTS AND FESTIVALS

The feast of the Assumption at Chrissopigí (40 days after the Orthodox Easter), the feast of Profítis Ilías (19 July), the Dormition of the Virgin all over the island (15 August), the feast of Ágios Simeon at Kamáres (31 August) and the the feast of Taxiárhis in Vathí (5 September).

Sýros★

Síros – Σύρος

A truly Greek island that remains largely undiscovered by foreign tourists, Sýros is a charming haven of tranquility for those who prefer to avoid the busier islands in the Cyclades.

A BIT OF HISTORY

In the 13C Venetian and Genoese settlers founded Ano Syra (Áno Sýros) here and introduced Catholicism. It remains a staunchly Catholic outpost.

Always an important shipping destination, Sýros welcomed thousands of Greek refugees in the early 19C. At one point the town of Ermoúpoli nearly became the capital of the newly established Greek kingdom. After the opening of the Corinth Canal in 1828, however, Ermoúpoli was eclipsed by Piraeus.

ERMOÚPOLI★★

Capital of the archipelago, Ermoúpoli is a charming town of medieval alleyways, monumental squares and Neoclassical buildings. The visitor arriving by boat gets an arresting view of the town's **site**★★. The 19C administrative and commercial centre occupies the waterfront area. Above it rise Áno Sýros *(left)*, the old Roman Catholic town dating from the 13C, and Vrondádo *(right)*, the Orthodox district.

▶ **Population:** 19, 782.
◔ **Michelin Map:** 86sq km/ 34sq mi – Michelin Map 737 K-L 10-11 – Cyclades – Aegean.
▣ **Info:** Tourist office on the ferry-port quayside. www.gosyros.com.
◖ **Location:** Sýros is 144km/ 78mi southeast of Athens.
⊛ **Don't Miss:** Find time to explore Ermoúpoli.
◔ **Timing:** The charm of Sýros is best appreciated slowly. Spend time soaking up the history and architecture in the capital and then hire a car to visit a couple of the southern beaches.

Fishing Port

This is one of the busiest parts of town, cluttered with banks, travel agents and shops. Café and restaurant terraces curve around the edge of the old port. Beyond the elegant marble façade of the customs house (1861) is a jetty marking the limit of the port, from here extends a good **view**★ of the town.

The Neoclassical Town★★

This is centred on marbled **Platía Miaoúli**★, a pleasant square of palm trees, cafés and arcades. The monumen-

Ermoúpoli

GETTING THERE AND GETTING AROUND

BY SEA – Daily mainland **ferries** to Piraeus *(2hrs 30min–5hrs)* and Lávrío *(2hrs 30min–5hrs 20min)*. Daily service to Tinos, Mýkonos, Paros and Naxos. Service to Santorini, Ios *(4/wk)*, Ándros *(3/wk)*, Serifos *(3/wk)*, Sífnos *(3/wk)*, Kéa *(3/wk)*, Amorgós *(2/wk)* and Mílos *(1/wk)*.

BY AIR – 4 flights/day between Athens and Sýros.

Vehicle Rentals – Several agencies near the port. **Sýros rent a car** ℘*22810 837 77. www.syosrentacar.com.*

---

tal **town hall**★ resembles the Athens Parliament building; its main chamber houses a collection of historical fire fighting equipment. Adjacent Neoclassical houses contain the Cyclades' archives and the Hellas cultural centre.

Behind the town hall, the **Archaeological Museum** (1834) displays funerary stelae, Cycladic idols, marble sculptures, an Egyptian black-granite statuette (8C BC) and ceramics from the third millennium BC *(⏰open Tue–Sun, 8.30am–3pm; ⊛no charge).*

Not far away, the precinct of the **Church of the Metamórfossis** (1824) is paved with stone from Rhodes and inside there are many fine icons donated by local guilds.

Below the Orthodox quarter are the fine **Apollo Theatre**★ (1864) and a scaled-down model of Milan's La Scala. Some of Europe's greatest theatre companies performed here for the local aristocracy *(⏰open daily 10.30am–1pm and 6–8pm; ⊛€2).*

The administrative district, **Nomarhía**★, *(around Odós Apólonos, climbing toward the Orthodox Cathedral)* is a peaceful area of Neoclassical buildings. Above is the Cathedral of Ágios Nikólaos (1870); inside is an iconostasis of Paros marble. Farther up is Vapória, an elegant residential district. Head down to the landing stage; the **view**★ of the town, Orthodox Cathedral, port, sea and islands is unforgettable.

As you head towards the port area, turn right on Odós Kitinou and enter the Church of **Kimissis**★. It contains an **icon**★ representing the Dormition of the Virgin by the famed painter Domenikos Theotokopoulos, also known as **El Greco** *(⏰open Apr–Aug 7.30am–noon, 5.30–6.30pm; Sept–Mar 7.30am–noon, 4.30–5.30pm).*

Sýros Industrial Museum

Odós Papandrou. ⏰Open daily except Tue 10am–2pm, Sun and Mon 10am–2pm and 6–9pm. ⊛€2.50, Wed no charge.

Aspects of the town's economic expansion at the dawn of industrialisation.

Vrondádo★

This lively quarter stretches from the Neoclassical section up to the Byzantine Church of Anástasi. The immense **flight of steps**★ to the church is a tiring climb up tall, irregular steps. From the top there are views of the sea, the port, the dockyards, the Neoclassical town and the Áno Sýros quarter.

Áno Síros★★ (Áno Sýros)

The old Catholic district dates from the 13C; typically Cycladic in feel, it is criss-crossed by steep and winding streets lined by chapels and convents. Side by side at the top of the hill are the bishop's palace and St George's Cathedral, built in 1843. From the terrace there is a **view**★ down the valley to Ermoúpoli and the harbour.

ÁNO MERIÁ★

This mountainous area north of the capital has beaches that are only accessible on foot *(bring strong footwear and plenty of drinking water)*. The two **northern beaches**★ *(Lía – 30min, Mármara – 1hr)* are accessible by paths from Kámbos, the village where the road peters out. It is also possible to take a boat from Kíni.

Ferikídi Grotto

Turn right along a track after Mítikas.
This rocky cave is said to have been occupied at one time by Pherecydes, one of Pythagoras' teachers.

Site of Halandrianí

Accessible by car, on a poor road which is signposted.
In a rocky landscape are the remains of an imposing Cycladic construction and a necropolis built in the third millennium BC. The **view**★ of the surrounding hillsides and out to the islands is impressive.

THE BEACHES★

Head west from Ermoúpoli up a hill crowned by a windmill. From here the view takes in both sides of the island. Then continue downhill; to the left is the Orthodox Convent of Agía Varvára, where examples of the nuns' weaving can be admired and purchased. The road ends at the popular and tamarisk-shaded beach of **Kinito**; to the north a narrow signed path *(10 mi)* leads across a promontory to the isolated bay and beach of **Delfini**.

On the west coast of Sýros, **Galissás** is the largest and most popular of its beaches. It is situated in a **bay**★ formed by a rocky peninsula. To the south a promontory is accessed by the steps to the left of the sea wall leading to a path which requires caution in places. At the top there is a chapel, from where the **view**★ in all directions is breathtaking*).* To the west of Galissás is the small beach of Armeós whose clear waters are popular with naturists.

South of Galissás, Fínikas is renowned for its marina, and the inland village of **Possidonía**★ (also known by its Venetian name, **Dellagrazia**), for its grand villas hidden among conifers. A small road leads to the sea at **Agathopés** which is the most fashionable destination of the island. Going east and then north are the less exclusive resorts of Achládi and Azólimnos and after that the road leads back to Ermoupoli.

ADDRESSES

🛏STAY

◙🛏 **Hotel Alkyon** – *Mega Gialos.* ℘*22810 61761. www.alkyonsyros.gr.* *25 rooms.* Tennis, swimming pool and garden available at this comfortable modern hotel.

◙🛏 **Espérance** – *Ermoúpoli, Odós Folégandrou and Akti Papagou.* ℘*22810 81671. www.esperance.gr. 32 rooms.* Tastefully done rooms in three Neoclassical houses. No breakfast.

◙🛏🛏 **Hermès** – *Ermoúpoli, Place Kanari, end of the quay.* ℘*22810 83011. hermes-syros.com/site. 71 rooms.* The "grand hotel" of Ermoúpoli, with balconied rooms overlooking the sea or a garden. Fitness centre. Open all year.

◙🛏🛏🛏 **Syrou Melathron** – *Ermoúpoli, 5 Odos Babagiotou.* ℘*22810 85963, www.syroumelathron.gr. 21 rooms.* Elegant historic structure (1850) in old Sýros. Internet access, terrace.

🍴EAT

◙ **Ioánnina** – *Ermoúpoli, on the harbour to the left of the Hermes Hotel.* A traditional spot with seafront terrace; grilled lamb a speciality. Good value.

◙ **Nisiotopoula** – *Ermoúpoli, street parallel to the port.* Delicious Greek cuisine includes tomatoes, courgette and honey yoghurt.

🚌TAKING A BREAK

IN ERMOÚPOLI

For teatime, stop in at lovely **Megaron**, just behind the port. Or grab a coffee in the café at the **Plastigga** bookshop. The Greek pastries at **Kanakari** are well worth sampling.

Sýros Casino – *Ermoúpoli, on the waterfront.* Roulette, blackjack and slots, plus a large restaurant and nightclub.

🎭EVENTS AND FESTIVALS

The biggest events take place on Good Friday. From mid-July to mid-August the Ermoupólia includes concerts, plays and exhibitions.

Santorini (Thira)★★★

Santoríni (Thíra) –
Σαντορίνη (Θήρα)

Santorini is the most spectacular island in the archipelago. The ancient volcanic crater or caldera, which for millennia has been submerged by the sea, is surrounded by giant, strangely-coloured cliffs. The huge caldera forms a large bay dotted with volcanic cones, reminders of the seismic catastrophe that engulfed the island in Minoan times.

A BIT OF HISTORY

Around 2000 BC a sophisticated civilisation, comparable to the Minoans of Crete, developed on Santorini. In the 17C BC a huge volcanic explosion devastated the island (👁 *see below*) and in the 3C BC renewed seismic activity split the north part of the island in two. Since the 16C seismic events have continued to transform the Santorini landscape, most recently in 1956 when a huge earthquake destroyed many structures and killed around 50 people.

Historians have speculated that Plato's reference of the continent of Atlantis which was submerged into the sea refers to the destruction of Thira that must have remained in folk memory. After the great eruption, several generations of Phoenicians, then Spartans occupied the island. The latter named it Thira, after their leader.

Venetian occupiers in the 13C called the island Santorini after a shrine to St Irene. After gaining independence

▷ **Population:** 13, 402.
🕐 **Michelin Map:** 83sq km/ 33sq mi – Michelin Map 737 L 11-12 – Cyclades – Aegean.
Info: www.santorini.gr.
▷ **Location:** The island is well served by ferries and by flights. The ferry port at Athinios is several miles south of the capital (bus and taxi services).
P **Parking:** Diabolically difficult at the height of the season.
Don't Miss: A boat trip in the caldera.
🕐 **Timing:** You'll need 4 days to visit Santorini.
Kids: There are open-air cinemas on the island.

GETTING THERE

BY SEA – Several daily **ferries** to Piraeus on the mainland *(3hrs 30min–13hrs depending on the vessel)*, Ios, Mílos, Naxos, Paros and Mýkonos. Also service to Sýros *(5/wk)*, Amorgós *(3/wk)*, Folégandros *(2/wk)*, Kýthnos *(2/wk)*, Serifos *(2/wk)*, Sífnos *(2/wk)*, and Lavrio *(1/wk)*.

BY AIR – Flights daily to and from Athens and European cities; intermittent air service to Mýkonos, Rhodes and Herákleion. Shuttle bus to Fíra from the airport.

Vehicle Rentals – Numerous agencies. Scooter-riders should always wear a helmet.

The White Wines of Santorini

The island's volcanic soil is particularly suitable for viniculture. Santorini produces a white wine with an unmistakeable bouquet which is among the best in Greece. The **assirtiko** vine produces a fairly fruity, medium-dry white wine, **vinsando** (made by leaving the grapes to supermaturation); **aidani** (known for its jasmine bouquet) and the rarer **nyhtari** are sweet fragrant wines. Surprisingly, the vines are grown in a spiral which makes them more resilient in the strong winds. Some tavernas and winemakers offer tastings, notably in Messariá and Megalohóri.

in the modern Greek State, the island officially resumed the name Thira (Thíra) but the majority of Greeks continue to call it Santorini.

BEACHES

The Santorini coastline is unlike any other in the Cyclades; the sea becomes deep very quickly (except at Monólithos) and the currents can be very strong. The finest beaches are to the south and east: Monólithos, **Kamári** (the island's main resort), Períssa, Vliháda (known for its forbidding rocks), Kókini, Lefkí Pigádia and Méssa Pigádia.

THIRA★★ (FIRÁ)

Occupying an extraordinary **site**★★★, the island's capital perches atop a precipitous cliff. Rebuilt after the 1956 earthquake, it lacks authentic charm, but there are magnificent views of the caldera, the volcanic cliffs, the lava islets and the vast sea.

Upper Town

This modern district of tavernas, shops and bars is dominated by the enormous white profile of the Orthodox Cathedral (1970). The area around Platía Theo-

tokopoúlou, near the bus terminal, is always lively and noisy.

Museum of Prehistoric Thira★★

🕐 Open Tue–Sun. 8.30am–7.30pm. 💳€3 (combined with the Archaeological Museum). 📞22860 23217.
Rightly famed for its unique 4 000-year-old frescoes, its golden figurine of an ibex and its masterpieces from Aegean Neolithic art.

Lower Town

Known as Káto Firá, the district is a maze of alleys. Among its houses are two whitewashed churches, Ágios Ioánnis and Ágios Minás, crowned by a lantern.

Catholic Quarter★

On the north side of the town, this is the best preserved part of Firá. Follow Agíou Miná street along the precipice overlooking the caldera, before wandering right into Ipapandis street and to the **Archaeological Museum** 🕐 Open Tue–Sun 8.30am–3pm. 💳€3 (combined with the Prehistoric Museum). 📞22860 22217. This museum picks up where the Prehistoric Museum leaves off and

Ágios Nikólaos near Imerovígli, just north of Firá

© www.santorini.gr

chronicles the Cycladic, Classical, Roman and Hellenistic eras with a display of idols and vases plus ceramics, statues and fragments. Follow Erythrou Stavrou street to The 17C mansion, **Gyzi Palace**, a commemorates life before the 1956 earthquake in photographs, prints, books, manuscripts, traditional costumes and objects (⏱*open Mon–Sat 10.30am–1.30pm and 5–8pm, and Sun 10.30am–4pm; ✍€3)*. To the right of the Gyzi Palace, is the restored former **Convent of the Sisters of Charity**★, now a carpet-weaving workshop. Nearby the **Church of Rosaria**★ is an extraordinary mix of Baroque art and Cycladic architecture. The Catholic cathedral of **Ágios Ioannis** was renovated in 1956. Follow the steps going down to Nomikos street to the Petros Nomikos Centre.

(⏱*Open daily 10am–6pm. ✍€3. ✆22860 23016. www.thera-conferences.gr)*. This features 3D reproductions of frescoes found in Akrotíri. To the north, Firá merges with the villages of **Firostefáni**★ and **Imerovígli**★. Near the latter, lies the 17C Monastery of Ágios Nikólaos. Around its paved courtyard is the abbey church. To the west of the village are the ruins of the much-photographed citadel of **Skáros**★ on a rocky promontory overlooking the caldera.

OÍA★★★

▶ *10km/6.25mi north of Firá. Access by bus or a 3hr walk along clifftop path.* The coast road can be steep in places and offers good views of the caldera. Oía, perched on the cliffs, is quieter than Firá. The **view**★★★ over the island, the

A Natural Disaster

In the mid 17C BC, the inhabitants of Santorini experienced powerful earthquakes over the course of several months. The volcano began to rumble and the population fled. Eventually the pressure in the mountain discharged with a huge eruption, destroying the centre of the island and sending an enormous column of ash and dust several miles into the sky. A tidal wave some 200m/650ft high devastated coastlines as far away as Crete. At the centre of the island the new crater was flooded by the sea. This eruption was one of the most violent ever experienced by mankind; archaeologists believe that it brought the brilliant Minoan civilisation to its end (⏱*see CRETE)*.

bay and its many islets is magnificent. This typically Cycladic settlement has pastel-coloured troglodyte dwellings, patrician houses and white churches.

The Ammoudi district of Oía was a prosperous port in the 19C, evidenced by its fine churches, opulent houses and marble squares. A small **Maritime Museum** (*open Wed–Mon 10am–2pm and 5–8pm; €3*) displays items from this period.

SITE OF AKROTÍRI★★

▶ *Southwest of the island.*
Open Tue–Sun 10am–5pm; €5.
22860 81366.

This Bronze Age (second millennium BC) city pre-dates the great eruption. Like Pompeii, it was buried in ash until being discovered in 1967. Miraculously preserved, Akrotíri retains its streets, paved squares and houses.

The huge jars *(pithoi)* in which stores were kept have been left where they were found. It seems the city must have been evacuated before the catastrophe because no human remains have been found.

ARCHÉA THÍRA★★★
(Ancient Thira)

▶ *East coast. Access from Perissa by a winding road; park the car at the top and take the path leading up to the ruins. Open Tue–Sun 8.30am–3pm. €2.*

Ancient Thira occupies a magnificent **site**★★★ above the Aegean Sea. Founded in the 9C BC, it thrived in Hellenistic times but was abandoned in the 13C. In the sacred entry enclosure there are unusual sculptures representing Artemidoros, the Lion of Apollo, the Eagle of Zeus and the Dolphin of Poseidon. The *agora* was divided into two parts: the first was overlooked by a Temple to Dionysos and the second by the Royal Portico. Beyond the *agora* is the theatre *(left)*; the Sacred Way leads to the Temple of Apollo, which was preceded by a court *(right)* flanked by two chambers.

On the way back, take the street by the theatre which climbs towards the Sanctuary of the Egyptian gods Isis, Serapis and Anubis.

BOAT TRIP IN THE CALDERA★★★

Departure from the old port (Skála) below Firá; trips also leave from Oía. A staircase leads down from Firá to Skála (20min). Those not wishing to walk can make the journey by donkey or by cablecar. Take sturdy shoes, water, a hat and a swimsuit. The trip described here takes about 3hrs. Tickets can be purchased at travel agents; around €15 for the boat trip; €20 including climb to Thriassia; add €2 to walk on the volcano. The view of the towering cliffs of the crater, the precariously sited villages, the bay and the volcanic outcrops is most

Ancient Thira

View of the caldera

© Roman Radomski/iStockphoto.com

impressive from the deck of a small boat. The first island approached from Skala is that cone of solidified lava which is **Nea Kameni**★★, only a few centuries old (where the 'Nea' – new – comes from). the island is still volcanically active and here and there, puffs of foul-smelling smoke burst from many fissures on the ground. *The climb to the crater summit takes about 30min.*

After Nea Kameni, the boat stops at the mouth of a cove at **Paleá (old) Kaméni**★★ where it is safe to swim. Towards the shore, the water grows warmer and is coloured red by volcanic mud. There are also hot springs containing gas bubbles that fizz to the surface. Both of these islands were formed by a series of eruptions between 1707 and 1956.

The final island around the caldera is the sparsely populated **Thirassía** whose volcanic landscape is unmatched. It is not as developed touristically and not as expensive as Santorini, which makes it ideal for those who want a more relaxing stay. The boat returns to Firá via the Skála of Oía (*see above*), skirting the forbidding cliffs of the crater.

🚗 DRIVING TOUR

THE CENTRE OF THE ISLAND★

Allow for 1 day's drive, including a dip in the sea.

▷ *Southeast from Firá; take the minor road to the right beyond Messariá.*

Vóthonas★

The village lies in a fold in the layer of *pozzolana* ash. All that can be seen above the surrounding countryside are a few domes and a church's bell-tower.

Episkopí Goniás★

Southeast of Vóthonas, near Méssa Goniá, a path runs south to the Church of Panagía Episkopís, one of the most beautiful on the island (11C). The frescoes date from about AD1100; note the reuse of ancient columns.

Pírgos

The highest village on the island is composed of concentric streets; there are several handsome Neoclassical houses and traces of a Venetian castle.

Prophet Elijah Monastery★ (Profítis Ilías)

From this 18C structure, there is a fine **view**★★ over the caldera and the island. The library and cellars house a museum of religious art and popular traditions.

▷ *Return to Pírgos and head towards the caldera.*

Megalohóri

Near this village stands St Nicholas' Chapel, a small white marble structure; it is an ancient funerary temple (3C BC), perfectly preserved.

Just outside **Emborío** lie the remains of a Venetian fortress (15C Church of the Virgin).

ADDRESSES

STAY

Santorini is among the most expensive islands in the Cyclades. The caldera side of the island features great views and nightlife, but is a good 30min trip to the beach. Some hotels have pools, but are priced accordingly. Prices are lower on the east side. If proximity to the sea is important, opt for Kamari or Perissa, which are linked by bus to Firá and Oía. In Firá, seek accommodations in Firostefáni, along the hillsides, or south of the Orthodox cathedral.

⊖ **Pension Galíni Ía** – *Oía, on the right-hand side on entering the village.* ✆ *22860 71396. www.galini-ia.gr. 17 rooms.* A charming traditional establishment, simple and comfortable. View over vineyards and sea; friendly welcome.

⊖⊖⊟ **Chez Sophie** – *Kamari.* ✆ *22860 33069. www.chezsophie.gr. 12 units.* Stunning villa complex in traditional design right by the sea.

⊖⊖⊟⊟ **Hotel Galini** – *Firostefáni.* ✆ *22860 22095. www.hotelgalini.gr. 13 rooms.* Nice rooms overlooking the caldera. Pleasant bar, warm welcome. Breakfast €7.

EAT

The island's cuisine has its own identity; look out for *kounéli tirávgoulo* (rabbit with onion and cheese), *fáva* (puréed broad beans), *domatokeftédes* and *pseftokeftédes* (vegetable fritters), *skordomakaronáda* (little garlic pastries) and *moshári tis panegíris* (literally, festive beef, a stew cooked in wine).

⊖ **Archipelagos** – *Firá.* www. archipelagos-santorini.com. Excellent fresh fish and giant salads.

⊖ **Thomas Grill** – *Oía, on the street between the bus stop and the church.* Unpretentious taverna popular with locals. Tasty, simple cuisine.

⊖⊖⊟ **Papagalos** – *Oía, along the cliff.* Sober, chic decor. Nouveau Greek cuisine; organic local produce and seafood.

⊖⊖⊟ **Selene** – *Firá, outskirts, near the Atlantis hotel. www.selene.gr.* Creative interpretations of Greek cuisine: Cyclades ham, *fáva* puree, rabbit and seafood. Varied wine list.

TAKING A BREAK

Kastro – *Firá.* Large bar on two levels, with superb views of the caldera.
Jazz Bar – *Firá, main street.* Good music and relaxing atmosphere.
Fanari Bar – *Oía, end of the village facing Thirassía.* Lounge atmosphere, great views.

Tinos★

Tínos – Τήνος

Tinos is an important centre of Christian pilgrimage, particularly during the feast of the Dormition on 15 August, when a long procession follows a miraculous icon of the Virgin as it is borne aloft by sailors. With its mountains, beaches and unspoilt coastlines, Tinos presents a landscape of great beauty.

A BIT OF HISTORY

Settlers were well-established enough by the 4C BC to build a sanctuary to Poseidon for his help in ridding the islands of snakes. The Venetians built a formidable fortress on the island which withstood attacks by Turkish forces only

▶ **Population:** 8, 574.
⚲ **Michelin Map:** 195sq km/ 77sq mi – Michelin Map 737 L 10 – Cyclades – Aegean.
🖪 **Info:** Kalypso Tourist Office, Odos Taxiarchon. ✆ 22830 25407. www.tinos.biz, www.tinos.gr.
◐ **Location:** Situated between Andros and Mýkonos.
◉ **Don't Miss:** The precious icon in Hóra's church.
◔ **Timing:** Enough to see to warrant a stay of 2 days.

to finally succumb in the early 18C and become the last addition to the Ottoman Empire. In 1822 a nun was directed by visions to a rock where a icon was found and this took on a nationalist significance given the context of the Greek War of Independence.

BEACHES

Ágios Márkos and **Ágios Fokás** are the island's busiest beaches; for quiet, head to **Kiónia**★, west of the port. The rocky cove of Stavrós (halfway between Ágios Márkos and Hóra) is sheltered enough to swim in safety even when windy.

Southeast coast

The strip of coastline facing Mýkonos has two fine beaches: sandy Ágios Ioánnis Porto and the superb crescent beach of **Pahiá Ámosa**★ *(access by footpath)*.

HÓRA★

The whitewashed capital of Tinos is a pleasant town and a busy port. There is an interesting **Archaeological Museum** *(Open Tue–Sun 8.30am–3pm; €2)*. where exhibits come from excavations in Boeotia and cover the region's civilisation from the Paleolithic to the post-Byzantine periods. Includes a colossal provisions vase from the 7C BC.

GETTING THERE

BY SEA – Mainland **ferry** service daily to Piraeus *(3hrs–5hrs 30min)*, Lavrio *(2hrs 20min)* and Rafina *(2hrs–3hrs 40min)*; daily service to Ándros, Mýkonos, Sýros, Máxos, and Paros. Also service to Serifos *(1/wk)* and Sífnos *(1/wk)*.

Church of Panagía Evangelístria★★

🕐*Open daily 9am–12pm.*
🎟*No charge.*

A broad steeply sloping street, which some pilgrims climb on their knees, leads up to the imposing white marble church (1823). The church was built after the discovery of a miraculous icon of the Virgin, object of pilgrimages by the sick and the faithful.

A ceremonial flight of steps approaches the church. In the nave is the holy icon, encrusted in jewels and hung with votive offerings.

On the left below the church are the "caves" where the icon was discovered; a neighbouring building contains a little **Museum of Religious Art** *(icons)* and an **art gallery** which displays works by well known local artists.

Horá with a view to the Church of Panagía Evangelístria

© Greek National Tourism Organisation

AROUND HÓRA
Kehrovouníou Convent★

▶ *6km/3.75mi northeast of Hóra.*
🕐 *Open daily 7–11.30am and 2.20–7pm; trousers or long skirts required.*

The convent (10–11C) is built on a steep hill with a beautiful view of the island, Inside, the Church of the Dormition features fine frescoes and a superb wooden iconostasis as well as several 18C and 19C icons and other sacred objects. Furthermore, visitors are allowed in the small, simple cell of St Pelagía who, as a nun here, experienced her visions in 1822 which led to the icon's discovery. She was canonised in 1970. Items made by the nuns such as candles, honey and small icons are available for sale.

Exómvourgo

▶ *9km/5.5mi north of Hóra, plus 1hr on foot there and back.*

This little mountain (553m/1814ft) is easy to climb. At its summit you can visit the ruins of a Venetian citadel built on the site of an ancient Acropolis. It is worth climbing for the lovely **view**★.

INLAND VILLAGES★
Allow a whole day.

There are many villages on Tinos, all packed close together. Their narrow alleyways and vaulted passages provided protection against the sun and wind, and against pirates.

Agápi

A good example of the classic medieval plan used in all the inland fortified villages; where peripheral houses formed the ramparts.

Arnádos

Close to the parish church, a **Religious Museum** displays icons and other objects.

Dío Horiá

Spend a little time in this pretty village (note the communal fountain), wandering the alleyways around the Church of Koímissis tis Theotókou (Dormition of the Virgin).

Koumáros

Traditional village on the slopes of Exómvourgo; lovely views of the island.

Loutrá

The imposing old college (17C) was a Jesuit seminary. Inside is a small Folk Museum (🕐 *open Tue–Sun, summer months only, 10.30am–3.30pm*); some of the original items of furniture remain *in situ*.

Méssi

Extraordinary church resembling the ecclesiastical architecture of central America.

Moundádos

This abandoned village is a network of paved whitewashed alleys; good views from the roof of the Church of Ágios Ioánnis tou Prodrómou *(flight of steps)*.

Skaládos

The church bell-tower is a good example of the local architecture. On the outskirts of the village is a café-grocery with a terrace that has a fine **view**★ over the valley down to the Gulf of Kolimbíthra.

Sklavohóri

The village has a remarkable communal wash-house dating from the early 19C.

Triandáros

In a verdant location, this village has a church (Ágioi Apostóli, built in 1887) with an impressive gabled façade. From here, a track leads to the pebble beach at Lihnáftia, 4.5km/2.8mi away.

Tripótamos

Follow the quiet alleyways to the Church of Isodia tis Theotoku (Presentation of the Virgin), which has rich marble decoration; lovely view over the valley and the sea.

Vólax

A right turn leads to this village lost in the meadows. Here and there, among its houses, are large boulders of volcanic origin.

Xinára

The seat of the Catholic see of Tinos; its cathedral is dedicated to the Virgin.

 DRIVING TOURS

ÉXO MERIÁ★

Allow half a day to visit the northwest of the island. This is a 70km/44mi round trip on a good road.

▷ *From Hóra, head northwest to Pánormos.*

Tarabádos Dovecots★★

Down in the valley *(from Kámbos, head to the nearby hamlet of Tarabádos)* are the finest dovecots on Tinos, some of them dating from the Venetian period.

Kardianí★

Amid the trees, the white houses of Kardianí look down over the sea. The village boasts two fine churches, Genéthliou tis Theotókou and Agía Triáda.

Istérnia

The large church sports ceramic tiled domes. The **Museum of Artists** displays the work of local artists (*open Tue–Sun 8.30am–3pm; no charge*).

▷ *Follow the road down to the other side of the island.*

Pírgos★

Below the town, Pírgos has several active sculpture workshops and there is a small **Museum of Tinian Artists** (*open Tue–Sun 10am–3pm; no charge*). A shop near the village square retails sculptures.

Pánormos

At the end of the road, this pretty little port sits in a sheltered rocky bay and you can while away time at one of the fish tavernas.

ADDRESSES

STAY

Eleana – *Hóra, 1 Odós Agio Ioannou.* ℰ22830 22561, www.eleana-tinos.gr. *17 rooms.* Tucked between two charming churches, this large hotel has impeccably kept rooms.

Boreádhes – *Hóra, after the church of Ágios Antónios.* ℰ22830 23845. www.voreades.gr. *12 rooms and 1 apt.* An attractive building in the traditional style and tastefully decorated (tester beds).

Golden Beach – *Agios Folkas, on the beach.* ℰ22830 22579. www.goldenbeachtinos.gr. *19 studios.* An attractive group of buildings situated in a large garden; nice tavern adjacent.

Tinion – *Hóra, east of the port.* ℰ22830 22261. www.tinionhotel.gr. *18 rooms.* An almost colonial feel to this white-painted historic residence.

EAT

Among the island's specialities, the veal *(moshári)* is the best in Greece. Also look out for rabbit *(kounéli)*, lamb *(arnáki)*, goat *(katsíki)*, either cooked in a lemon or tomato sauce or roasted, and potato and pork omelette *(froutaliá)*.

Arkyra – *Hóra, near the port.* Small family-run *ouzerie* serving very good fried fish and excellent local cheese.

Kapilio – *Hóra, Odós Aristidou Kodogiorgi.* Come for live Greek music on Saturday evenings, and to sample the tasty pork in mustard sauce.

To Thalassaki – *Isternia, turn left toward the beach.* An excellent spot for sampling fine local cuisine. Tasty fresh *mezes*, impeccable grilled fish, and sublime halva with honey and pistachios.

TAKE A BREAK IN HÓRA

For cocktails try **Sympossio** for its lounge atmosphere; **Mycro Café** for a more upbeat experience.

EVENTS AND FESTIVALS

Tinos has no shortage of events, ranging from saints' days to raki festivals. Among such festivals are Kardianí (mid-June, 50 days after Easter), Agía Paraskeví in Istérnia (26 July), Agía Marína in Pírgos (17 July), and Ágios Ioánnis in Kómi.

THE DODECANESE

Dodekanisa–Δωδεκάνησα

Dotting the southern Aegean Sea just a few kilometres off the Turkish coast, this archipelago is composed (as the name suggests) of 12 main islands and roughly 150 smaller islets. Mountainous and picturesque, the Dodecanese Islands played an important role in antiquity and during the Middle Ages, when they were the front line of the Christian world as it faced the threat of invasion by Turkey (the islands finally succumbed in the 16C). The islands were occupied by Italy in 1912 and joined the Greek State in 1947–48.

A Bit of History

Early Times – The first known settlers came from Caria, a region in Asia Minor (now the west coast of Turkey), and there was an early connection with Minoan Greece. After the collapse of Minoan civilisation the islands came under the influence of the Myceneans and in this regard the Dodecanese contributed their share of ships to the armada that sailed to Troy. Other seafaring groups arrived in due course but it was the Dorians who made their presence really felt. The islands of Rhodes and Kos became important and prosperous enough to be able to send out their own settlers to found colonies in the western Mediterranean.

In the aftermath of the defeat of the Persians (who captured the Dodecanese) the main islands joined the Athenian-led alliance that eventually turned into an empire. The physical distance from Athens, however, enable the Dodecanese to develop their own sense of identity and culturally this was a flourishing time for the islands. During the Peloponnesian War, when Athens was fighting Sparta, the islands were able to remain neutral most of the time. The islands allied themselves with Rome in the 2C BC while maintaining a degree

of autonomy to which they had become accustomed. This came to an end after the assassination of Julius Caesar in 44 BC; Cassius invaded the islands and they were incorporated into the Roman Empire.

After the east/west split in the Empire in AD 395, the islands gradually became part of the Greek Byzantine Empire and remained so for nearly a millennium.

Knights of St John – Crusaders found the Dodecanese a useful watering hole on their sea route and the islands became even more significant after the fall of Jerusalem to the Ottomans in the late 13C. The Knights of St John, an aristocratic order who ran a hospital in the Holy Land, were forced to decamp and find a new base. They purchased the Dodecanese from a pirate who claimed ownership of them and set up their headquarters on Rhodes. Neighbouring islands were fortified and Muslim ships attacked until Sultan Suleiman the Magnificent captured Rhodes in 1522. The population of the islands remained predominantly Greek (the Ottomans were not harsh masters) and it was only Rhodes and Kos that developed Turkish communities. However, following Greece's declaration of independence in 1822, the islanders did not join the war of Independence. A history of relative autonomy remained in place and allowed Greek merchants to continue their activities within the Ottoman Empire.

Modern Times – Turkish rule continued until 1912, when the Italians became the new rulers – a blatant act of expropriation that was sanctioned by the second Treaty of Lausanne in 1923. The Italians under Mussolini's fascism set about

GETTING THERE

BY AIR - Flights link Astipalea, Kalimnos, Karpathos, Kos, Leros and Rhodes to Athens, and Rhodes to Thessaloniki. Kos and Rhodes are also linked to many European airports.

BY SEA - Boats serve the Dodecanese from Piraeus and Thessaloniki via the Cyclades but the journey is a long one. The **ferries** stop at Astipálea, Kálimnos, Leros, Pátmos, Kos, Níssiros, Tílos and Sými and Rhodes; and some go on to Karpathos. Another service links Crete to Rhodes, and there are numerous inter-island ferries within the Dodecanese.

making the islands their own and imposed their language (the medium of instruction in schools became Italian) and religion on the islanders. This came to an end with the defeat of Italy in the Second World War – the islands were the scene for many fierce battles with British forces in 1943–44, but only after nearly all 6 000 Jewish inhabitants were removed and murdered. It was not until 1948 that the Dodecanese became formally attached to Greece; for 700 years the islands had been under non-Greek rule. Given that the islands are far closer to Turkey than Greece it is understandable why this arrangement was disputed for a long time. Even today, with Turkey less likely to reignite old passions, the Greek government has a military presence on the islands. The cultural legacy left by the classical Greeks, Byzantines, Crusaders, Ottomans and Italians has been a rich one, especially in the form of architecture. The Italians were especially concerned to make their presence felt and lavished money on grand public buildings.

Today, the administrative capital is in Rhodes Town, and the 12 main islands are Rhodes, Pátmos, Kos, Léros, Kálimnos, Nissiros, Tílos, Sými, Astipálea, Kastelório, Kárpathos and Kássos.

To these are added numerous smaller islands such as Hálki near Rhodes, Lipsí and Arkí near Pátmos, and Télendos and Pserimos near Kálimnos. There are 163 islands in total, 26 of which are inhabited.

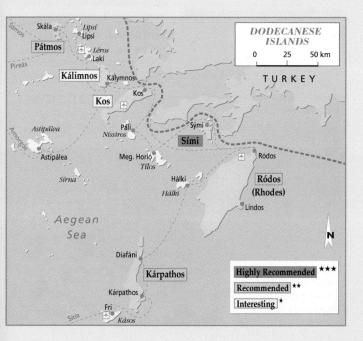

Astypálaia

Astipálea – Αστυπάλαια

Astypálaia is mountainous, yet relatively fertile. The capital is a pretty village of white houses scattered around a Venetian fortress. Because of its isolated location, the island is little visited, even in high season. It is renowned for being shaped very like a butterfly, and its almost-Cycladic architecture suggests it is flying between the Dodecanese and the Cyclades.

▶ **Population:** 1, 240.
⚹ **Michelin Map:** 737 N-O 12-13 – Dodecanese – Aegean.
▤ **Info:** At Hóra. ✆22430 61412. www.astypalaia.com
▶ **Location:** 45km/28mi from Amorgós.
🕐 **Timing:** Book accommodation in advance for mid-July to early September.

ASTIPÁLAIA TOWN (HÓRA)

This attractive coastal village has many old houses dating from the Venetian period. Below is the Convent of Panagia Portaitissa. The **Archaeological Museum** includes objects from the Mycenaean tombs as well as many architectural fragments from the classical and Hellenistic periods (🕐*open Jul–Oct Tue–Sun 11am–1pm, 5–10.30pm; Nov–Jun Tue–Sun 8.30am–2.30pm;* 🎫*€2;* ✆*22430 61500).*Pleasant excursions from Hóra include **Analipsi (Maltezana)** *(9km/6mi)*, with

fine sea caves in its sheltered bay; **Vathy** *(20km/12mi east)* with intriguing sea caves; and **Livadi** *(1km/0.6mi south)*, a seaside resort with a fine beach.

ADDRESSES

🍴STAY / 🍽️EAT

🛏️ **Paradissos** – *Hóra, on the quayside.* ✆*22430 612 24. www.astypalea-paradissos.com. Open Apr–Oct.* Renovated, clean rooms.

🛏️ **Akti** – *Hóra, on the quayside.* ✆*22430 611 14. www.aktirooms.gr.* Small, pleasant terraces; typical Greek cuisine.

🍵TAKING A BREAK

Toxotis – *Hóra, on the quayside.* In an agreeable spot (with roof terrace), this establishment is also a restaurant.

GETTING THERE

BY SEA – **Ferry** to Piraeus *(4/wk; 8–13hrs).* Also service to Kalymnos *(3–4/wk)* and Amorgós *(2/wk)* and other Dodecanese and Cyclades Islands .
BY AIR – Flights to Athens *(several each week; 1hr).*

📷EVENTS AND FESTIVALS

The Feast of the Assumption takes place on 15 August.

View of Hóra

Traditional windmills of Kárpathos

© Phototravellers/MICHELIN

Karpathos★

Kárpathos – Κάρπαθος

Kárpathos stretches from north to south like a huge sea serpent at the frontier between east and west. Located in the southeast of Kárpathos, the capital and port of Pigádia is an attractive town. Numerous hotels have been built by returning expats, and fish restaurants cater to both locals and visitors. Amopi Beach lies 6km/4mi to the south.

THE EAST COAST AND NORTH OF THE ISLAND★★

◐ *Heading north from Pigádia, a road to the right leads 3km/2mi to the beautiful Aháta Beach, bordered by arid cliffs.*

The **Apéri-Spóa**★★ stretch of road requires a four-wheel drive vehicle, or can be walked. It offers fine panoramic views over the island. Kirá Panagía, Apéla and Ágios Nikólaos are the finest beaches on the island.

Between Spóa and Ólimbos, another road leads to the north of the island. To the right are the superb, deserted beaches of Ágios Minás and Forókli.

Diafáni

This pleasant little town sits on the northeast coast of Kárpathos and is where ferries arrive bringing visitors to the dramatic inland village of Ólimbos.

▶ **Population:** 6, 511.
⚲ **Michelin Map:** 300sq km/ 117sq mi – Michelin Map 737 P 14-15 – Dodecanese – Aegean.
▤ **Info:** ☏ 22450 23835. A nominal information bureau on the quayside in Jul-Aug.
▷ **Location:** Located between Crete and Rhodes.
⚐ **Don't Miss:** The west coast and the mountain villages.
◔ **Timing:** Plan for 2 nights at least.

GETTING THERE

BY AIR – The airport is at the southern end of the island, 18km/11mi from Pigádia. Service to Rhodes *(2/ day)*, Crete *(several/wk)* and Athens *(5/ wk; 3/wk in winter)*.
BY SEA – **Ferry** service to Piraeus via Crete, Santorini and Mílos *(2/wk)* and Rhodes via Diafani *(3/wk)*.

Ólimbos★

This high, fortified village overlooked by windmills is little changed since the 15C. Elderly women still wear the traditional garb of long black dress and scarf, with the neck and cuffs embroidered in coloured patterns; the very ancient local dialect is also still in regular use. A **traditional house** is open to the public; its sole room is centred around a pillar, with folding beds, icons, photos and personal effects.

THE WEST COAST★

From the well-maintained coast road there are fine **views**★ of the mountains, the sea and the island of Kássos. Near the pleasant village of Arkássa and the beach of Ágios Nikólaos is the Agía Sofía Basilica, some 15 centuries old. Inside are mosaics and artefacts dating from the paleo-Christian era.

THE MOUNTAIN VILLAGES★

The mountain villages, with white-washed houses, seem unchanged by time. Worth a stop is **Othos**, a busy community with grand houses, a modest market and numerous tavernas which serve the celebrated local wine. It's the highest village on the island, on the slopes of Mount Kalilímni. Local artist Saunis Hapsis holds the keys of the **Ethnographic Museum** and he can usually be found either in the museum or in the gallery where he works and exhibits his paintings of local scenes and traditions.

EXCURSION
Island of Kássos

Accessible by ferry from Kárpathos or by plane; accommodation at and near the harbour in the unusually-named port of Fri.

This island is very close to Kárpathos but little visited. The capital, Fri, is a small port with numerous waterside restaurants; excursions depart from here to the island of **Armathia**, which has magnificent beaches. Fri also has a tiny **Archaelogical Museum** (✆22450 41865; 🕐open daily 9am-3pm in summer only; 🚫no charge) which displays the island's scant archaeological finds. Near Fri are four charming villages, and many inlets; the most striking of these is **Kelatros** (*15km/9mi from Fri*).

ADDRESSES

🛏STAY

⊖ **Hotel Aphrodite** – *Olimbos, top of the village.* ✆22450 51307. 4 rooms. Pleasant small rooms in a good location.

⊖ **Hotel Dolphin** – *Above the port of Diafáni.* ✆22450 51354. www.dolphin studios.gr. 6 rooms, 4 apts. 🍴 Light, spacious rooms in a charming lane leading to two isolated chapels at the end of the bay. No breakfast.

⊖ **Pine Tree** – *Adia Beach.* ✆22450 29065. www.pinetree-karpathos.gr. 9 rooms, 3 apts. Open May–Oct. 🍴 Isolated in Adia Bay on the pine-covered slopes of Kalilímni. Fresh, local fruit served at breakfast.

⊖⊖ **Krínos** – *Lefkós.* ✆22450 71410/71412. www.hotel-krinos.com. Open Apr–Oct. 42 rooms. 🍴 Comfortable hotel overlooking the sea; all rooms have balconies with views. Greek dancing.

🍽EAT

⊖ **Ánixis** – *Diafáni, near the church.* ✆22450 51226. Open May–Oct. 🍴 Simple, authentic and tasty dishes that depend on the day's catch. Specialities include *dolmades* made with hibiscus leaves and delicious *loukoumádes*.

⊖ **To Ellinikon** – *Pigádia, Odós Apodimon Karpathion.* ✆22450 23932. In the kitchen, choose a variety plate of fresh vegetables, or the *makarones* pasta with goat cheese.

⊖ **The Milos** – *Ólimbos, end of the village near the windmills.* ✆22450 51333. Open May–Sept. 🍴 Choose a table with a sea or mountain view. Wide variety of dishes (some cooked in view of the tables in the traditional oven). .

🎉EVENTS AND FESTIVALS

Local feasts – On Kárpathos, Easter is a huge celebration. On the Tuesday of Holy Week the men go on an icon procession through the villages. Lamb feast on Easter Monday with music (*tsaboúna*, bagpipes, and *láouto*, lute).

🏖BEACHES

Some beaches are accessible only by footpath or by water-taxi. Some of the best are on the east coast: Kira Panagia, Ágios Nikólaos (Spoa) and Apela.

Kos★

Kós – Κώς

Close to the shores of Turkey, Kos is a mountainous island rich in agricultural resources. The resorts at Kos Town and Kardámena are among the largest in Greece, and away from Kos Town and its renowned nightlife, the island has many other popular resorts and some of the finest beaches in the country.

KOS TOWN★

Capital of the island and its main resort, charming Kos Town offers terraced cafés, palm-lined walks and gardens of flowering hibiscus. There are some **ancient ruins** in the port quarter, including foundations and columns of a temple to Aphrodite. The vast **archaeological site** *(Odós Grigoriou, south of the town; open daily 8am–2pm, free of charge)* includes traces of a Temple of Dionysos, a colonnaded *palaestra*, baths, houses decorated with **mosaics**★ and frescoes. At the **Archaeological Museum** *(Platía Eleftherías; ⏱ open Tue–Sun 8am–2.30pm; ⊜€3)* you'll see an interesting

- ▸ **Population:** 26, 379.
- ⏱ **Michelin Map:** 290sq km/113sq mi – Michelin Map 737 P 12 – Dodecanese – Aegean.
- ▤ **Info:** Vasileos Georgiou, by the hydrofoil terminal. ℘ 22420 24460. Open Mon–Fri 8am–8pm (2.30pm off-season). www.kosinfo.gr.
- ◗ **Location:** Close to Bodrum in Turkey.
- ⌾ **Don't Miss:** A day trip to Kálimnos.
- ♟ **Kids:** The volcanic crater.

collection of Hellenistic and Roman sculptures.

Plane Tree Square★ (Platía tou Platánou)

The centre of the town takes its name from the enormous plane tree beneath which Hippocrates, the famous doctor, is said to have taught. Next to the tree stands a covered Turkish fountain

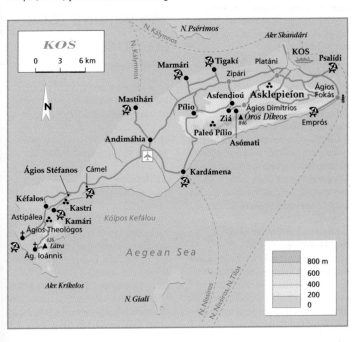

GETTING THERE

KOS

BY AIR – Service to Athens *(daily)*, Crete *(3/wk)* and Rhodes *(2–3/wk)*. The airport is 25km/17mi southwest of Kos Town; ✆22420 51229.

BY SEA – **Ferry** service (Kountouriotou dock, behind the Kastro) to Piraeus *(daily)* via Kalimnos *(6/wk)*, Pátmos *(6/wk)*, Amorgos *(1/wk)* and Siros *(2/wk)*. Also service to Rhodes *(daily)* via Sými *(1–3/wk)*. For information ✆22420 28507. Day trips to Bodrum in Turkey.

KÁLIMONOS

BY SEA – From Póthia, ferry service to Piraeus *(daily; 14hrs)*, to Kos *(2/day)*, and to Rhodes *(2/day)*. Also ferry or hydrofoil service to Pátmos *(9/wk)*, Léros *(6/wk)*, Kárpathos and Lipsí *(2/wk)* and Mykonos, Amorgós, Astipálea and Kastelórizo *(1/wk)*.

BY AIR – Flights to Athens *(daily)*.

NÍSSIROS

BY SEA – Ferry services from Kos *(daily)*, Rhodes *(2–3/wk)*, Tílos *(1/wk)* and Piraeus *(1/wk)*.

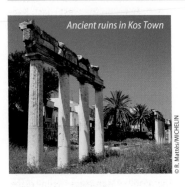
Ancient ruins in Kos Town
© R. Mattes/MICHELIN

built from older materials; note also the nearby sarcophagus converted into a basin. The Mosque of the Loggia (18C) has a tall minaret.

Kástro★ (Knights' Castle)

Access: Over a bridge from Platía tou Platánou. ◷*Open Tue–Sun 8am–2.30pm.* ⊛€4.

The castle's two concentric sets of walls, (1450–1514) are constructed with pieces taken from ancient buildings: note the Hellenistic frieze over the entrance door. The parapet walk gives a succession of picturesque views of the town, the harbour, the sea and the Turkish coast.

BEACHES AND RESORTS

Kardámena

This large resort teems with people in summer and is virtually deserted in winter. At night, the music from the bars, pubs and discos is deafening. From the port, there are excursions to Níssiros, renowned for its volcano.

Kéfalos Bay (Kólpos Kéfalou)

Enclosed by Mount Látra, this submerged section of a volcanic crater is bordered by fine sandy beaches, notably **Parádissos**★ (Paradise Beach) and **Camel**★. Near the beach at Kamári is a rock terrace above the Club Med beach; here lie the ruins of a palaeo-Christian basilica, **Ágios Stéfanos** (5C).

To the west of Kos Town lie dune-fringed resorts of Mastihári, Marmári and Tingáki.

🚗 DRIVING TOUR

ACROSS THE ISLAND★

86km/54mi round trip.

Following a scenic road that runs the length of Kos this route takes in ancient remains and traditional villages.

▷ *Drive 4km/2.5mi southwest of Kos Town to the ancient site of Asklipiío.*

Asklipiío★

◷*Open Tue–Sun 8am–7.30pm (3pm in winter).* ⊛€4.

This important sanctuary (4C–BC) commemorating the skills of Hippocrates occupies a magnificent **site**★★ overlooking the Kos Plain. Complete with healing sulphurous waters, it served as both a place of worship and a treatment centre. Climb up the successive terraces past the monumental entrance *(propylaia)*, altars and temples to the top terrace, where the great Temple of Asklepios stood. From here there are magnificent **views**★★ down over the sanctuary and the surrounding woods to the town of Kos and across the sea to the Turkish coast.

From the village of **Asfendioú** *(8.5km/ 5mi from Kos Town, turn left onto a little mountain road)* there is a good view over the island and out towards Kálimnos.

▶ *From Asfendioú head due west for a 20min drive to the village of Andimáhia.*

Andimáhia

This village is adjacent to a Hospitallers' fortress (take the path to the left before the village), with ruins of churches, houses and cisterns.

▶ *Another 20min southwest of Andimáhia is Kéfalos.*

Kéfalos★

The old village of Kéfalos lies above the ruins of its castle. From the foot of the wall there is a splendid **view**★★ over the vast Bay of Kéfalos to the east and beyond. Further on from here is some of the most dramatic scenery on the island, far-removed from the bustle of the beach resorts.

KÁLIMNOS★

▶ *Island northwest of Kos.*

♿ *For getting there, see Address Book.*

The influx of visitors has made the island prosperous, but it retains its wild grandeur: striking rockfaces, attractive beaches, and paths bordered by fragrant flora.

Along the quayside and scaling the hillside of the main town rise tall houses, often painted in the national colours of white and blue and built in the Neoclassical style. There is a small **Maritime Museum** (🕐*open Mon–Fri 8am–1.30. pm, Sat–Sun 10am–12.30pm, summer only; ✆€2)* where you can find out how islanders set about about spongediving, and about the Allied liberation of the island in 1945.

There is also a new **Archaeological Museum** (🕐*open Tue–Sun 8.30am–* 2.30pm; ✆ 22430 23113; ✆€5) with finds dating from the early Bronze Age and after.

To the northeast, the **Vathis Valley**★ is an oasis of coolness. Rina is an attractive village, and the port of Vathís nestles in the curve of a bay as steep-sided as a fjord.

Péra

▶ *Northeast of Horió.* 🕐*Open every day 8.30am–3pm.* ✆*No charge.*

The steep climb to Péra Castle (once used by the Knights of St John) is worthwhile for the superb **view**★. There are fine beaches on the west coast: Kandoúni, Linária and Platís Gialós.

The Northern Tip★

North of Mirtiés, Emporiós is a charming coastal village and although the beach does not look immediately inviting it becomes more sandy at the western end.

NÍSSIROS★

This island south of Kos is a partially active volcano.

The village of **Mandraki**★, is one of the most beautiful places in the Dodecanese, is dominated by an ancient defensive wall and a medieval castle; inside is the Monastery of Panagía Spilianí and its rock church. Also worth a visit is the **Folk Museum**. Nissiros' **beaches** are of black sand; the finest are to be found at the northern end of the island.

Volcano★

Wear strong shoes. Bus from Mandráki, or on foot from the village of Nikiá.

Above the coastal villages of **Loutrá** and **Páli** (curative hot springs) lies the Láki plateau. You can walk down into the smoky, sulphurous Stéfanos crater. To the west of the main crater there is an equally remarkable double crater which can be reached on foot along a clearly defined pathway. Look out for the small blowholes emitting jets of steam. These jets and the colours and crystals and, in summer, the intense heat make the experience feel like a visit to another planet.

ADDRESSES

🛏️STAY

KOS

🛏️🍽️ **Hotel Maritina** – *Kos, 19 Odós Vironas.* ☎22420 23511. www.maritina.gr. *81 rooms.* Fine establishment with very comfortable rooms facing the Temple of Dionysos.

🛏️ **Panorama Studios** – *Kéfalos Bay.* ☎22420 71924. www.panorama-kefalos. gr. *17apts. May–Oct.* Gorgeous views over the bay from this isolated spot.

🛏️ **Syrtaki** – *Kéfalos Bay.* ☎22420 72139. *6 apts. Open May–Oct.* 🍽️ Excellent value, and a warm welcome from the owner. Rooms and studios face the sea.

KÁLIMNOS

🛏️ **Panorama** – *Póthia, on the left heading up from the port.* ☎/Fax 22430 23138. www.panorama-kalymnos. gr. *13 rooms.* In an elevated location overlooking the port (good view of the bay), this tranquil establishment has clean, comfortable rooms, and offers friendly, welcoming service.

🛏️ **Villa Melina** – *Póthia, northeast part of the town.* ☎22430 22682. http:// villa-melina.com. *23 rooms.* 🍽️ All the charm of a 19C mansion, conveniently yet quietly located in town. Pleasant garden.

NÍSSIROS

🛏️ **Pofyris** – *Mandráki, centre of the village.* ☎/fax 22420 31376. www.porfyris-nisyros.com. Modern rooms; salt-water swimming pool.

🍽️EAT

KOS

🍽️ **Agios Theologos** – *Agios Theologos, above the beach.* 🍽️ Tasty dishes made with fresh farm products.

🍽️ **Mummy's Cooking** – *Kos, 27 Odós Bouboulinas.* 🍽️ Popular spot, with Greek music.

🍽️ **Seaside** – *Mastihári, at the beginning of the beach facing west.* ☎22420 59284. Dine in the cool of a sea breeze. Friendly welcome; open all year for lunch and dinner.

🍽️ **Stamatia** – *Kéfalos Bay, on the beach.* ☎22420 71245. Homemade specialities with fruit, vegetables and chicken. Glorious bay window.

KÁLIMNOS

🍽️ **The Harbour Taverna** – *Vathís, on the quayside to the right.* ☎22430 3106. Good atmosphere and friendly welcome. Fresh fish depending on the catch, and traditional Greek fare served in a typical lively taverna.

🍽️ **Xeftéries** – *Póthia, in the street to the right of the cathedral.* ☎22430 28642. 🍽️. Simple but appetising food in generous portions. Pleasant open-air dining in the shade. Greek specialities, but no fish. Good value.

NÍSSIROS

🍽️ **Níssiros Taverna** – *Mandráki.* A good menu offering local specialities; excellent value.

🚶SPORTS AND LEISURE

Boat trips – To other islands including Kálimnos, Pséissiros, and also to Turkey, as well as day cruises around the Kos coastline to remote beaches. *Departures daily usually between 8.30–9.30am; enquire at the port.*

Diving – Several boats depart from the port at Kos and there are also several diving clubs in Kos Town, as well as around the island, where lessons can be taken and dives organised. **Kos Diving Centre,** *5 Odós Mitrop Nathanail (south of the agora),* ☎22420 20269.

Thermal baths – At **Empros,** 12km/7.5mi southwest of Kos Town. Here a natural warm spring gushes from a grotto and the waters flow down into a man-made pool alongside the sea, The pool's rocks and boulders are heated by the water and they in turn heat the seawater.

🎭EVENTS AND FESTIVALS

Easter Sunday sees traditional celebrations in Póthia's main square. Sunday is merely the culmination of many celebrations that go on throughout the town, and the whole island, in the days building up to Easter. Mass is celebrated on Saturday night, with a dramatic climax at midnight.

Pátmos★★★
Pátmos – Πάτμος

The tiny, arid island of Pátmos derives its extraordinary renown from its association with St John the Divine, the apostle who wrote the Book of Revelation in the Christian Bible, and from its 11C monastery, an important shrine of the Orthodox Church. The houses surrounding the monastery form the finest architectural group in the Aegean.

A BIT OF HISTORY

The author of the Apocalypse, by tradition identified as St John the Divine, was said to have been banished to Pátmos in AD 95 for preaching the Gospel at Ephesus. At the end of the 11C, the Emperor **Alexis I Comnenos** ceded the island to the monk **Christódoulos** for him to found a monastery dedicated to the saint.

Beginning in 1089 Christódoulos and his companions built massive walls to protect the monastery from pirate and Turkish raids, but shortly thereafter were forced into exile. Nonetheless, the community received extraordinary support: Christodoulos' relics were eventually returned to Pátmos, pilgrims soon thronged the monastery, and emperors and patriarchs donated the profits of arable land to the monastery. The library founded by Christódoulos enriched its collections and the monastic community produced many scholars.

At the end of the 13C the lay population resettled for protection at the base of the monastery's wall and founded the capital, Hóra.

In 1948, after centuries under Norman, Turkish and Italian rule, Pátmos finally became a part of Greece.

The development of tourism in Pátmos in recent years has not affected the great moral and spiritual influence of the Monastery of St John, and religious festivals continue to be of great relevance to the lives of the inhabitants. A text recounting the saint's voyages and miracles is

▶ **Population:** 3, 044.

Info: EOT; white building facing the ferry landing. ℘22470 31666. Open daily 9am–10pm, Jun–Aug only. www.12net.gr.

Location: The northern-most of the Dodecanese, Pátmos is also one of the smallest islands in the Aegean Sea.

Don't Miss: The monastery of St. John; Holy Week activities.

Timing: Plan a 2-day visit, in Holy Week if you can. Visit nearby Lipsí to truly get away from it all.

GETTING THERE
PÁTMOS
BY SEA – Ferry services to Piraeus *(6/wk)* via Naxos *(3/wk)* and Páros *(2/wk)*. Links to **Rhodes** *(6/wk)* via Kálimnos *(5/wk)*, Kos *(6/wk)* and Sými *(1–3/wk)*. Links to Limnos via Samos, Chios and Lesbos *(1/wk)*. During the summer months, the Dodecanese are well served by hydrofoil services.

LÉROS
BY SEA – Daily services from Kos, Kalimnos, Rhodes, Samos and Lipsi. From Piraeus, ferry service daily in summer *(11hrs)*.
BY AIR – Daily flight from Athens *(1hr)*. The **airport at Partheni** is around 10km/6mi from the capital, and is linked by taxi and bus services.

LIPSÍ
BY SEA – Hydrofoil services depart from Pátmos and Leros *(20min)*. From Piraeus, ferry service several times a week *(11–17hrs)*

illustrated on the walls of the monastery and of many other shrines; several places on the island are associated with the saint.

BEACHES
Psiliámo Beach★
South of Hóra, this beach may be the most beautiful on the island, and is often deserted.

Gríkou Bay★
By bus or 45min on foot from Hóra.
Traoníssi Islet rises at the far end of the curving bay; just to the south is Pétra Beach, a sandy crescent fringed by marshland. Close by is Kalíkastrou Rock, honeycombed with caves, and beyond is a tiny fishing port.

Kámbos and Lámbi
By boat or by bus to Kámbos and its beach, then about 35min on foot to Lámbi.
Kámbos is a large village overlooking a fertile valley. The vast and shady **Kámbos Beach** *(sand and pebbles)* is very popular in summer. The windswept **Lámbi Bay** *(2km/1mi north)* is famous for its coloured pebbles.

SKÁLA
The biggest town on the island, and home to the vast majority of its population, Skála is an attractive port with white cube houses; most of Pátmos' hotels, guesthouses and restaurants are located here. Boats run to many Pátmos beaches. For religious pilgrims, Skála is also known as the place where St John baptised the local people to convert them to Christianity.

View over Skála harbour

© Pierdelune/Dreamstime.com

Kastéli Hill★★
20min on foot, west of Skála.
There are traces of a Hellenistic wall and a small chapel, with a magnificent view of Skála harbour, Hóra, St John's Monastery and the neighbouring islands.

ÁGIOS IOÁNNIS THEÓLOGOS★★★
Between Skála and Hóra (just outside the latter). Access by bus or taxi, or on foot (about 30min) by an old mule track from Skála. ◷*Open daily 8am–1.30pm (Sun, Tue, Thu also 4–6pm).* ◈*No charge.*

Exterior Walls★★
Brooding over the white houses below, the circuit wall was built on a polygonal plan in the 11C–12C by the Blessed Christódoulos; its massive canted buttresses were added in the 17C. The terrace at the entrance affords a good **view**★ of Skála Harbour.

Central Courtyard
Beyond a dark zigzag passageway, the monastery's fortress-like appearance gives way to a maze of courtyards, stairs and domed white buildings with stone arcading. At the far end on the left is a huge jar in a round cistern, previously used to store the monastery's wine.

Main Church★ (Katholikón)
The 17C outer narthex (frescoes of the life of St John) leads to the 12C inner narthex. The **Chapel of the Blessed Christódoulos** was constructed in the 16C as the final resting place of the monk's relics, contained in an 18C wooden reliquary.
The main church is the oldest part of the monastery. Note its grey-and-white marble floor and heavy gilt-clad wood iconostasis (1820). Most of the frescoes on view were painted in the 19C on top of 17C murals.
Accessed from the main church, the **Chapel of the Virgin** has admirable late-12C **frescoes**★ that were uncovered during restoration work, and portray biblical scenes. The remaining murals depict, in the main, oriental saints and

Monastery of St. John

© Greek National Tourism Organisation

patriarchs. The chapel also contains a fine Cretan iconostasis in painted wood (1607) with an antique threshold step.

Old Refectory★

It contains two long stone tables faced with marble with niches in the bottom for the monks' cutlery. The floor comprises fragments from the ancient foundations and the early-Christian basilica. The style of the late 12C–13C **frescoes**★ on the upper west wall is more expressive than the 18C murals from the Chapel of the Virgin on the east wall (opposite the entrance). The earliest murals appear on the tympanum of the north arch (left of the entrance).

▷ *Return to the main courtyard by the vaulted passage.*

The old storerooms with the monks' cells (⊶*not open*) behind are on the left on the south side; the museum and shop are on the west side of the courtyard.

Museum★

⊙*Same opening hours as the monastery.* ⊷*€3. Some objects may not be on display because of exhibitions and religious ceremonies.*
The museum displays the most precious articles from the monastery's library, archives and treasury. The icon collection includes a rare 11C icon in mosaic of St Nicholas, probably from Asia Minor.

The treasury dates mostly from the 17C and is made up of donations from priests and patriarchs who were born or who studied in Pátmos, including a cross and medals given by Catherine II of Russia.

Terraces

Access from the first floor in the museum or from the courtyard.
The lower terrace, where the Chapel of the Holy Cross stands, provides an interesting bird's eye view of the main courtyard and part of the island.
⊶*At present the upper terraces are not accessible to visitors.*

HÓRA★★

The white houses of Hóra, which is also called Pátmos Town, form a sparkling necklace around the dark fortress. The houses (the oldest probably dates back to the 16C) line a maze of steps and lanes; traces of the walls of the fortified town are visible in the town centre.
The corbelled houses built by refugees from Constantinople stand in the Alótina district west of the monastery.
In the 17C Cretans settled in Kritiká to the east; in the 17C and the 18C prosperous families built their mansions on the hillside to the north. High walls screen the courtyards and façades, but the Neoclassical doorways decorated with carvings and mouldings, pedimented windows and, more rarely, balconies, can be seen from the street.

The town hall, a fine Neoclassical building, stands in **Lozia Square** *(Platía Lozia)*; from here there is a beautiful **view**★★ of the Convent of the Apocalypse on the north face of the hill and of Skála Harbour.

To the west of the town, the **Convent of the Source of Life (Zoodóhos Pigí)** is decorated with frescoes dating from 1607. The church is surrounded by courtyards bright with flowers.

Panorama★★★

From Pátmos Town head east to the three windmills overlooking the Gríkos road.
The area around the windmills provides admirable views of the island and the archipelago: west, Hóra and the monastery walls; Skála Harbour and Mérika Bay beyond the isthmus; on the horizon *(left to right from Hóra)* the elongated shape of Icarus and the islands of Foúrni; north, Kerketéas, the tallest peak on Sámos; between the mainland and the northeast tip of Pátmos, the islands of Arkí, Lipsí and Léros.

Cave of the Apocalypse★

15min on foot by a mule track going down from Hóra or up from Skála. There is a request bus stop near the convent.
🕐*Open daily 8am–1.30pm (Sun, Tue, Thu also 4–6pm).* ⊗*No charge.*
17C chapels and monks' cells line charming courts bedecked with flowers on the way down to St Anne's Chapel, which was founded in 1090 and rebuilt in the early 18C. According to a local tradition, it is in this grotto that St John had his vision of the world's end and the guide points to the rock which served as a desk where he wrote the Apocalypse.

EXCURSIONS
LIPSÍ

Lying to the east of Pátmos, this little island is unspectacular, but its beaches are peaceful, its paths attractive and its villages charming. The quayside tavernas serve the squid and fish caught by local fishermen each morning.

Lientou

Nestled in a small bay near a popular beach, this attractive little port is Lipsí's capital. In the Church of **Panagia tou Charou** is a fine icon representing the Virgin bearing the crucified Christ.

From the port, boats serve neighbouring islands and the **beaches**★ of Lipsí: **Platís Gialos** (north) and **Monodendri** (east).

A network of undemanding and excellent **walks**★★ *(maps available in the village)* allow visitors to explore the island's peaceful landscape. With only 700 inhabitants and a handful of visitors, Lipsí is one of the few islands that offers a taste of the old-fashioned island life.

LÉROS

Made up of three peninsulas, this island lying to the southeast of Pátmos has seven deep bays with beaches sheltered from the wind and the waves. Traditionally Léros has been an island of exile, and its bleak reputation, coupled with the existence of a huge psychiatric hospital, has not helped tourism to develop. It is, however, an attractive place popular with many Greek visitors, who appreciate its seascapes and hillsides planted with tobacco, fruit trees, olive groves and vineyards.

Bordered by the neighbouring villages of Pandeli and Ágia Marina (which is the point of arrival for many tourist boats and merchant vessels), **Platanos** is the capital of the island. A large Byzantine fortress which serves as a military observatory dominates the town.

Around Platanos

East of the airport *(9km/6mi north of Platanos)*, **Blefouti Beach**★ is the finest beach on the island, with only a solitary taverna open in summer by way of facilities.

To the north of Platanos, **Alinda,** made up of modern buildings along the beachfront, is the island's main resort. Its beach vies with Blefouti for being the loveliest on the island, and there is also a small Historic and Ethnographic Museum to explore *(🕐open Tue–Sun 9am–12.30pm and 6.30–9pm. €3).*

West of Platanos **Ágios Isidoros** church, the symbol of Léros, sits on a rocky outcrop linked to the rest of the island by a narrow isthmus.

Lakki

Situated in a bay, this was the site of an Italian naval base in the Second World War and in fact was only built in the 1930s to house the families of the workers at that naval base. Its imposing buildings are mostly deserted although a restoration programme is currently underway to restore them to their former glory.

To the west of Lakki are the two fine beaches of **Koulouki** and **Merikiá**, with Merikiá also the site of the island's fascinating War Museum (*open daily 10am–1pm. €3*).

ADDRESSES

STAY

PÁTMOS

○ **Sydney** – *Skála, yacht harbour, head up the alley to the left behind and above the Australis Hotel.* 22470 31689. *11 rooms. Open Apr–Oct.* Inexpensive guesthouse; warm welcome; comfortable rooms with fridges.

○ **Australis** – *Skála, after the first yacht moorings head up the alley to the left.* 22470 31576. *www.patmosaustralis.gr. 20 rooms, 4 apts. Open Apr–Oct.* Set in a magnificent garden, this hotel has comfortable, well-equipped rooms. Apartments for up to six people with kitchens.

LIPSÍ

○ **Hotel Aphrodite** – *Lientou, near the landing stage.* /Fax 22470 41000. *www.hotel-aphrodite.gr. 30 studios and apartments.* Attractive modern studio accommodation looking onto the beach.

LÉROS

○○○○ **Hotel Angeloux** – *Álinda.* 22470 22749. *www.hotel-angelou-leros.com. 9 rooms. Open May–Oct.* Housed in a Neoclassical mansion, this intimate hotel offers breakfast in a delightful garden and all rooms have ensuite showers.

EAT

PÁTMOS

○ **Khilimodi** – *Skála, second alley to the left of the road to Hóra.* 22470 3480. *Open all year, evenings only.* In a narrow street next to a small garden, this traditional little taverna is modest yet pleasant. Simple but tasty dishes and a warm welcome.

○ **Lampi** – *Lampi, on the beach.* 22470 31490. *Open Easter–early Oct.* Tables and chairs on the beach! Lobster, mackerel and cod on the menu.

○ **Loza** – *Hóra, lane leading to the town hall square.* 22470 32405. Prettiest terrace in Hóra, overlooking the north of the island. Creative, tasty dishes.

LIPSÍ

○ **Café du Moulin** – *Lientou, on the church square.* Local specialities.

LÉROS

○ **O Neromilos** – *Ágia Marina, on the Alinda road.* Fine regional cuisine in an exceptional setting.

EVENTS AND FESTIVALS

Holy Week is marked by fasting across Pátmos and on Maundy Thursday the Bishop re-enacts the washing of the disciples' feet in front of a huge crowd.

In **Kámbos** there are major festivals on 6 August (the Transfiguration) and 15 August (the Assumption).

23 to 26 August: **pilgrimage** to Lientou Church and village festival.

Around 10 August: **wine festival** – Pátmos, along with Sámos, Santorini and several other Greek islands, makes some good wine, and this exuberant wine festival is the perfect way to sample some tastings.

TAKING A BREAK

PÁTMOS

Bar Le Faros – *Ágia Marina.* Underground bar with music.

Rhodes★★★

Ródos – Ρόδος

Close to the shores of Turkey, the island of Rhodes is popular with visitors all year round. The landscape is varied and often mountainous (Mount Atáviros reaches a height of 1 215m/3 986ft). Renowned for its plant life, the "island of roses" is covered with conifers, semi-tropical shrubs, red hibiscus, mauve bougainvilleas and white scented jasmine.

A BIT OF HISTORY

The Island of Helios – According to Greek myth, Rhodes was given to **Helios** the sun god, and his descendants founded Ialyssos (near Filérimos), Líndos and Kámiros. According to historians, it was the Minoans who first colonised the island and worshipped the moon at these three locations and it was the Myceneans who later took over the island.

In the 7C BC these three cities were already trading throughout the Middle East as far as Egypt and founding colonies elsewhere. In 408 BC the three cities jointly founded the city of Rhodes, which rapidly eclipsed them.

The new town was a planned city, laid out on a grid, and admired throughout

- ▶ **Population:** 117, 007.
- ⚲ **Michelin Map:** 1 400sq km/ 540 sq mi – Michelin Map 737 Q-R 13-14 – Dodecanese – Aegean.
- ▯ **Info:** Dodecanese Islands Tourist Office: Corner of Odós Arhiepiskopou Makariou and Odós Papagou. ✆ 22410 44333. Open Mon–Fri 8am– 2.45pm. www.ando.gr/eot. Municipal Tourist Office: Platia Rimini, ✆ 22410 35945. Open Jun–Oct 9am–8pm.
- ▶ **Location:** Situated near Turkey, Rhodes is the fourth-largest Greek island.
- ▯ **Parking:** Limited space makes parking very difficult and parts of the town centre are closed to traffic (except taxis).
- ⊗ **Don't Miss:** The splendid citadel of Rhodes Town; Monolithos Castle; Lindos.
- ◷ **Timing:** Plan a 5-day stay on the island; you'll need 3 of those days to see all of Rhodes Town.

GETTING THERE AND GETTING AROUND

RHODES

BY AIR – During the summer there are many flights to Rhodes from most European capitals. Several flights a day from Athens *(1hr)* and Crete *(55min)*. The airport is near Paradisi on the northwest coast, 16km/10mi from Rhodes Town; regular bus service.

BY SEA – Rhodes is an important hub of maritime traffic. Service from Piraeus *(22/wk)*, Kos *(29/wk)*, Kálimnos *(28/wk)*, Pátmos *(11/wk)*, and many more. **ANES**, 88 Odós Australias. ✆ 22410 37769/77760. www.anes.gr. **Blue Star Ferries**, 111 Odós Amerikis, ✆ 22410

22461, www.bluestarferries.com. **Dodekanisos Seaways**, *3 Odós Australias*, ✆ 22410 70590, www.12ne.gr. Travel agencies sell tickets for most companies, but not always, so check with more than one; The EOT, local tourist office and harbourmaster's office all have timetables.

HÁLKI

BY SEA – From Skála Kámírou, southwest of Rhodes Town *(daily)* and Rhodes Town *(4/wk)*. Also from Piraeus *(2/wk summer; 1/wk winter)*.

KASTELÓRIZO

BY SEA – **Ferry** service from Rhodes *(3/wk in summer)*.

BY AIR – Service from Rhodes *(6/wk)*.

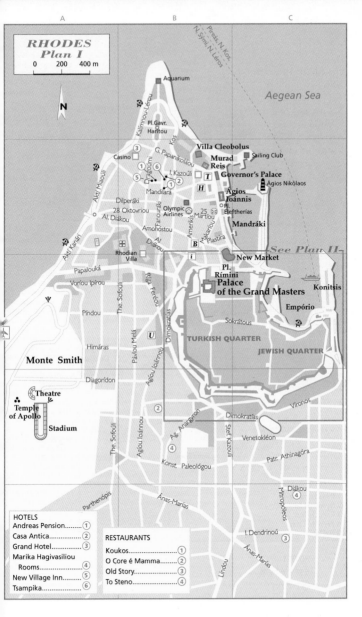

RHODES
Plan I
0   200   400 m

Aquarium

Aegean Sea

Pl. Gavr.
Harítou

Villa Cleobolus

Casino

Murad
Reis

Sailing Club

G. Papanikoláou

Governor's Palace

I. Kazoúli

Agios Nikólaos

Agios
Ioánnis

Mandilará

Olympic
Airlines

Dilperáki
28 Oktovríou
Al. Diákou

Eleftherías

Amohóstou

Mandráki

Rhodian
Villa

New Market

Papalouká

Pl.
Rímini
Palace
of the Grand Masters

Voríou Ipírou

Konitsís

Píndou

Empório

Sokrátous

Himáras

TURKISH QUARTER

JEWISH QUARTER

Monte Smith

Diagorídon

Theatre
Temple
of Apollo

Stadium

Víronos

Dimokratías

Konst. Paleológou

Venetokléon

Patr. Athinagóra

Diákou

Parthenópis

Ánas-Marías

I. Dendrinoú

Ánas-Marías

HOTELS	
Andreas Pension	①
Casa Antica	②
Grand Hotel	③
Marika Hagivasiliou Rooms	④
New Village Inn	⑤
Tsampika	⑥

RESTAURANTS	
Koukos	①
O Core é Mamma	②
Old Story	③
To Steno	④

the ancient world as a model design for a modern metropolis. During the 3C and the 2C BC, the island became the main maritime power in the eastern Mediterranean because of its fleet and its wealth. The arts flourished, particularly a school of sculpture, as immortalised by the famous **Colossos** of Rhodes. This great wonder was built by recycling the material of giant siege machinery that had been used in a year-long siege of the island following the death of Alexander the Great and a squabble for possession of the island by his generals.

Front Line of Christianity – From 1306 until 1522 the island was a Christian bastion under the very noses of the Turks, and the Knights of St John of

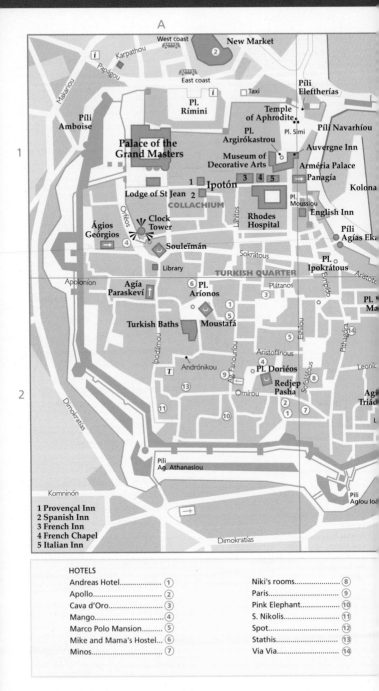

A

West coast

New Market

Karpathou

Papágou

Makaríou

East coast

Taxi

Píli
Eleftherías

Pl.
Rímini

Temple
of Aphrodite

Píli Navarhíou

Píli
Amboise

Pl.
Argirókastrou

Pl. Simi

Auvergne Inn

**Palace of the
Grand Masters**

Museum of
Decorative Arts

Arméria Palace

Panagía

Kolona

1 Ipotón 3 4 5

Lodge of St Jean 2

COLLACHIUM

English Inn

Orféos

Rhodes
Hospital

Pl.
Moussíou

Ágios
Geórgios

Clock
Tower

Láhitos

Píli
Agías Eka

Souleïmán

Sokrátous

Pl.
Ipokrátous

Library

TURKISH QUARTER

Aristote

Apoloníon

Agía
Paraskeví

Pl.
Aríonos

Plátanos

Pl.
Ma

Turkish Baths

Moustafá

Eshiliou

Evripído

Pithagóra

Aristofánous

Leoníc

Andrónikou

Apollonúou

Pl. Doriéos

Sofokléous

Ag
Triád

Omírou

Redjep
Pasha

Dimokratías

Píli
Ag. Athanasíou

Komninón

Píli
Agíou Ioa

1 Provençal Inn
2 Spanish Inn
3 French Inn
4 French Chapel
5 Italian Inn

Dimokratías

HOTELS

Andreas Hotel.................... ①
Apollo.............................. ②
Cava d'Oro....................... ③
Mango............................. ④
Marco Polo Mansion.......... ⑤
Mike and Mama's Hostel... ⑥
Minos.............................. ⑦

Niki's rooms..................... ⑧
Paris............................... ⑨
Pink Elephant.................. ⑩
S. Nikolis........................ ⑪
Spot............................... ⑫
Stathis............................ ⑬
Via Via........................... ⑭

Jerusalem who served here constructed many buildings with French influences. In 1523, the Knights fell to Suleiman the Magnificent; the Turks were to stay for nearly four centuries. Ruled in the 20C by Italians, Germans and lastly the British, Rhodes became part of the Greece on 7 March 1948.

B

Konitsis

Píli
Mílon

Empório

Archbishopric

③

JEWISH QUARTER

✡

⑫

Pl.Gavr.
Haritou

Vironos

RHODES
Plan II

0   100   200 m

RESTAURANTS

Despina's............................ ①
Isimi..................................... ②
Lefteras............................... ③
Mama Sofia.......................... ④
Sea Star............................... ⑤

RÓDOS★★★
(RHODES TOWN)

The city is situated at the northeastern end of the island, facing the Turkish coast. The superb medieval "Old Town" was restored by Italian architects early in the 20C, and the modern town attracts visitors to its beaches, hotels, nightclubs and countless boutiques. This is a resort of international repute, popular in both summer and winter. Many cruise ships also come to visit, giving the New Town a prosperous, cosmopolitan feel, and it is one of the most enjoyable capital cities in the whole of the Greek islands.

OLD TOWN★★★
This World Heritage Site has to be explored on foot, and while packed with people in some places, there are also quieter areas.

Citadel★★
Despite its troubled history and restoration works of varying success, the citadel remains an imposing sight. The knights and their attendants lived in this part of the city, which was fortified on all four sides and called **Collachium.**

Píli Amboise (Amboise Gate)
An arched bridge over a moat stood at the approach to the gate (1512). A passage leads to St Antony's Gate which opens into the Palace Square.

Paláti Megálon Magístron★
(Palace of the Grand Masters)
🕐Open Tue–Sun 8.30am–7.30pm, Mon 12.30–7.30pm, off-season Tue–Sun 8.30am–3pm, Mon 12.30–3pm. ⊛€6 (combined ticket for the palace, and the Byzantine, Archaeological and Decorative Arts museums: €10).
On the site where many scholars think the Colossus probably stood, the Grand Masters' residence (14C) more closely resembles a palace than a fortress. It was protected by a moat, crenellated walls and towers, and a keep, and had three underground floors of storerooms to hold victuals and munitions.

Odós Ipotón★★ (Knights' Street)
This medieval cobbled street is lined with Inns, the 15C and 16C Gothic buildings in which the knights lived according to their nationality.

Colossos of Rhodes

Nothing remains of the Colossos of Rhodes, the huge bronze statue of the sun god Helios that came to embody the island's power. Created by Chares of Líndos around 300 BC, it ranked among the Seven Wonders of the Ancient World. Believed to have been 30m/98ft high (the Statue of Liberty measures 46m/150ft), the statue was destroyed by an earthquake in 225 BC. It lay in ruins for 800 years before being removed by a Syrian merchant who needed 900 camels to carry away all the pieces. Its exact location is a topic of debate: was it at the harbour mouth, on the shoreline, or in the town itself?

Panagía Kástrou

🕑*Open Tue–Sun 8.30–2.45pm.* 🎫*€2.*
St Mary's Church (12C) was transformed into a Latin cathedral by the Knights, who incorporated it into the ramparts. Later the Turks turned it into a mosque; today it houses the Byzantine Museum *(frescoes, mosaics).*

Katálima Anglías

The **English Inn** was built in 1483 but later demolished; it was rebuilt in 1919.

Nossokomío Ipotón★

🕑*Open Tue–Sun, 8.30am–2.45pm.*
📞*22410 25500.* 🎫*3€.*
The impressive Knights' Hospital was completed in 1505. Beyond the door a vaulted passageway leads into an inner court; there were shops on the ground floor. Today it houses the **Archaeological Museum**, featuring the **Aphrodite of Rhodes★**. The hospital proper was on the upper floor. The Great Ward of the Sick could accommodate about 100 patients. Note the chapel entrance, which is carved with festoons, and the alcoves where those with contagious diseases were isolated.

Katálima Overnis

Leave Hospital Square by the northwest corner, passing in front of St Mary's Church to reach Platía Alexándrou, a small square containing the **Auvergne Inn** (14C).
Pass under the arch into another square; the fountain at the centre was created out of Byzantine baptismal fonts.

Arméria (Arsenal)

One wing of the main building (14C) contains the **Museum of Decorative Arts** (Diakosmitikí Silogí): furniture, costume and a beautiful collection of Rhodian ceramics (🕑*open Tue–Sun 8.30am–2.40pm;* 🎫*€2*).
Continue north to the ruins of a **Temple to Aphrodite** and then turn right *(east)* through the Arsenal Gate (Píli Navarhíou) onto the harbour quay.

Embório★ (Harbour)

In the days of the Hospitallers the entrance was closed by an enormous chain strung between the square Naillac Tower (Pírgos Naillac), and the Mill Tower (Pírgos Mílon).From the waterfront on the seaward side of the Arsenal Gate there is a fine perspective *(south)* of the ramparts, and the minarets of the Turkish district.

Píli Agías Ekaterínis★

Impressive **St Catherine's** (or **Marine) Gate** (1478) has four machicolated towers.

Town★

Bear left through the gate into **Platía Ipokrátous** with its Turkish fountain; on the far side stands the **Lódzia Embóron** (Merchants' Loggia); behind it *(southeast)* lay the Jewish district.

▷ *Turn west along Odós Sokrátous which marks the northern limit of the Turkish district.*

Turkish District★

After the Aga Mosque turn left on Odós Fanouríou, one of the oldest and most picturesque streets; take the second turn on the right which leads to Platía Aríonos to see the 18C **Mustapha Mosque** (Dzamí Moustafá) and the

Turkish Baths (16C). Take Odós Arhe-láou and Odós Ipodámou *(northwest)* past the 15C Church of **Agía Paraskeví** *(left)* to reach the **Suleiman Mosque** (Dzamí Souleimán). Turn off into Odós Apoloníon to visit **St George's Church** (Ágios Geórgios) *(no. 18)*.

◯ *Return along Odós Apoloníon and turn left into Odós Orféos passing beneath the Clock Tower or belfry to return to St Anthony's Gate and Amboise Gate.*

RAMPARTS WALK★★

The walk on the ramparts *(○━ currently closed for restoration work)* covers four sections called "boulevards", and assigned respectively to Germany, the Auvergne, Spain and England; the next two boulevards running east to the shore were assigned to Provence and Italy. Ask locally for details of when sections of the ramparts may be re-opened.

MANDRÁKI★

On either side of the entrance to this protected harbour, the Italians erected a column supporting two bronze deer (a buck and a doe), the symbolic animals of Rhodes. According to tradition this was originally the site of the Colossos of Rhodes, though this isn't backed up by any archaeological evidence. The east mole (three windmills), ends in St Nicholas' Tower (Ágios Nikólaos).

MODERN TOWN

The northern part of the town west of Mandráki was built during the Italian period (1912–1943). Liberty Square (Platía Eleftherías), a lively stretch of waterfront with pleasant gardens, is closed at the southern end by New Market (Néa Agora), and on the north by St John's Church (**Ágios Ioánis**). Platía Vassilíou Georgíou, the administrative centre, is bordered by the **Governor's Residence** (Nomarhía), the Town Hall (Dimarhío) and the theatre. Farther north, the charming **Murad Reis Mosque**★ (Dzamí Mourát Réïs) is surrounded by Muslim tombstones; the graves of the men are distinguished

by a turban *(○open daily 1–2pm; ∞no charge).* To the west are a number of pedestrianised streets with hotels and restaurants.

Rodíni Park
2km/1.3mi south: access by no. 3 bus near New Market.
This large, pleasant park is perfect for strolling; there is a small zoo.

AKRÓPOLI (Mount Smith)
4km/2.5mi or 1hr 30min on foot there and back; no. 5 bus from the New Market.
Several elements of the ancient city (5C BC) still exist; the theatre (2C BC) – only the lower terrace is authentic – the stadium (2C BC) and the Temple to Pythian Apollo.
From the top of Mount Smith there are superb **views**★★, particularly at sunset.

THE INTERIOR
Petaloúdes★ (Butterfly Valley)
◯ *24km/15mi from Rhodes Town.*
○*Open 8am–dusk.* ∞*Apr no charge; May–mid-Jun & Oct €3; mid-Jun–Sept €5)* ○*Closed off-season. Parking a little out of the way.*
From June to September this shady rock-strewn valley is filled with orange and black butterflies. A path climbs up the valley and is carried on wooden bridges over the narrow stream which tumbles in cascades and waterfalls.

Profítis Ilías (Mount Elijah)
◯ *49km/31mi from Rhodes Town.*
A small summer resort has been built on the upper slopes. To the east, 2km/1.25mi before reaching Eleoússa, is the Church of **Ágios Nikólaos Foun-touklí** with some medieval frescoes.

Émbonas
◯ *62km/39mi from Rhodes Town.*
Émbonas has kept its traditional ways: women in local dress can be seen spinning, or working the fields. In some houses walls are hung with **Rhodes faience**. In Émbonas you can arrange to climb **Mount Atáviros** with a guide *(6hrs on foot there and back)*; from the

top, where a Sanctuary to Zeus once stood, there is a fine **view**★.

Monastery of Thári

70km/44mi from Rhodes Town. No charge; appropriate clothing available.

The church has medieval frescoes; fine liturgical chants may often be heard here.

🚗 DRIVING TOUR

TOUR OF THE ISLAND★★

Around 200km/125mi round trip from Rhodes Town. Allow 2 days.

There are good hotels in Líndos and Monolithos. The best beaches are marked on the map and the tour takes in monasteries, ruined castles and archaeological remains.

Drive 15km/9mi along the coast road south, at first through several holiday resorts.

Kalithéa Spa★

The waters here were recommended by Hippocrates. In 1929 the Italians built a little spa with white pavilions (no longer in use). There is a charming sandy beach.

Beach and Monastery of Tsambíka

Views extend along the coast from the monastery overlooking the sandy beach.

Drive through the hamlet of Haráki and look for the castle ruins.

Feraklós Castle

45min on foot there and back from the foot of the hill (where you can leave the car).

Only a few ruined walls remain of one of the largest castles built by the Knights of St John, but there is a fine **view**★★ of the bays on either side of the promontory.

Continue on south and around the bay which leads to Líndos.

Líndos★★

Leave vehicle at the upper parking area, to the right on arrival.

Líndos is a spectacular **site**★★★ bearing the mark of three civilisations – ancient, Byzantine and medieval Greek. There is also a fine **beach**★ here.

With its two natural harbours and its easily defended hill, Líndos has been inhabited since the prehistoric era. After the Byzantines and the Genoese came the Knights Hospitaller who built an imposing fortress (1503).

Souvenir shops and white houses line the narrow streets of the **town**★; the most beautiful houses were built for wealthy ship owners or sea captains in the 16C and the 17C. Some of the internal courtyards have a black and white pebble pattern. The Church of the Virgin (Panagía) in the town centre has 17C and 18C frescoes.

Acropolis and Citadel★★

Access by a path and steps (1hr on foot or by donkey there and back). Open Tue–Sun 8.30am–2.40pm. €6.

A long flight of steps and a vaulted passage emerge near St John's Chapel. Take a second vaulted passage under the Governor's palace on the left which emerges below the **acropolis** excavated in the early 20C. About 20 columns mark the position of the great Doric portico *(stoa)* which was preceded by a great staircase leading up to the entrance *(propylaia)* to the ancient **Sanctuary to Athena Lindia** (4C BC). From the hilltop there are splendid **views**★★★ of the headland and the coast.

Continue south through Péfkoi and turn inland to Asklipiío.

Asklipiío

This is an interesting village because of its site, its old houses and its fortress. The church (1060), is decorated with fine frescoes *(for access, enquire at the museum).*

The itinerary continues across a wilder landscape. If time permits, head south of Kattavia; the beach at **Prassonissi** is popular with windsurfers.

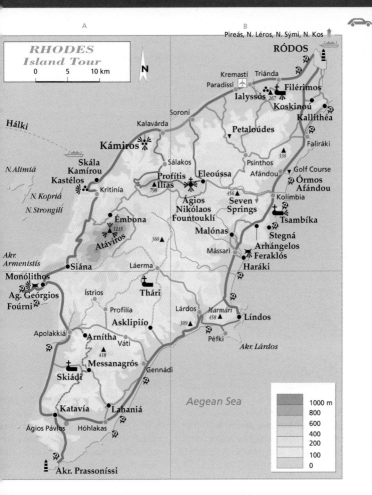

RHODES
Island Tour

0   5   10 km

RÓDOS

Kremastí Triánda
Paradíssi
Ialyssós   Filérimos
267
Koskinoú
Kallithéa
Soroní
Kalavárda   Petaloúdes
Hálki   Faliráki
Kámiros
330
Sálakos   Psínthos
Skála   Afándou   Golf Course
Kamírou   Profítis   Eleoússa
N. Alimiá   Íllias   Órmos
Kastélos   Kritinía   798   456   Kolímbia   Afándou
N. Kopriá   Ágios   Seven
N. Strongílí   Nikólaos Springs
Émbona   Fountouklí   Tsambíka
1215   Malónas   Stegná
Atáviros   360   Arhángelos
Akr.   Mássari   Feraklós
Armenistís   Siána   Láerma   Haráki
Monólithos
Ístrios   Thári
Ag. Geórgios
Foúrni   Profília   Lárdos   Marmári
309   458   Líndos
Apolakkiá   Arnítha Váti   Péfki
418   Akr. Lárdos
Messanagrós   Gennádi
Skiádi
Aegean Sea
Katavía   Lahaniá
1000 m
Ágios Pávlos   Hóhlakas   800
600
400
200
100
Akr. Prassoníssi   0

Otherwise head west across the island to the village of Apolakkiá and its nearby monastery.

Monastery of Skiádi

This restored monastery is of Byzantine origin, dating mainly from the 18C, and there are impressive coastal views from here.

Head back north up the west coast. There is a narrow turning north of Monólithos village.

Monólithos Castle★★

The Knights of Rhodes built Monólithos Castle on a spectacular **site★★** at the top of a rocky escarpment. A path leads up to the fortress; the view extends

across the sea to Hálki Island. Nearby is the attractive beach of **Ágios Georgios**.

30min drive north.

Ruins of Kritinía Castle★

Access by road for 1.2km/0.75mi, then 15min on foot.

On a spur over the sea are the ruins of Kritinía Castle; **views★** from the site.

A very short drive from the castle are the ruins of Kámiros.

Ancient Ruins of Kámiros★

Open Tue–Sun 8am–6.40pm (off-season 8.30am–3pm). €4.

In antiquity, Kámiros was one of the three great cities of Rhodes. Excavations

429

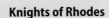

Knights of Rhodes

Founded in the 11C to protect pilgrims in the Holy Land, the Order of the **Hospitallers of St John of Jerusalem,** was both a religious and a military body. In 1291, the Knights of St John had to leave the Holy Land; they moved first to Cyprus then to Rhodes, a Genoese possession, which became their main base in their struggle against the Turks in the eastern Mediterranean.

The Knights were divided along national lines – France, Provence, Auvergne, Aragon, Castille, Italy and England. The Order was ruled by the Grand Master; French and Latin were the official languages. The Knights took vows of poverty and chastity and were assisted by squires.

When the Knights Templar were suppressed in 1312 and their possessions and duties passed to the Hospitallers, the latter built a fleet which took part in the papal crusades. In 1331 the Hospitallers signed a treaty with the French, the Italians and the Byzantine Emperor against the Turks.

In 1444 and again in 1480 Rhodes was besieged by the Turks but without success. A third siege in 1522 was to signal the end for the Knights on Rhodes. For a good six months, 650 Knights and about 1 000 auxiliaries held out against an army of 100 000 Turks led by **Suleiman the Magnificent** before surrendering. On 1 January 1523, the Grand Master, **Villiers de l'Isle-Adam** (1464–1534) and the 180 Knights who had survived left Rhodes for Malta.

---

have brought to light traces of a 3C BC sanctuary consisting of a Doric temple; lower down there is a semicircular seat *(exedra)*, and an area for sacrificial altars; Hellenistic houses, several with peristyles; an *agora* lined by a long 3C AD portico *(stoa)*, and a temple dedicated to Athena Kamíria, dating from the 5C BC.

▶ *It is almost 1 hour's drive north along the west coast to yet more impressive remains.*

Iálissos and Mount Filérimos★
Founded by the Phoenicians, the ancient city of **Iálissos** stands on Mount Filérimos, overlooking the coastal plain. On the acropolis are the foundations of a 4C BC temple and a palaeo-Christian basilica. The Gothic monastery (◷open Tue–Sun 8am–7pm; off-season 8.30am–2.45pm; ⊜€4) was restored in the early 20C; from here there is a vast **panorama**★★ of the northern end of the island.

EXCURSIONS
Hálki
Lying to the west of Rhodes, this little island has become prosperous as emigrants return, bringing the results of their financial success with them. The restored **harbour** is largely Neoclassical in style. The walk to the abandoned **Monastery of Ágios Ioannis** (⏱6h. there and back on foot by a road which becomes a track and then a path; take plenty of water and a hat) is delightful. From Hálki, you can take a boat to the untouched island of **Alimia**.

Kastelórizo (Megísti)
Just a kilometre from the Turkish coast, the island is striking for its attractive beaches and sea caves. The fortified **harbour,** a charming settlement of around 50 neo-Classical houses is dominated by a citadel built by the Knights of Rhodes and the nearby Megisti Museum displays Byzantine and folk art. ◷Open Tue–Sun 7am–2pm. ☎22410 49283. ⊜No charge. Accessible by boat from the harbour. **The Blue Grotto**★ is a magnificent sea cave with a phosphorescent blue tinge. The stalactites look magical at dusk.

ADDRESSES

🏠STAY

RHODES

🛏 **Mango Rooms** – *Rhodes, Old Town, Dorieos Sq. www.mango.gr/accomodation.htm. 6 rooms.* 🍴. Youth hostel open to all; bar and internet access downstairs.

🛏–🛏 **Pension Minos** – *Rhodes, Old Town, 5 Odós Omírou.* 🕿*22410 31813. www.minospension.com. 15 rooms.* Clean, renovated guesthouse with spacious rooms; roof garden offering panoramic views over the Old Town.

🛏 **Pink Elephant** – *Rhodes, Old Town, 9 Odós Timakida.* 🕿*22410 224 69. www.pinkelephantpension.com. 10 rooms. Apr–Oct.* Near the walls in the southern part of the town, in a quiet area. Attractive and well-kept, with pretty decor.

🛏 **Thomás Hotel** – *Monólithos.* 🕿*22460 61291. 10 rooms.* 🍴. Quiet, modern hotel with clean, comfortable, spacious, rooms with terraces and good views. Ideal base for excursions.

🛏🛏 **Maria's Rooms** – *Rhodes, Old Town, 7 Odós Menekleous.* 🕿*22410 22169. 8 rooms.* 🍴. *Apr–Oct.* In a quiet quarter of Old Town, Maria offers simple but very clean and inexpensive accommodation

🛏🛏 **Hotel Via Via** – *Rhodes, Old Town, 45 Odós Pithagóra.* 🕿*22410 77027/69485 22081. www.hotel-via-via.com. 9 rooms.* 🍴. Designer decor in glorious colours; attractive rooms. Rooftop terrace with views of Old Town and the harbour.

🛏🛏 **Marco Polo Mansion** – *Rhodes, Old Town, 40–42 Odós Agíou Fanouríou.* 🕿*22410 255 62. www.marcopolomansion. gr. 7 rooms. Apr–Oct.* The most charming hotel in the Old Town. Occupying an old Turkish house with its own *hammam* (Turkish bath).

HÁLKI

There are private rooms, apartments and hotel accommodation, but booking in advance is essential.

🛏 **Hotel Hálki** – *At the harbour.* 🕿*22460 453 90. 29 rooms.* Balconies with fine views and direct access to the seashore.

KASTELÓRIZO

🛏🛏 **Megisti** – *At the harbour.* 🕿*22460 49272. www.megistihotel.gr. 19*

rooms and suites. The only hotel on the island (the other accommodations are guesthouses) and very well maintained. Good view of the Turkish coast from some rooms. Sun deck runs along the shoreline providing direct access to the sea.

🍴EAT

🍽 **L'Auberge** – *Rhodes, Old Town, 21 Odós Praxitélous.* 🕿*22410 34292.* 🍴. Slightly off the beaten track in the north of the Old Town. Excellent cuisine and a fine choice of French and Greek wines, impeccable service and a friendly welcome.

🍽 **Baki Brothers** – *Émbonas, upper village.* 🕿*22460 41247.* 🍴. Traditional dishes; meats are the speciality. Try the lamb cutlets, veal *souvlaki* or the steak.

🍽 **Broccolino** – *Lindos, east of town.* 🕿*22440 31688.* Italian–American proprietors run this charming, artistic restaurant. Homemade pastas, excellent cheeses.

🍽 **Chalki** – *30 Odós Kathopouli.* 🕿*222410 31235.* 🍴. *May–Oct.* Traditional tavern with icons, old photos on the walls; excellent dishes, including marinated tuna and aubergine stuffed with tomato.

🍽 **Mezedákia** – *Genádi, 500m/550yds out of town on the Rhodes Town road.* 🕿*/Fax 22440 43627.* 🍴. A fish restaurant, very popular with locals on Sundays. Very good food and friendly welcome.

🍽🍽🍽 **Alexis Taverna** – *Rhodes, Old Town, 18 Odós Sokratous.* 🕿*22410 29347.* An Old Town institution serving the best fish around and an inventive menu; fantastic atmosphere and booking is essential.

🍽🍽 **Old Story** – *Rhodes, Modern Town, 108 Odós Mitropóleos.* 🕿*22410 32421.* Very popular with locals; pleasant setting, original decor and attentive service. A good wine list accompanies the carefully prepared, modern Greek cuisine. Reservations essential.

HÁLKI

🍽 **Maria** – *At the harbour.* Good taverna offering local specialities.

KASTELÓRIZO

🍽🍽 **Lazarakis** – *At the harbour.* Attractive location. Seafood and fish.

🚌 TAKING A BREAK

Marco Polo Café – *Rhodes, Old Town, 40–42 Odós Agíou Fanouríou. 🕾22410 37889.* Steps lead to a quiet garden in a courtyard where good cocktails are served.

Lovía Lounge – *Platía Arionos.* Relaxed ambience in the lounge; lively concerts in the room at the back.

Haraki Dreams – *Haraki, waterfront.* Internet café, perfect for an afternoon break to drink in views of bay and kástro.

HÁLKI

Café Theodosia – *On the harbour.* Ice cream and cakes.

🤸 SPORTS AND LEISURE

Watersports – The island of Rhodes offers excellent watersports; there are several diving clubs based in Rhodes Town (Mandráki Harbour).

Golf – 18-hole course at Afandou, *🕾22410 85513. www.afandougolfcourse.com.*

Turkish Baths – *On Platía Aríonos in the Old Town. Open Mon–Fri 10am–5pm, Sat 8am–5pm. €5.* Separate baths for men and women; bring flip-flops or sandals.

Sound and Light Show – Every evening in the municipal garden; information at the tourist office.

Shows of folkdancing and folksongs in traditional costume. *Odós Androiko, May–Oct Mon, Wed, Fri evenings.*

🛒 SHOPPING

Local arts and crafts – Jewellery (gold and silver), goldware, leather and ceramics is of good quality. There are plenty of shops around **Platía Kíprou** and **Odós Griva** in the modern town. Look for Oriental rugs at Afántou, embroideries at Líndos, leather boots at Archángelos.

🎭 EVENTS AND FESTIVALS

HÁLKI

On 29 August, the island celebrates its feast day at the monastery of Ágios Ioannis Alargas.

Sými★★

Sými – Σύμη

Less than 5km/3mi from the Turkish coast, Sými is a charming, peaceful island. Its rocky mountains rise dramatically from the sea and give it a wild appearance. The island has attractive bays that encourage the visitor to linger and many fine Neoclassical houses.

A BIT OF HISTORY

According to Homer, Sými sent a contingent of three ships to join the Greek flotilla sailing for Troy. The ships were commanded by the island's king, Nireus, famous for his manly beauty that was only outmatched by Achilles himself. Following this illustrious start, little is then heard of the island although the Romans and Byzantines both dropped by and stationed troops there until the Knights arrived and turned it into a useful outpost for their headquarters at Rhodes.

> ▶ **Population:** 2, 606.
> 🕗 **Michelin Map:** 57sq km/ 22sq mi – Michelin Map 737 Q 12 – Dodecanese – Aegean.
> ℹ **Info:** A Visitor Office opens on the harbour in summer, irregular hours; www.symi.gr.
> ▷ **Location:** Sými lies 20km/12mi northwest of Rhodes. Most beaches are accessible only by boat.
> 🚩 **Don't Miss:** Sými Town; a swim in a deserted bay or beach.
> 🕐 **Timing:** Plan a 2-day stay.

Prosperity came in the wake of Ottoman rule when Suleiman the Magnificent was persuaded not to ransack the island in return for an annual tribute of sponges. By all accounts, the quality of the sponges was exceptional and the urks allowed the island to become a free port and promoted its trade in sponges. This was the basis of Sými's prosperity and the population increased significantly as a result. What brought all this to an end was the Italian occupation in the early 20C and the development of synthetic sponges which destroyed its lucrative trade (the ones you see on sale everywhere are imports).

SÝMI TOWN★★

The island's little capital is a triumph of harmony and beauty. Protected by the archaeological authorities, it is composed of two districts: the lively and colourful harbour area, and the upper town with its fine pastel-coloured houses. As you walk around, look for the ruined old mansions that date back to the 19C when sponge merchants became rich and lavished their profits on the building of fine houses.

Harbour (Gialós)★★

The focus for tourist visitors with many shops, restaurants and hotels. The daytrip boats from Rhodes all arrive around mid-morning and the place becomes mildly frenetic for a few hours.

Behind the harbour front is a small **Maritime Museum** with some fine model ships and examples of the equipment once used in sponge-diving. *Open Tue–Sun 11am–4pm. €2.*

Sými harbour

© Matej Micheliza/iStockphoto.com

GETTING THERE

BY SEA – Frequent **ferry** service to Rhodes and Kos, in addition to catamarans (all year) and hydrofoils (summer). Also ferry links to Piraeus (2/wk) via Kos, Kálimnos and Pátmos.

There is some lovely domestic architecture that dates back to the pre-Italian period; look for the decorative details to be found on some of the window frames and doorways. The old 19C pharmacy is sure to catch your eye and there are many churches to admire.

Upper Town (Horió)★★

A steep stairway of some 400 steps leads up to this cluster of 18 and 19C Neoclassical houses. The **Sými Museum** *(open Tue–Sun, 10am–2pm; €2)* displays palaeo-Christian statuary, 12C and 13C Byzantine pottery, fine icons and traditional costumes. The museum's annexe is housed in a grand old mansion that was built in 1800, one of the best to be seen in a restored state, and it is home to an impressive collection of decorated old wooden chests that once belonged to the well-off families who lived in houses like this one.

Castle

At the top of the hill, the original island acropolis, this fortress with its church was built by the Knights of Rhodes. The original church was blown up by the Germans in the Second World War after a secret cache of arms was found inside it. When the church was rebuilt, a grim reminder of the war was incorporated into the bell-tower by using the nose-cone of a thousand-pound bomb as one of the bells. From here, there are fine **views**★★ of the sea and the town.

OUTSKIRTS OF SÝMI★

The lovely **bay** and **village of Emboriós**★★ *(4km/2.5mi west of Sými Town, 1hr 30min there and back on foot, or by water taxi 10am–2pm, 4–6pm)* offer pleasant walks, and swimming directly off the quay.

Also worth a stop is **Pédi**★ *(2km/1.25mi east of Sými Town)* with its charming fishing port and beach.

From Gialós, boats serve the **beaches**★ of Pédi, Georgios Dissalonas, Nano, Marathounda, Ágios Vassilios, and Sesklio. Good **walks**★★ along the rocky coast.

MONASTERIES

The island is richly endowed with monasteries. Some are huge, others tiny. There are some remarkable frescoes to be seen; in the 18C Sými was the centre of a renowned school of religious painting. There are also around 60 chapels.

St Michael Roukouniótis (Ágios Mikhaíl Roukouniótis)

1hr on foot from Sými Town, or by vehicle. ☏69777 09327.

This small monastery has some great treasures; its 14C church (rebuilt in the 16C) is the oldest religious building on the island and houses a fine iconostasis of St Michael made of solid gold and silver.

St Michael of Panormítis (Moní Taxiárhou Mihaíl)

▶ *South end of the island.*

Access by boat (1hr) from Sými Town, departing between 10am and 12pm, returning around 4–5pm. Road access is difficult. If coming to Sými on a day trip from Rhodes, your boat may stop here first.

This huge monastery dedicated to St Michael, patron saint of Sými, is a pilgrimage site that receives very high numbers of visitors during the main religious festivals (Pentecost and 8 November). It is possible to stay here. The 18C monastery is now surrounded by modern buildings. The church has a fine wooden iconostasis and a **Museum of Religious Art** (○*opens to coincide with the boat trips,* ✆€1.50), located in a corner of the inner courtyard. There are no great treasures to be seen because the monastery was thoroughly ransacked during the Second World War. There is a bakery and a taverna near the monastery. The memorial that stands near the taverna commemorates the

death by execution of three Greek me by the Germans in 1944 for aiding Britis commandos.

ADDRESSES

🏠STAY

🛏 **Pension Catherinettes** – *Gialós, west quay.* ☏22460 71671. marina-epe@ rho.forthnet.gr. *6 rooms.* 🍴. Elegant, patrician residence. Painted ceilings, balconies offering one of Sými's best views.

🛏 **Marika** – *Gialós, west quay.* ☏22460 72750/69445 44981. *May–Oct. 5 rooms.* 🍴 Small house just steps from the quay, near the clocktower. No breakfast.

🛏 **Hotel Albatros** – *Gialós, alley at centre of the harbour.* ☏22460 71 829/71 707. www.albatrosymi.gr. *Open Apr–Oct. 5 rooms.* 🍴. Recently renovated, this small hotel is spotlessly clean. Helpful management.

🛏 **Hotel Fiona** – *Horió, on the left up the large staircase.* ☏/Fax 22460 72088. www.fionahotel.com. *11 rooms.* 🍴. This quiet, clean hotel is in a pleasant location overlooking the sea.

🛏🛏🛏 **Villa Thalassa** – *Gialós, eastern quayside; enquire at the Hotel Albatros.* ☏22460 71829/71707. www.albatrosymi.gr *5 apts.* 🍴. Restored Neoclassical villa, split into a number of apartments (accommodating from two to five persons).

🍴EAT

🍽 **Mythos Meze** – *On the harbour (Gialós), east quay.* ☏22460 71488. One of the best restaurants on the harbour. Fresh fish, along with imaginative and carefully prepared dishes.

🍽🍽 **Mylopetra** – *To the left of the square, behind the little bridge.* ☏22460 72333. www.mylopetra.com. A peaceful and attractive establishment occupying an old mill. Traditional and modern Mediterranean cuisine. Evenings only.

Tílos

Tílos – Τήλος

Tílos is virtually deserted and largely overlooked by tourists. Fairly mountainous, the island has two villages, some Byzantine churches, and sand and shingle beaches. The traditions of religious festivals and folk dances are very much alive here. With only 500 or so residents, it may look unexciting at first but it is a relaxing and interesting place that welcomes visitors and rewards a longer stay.

LIVADIA

This little village has a shingle beach, and a tiny harbour that's used by fishing boats and the occasional ferry. There is a track that leads out of the village and follows the coastline to a pebbly beach at Lethrá. It will take about an hour to walk there so bring provisions because there are no amenities at the cove and you may be the only one there. It is also possible to walk to the south coast of the island from Livadia.

MIKROHORIO

▶ *2km/1.2mi from Livadia by the island's only road.*

The abandoned houses of this eerie village were occupied until the 1950s. The village used to have around 1 000 inhabitants.

MEGALO HORIO

▶ *5km/3mi from Livadia.*

The old "capital" of Tílos was built on a hill for strategic reasons, safe from marauding pirates. It is dominated by a ruined fortress. Allow at least half an hour to walk there from the village. A small museum (🕐 *open daily 8.30–2.30, summer only*) includes dwarf-elephant tusks discovered in the nearby Harka-dio Cave (⊶ *closed to the public*). Below the village is the little harbour of **Ágios Antonios**.

BEACHES

In addition to the one at Livadia, there are two other pleasant beaches. Plaka

- ▶ **Population:** 533.
- 📐 **Michelin Map:** 63sq km/ 25sq mi – Michelin Map 737 P 13 – Dodecanese – Aegean.
- 🛈 **Info:** There is no tourist information office but Tílos Travel (www.tilos travel.co.uk) by the harbour is a useful source of local information.
- ◑ **Location:** The island lies to the northwest of Rhodes.
- 🕐 **Timing:** A day trip may be disappointing but a longer stay allows the quiet charms of the island to emerge.

GETTING THERE

BY SEA – Ferry service from Rhodes *(2–6wk)* and Kos *(2/wk)*. Also service from Piraeus *(1/wk)*.

runs to the west of Ágios Antonios. Eristos, to the south of Megalo Horio, is the largest beach on the island. There are two inlets south of Livadia, at the head of deep bays.

ADDRESSES

🛏 STAY / 🍽 EAT

🍴🍴 **Blue Sky** – *Livadia, on the harbour.* Good quality local cuisine. Apartments to rent too.

🍴🍴 **Hotel Irini** – *Livadia, set back from the harbour.* 📞*4104 4238. www.tilos holidays.gr. Open Apr–Oct.* This simple and well-run hotel has an attractive garden with swimming pool.

🎉 EVENTS AND FESTIVALS

25 to 27 July: **Religious festival** at the Monastery of Ágios Pandeleimonas, to the west of Plaka Beach. Because Tílos is a small and mostly quiet place, they make the most of festivals like this and visitors are welcome to join in the fun.

IONIAN ISLANDS ★★

Iónia Nisiá – Ιόνια Νησιά

The landscape of these seven fairly mountainous islands is reminiscent of Italy, with cypresses, vineyards, olive groves and fragrant citrus trees. They lie to the south of the Otranto Channel separating the Adriatic from the Ionian Sea. Well placed for access from the rest of Europe, the Ionians attract visitors year-round to their spectacular coastlines, luxuriant flora, white-sand beaches, warm sea temperatures and pleasant climate. Cruising in the Ionian Sea is a great way to discover this region, one of the most beautiful that Greece has to offer.

Highlights

1 The **Old Town** in Corfu Town (p441)
2 Paleokastrítsa on **Corfu** (p444)
3 Mírtos Beach on **Kefalonía** (p448)
4 **Ithaca** (p455)
5 Blue Caves on **Zakynthos** (p460)

The Islands Today

The best known and by far the most tourist-developed of the islands is Corfu. In the 1960s it became one of the first places in Greece to attract package holidaymakers. Zakynthos, or at least its southern half, is the next most visitor-orientated of the islands – primarily due to its superb beaches. Each of the other five islands has its own claim to fame and while Kefalonía, Ithaca and Lefkada are geographically the most amenable to island-hopping, they retain their individualities. Kefalonía does not depend on tourism and this is part of its appeal; Ithaca lacks sandy beaches but compensates by way of its putative Homeric legacy; and Lefkada has retained a traditional feel while also boasting some gorgeous beaches. Small is beautiful in the case of tiny Paxós, which is classy in a way that Corfu once was. Kythera is the oddball of the Ionian islands, geographically separate by way of its location at the bottom of the Peloponnese yet historically very much a part of the group. The Ionian islands are culturally and physically different from the islands in the Aegean and in some respect resemble Italy more than mainland Greece. There are reminders of French and British rule and if your first sight of the islands is from the air you look down on green and fertile lands (the highest rainfall in Greece is on Corfu) that could never be confused with the starker look of the rocky Aegean isles. Winters tend to be mild but wet while the summer months are very hot indeed; the islands do not benefit from the *meltemi* wind that cools the Aegean Islands and in the middle of summer temperatures reach as high as 40°C (104°F).

A Bit of History

According to Homer the Ionian Islands were the territory of Odysseus and

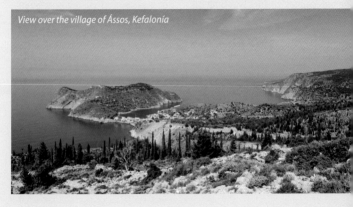

View over the village of Ássos, Kefalonía

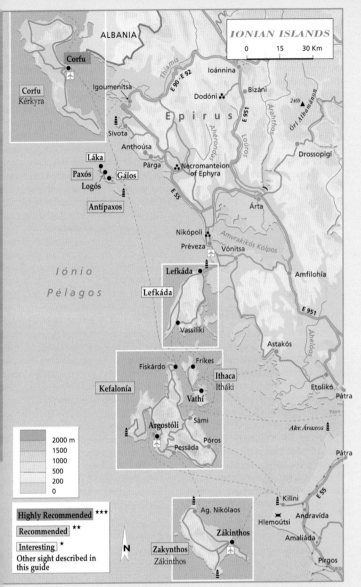

...e was born on one of them, named Ithaca. It was here that Odysseus had his home and it was to here that he finally returned following his years of exile and wandering after the defeat of Troy. One of the seven islands is named Ithaca but, while the description of Ithaca provided by Homer bears a convincing resemblance to the island that now bears this name, the claim that Odysseus's palace has been identified is a suspect one.

The city of Corinth colonised the islands in the 8C BC. One of them, Corfu, became so powerful that three centuries later it was able to challenge the mother city and defeat it in battle. This led to an Ionian alliance with Athens and then the Peloponnesian war when Sparta felt threatened by this expansion of Athenian power into its part of the Greek world. In this way, one of the Ionian islands acted as a trigger for the

GETTING THERE

BY SEA – The archipelago is accessible from various Greek ports: Igoumenítsa for Corfu and Paxós, Astakós for Ithaca, Kilíni for Kefaloniá and Zakynthos, Patras for the majority of the islands, Gíthio and Nauplion for Kythera. Hopping from island to island can be awkward though. There are numerous services each week from Italy (Ancona, Brindisi, Venice) to Corfu, and you can travel from Kythera to Crete (Kastéli). Lefkada is linked to the mainland by a bridge.

BY AIR – The airports on **Corfu, Kefaloniá and Zakynthos** have flights from Athens and Préveza; they also have many international flights to Europe in summer.

destructive war between the two superpowers of the ancient Greek world; on a broader historical canvas, however, the Ionian Islands were never influential players in their own right and the history of ancient Greece largely ignores their existence. In the 4C BC they were quietly absorbed into the Macedonian empire and this remained more or less the case until Rome arrived on the scene. There followed four centuries of uneventful Roman rule before the islands became part of the Byzantine Empire. There was then nearly a millennium of Byzantine rule until, following the destruction of Constantinople during the Crusades, European powers began to express an interest in this corner of the world.

Between 1386 and 1797 the Venetians were in charge but the majority of islanders retained their Greek identity and language. The rise of Napoleon in the late 18C led to the islands being fought over by French and Russian–Turkish forces. After the defeat of Napoleon in 1815 the British claimed neutrality for the islands during the course of the Greek War of Independence. The British then stubbornly held on to the islands as useful territory for naval bases in their ongoing dispute with Russia and it was not until 1864 that the Ionian Islands were finally integrated into a Greek national state.

In 1941 when Axis forces occupied Greece, the Ionian Islands (except Kythera) were gifted to Mussolini's Italy. Over the course of the next three years the Italians tried unsuccessfully to Italianise the population of Corfu. The Nazis later took control and were only too successful in rounding up the island's Jewish population of 5 000 and sending them to Auschwitz.

Difficult times affected some of the Ionian islands in the 1940s and 50s when earthquakes devastated Lefkada, Kythera, Kefaloniá, Ithaca and Zakynthos. Despite the severe damage the islands rebuilt themselves and now prosper thanks to tourism and agriculture.

Cricket in Greece

The first game of cricket in Greece was played on Corfu in April 1823 between officers of the Royal Navy and officers of the garrison, who were stationed there under the British Protectorate of the Ionian Islands (1814–63). Twelve years later there were two Corfiot teams to challenge the British visitors.

After the Second World War, amateur teams began scheduling regular matches in Corfu and the Anglo–Corfiot Cricket Association was founded in 1970–71. The season runs from April or May, depending on the weather, to the end of October. During those months there is a daily game; matches against visiting teams are usually played on Monday, Wednesday, Saturday and Sunday between 3pm and 8pm (2pm and 7pm in April and October).

There are now quite a few cricket clubs in Greece, 13 of them on Corfu, and even an international Greek cricket team. Since 1966 Greek cricketers have competed successfully in the Mediterranean Cricket Festival, the European Clubs Champions Cup, European Nations Cup and European Indoor Championship.

Corfu★★★

Kérkyra – Κέρκυρα

Corfu, which lies between the Italian Peninsula and the Greek mainland, is the jewel of the Ionian Islands: luxuriant gardens, rocky bays, large sandy beaches, and a mild climate make it a popular year-round destination. Fashionable in the 19C with the European aristocracy (notably Empress Elisabeth of Austria), it has retained its cosmopolitan character.

A BIT OF HISTORY

In the *Odyssey* Homer tells how Odysseus, marooned on Corfu, was feted before his return to Ithaca. In the 8C BC the Corinthians founded a colony on the island, which became known as **Corcyra**. It came under Venetian control in the 14C. For some three centuries the Venetians imposed their rule on Corfu, beating back several incursions by the Turks. Italian became the official language, Roman Catholicism held a privileged position, and many of the monuments visible today were erected.

- ▶ **Population:** 107, 879.
- **Michelin Map:** 593sq km/ 237sq mi – Michelin Map 737 K 9 – Ionian Islands.
- **Info:** Ionian Islands Tourism Directorate, Rizospaston/ Polila. ☎26610 37520. www.agni.gr.
- **Location:** Corfu lies at the northern end of the archipelago near Albania. There are ferries from Patras, Igoumenítsa and numerous Italian ports (Otranto, Brindisi, Venice).
- **Don't Miss:** Corfu Old Town, the Achilleion (Ahílio).
- **Timing:** Plan 4 days to see the main sights.
- **Kids:** A choice of superb beaches, some with organised activities suitable for older children.

France, Russia and Turkey all vied for control until 1818, when the Ionian Islands were granted independent status as a British protectorate. In 1863, the islands were ceded to Greece.

GETTING THERE

CORFU

BY SEA – The ferry port is to the north of the Old Town. Ferries serve Igoumenítsa (hourly), Patra (several/ day) and Paxos (1/day summer); hydrofoil service to Paxos (3/day summer/ 1/day winter). Numerous ferry links exist with Italy: Venice (2–3/ week), Ancona and Brindisi (several/ day) and Bari (2–3/daily). Tickets can either be purchased at the port, or from travel agencies in town.

BY AIR – The international airport is just to the south of Corfu Town. ☎26610 89600. There are several Athens flights each day (60min), and many direct charter flights from the big European cities in summer. Taxis and buses to the airport leave from various parts of town.

PAXOS

BY SEA – Flying Dolphins offers hydrofoil service from Corfu Town (3/day summer, 1/day winter); the same hydrofoil sometimes runs to Igoumenítsa. There is a daily ferry service (passengers and cars) from Corfu (1/day summer). A passenger-only boat runs between Gáïos and Párga (1/day). There is a ferry and bus link between Gáïos and Athens (3/week). Hours vary, so consult a travel agency or the harbour police, ☎26620 32259. For general information see www.paxos-greece.com.

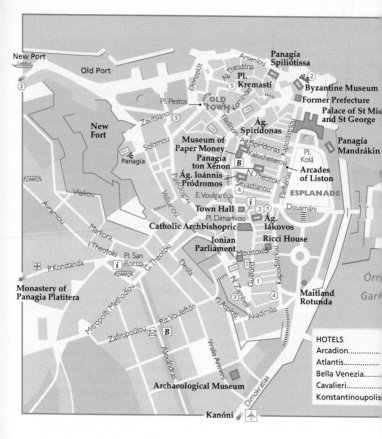

In the late 19C, Corfu became a playground for Europe's aristocracy, including Empress Elisabeth of Austria. Her fine residence (the Achilleion) is open to visitors.

KÉRKYRA★★
(CORFU TOWN)

The capital of the Ionian Islands is one of the most cosmopolitan of Greek island towns. The old town, standing between two huge citadels, has narrow streets, tiled roofs and cypress trees, evocative of Italy. There is also a significant British influence, especially around the Spianáda, which is the hub of activity in Corfu Town.

Palace of St Michael and St George

Open Tue–Sun 8.30am–7pm (2.30pm in winter). €4. 22610 30443.

Built in 1819 as the British High Commissioner's official residence, the palace features a fresco cycle depicting the *Odyssey*, a throne room and banqueting hall. Today it houses the **Museum of Asiatic Art,** containing urns, bronzes, rare lacquers, ceramics, engravings and Japanese screens; also beautiful 17C and 18C icons.

From the seafront head left around the palace; this leads into an attractive parade of old houses, looking northwards out to sea and the shores of Albania and Epiros.

Byzantine Museum (Vizandinó Moussio)

Open Tue–Sun 8am–7pm (8.30am–2.30pm in winter). €2 (combined ticket with Asiatic and Archaeological Museums and Paleó Froúrio: €8). 26610 38313. In the Church of Panagía Antivouniotissa.

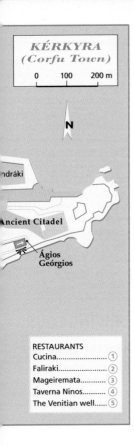

N

ndráki

Ancient Citadel

Ágios
Geórgios

RESTAURANTS
Cucina....................... ①
Faliraki....................... ②
Mageiremata.............. ③
Taverna Ninos........... ④
The Venitian well...... ⑤

A very fine collection of 16C and 17C
icons.

New Fort (Néo Froúrio)

🕒Open 9am–9pm. ⊚€3.
☏22610 27330.

Built on a hillside in the 16C and 17C,
the Néo Froúrio is worth the climb for
its views over the Old Town.

Old Town★
(Paleá Póli)

This district has enormous charm: narrow streets, little paved squares, elegant church façades and high arcaded
houses.

Follow Odós Solomou, then the shopping street Odós Nikifórou Theotokí,
at the top of which is the 14C Church
of Ágios Andónios (inside is a fine 18C
baroque iconostasis). Turn left halfway
along this street.

Ágios Spiridónas

A chapel houses the silver coffin containing the mummified body of **St Spiridon**,
a 4C Cypriot bishop who became the
patron saint of Corfu.

Panagía ton Xénon

Southeast of St Spiridon's Church is a
charming little square flanked by the
Church of Our Lady of Strangers, featuring a fine decorated ceiling.

Town Hall

In Platía Dimaríhou, this 17C building,
formerly the theatre, is decorated with
carved medallions and is one of the finest Venetian monuments on Corfu.

Return towards the seafront, passing the
remarkable Ricci House, a fine Venetian
residence.

Esplanade (Spianáda)★

Once an open space for drilling soldiers, the Spianáda (or Platía) is liberally
adorned with commemorative monuments and statues. To the south are fine
views★ of the old citadel, the sea and
the coast of Epiros.

The west side of the Spianáda is lined by
the **"Liston"**, an arcaded terrace housing restaurants and bookshops; it was
inspired by the rue de Rivoli in Paris and
the cafés are always busy, especially in
the evenings.

The Spianáda also incorporates the
Corfu **cricket pitch**.

Paleó Froúrio★★

🕒Open daily 8.30am–7pm in summer,
8.30am–3pm in winter. ⊚€4 (combined
ticket with Archaeological, Byzantine
and Asiatic museums: €8). ☏26610
48310.

Separated from the Spianáda by a canal,
the **ancient Citadel** is sited on a rocky
promontory. By the Middle Ages fortifications were already established here.
The Church of **Ágios Geórgios**, resembling a Doric temple, was built in 1830,
and the barracks (Venetian) dominate
the little port of Mandráki.

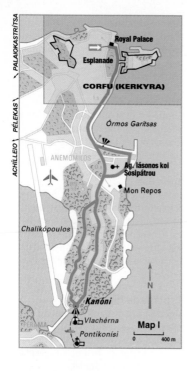

Map I

0   400 m

Additional Sights

Archaeological Museum★

Vraila 5, south from the Asiatic Museum.
Open Tue–Sun 8.30am–3pm. €4.
26610 30680.

Star of the collection is an Archaic **pediment**★★ from the Temple of Artemis, known as the Gorgon Medusa and an impressive piece of carving. See also the 7C BC Lion of Menekrates from the Tomb of Menekrates, a few streets away.

Monastery of Panagía Platitéra

To the west of the town, Odós Polihroníou Konstandá.
This 19C structure is the burial place of Ioánnis Kapodístrias, first President of Greece; there are also some fine **icons**★ here.

WALKING TOUR

To Kanóni★★

4km/2.5mi south of Corfu Town.
Follow the attractive curve of Garítsa Bay as far as the suburb of Anemómilos, where the villas are surrounded by gardens. From here, there is a fine **view**★★

over the bay, the ancient citadel and the coasts of Albania and Epiros.

Bear right into Odós Iássonou Sossipatrou which leads to a 12C Byzantine church, **Ágios Iássonas-Sossípatrou** (*Open daily 9am–3pm; no charge*). In the narthex are four fine 17C icons. The road, which is narrow and congested, skirts the villa known as **Mon Repos** (*open 8am–7pm summer, 8am–5pm winter; no charge*) surrounded by a park and standing on the site of the ancient acropolis of Corcyra. From the southern tip of this peninsula there is a **view**★★ down onto the Monastery of Vlahérna (17C) and beyond it to the circular Mouse Island (Pondikoníssi) which also has a monastery. Vlahérna is accessible on foot, and Pondikonísi by boat from Vlahérna.

DRIVING TOURS

SOUTH OF THE ISLAND★★

Around 75km/45mi round trip if you include only Ágios Geórgios beach. Allow half a day; more time if you intend to visit other southern beaches.

Less mountainous than the north, this part of Corfu features many beaches, some excellent panoramic viewpoints and the Achilleion, Empress Sisi's villa.

▷ *Drive 12km/7mi south of Corfu Town.*

Ahílio (Achilleio)★★

Open daily 8am–7pm. €6.
26610 56210.

An imposing Neoclassical villa, the **Achilleion** was built in 1890 for Empress **Elisabeth of Austria**, who in 1898 was assassinated by an Italian anarchist. It is dedicated to Achilles, hero of the *Iliad*. Its large rooms are decorated with frescoes and ancient motifs, and there are many items associated with the Empress on view.

The Italian terraced gardens are adorned with statues including *The Dying Achilles* (1884) by the German sculptor Herter, and a huge bronze of *Achilles the Victor*.

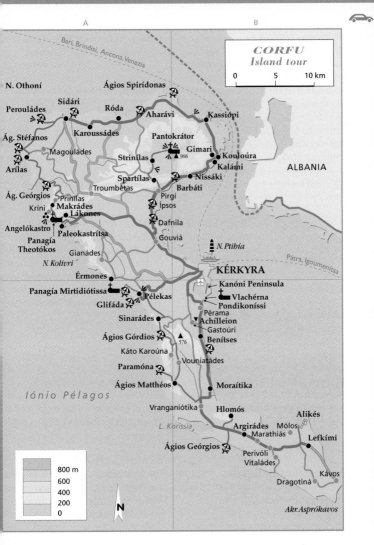

CORFU
Island tour
0   5   10 km

N. Othoní
Ágios Spirídonas
Sidári   Róda
Perouládes   Aharávi   Kassiópi
Ág. Stéfanos   Karoussádes   Pantokrátor
          Magouládes   Gimari   Kouloúra
Arílas   Strinílas   ▲906   Kalámi
                        Spartílas   Níssáki   ALBANIA
          Troumbétas   Barbáti
Ág. Geórgios   Prinílas   Pirgí
Krini   Makrádes   Ípsos
       Lákones
Angelókastro   Dafnila
         Paleokastrítsa
Panagía   Gouviá
Theotókos
         Gianádes   N. Ptihía
N. Kolívri
                         KÉRKYRA
Érmones
                         Kanóni Peninsula
Panagía Mirtidiótissa   Pélekas   Vlachérna
                                    Pondikoníssi
Glifáda   Péraro
                              Achílleion
Sinarádes   Gastoúri
                             Benítses
Ágios Górdios
       Káto Karoúna   ▲576
Paramóna   Vouniatádes

Ágios Matthéos   Moraítika

Ióni o Pélagos
          Vranganiótika   Hlomós   Alikés
                                    Mólos
                      Argirádes   Lefkími
                         Marathiás
          Ágios Geórgios   Perivóli
                         Vitaládes
                                    Kávos
                         Dragotiná
                         Akr.Asprókavos

800 m
600
400
200
0

N

◐ *Return to the coast and drive south to Benítses.*

Benítses

Typical fishing village and seaside resort. There is also the head of an aqueduct built by the British to supply water to Corfu Town.

◐ *Continue to one or more of the southern beaches before rejoining the road towards Pélekas.*

Pélekas★★

Stop to admire the superb **panoramic view**★★ of the centre of the island.

◐ *From here it is a short 20min drive back to Corfu Town.*

NORTH OF THE ISLAND★★

The north of the island is the mountainous half, with some magnificent scenery and driving. This circular route is a good full day's excursion of about 150km /94mi. Drive 25km/16mi northwest of Corfu Town.

Paleokastrítsa★★

This very popular seaside resort is located in a magnificent **bay**★★ at the foot of a steep hillside. The road runs to the end of the promontory where the monastery of Paleokastrítsa was founded in the 13C; the present buildings date from the 18C. ◷ *Open daily Apr–Oct 7am–1pm, 3–8pm; appropriate attire provided.*

▷ *Head back along the Corfu Town road; turn left towards Lákones.*

A terrace beyond the village of **Lákones** (sign "Parking") provides an extraordinary **view**★★ of the many rocky inlets in Paleokastrítsa Bay.

▷ *Continue towards Kríni.*

Before entering the village bear left into a narrow road to Angelókastro, which leads to a hamlet and then to a restaurant.
Leave the car here and take the path to the ruins of **Angelókastro** *(1hr there and back on foot)*, a 13C Byzantine fortress, from which stretch splendid **views**★★ of the coast.

▷ *North of Paleokastrítsa.*

Ágios Geórgios Beach

In a rocky bay, this sandy beach is one of the island's finest.

▷ *The drive north takes you through several hill villages before emerging at the coast.*

Sidári★★

This busy resort at the northern end of the island is on a stretch of coast unusual for its curious **rock formations**★★.
The sea has caused erosion, creating rocky inlets, some with little beaches, islets and promontories resembling piles of ruins, and caves and caverns where the sea rushes in.

Kassiópi★

This fishing port and bustling resort is approached by a spectacular **corniche road**★ which goes to **Koloúra**. Remark able views of the Albanian coast.

▷ *Take the coastal road all the way around the northwest corner of Corfu.*

Spartylas★

The road loops its way up through the olive groves, providing fine views of the island scenery and the Epiros Coast.

▷ *Keep driving right to the top of Mount Pandokrátor.*

Pandokrátor Monastery

◷ *Open daily Apr–Oct 7am–12.30pm, 2.30–8pm. Appropriate attire provided.*
On the island's highest point, the monastery has a marvellous **view**★ over desertlike, almost lunar, plateaux to one side; sea, coastline and Albanian lake to the other.

▷ *Descend back to the east coast and south towards Corfu Town via Ípsos.*

Ípsos (Ypsos)★

This pleasant resort is situated on the edge of a huge sandy bay that is ideal for all watersports: bathing, sailing, waterskiing etc.

BEACHES OF CORFU

The beaches of Corfu are numerous and magnificent, but very busy in summer, the majority of them disappearing under parasols and sun loungers. Watersports are very popular. Those listed below are some of the island's finest; they are marked on the map and appear here in clockwise order starting from Corfu Town.
Benítses: A popular tourist beach facing the coast of Epiros.
Vitaládes: A long strip of sand at the foot of a cliff, more used by locals than visitors.
Ágios Geórgios: Sandy beach with compacted, rocklike dunes.
Paramóna: West-facing beach below the attractive village of Ágios Matthéos.
Ágios Górdis: 5km/3mi-long beach with facilities and watersports.

Pélekas: Below the village of the same name, and surrounded by rocks.

Mirtidiótissa: This inaccessible little beach lies in an attractive bay.

Paleokastrítsa: Numerous beautiful coves but very busy in summer.

Ágios Geórgios: Not to be confused with the southern beach of the same name.

Arílas, **Ágios Stéfanos**: Windy beaches set among rocks and green hillsides.

Perouládes: The main beach is a narrow strip of sand dominated by dramatic grey and ochre cliffs, and there are bigger beaches nearby.

Sidári: Many coves in a beautiful rocky setting and surreal rock formations.

Ágios Spirídonas: Facing nearby Albania, a wild and striking beach.

Ipsos, **Dassiá**: Big resorts with fine beaches and plenty of watersports.

EXCURSIONS

Paxós★

Lying to the south of Corfu, this quiet island is one of the smallest (25sq km/10sq mi) in the Ionian archipelago. Popular but not teeming, it is renowned for its olive oil, and the slopes of its hills are covered by olive groves. The pebble beaches are never crowded, even in high summer.

Gáïos

With beautiful houses, a carefree atmosphere, and yachts dotting the bay, Gáïos is wonderfully relaxed. The bay is protected by two tiny islands: **Ágios Nikólaos**, a nature reserve with the ruins of a Venetian chateau; and Moní Panagía, with its small monastery, *(reached by boat; only open on 15 August)*.

Laka

Situated at the far end of the island, this charming little port features authentic tavernas and a small-scale aquarium.

Antípaxos★

❯ *South of Paxós. Access by boat (2hrs) from Gáïos.* ⏰*Daily departures in summer; information available near the port.*

The **boat trip★★** to Antípaxos offers a marvellous chance to see Paxos' magnificent setting: pebbly beaches, cliffs, rocky outcrops, marine caves and arches carved out by the waves.

Given over to vineyards and market gardening, Antípaxos is Paxós's garden. There are also some fine sandy **beaches★**.

ADDRESSES

🛏️STAY

CORFU

⊜🖥️💾 **Hotel Bella Venezia** – *Corfu Town, 4 Odós N Zambélli.* ℘*26610 46500/ 44290. www.bellaveneziahotel.com. 31 rooms.* A charming hotel with smart Italianate decoration (coffered ceilings, some rooms with four-poster beds) occupying an attractive 19C residence with a pleasant planted terrace.

⊜🖥️💾 **Hotel Golden Fox** – *Lákones, to the northwest of Corfu Town.* ℘*26630 49101/2. www.corfugoldenfox.com. 10 apartments. Open May–Oct.* This white-painted hotel overlooking Paleokastrítsa has comfortable apartments with kitchenettes and balconies (superb views). Book in advance. Restaurant, shops and a pool with a fantastic view.

⊜🖥️💾 **Hotel Neféli** – *Dafníla, northwest of Corfu Town.* ℘*26610 91033, www.hotelnefeli.com. 45 rooms.* A charming ochre-and-white NeoClassical hotel set among olive trees. Spacious rooms with balconies overlooking the sea or the hills. Close to the beach, good value.

⊜🖥️💾 **Levant Hotel** – *Pélekas, west of Corfu Town.* ℘*26610 94230. www.levantcorfu.com. 25 rooms.* On the hillside behind "Sunset" village. A charming hotel occupying a beautifully presented Neoclassical villa. Warm welcome, good restaurant, romantic, cool rooms and fantastic views. Beaches 3km/2mi away, golf and riding 4km/2.5mi away. Four-bed rooms to accommodate families.

⊜🖥️🖥️💾 **Hotel Cavalieri** – *Corfu Town, Odós Kapoditríou 4.* ℘*26610 39041. www.cavalieri-hotel.com. 50 rooms.* Luxurious "A" Class hotel, occupying a

17C building decorated in Anglo-Venetian style. Splendid sea view, and a panoramic bar and roof garden.

⊖⊜🖥🖻 **Érmones Golf Palace Hotel** – *Érmones, west of Corfu Town.* ☏*26610 94 045/94226. 41 rooms.* Two attractively decorated buildings laid out around a pleasant swimming pool. Big rooms with balconies and sea views, just up from the beach.

⊖⊜🖥🖻 **Menigos Resort** – *Glifáda, west of Corfu Town.* ☏*26610 950 74. www.corfu-glyfada-menigos-resort.com. 163 apartments.* Large bungalows built on terraces above the beach, some with big gardens. All are different, furnished and well-equipped; balconies with sea views. Small swimming pool, supermarket, snack bar, and tennis courts available at nearby hotel.

PAXÓS
Private rooms are available in Gáios, Logós and Láka. Booking is essential; prices are high in season. Everything closes from October to April.

⊖⊜🖻 **Hotel Paxos Beach** – *1km/0.6mi from Gáios.* ☏*26620 32211. www.paxosbeachhotel.gr. 42 rooms.* Peaceful stone bungalows set among trees by a private beach. Bright, clean rooms with rattan furniture. Reservations essential. Mini-golf and games area.

🍴/EAT
CORFU
⊖⊜ **Taverna Ninos** – *Corfu Town, 46 Odós Sebastianoú (corner of Odós M Theotóki).* ☏*26610 46175. Closed Sunday.* On a terrace in a small street parallel to Odós Kapodistríou. Simple, fresh food and generous portions: *sofrito, pastitsad*, and a tasty andouillette (*gargouma*). Popular with locals and lively in the evenings, with a well-known local singer performing.

⊖⊜ **Taverna O. Boúlis** – *Lákones. Open daily Apr–Oct.* ☏*26630 49429.* Simple taverna serving generous portions of freshly prepared dishes indoors or outside on a terrace: *tzatzíki, keftédes* (rissoles), *saganáki* (fried cheese in breadcrumbs), delicious chicken and perfectly barbecued meats.

⊖⊜ **Taverna Lagoon** – *Ágios Spirídonas. Open May–Oct.* ☏*26630 98333.* A large beachfront terrace serving up excellent fresh-fish kebabs and grilled fish dishes. Fine views of the nearby Albanian coast.

⊖⊜ **Taverna Kouloúra** – *Kouloúra, northeast side of the island.* ☏*26630 91253. Closed late Oct–early April.* An attractive terrace overlooking the peaceful harbour. Delicious fish specialities. Pleasant welcome and ambience.

⊖⊜🖻 **The Venetian Well** – *Corfu Town, Platía Kremastí.* ☏*26610 44761. Closed Sunday.* Overlooking a small, flower-filled square, this has to be the most attractive restaurant terrace in Corfu. Refined menu, an excellent combination of Greek and Italian gastronomy. Delicious swordfish kebabs with walnut… ideal for a romantic dinner. Booking essential.

PAXÓS
⊖⊜ **Taverna Basílis** – *Logós.* ☏*26620 30062.* In a pretty yellow house with stone floors. Fish, lobster and mussels served on the waterfront terrace.

🚃 TAKING A BREAK

In Corfu Town, stop in at **Ta Olympia**, *(open daily 7am–2am)* with grand woodwork and Art-Deco furnishings. Also stop at **Arte Cafe** *(garden of the Palace of St. Michael and St. George, daily 9am–1pm)*, a lovely terrace amid cypress and jasmine; a good place to sample salads or cold dishes.
Hotel Cavalieri – *Corfu Town, 4 Odós Kapodistríou, to the south of the seafront in the direction of Garítsa Bay.* The panoramic sixth-floor terrace has splendid views over the town and the sea (especially striking at dusk). Open from 6pm; dress code (no shorts).
Nightclubs – All the trendy techno-music clubs are located in Corfu Town's northern suburb of Mandoúki, beyond the new port. Some are worth a visit for their ambitious decor, particularly the extravagant **Apocalypsi**.

Kefaloníá★★

Kefaloniá – Κεφαλονιά

The largest of the Ionian Islands, Kefaloníá is formed of jagged hilly limestone. Its landscape is varied: peninsulas, rocky headlands, deep gulfs and sandy beaches. The landscape also includes fertile terraces by the sea and busy beaches on the south coast. The dark peak of Mount Énos (Ainos), one of Greece's highest points, is covered by a type of spruce peculiar to the island.

A BIT OF HISTORY

Archaeological evidence speaks of habitation here 50 000 years ago; in the 5C BC, Thucydides records four large cities here. From the Middle Ages to the mid-19C, in common with the other Ionian islands, dominance of Kefaloníá passed among French, Turkish and Italian occupiers. Some of Kefaloníá's inhabitants became such noted travellers around the globe that the island could make a case for being the spiritual home of Odysseus himself. In the 16C, the explorer known as Juan de Fuca (seeking the Northwest Passage for Spain) was actually a Greek from Kefaloníá and another wealthy islander ended up as a Regent of Siam. In the field of archaeology, a Mycenean tomb has been unearthed on the island and this gives some credence to the possibility that the island may indeed be Homer's true Ithaca.

Louis de Bernieres' popular novel, *Captain Corelli's Mandolin* (film by John Madden), records the Second World War history of Kefaloníá. Italian and German troops occupied the island early on in the war but then came the Italian armistice in September 1943.

The Germans insisted on the surrender of Italian weapons and brought in reinforcements to back up their demand. The Italian soldiers chose to fight and over the course of one week some 1300 died in an armed struggle. Thousands more were executed afterwards by the Germans.

▶ **Population:** 36, 400.

Michelin Map: 737sq km/ 295sq mi – Michelin Map 737 C 8-9 – Ionian Islands.

Info: On the quayside in Argostóli. ℰ 26710 22248. www.ionion.com.

Location: Kefaloníá is served by ferries from Patras and there are numerous links with neighbouring islands, notably Ithaca and Lefkada. Note that there are several ports. It's best to rent a car to explore the island.

Don't Miss: A swim at Mirtós or Pétani; a climb up Mt Énos.

Parking: Outside of the towns the roads are very quiet and you can stop anywhere you like along the way. There are plenty of spaces in the towns and at beaches and sights.

Timing: Allow 4 days.

Kids: Experimenting with echoes in Melissáni Cave.

GETTING THERE

BY SEA – Ferry service to Patras (*2/day summer 1/day winter*), to Kilini (*several/day*), and to Corfu (*1–2/week*). Boats for Zakynthos leave from Pessáda (*2/day summer, 1/week winter*). For Ithaca (*departing from Sámi*): links with Pisso Aetós and Vathí. There are several boats a day from Fiskárdo to Vassilikí or to Nidri, on Lefkada. Timetables vary over the course of the year; information is available from travel agents.

BY AIR – ℰ *27610 42000*. There are flights to Athens (*2/day*), Zakynthos (*3/wk*), Corfu (*several/wk*) and Paxos (*several/wk*). Taxi service between the airport and Argostóli.

In 1953 an earthquake caused severe damage throughout the island; only the village of Fiskárdo was left with its traditional Venetian architecture intact. Afterwards, a large number of inhabitants moved to the mainland to escape further disasters. Not surprisingly, regulations were introduced to restrict the height of all future buildings.

🚗 DRIVING TOURS

AROUND THE ISLAND★★
Allow 2 days. Around 200km/125mi.

The drive takes in many of the island's highlights, including beaches and caves and the pretty town of Fiskárdo.

Sámi
On the east coast, the port of Sámi has connections with Corfu, Paxós, Lefkada and Patras. Destroyed in the 1953 earthquake, it was subsequently rebuilt, and nestles in a gently curving bay.
There is a fine view of the narrow entry to the bay and of the stark coast of Ithaca. Sámi was the island's capital in ancient times and with the burgeoning ferry links the place is beginning to recapture some of its past importance. The local beach is not spectacular but it is sandy and the tourist infrastructure is modest enough to make Sámi worth considering for a 1-night stopover, especially with two caves worth visiting in the vicinity.

◐ 2km/1.25mi southwest of Sámi; take the road to Argostóli and after 2km/1.25mi turn right into a track.

Drogaráti Cave
◔*Open May to Oct 8am–8pm.* ✆€5.
A flight of 166 steps leads down into this cave, which is easy to explore. Among the beautiful creations are some enormous stalagmites. The cave's acoustics are of such a quality that concerts occasionally take place here (Maria Callas once made an appearance).

◐ Head towards the northeast coast.

Melissáni Cave★
◔*Open daily May to Oct 8am–8pm; winter, weekends, 10am–4pm.* ✆€7.
✆ 26740 22997.
This underground lake, which receives its water via subterranean passages from the swallowholes near Argostóli (✆*see below*), is explored by boat. The intensity and variety of the colours of the water, and the resonance and echo make for a surreal effect.
Just before reaching Fiskárdo, the route from Sámi offers a magnificent **view**★★ over the sea and of Ithaca and Lefkada.

Fiskárdo★
This charming sheltered port at the extreme north of the island was largely spared by the earthquake in 1953 and has therefore kept its character.
Heading south, the road as far as Ássos has remarkable views, taking in both the sea and the mountains.

Port of Fiskárdo

Ássos★
This fishing village on the west coast, **in a lovely location**★★, lies at the neck of a hilly peninsula crowned with a Venetian fortress (16C). The little port and its square, surrounded by flower-bedecked houses, with a mountainous backdrop, make Ássos one of the most charming places in Kefalonía.
Further on, the winding corniche road has fine **views**★★ of the Ássos Peninsula, Gulf of Mirtós and the Ionian Sea.

Mirtós Beach
Probably the best on the island (*very busy in summer*) with turquoise waters set against majestic white cliffs.

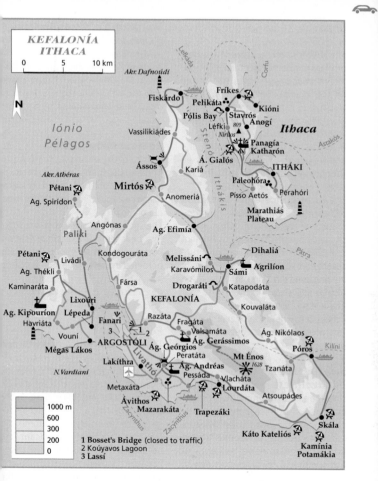

KEFALONÍA
ITHACA
0   5   10 km

▷ *3km/2mi after Angónas, turn right towards the Paliki Peninsula.*

Known as the Garden of Kefalonía, this is a landscape of vineyards, olive groves and fruit trees.

Lixoúri

The island's second town, with a busy port dating from the 1960s. Behind its modern seafront, the streets are lined with restaurants and shops.

Pétani Beach★★

To the northwest of Lixoúri, this attractive bay is tucked between tall white cliffs.

Monastery of Ágios Kipouríon

Occupying a magnificent site on the edge of a precipice, this little monastery is surrounded by vineyards and olive groves.

Argostóli★

The capital of the island since Venetian times is located on a promontory in a fjord-like bay. The main approach is over a bridge *(now closed to traffic)* which crosses the Koútavos Lagoon.

After the earthquake in 1953 Argostóli lost its Greco–Venetian atmosphere, though it still features an attractive seafront and a large pedestrian area. The **Church of Ágios Spirídon** has a fine iconostasis in carved wood. A small **Archaeological Museum** displays local

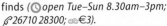

finds (○ *open Tue–Sun 8.30am–3pm; ℘26710 28300; ⊚€3*).

The **History and Folklore Museum**★ displays costumes, documents (including Venetian ones relating to their rule on the island), decorative arts and fascinating old photographs (○ *open Mon–Sat and public holidays 9am–2pm; ℘26710 28835; ⊚€4*). As ethnographic museums go, this is an exemplary one and well worth a visit, especially to see the photographs of the island before the terrible earthquake of 1953.

The **Focas-Cosmetatos Foundation** (○ *open Mon–Sat 9.30am–1pm, and in summer Tue–Sat 7pm–10pm; ⊚€3*), situated opposite the local government building, has a collection of furniture that dates back to the 19C when Britain administered the island; lithographs on display inlcude works by Edward Lear and Joseph Cartwright.

Admission will also cover a visit to **botanical gardens** just outside of town to the south.

Swallowholes (*katavóthres*)

Near the end of the promontory the sea flows into a fissure, reappearing on the other side of the island in the Melissáni Cave. The hydraulic power thus created was harnessed to power mills; one of these, with paddle wheel, is on view.

The Livathó Plain

Ancient olive groves cover this area of innumerable small villages lying to the south of Argostóli. Along the coast are a number of busy beaches.

Ágios Geórgios★

○ *Open Tue–Sun 8.30am–3pm.*
⊚*No charge.*

Until 1757 **St George's Castle** was the Venetian capital of the island; among the ruins are traces of St George's Collegiate Church. From the castle there are fine **views**★ of the Livathó Plain, the Lixoúri Peninsula and Zakynthos. In the nearby village of Peratáta, the poet Byron lived for a short while.

Monastery of Ágios Andréas

○ *Open daily 9am–1.30pm and 5–8pm.*
⊚*No charge.*

South of Peratáta, this monastery (also called Moní Milapidíon) has a remarkable church with frescoes, a fine iconostasis and icons painted on wood and metal.

Ruins of Mazarakáta

Close to the monastery of Ágios Andréas, this is the only ancient site of significance on the island. This Mycenaean necropolis has many tombs hewn out of the rock.

The southeast of the island has some fine beaches: Káto Kateliós, Kamínia Potamákia and most importantly Skála, bordered by dense pine woods.

▷ *Head north along the coast road to Poros.*

Poros

This resort town with a small ferry port is located in a rocky bay. There is a walking trail from the town that passes the village of Tzanáta (*also accessible by car or motorcycle*) and it was here, in the early 1990s, that a team of archaeologists excavated a Mycenean tomb. It is regarded as a highly significant find because nothing similar in terms of size has been discovered in western Greece. It raises the possibility that this was the last resting place of a royal household dating back to the time of Odysseus.

THE MOUNTAIN★★

A 40km/25mi round trip from Sámi.

This drive/walk to the top of Mount Énos shows a very different side of the Greek Islands.

▷ *Take the Argostóli road which heads over the mountain. After about 10km/6mi turn left towards Mount Énos*

Mount Énos

2hrs there and back on foot from the TV masts.

Hikers and lovers of scenery will enjoy ascending this mountain, one of the highest in Greece (1 628m/5 941ft). The area is Greece's smallest national park. The route passes an observatory, then leads up to the gates of the nature reserve *(allow 35min of gentle climbing)*. Leave vehicles at the bend opposite the transmission masts and take the path to the south *(left)*. At the next signpost on the right, a well marked footpath *(yellow and green)* makes its way up. From the summit *(marked by a cairn)* the **view★** of the island is breathtaking. It is a stiff climb and you may want to drive some of the way because roads lead almost to the summit; whatever your mode of transport be sure to bring water because there are no amenities at the top.

Ágios Gerássimos

Between Valsamáta and Mikhata, to the south of Mount Énos. ◷*Variable opening hours, 8am–1pm, 4–8pm.* This restored 16C monastery occupies an impressive site on the mountainside. The modern church, built in the Byzantine style, is decorated with frescoes.

ADDRESSES

🏠 STAY

◉◉◉ **Hotel Olga** – *Argostóli, 82 Odós Antoni Tritsi.* ☏*26710 24981-984. www.olgahotel.gr. 42 rooms.* A blue-shuttered façade, well situated behind the palm trees that line the promenade. Friendly welcome; spotless and spacious rooms with pleasant little balconies. Buffet breakfast. Bar. Good value.

◉◉◉ **Hotel Mirabel** – *Argostóli, Platía Valiánou.* ☏*26710 25381-3. www.mirabelhotel.com. 33 rooms.* A well-located hotel with clean, spacious and pleasantly furnished rooms each with a terrace (some overlook the square and can be noisy). Friendly welcome from the proprietor; open year-round.

◉◉◉ **Hotel Oceanis** – *Poros.* ☏*26740 72581-2. www.hoteloceanis.gr. 16 rooms.* Perched on the rocky promontory beyond the ferry port, this hotel has superb views. Friendly management; spacious and bright rooms with balconies and fridges.

◉◉◉ **Hotel Sámi Beach** – *Karavómilos, to the west of Sámi, at the far end of the large beach.* ☏*26740 22802-22824. Fax 26740 22846. www.samibeach hotel.gr. 94 rooms.* A lovely place to stay; family atmosphere, despite the size and luxury of the place. The bright, pleasantly furnished rooms are well presented and comfortable, with good bathrooms. Large swimming pool, bar and table-tennis; games for kids.

◉◉◉ **Kanakis Apartments** – *Assos.* ☏*27640 51631. www.kanakis apartments.gr. 6 rooms.* Spacious apartments for 2–4 guests; tastefully decorated. Terrace with splendid views of the sea and the fort. Swimming pool.

🍽/ EAT

◉ **Zorbas** – *Lixoúri, corner of Odós Grigoríou and Odós 25 Martíou.* This establishment benefits from a large, shady courtyard. Attentive service. Greek cuisine including fried fish, *skordaliá, saganáki* and other specialities.

◉◉ **To Arkotikon** – *5 Odós Pizospatou.* ☏*2710 27213.* On Platía Valianou, this pretty restaurant serves up fresh, tasty dishes. Swift service, and a large selection of Greek wines.

◉◉ **Fótis** – *Poros, in a corner of the seafront square.* ☏*27640 72972. Open May–Oct.* A delightful two-storey terrace, looking directly onto the beach and the square. Good home-cooking and friendly welcome. Rooms to let at the other end of the beach.

◉◉ **Tselendí** – *Fiskárdo, set back from the harbour in a pleasant little square.* Occupying one of the finest houses in the village; magnificent dining room with an excellent bar. A good place for breakfast too.

🚋 TAKING A BREAK

In Argostóli, the **Rock Café** *(on the quayside just before the promenade lined with palm trees)* has modern decor. More authentic cafés are to be found in the pedestrian precinct *(Lithóstrotos)* including **Café K**, the **Metropolis** and the **Antika**, or in Platía Valiánou, which is very lively at night.

🛒 SHOPPING

Market – Lively open-air market daily in summer near the quayside.

Kythera★★

Kíthira – Κύθηρα

Mythical home of Aphrodite, goddess of love, Kythera presents two differing faces. Its northern landscape is composed of heath and pine woods; in the south there are wild gorges full of myrtles. Villages on Kythera have the striking whitewashed walls which are the norm in the nearby Cyclades.

A BIT OF HISTORY

The cult of Aphrodite, goddess of love, seems to have arrived on Kythera with the Phoenicians, who came here to collect the murex, a shellfish which yields a purple dye. Several temples to Aphrodite were built, but almost nothing remains. Kythera has been a rich source of inspiration for numerous artists and poets, including Watteau and Baudelaire.

To the south, in the waters off the island of **Antikythera**, an ancient wreck was discovered in 1900; the ship contained the famous Ephebe of Antikythera (4C BC), now in the Athens Museum.

BEACHES★★

The best of Kythera's many beaches are marked on the map; popular with families are the two beaches at Kapsáli, near Hóra (the only ones to get really crowded in summer), and the beaches around Agía Pelagía to the northwest, most of which have beautiful golden sand.

The fine red-sand beach at Firí Amos *(southwest of the island, not accessible by car)* is for naturists.

On the east coast, the beaches at Kalsadi, Avlémonas and Diakófti are attractive; the west-coast beaches are much less accessible and therefore less crowded.

KYTHERA TOWN★★

The capital of the island occupies a very beautiful **site★★** overlooking a magnificent natural harbour on the south coast. The islet that can be seen out to sea is the legendary home of Aphrodite. The bright white walls of its houses show a Cycladic influence which combines with

▸ **Population:** 3, 354.
◔ **Michelin Map:** 284sq km/ 114sq mi – Michelin Map 737 H 13 – Ionian Islands.
▯ **Info:** www.kythera.gr; www.kythira.net.
◑ **Location:** Kythera lies just off Cape Malea (Ákri Maléas). There are three ports: Agía Pelagía (to the north), Diakófti (northeast) and Kapsáli (south).
◌ **Don't Miss:** The ruins at Milopotamos and Paleohóra; Agía Sofía cave.
◔ **Timing:** It's best to have a car here; plan 3–4 days to visit.
⣿ **Kids:** Don a hard hat and equip them with a lamp to explore the cave of Agía Sofía.

GETTING THERE

BY SEA – It is sensible *(and obligatory in summer)* to book cars onto ferries in advance. Ferry service to Athens *(2/wk in summer)* and Crete *(several/wk in summer)*. There is also intermittent service from Gíthio, on the east coast of Máni *(frequency and timetable vary)*.
BY AIR – Service to Athens *(1/day in summer)*; the airport is 15km/9mi northeast of the capital.

the ochre colours of Venetian architecture.

The 16C Venetian citadel is sited on rocky peak with a panoramic view of the town and the twin bays of Kapsáli. There are four Byzantine churches, a former aristocratic residence and numerous cannons. The small **Archaeological Museum** (Arheologikó Moussío) has examples of Minoan and Mycenaean finds from the island, including a pitcher an Archaic lion and a dog's head (◔open Tue–Sat 8.30am–3pm, Sun 9.30am–1pm ⌫no charge).

Backstreet in Kythera Town

© M. Guillochon/MICHELIN

AROUND KYTHERA TOWN
Kapsáli★

To the east lie two bays separated by a rocky promontory. The little port of Kapsáli, which becomes busy in the evenings, is a popular yacht-mooring as well as being the resort of choice on the island. Tavernas are concentrated in the larger of the two bays and this is the place to hire a vehicle.

Monastery of Ágios Ioánnis

⊳ *North of Hóra, in the direction of Livádi.*
This 16C monastery sits atop a cliff overlooking pine woods.

Livádi

This former retreat for 19C British administrators includes the Church of Ágios Andréas (12C) and Kythera's largest bridge, which was built by the British and has 13 arches.

Poúrko

This village features the church of Ágios Dimítrios, decorated with 12C frescoes.

AGÍA SOFÍA AND WEST COAST
Milopótamos

⊳ *West island.*
Not without charm, this village has Neoclassical houses with ornate balconies. A little to the west lies the site of **Káto Hóra**★★, a ruined town dating to Byzantine and Venetian times with a gateway surmounted by the Lion of St Mark.

Cave of Agía Sofía★★

◔ *West island.* ◷*Open Tue–Sun 10am–5pm. Guided tours (hard hats and lamps).* ✎€3.
Chambers within this cave were used as chapels (fresco decoration and flooring). There are also galleries with stalactites, stalagmites and underground lakes.

EAST COAST
Avlémonas

◔ *East coast.*
At the harbour mouth of this fishing village stands a Venetian citadel. More dubious in terms of its historical authenticity is the spot known as Helen's Throne, where Paris of Troy is said to have first met with Helen, setting off a trail of events that led to the Greek expedition to rescue her. The neaby beach, Kaladi, is probably the best on the island and it takes less than half an hour to walk to.

Diakófti

◔ *East coast.*
From this town *(modern port and good sandy beach)*, a road leads to the abandoned **Monastery of Agía Moní**★ (1840), occupying a splendid site.

The Ruins of Paleohóra★★ and North of the Island

In the far north, on a steep slope, the little village of **Karavás**, with its fast-running stream, is located in the greenest part of the island. A little farther north

453

is the Moudari Lighthouse. From here on a clear day it is possible to see the Máni Peninsula, some 20km/13mi away. A little further south is **Potamós**, the most commercially active town on the island, but still a low-key place in terms of visitor numbers. Potamós reveals a pleasant main square and little streets lined with attractive Neoclassical houses. Less than 1km/0.6mi to the south is the white monastery of Ágios Theódoros; the medieval church has a whitewashed façade and a fine painted wooden iconostasis. The nearest place for a swim, off the rocks, is a short way to the south, reached by an unpaved road from Logothetíanika.

The taverna at Logothetíanika is popular at weekends for its live musical entertainment.

Ruins of Paleohóra★★

North of the island; access by a poorly maintained road, signposted off the main road from Potamós, or on foot from the village of Trifyliánika near Potamós along a poorly maintained path.

In a spectacular mountain cirque above the Langáda Gorge lie the impressive but little-known ruins of the Byzantine capital (12C). The peaceful community came to a catastrophic end in 1536 when the pirate Barbarossa sacked the town and massacred the inhabitants.

ADDRESSES

⌂ STAY

🍴🛏 **Hotel Margarita** – *Hóra, in an alley leading to the right off the main street.* ℰ*27360 31711. www.hotel-margarita.com. 12 rooms.* A 19C house, renovated to create a charming hotel in the heart of the capital. Breakfast on one of two peaceful terraces overlooking the countryside.

🍴🛏 **Pitsinades** – *Pitsinádes.* ℰ*27360 33877. www.pitsinades.com. 6 rooms. Open Apr–Oct.* Lovely rooms with vaulted ceilings in a charming old house. Rooms (2 with kitchenettes) open onto a common patio.

🍴🛏 **Ta Sfentónia** – *Pitsinádes.* ℰ*27360 33570. 4 studios.* Spacious and cool studios with kitchen facilities in two magnificently restored old houses decorated with old tools and implements. The private terraces look out over peaceful countryside, and the owner, Anna, is very hospitable.

⌾/EAT

🍴 **Hydragogío** – *Kapsáli.* ℰ*27360 31065.* With a good view over the harbour, this is the best taverna in Kapsáli; tables sit in the shade of a vine-covered arbour. The young proprietors create lively and inventive dishes, with tasty honey doughnuts to finish off the meal. Arrive before 8.30pm to ensure a table.

🍴 **Panaretos** – *Potamós, in the main square.* ℰ*07360 34290.* An open-air restaurant offering local cuisine, such as *loukánika* (sausages) and excellent oriental pastries.

🍴 **Taverna Salonikios** – ℰ*27360 31705.* Family atmosphere, delicious and healthful traditional cuisine.

🍴 **Zephiros** – *Diakófti, opposite the hydrofoil port.* ℰ*27360 34290.* Right on the beach, looking out over a blue sea, this taverna serves Greek fare and grilled-fish dishes.

☕ TAKING A BREAK

Ouzerí Selana – *Potamós, on a terrace in the main square.* Shaded by large pine trees, this is the best place to enjoy an ouzo and grilled octopus with the locals. **Amir Ali** – *Karavás.* Café-bar near the rushing river.

⌖ EVENTS AND FESTIVALS

12 May – Feast day of the Monastery of Ágios Theódoros.

In early August, there are two festivals with singing, dancing and feasting: the wine festival at Mitáta, and the Portokália (orange tree) festival at Karavás.

15 Aug – Potamós festival.

20 Sept – Feast of Agía Pelagía.

thaca★

Itháki – Ιθάκη

little removed from the tourist
nainstream, Ithaca is made up of
wo mountain massifs connected
y an isthmus. The steep west coast
ontrasts with the eastern shoreline,
vhich is less rugged and more
velcoming. The island corresponds
o descriptions in Homer's *Odyssey*:
nountains rising out of the sea,
leasant seascapes, and welcoming
oves. Excavations, it is claimed,
ave identified the places where
dysseus, his father Laertes, his wife
enelope and their son Telemachos
ved. Nothing of ancient Ithaca
emains today.

> ▶ **Population:** 3, 100.
> ⌖ **Michelin Map:** 96sq km/
>   38sq mi – Michelin Map 737
>   C 8 – Ionian Islands.
> ▯ **Info:** ithacagreece.com
> ▶ **Location:** Off the northeast
>   coast of Kefalonía.
> ⌔ **Don't Miss:** Unhurried
>   walks in the countryside.
> ⏱ **Timing:** A couple of days
>   are needed to soak up the
>   relaxing atmosphere.

GETTING THERE

BY SEA – Ferry service from Patra:
(2/day, 1 to Aetos, 1 to Vathí). From
Kefalonía: Sami to Aetos *(5/day)*;
Sami to Vathí *(2/day)*; Fiskárdo to
Fríkes *(1/day)*. From Lefkada: Vasiliki
or Nidrí to Fríkes via Fiskárdo *(1/day)*.
Timetables vary over the course of
the year, with increased services in
summer; enquire at travel agencies or
at the harbourmaster's office in Vathí
☏ *26740 32909.*

VATHÍ (ITHÁKI)

he port and resort town of Itháki, widely
nown as Vathí, occupies a charming
ite at the head of a deep and narrow
nlet; the green slopes on either side are
otted with smart white houses built
fter the 1953 earthquake. The two
uined forts that stand by the entrance to
ne harbour date back to Venetian times.
here are several fine **beaches** nearby,
ome accessible only by boats which
perate from the harbour. Make a quick
top at the **Museum of Folk Art and
he Sea** (⏱*open Tue–Sat 10am–2pm,*
–9pm; ☞*€1.50*) to see some recon-
tructed interiors; the **Archaeological
luseum** (⏱*open Tue–Sun 8.30am–3pm;*
no charge) displays ancient ceramics.

☞*no charge)* displays figurines, ceramics, statuettes, vases and oil lamps dating from the Mycenaean period.

Pólis Bay

1hr 30min on foot there and back.
A path leads down to this charming bay
(pebble beach) where the port is thought
to have been in Odysseus' day; in the
cave sanctuary of Loizos *(closed)* on the
north side of the bay, numerous Mycenaean artifacts have been found.

NORTH OF THE ISLAND

Stavrós

he village is reached from Vathí by a
oad★★ built high on the cliff face pro-
iding fine views; it is the starting point
or two walks.

Pelikáta

Omin on foot there and back.
xcavations here have uncovered
Mycenaean remains. There are also
ood views over the island. The small
elikáta Archaeological Museum
*km/0.6mi from Stavrós, on the Fríkes
oad;* ⏱*open Tue–Sun 9.30am–2.30pm;*

Fríkes

This little port with its clear waters is
charming; old windmills, tavernas and
houses line the quayside, the slopes of the
mountain behind covered by olive groves.

Kióni★

Close to a number of ruined windmills
and far from the tourist routes, this
serene little harbour iies at the foot of
three hills.

Ithaca on Foot★★

The island is ideal for keen walkers; detailed itinerary maps are available in Fríkes and, unsurprisingly, a number of them feature locations identified with the *Odyssey*. The trail to the Cave of the Nymphs (where Odysseus, on his return and while still in disguise, hid the gifts he had been given by King Alcinous), is signposted on the hill above Dhéxa Beach and takes about 40min. There is another pleasant pathway (to the Fountain of Arethoussa) that begins next to the telecoms office at the seafront; this one takes twice as long and requires a degree of stamina.

ADDRESSES

⌂ STAY

⊜⊜ **Hotel Nostos** – *Fríkes outskirts.* 𝒫*26740 31644 (31476 out of season). www.hotelnostos-ithaki.gr. 31 rooms.* This large cream-coloured hotel with red shutters has bright and spacious room with balconies. Family atmosphere and good restaurant. Swimming pool.

⊜⊜⊜ **Hotel Mentor** – *Vathí.* 𝒫*26740 32433/33033. www.hotelmentor.gr. 36 rooms.* Situated near the harbour, this white-and-cream painted hotel ha rooms with balconies overlooking the sea. Breakfast available *(€6)*.

♈/EAT

⊜ **Taverna Kalnakis** – *Vathí, Platia Polixetion.* Popular with locals, this taverna serves generous portions of traditional Greek dishes.

⊜⊜ **Restaurant Calipso** – *Kióni, large terrace on the harbour. Open May–Oct.* A gourmet experience. The creator of the Ionian paté (three cheeses, cream, cured and smoked ham), which is widely, though poorly, imitated elsewhere. Fresh fish, artichoke soufflé and a delicious lamb pie *(kleftiko)*. The best restaurant on the island.

⊜⊜ **Restaurant Pementzo** – *Fríkes, on the harbour.* 𝒫*26740 31719.* Good-quality local cuisine.

Lefkada★

Lefkáda – Λευκάδα

Lefkada is a fairly mountainous island (high point: Mount Eláti at 1,158m/3,799ft) with several fertile valleys where wheat, olives and citrus fruit are cultivated. Its villages, white cliffs and vast beaches make it a beautiful island to explore, and it still has a number of its old houses with wooden balconies.

TOWN AND LAGOON

This peaceful port town appears Venetian thanks to its paved streets lined by low houses. The Church of **Ágios Minás**, at the end of the main street, has a very fine 18C painted ceiling.

There are several small museums: the **Ethnographic Museum** (⚬ *closed for renovation*), the **Phonograph Museum** (🕒 *a small private enterprise, open in the evenings*), and most importantly the

▶ **Population:** 22, 879.

⚲ **Michelin Map:** 305sq km/ 122sq mi – Michelin Map 737 C 8 – Ionian Islands.

▤ **Info:** www.lefkas.net.

◖ **Location:** Lefkada is linked to the mainland by a narrow strip of land and, since 1987, by a bridge.

🅿 **Parking:** A vehicle is needed to appreciate the island and this makes for busy roads; take care when parking by the side of a road.

🕒 **Timing:** The island hosts the International Folk Dancing Festival in the last two weeks of August.

👥 **Kids:** Boat trips from Nidrí.

Archaeological Museum (*open Tue–Sun 8.30am–3pm, €3*); terracotta wares, statuettes, archaic milling tools, and Hellenistic funerary *stelae*, displayed in a recently renovated environment. Fairly shallow, the **lagoon** (only 1–2m/4–6ft deep) is used for fish farming and salt extraction. Drive around the north branch to enjoy beaches, windmills, and stunning view of Lefkada Town. **Faneroméni Monastery** (*3km/2mi southwest*) also provides **views** of Lefkada Town and the lagoon.

EXCURSIONS

Santa Maura Fort

Constructed on a narrow island, this old fort (14C) was originally surrounded by water. Inside the curtain wall are traces of the town of Santa Maura. From the ramparts there is an attractive view of Lefkada Town and the lagoon. On the mainland opposite stands Grivas Castle, built during the War of Independence.

The Mountain★

To the south of Lefkada Town, a road to the right leads to Kariá, a charming village hidden on an olive-grove and cypress-covered mountainside. The road offers fine **views**★ as it winds over empty high plateaux.

 **DRIVING TOUR**

THE ISLAND★★

Around 100km/63mi. Allow one day.

The road from Lefkada Town skirts the west side of the lagoon, with a view across to Fort St George (17C). It then follows the east coast of the island facing Etolía. On reaching Nidrí turn left to visit the harbour.

West Coast★

A road heads west from Lefkada Town and, at the village of **Tsoukaládes**, leads south to a pebble beach at **Kalímini**. Further south, **Ag. Nikítas** is a delightfully low-key destination where the narrow streets made parking such a headache that it is now off-limits to cars; the

GETTING THERE

BY BUS – There is one Athens–Lefkada service a day, and four or five a day to Préveza and Áktio airport.
BY AIR – There is a daily flight from Athens to Préveza (*bus or taxi from there*).
BY SEA – From Vassilikí and Nidrí, daily **ferry** service to Fríkes and Písso Aetós (*Ithaca*), Fiskárdo and Sámi (*Kefalonía*). Timetables are subject to change so check at the port.

nearby pebble beach has better parking space and there is a taverna here. For a sandy beach (*with a nudist section*) head a little further south to **Kalamitsi**; from here the road heads inland to the photogenic village of **Chortáta** and just south of here there is a choice of roads: to access the southwest peninsula and its attractive beaches (**Gialós**, **Egrémni** and **Porto Katsíki**) take the right fork. At the tip of the southwest peninsula are the cliffs from where in the 6C BC Sappho is said to have hurled herself into the sea after being rejected by her lover. The spot is called **Lefkada Leap**★. The headland (Ákri Doukáto) bears traces of a Temple to Apollo and apparently the priests here used to select candidates to act as sacrificial scapegoats for the islanders' sins; the poor scapegoats were then thrown off the cliffs. According to another version of the legend, the priests themselves leapt into the sea and their suicidal cult lasted into the Roman era. Nowadays you may see hang-gliders gather on the cliffs each July for their jumps.

Viewed from the sea, the site is impressive, and the view towards Kefalonía and Ithaca is memorable (the same view can be seen from the Corfu–Patras ferry). Byron sailed past the headland when he first visited Greece and a description of the view is in *Childe Harold*.

Nidrí Bay★

The main resort of the island, attractive Nidrí is very popular with tourists and the waterfront teems with people day and night. The **bay**★ sheltered by a screen of little tree-covered islands, is an enchanting sight.

Departing from Nidrí, boat trips skirt the bay and its islands: Madourí, Spárti, Meganíssi and Skorpiós (formerly the home of shipping magnate **Aristotle Onassis**, who was married on the island to Jacqueline Kennedy in 1968). **Meganíssi** is the most attractive of these small islands and from its port it is only a 10min walk to the main village of Katoméri; from here there are pathways leading to beaches *3km/2mi west of Nidrí*, a path leads up to two refreshing waterfalls on the mountainside.

Vlihó Bay

All around this deep, narrow-mouthed bay are vertiginous views down onto the sea. The village of the same name is well known for its attractive fishing port.

▷ *Return to the main coast road and continue on south.*

Poros

Picturesque inlet below a village sitting on an olive grove-covered hillside.

▷ *About 20 minutes west of here is the popular resort of Vassilikí.*

Vassilikí★

Charming village on the edge of a fertile plain with a beach to the north that has developed into the island's centre for watersports, especially windsurfing. Lessons for learners usually take place in the mornings when winds are gentle; by the afternoon only experieneced windsurfers venture into the sea. Fortunately, the wind dies down by the evening and there is no shortage of tavernas and bars with tables on the beach. There are many places offering a room for the night.

There are boat trips from Vassilikí to **Lefkada Leap★**, The headland is also accessible by a poorly maintained road and then by a track from Komilió, about 10km/6mi north of Vassilikí.

ADDRESSES

🛏 STAY

🛏 **Katina's Place** – *Vassilíki.* 📞 26450 31262. 8 rooms. Simple, comfortable rooms in one of the town's oldest houses; bathrooms on each floor. Striking views, warm welcome.

🛏🛏 **Hotel Santa Maura** – *Lefkada Town, near Platía Ágios Spirídonas.* 📞 26450 21308. www.santamaura.gr. 14 rooms. This renovated hotel in the town centre occupies a historic yellow residence. Cool rooms, some of which overlook the garden.

🛏🛏 **Hotel Athos** – *Nidrí.* 📞 26450 9284. athos@otenet.gr. 43 rooms. A white hotel at the end of the harbour. Cool rooms with balconies, housed in several different buildings. Jacuzzi; evening entertainment and excursions to the islands of Skorpiós and Meganíssi.

🛏🛏🛏 **Hotel Nefeli** – *Agios Nikitas, near the beach.* 📞 26450 97400. www. nefelihotel.gr. 20 rooms. Open May–Oct. Charming hotel with green shutters; bright, cool rooms, some with sea views.

⚊/EAT

🍽 **Restaurant Iónion** – *Nidrí, at the end of the harbour.* 📞 26450 93094. Good local cuisine accompanied by dry local wines and a quiet pergola terrace.

🍽 **Taverna Romantica** – *Lefkada Town, 11 Odós Mitrópoleos.* 📞 26450 22235. Open 8.30am–1am. This popular family taverna serves good local cuisine (fish, *pastítsio* and *maridópita*, a sort of pizza with fried fish). Live music.

🍽🍽 **Taverna Leftéris** – *Ágios Nikítas, in the main street.* 📞 26450 97495. Open May–Oct. Excellent freshly prepared dishes served on a large airy terrace. Specialities include fish, spaghetti with prawns; friendly welcome.

🍽🍽 **Taverna Stéllios** – *Vassilikí.* 📞 26450 315 81. Open May–Oct. Attractive, shady waterside terrace, the ideal spot for grilled fish.

🍽🍽 **Light House Tavern** – *Lefkada Town, 14 Odós Philarmoníki.* 📞 26450 25117. Open Apr–Oct. Excellent food: grilled dishes, fresh fish, and simple freshly-prepared starters. The tables are laid out under a pretty, ivy-covered arbour, steps from the open-air theatre.

Zakynthos★

Zákinthos – Ζάκυνθος

Despite being shaken by earthquakes, Zakynthos is praised for its gentle climate, luxuriant flora, fertile soil and fine sandy beaches (the one in Shipwreck Bay is one of the most famous in Greece). The island rises in the west in a chain of limestone peaks, but levels out to the east in a fertile plain producing olives, citrus fruit and grapes for wine. Protected sea turtles nest on several of the island's beaches.

A BIT OF HISTORY

From 1489 to 1797 Zakynthos belonged to Venice. When Crete fell to the Turks in 1669 many artists moved here and contributed to the Ionian School of painting, which combined the Byzantine tradition and the Venetian Renaissance. Local architecture was also marked by the Venetian influence. In the late 18C and early 19C Zakynthos became a breeding ground for poets, whose work was a blend of the Hellenic and Italian cultures, among them **Ugo Foscolo** (1778–1827) and **Dionysios Solomós** (1798–1857), author of the Greek national anthem.

ZAKYNTHOS TOWN★

One of the most picturesque towns in the Ionians, Zakynthos Town was rebuilt in the Venetian style after 1953 with pretty churches, palaces and arcaded squares. Visitors to the island without their own transport should base themselves here because the only bus station is located in the town.

At the palm-shaded main square, Platía Dhionísios Solomós, you can visit wthe **Museum of Byzantine Art** (Ⓛopen Tue–Sun 8.30am–3pm; ⊛€3) with its collection of icons and religious art. The square is named after the Greek poet, writer of the words for his country's national anthem, who was born on the island. Zakynthos was also home to the novelist Grigorios Xenopoulos (see the dedicated museum in town).

▸ **Population:** 41, 500
☖ **Michelin Map:** 406km2/ 162sq mi – Michelin Map 737 C-D 9-10 – Ionian Islands.
▯ **Info:** www.zanteweb.gr.
◖ **Location:** The third largest of the Ionian islands, to the south of Kefalonía.
⊛ **Don't Miss:** Shipwreck Bay.
Ⓛ **Timing:** At least a couple of days should be set aside for Zakynthos. If you are short on time, take a delightful coastal boat trip.

GETTING THERE

BY SEA – **Ferry** service from Kilíni *(8/day in season, 5/day winter)*. Ferry service *(2/day)* from Pessáda on Kefalonía, arriving at Ágios Nikólaos at the northern end of the island. From here, taxis are the only transport to the capital.
BY AIR – There is a daily flight from Athens to the island (airport south of Zakynthos Town on the Lithakiá road; bus and taxi service from there. *℘26950 28322*) and to Corfu *(several/wk)*, Kefalonía *(several/wk)* and Prevéza *(several/wk)*.

Near the ferry port, the seafront promenade (**Strata Marina**) is very popular, and the church dedicated to the island's patron saint, Dionysios, is well worth visiting for its frescoes and ornate decoration.

Kástro★

Ⓛ*Open Tue–Sun 8.30am–2.30pm (7pm in summer)*. ⊛€3.
The old Venetian citadel set on a hill survived the earthquake and provides an extended **view**★★ of the town, the bay and the Peloponnese coast. It makes an idyllic spot for a picnic.

BEACHES★★

The beaches of Zakynthos are among the best in the eastern Mediterranean. Those listed below are some of

Shipwreck Bay

the island's finest; they appear here in clockwise order starting from Zakynthos Town. Other resort beaches dot the east coastal plain *(salt marshes, orchards)* between Alikés and Zakynthos Town.

Banana Beach★
▶ *East coast.*
This long strip of sand is bordered by dunes, rocks and pine trees.

Pláka
▶ *East coast.*
Neighbouring the above beach, and before the rocks of Cape Ágios Nikólaos.

Pórto Róma
▶ *East coast.*
An attractive inlet with low cliffs; a very good taverna here and lovely views.

Gérakas★
▶ *South coast.*
A vast crescent of sand, part of which is covered by sunbeds; the beach is bordered by curious tufa rocks.

Dafni
▶ *South coast.*
This wild beach is a longtime nesting site for endangered loggerhead turtles.

Cape Kerí★★
▶ *West coast.*
Ideal place to watch the sunset against the backdrop of the tall cliffs.

To the south lie the twin reefs of the Mizíthres, two slivers of white stone.

Shipwreck Bay★★★
▶ *West coast.*
One of Greece's most famous land-marks acquired its nickname after the *Panayótis* was wrecked here in the 1960s.
A viewing platform has been built (signposted "Shipwreck"), from which the **view**★★★ is breathtaking. *The only way to reach this idyllic spot is by boat from Pórto Vrómi (5km/3mi to the south), Límni Kerí, Kokínou or Zakynthos Town.*

Cape Skinári★★
Beyond Korithi, Cape Skinári has stunning views towards Kefalonía.

Kokínou
▶ *East coast.*
From this tiny harbour, boats depart for the famous **blue caves**★, a fine series of arches gouged out of the cliffs. Refracted light turns the sea turquoise.

Makrís Gialós
▶ *East coast.*
A charming beach among white rocks.

Alikés
▶ *East coast.*
This resort with its fine sandy beach has excellent views of Kefalonía.

BOAT TRIPS★★★

In addition to the excursions mentioned above leaving from Pórto Vrómi and Kokínou, the following are recommended.

Tour of the Island★★★

Around €20 (prices vary from one boat to another). Choose one of the smaller vessels, like the Dias, from opposite the Pilot J agency in Zakynthos Town. The trips head north and round Cape Skinári before the impressive **cliffs**★★★ of the west coast come into view, interspersed here and there by delightful beaches.

Marathoníssi★

There are boats from Límni Kerí, at the southern end of the island, which take sightseers to the nearby sea caves *(2hrs, departures on the hour every hour from 9am to 6pm, €15)* and to the island of Marathoníssi. This tiny and private island is uninhabited, and is one of the places where the endangered loggerhead turtles go to breed. You may get a sight of the turtles on the boat trips, and because of the turles the island is part of a protected Marine Park.

ADDRESSES

🛏 STAY

◉🛏 **Villa Christina** – *Keri Lake, near village entrance.* ℘26950 35474. www.villachristina.gr. 6 rooms, 4 studios. Charming little building with comfortable apartments, prettily appointed with garden-style furniture and balconies. Open Apr–Oct; no breakfast.

◉🛏 **Geórgios Zourídis** – *Zakynthos Town, 30 Odós L. Karrer.* ℘26950 44691. 14 rooms. Look for the "Rooms to let" sign on the façade. The ground floor has a pleasant split-level lounge area. Upstairs, the bright, comfortable and spacious rooms (two with air-conditioning) all have kitchen facilities. Excellent value. Open all year; no breakfast.

◉🛏 **Seaside** – *Límni Kerí, on the harbour.* ℘26950 22827. www.seaside.net.gr. Four apartments for 3–5 persons, and four studios for 2 persons. A truly charming place to stay. Olympia, an English-speaking artist, welcomes guests to this renovated property with spacious, clean rooms with terraces. Unbeatable price, especially in winter *(open on request).*

◉🛏 **Villa Fínikes** ("Phoenix") – *Límni Kerí, set back from the harbour.* ℘26950 26513. www.villa-phoenix.com. 9 apartments. A real haven of tranquility; the studios are set in a well-tended garden planted with olive trees. Spacious, well-equipped and very quiet; all with terraces overlooking the countryside. Booking essential.

🍷 EAT

◉ **Arékia** – *Zakynthos Town, north side of town.* ℘26950 26346. A small roadside taverna with terrace opposite overlooking the sea. Very popular with locals but little-frequented by tourists. Good, simple Greek cuisine and singers performing *arékia* (traditional ballads).

◉◉ **Amos** – *Ágios Nikólas Beach.* ℘26950 35000. Under a huge straw canopy, this bar is a pleasant spot for a meal or a drink, with a good selection of music (Greek, international, jazz).

◉◉ **To Pósto** – *Límni Kerí, on entering the village.* ℘26950 26243. Dining under the trees in a pleasant garden. The á la carte menu features traditional Greek dishes. Open evenings only.

◉◉ Mantalena – *Alykanás.* ℘26950 83550. www.mantalena.com. Long-established family-run restaurant, and locals will travel for miles to sample the traditional dishes. Always packed with visitors in summer.

🚋 TAKING A BREAK

Rock Café – *Límni Kerí, on the harbour; next to the Seaside apartments.* A stylish modern building in stone and wood which has been tastefully furnished. The terrace is the ideal spot for an iced coffee, an ouzo or a fresh orange juice. Good local and international music.

Logós Café Bar – *among pine trees on the Vassilikós–Ágios Nikólaos road.* Disco which opens every night at 10pm.

EASTERN AEGEAN ISLANDS

Nisiá Anatolikoú Aigaioú –
Νησιά Ανατολικού Αιγαίου

Thassos and Samothrace are part of the eastern Macedonia and Thrace region. Chíos, Icaria, Lésvos, Límnos, Sámos and adjacent small islands form the Eastern Aegean Islands region. On the very frontier between East and West, each island is its own little world, with unique landscapes and histories. The two nearby islands situated towards the Dardanelles form part of Turkey.

Highlights

1 A drive through the mastic villages of **Chíos** (p464)
2 Living the quiet life on Fourni off the coast of **Icaria** (p467)
3 Following the coast of **Sámos** (p469)
4 The picturesque artistic town of Molívos on **Lésvos** (p474)
5 The bays and villages of volcanic **Límnos** (p476)

GETTING THERE

BY SEA – The islands are served by **ferries** from various mainland ports, most importantly Kavála *(not far from Thassos)*, Alexandroúpoli *(north of Samothrace)* and from Piraeus via the Cyclades. In high season there is a link between Chíos and Turkey *(boats from Cesme, near Izmir)*. The remoteness of some islands can make the crossing very long and it is preferable to fly. Numerous airports link the islands to the rest of Greece, most notably Athens and Thessaloniki. Chíos, Lésvos, Límnos, Sámos and Icaria all have airports.

The Islands Today

The islands are off the coast of Turkey, with the exception of Thassos, which lies off the coast of Thrace but is part of Macedonia. Ferries from the mainland arrive at Thassos regularly. Chíos and Lésvos also have airports and Lésvos receives some international flights. Generally speaking, the islands are less touristy than the Cyclades and Dodecanese; they also tend to be larger in size. Like so many of the Greek islands, they boast some superb beaches and, because they are not overwhelmed with visitors, retain much of their traditional charms.

A Bit of History

Greek Colonies – It was around the 12C BC that the first colonists arrived on these islands from mainland Greece. These early colonists were searching for a new home in the wake of the invasion of their own lands by the Dorians from the north. By the 6C the colonised cities had become vitally important players in the mercantile life of ancient Greece, supplying olive oil and wine in large quantities.

Poets, Philosophers and Amazons – Culturally and socially the Eastern Aegean islands developed rich and creative environments and a number of famous figures in the arts emerged from them. Pythagoras, Epicurus and Aesop came from Sámos. Sappho, Alcaeus and Pittacus were from Lésvos and Homer himself is said to have hailed from Chíos. The island of Límnos was known as the home of the Amazons; indeed, legend has it that only women inhabited Límnos, a fact that surprised the Argonauts when they landed here on their way to the land of Colchis to find the golden fleece. The all-female islanders, though attired in full battle dress, received the Greek Argonauts with kindness and goodwill. They told their visitors that the island's menfolk had been killed in battle (they had actually been slain by their wives) and invited the Argonauts to take their place. Just as well, then, that the Greeks declined and went on their way towards the Black Sea.

Chíos★

Híos – Χίος

Homer's birthplace is dominated by volcanic mountains, the highest of which, Mount Pelinéo, reaches 1 297m/4 255ft. Aromatic resin from the mastic tree (Pistacia lentiscus) is used to make alcoholic drinks, chewing gum and sweets. Chíos has lovely beaches, an unspoilt local culture, Byzantine art and history.

A BIT OF HISTORY

Mediterranean Maritime Trading Centre – Situated on major shipping routes, Chíos played a major role between East and West from antiquity to the 19C and enjoyed its first cultural and economic heyday in the 6C. The Persian invasion in 493 BC brought an end to the island's prosperity. After centuries of decline, it resumed its pivotal role during the Venetian period (12C). The port handled commodities from throughout the Mediterranean, especially the local mastic, and alum from Anatolia, which was essential to the dyeing process and exported mainly to Bruges.

The Turkish occupation of Chíos did not damage the island's trade. In the 19C Chíos's merchant fleet rivalled those of Hydra, Spétses and neighbouring Psará.

Chíos Massacres – At the beginning of the War of Independence, in 1822, the island rose against the Turks, but the revolt failed and the Turks exacted a terrible vengeance: thousands of Christians were massacred or enslaved. The event aroused intense emotion, particularly in France: Delacroix's famous painting *The Massacres in Chíos* and Alfred de Vigny's poem *Helena* were inspired by it. Chíos became part of Greece in 1912.

HÍOS TOWN★ (CHÍOS TOWN)

This small harbour town facing the Turkish coast retains a certain charm. Cafés and restaurants border the lively and colourful **port**★. Behind the business area parallel to the quayside is **Platía Vounáki**, the town centre; on the north side of the square is a charming **Turk-**

▶ **Population:** 52, 000.

Michelin Map: 842sq km/ 337sq mi – Michelin Map 737 N 8 – Northern Aegean Islands.

Info: Chíos Town, Odós Kanari 18, corner of Odós Roïdou. 𝒫22710 44389. www.chiosonline.gr, www.chios.gr.

Location: One of the larger Greek islands, situated 7km/ 5mi off the Turkish coast.

Parking: The roads are generally wide and parking is not usually a problem.

Don't Miss: Kámbos Plain.

Timing: 2–3 days.

GETTING THERE

BY SEA – **Ferry** service from Piraeus, *(2/day)*, Mitilini *(2–3/day)*, Sámos *(3/ wk)*, Límnos *(5–6/wk)*, and Rhodes via Kalímnos and Kos *(1/wk)*. Also ferry service to Cesme in Turkey *(daily; purchase tickets the day before travel, passport required, visa issued on arrival in Turkey)*.

BY AIR – The airport is 4km/2.5mi from Chíos Town. There are several flights a day to Athens, and several per week to Thessaloniki, Lésvos, Límnos, Rhodes and Sámos.

ish fountain★ (1768) decorated with floral reliefs.

Near the port, stop in at the **Archaeological Museum**, *(Odós Mihalou, near the University of the Aegean;* ⏱ *open Tue–Sun 8.30am–2.45pm;* €⊜2) to see objects recovered from the island's archaeological sites.

Kástro (Citadel)

North of the harbour and of Platía Vounáki. The formerly elegant old town is still surrounded on three sides by ramparts built in the 14C. Today it is a quiet area, somewhat rundown. Inside the **main gate** on the right is the dark basement room of the keep, formerly used as a dungeon.

Opposite the Kástro gate the **To Palatákia (Small Palace)** (*open Tue–Sun 8.30am–3pm; €2)* 15C mansion houses a small collection of **Byzantine art**; a fine mosaic (5C AD) found in the modern town and Byzantine and post-Byzantine icons and frescoes.

Nearby is the **Fort Museum** (*same times and charges as To Palatákia)* which displays artillery pieces, most notably French cannons.

To the left as you exit lies the tiny old **Turkish Cemetery**. The **Odós Frourio** road runs through the *kástro* district and up a bare hill from where there are fine **views**★ over the town and the sea. Clearly visible is the rooftop of the old Turkish Baths: four terracotta domes dotted with small holes and overrun with greenery.

Koraïs Library and Argentis Museum★

Junction of Odós Koraïs and Odós Argendis near the cathedral. Open Mon–Thu 8am–2pm Fri 8am–2pm and 5pm–7.30pm, Sat 8am–12.30pm. No charge to enter the hall, €3 for the galleries. 22710 44246.

100 000 books collected by the writer **Adamántios Koraïs**, a small **Ethnographic Museum** and collection of **portraits** of the Argentis family.

ISLAND CENTRE★★

A superb **panoramic road** climbs the foothills of Mount Épos to the village of **Anávatos**. Perched on a rocky spur, the village was probably built to defend the east coast against the Turks. Today it is deserted and a delight for lovers of solitude. The village boasts a fine **view**★ of the west coast. Nearby, the monastery of Néa Moní stands in a wooded valley guarded by cypress trees.

Néa Moní Monastery★★

Open dawn to dusk; closed from 1pm–4pm. No charge. 22710 79391, www.neamoni.gr.

A UNESCO World Heritage Site, this is one of the most important buildings of the Byzantine era. It was built in the 11C and is the work of architects and painters from Constantinople. The **exterior** is protected by a layer of plaster.

The octagonal church is the best surviving architectural example of its age. Its large triple-domed **exonarthex** was originally faced in red marble painted with post-Byzantine frescoes; only the Last Judgment on the south wall remains. The austere figures and expressive features of the brightly coloured 11C **mosaics**★ in the narthex and the nave show great unity of style. The tall dome of the **nave** and the mosaic of the Pantocrator were restored in 1900.

NORTHERN VILLAGES
Mármaro
27km/17mi.

Lying in a deep bay, Mármaro is the harbour for neighbouring Kardámila. A little farther on, **Nagós** and its environs boast the island's finest **beaches**★★.

Pitioús
28km/18mi.

As with Volissós, Pitioús claims to be Homer's birthplace. Its medieval fortress has a yellow Byzantine church.

Volissós
46km/29mi.

This village at the foot of a medieval fortress has a fishing harbour at Límnos. 6km/4mi to the north is a fine **beach** by the Monastery of Agía Markéla. The road back to Chíos Town has vertiginous **views**★ of the west coast.

🚗 DRIVING TOUR

MASTIKOHÓRIA★★ (Mastic Villages)
90km/56mi round trip, south of Chíos Town.

This region covers all the southern part of the island from Armólia and comprises some 20 villages. This is where the **lentis** grows; the tree's resin (**mastic**) is collected in the early autumn. Chíos is the only place where the resin solidifies naturally.

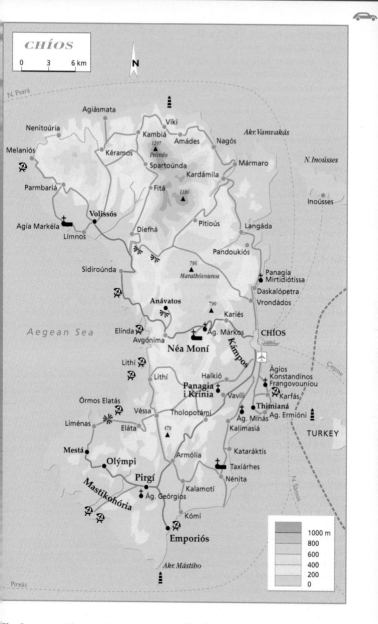

CHÍOS

0   3   6 km

N

N. Psará

Agiásmata

Nenitoúria

Víki

Kambiá
1297
Pelinéo

Amádes   Nagós

Akr. Vamvakás

Melaniós

Kéramos   Spartoúnda   Mármaro

N. Inoússes

Parmbariá   Fitá   Kardámila

1186

Inoússes

Volissós   Diefhá   Pitioús   Langáda

Agía Markéla
Límnos

Pandoukiós

Sidiroúnda   *796*
Marathóvounos   Panagía
Mirtidiótissa

Daskalópetra

Anávatos   *790*   Vrondádos

Kariés

Aegean Sea   Elínda   Ag. Márkos   CHÍOS

Avgónima   Néa Moní   Kámpos

Lithí   Çeşme

Lithí   Halkió   Ágios
Konstandínos
Frangovouníou

Panagía
i Krína   Vavíli   Karfás

Órmos Elatás   Thimianá   Ag. Ermióni

Véssa   Tholopotámi   Ag. Minás

Liménas   Eláta   *479*   Kalimasiá   TURKEY

Mestá   Kataráktis

Olýmpi   Armólia   Taxiárhes

Pirgí   Nénita

Mastikohória   Kalamotí   Ág. Geórgios

N. Sámos

Kómi

Emporiós

Akr. Mástibo

Pireás

1000 m
800
600
400
200
0

The Byzantine Church of the **Panagía i Krina** (12C or 13C) may be visited on the way *(access from Vavíli, 1km/0.6mi on the Sklaviá road, then about 15min on foot by a track – right – through an olive grove)*. Its frescoes are in the Palatákia Museum in Chíos.

Pirgí★

A tower dominates the medieval village, although the walls have been razed. The geometric *sgraffito* decoration of the houses and churches is an unusual feature; the technique known as *xistá* or *skalistrá* is still in use today.

A covered passage northeast of the square leads to the Church of the **Holy**

Apostles (Ágii Apostóli, c.1200) with its typically Byzantine exterior. The interior is decorated with frescoes (1665). The 17C Church of the Dormition in the square contains fine carved furnishings.

> ⟲ *6km/3.5mi south of Pirgí.*

Emboriós★

A small square bordered by houses gives onto the sea. To the south of the port, a path leads to two black pebble **beaches** ★★ tucked away under volcanic cliffs.

> ⟲ *Beyond medieval Olímbi is one of the most unusual vMastic villages.*

Mestá★

It is pleasant to stroll through the old lanes and vaulted passages. The church and the main square have replaced a defensive tower. Farther along the old Byzantine **Taxiarchs Church** (Paliós Taxiárhis) contains a beautifully carved iconostasis (18C). Return to Chíos Town via Liménas, Mestá's port, and the Véssa road, which offers at the start extensive **views**★ of the barren and jagged west coast.

THE KÁMBOS PLAIN★

⟲ *The Kámbos Plain is a large fertile area in central Chíos, southwest from Chíos Town.* From the 15C to the 19C some 200 houses **(arhondiká)** and mansions were built in this fertile plain by wealthy merchants for use as summer residences. The 10 or so that survive evoke a bygone age. Houses occasionally open to the public include the Neoclassical **Zigomalas House**, which has a fine courtyard *(beginning of the road, about 800m/0.5mi after the bridge over the River Parthenis);* and the well-preserved **Argenti House** *(about 5km/3mi farther in a parallel road to the west, Odós Argentis).*

ADDRESSES

🛏 STAY

CHÍOS TOWN

🛏 **Alex Rooms** – *Chíos Town, 29 Odós Livanou, near the harbour. ℰ/Fax 22710 26054. roomsalex@chi.forthenet.gr.*

6 rooms. Shared bathrooms. The owner is a very cordial retired sea captain, and all guests are treated as family. Sober decoration in comfortable rooms.

🛏 **Chíos Rooms** – *Chíos Town, at the harbour. ℰ22710 20198. www.chios rooms.gr. 10 rooms.* 🍴. Charming old building; half the rooms have en suite facilities and several have balconies.

VOLISSOS

🛏 **Kyriaki House** – *Volissos; follow the "Artemis Apartments" sign. ℰ22740 21941. 2 apts.* 🍴. Two comfortable studios; magnificent terrace with sea views.

🛏🛏 **Perivoli** – *Kámbos, a little out of Chíos Town. ℰ22710 31513. 15 rooms.* A fine building in typical island style. Try to book one of the four larger rooms with high ceilings, which are comfortable even in high summer.

🛏🛏 **Volissos Travel** – *Volissos, various houses in the upper part of the village. ℰ22710 21421. www.volisso travel.gr.* Historic stone houses, all two-storey; kitchen downstairs, bedrooms above.

🍽 EAT

CHÍOS

🍴 **Byzantio** – *Chíos Town, market district, Odós Rali. ℰ22710 41035.* 🍴. This restaurant always has several daily specials. The cuisine is tasty and served in a characteristic local setting.

🍴 **Meliotiko Ouzerie** – *Chíos Town, at the port. ℰ22710 40407.* 🍴. Traditional place, renowned for its huge helpings, and handy for the ferry terminal.

KÁMBOS

🍴 **Restaurant Perivoli** – *Kámbos, a little out of Chíos Town. ℰ22710 31973.* In the gardens of the pleasant hotel of the same name. Try the veal in wine.

VOLISSOS

🍴 **O Zikos** – *Volissos, at the harbour. ℰ22710 22040.* 🍴. The ideal spot for sampling seafood: mussels, lobster pasta, swordfish, etc.

🎉 EVENTS AND FESTIVALS

Volissos – The village hosts an unusual Easter tradition: a fireworks "battle" between the two main churches.

Pirgi – **15 August**, village festival.

caria

Ikaría – Ικαρία

ccording to myth, Icaria drowned
ear the island's shores when the
un melted his wax wings after he
ad escaped the Labyrinth with
is father, Daidalos (see Knossós).
rapes cultivated here produce a red
ine mentioned by Homer.

- ▶ **Population:** 8, 312.
- **Michelin Map:** 267sq km/
  107sq mi – Michelin Map
  737 N 10 – Northern
  Aegean Islands.
- **Info:** www.greekisland.
  co.uk/ikaria/ikaria.htm.
- **Location:** This island
  lies between Sámos and
  Mýkonos in the Cyclades.
- **Don't Miss:** The beaches
  on the northern coast.

GETTING THERE

BY SEA – Ferry service from Piraeus,
(3/wk, usually Mon, Thu, Fri). Some
boats dock at Ágios Kírikos (south
coast) or Évdilos (north coast). In
summer, ferries link the island to
Pátmos, Páros, Chíos, Léros, Sámos,
Mýkonos, Kos, KáLímnos and several
other islands.

GIOS KÍRIKOS

his small fishing town has typical
wo-story houses around its port. A bit
arther west along the coast lies **Thé-
ma Lefkádas**, a resort famous for its
ot springs. Farther still lies the stun-
ing **Evangelistria Monastery** (17C)
ear Xylosirtis. A chief attraction on the
sland, a short distance from the port
rea, are the spas. The spa of **Thérma**
s the oldest and its claim to have the
nost radioactive hot springs in Europe
oes not put people off. More attractive
pas for visitors, in terms of the facilities,
re the ones at **Thérma Lefkádhos** and
sklípiou.

NORTHERN COAST★

With its hilly terrain and cool climate, the
orthern coast holds more interest for
he visitor. The majority of the island's
eaches are found here; they are quite
mall in size, with a couple of exceptions
nentioned below.

he surfaced road from Ágios Kírikos
oes through the pleasant village of
aravostamo, dominated by a splen-
id Byzantine chapel, Ágioi Pantes, and
rrives at **Évdilos** with its small port.
eyond, an unsurfaced road leads to
ampos; its archaeological museum
ouses objects found at the ancient
ite of Oinoe, once the island's capital.
Pigi, there is a lovely **monastery**; its
escoes recall those at Mount Áthos.
fter Kampos, head towards the loveli-
st part of the island, which stretches
eyond **Armenistís**. Nearby are the two
arge and sandy beaches of **Livadi** *(5min
n foot)* **Messachit** *(a 15min walk away)*.
he beaches are superb but take heed of
he signs warning bathers of the danger
osed by strong currents. Armenistís is

the most popular destination for visitors
and there a number of hotels and tavernas
to choose from. This is also the best place
for hiring a bicycle, a scooter or a car.
Near the attractive village of **Christos
Raches** there are splendid views of the
coast and a number of lively tavernas.
From the village there are several walks
that can be enjoyed – a locally-produced
map showing various routes is readily
available – and one of the most popular
heads east towards a medieval convent
at **Moundé**.

To the west of Armenistís, at **Nas**, there is
a pathway that leads to the island's main
nudist beach and the ruins of a temple
that dates back to the 5C BC. As with
the beach at Armenistís, take care when
swimming and do not venture beyond
the line of buoys placed in the water to
mark a safety line.

Beyond Nas, the village of **Vrakádes**
makes for a pleasant destination and
there are a couple of cafés serving food
and drinks. A day's drive could be completed by moving on to the village of
Karkinágri from where boats depart for
Ágios Kyriikos.

FOURNI★

There are three islets off the coast of Icaria, and Fourni is the main one that receives summer visitors. Rooms can be rented but it is also possible to go on a day trip from Ágios Kyríikos. Social life is concentrated around the port and there is a pleasant walk from here to small coves at Kambi where tavernas serve food at tables on the sand. You can continue walking around the islet, discovering deserted coves and places to swim. The only paved road leads from the port to the south of Fourni where there are more small beaches but with no facilities.

⌂STAY / ⟨EAT

ÁGIOS KÍRIKOS

⌂ **Hotel Akti** – *Ágios Kírikos, opposite the harbour.* ℘*22750 23905*. This budget hotel occupies a house perched on a rock above the island's main port. Fine sea view from the terrace.

ÉVDILOS

⌂ **Rooms Spanos** – *Évdilos.* ℘*22750 31220*. These rooms are basic but all have their own bathroom.

Hotel Karras – *Ágios Kíriko.* ℘*22750 22494*. This quiet and simple hotel is 6km/4mi from the port at Évdilos .

⌂ **Taverna** – *Karavostamo.* This large, pleasant restaurant has tasty cooking and a friendly proprietor.

Sámos★

Sámos – Σάμος

A narrow strait separates Sámos from the Turkish coast. The island's beaches, coves and indented coastline, together with its interesting archaeological remains, make Sámos a pleasant place for a prolonged stay; excursions to Ephesus (Efes) in Turkey are an added attraction. On Sámos itself, the Temple of Hera is one of the most ancient in all Greece.

A BIT OF HISTORY

In the Archaic period the island flourished, reaching its apogee in the middle of the 6C BC under the rule of **Polycrates.** The enlightened tyrant caused construction of a long breakwater to protect the port, and an underground aqueduct, one of the wonders of the ancient world. Sámos retained its prosperity until the Roman period.

Famous sons of ancient Sámos include the mathematician **Pythagoras** (6C BC), the sculptor **Pythagoras** (5C BC), the philosopher **Epicurus** (4C BC) and the astronomer **Aristarchos** (3C BC), who anticipated the findings of Copernicus and Galileo in discovering that the Earth revolves round the sun. Under the Byzantine Empire, Sámos fell

▶ **Population:** 33, 814.
🜂 **Michelin Map:** 477sq km/ 191sq mi – Michelin Map 737 O 10 – Northern Aegean Islands.
▪ **Info:** 107 Themistoklí Soufoúlí ℘22730 28582. Another office in Pithagório. www.samos.gr, www.pythagorion.net.
▶ **Location:** Sámos is south of Chíos and north of Patmos; the western coast of Turkey is not far away.
◈ **Don't Miss:** The fine taste of the island's wines.
◷ **Timing:** Stay for a week with a couple of days in Sámos Town.

into decline. The Venetians occupied i several times. When the island fell to the Turks in 1475, the population emigrated to Chíos and Lésvos.

In 1821 Sámos took an active part in the national liberation movement. The Turkish fleet was sunk in 1824 near Pithagório. Despite being excluded from the new Greek State under the 1830 London Accord, Sámos was reunited with Greece in March 1913.

GETTING THERE

BY SEA – Most **ferries** arrive at Sámos Town. Ferries link Sámos to Piraeus *(daily)*, Syros *(6/wk)*, Mýkonos *(4/wk)*, Chíos *(3/wk)*, Límnos, Lésvos, Naxos, Paros *(2/wk)*, Rhodes and Kos *(1/wk)*. Also service to Pithagório from Kalímnos, Pátmos *(3/wk)*, Piraeus *(daily)* and, in season, to Rhodes and Kos.

BY AIR –The airport is located 4km/2.5mi from Pithagório; there are daily flights to Athens, and several a week to Crete and Thessaloniki.

SÁMOS TOWN★

The island capital occupies an attractive **site**★★ in the Bay of Vathí (meaning deep). The lower (and newer) town is the business and administrative centre. In Platiá Pithagória a great marble lion symbolises the people's bravery during the liberation movement.

The **Municipal Gardens,**★ set back from the quayside, are the town's most attractive spot. The only beach is at Gangos, 1km/0.6mi from the jetty. In the **Archaeological Museum**★ *(◷open Tue–Sun 8.30am–3pm; €3; 22730 27469)* there is a remarkable collection of artefacts from the Heraion and from ancient Sámos, including a marble *kouros* and fine bronzes. You can also visit the small **Paleontology Museum** *(◷open Apr–Oct, Tue–Sat 9am–2pm, Sun 10am–2pm; €3)* with its collection of fossils; some are 10 million years old.

Áno Vathí

The old town *(Áno Vathí – the upper town)* spreads up the hillside behind the port. Walk up Odós Smirnis to explore the picturesque streets lined with Turk-

ish corbelled houses. **Ágios Gianákis,** a lovely Byzantine church dedicated to St John and St Theodore, nestles in a hollow on the hillside to the east.

Zoodóhos Pigí Monastery

▶ *8km/5mi east.* ◷*Open daily except Fri, 10am–1pm and 3–8pm.* ⊜*No charge.*

Founded in 1755, the **Monastery of the Source of Life** crowns a wooded hill on the Prasso Headland.

The church columns are probably from ancient Miletus in Asia Minor. Extensive **views**★★ of the Turkish coastline.

Ruins of the Temple of Hera, Heraion

© John Sfondilias/Bigstockphoto.com

On the way back, in Kamára, turn left into a small road leading to the village of **Agía Zóni**. The monastery (1695) contains late-17C frescoes and an iconostasis (1801).

Psilí Amos

▶ *12km/8mi east.*

The attractive beach of Psilí Amos ("fine sand") looks out towards Turkey's Cape Mycale. The narrowest point between Greece and Turkey (1 300m/1 430yds) is 1km/0.6mi east of here.

🚗 DRIVING TOUR

TOUR OF THE ISLAND
Around 140km/88mi. Allow a full day.

The route covers the north and south coasts, the Temple of Hera, and Pithagório. It reveals just how beautiful an island Sámos is.

NORTH COAST★

Kokári

This fishing village and lively resort boasts a nice harbour and pebbly beach to the west.

The road then overlooks the beaches of Lemonákia and **Tsamodoú** and continues to Avlákia for a splendid **view**★★ of Cape Kótsikas and of Kokári and its promontory.

Vourliótes★

▶ *Beyond Avlákia bear left for 4km/2.5mi.*

A wine-growing village with traditional houses. Continue 2km/1.25mi to the southeast to reach **Vrondianí Monastery** (1566), the oldest on the island. The road winds through vineyards, giving **views**★★ of the island's coastline.

Aïdónia Gorge★

Turn left after the bridge at Platanákia and drive through the valley of the fast-flowing Aïdónia River where the occasional song of nightingales – *aïdónia* – breaks the silence. The road climbs to the village of **Manolátes,** overlooking the Aïdónia Gorge.

Karlovássi

Paleó Karlovássi overlooks the harbour area and its churches and old houses. The 11C **Church of the Transfiguration** (Metamorfóssis), its dome resting on four ancient columns, nestles near the beach at **Potámi**.

Head south across the island, passing through mountainous country.

THE SOUTH★

Take the road leading to MarathóKámbos.

MarathóKámbos

The harbour, Órmos Marathokámbou, is also a resort *(large beach and excursions by boat to Samiopoúla and Pátmos)*. Numerous fine beaches in the area.

▶ *Return to the main road and head towards Pithagório (right).*

At first the road affords lovely **views**★ over Marathókambos Bay, then cuts through the forest to the villages of **Pírgos** and **Koumaradéi**; at the latter, bear right.

Megáli Panagía

Founded in 1586 in a wooded valley, the Monastery of the Great Virgin was rebuilt in the 18C after a fire. It was again damaged by fire in 1988.

▶ *Return to the main road. After 5km/3mi turn left to the Monastery of Timíou Stavroú.*

Timíou Stavroú

🕐 *Open daily 9am–noon, 5pm–sunset.* 🚫 *No charge.*

The Monastery of the Holy Cross was founded in the 16C after an icon of the Crucifixion was found on the spot.

Iréo★ (Heraion)

🕐 *Open Tue–Sun 8.30am–3pm.* 💶 *€4.* 📞 *22730 95277.*

Facing the sea are the meagre ruins of the celebrated Shrine of Hera, wife of Zeus. Several shrines have been built on this spot from the Bronze Age to the end of the Roman Empire; it is the earliest

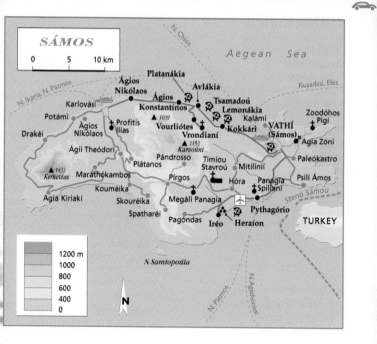

known Greek temple. Walk past the foundations of the enormous **Temple of Hera** (6C BC).

The gigantic scale of the building (twice the size of the Parthenon) can be deduced from the single standing column, although it is only half its original height of 20m/65ft. Note the three headless **korai**★ *(originals in the Archaeological Museum in Sámos Town)*. Farther to the left are traces of a **Christian basilica** built in the 5C or 6C. Beyond a paved street lie the remains of the **altar** dedicated to Hera. Beyond is the **Sacred Way**, which linked the sanctuary with the town of Sámos.

Pithagório★

This popular port was renamed in 1955 in honour of the mathematician and philosopher **Pythagoras**, born on Sámos. Two beaches, and Potokáki Beach *(west)*.

Logothetis Castle

Built in the early 19C, its tower soars above the town. There are extensive **views**★ to Cape Mycale in Turkey, Agathoníssi Island (south) and Cape Foniás (east).

Efpalínio★ (Eupalinos' Aqueduct)

◐ *1.5km/1mi north of Pithagório.*
◷ *Open Tue–Sun 8.45am–2.45pm.*
◉ €4. ✆ 22730 62811.

According to Herodotus the historian and geographer (5C BC), this aqueduct hewn through the mountain was one of the wonders of his time. It provided Sámos with fresh water from the Agiádes Stream on the other side of the mountain.

Ancient Wall

One of the best preserved sections of the ancient circuit wall rises about 100m/328ft west of the tunnel entrance. Other sections can be seen by the side of the road to the west, and above the road to Sámos Town on leaving Pithagório to the east.

Thérma (Roman Baths)

◐ *To the west of Pithagório.* ◷ *Open Tue–Sun 8am–2.45pm.* ◉ *No charge.*
The Romans converted a large Hellenistic gymnasium into these baths.

471

ADDRESSES

🛏 STAY

SÁMOS TOWN

🛏 **Pension Dreams** – *9 Odós Areos (north of Pithagório Square).* 𝒫*22730 24350. 11 rooms.* At the top of a hill overlooking the bay; clean, high-ceilinged rooms.

🛏 **Mirini Hotel** – *Odós Kallistratoús . Sámos Town, up from the landing stage.* 𝒫*22730 28452. www.mirini.com. 34 rooms. Open May–Oct.* Well-presented rooms; dramatic views from all rooms over the rocky coastline.

🛏🛏 **Aeolis Hotel** – *33 Themistoklí Soufoúlir.* 𝒫*22730 28904. www.aeolis.gr. 50 rooms.* The town's best hotel in this category, well kept and stylish. Swimming pool.

PITHAGÓRIA

🛏 **Pension Déspina** – *Platía Irínis* 𝒫*22730 61677. 3 rooms, 6 apts.* Clean, bright rooms; studios overlooking the square or a verdant courtyard.

🛏 **Pension Daphné** – *Pithagória, to the left of the museum.* 𝒫*22730 61529. 5 rooms.* Some rooms have balconies overlooking the attractive square.

🛏 **Paris** – *Pithagória, coast road.* 𝒫*22730 95397/69472/08300. 7 apts. Open May–Oct.* Diminutive guesthouse just steps from the sea. Balconies.

🍴 EAT

SÁMOS TOWN

🍴 **Next** – *Sámos Town, on the bay.* 𝒫*22730 27719.* Italian cuisine, devoured by a youthful clientele.

🍴 **To Ostraki** – *Sámos Town, on the bay.* 𝒫*22730 27070.* Wide variety of excellent fish and seafood.

PITHAGÓRIA

🍴 **El Coral** – *Pithagória, at the harbour.* 𝒫*22730 61193.* Meat-based specialities (pork, lamb) dressed with sauces according to your preference.

🍴 **Notos** – *Pithagória, on the beach near the Kástro.* 𝒫*22730 62351. Open May–Oct.* Salads and *souvlaki* served on a pleasant terrace on the beach.

Lésvos (Mýtilini)★

Lésvos (Mitilíni) – Λέσβος (Μυτιλήνη)

Close to Turkey's Anatolian Coast, Lésvos is renowned for its beautiful villages, its countless beaches, its mountainous and wooded landscapes, and its huge gulfs. Sometimes called Mýtilini, the name of its capital, Lésvos has a large population and its size makes it the third-largest island in Greece after Crete and Euboea. The fertile soil supports over 11 million olive trees, the island's most important crop. There are several distilleries producing the best *ouzo* in Greece, spas, and a flourishing tourist sector.

A BIT OF HISTORY

A Poetess Renowned The World Over – Artist, genius and free spirit, **Sappho** is the most famous person to have come from Lésvos. Her poetic works were

▸ **Population:** 90, 643.

◔ **Michelin Map:** 1 633sq km/ 653sq mi – Michelin Map 737 N 6 – Northern Aegean Islands.

▯ **Info:** North Aegean Islands Tourism Directorate, 6 Odós Aristarcho, near the harbour. 𝒫 22510 42511. Open Mon–Fri 8am–2.30pm, www.lesvos-travel.com, www.mithymna.gr.

▶ **Location:** Located between Límnos and Chíos.

◬ **Don't Miss:** Mólivos.

◷ **Timing:** 2–3 days

highly regarded in antiquity. Whether it was odes, hymns or songs, all of Sappho's verses spoke of love and beauty in a style that particularly touched female sensitivity. She committed suicide in Leukas.

MÝTILINI★

The island capital is on the east coast facing Anatolia. The district on the isthmus between the two harbours, which was the centre of town during the Turkish occupation, has retained some fine houses, the remains of a mosque and the cathedral, which contains a very fine post-Byzantine iconostasis.

There are two small museums: the **Byzantine Museum** (◷open May–Oct Mon–Sat 9am–1pm; ⊜€2; ☏22510 28916) housing precious icons from the 13C to the 17C; and the **Archaeological Museum** (◷open Tue–Sun 8.30am–3pm (7pm in summer); ⊜€3; ☏22510 28032) with fine ceramics, Greek sculpture and Roman mosaics. The ticket also gives admission to the nearby New Archaeological Museum.

House of Lésvos (Lesviakó Spíti)

Collections of art and popular traditions; adjacent small museum.

Kástro

◷Open Tue–Sun 8am–2.30pm (7pm in summer). ⊜€2.

The castle (rebuilt 14C) stands on a promontory projecting seawards beyond the town and overlooking the two harbours. Note above the gate the arms of the Palaiologos Emperors of Byzantium, the horseshoe of the Gatteluzzi and Arabic inscriptions.

GETTING THERE

BY SEA – **Ferry** service to Piraeus (daily in summer); and neighbouring islands, notably Límnos, Sámos and Rhodes (several/wk). There are occasional services to Turkey.

BY AIR – The airport is 8km/5mi south of Mýtilini; regular flights to Athens (several/day in summer); also to Thessaloniki, Límnos and Chíos.

Hellenistic Theatre

◷Open Tue–Sun, 8.30am–2.30pm (7pm in summer). ⊜No charge.

Northwest of the old district lie the remains of a Hellenistic **theatre**; most of the terraces have disappeared. The size of the theatre (it seated 15 000 spectators) indicates the cultural importance of Lésvos in antiquity. From the upper terraces there is a fine view of the old town, the castle and the Turkish coast.

AROUND MÝTILINI

Variá (4km/2.5mi south along the coast has the Theophilos Museum which houses many works by the famous naive painter Theophilos (1873–1934), who was born here; the paintings are brightly coloured representations of popular scenes or incidents in Greek history. On the same site, under the olive trees, stands the Teriade Museum, which contains a rich library and engravings and lithographs by Chagall, Picasso, Fernand Léger, Matisse and Giacometti.

Festivals on the Island

Religious festivals are celebrated on Lésvos with great enthusiasm and sometimes incorporate very ancient elements such as ritual sacrifice (only tolerated by the Church). The feast of St Michael the Archangel, patron saint of the island, is celebrated on the third weekend after Easter at **Mandamádos** (34km/21mi northwest of Mýtilini). During the festivites, several animals are sacrificed and spectators mark their foreheads with the blood to protect themselves from illness. Worshippers throng the monastery to kiss a very old terracotta icon of the Archangel Michael.

A similar celebration takes place during the last week in May near the town of **Agía Paraskeví**. After a colourful procession, a bull is sacrificed on Saturday evening . On Sunday, after the service and the distribution of the meat, there is horse racing.

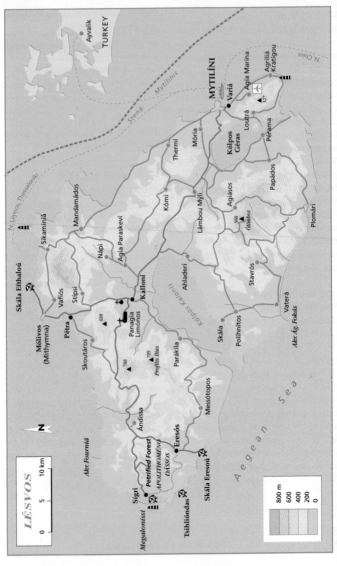

To the southwest of Variá, **Thermí** boasts the popular spa of Loutropóli Thermís; its curative waters were renowned even in antiquity. South of Thermí and west of the village of Mópia are traces of an impressive Roman aqueduct.

SOUTH OF THE ISLAND
Agiássos
◯ *25km/16mi.*

The wooded lower slopes of the highest peak on the island (Mount Olympus,

968m/3 235ft) frame this charming unspoilt town.

Plomári
◯ *42km/26mi.*

Plomári is famous throughout Greece for the high quality of its aniseed liqueur (ouzo).

Tucked in a hollow in the cliff face, it is scarcely visible from a distance. The modern seafront provides cafés, restaurants and a tiny beach. East o the town is a shingle beach, **Ágios Issídoros**, which is very popular.

Vaterá
▶ *52km/32mi.*

This is the most beautiful beach on the island, and one of the loveliest in Greece. It extends for several kilometres, and for most of the year it should be possible to find quiet stretches which you can have all to yourself.

WEST OF THE ISLAND
Eressós and Skála Eressoú
▶ *90km/56mi.*

Skála Eressoú, which is the port for the larger village of Eressós, attracts many holidaymakers to its long sandy **beach★**. **Ancient Eressós**, on a hill to the east of the village, is thought to be the birthplace of Sappho.

Petrified Forest (Apolithoména Déndra)
🕐*Open Jul–Sep: daily 9am-5pm. Oct–Jun: Tue-Sun 8.30am–4.30pm.* ✆€5. 𝟸22530 54434. www.petrifiedforest.gr.

Between Sígri and Eressós there is a petrified forest of fossilised trees that were buried in volcanic ash millions of years ago. The trees reach up to 10m/33ft in height and the trunks measure about 8m/26ft round the bole. The most accessible trees are to be found on the south side of the Ándissa to Sígri road (about 7km/4mi from Ándissa). The **views★★** from the highest point of the "forest" are stunning.

Mólivos★ (Míthimna)
▶ *64km/40mi.*

Picturesque little town favoured by artists; pebble beach and fishing port. The handsome houses, painted in pastel shades, climb the steep slope towards an impressive 14C Byzantine–Genoese castle (🕐*open Tue–Sun 8.30am–7pm;* ✆€2; 𝟸22530 71803), which offers views of the town and the coast, and across the sea to Turkey. Apart from the views there is not a lot to see, but the castle is used to provide a dramatic setting for an annual summer drama fes-

tival. A radioactive spring (46.8°C/124°F) beyond the beach at Eftaloú *(3km/2mi east of Mólivos)* is captured in a covered bath before warming the sea water off the shingle beach (🕐*open daily 9am–6pm;* ✆€5). There is also an older bathhouse *(open daily 6am–8am and 6am–10pm,* ✆€3.50).

ADDRESSES

🛏STAY

MÓLIVOS
🛏 **Mólivos Camping** – *Efthalou road.* 𝟸22530 71169/71079. 88 sites. May–Oct. Shady sites; clean common areas.

🛏 **Nassos** – *Mólivos, up the main street from the tourist office.* 𝟸22530 71232. www.nassosguesthouse.com. Open Mar–Dec. 7 rooms, 1 apt. No breakfast. Charming, rustic home in the older part of town, which organises Greek dancing and yoga workshops.

🛏 **Paradise** – *Mólivos, village entrance.* 𝟸22530 71778/69454 03236. 6 apts. Simple, clean studios with views of the kástro and the village.

MÝTILINI
🛏 **New Life Rooms** – *Odós Ermou 68.* 𝟸22510 23400. 9 rooms. Tastefully decorated budget guesthouse; shady garden to the side for relaxing.

🛏 **Pension Thalia** – *Odós Kinikiou 1. 3 rooms. 1apt.* Simply decorated; several rooms with private bath. Reserve in summer.
Hotel Erato – *Odós Vistani 2.* 𝟸22510 41160. 20 rooms. Handy for the port, many rooms with balconies, all with private bathrooms.

🍽EAT

MÝTILINI
🍴 **Matzourana** – *Mýtilini Odós Komninaki.* 𝟸69485 80463. Open evenings. Contemporary bistro serving up inventive dishes presented with care. Try the honey beef or the stuffed peppers.

MÓLIVOS
🍴 **Panorama** – *Mólivos, opposite the entrance to the citadel.* Typically Greek dishes and pastries which will delight.

Límnos★

Límnos – Λήμνος

The volcanic island of Límnos has an astonishing variety of landscapes. Historical sites are in fertile plains to the east, while the barren mountain chains with cultivated valleys to the west form a rugged coastline indented with bays and sandy coves. The main resort is the capital, Mírina, with its Genoese citadel. The distance separating the island from the rest of Greece means it is little frequented by tourists.

A BIT OF HISTORY

Pocked with volcanoes and sulphurous springs, Límnos was the mythological home of **Hephaïstos** (Vulcan), who landed here when he was cast off Mount Olympus by his angry father, Zeus. Afterwards, the god of fire lived on the island and toiled at his forges (the Límnos volcanoes), and instructed the islanders in the art of metalworking.

MÍRINA★

Quiet and pleasant, the island's capital has a charming fishing harbour in a bay to the south. Beyond the harbour is the Turkish Beach (Toúrkikos Gialós) and to the north lies the fine sandy "Greek" beach, Roméïkos Gialós, where there is a small Archaeological Museum and Rihá Nerá (a low-tide) beach. The musuem is housed in an impressive old building from Ottoman times.

Also worth a visit is the **Kástro**★. The climb to the fortress gates affords good views of the harbour and the south side of the bay; consider making your climb on an evening when the sky is clear, because the views can be tremendous. The foundations of an ancient wall are the only traces of a Temple to Artemis and a town which stood on the jagged headland. Beyond the gates, a track on the left leads to the top of the south wall. From this spot and from the tip of the headland there are splendid **views**★★★, especially at sunset, of Kástro Bay, the indented west coast, and on the horizon Mount Áthos rising from the sea.

▶ **Population:** 18, 104.
⊙ **Michelin Map:** 477sq km/ 191sq mi – Michelin Map 737 L 5 – Northern Aegean Islands.
▯ **Info:** At the ferry port.
◐ **Location:** Between Mount Áthos and the Turkish coast.
⊛ **Don't Miss:** Káspakas Bay.

GETTING THERE

BY AIR – The airport is located in the middle of the island, 22km/14mi from Mírina. Flights from Athens *(daily)*, Thessaloniki *(several/wk)*, Lésvos and Rhodes *(4–5/wk)*.

BY SEA – **Ferry** service to Piraeus *(1/wk)*, Lavrio *(2–3/wk)*, Lésvos (several/wk), Chíos *(several/wk)*, Sámos *(several/wk)* And several other islands.

AROUND MÍRINA

Káspakas Bay★★ (Ormos Káspaka)

◐ *11km/6.5mi north of Mírina.*
After Cape Pétassos the road skirts the **Avlónas Coast** (bays and coves). The vast **bay**★★ with Cape Kalógeri at the far side comes into view before the village of **Káspakas**★ nestling on the mountainside. Beyond the village a side road runs down to the beach and hamlet of Ágios Ioánis. There are fine sandy beaches north of the bay.

Platí and Ágios Pávlos Bays

◐ *About 15km/9mi south of Mírina.*
A large sandy beach stretches below the mountain village of **Platí.** To the south of the village, just after Thános, lies the vast Ágios Pávlos Bay.

Moúdros Bay★ (Kólpos Moúdro)

◐ *20km/12mi northeast of Mírina.*
This immense bay is one of the most important natural anchorages in the Aegean. There are numerous, virtually deserted little villages, notably **Fana**

↓ N. Ágios Efstrátios

raki. From the village of **Kalithéa**, to the south of Livadohóri, there are fine views. To the east of Moúdros Bay is the Commonwealth War Cemetery, dating from the Dardanelles campaign.

Polióhni★

➲ *37km/23mi northeast of Mírina.*

A 4C BC village with oval huts was replaced in the 3C BC by a fortified town built in four stages *(indicated in blue, green, red and yellow on the site).* According to archaeologists, the earliest city (c.2800–2550 BC) is more ancient than Troy in Anatolia. Finds from the later "yellow" period (2200–2100 BC) include human skeletons, pottery and gold jewellery.

Settlement on a more modest scale continued until about 1275 BC, probably just before the Trojan War. There are scant remains, but the streets, wells, rectangular houses and wall sections are well presented and explained. The small museum at the site explains the significance of the ruins.

To the south is the Monastery of **Ágios Sózon**, situated amid sand dunes.

Ifestía (Hephaistia)

➲ *36km/22mi northeast (only accessible by car or scooter).* ◷*Open daily 8am–7pm (3pm in winter).* ⊗*No charge.*

Hephaistia was inhabited in the pre-Hellenic era and was Límnos' principal city in the classical period until it was destroyed by a landslide. The **site★** was particularly well chosen on a little promontory jutting out to sea. A sign shows the site of an *agora* with a shrine above and a small theatre below. From the hilltop above the sanctuary there is a **view** of Pourniás Bay and Kavírio-Hlói.

Kavírio-Hlói★

(Sanctuary of the Kabeiroi) 41km/26mi north of Mírina. ◷*Open daily 8am–7pm (3pm in winter).* ⊗*No charge.*

As on the island of Samothrace, the **Kabeiroi,** the mysterious gods of the Underworld, were venerated during the Hellenistic period with huge nocturnal ceremonies. Before the sanctuary, climb up to the top of a hill *(indicated by a white column on the left)* to enjoy a magnificent **panorama**★★ over Pourniás Bay. The ruined Kabeirion in its lonely majestic **site**★ overlooking Pourniás Bay dates from a later period. Eleven columns of a vast Hellenistic *telestrion* (where the mysteries were enacted) remain on the upper terrace. The earliest section of the sanctuary (8C–7C BC) on the lower level included a temple, a portico and a telestrion.

ADDRESSES

STAY

⌂ **Apollo Pavillion** – *Mírina Odós Garofalidi, behind the cinema.* ℘22540 23712. 11 apts. Unabashedly kitschy decor; beautiful terrace; attentive service. Some rooms for 5 people.

⌂ **Poseidon** – *Mírina, at the end of Roméikos Gialós Beach.* ℘22540 24821/ 69449 19664. 20 apts. A comfortable and well-run hotel, located in a quiet setting on the edge of town. The airy rooms have fridges and balconies; warm welcome.

⌂ **Petradi** – *Thanos, on the beach.* ℘22540 29905. www.petradistudios.gr. 12 apts. Open May–Sept. Clean studios with sunset-facing balconies, isolated at the end of the beach.

⌂⌂ **Sunset** – *Agios Yannis, above the main street.* ℘22450 61555/61593. www.sunsetapartments.gr. 14 apts. Jun–Sept. Magnificent views of beach, cliffs and hills. Several studios.

EAT

⌂ **Gláros** – *Mírina, at the fishing harbour.* ℘22540 222 20. Open Mid-Apr–Nov. Incomparable setting; Fresh *dorade*, sardines and mackerel.

⌂ **Plátanos** – *Mírina, Odós Karatza.* ℘22540 220 70. Typical Greek spot; very popular. Dishes may be selected directly from the kitchen; no fish, but tasty meat in sauces, pasta, vegetables.

TAKING A BREAK

Karagkiozis – *Mírina, on Romeikos Gialos beach.* Local watering hole: one room with DJ, one quiet lounge, one charming terrace. Choice of whiskies.

Thassos★★

Thássos – Θάσσος

Lying just off the coast of eastern Macedonia, Thassos is a wooded island, mountainous and beautiful. The island was famed in antiquity for its gold and marble. In addition to its mountains and archaeological treasures, Thassos has golden beaches which attract holidaymakers seeking silence and space.

A BIT OF HISTORY

In antiquity, particularly from the 7C to the 5C BC, Thassos was of considerable economic importance because of its exports of oil and wine, of white marble and of gold and silver; the metal was used to mint money throughout the Mediterranean.

▶ **Population:** 13, 765.
Michelin Map: 380sq km/ 152sq mi – Michelin Map 737 K 3 – Northern Aegean Islands.
Info: www.thassos-travel.com
▶ **Location:** Northernmost Greek island, Thassos lies 20km/12mi from Kávala.
Don't Miss: The splendid coastline (see by boat or car) or the ruins of Thassos.
Timing: Plan a 4-day visit.
Kids: A boat trip around the island and fishing.

The Persians made a point of stopping off to raze the island on their way to invade the Greek mainland in 490 BC

They tried to do the same in 480 BC when making their second attempt to conquer the Greeks but this time the islanders laid on a lavish feast for them and wished the invaders every success. The ruse, if that is what it was, worked and the Persians left them in peace. The Athenians were keen to make Thassos part of their empire because of the island's valuable natural resources but it was after an extended siege that the islanders finally capitulated.

In the 15C Thassos was occupied for a period by the Genoese, who set up a trading post under the Gatteluzzi, the lords of Lésvos and Samothrace. After the Genoese came the Turks and they remained in charge from 1460 to 1770. Then it was the turn of the Russians, though only for 4 years. The island then came under the power of Egypt but this proved to be a period of enlightened rule and the island prospered and enjoyed a substantial degree of autonomy. During the Second World War, Thassos was occupied by Bulgarian forces. Interest in Thassos was renewed in 1971 when oil was discovered offshore.

LIMÉNAS★ (THASSOS TOWN)

Thassos Town, also known as Liménas, is the island's capital and one of its two main ports. If taking the ferry to or from Thassos, it's important to know which port you're using. Liménas is mostly a modern town but it does have traces of its ancient Greek civilisation. These are spread over a vast area enclosed within a marble wall (5C BC); a few of the gates are decorated with low-relief carvings.

Agora

The *agora* was not far from the harbour. Surrounded by porticoes and studded with monuments, it was linked to the neighbouring shrines by the **Ambassadors' Passage**, which was decorated with low-relief sculptures. Most of what you see today dates from Roman times. Remains of three porticoes frame the *agora*: within the open space lie the remains of a *thólos*, an altar dedicated to the deified Theagenes, a Thassian athlete who had been victorious in the

GETTING THERE

BY SEA – **Ferries** from Kavála to Skála Prínos *(several/day)*. In summer, link from Keramotí to Liménas every hour. Hydrofoil service *(several/day)* between Liménas and Kavála. Timetables at the harbourmaster's office.

Olympic Games, and some round stone benches *(exedrae)*.

The remains of a Roman street are to be seen near the *agora*, as well as a number of assorted other ruins which will appeal more to specialists than the average visitor. What is worth seeing is the theatre from the Hellenistic era, though unless you visit when the annual summer drama festival is on, you can only view from the outside.

Eastern Ramparts and the Acropolis★

🚶 *2hrs on foot there and back.*

Starting behind the long Turkish building overlooking the caique harbour, the path runs inside the ramparts, then climbs above the **ancient port**; the outline of the old jetties can be traced beneath the water. A little way offshore lies the islet of Thassopoúla. After passing the remains of a 5C palaeo-Christian **basilica** set on a promontory, the path climbs up by the wall, which is superbly constructed in places with polygonal blocks. Halfway along is the **theatre**; it was built in the Hellenistic period but remodelled by the Romans as an arena for wild-animal fights.

The **acropolis**★ comprises three peaks in a line separated by two narrow saddles. On the first peak stood a Sanctuary to Pythian Apollo, which was converted into a fortress. The second peak boasted a Temple to Athena: the 5C foundations are still visible. At the base of the third is a small rock sanctuary dedicated to Pan; from the peak there are beautiful **views**★★ of Thassos and the Aegean Sea as far as Samothrace.

In the **Archaeological Museum** (🕐*open 15 Jun–15 Sept Tue–Sun 9am–7pm, rest of the year 9am–3pm; ⊚€2;*

25930 22180) you'll find various objects from the excavations: note the ivory **lion's head** from the 6C BC★ and the depiction of Bellerophon astride Pegasus in the act of slaying the Chimera that dates to the 7C BC.

🚗 DRIVING TOUR

TOUR OF THE ISLAND★★
Around 80km/50mi round trip heading clockwise from Liménas.

Those seeking something other than archaeology can discover the island's splendid coastline. There is a good road that hugs the coast, remaining fairly close to the shore. It passes inlets and beaches, crosses tiny coastal basins or cuts into the cliff face.

Panagía
Leaving Liménas in a southeasterly direction the road first climbs to **Panagía**, the ancient capital of the island; the picturesque houses have balconies and schist roofs.

▷ *Follow the road down the valley to the next major stop, Potamiá.*

Potamiá
Not as popular as Panagía but worth a visit for the two museums in this village: a Folk Art Museum (🕐*open Wed–Mon 9am–2pm;* ⊜*no charge*) and the Polygnotos Vagis Museum (🕐*open Tue–Sat 8.30am–noon, 6–8pm, Sun 8.30am–noon;* ⊜€3; *25930 61400*), named after the sculptor who was born on the island and who made a name for himself in the USA (he died in the 1960s). The local beach is one of the best to be found anywhere on the island but it retains a low-key character despite the accommodation on offer and the tavernas welcoming guests.
From Potamiá, a track leads to the summit of **Mount Ipsári** but this is a tough climb and takes at least 3 hours up and almost as long to come down again. A more sensible option is to set off with picnic food and climb for about an hour.

Kínyra
The sprawling village of Kínyra has little to recommend it, although accommodation is available, but it is convenient for accessing some good beaches in the vicinity. The best one is probably Makryammos (popular with nudist bathers) although the amenities are poor and there is nowhere to enjoy a meal.

▷ *Another 10min of driving takes you onto the south coast.*

Alikía
On the south coast, this village is built at an attractive site on the neck of a peninsula consisting entirely of marble quarries, which seem to have been abandoned only yesterday. There was an ancient city here, proved by the remains of a double sanctuary; the edge of the hill bears traces of two palaeo-Christian basilicas. The village itself is very attractive due to the vernacular style of architecture which studiously avoids any touch of the modern in favour of traditional design and simple colours. There are two local beaches and opportunities for snorkelling, with some good tavernas dotted about and rooms for rent.
A little way to the west of Alikía is the **Convent of Arhangélou Milaíl**, normally open to visitors during the day, set in a splendid location on a cliff top.

Limenária
To the southwest, this is a fishing village and a lively summer resort with some good beaches nearby (the best one is Trypití to the west). There are a number of small hotels, a dozen or so rooms for short or long rentals, no shortage of bars and some good tavernas.
The town also has an interesting history: beginning in the last decade of the 19C, the Ottomans wanted to encourage German businessmen to Thassos in order to oversee mining operations and so they built houses here for their accommodation, and that is how Limenária was founded. Along the west coast the road passes many fishing villages and there are fine views of the Macedonian coast. If there is time make a detour to **Mariés**

(29km/18mi there and back), a pretty village which is close to Mount Ipsári.

Astrís

The southern tip of the island has a good beach, although there is little else that makes the journey here worthwhile. Nearby **Potós** has an even better beach although there is rampant tourist development in progress and it may not remain an idyllic spot for much longer.

BOAT TRIPS★★

The *Eros* and the *Zorbas* offer day-long circuit trips of the island, stopping at some of the most beautiful spots to allow swimming and fishing (*depart Liménas around 9.45am and return around 5.45pm*).

The *Angetour*, based in the old port at Liménas, offers sea-fishing trips.

EXCURSION

Samothráki (Samothrace)

A taste of a real island retreat. www.samothraki.com.

A short distance from the maritime boundary between Greece and Turkey, Samothrace is a wild island, rarely visited for lack of safe harbours, but there are interesting traces of the past. Mount Fengári rises to 1 611m/5 285ft.

Ruins of the Sanctuary of the Great Gods★

Open Tue–Sun 8.30am–4pm. €3. Museum. 25510 41474.

The sanctuary, in a ravine above Paleópoli, was dedicated to two mysterious subterranean divinities known as the **Kabeiroi**.

The Anaktoron, the Hall of Princes (1C BC), was built of polygonal masonry and used for initiation ceremonies. The **Arsinoeion**, the largest rotunda in Greece, dates from about 285 BC. A rectangular precinct *(temenos)* whose foundations date from the 4C BC contained an allegorical statue of Desire by the great sculptor Skopas. The **Hieron**, a 4C BC temple with a Doric doorway and an apse, was used for sacrifices.

Near the theatre, of which little remains, was the Victory Fountain, set in a rocky

niche and decorated with the famed **Winged Victory of Samothrace**, a masterpiece of Hellenistic art (3C BC), now in the Louvre in Paris. The Ptolemaion was erected by the ruler of Egypt, Ptolemy Philadelphos (280–264 BC) as a monumental gateway to the sanctuary.

ADDRESSES

STAY

Dionysos – *Skála Panagia. 25930 61822. www.hotel-dionysos-thassos.gr. 33 rooms.* Simple, bright, comfortable rooms; lovely views.

Mironi Hotel – *Liménas, Odós K. Dimitriádou. 25930 23256. 10 rooms.* A huge marble lobby leads to large, spotlessly clean rooms (with fridges).

Timoleon Hotel – *Liménas, on the harbour, near the bus stop. 25930 2217. www.hotel-timoleon.gr. 30 rooms.* A large building, comfortable rooms with balconies overlooking the harbour. Bus service to Isteri Beach.

Hotel Vicky – *Liménas. 25930 22314. www.vickyhotel.gr. 21 rooms.* Bright, comfortable rooms in a small three-storey building. Most rooms have kitchen facilities; a good place to stay.

Hotel Victoria – *Liménas, Odós K. Dimitriádou. 25930 23256. 12 rooms.* A small building with spacious rooms, equipped with fridges.

EAT

Christos – *Ágios Geórgios.* A pleasant little fish restaurant under a pergola.

Pachys – *Pahís Beach.* Shady terrace near the beach; excellent fish.

Takis – *Odós Polignotou Vagi.* International and Greek cuisine.

Restaurant Vigli – *Northern end of Golden Beach.* Superbly situated; enjoy *meze*, grilled dishes, pizzas and seafood.

TAKING A BREAK

Anonymous Café – *Liménas, Odós 18 Oktovriou.* Eclectic selection of music.

SARONIC GULF ISLANDS

Nisiá Saronikoú Kólpou – Νησιά Σαρωνικού Κόλπου

These five easily accessible islands (Aegina, Hydra, Poros, Salamis and Spétses) are sometimes called the Argo-Saronic Islands because of their proximity to the Argolid. Greeks regard them as a little paradise just off the mainland coast. They are all easily reachable by ferry from Athens, and some Athenians commute from the closer islands into the city. Others escape to them on summer weekends, and all the islands are delightfully different.

Highlights

1 The Temple of Atéa on **Aigina** (p483)
2 The Port of **Hydra** (p484)
3 The Beaches on **Spétses** (p491)

The Islands Today

All the islands have their quirks and charms: for example, Hydra still has no vehicles, apart from a dustcart. Even bicycles are banned here. Poros is favoured by the yachting crowd, and all rely to a great degree on tourism too. Even though they are so close to the Greek capital, they still maintain the feel of true Greek islands, each with their own culture and identity. This is especially noticeable if you get out of the main port towns and go exploring inland. Visiting in summer, especially on weekends, is not recommended, as ferries are crowded, restaurants and hotels too, and these places are best seen in spring or autumn, when their beaches, tavernas, hikes and handful of archaeological sights can be more easily enjoyed.

A Bit of History

The geography of the islands, between Attica and the Peloponnese, ensured them a significant role in an ancient Greek world where maritime considerations were always of strategic importance. As early as the 9C BC, Aegina had joined one of the first confederations of Greek states and a century later it was minting its own coins – a clear reflection of its commercial and political power. This inevitably led to conflict with Athens because the major power in Attica was not going to willingly tolerate a rival in its backyard. The arrival of the Persians in 490 BC caused a dilemma for Aegina so that first it sided with the invaders but then thought better of it and dispatched a fleet to aid the Athenians at the battle that took place off the neigbouring island of Salamis. After the war, though, Athens used its increased power to subdue the island and enforce its submission. When the Peloponnesian War broke out, Athens knew well that the island would side with Sparta and, in a pre-emptive strike, deported all its citizens. After the war, victorious Sparta helped the exiles regain their homeland but Aegina never recovered its former importance.

The three islands of Poros, Spétses and Hydra are not naturally well-endowed with fresh water and their patterns of settlement were never the conventional ones for the ancient world. It was not until the 15C AD that the first Greeks, and some Albanians, came to live on Hydra and that was only because they were fleeing anti-Christian persecution. They depended on maritime trade for a means of making a living. Poros served as a base for fleets in the ancient world and had an important sanctuary to the god of the sea, Poseidon.

Of all the Saronic Gulf islands it is Salamis that has gone down in world history as the scene for a decisive battle between the Greeks and the Persians in 480 BC. The Athenians fled to the island in the face of the numerically far stronger Persians and watched the smoke rising from their home city as the invaders set fire to their sacred buildings on the Acropolis. The Athenian General, Themistocles, was able to deceive Xerxes into thinking that the Greeks had lost heart and that the allies of Athens were preparing to sail home. Xerxes quickly moved to block the two sea lanes from Salamis and fell into the Greek trap. It was a momentous victory and one that the Greeks, ancient and modern, would never forget.

Aegina★

Égina – Αίγινα

The isle of Aegina comprises a series of volcanic heights culminating in Mount Zeus, now known as Mount Profítis Ilías. In the Archaic era (7C–6C BC) Aegina was a powerful maritime state that rivalled Athens, but was eventually eclipsed by its neighbour. Today, it is almost a leafy suburb of the Greek capital, and a popular weekend escape from the big city noise and heat. The tasty pistachio nut is grown in huge quantities on the coastal plains.

▶ **Population:** 13, 552.
Michelin Map: 83sq km/ 32sq mi – Michelin Map 737 I 10 – Attica.
Info: www.aegina greece.com.
Location: South of Athens.
Parking: Always a problem during the summer and especially at weekends.
Don't Miss: Temple of Aféa.
Timing: Allow for at least 1 night's stay. The Agios Nektarios Festival takes place on 9 November.

AEGINA TOWN★★

▶ *Western end of the island.*

The town enjoyed a brief moment of glory during the struggle for independence from 1827 to 1829, when it was the capital of the new Greek state. Pink-and-white houses cluster around the little harbour overlooked by a charming chapel dedicated to **St Nicholas**, the patron saint of sailors. From the harbour, there is a magnificent **view**★★ over to the islets in the Saronic Gulf and the Peloponnese. The shops along the waterfront sell the local specialities: pottery, pistachio nuts and marzipan.

Temple of Apollo

▶ *North of Aegina Town.* ◷*Open Tue–Sun, 8.30am–3pm.* ⊛*€3 (includes museum).*

On **Cape Kolóna** stands a fluted column crowned with a capital, once part of a Temple to Apollo erected in the 5C BC; a small **Archaeological Museum** displays items found on the island.

EXCURSION
Paleohóra★

▶ *In the centre of the island, halfway between Aegina Town and Temple of Aféa.*

Paleohóra was the capital of the island under the Venetians and the Turks. The houses are gone but the cathedral, a basilical building, and the churches and chapels have been restored; some are adorned with interesting frescoes and iconostases.

GETTING THERE

BY SEA – Many **ferry** companies offer daily service to Piraeus, Méthana, Poros and, via Poros, to Hydra and Spétses. Ferries also run to the Cyclades in Jul–Aug. Daily shuttles link Aegina Town and Agía Marína.

The Venetian castle on the hilltop provides a good view of Mount Zeus and the northwest coastline.

▶ *A few miles east is the Temple of Aféa.*

Temple of Aféa★★★

◷*Open daily 8am–7.30pm in summer, 8.30am–5pm in winter.* ⊛*€4 (includes museum).* ✆*22970 32252.*

This Doric temple is one of the best preserved in Greece. It stands on a magnificent **site**★★ on the summit of a wooded hill overlooking the Bay of Agía Marína, the rocky coastline, Athens, Salamis and the Peloponnese *(north and west)*.

Dedicated to Aphaia, a local divinity, the temple (5C BC) has 22 monolithic limestone columns. Its pediments of sculpted marble, known as the Aegina Marbles, were bought in 1812 by Prince Ludwig of Bavaria, and displayed in Munich.

To the west of the temple, there is a small **Museum** which attempts to reconstruct the second Temple of Aféa (destroyed by fire in 510 BC) using original fragments, most notably the polychrome façade.

SOUTHWEST OF THE ISLAND
Pérdika
▶ *10km/6mi south of Aegina Town.*
This charming fishing harbour affords a good **view** of Moní Island. Excursions by boat can be made to the island *(old monastery, beach)* in summer. There are two fine beaches between Aegina Town and Pérdika: **Faros** and **Marathonas**.

Mount Zeus
4hr round trip from Marathonas Beach.
The highest point on the island (532m/ 1 745ft); from here on a clear day it is possible to see Poros, the mountains of the Peloponnese, the isthmus of Corinth, Salamis, the Athens conurbation and the coast as far as Cape Sounion.

NORTH COAST
There are many beaches and pleasant inlets looking out towards Salamis. The northern part of the island consists mostly of fertile plains, where crops such as almonds, figs, olives and grapes are grown, alongside the pistachio nuts for which Aegina is famous.

ADDRESSES

🏠STAY
⊖⊖ **Hotel Plaza** – *Aegina Town, left of the landing.* ☎22970 25600. www.plaza-aegina.gr. *37 rooms.* One of a group of three hotels; rooms all across the price range (the cheapest are among the island's least expensive).

⊖⊖ **Nafsika Hotel Bungalows** – *Aegina Town, 55 Odós Kazantzaki, north of the port.* ☎22970 22333. *Open mid-Apr–mid-Oct. 34 rooms.* Peaceful bougainvillea-draped bungalows, almost invisible from the road.

🍴EAT
⊖ **Areti** – *Aegina Town, opposite the Hotel Plaza.* This seafront spot serves specialities of fish caught the same day.

⊖ **Argyris** – *Messagrós, road out of the village.* Popular with locals, this taverna serves the freshest grilled fish, and a tasty local retsina. Try the spinach pie.

⊖ **Kostas** – *Álones, south of Agía Marína.* Under a shady pergola, this taverna (like its neighbour Takis) serves authentic Greek fare in a village atmosphere.

Hydra★★

Ídra – Ύδρα

The Gulf of Hydra separates the island from the Peloponnese. From the 15C it was one of the most important ports in Greece. Today Hydra is a popular tourist destination.

A BIT OF HISTORY
Hydra was once much greener and more abundantly supplied with water than it is now, hence its name (the Greek for "water"). Pine forests covered the slopes, and gardens flourished with water channelled from huge underground cisterns. Gradually the surface water grew rarer, the forests were over-exploited for shipbuilding and the cultivated terraces

▶ **Population:** 62, 719.
🌏 **Michelin Map:** 86sq km/ 34sq mi – Michelin Map 737 I 11 – Attica.
ℹ **Info:** On the quay, at the Manessi Hotel. www.hydra-island.com.
▶ **Location:** In the Saronic Gulf south of Athens.
👁 **Don't Miss:** Hydra Town, charming and scenic; walking in the interior.
🕐 **Timing:** A good choice for a day trip but busy midsummer best avoided.
👪 **Kids:** The sandy beach at *Mandráki*.

were abandoned. Since 1960 water has been imported from the mainland by tanker.

HYDRA TOWN★★

The little port of Hydra, which is packed with yachts in the season, occupies an extraordinary **site**★★★, hidden in a rounded inlet and bordered by old houses which fan out up the rocky hillside like seats in a theatre. Lively crowds stroll the **quayside**★★, past cafés, tavernas, restaurants and souvenir shops. Near the port, the **Museum of Historical Archives** (⏱open Jul–Aug Tue–Sun 9am–4pm, 7.30–9.30pm; Sept–Jun Tue–Sun 9am–4pm; ☎22980 52355; www. iamy.gr; ☞€5) traces Hydra's maritime history.

Monastery of the Assumption

A large clock tower marks the entrance to this monastery, built in 1643, and restored in the 18C after earthquake damage. Its two marble courtyards form a tranquil haven. In the basilica (nave and two aisles) there is a fine marble iconostasis and a gilt icon of the martyr Constantine the Hydriot. Note also the decorated chandeliers.

At the exit of the church, a stairway leads to the small **Byzantine Museum** (⏱open Tue–Sun 10am–5pm, summer only; ☞€2; ☎22980 54071); collection of liturgical objects, icons.

Belvedere

To the west of the port, a shady promenade offers a good view of the island of Dokós and the mainland. Cannons from the 19C guard the entry to the bay.

Upper Town★★

Cool and quiet, the upper town offers impressive views over the port below. The area's **ship-owners' houses**★ were mostly built in the 19C, often in imitation of Venetian palaces (loggias, internal courtyards). Many of these noble residences have remained in the same families. Three on the west side of the harbour are worth noting: the Voúlgaris House (far end of the waterfront), the Tombázis House (farther up), now a

Hydra Town

© Greek National Tourism Organisation

GETTING THERE

BY BOAT – Several hydrofoils a day run from Piraeus; also ferry services to Ermióni on the Peloponnese coast, to Poros and to Spétses. Service to the Cyclades in Jul–Aug. Daily water taxis link the beaches.

School of Fine Arts, and the Koundouriótis House (halfway up the hillside).

AROUND HYDRA★
Monasteries of Profítis Ilías (Prophet Elijah) and Agía Efpraxía (St Euphrasia)

▶ 2hrs on foot there and back by Odós Miaoúli and the valley.

These two convents, one for men, the other for women, were built near a pine forest. There are fine **views**★ of Hydra, the coast and the other Saronic Gulf Islands.

Kamínia

▶ 45min on foot there and back following the harbour quay round to the west.

Beyond the fort the coast path continues to **Kamínia**, a quiet fishing hamlet with a shingle beach.

Vlichós

▶ West of Hydra, beyond Kamínia.

The red pebble beach contrasts with the immaculate white of the houses.

485

Port of Kamínia

© Greek National Tourism Organisation

Mólos Bay

▶ *West of Hydra, beyond Vlichós.*
Yachts at anchor in this wide bay make for an attractive scene.

Cape Bísti

▶ *West of Hydra.*
This wild spot is accessible by boat or on foot and is a good place for a swim.

Mandráki

▶ *1hr on foot there and back or by taxi-boat or caique.*
Follow the quayside round to the east past the Merchant Navy Captains' School, which occupies an old ship-owner's house. The road continues to Mandráki Bay *(sandy beach)*, former site of the 19C shipyards. Most of the Hydriot fleet used to anchor in the bay. The **sandy beach** here is very pleasant.

ADDRESSES

🏠 STAY

⊜ **Hotel Nefeli** – *Hydra Town, at the top of the town.* 𝄘22980 53297. *www.hotelnefeli.eu. 8 rooms.* If you have lots of luggage, use the services of a donkey to get here. Simple rooms arranged tastefully. Lovely view of the town from room 15.

⊜⊜⊜ **Miramare** – *Mandráki.* 𝄘22980 52300. *www.miramare.gr. 28 rooms.* Cool bungalows with terraces and fridges on the edge of Mandráki Beach, 5min by boat from the centre of town (service until 3am). Various watersports and children's pool; island tours in the hotel boat.

⊜⊜⊜⊜ **Miranda** – *Hydra Town, Odós Miaoúli.* 𝄘22980 52230. *www.mirandahotel.gr. 14 rooms.* This fine historic residence, built in 1810 for a sea captain, retains its shady courtyard garden and its antique decor.

⊜⊜⊜⊜ **Orloff** – *Hydra Town, near public gardens.* 𝄘22980 52564 and in *Athens 21052 26152. www.orloff.gr. 9 rooms.* Will appeal to lovers of authentic architecture; gracious welcome.

🍴 EAT

⊜ **Gitonikon** – *Hydra Town, behind and to the right of Xerí Eliá taverna.* 𝄘22980 53615. This restaurant on two floors (with terrace) serves forth carefully prepared dishes of the freshest ingredients. Great value.

⊜ **To Steki** – *Hydra Town, Odós Miaoúli.* 𝄘22980 53517. This taverna offers meals including ouzo and dessert at reasonable prices. Very busy in the evenings.

⊜ **Xerí Eliá (Douskos)** – *Hydra Town, in the centre.* In a pretty square of white houses, with tables set out under two old trees. Try the stuffed squid with wine straight from the barrel, accompanied by Greek music.

⊜ **Mertazani Zoi** – *Near Mandráki.* An unpretentious restaurant where the tomatoes come fresh from the vegetable garden and the fish from the sea just below.

⊜ **Bratsera** – *Hydra Town, in the hotel of the same name.* 𝄘22980 52794. The best restaurant in town with magnificent decor. Traditional dishes as well as international cuisine (*tabbouleh*, Caesar salad) and a good selection of pasta.

Poros★★

Póros – Πόρος

Poros' pleasant climate and verdant landscape make it an agreeable place to visit. A canal divides the island in two: the major part, called Kalavría, is a limestone ridge; the other half is a volcanic islet called Sfería and is home to Poros Town, the main port.

VISIT

Arriving by boat gives lovely **views**★★★ of the bay, the little white town, and of the green shores of the mainland. From **Galatás** on the mainland, there are also great views of Poros Town reflected in the calm waters of the strait.

Poros Town★

Poros Town stands in a sheltered spot facing the Peloponnese.

The white cuboid houses mount the slopes of the promontory towards a blue painted bell-tower; from the top there is a **view**★★ of the town, and the busy strait.

A stroll along the quay opens up a picturesque view of Galatás. In the typical fishermen's district *(east)* the cafés and tavernas are decorated with naive paintings. The old arsenal *(west)* now houses an important Greek naval college.

▶ **Population:** 4, 348.

ⓘ **Michelin Map:** 33sq km/ 13sq mi – Michelin Map 737 I 10 – Attica.

▤ **Info:** www.travel-to-poros.com

◗ **Location:** A mere few hundred metres separate the island from the Peloponnese; excursions from the Argolid Peninsula are an easy hop.

⊙ **Don't Miss:** Kalavría, the lemon groves on the nearby mainland

◷ **Timing:** Stay a few days, alternating beach time with visits to nearby historic sites (Nauplion, Epidaurus, Corinth, Tirinth, Mycenae).

👪 **Kids:** A choice of sandy beaches.

GETTING THERE

BY SEA – Many **ferry** and **hydrofoil** services to Piraeus, Méthana and Galatás *(from where a car ferry operates all day)*, and to the other Saronic Gulf islands. If you plan to just visit Poros Town, leave your car in the car park at Galatás and take the shuttle.

Poros viewed from the mainland

© R. Mattès/MICHELIN

Poros Town

© Nikita Rogul/Dreamstime.com

The small **Archaeological Museum**, *(Platiá Alexis Korizis; ○open daily 9am–3pm; ⊜€2)* displays architectural fragments and statuettes dating from 4C–3C BC.

Kalavría★

▶ *Across an isthmus and over a canal is the major part of Poros, called Kalavría.*
A magnificent forest covers this part of the island, which can be surprisngly quiet in places despite the bustle of Poros Town. The road climbs to the ruins of a **Sanctuary to Poseidon (Naós Possidóna)** *(○ open daily, dawn–dusk; no charge)* dating from the 6C BC; only the outline remains, but it is on a superb site overlooking the island and the Saronic Gulf. From the temple follow the road downhill to the **Zoodóhos Pigí Monastery★**, a white building set in a valley refreshed by many springs. The cloisters with their noble cypress trees are open to the public *(○open 9am–4pm winter, 9am–9pm summer; no charge)*.

BEACHES

There are several pleasant sandy beaches, including Kanali Beach, Neorio and Askeli. These are all on the south side of Kalavría, and can be reached on foot from Poros Town.

ADDRESSES

⌂STAY

⊜⊜ **Manessi** – *Poros Town, almost directly opposite the ferry dock.* ℘22980 22273. www.manessi.com. 15 rooms. An elegant building with a white- and- blue façade and a pleasantly old-fashioned interior.

⊜⊜ **Seven Brothers** – *Poros Town, near the shuttle landing.* ℘22980 23412. www.7brothers.gr. Pretty, modern hotel; some rooms have balconies.

⊜⊜⊜ **Poros Hotel** – *Neório Bay.* ℘22980 22216 or in Athens. ℘21094 00580. Open mid-Apr–late Oct. 100 rooms. A recently renovated complex with large, bright rooms; good views over the harbour. Private beach.

⊜⊜⊜ **Sirene** – *Monastiri Bay.* ℘22980 22741 to 43. This luxury hotel stands on a cliff between the road and the sea. Attractive rooms (the best overlook the sea), restaurant, dance hall, private beach, two swimming pools. Open mid-Apr–mid-Oct.

ⴠ/EAT

Caravella Restaurant – *at the port, Poros Town,* ℘22980 23666. Very busy with visiting Athenians, this portside place serves everything from souvlaki to fresh lobster.

Taverna Karavolos – *Near the harbour, Poros Town.* ℘22980 26158. www.karavolos.com. The taverna's name means "the big snail" and that island speciality is here cooked in onions, garlic and tomato sauce.

⥴TAKING A BREAK

Poseidon Music Club – *Between Poros Town and the Temple of Poseidon.* Great views over the harbour and Galatás; bar with pool open in summer with concerts of Greek and international music.

ⴖEVENTS AND FESTIVALS

In May there is an annual International Yachting Symposium, when the island is incredibly busy. Summer sees a watersports week, including lots of regattas.

Salamis

Salamína – Σαλαμίνα

Fringing the Bay of Eleusis, Salamis is the closest island to Athens and the largest in the Saronic Gulf. Easily accessible, it is very popular with Athenians. Its name is inextricably linked with one of the greatest sea battles in history.

▶ **Population:** 38, 000.
◔ **Michelin Map:** 96sq km/ 38sq mi – Michelin Map 737 I 9 – Attica.
▤ **Info:** www.salamina.gr.
▷ **Location:** Minutes away from Athens by ferry.
◉ **Don't Miss:** Reminding yourself on the ferry that you are crossing the strait where the Greeks defeated the Persians in 480 BC.
▣ **Parking:** Use the municipal car parks.
◷ **Timing:** A day visit is sufficient.

View of Salamis

© banglds/Fotolia.com

GETTING THERE

BY SEA – Numerous **ferries** to the mainland (Piraeus, Pérama and Mégara). Between Pérama and Paliouka, there is a service every 15min by day and every hour by night.

VISIT

The island is largely a weekender's sub-urb, composed of second homes belonging to Athenians. The resort of **Selinia** to the east is quite busy. The south of the island is more mountainous and offers fine views of Aegina and the Peloponnese Coast. For visitors who want a break from urban blues in Athens the island offers some peace and quiet – though to make this possible you need to get out of Salamis Town as soon as possible and head south towards Eandio.
On the way there are places to swim and tavernas are dotted along the roadside.

Eandio has its own organised beach but it lacks sand. One road continues south-west to Kanakia but a better bet is to take the road that heads due south to the resort areas of Perani and Peristéria.

Monastery of Faneroméni

▷ *Western end of the island, 1.5km/ 1mi from the arrivals dock for the Mégara ferry.*
Built in the 17C, the church here has some fine 18C frescoes (Last Judgment). The Virgin is said to have appeared here, and the monastery attracts many pilgrims.

The Battle of Salamis

Having occupied Athens and Attica in the Second Persian War, the Persian fleet gathered in the Saronic Gulf as the Persian King Xerxes looked on from shore. A large number of Persian ships engaged the Greeks in the narrow straits off Pérama, but were unable to manoeuvre in such a small space. The Greek *triremes*, fitted with bronze prows, rammed the enemy vessels. The engagement is described by Aeschylus, an eyewitness, in his play *The Persians* (472 BC), and by the historian Herodotus.

Spétses★★

Spétses – Σπέτσες

Popular with the Athenian middle class, many of whom own houses here, Spétses is an attractive island bathed in a gentle light and scented with jasmine. There is only one town, which stretches along the coast facing the Argolid Peninsula. The rest of Spétses is given over to a vast forest of Aleppo pines. Like its rival Hydra, Spétses grew rich through trading in the Mediterranean during the 18C and 19C. When the War of Independence began in 1821, the islanders converted merchant vessels into powerful warships, and played an active role in the conflict, destroying the enemy admiral's flagship.

▶ **Population:** 3, 900.
 Michelin Map: 22sq km/ 9sq mi – Michelin Map 737 H 11 – Attica.
 Info: www.spetses direct.com.
 Location: Spétses lies just 3km/1.9mi from the Peloponnese coast. Only locally-owned vehicles are allowed on the island.
 Don't Miss: Bouboulina's House.
 Timing: A good day-trip destination.

A BIT OF HISTORY

Born in a Turkish prison in 1771, Lascaŕina Pinótzis (called Bouboulina) was married twice; first to a Spetsiot sea captain (killed when his ship was sunk by pirates), and then to another sailor (also killed by pirates).

Her husbands' deaths made Bouboulína the owner of shipyards and a fleet of brigs and schooners. She took part in naval engagements between 1821 and 1824, leading her crews in person.

A national heroine, she died violently in a family dispute in 1825.

SPÉTSES TOWN★★

Spétses consists of two districts round the harbour, Dápia and Paleó Limáni, as well as the upper town, Kastéli. It has become a fashionable destination and is particularly popular with the British.

Dápia★

The modern port is a lively place. The waterfront is lined with shops and restaurants, but the nearby alleys, with their ship-owners' houses, are quiet. It is pleasant to stroll past the shipowners' and sailors' houses set in their gardens *(note the thresholds decorated*

GETTING THERE

BY SEA – Spétses is 1hr 10min from Athens by hydrofoil. There are also plenty of **ferries** to Kósta on the Argolid mainland. There are moorings for pleasure craft and yachts in the old harbour and at Portohéli and Tolo.

with pebble mosaics). You can visit **Bouboulina's House** (◔*open daily 10am–9pm in summer only; guided tour only. 22980 72416. www.bouboulinamuseumspetses.gr.* ◌*5€),* now a house museum; or the **Maison Mexis, home of the Spetsai Museum** (◔*open Tue–Sun 8.30am–2.30pm;* ◌*3€),* for a glimpse of the fabulous interior decor of a ship owner's house.

West of the port, the waterfront is bordered by a pleasant **residental quarter** with lovely villas. The **Hotel Posidonion** (1914) overlooking the sea has a magnificent façade flanked by two towers. Also note the former **Anargirios-Orgialenios** School (now a conference centre), for boys of the Greek aristocracy.

Upper Town★ (Kastéli)

The upper town above Dápia was fortified by the Venetians in the 16C.
The largest church, **Agía Triáda** (Holy Trinity), contains a beautiful carved-wood iconostasis.

Old Port★ (Paleó Limáni)

The old port is composed of many inlets filled with the vestiges of 18C marine facilities. This quarter is less developed than Dápia and has some pleasant restaurants.

St Nicholas' Monastery (Ágios Nikólaos)

Not far from the old port is the bell-tower of the island's cathedral. The war memorial with two cannons marks the place where the first flag of independence was flown in 1821. The dimly lit church interior contains a fine wood iconostasis.

Walk to the Lighthouse★

Located on a promontory to the east of the town. The walk along the seafront *(30min there and back)* is pleasant; along the way is the Chapel of Panagia Armata, erected to commemorate the destruction of the Turkish admiral's flagship on 8 September 1822 *(large painting of the event)*. From the lighthouse there is a fine view of Spétses and the Peloponnese coast.

BEACHES

Kaiki Beach

1km/0.6mi west of Dapia.
Near the Anárgyros-Orgialénios College, this beach is busy but attractive.

Órmos Zogeriás★★ (Zogeriá Bay)

Take the coast road northwest *(5hrs on foot there and back; 2hrs by bicycle there and back)*. There are also boats from Dápia.
The road climbs through forests of Aleppo pines until it reaches the huge bay at Zogeriá, a beautiful site★★ facing north towards the Bay of Nauplion.

Agía Marína Beach

This attractive beach is to the south of the old harbour.

Ágioi Anárgiri Beach★

13km/8mi west of the town (bus from Agía Marína).
Magnificent beach bordered by pine trees and scrubland.

ADDRESSES

🏠 STAY

Armata – *Dápia. From the port take Odós Santou, the left into a small square.* ☎22980 72683. www.armata hotel.gr. *20 rooms.* An authentic Spetsiot house converted into a boutique hotel with pleasant rooms giving onto a garden; breakfast by the pool.

Posidonion – *On the seafront to the right of Dápia.* ☎22980 74553. www.poseidonion.com. *453 rooms and 73 suites.* The atmosphere of the Roaring Twenties lingers in this palatial establishment; marble staircase, high-ceilinged rooms and a huge shaded terrace. Charming.

🍴 EAT

Mourayo – *Far end of the old harbour.* ☎22980 73700. www.mourayo spetses.gr. Peaceful restaurant with terrace overlooking the sea. Quality cuisine: fish à la Spétses and French dishes. Greek music and piano bar until 2am.

Tassos Taverna – *Ágioi Anárgiri Beach, western part of the island.* Good choice for oven-baked dishes.

Orloff – *Halfway between Dápia and the old harbour.* A trendy spot; views over the water. Good choice of *meze*, and pricier fish dishes.

Patralis – *beyond the Posidonion Hotel.* ☎22980 74441. www.patralis.gr. Excellent fish restaurant, refined atmosphere. Terrific views over the Argolid Coast.

🚌 TAKING A BREAK

Figaro – A disco in the old harbour.
Papagayo – For dinner or cocktails. Band on Friday, Saturday and Sunday.
Politis – *Not far from the Papagayo.* Don't miss the almond cakes here.

🎉 EVENTS AND FESTIVALS

26 July – Traditional festival at the Church of Agía Paraskeví, on the beach of the same name.
2–8 September – commemoration of the victory of the Spetsiot ship-owners over the Turks, with dancing, singing and fireworks (on the Saturday).

SPORADES★★

Sporádes – Σποράδες

These four islands – Skiathos, Skopelos, Alonnisos and Skyros – lie close to the mainland and are invaded each summer by tourists drawn to their beaches, their icon-filled monasteries, their little fishing ports and their villages of shady alleys. Skiathos is the nearest to the mainland and the most visited; Skíros, set apart somewhat from the other islands, is the most secretive. *Sporades* means "scattered", a fitting name for these islands and islets.

Highlights

1 The marine park around **Alonnisos** (p493)
2 The beaches of **Skiathos** (p494)
3 **Skyros Carnival** (p495)

GETTING THERE

BY SEA – **Ferries** run year-round from Vólos and Kimi; there are also links to Lemnos and Thessaloniki, as well as between the Sporades islands.
BY AIR – There's air service from Skiathos and Skyros to Athens and some European cities in summer; there is a year-round Skíros-Thessaloniki service (several/wk).

A Bit of History

Ancient Times – In Minoan times, around 1600 BC, colonists from Crete came to the Sporades and brought civilisation with their knowledge of how to farm olive trees and vineyards. In legend, the colonists were led by Staphlylos (the word *staphlyos* means "grape" in Greek), the son of Dionysus and Ariadne. The remains of a tomb excavated on Skopelos is said to be the place where he was buried (a golden sceptre was found inside the tomb). By the classical era the islands had developed a maritime identity and this inevitably brought conflict with the rising power of Athens. In 476 BC the islands' fleet was attacked and destroyed by an Athenian force and the Sporades duly fell in line with the regional superpower. When Athens was defeated by Sparta in the Peloponnesian War, the islands came under Spartan dominance. Later, with the rise of Macedonian power, the Sporades fell to the army of Philip II.

Byzantine and Ottoman Rule – In the Byzantine era, beginning in the 4C AD and lasting some eight centuries, little is known about the Sporades. Beginning in the 13C, the islands were passed from one local power to another before being absorbed into the Ottoman Empire. Turkish rulers paid scant attention to the Sporades, and never tackled the pirates that ruled the seas.

In the 18C the spirit of Greek nationalism spread to the islands and early fighters against the Turks used the Sporades as places of refuge. The islands became part of Greece in 1830, suffered occupation by the Italians and Germans in the Second World War, and only emerged from poverty with the rise of tourism in the last quarter of the 20C.

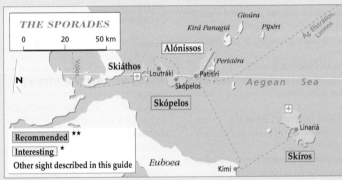

Alonnisos

Alónnisos – Αλόννησος

The island has a rugged topography of pine-covered hillsides, and pebble or sand beaches. Curiously undiscovered, it is in a rich wildlife reserve for endangered monk seals and dolphins.

VISIT

Patitíri

▶ *In the far southeast corner of the island.*
The principal port and capital of the island, Patitíri is a large modern town. It is located in a bay dominated by promontory covered by pine trees and a few hotels. At the **Folklore Museum** (🕐 *open daily Jun–Aug 11am–9pm, May and Sep 11am–6pm; 𝄞 24240 66250; www.alonissosmuseum.com; ⌕ €4*) tools and other objects of daily life offer a peek at life in centuries past; a display of photographs shows what the place looked like before an earthquake in 1965 destroyed most of the old town.

Modern Patitíri was the result of hasty rebuilding and consequently suffers from a lack of character; nevertheless, it is a possible base for a short stay on the island because there are good bus routes from the town and this is also the best place to arrange car rental.

The island offers some great **walks**★. The Anavasi 1:40 000 Map *(available from travel agencies in Patitíri)* shows the main footpaths.

Alonnisos★

▶ *Uphill from Patitíri.*
Perched on a hill, this is a charming village of white and blue houses with tile or slate roofs. From the top of the village there is a fine view over the sea and there are a number of pleasant walks to beaches in the vicinity. The town walls date back to Byzantine times although they were extensively rebuilt in places by the Venetians.

More rebuilding took place after the devastating earthquake of 1965, when the local people were forcibly moved out down to Patitíri, and their ruined houses sold mostly to foreign visitors,

- ▶ **Population:** 2,700.
- ⚲ **Michelin Map:** 65sq km/ 26sq mi – Michelin Map 737 J 6 – Thessaly.
- ▤ **Info:** http://alonissos travel.com.
- ▷ **Location:** This northern-most island of the Sporádes has connections by ferry and hydrofoil with Skopelos and the mainland.
- ⊘ **Don't Miss:** Alonissos village.
- 🕐 **Timing:** One or two nights should be spent on the island.

who still make up a majority of the population.

BEACHES

Beaches accessible from Alonissos, include Megálo Mourtiá, Mikro Mourtiá *(45min walk)*, Marpoúnda and Vtysítsa *(35min walk)*. Farther north, there are numerous (mostly pebble) beaches which can be reached by boat or on foot. Those seeking a sandy beach should try Hrysi Miliá. At the northern end of the road is the pebble beach at Gérakas.

🧍‍♂️NATIONAL MARINE PARK★

Boat trips from Patitíri (the Kassandra) leave daily at 11am, returning at 5.30pm.
The sea to the north of the island, where there are a number of mostly uninhabited islets, is a protected area. Here it is possible to see endangered monk seals, Audouin's gulls, shags and dolphins.
The monk seal (Monachus monachus) is a seriously endangered species because of fishing fleets that regard the seal as a rival; the species is now only found in certain spots around the Mediterranean. Their existence and maintenance of the National Marine Park owes a lot to the Society for the Study and Protection of the Monk Seal and the organisation's headquarters are on Alonissos (🕐 *open daily 10–8pm in summer, 𝄞 24240 66350, www.mom.gr).*

Skiathos

Skíathos – Σκίαθος

Like its neighbour Skópelos, an offshore extension of the Pelion massif, Skiathos is covered by pine trees and olive groves. The island has many coves with turquoise water, and a beautiful lagoon with fine sand at Koukounariés Beach, one of the best anywhere in Greece. It is a popular year-round destination, appealing to those seeking both its tranquility and its nightlife.

▶ **Population:** 6, 160.

◔ **Michelin Map:** 50sq km/ 20sq mi – Michelin Map 737 I 6-7 – Thessaly.

🛈 **Info:** The Tourist Police have a booth at the port.

◐ **Location:** East from the Pelion Peninsula in northern Greece.

◶ **Don't Miss:** Skiathos Town; the island's stunning beaches.

◕ **Timing:** Allow for a couple of days at least.

SKIATHOS TOWN★

▶ *On the east coast, Skiathos Town is the island's main port.*

Skiathos is the capital of the island; a charming place, its white houses with red roofs scale two hillsides. Its two harbours are separated by a pine-covered islet (Boúrdzi). Although quiet in winter, it gets extremely busy in summer with its many bars, restaurants and shops, making for very lively evenings.

Skiathos is a decidedly hedonistic kind of place but there is a little culture in the **Papadiamantis Museum** (⊙open Tue–Sun 9.30am–1.30pm, 5pm–8.30pm; ℘24270 23843; ⊷€1), dedicated to the modern Greek writer who lived here. The upper part of the museum building (it was built by the writer's grandfather) is furnished the way it was when the young Papadiamantis was growing up here; the ground floor is a bookshop with exhibition space for art and craft items still made by the islanders.

☙WALKS

The best way to see the island is on foot.

Kástro★

◐ *North coast.*

Access by boat (1hr 30min) or on foot (4hrs round trip) from Skiathos Town.

The path passes two monasteries – **Evangelístria** *(a beautiful iconostasis of carved wood in the church)* and **Ágios Harálambos** – before reaching the ruins of the medieval fortress (Kástro). It stood on a promontory, accessible only by a drawbridge. Two of its houses (which

numbered 300) are well-preserved and the largest of its four remaining churches contains a 17C carved wooden iconostasis.

Monastery of Panagía Kounístra★

3hrs round trip from Fteliá.
Also accessible by car.

This walk provides superb views of the island. From the monastery, the **view**★ takes in the entire coastline.

BEACHES

Renowned for their fine sand and crystal-clear water, the beaches of Skiathos are one of the island's main attractions. There are around 60 to choose from, and most of them get busy in summer. The quietest are on the north coast *(Lalária, Nikotsára, Xánemos)* and are accessible by boat. Lalária is the most famous and beautiful of these, right at the northern tip of the island and only accessible by boat. It's a long strip of white pebbles, backed by dramatic cliffs.

At the southwest end of the island, **Bananá Beach** *(official name Krassás)* is extremely busy in the summer, with plenty of watersports activities, and several bars. Mandráki is a glorious carpet of fine sand.

The most famous and busiest is **Koukounariés Beach**★★ on a pine-fringed lagoon that seems more Polynesian than Greek and it is in a protected nature reserve. There are also several other beaches around **Koukounariés**.

Skyros★

Skíros – Σκύρος

Facing Euboia, Skyros is the largest of the Sporades. It is composed of two mountainous outcrops connected together and has a wilder character than the other islands in the archipelago. The southern part, called Vounó ('mountain'), provides grazing for half-wild goats and sheep, and small native horses. The northern part, Méri, is covered with pine trees and agricultural land. All around the coast are deserted coves with turquoise waters and beautiful seascapes.

▶ **Population:** 2, 602.
⚲ **Michelin Map:** 223sq km/ 89sq mi – Michelin Map 737 K 7 – Central Greece.
▣ **Info:** www.skyros.gr
▷ **Location:** The most south-easterly of the Sporades, in the Aegean Sea.
☺ **Don't Miss:** The dramatic scenery in the south of the island.
◷ **Timing:** Give yourself 2–3 days.

HÓRA★ (SKYROS TOWN)

▶ *On the eastern coast of Méri.*

The main town, Hóra, has tiny white cuboid houses, more typical of the Cyclades. It is a pleasure to stroll through the network of narrow alleyways and steps, which pass under arches and open into courtyards. The interior of a house may be viewed at no. 992 of the **Agora** (narrow pedestrian street with shops). On a bastion on the northeast edge of the town stands a statue in memory of **Rupert Brooke** (1887–1915). The poet's grave lies in a valley on the southern shore of the island in Trís Boúkes Bay *(1hr by road from Hóra or by boat from Linariá)*. Aged 27, the poet was on the way to to fight at Gallipoli when he contracted blood poisoning and died. At the **Faltaïts Museum of Folk Arts** *(◷ open summer 10am–2pm, 6–9pm; winter 10am–6pm; ℘22220 91327; www.faltaits.gr; ⌗€2)* you can see local crafts, both modern and traditional. Hellenic and Roman period artefacts are on view at the **Archaeological Museum** *(◷ open Tue–Sun 8.30am–3pm; ⌗€2; ℘22220 91327).*

Kástro

○━ *Closed for restoration.*

The Venetian fortress was built on the old acropolis where **Achilles** is supposed to have been brought up disguised as a girl. There is an unusual **view**★★ over Hóra. Adjacent to

GETTING THERE

BY SEA – The port is at Linariá on the west coast. There are two **ferries** to Kími (Euboea) a day in summer. Hydrofoil service *(Jun–Sept)* links the island to Alonnisos, Skópelos, Skiathos, Vólos and Thessaloniki.
BY AIR – The airport is at the northern end of the island; service to Athens and Thessaloniki in summer.

the Kástro is the monastery of Ágios Nikólaos with its 10C church, perched on a rocky outcrop above the town.

NORTH PENINSULA (MÉRI)★

This part of the island has numerous beaches: Magaziá and Mólos (just north of Hóra); Kyrá Panagiá and Atsítsa (west coast); and Ágios Fókas, near a pine forest (southwest coast).
There are also three ports: Péfkos, Ahérounes and Linariá (where the ferries dock).
On a hill above Péfkos is the Chapel of Ágios Pandeleímonos, from where there is an excellent **view**★ of the island.
In the northeast of the island, **Palamári** is the site of a Bronze Age settlement which has been dated to between 2500 BC and 1800 BC. Excavations have unearthed clear evidence of an organised city, and hearths and ovens have been discovered in the rooms of buildings *(some of the artefacts are on display in the Archaeological Museum in Hóra).*

Visitors can wander through the site and there is a lovely little beach nearby.

SOUTH PENINSULA (VOUNÓ)★
Beyond the little resort of Kalamítsa and the beach at Kolibádas Bay, the road traverses a desert-like landscape and passes some beautiful **cliffs**★★ bordering a gulf, across which are scattered numerous islets. It is near here at Trís Boúkes that the grave of the poet Rupert Brookes can be found.

ADDRESSES

STAY
⊝ **Domátia Anna Kiriazi** – *Hóra, above the agora, fork left and then head up to the museums on the right.* ℘22220 91574. Charming traditional house with fireplace, ceramics and terrace.

⊝⊜⊜ **Hotel Nefeli** – *Hóra, outskirts of town.* ℘22220 91964/92063. www.skyros-nefeli.gr. 16 rooms. Apartments and rooms in an attractive building with fireplaces and antiques. The bar is very pleasant. Breakfast €6.

⊝⊜⊜ **Hotel Hydroussa** – *Magazía, beach north of Hóra.* ℘22220 92063 to 65. www.hydroussahotel.gr. 22 rooms. The main hotel on the beach. Balconies with sea views. Open Jun–Sep only.

⚟/EAT
⊝ **Taverna Metopo** – *Main street.* Tasty, varied cuisine (lasagne, fresh vegetables, lentil soup), quick service and a shady terrace.

EVENTS AND FESTIVALS
Festivals – In February don't miss the famous **Skyros Carnival**, an amazing mix of pagan rites and renowned throughout Greece. In the first three weeks of August is the **Faltaïts Festival** (theatre, music, dance); details available from the Folklore Museum (*shows around 9pm; tickets €4–5*).

Skopelos★★
Skópelos – Σκόπελος

The most densely inhabited of the Sporades and also the most fertile, this orchard island is covered by pine trees, olive groves, almond trees and plum trees; the fruit of the plum trees makes excellent prunes when dried. The island has many churches and chapels, as well as several monasteries dating from the 17 and 18C. Tourists appreciate its coves with sandy beaches and emerald waters.

▸ **Population:** 4, 700.
Michelin Map: 97sq km/ 39sq mi – Michelin Map 737 I 6 – Thessaly.
Info: At the port. ℘24240 23231. www.skopelos-greece-vacations.com.
Location: Tucked between Skiáthos and Alonissos in the Aegean.
Don't Miss: The beaches on the west coast.
Timing: A minimum of 2 nights.

SKOPELOS TOWN★★
This attractive hillside settlement, set deep in a wide bay, is protected by a sea wall. Pleasantly shaded by the plane trees and flanked by houses with tiled roofs and little chapels, the alleyways make for a lovely stroll.
The medieval **fortress** (*Kástro*) contained many houses and religious buildings. St Athanasius' Chapel was built in the 9C on the foundations of an ancient temple, and contains a sumptuous polychrome iconostasis. From the top of the ruins there is a fine view of Skopelos Town, the island and the Sporades archipelago.

MONASTERIES OF MOUNT PALOÚKI★
Like a lesser Mount Áthos, Mount Paloúki is an important monastic site.

The summit is a superb viewpoint over the island and beyond.

Evangelístria Monastery

🕐 *Open daily 8am–1pm and 4–7pm.* ✎*Donation.*

A nun will show visitors the gold-plated iconostasis, which dates from the 14C and was brought here from Constantinople. There are also stunning views over the island and of Skopelos Town from this 18C monastery, which was was founded by monks from Mount Athos.

Metamórfossi Monastery

🕐 *Open daily, 8am–1.30pm and 5–8.30pm, summer only.* ✎*Donation.*

This dates from the 16C and has a church in its attractive courtyard. *It's found at the top of a ravine and has one monk who stays there in the summer to welcome those visitors who make the effort to get there.*

Metamórfossi Monastery
© P. Longin/MICHELIN

Pródromos Convent

🕐 *Open daily 8am–1pm and 5–8pm.* ✎*Donation.*

This convent is cut off from the outside world with only a handful of nuns living here now, and it also has a church with a wonderful iconostasis, and superb views. It rewards the long walk to reach it, as it is one of the most beautiful of the convents and monasteries on Skopelos.

GLÓSSA★
AND THE NORTH

The second town is Glóssa, to the north of the island and reached by bus from Skopelos Town in under an hour. It has an unspoilt authenticity, with its old church, its white houses and its network of alleyways. A good base for a night's stay, it is a low-key place but accommodation and good food is available. A road leads down to **Loutráki**, its port, where there are a number of pleasant restaurants. There is also a pathway that leads from Glóssa to a **monastery** dramatically perched on a clifftop; it takes an hour to walk here and part of the reward in making the trek is a neat little sandy beach that is often empty.

A road south from Glóssa accesses the small harbour of **Agnóndas**, named after a Greek athlete who achieved victory in the 569 BC Olympics. The beach is not sandy but the water is clean.

A pleasant coast **road**★ runs south from Loutráki along the eastern coast giving some wonderful views.

BEACHES★

There are many attractive beaches, some pebble, others sand. The finest are on the south and southwest coasts. **Miliá**, on the west coast, is one of the most popular, and has very good swimming, as does the neighbouring beach of Kastaní.

Nearer to Skopelos Town is Stafylos Beach, a mixture of sand and pebble, and next to this is Velanio Beach, known for the good snorkelling in its crystal-clear waters.

ADDRESSES

🏠STAY

Adrina Beach Hotel – *Panormos,* ☎*24240 23371. www.adrina.gr. 52 rooms.* One of the island's best hotels, in a resort town on the west coast. Private beach, huge swimming pool, restaurant, surrounded by woodland.

🍴/EAT

Taverna Agnanti – *Glossa,* ☎*24240 33076.* Traditional taverna that serves exceptionally good versions of local dishes, and with a view to die for; occasional live music too.

INDEX

INDEX

INDEX

INDEX

🍴/EAT

MAPS AND PLANS

Island Maps

Many of the Greek islands
share their name with that of
the main town. To distinguish
between the two, the maps
show the island name prefixed
with 'N' meaning Nesos, or in
English, island.

MAP LEGEND

	Sight	Seaside resort	Winter sports resort	Spa
Highly recommended	★★★	♨♨♨	❄❄❄	♰♰♰
Recommended	★★	♨♨	❄❄	♰♰
Interesting	★	♨	❄	♰

Selected monuments and sights

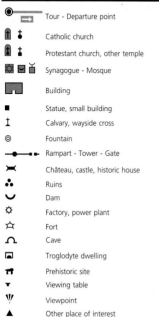

	Tour - Departure point
	Catholic church
	Protestant church, other temple
	Synagogue - Mosque
	Building
	Statue, small building
	Calvary, wayside cross
	Fountain
	Rampart - Tower - Gate
	Château, castle, historic house
	Ruins
	Dam
	Factory, power plant
	Fort
	Cave
	Troglodyte dwelling
	Prehistoric site
	Viewing table
	Viewpoint
	Other place of interest

Abbreviations

H	Town hall
M	Museum
T	Theatre

Sports and recreation

	Racecourse
	Skating rink
	Outdoor, indoor swimming pool
	Multiplex Cinema
	Marina, sailing centre
	Trail refuge hut
	Cable cars, gondolas
	Funicular, rack railway
	Tourist train
	Recreation area, park
	Theme, amusement park
	Wildlife park, zoo
	Gardens, park, arboretum
	Bird sanctuary, aviary
	Walking tour, footpath
	Of special interest to children

Special symbols

	Metro
	Olympic Airways
EΛΠA *ELPA*	Greek Automobile-Club
	Ancient site
	Ancient theatre
	Christian cemetery
	Muslim cemetery
	Monastery
	Beach
	Olympic sites 2004

Map Legend continued overleaf

Additional symbols

🅩	Tourist information	
═══ ═══	Motorway or other primary route	
❶ ❶	Junction: complete, limited	
═══ ═══	Pedestrian street	
⊥═══⊥	Unsuitable for traffic, street subject to restrictions	
····· ----	Steps – Footpath	
🚆 🚉	Train station – Auto-train station	
🚌 🚌 S.N.C.F.	Coach (bus) station	
┄┄	Tram	
Ⓜ	Metro, underground	
🅿	Park-and-Ride	
♿	Access for the disabled	

⊠	Post office
☎	Telephone
▭	Covered market
·╳·	Barracks
△	Drawbridge
∪	Quarry
✗	Mine
Ⓑ Ⓕ	Car ferry (river or lake)
⛴	Ferry service: cars and passengers
⛵	Foot passengers only
③	Access route number common to Michelin maps and town plans
Bert (R.)...	Main shopping street
AZ **B**	Map co-ordinates

508

COMPANION PUBLICATIONS

MICHELIN MAP 737
On a scale of 1:700 000, the whole Greek road network, islands and mainland (including Crete), with names indicated both in Greek letters and their Latin transcription.

TRAVELLING TO GREECE
Michelin Road Atlas Europe
With an index of place names, 73 town and city plans.

INTERNET
Internet users can access personalised route plans, Michelin maps and town plans, and addresses of hotels and restaurants featured in the *Michelin Guide Europe* through the website at: **www.viamichelin.com and www.travel.viamichelin**

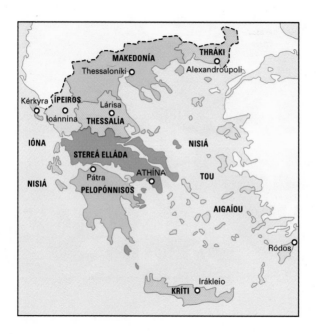

YOU ALREADY KNOW THE GREEN GUIDE, NOW FIND OUT ABOUT THE MICHELIN GROUP

The Michelin Adventure

It all started with rubber balls! This was the product made by a small company based in Clermont-Ferrand that André and Edouard Michelin inherited, back in 1880. The brothers quickly saw the potential for a new means of transport and their first success was the invention of detachable pneumatic tires for bicycles. However, the automobile was to provide the greatest scope for their creative talents. Throughout the 20th century, Michelin never ceased developing and creating ever more reliable and high-performance tires, not only for vehicles ranging from trucks to F1 but also for underground transit systems and airplanes.

From early on, Michelin provided its customers with tools and services to facilitate mobility and make traveling a more pleasurable and more frequent experience. As early as 1900, the Michelin Guide supplied motorists with a host of useful information related to vehicle maintenance, accommodation and restaurants, and was to become a benchmark for good food. At the same time, the Travel Information Bureau offered travelers personalised tips and itineraries.

The publication of the first collection of roadmaps, in 1910, was an instant hit! In 1926, the first regional guide to France was published, devoted to the principal sites of Brittany, and before long each region of France had its own Green Guide. The collection was later extended to more far-flung destinations, including New York in 1968 and Taiwan in 2011.

In the 21st century, with the growth of digital technology, the challenge for Michelin maps and guides is to continue to develop alongside the company's tire activities. Now, as before, Michelin is committed to improving the mobility of travelers.

MICHELIN TODAY

WORLD NUMBER ONE TIRE MANUFACTURER

- 70 production sites in 18 countries
- 111,000 employees from all cultures and on every continent
- 6,000 people employed in research and development

Moving
for a world

Moving forward means developing tires with better road grip and shorter braking distances, whatever the state of the road.

RIGHT PRESSURE

- Safety
- Longevity
- Optimum fuel consumption

-0,5 bar

- Durability reduced by 20% (- 8,000 km)

-1 bar

- Risk of blowouts
- Increased fuel consumption
- Longer braking distances on wet surfaces

forward together
where mobility is safer

. also involves helping motorists take care of their safety and their tires. To do so, Michelin organises "Fill Up With Air" campaigns all over the world to remind us that correct tire pressure is vital.

WEAR

DETECTING TIRE WEAR

The legal minimum depth of tire tread is 1.6mm. Tire manufacturers equip their tires with tread wear indicators, which are small blocks of rubber moulded into the base of the main grooves at a depth of 1.6mm.

Tires are the only point of contact between the vehicle and road.

The photo below shows the actual contact zone.

If the tread depth is less than 1.6mm, tires are considered to be worn and dangerous on wet surfaces.

NEW TIRE

WORN TIRE
(1,6 mm tread)

Moving forward
means sustainable
mobility

INNOVATION AND THE ENVIRONMENT

By 2050, Michelin aims to cut the quantity of raw materials used in its tire manufacturing process by half and to have developed renewable energy in its facilities. The design of MICHELIN tires has already saved billions of litres of fuel and, by extension, billions of tons of CO2.

Similarly, Michelin prints its maps and guides on paper produced from sustainably managed forests and is diversifying its publishing media by offering digital solutions to make traveling easier, more fuel efficient and more enjoyable!

The group's whole-hearted commitment to eco-design on a daily basis is demonstrated by ISO 14001 certification.

Like you, Michelin is committed to preserving our planet.

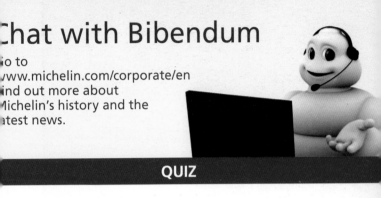

Chat with Bibendum

Go to
www.michelin.com/corporate/en
find out more about
Michelin's history and the
latest news.

QUIZ

Michelin develops tires for all types of vehicles.
See if you can match the right tire with the right vehicle…

A
B
1
2
3
C
4
D
E
5
F
6
G
7

Solution : A-6 / B-4 / C-2 / D-1 / E-3 / F-7 / G-5

Michelin Travel Partner

Société par actions simplifiées au capital de 11 629 590 EUR
27 cours de l'Ile Seguin - 92100 Boulogne Billancourt (France)
R.C.S. Nanterre 433 677 721

No part of this publication may be reproduced in any form
without the prior permission of the publisher.

© 2013 Michelin Travel Partner
ISBN 978-1-907099-85-4
Printed: July 2012
Printed and bound in France : Imprimerie CHIRAT, 42540 Saint-Just-la-Pendue - N° 201207.0282